THE HISTORY OF THE ORGAN
IN THE UNITED STATES

THE
HISTORY
OF THE
ORGAN
IN THE
UNITED
STATES

ORPHA OCHSE

INDIANA UNIVERSITY PRESS
Bloomington & London

Published in Canada by Fitzhenry & Whiteside Limited,
Don Mills, Ontario
Manufactured in the United States of America

Library of Congress Cataloging in Publication Data
Ochse, Orpha Caroline, 1925–
The history of the organ in the United States. *See slip*

Bibliography: *p. 440–463.*
1. Organs—United States. 2. Organ—History.
3. Organ-builders. I. Titles.
ML561.03   786.6'273   73–22644   ISBN 0–253–32830–6

Dedicated
to the memory of
Ruth and Clarence Mader

It roars louder than the lion of the desert, and it can draw out a thread of sound as fine as the locust spins at hot noon on his still tree-top. It imitates all instruments; it cheats the listener with the sound of singing choirs; it strives for a little purer note than can be strained from human throats, and emulates the host of heaven with its unearthly "voice of angels." Within its breast all the passions of humanity seem to reign in turn. It moans with the dull ache of grief, and cries with the sudden thrill of pain; it sighs, it shouts, it exults, it wails, it pleads, it trembles, it shudders, it threatens, it storms, it rages, it is soothed, it slumbers.

—Oliver Wendell Holmes

CONTENTS

Part Five: Organs in the Twentieth Century

Illustrations

PREFACE

Dependence on trans-Atlantic models is a thread that runs through most of the fabric of American organ history. But while we have copied English church music, French reeds, and German Rückpositivs, we have neglected to mimic the admirable North European enthusiasm for documenting organ history. One could collect dozens of small books and some larger volumes containing pictures, specifications, and histories of the organs in various locales of Holland or Germany.

The European organ historian has at his doorstep a selection of instruments that are interesting because they are old, visually exciting, representative of an important style of tonal design, originally built (or later rebuilt) by a famous organ builder, or any combination of these characteristics. The same ingredients are available in America, although the historian may have to do some long-distance commuting to gather them together.

We have been slow to recognize the fact that the United States has been the home of organ builders whose work is of first-class quality. We should be thankful that the Organ Historical Society, the Boston Organ Club, and the Organ Clearing House have made heroic efforts to preserve our important old instruments. These organizations have also collected and published much valuable information about early instruments and builders.

The major objectives of this book are to provide a chronological history of the organ in the United States and to supply much of the available information in its most useful form. Within that framework technical information and source material have been included as a starting-point for the specialist doing research in a specific area of organ history. The analyses of the circumstances that effected stylistic change, the attitude of organists to trends in organ design, foreign influences on organ design, and influences other than those directly related to the organ industry and organ profession are of more general concern, not only to organists, but also to those interested in other aspects of American history and other phases of music history.

Lastly, the history of the organ in the United States is intrinsically interesting, and its recital probably requires no external justification. One has only to think of the Moravian pioneers showing their little organ to the Indians, or imagine the utter chaos of the opening of Trinity Church's new Erben organ, or read of the experiments presented as evidence in the Hammond hearings to realize that there is a unique, free-wheeling spirit of adventure in the story of the organ in the United States. If a reverence for tradition has sometimes been in short supply, there has been no lack of enterprise and initiative.

Most sources used are identified in the text by numbers in square brackets that refer to entries listed in the Bibliography. For example, [5, p.5] refers to Myron Angel's *History of Nevada,* page 5. References numbered below 200 are books, dissertations, and pamphlets, while those numbered 200 and above are periodicals.

Two sources are identified by abbreviations. The *Boston Organ Club Newsletter* contains a wealth of material on American organs collected and edited by Edgar A. Boadway. Issues of this periodical are indicated by *BOC,* the whole number of the issue, and the page or pages. Convention program brochures of the Organ Historical Society contain specifications and other information about the organs heard at the conventions. They are identified by *OHS* and the year of the convention, e.g., *OHS 1970 Convention Program.*

Pitch designations used are:

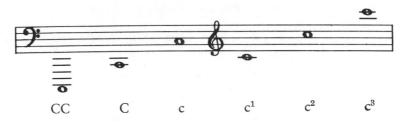

CC   C   c   c^1 c^2 c^3

These symbols correspond to the written pitch. Thus, the lowest note on the pedals as well as on the manuals of the modern organ is C. Exceptions to the above designations occasionally occur in direct quotations, where the terminology of the original source is retained.

Acknowledgments

The completion of this book depended on the help of many friends and associates. I am most grateful for their encouragement and patience during the years the manuscript was in preparation. Those who made major contributions in information, pictures, advice, hospitality, typing, and proofreading deserve a special word of thanks. They are: Ruth Banbury, Lois and Donald Battersby, Alan Beetle, Edgar Boadway, Charles Bradley, Linda Bradley, Alzie and Ray Brown, Priscilla and Willard Brown, William Dale, Donald Dierks, James Duncan, Mary Gallatin, Robert Glasgow, Catharine and Harold Gleason, Ann Goodman, Earland, Lucile, and Donna Hanson, Cheryl Haskell, Charles Lauer, Alan Laufman, Jim Lewis, Charles and Elaine Lutz, Lawrence Moe, Thomas Murray, Michele McCartney, David McVey, Eunice Newton, Barbara Owen, and Kenneth Simpson.

Clarence Mader followed closely the progress of this project from its inception until his death in 1971, and it was he who first read the manuscript. Those who knew him can well imagine the generosity of his help and the insight that formed the basis of his advice.

Funds for the completion of this book were made available through a faculty research grant from the Professional Interests Committee of Whittier College. I greatly appreciate the interest my colleagues have shown in this project.

PART ONE

Organs in a New Land

1524—1760

I

THE SPANISH MISSIONS

Church Music in Mexico

EAGER to convert the New World Indians to Christianity, Spanish missionaries recognized early the value of music in religious rituals and ceremonies. It was a common meeting ground understood by padre and pagan alike, and the Indians applied themselves with enthusiasm to learning the songs and charts of the Catholic church and to playing instruments of European origin.

Almost a hundred years before the first permanent colony in New England, the Spaniards were establishing music schools in Mexico. The first one was founded in 1524 at Texcoco by Pedro de Gante. With twelve Franciscan missionaries, he initiated a course of music instruction to teach European notation and technique to the natives. The purpose was to train musicians to perform the liturgical music of the church [35, p.258]. Instruction in music was only one of the functions of the Texcoco school, however. The Indians also learned many arts and crafts, including leatherwork, woodcarving, bell casting, and instrument making. Schurer relates that the first organs made in Texcoco were installed in churches in 1527 [137, p.34].

Additional schools were opened, and participation in church music became so popular among the Indians that by the middle of the sixteenth century the Spaniards had to place some restrictions on musical performance. A church council was called in 1555 by Archbishop Alonso de Montúfar. Actions taken, published the following year, stated that no more trumpets should be bought and that those in existence should not be played in churches during divine services, but should be used only in outdoor processions; that chirimías (shawms), flutes, viols, and other instruments should be stored and only distributed for use on special days; further,

> we urge all the clergy to install organs everywhere so that indecorous and improper instruments may be banished from the church. The organ is the correct instrument for use in the church, and we wish its use to become universal in Mexico. [Cited in 146, p.63.]

Such action, of course, was a great stimulant to organ building, and by 1616 a chronicler could write:

> Organs have also been installed here in nearly all the churches which are administered by the orders. However, with these, not the Indians but rather Spanish builders have taken charge of construction, since the Indians do not have capital for such large enterprises. The Indians make the organs under supervision, and they play the organs in our monasteries and convents. [Cited in 146, p.68.]

Organs in the Early Missions

With organ builders active in Mexico throughout the seventeenth and eighteenth centuries, and with the encouragement of the church hierarchy, it was natural that missionaries moving to the north should attempt to procure organs for their new churches.

Although earlier explorations had been made, it was not until 1598 that the conquest and colonization of New Mexico was begun by Juan de Oñate. It was probably as a member of Oñate's colony that a Franciscan missionary, Cristóbal de Quiñones, entered this territory some time between 1598 and 1604. So far as present records show, de Quiñones holds the distinction of installing the first organ within the boundaries of what is now the United States.[1] By the time of his death in 1609, he had "learned the language of the Queres Indians, erected the church and monastery at San Felipe, installed an organ in the chapel there, and taught many of the natives so successfully that they were skilled singers of the church service" [475, p.29].

In 1630 Friar García de San Francisco y Zúñiga was put in charge of the church and monastery at Senecú, and he installed an organ in the church [475, p.30]. Later Friar García established the mission of Nuestra Señora de Guadalupe at El Paso, where he remained from 1659 until after 1671. Although there is no record of his having placed an organ in this church, it was certainly a possibility, considering both his interest in music and the number of organs that existed in the Spanish settlements by this time.

A document copied in Madrid in 1664, referring to conditions as they existed in about 1641, described twenty-seven of the New Mexico missions, their churches, and their convents. According to this source, seventeen missions had organs. One of them, at Ácoma, was later described as "an excellent large organ" [477, p.16].

The origins and builders of the New Mexico organs pose an interesting problem. Supply lists of 1626 and 1631, giving materials to be transported from Mexico to the northern settlements, specifically include shawms, bassoons, and trumpets, but according to Spiess, none of the seventeenth-century lists mention organs [477, p.16]. On the other hand, we have no sources that describe the construction of organs in New Mexico, although several refer to the purchase of organs or to organs being brought to the missions.

Supply caravans, requiring a year and a half for the round trip from Mexico City, arrived regularly once every three years during the period from 1631 to 1656, and on one trip a 200-pound bell was transported [137, p.37]. Surely the inclusion of a small organ in the caravan inventory was within the realm of possibility [see also 476]. Whether or not it was "practical" in the modern sense of the word was not always a determining factor. As we have seen, the organ was regarded as an important and valuable piece of equipment for missionaries working with the Indians, rather than as a luxury item.

We have no description of the New Mexico organs, but must assume that they reflected their Spanish ancestry. Certainly most of them must have been of modest size, although the instrument at Ácoma was described as "large." A little Mexican positive organ in the church of Santo Domingo in Zacatecas may be similar to the organs used in the missions. According to Schurer it consists of three stops, "probably a Gedeckt 4', a Flute 2' and a Quinte 1'" [137, p.35].

Conflict between Church and State

The pattern of mission development was not destined to continue for long. Rivalry between the clergy and government officials resulted in serious conflicts by the middle of the seventeenth century. Even as early as 1610–14, during the administration of Don Pedro de Peralta as governor of New Mexico, some controversies arose that were to last throughout the rest of the Spanish occupancy of New Mexico, eventually breaking the hold of Spanish influence. Church authorities were accused of misuse of funds. In 1639 the viceroy of Mexico received a complaint from the cabildo of Santa Fe: "they say that an altar ornament, an organ, and other things have been given, but they are not there" [475, p.33].

The most powerful weapon the clergy had in response to such accusations was the Holy Office of the Inquisition. Established by the crown in Spain twelve years before the discovery of America, the Holy Office located Tribunals in Mexico City (1569), Lima (1569), and Cartagena (1611). The commissary of the Inquisition in the provinces was often the prelate or custodian of the Franciscan missions of the region.

The disputes reached such a point that the governor of New Mexico, Bernardo López de Mendizábel, was impeached and taken to Mexico City for trial by the Holy Office of the Inquisition. Documents of the trial, dating from 1659 to 1662, contain some interesting information about organs in New Mexico. A letter of November 11, 1659 to the viceroy of New Spain, signed by Fray García de San Francisco, vice-custodian, Fray Francisco de Salazar, Fray Benito de la Natividad, and Fray Joseph de Espeleta, *definidores,* accuses the governor of enslaving some Indians and of taking other Indians off the farms to serve in the army. It further states:

> Another charge is brought against us [the clergy], it being said that in some places the religious receive a few antelope skins in exchange for sustenance or for the crop; we do not deny this charge, as they call it, but indeed it is in very few places that this occurs, and where it happens it is done for the purpose of obtaining for the value of the skins certain ornaments, trumpets, and organs. For one hundred and fifty pesos a year are not sufficient for this, as we have to buy wine, wax, oil, incense, and other things; nor would it be fitting, since we can obtain these extra things by this means, for us to insist that everything should be given to us by his Majesty, who is in such great need. The same kind of a calumny is current this year, for God is good enough to allow certain pine-nuts to grow in the forests of five or six pueblos in this country, and the minister is accustomed to ask his parishioners to gather some of them for their churches, giving them abundant sustenance while they are doing so. From the pine-nuts which are gathered and sent to Mexico the proceeds are given to God (for instance, recently there was brought a fine organ for the convent of Abó, and certain things used in the divine cult for the convent of Cuarac) and there have been brought very curious altar-cloths and ornaments from the proceeds of this fruit.
>
> [Cited in 71, I, p.192.]

The governor was also accused of mistreating the singers, and as a result the clergy could no longer get enough singers for the Mass. In his reply to this charge, Don Bernardo de Mendizábel stated that "they had all the volunteer singers they wanted or could use, namely, a cantor and a sacristan, and where there was an organ they had an organist. These persons by order of the royal [audiencia] were excused from the tribute and from labor" [cited in 71, II, p.212].

Further pointing out his piety and devotion to the Church, the governor's defense noted:

> And as soon as he [the governor] reached Sante Fé, he saw that the church was without an organ, which seemed to him very improper, and so he said to Fray Juan Ramirez, custodian, and to Fray Miguel Sacristán, *guardián* of the villa, that an organ ought to be brought there, and that if it was too expensive to do so, [he], the accused, would pay half the cost, and if the expense was moderate, he would bear it all. [Cited in 71, II, p.213.]

Through the long years of controversy, the real victims were the Indians. No doubt some of the accusations of corruption and poor treatment of the Indians were true. Certainly the disputes hampered educational efforts and any feeling of loyalty they might otherwise have held. In 1680 the Indians finally rose in rebellion, killing many of the Spaniards, burning homes, missions, and churches, and driving away the survivors. Most of the Spaniards who escaped made their way to El Paso, which became a center of activity, and new missions were established in Texas.

However, the era of the organ in the Spanish missions was virtually at an end. Spain, past the height of her wealth and power, no longer had the resources to furnish the missions with supplies and money as before. Missions in New Mexico were rebuilt after the Spaniards were again in control in 1696, but the organs destroyed in the uprising were not replaced, and if any survived, evidence of them has long since disappeared. There are no known records of organs being placed in the Texas missions. Schurer tells of the isolated case of a portable organ that Padre López is said to have taken along on the Mendoza expedition to San Angelo in 1683 [137, p.40].

"New California"

In the light of these conditions, the lack of organs in the later California missions is somewhat explained. Dating from 1769 to 1823, the chain of missions extended from San Diego to San Francisco. At the completion of Mission Dolores (San Francisco) in 1776, musical instruments were lacking for the celebration, but there was no want of noise. Fray Francisco Palóu wrote: "The function was celebrated with repeated salvos of muskets, rifles, and the swivel-guns that were brought from the bark for this purpose, and also with rockets" [119, IV, p.133]. Palóu, the founder of Mission Dolores and later the president of all the missions in "New California," was quite thorough in listing supplies. It is unlikely that he would have failed to mention an organ had one

existed in the California missions during the early period covered by
his *Memoirs* (1769–83).

As time passed, small instrumental ensembles were formed, and a
few missions had orchestras of as many as thirty or forty players.
Violins, cellos, flutes, trumpets, guitars, and various percussion instruments could be found in the orchestras of San Gabriel, San Jose, and
San Luis Rey missions [98, pp.7–8]. But all of them were eclipsed by
the skill and splendor of the orchestra in the Santa Clara Mission.

The existence of an organ in this mission, as well as a colorful picture of tradition-scorning musical practice was recorded by the French
explorer De Mofras when he visited Santa Clara. The little organ had
been imported for the mission from France. The musicians of the orchestra wore "resplendent French uniforms" and were likely to play
martial airs, polkas, or waltzes to accompany the most solemn occasions. When he attended Mass, De Mofras was amazed to hear the
orchestra give a rousing chorus of "La Marseillaise" during the Eleva-
tion of the Host. No less was his surprise that the procession was
accompanied by "Vive Henri Quatre" [98, p.8].

The only other organ mentioned in accounts of the missions in
California[2] was a barrel organ with three cylinders that was in the San
Juan Bautista mission by 1829. The instrument was made in London,
and may have been given to the mission by visiting British sailors. With
a somewhat idealized view of mission music, Engelhardt wrote:

> There is no evidence that the thing was ever put to use in the church.
> Its lively tunes could not harmonize with the stately Roman plain
> chant, nor with the devotional Latin and Spanish hymns sung by the
> congregation. [52, p.42]

If the music at San Juan Bautista was in any way similar to that at Santa
Clara, we may imagine that the mechanical instrument contributed in
its own manner to the spirit of the services.

In considering generally the musical endeavors of the Spanish missionaries (without reference to the exploitation of the Indians), it is
indeed unfortunate that there was not a greater or more lasting effect
from this period of our music history. There were, in all, perhaps
twenty or more organs installed in what is now the United States.
That no organ-building tradition, no surviving schools of church music
grew out of this background is a great loss. If we view the influence
that Spanish mission architecture has exerted through the centuries on
building styles in the Southwest, we can imagine the extra dimension
that a strong and continuous Spanish church-music tradition might
have added to the history of the organ in this country.

II

THE BRITISH COLONIES

Introduction

The Town-Centered North

BY the opening of the eighteenth century, when organ history in the British colonies began, patterns of immigration had helped to establish rather definite regional characteristics in church music. These characteristics are traceable to the very beginnings of colonization, and were influenced not only by the churches themselves, but also by social and political factors.

In New England the town was the hub of activity. Life was community-centered as schools were opened, churches built, and trade and commerce encouraged. The town was a place where craftsmen could find markets for their work, and many of them were attracted to New England for this reason. Boston was the early leader in shipbuilding, lumbering, and other industries, and held the distinction of being the largest city in the colonies. By 1730 the population of Boston reached 13,000, while Philadelphia and New York each had about 8,500.

Organ builders, most of whom relied on some other activity for a livelihood, naturally were drawn to the population centers. Some of them were cabinetmakers who found an outlet for their products in the cities and towns, building organs only as a sideline.

Church Music

"Dissenting" churches were in the majority in New England. The Puritans held strict views about the introduction of anything "popish" in the ritual, and organs fell into this classification. Many clergymen roundly denounced the organ, and some of the more determined churches remained without organs until the middle of the nineteenth century. Meanwhile, singing was accompanied by a bass viol or by a combination of instruments that, for some reason, were considered "non-popish," such as flute, bassoon, and cello. Fisher relates that the instruments in use in one Boston church in 1845 were a clarinet, a double bass, and an ophicleide [54, p.9]. The tuning fork had its brief moment of glory in some churches in which instruments were either not available or not tolerated.

Anglican churches presented a much different situation, not only in New England but throughout the colonies. Here organs found an early welcome. The influence that this attitude exerted on the development of our organ and church-music history can hardly be overestimated. During the colonial period most of the organs for Anglican churches were imported from England, and when local musicians were found inadequate, English organists were engaged. Traditions were established here that caused American church musicians to turn to England for models and ideals—traditions that continued long after our concert music came under the domination of Continental European styles. Here lie the roots of some of the stylistic and technical distinctions that persist today between our church and concert music, over and above the distinctions of sacred and secular.

The Church of England dominated church music in New York as well as in New England. Settled by the Dutch, New York became an English colony in 1664. Although the Dutch Reformed Church was the "Mother Church" in New York City, the English church soon gained ascendency. The old church in the Fort, originally Dutch, was renamed The King's Chapel [69, p.60]. Trinity Church (1696–98) and the Old Dutch Church (1692–96) completed the roster of seventeenth-century New York churches.

The Plantation-Centered South

In the southern colonies also, the Church of England held a position of authority. In Virginia, the Carolinas, and Georgia, it was the state church and was tax-supported. Here one might have expected organ building to flourish, had other things been equal. However, in these colonies the center of activity was the plantation instead of the town. The owner of the plantation often employed a tutor for the early schooling of his children, and relied on sending them to England for higher education. He depended largely on his plantation workers to supply his needs so far as crafts and construction were concerned. One may read, for example, of a large brick plantation home for which all the bricks had been made on the plantation.

With this kind of organization, life for a craftsman was much more difficult. The clockmaker, cabinetmaker, or organ builder depended on a commercial center for his livelihood and on townsmen for his customers. Of course, the southern seaport cities attracted a fair share of craftsmen. The plantation system similarly imposed particular difficulties on the churches. It was not easy to minister to a congregation scattered over a large area; clergymen were scarce, and many of them served more than one parish. The fact that there was no American bishop to encourage and supervise the growth of the church reduced further the potential authority of the southern churches.

As a reflection of these conditions, we find that there were some early organs in the population centers of the South, and occasionally one was placed in a rural church, but the number of people who actually engaged in organ building does not compare with the activity in the North. One looks in vain for the seedling organ industry already appearing in Massachusetts and Pennsylvania.

German Settlers in Pennsylvania

Pennsylvania presented a unique picture among the early colonies. Religious tolerance attracted large numbers of immigrants who sacrificed their homes and countries for the sake of their beliefs, and who represented sects that were unpopular or not tolerated in other colonies. German Protestants flocked to William Penn's colony. Between 1710 and 1770 an estimated 225,000 to 250,000 Germans arrived in America. More than 70 percent of them settled in New York, Pennsylvania, and New Jersey, and of this number, 110,000 settled in Pennsylvania. Fewer than one percent made their homes in New England[1] [161, p.167].

Prominent among the Germans were large groups from the Palatinate, where the Protestants had been subjected to particular hardships. For many of them, however, their hardships were not over when they left home. Those who did not have money for their passage to America entered into an agreement that bound them as servants for an undetermined period of time. When the ship arrived in America, the future labor of the immigrant was auctioned off for a number of years to anyone who would pay the price of the passage. The poor immigrant had no voice in fixing the length or terms of his service, and had no choice but to accept payment of his passage in this way. The position of an indentured servant from England was different, for he left home with a contract stating the terms and conditions of his future service[2] [107, pp.x–xi].

Many German Lutheran and German Reformed churches were established in Pennsylvania. In the rural areas and small communities these two denominations usually used the same building, and today one often finds a church bearing two names: one for the

Lutheran congregation and another for the Reformed congregation.

The German migration also included groups of Dunkards, Mennonites, Moravians, and Schwenkfelders. These groups formed closely knit communities, regulating the membership in ways that seem restrictive today, but which often resulted in well-ordered and productive societies. In the Moravian communities, for example, the church leaders not only had jurisdiction over the social conduct of their members but also determined what business or craft they could pursue. Competition, in other words, was not allowed. Each member had his contribution to make to the community, and he was not to interfere with the work of others. When the Moravian organ builder David Tannenberg complained to the elders of the church that John Antes was beginning to make keyboard instruments, thus threatening his own business, the elders agreed that Antes should confine himself to making stringed instruments [6, p.17].

The importance that was attached to the organ and organ music in Germany had its effect on church music in Pennsylvania. Lutheran and Reformed churches in the most unlikely rural areas installed organs as soon as their church buildings had advanced beyond the log-cabin stage. Like the New England dissenting churches, some of the other sects outlawed organs in their churches. In contrast, the Moravians encouraged the use not only of organs but of a variety of other instruments, and established a tradition of church music unique in our colonial history.

The eighteenth-century German organ style was not destined to have a continuous effect on American organ building. In some respects this phase of organ history resembles that associated with the Spanish missions: an interesting interlude, regionally important, but outside the mainstream of developments. In other respects, however, this analogy is not valid. The Spanish organs have disappeared, while at least a few of the Pennsylvania German organs are extant and playable. Some, in fact, have continued in use to the present time. They remain a part, however small, of our present heritage, and the twentieth-century style, which derives many of its features from German principles of organ building, gives a new perspective to this heritage. While the Pennsylvania organs hold particular interest for the organist today, one should note that German influence of a later period appeared in the early organs of the Midwest and Texas, as well as in the Boston Music Hall organ and other instruments in the East.

Characteristics of the Organs

For the most part, only scant information is available about the earliest organs in the British colonies. What reports we have reveal little about the quality or the characteristics of the instruments. In most cases the craftsmanship can be evaluated only by the organ's longevity, but that indicates nothing about its musical worth. Even in the matter of specifications, one can often find only a partial list of stops or just an indication of size.

Most of the organs were small. Klemm's organ for Trinity Church, New York, and the imported organ of King's Chapel, Boston, were the only known three-manual organs of this period. One-manual organs were in the majority, and when a second manual was included, it was usually a "short" keyboard of treble stops. This division, if unenclosed, was sometimes called Choir and sometimes Echo. The term Swell was used, as today, for a division in an expression, or swell, enclosure.

Manual keyboards were shorter than our present standard of sixty-one notes. The single manual of the Brattle organ (see p.20) for example, contains forty-nine keys. The original compass was C to c³, with C♯ sounding AA. During this period, no organ in the colonies had pedals, although Trinity Church contemplated the addition of a pedal clavier.

Stop names were often given without a pitch designation. However, the basic plan was so standard that there is little room for confusion. The Open Diapason and Stopped Diapason were at 8′ pitch, and stops called Principal and Flute were at 4′ pitch. Higher-pitched stops are usually self-explanatory. A reed, if included, would be at 8′ pitch.

Manual stops were often divided, permitting the organist to use a solo and accompaniment registration. Sometimes the higher-pitched stops were divided, while 8′ and 4′ stops were "whole," i.e., one stop for the entire manual compass. In chamber organs, the Open Diapason was characteristically only a treble stop, omitting the larger pipes in the bass, and one would have to use it in conjunction with the Stopped Diapason to play in the lower register. If the Stopped Diapason were a divided stop, its lower register would be used as a common bass for both the Stopped and Open Diapasons. The Open Diapason could also be used as a solo stop, accompanied by a different stop in the bass.

Many of the organs of this period were imported from England, although a few were brought from Germany. The names of some early builders in the colonies come to us in connection with only one organ each, while a greater scope of activity and the beginning of professional organ building in this country are seen in the work of Johann Klemm and Thomas Johnston. David Tannenberg also entered the picture toward the end of this period, but his major work belongs to a later time.

Pennsylvania

The First Organ in the British Colonies

German pietists in a Swedish Lutheran church were responsible for the first recorded use of an organ in the British colonies. In 1694 Johannes Kelpius arrived in Pennsylvania with a group of forty followers. Kelpius, then only twenty-one, was both a philosopher versed in Oriental studies and a hymn writer. He and his followers went first to Germantown for a short time. They then settled near Philadelphia on the banks of the Wissahickon, where they became known as the Hermits or the Mystics of the Wissahickon. Evidence of their interest in music is found in the assortment of instruments they brought with them and in Kelpius's account of prayer services during their voyage to America. These services included the singing of hymns, accompanied by instruments.

On November 24, 1703, nine years after their arrival in America, the Mystics participated in the ordination service when Justus Falckner became pastor of the Gloria Dei Church of Philadelphia, the first ordination of a Protestant clergyman in America. The service "opened with a voluntary on the little organ in the gallery by Jonas the organist, supplemented with instrumental music by the Mystics on the viol, hautboy, trumpets, and kettle-drums" [36, I, p.176]. Although a hymn and an anthem were also included in the service, no further mention is made of the organ, nor is Jonas, the organist, identified.

It is possible that the Mystics supplied the organ, as well as the other instruments, either having brought it with them or having built it later. Another possibility is that an organ was already in the church. Two years earlier, Falckner, who evidently had some musical interest himself, had written to Heinrich Muhlen of Holstein asking for assistance in procuring an organ. The letter, dated August 1, 1701, is an interesting reflection of one aspect of life in the new land.

> I will here take occasion to mention that many others beside myself, who know the ways of this land, maintain that music would contribute much towards a good Christian service. It would not only attract and civilize the wild Indian, but it would do much good in spreading the Gospel truths among the sects and others by attracting them. Instrumental music is especially serviceable here. Thus a well-sounding organ would perhaps prove of great profit, to say nothing of the fact that the Indians would come running from far and near to listen to such unknown melody, and upon that account might become willing to accept our language and teaching, and remain with people who had such agreeable things; for they are said to come ever so far to listen to one who plays even upon a reed-pipe: such an extraordi-

nary love have they for any melodious and ringing sound. Now as the melancholy, saturnine, stingy Quaker spirit has abolished all such music, it would indeed be a novelty here, and tend to attract many of the young people away from the Quakers and sects to attend services where such music was found, even against the wishes of their parents. This would afford a good opportunity to show them the truth and their error.

. . . And it may be assumed that even a small organ-instrument and music in this place would be acceptable to God, and prove far more useful than many hundreds in Europe where there is already a superfluity of such things. . . .

. . . There are in Europe masters enough who build such instruments, and a fine one can be secured for 300 or 400 thalers. Then if an experienced organist and musician could be found, and a curious one who would undertake so far a journey, he would be very welcome here. In case this could not be, if we only had an organ, some one or other might be found who had knowledge thereof. [134]

Johann Gottlob Klemm

While occasional references to small organs owned (and possibly built) by colonists may be found, a generation elapsed between the time that Falckner wrote his letter and America's first professional organ builder arrived in the Philadelphia area. Born in a village near Dresden, Johann Gottlob Klemm (John Clem, 1690–1762) had studied theology for two years at the University of Leipzig before he decided against going into the ministry, turning instead to organ building. Some writers have suggested that he learned the art from either Gottfried or Andreas Silbermann. If so, Klemm's Dresden birthplace and residence would make it more likely that Gottfried Silbermann was his teacher.

In 1724 Klemm met Count Zinzendorf, the patron of the Moravian Brethren. Through his association with the count, Klemm traveled to Berthelsdorf to repair the organ, and in 1726 moved to the Moravian settlement at Herrnhut. Although he was recognized as a spiritual leader and teacher in the community, Klemm became disillusioned with Herrnhut, and in 1733 he and his wife decided to travel to America with a group of Schwenkfelders [6, p.13].

In September of that year they arrived in Pennsylvania and settled near Philadelphia. In 1739 Klemm was engaged to construct "one of the largest and most significant instruments built in Colonial America in the eighteenth century" for Trinity Parish, New York [42, p.104]. Klemm's other professional activities during this period included the construction of at least one harpsichord.[3]

In 1746 Klemm installed an organ in the Moravian Church in Bethlehem. A series of letters and receipts identifies Klemm's association in this transaction with Mons Gustaff Hesselius (d.1755), a Swedish portrait painter who had immigrated to the colonies in 1712. The origin of the organ has not been established.

To the Reverend Mr. Pyrlaeus, Bethlehem.
Philadelphia, May 28, 1744.

My dear Brother: I salute you heartily. I am glad to hear of your welfare. I hope Mr. Klemm will see the Organ all safe to your hands. If you please to pay him the remainder of the money, which is 14 pd. 9 sh., I shall be very much obliged to you. The rest of the money, the eleven pd., for my part, you may send it to me when you can and have opportunity. My love to you and all the Brethren.

I remain your humble servant and poor Brother,
G. Hesselius.

Received June 9, 1746, of Jasper Payne, Four pounds, viz. Three pounds for the half set of pipes, and one pound for coming and putting the organ up.
John Clem, Organmaker.

Received June 10, 1746, of Jasper Payne, Fourteen pounds Pennsylvania Currency for Gus. Hesselius.
John Clem, Organ Maker.

Philadelphia, June 26, 1746. Received of the Brethren in Bethlehem eleven pd. currency for an organ, being in full of all accounts. Witness my hands.
Gustavus Hesselius.

[Cited in 36, II, p.271.]

This organ was repaired in 1751 by Robert Harttafel,[4] and in 1761 was taken to Lititz by Tannenberg and installed there. The organ restored and now preserved in the Moravian Historical Society Museum at Nazareth is said to be this organ, but it is probably a later instrument.[5]

Klemm moved to New York in 1746, evidently after the Bethlehem installation, but he continued his activities as an organ builder in Pennsylvania. In 1752 he built an organ for Christ Lutheran Church, Berks County, Pennsylvania. He also enlarged an instrument in the Trappe Augustus Lutheran Church, Montgomery County, Pennsylvania.

Klemm and Tannenberg

Finally, in 1757, at the age of sixty-seven, Klemm decided to return to Bethlehem. Armstrong describes the last years of Klemm's life and his association with a man who became known as one of America's most important early organ builders, David Tannenberg:

> In 1745 or 1746 Klemm's wife had died and he had moved to New York City where he had renewed his associations with the Moravians. A visitor from Bethlehem told him of the need for a new organ in Nazareth and Klemm wrote to Bishop Spangenberg, asking permission to spend his last days in Bethlehem and offering his services as an organ builder. Permission was granted and Klemm arrived in Bethlehem on November 25, 1757. He was soon put to work repairing the Bethlehem organ.
>
> The first reference to Tannenberg's association with Klemm appears in the Bethlehem diary for January 15 of the following year when Tannenberg traveled to Philadelphia to buy boards for an organ. Then on March 1, 1758, Klemm, Tannenberg, and Tannenberg's family left Bethlehem for Nazareth to take up residence in Nazareth Hall and begin the construction of two organs, which were completed by the end of the year. [6, p.15]

One of the two organs mentioned by Armstrong was for the chapel of the Moravian congregation in Nazareth Hall. It was used there until 1793, when it was sold for thirty pounds to the Moravian congregation at Emmaus, Pennsylvania [6, p.86]. The second organ was a small positive which was used in another room in Nazareth Hall.

In 1759 Klemm and Tannenberg built an organ for the chapel of the Moravian congregation in Bethlehem. It was evidently a small one, since it was transported to Bethlehem on January 29, 1759 and was played for the first time the same evening [6, p.86]. According to an account written in 1799, the organ had a reversed console—a technique Tannenberg used to good advantage later:

> The organ in the gallery, is placed contiguous to the wall, and the organist is seated in the front, with the keys before him, and his face towards the congregation. The wires and communications with the pipes pass under his feet, secured by the platform, which elevates him a few inches. [113, p.34]

In July 1760, Klemm and Tannenberg completed an organ for the chapel of the Moravian congregation in Christian's Spring, Pennsylvania. Shortly afterward Klemm and the Tannenbergs moved to a house outside Bethlehem. Here they may have built the little one-rank organ that was taken by a group of Moravian settlers to Bethabara, Forsyth County, North Carolina.

Klemm died on May 5, 1762, having passed his last years in the house he shared with the Tannenbergs near Bethlehem. With the possible exception of the 1746 Bethlehem Hesselius-Klemm organ, none of his works remain for us to see today.[6]

Gottlieb Mittelberger

> In the month of May 1750 I left my birthplace Enzweihingen in the district of Vaihingen for Heilbronn, where an organ was waiting for me, ready to be shipped to Pennsylvania. With this organ I took the usual route down the Neckar and the Rhine to Rotterdam in Holland. [107, p.7]

Gottlieb Mittelberger traveled to Pennsylvania on the ship *Osgood* with almost five hundred other passengers, arriving in September 1750. The organ he mentioned had been built by Johann Adam Schmahl (1704–1757) of Heilbronn, and was destined for St. Michael's Church, Philadelphia. In spite of his claim, Mittelberger apparently had no official connection with the organ shipment, which was entrusted, rather, to Johann Georg Landenberg(er) [518a, p.9].

The dedication of this instrument in St. Michael's on May 12, 1751 attracted a large crowd, and contemporary accounts lauded the organ of twenty registers, reputed to be the largest and best in Philadelphia at that time. Mittelberger's own account of the consecration is somewhat exaggerated:

> At this great and joyous festival there appeared fifteen Lutheran preachers as well as the entire vestries of all the Evangelical churches. The number of people present was immense. Many people came a great distance, ten, twenty, thirty, forty, up to fifty hours' journey in order to see and hear this organ. The number of people listening, standing inside and outside the church, German and English, has been estimated at several thousand. On the second day of this solemn and joyous festival all the assembled Lutheran preachers and vestries held a conference in the course of which I was appointed schoolmaster and organist. As I became better and better known in Pennsylvania, and people found out that I brought fine and good instruments with me, many English and German families came ten, twenty, up to thirty hours' journey to hear these instruments and to see the organ. And they were greatly surprised, since they had never in all their lives seen or heard an organ or any of these instruments.
> [107, pp.87–88]

According to Eugene McCracken, Mittelberger brought four organs to America for use in Lutheran churches [383, p.1], one of which was for the Old Trappe Church (Augustus Lutheran, at Trappe, Pennsylvania). A pamphlet issued by Augustus Lutheran Church throws further light on Mittelberger's activities:

By 1752 the interior of the church building was completed as it appears today with the erection of the east gallery and the installation of a pipe organ. The organ was secured through the efforts of Gottlieb Mittelberger, who came to Providence [Trappe] in 1751 to be the schoolmaster. There was gradually added to his duties the responsibilities of organist, choirmaster, and sexton of the church. [114]

Other Organs and Builders in Pennsylvania

There were other organs in the Philadelphia area during the early eighteenth century, but little information about them is available. For example, in a will made in 1734, Matthias Zimmerman bequeathed an organ he had built. Another organ, valued at forty pounds, was listed among the possessions of Dr. Christopher Witt (1675–1765) at the time of his death.[7]

In 1728, Christ Church, Philadelphia, elected to purchase an organ from Ludovic Sprogel (Ludowick Sprogell, died c.1729). The vestry records for September 2, 1728 hint that the organ was imported:

> A committee, having been appointed by the vestry to treat with Mr. Lod. C. Sprogel about an organ lately arrived here, report that they had done the same, and that he insisted on 200 pounds for said organ. . . . [Cited in 378, p.9.]

A small new organ was installed in the Gloria Dei Church between 1737 and 1741; two organs were in the First Moravian Church of Philadelphia as early as 1743; and St. Joseph's Church, Willings Alley, Philadelphia, acquired an organ between 1748 and 1750.

In his journal entry for June 1, 1744, William Black[8] noted the existence of an organ in Germantown:

> German Town about 6 miles from Philadelphia, is a Continued Row of Houses in each side of a Public Road, for more than a Mile and a half, the Inhabitants are Chiefly Dutch, and has a very Good Church with Organs in the Town. [226, p.408]

The Reverend Peter Brunnholtz of St. Michael's Church mentioned three of these organs, as well as one in Lancaster, in a letter of 1752:

> I knew: (a) Before I came here a Germantown congregation purchased an organ or little positiv for £ 70 and had to pay £ 7 annually on it until 1750. The same truly is not worth more than £ 10 and provides poor service. (b) The organ in the Swedish church [Gloria Dei] cost £ 80 and is still only a modest positiv. (c) The Lancaster organ, also, had cost £ 80; however, it is also small and a noisy patchwork. Likewise the Catholics [St. Joseph's Church]. [Cited in 518a, p.9.]

Although Mr. Brunnholz's evaluations may have been valid, it should be noted that his letter was written to his superiors to justify the purchase of the new organ for St. Michael's Church.

This section would not be complete without mentioning the organ in the Hershey Museum, Hershey, Pennsylvania. According to the information furnished by the curator of the museum, the organ was built about 1735 by Mr. Dyer, a cabinetmaker in Manheim, Pennsylvania. The little four-stop organ has four octaves of keys, minus low C-sharp. A thorough examination may assign it a somewhat later date than 1735.

New England

King's Chapel, Boston: Two English Organs

The history of organs in Boston opens with the long and colorful story of the Brattle organ. Built in England, this one-manual organ was imported in the late seventeenth century or in the early years of the eighteenth. Although the exact date of its arrival is not known, it was in Boston by 1708, and was the property of Thomas Brattle [233, p.5]. It is mentioned in the September 3, 1708 entry in the diary of the Reverend Samuel Sewall,[9] and again by another diarist, the Reverend Joseph Green, who wrote on May 29, 1711: "I was at Mr. Thomas Brattle's; heard ye organs and saw strange things in a microscope" [68, p.90].

In 1713 Brattle died, leaving the organ to the Brattle Square Church. The subsequent events are told by Fisher:

> When in 1713 Thomas Brattle, Esq., of Boston, willed the Brattle Square Church an organ, they declined it. He had provided, however, that in this event it was to be given to Queen's Chapel (known since the reign of Queen Anne as King's Chapel), but so great was the prejudice that the organ remained seven months in the porch of the church before it was unpacked. This instrument, set up in 1714, was the first pipe organ used in a church in the Colonies, and it was bitterly denounced by Dr. Cotton Mather and other dignitaries of the day.[10] [54, p.8]

After its installation, William Price played the organ until the arrival, some months later, of the English organist Edward Enstone. Enstone was awarded the less-than-handsome salary of thirty pounds yearly, which he supplemented by teaching music and dancing [14, p.126].

By 1756 the old wooden building of King's Chapel had been replaced by a new stone building (the present structure), and a new organ had been imported from England. The old Brattle organ, having served the church for forty-two years, was sold and moved to St. Paul's Church, Newburyport. It remained in use there until 1836, when it was sold to St. John's Church, Portsmouth, New Hampshire, for $450.

After surviving periods when it was not playable and occasional repairs, a new chapter in the story of this famous old organ opened with its restoration in 1965 by Charles B. Fisk, Inc., of Gloucester, Massachusetts. The report of the restoration and specification appeared in *The Tracker* in 1966:

> Most of the wooden pipes are original, but several were missing and have been skillfully replaced by Douglas Brown, another member of the firm.
>
> The Fifteenth is comprised of 8 original pipes and 41 new. The restored Sesquialtera is entirely new, but is of the scale, composition and material prevalent in England 300 years ago. The final voicing and tuning were done by Mr. Fisk.
>
> The specifications are:

Stopt Diapason 8'	49 Wood Pipes
Principal 4'	49 Open Wood Pipes
Fifteenth 2' Bass	25 Metal Pipes
Fifteenth 2'Treble	24 Metal Pipes
Sesquialtera II Bass	(19th–22nd)
Sesquialtera II Treble	(12th–17th)

[233, p.5]

Particularly worthy of note is the gentle quality of the wooden Principal 4' and the refined tonal balance of the entire instrument, which probably do credit to the recent restorer as much as to the original builder.

The English builder Richard Bridge was selected to construct the second organ installed in King's Chapel, Boston. In August 1756 the arrival of the new instrument was heralded by the *Boston Gazette and Country Journal:*

> We hear that the organ, wh. lately arrived from London, by Capt. Farr, for King's Chapel in this Town, will be opened on Thursday next in the Afternoon; and that said organ (wh. contains a variety of curious stops never yet heard in these parts) is esteemed by the most eminent masters in England to be equal, if not superior, to any of the same size in Europe. [Cited in 117, p.7.]

The organ had been inspected and approved by the well-known London organist-composer John Stanley, and both its size and quality placed it in the forefront of Boston organs, a position it retained for many years.

The specification is of particular interest because three-manual organs in America in the eighteenth century were very rare. Klemm had built one for Trinity Church, New York, in 1739, the only one known to have preceded the Bridge organ. But aside from mere size, the organ contained some noteworthy characteristics. The Great manual had two mixtures: a Cornet IV and a Sesquialtera IV. In both of them each rank could be drawn separately, giving an unusual number of registration possibilities to this division. In addition, the Great had a full complement of mutations up to the 1⅗'. Great and Choir manuals of fifty-seven notes each extended from GG to e³, omitting GG♯. The Swell extended down only as far as tenor f or g. Originally there were no pedals, but a Sub Bass of eighteen notes was added in 1824.

King's Chapel, Boston, Massachusetts
RICHARD BRIDGE, 1756

Great		Swell	
Open Diapason	8'	Open Diapason	8'
Stop Diapason	8'	Stop Diapason	8'
Principal	4'	Principal	4'
Twelfth	2⅔'	Hautboy	8'
Fifteenth	2'	Trumpet	8'
Tierce	1⅗'		
Cornet (treble, c¹)	IV	*Choir*	
(ranks drawing separately)		Open Diapason	8'
Sesquialtera	IV	Stop Diapason	8'
(ranks drawing separately)		Dulciana	8'
Trumpet	8'	Principal	4'
		Flute	4'
		Vox Humana	8'

[117, p.36]

This organ was used for more than a hundred years in King's Chapel. When it was replaced in 1860 by Simmons and Willcox, the original case and eleven of the stops were retained in the new organ. Two new organs and an extensive rebuild later, only the pipe shades and some case details of the original instrument remain in the present installation, a 1964 organ built by Charles Fisk.[11]

Old North, Boston: The Claggett Organ

An organ installed in Old North Church (Christ Church), Boston, in 1736 was purchased for 320 pounds from William Claggett, a clockmaker in Newport, Rhode Island. Claggett may have constructed the instrument himself, or it may have been imported. Preparations for the installation have been described by Babcock:

An organ by Richard Bridge, 1756. King's Chapel, Boston. *Photo courtesy Essex Institute, Salem, Massachusetts.*

An organ by Charles Fisk, 1964. King's Chapel, Boston. Pipe shades, impost carvings, crown, and mitres remain from the 1756 organ. *Photo courtesy C. B. Fisk, Inc.*

By a vote of the vestry, October 5, 1736, it was resolved "to gett the front gallery prepared after the best manner for the reception of the Organ," and it was specified that the committee should "add what is proper in the Beautifying and fixing up said Organ in the church."

It was fortunate that, as usual, the vestry did not foresee into what multitudinous expenses this was to lead the parish. First, there was the work of carpenters and painters who had to alter the gallery by removing the pews; second, the organ had no case, which had to be designed and constructed, the pipes gilded and ornaments designed to be carried out on each side, perhaps to give a more imposing front to the instrument which must have been small, as a comparison with the King's Chapel organ of 1713 now at St. John's Church, Portsmouth, New Hampshire, will show; but most essential, an organist and an organ blower. [14, pp. 125–26]

In all, the preparations cost 522 pounds in addition to the 320 pounds for the organ.

William Price, who had previously played the organ at King's Chapel, volunteered to play the organ free for one year at Christ Church if he were engaged to play for five years, a clever arrangement that was accepted by the wardens and vestry. Price remained in this post until 1743.

Various bills for the repair of the organ are noted in the vestry records, and finally, on August 11, 1752, the vestry voted to replace the organ with a new one to be built by Thomas Johnston.

Trinity Church, Boston: An English Organ

An article in *The New-England Magazine* for March 1834 states that Trinity's "first and only organ was imported from London in 1737" [400, p.27]. Another issue of the same publication clarifies:

It was then [1737] an old organ, and is said to have stood, previously, either in Salisbury cathedral, or in some other church in Salisbury. It is of moderate size, with two rows of keys, and consists of a great organ and swell. When played full, it has a good body of tone, and all the stops mix well. But the solo stops, played as such, are not good, especially the reeds. This organ was put up again in the new edifice, where it still remains; but it is altogether insufficient in power, as well as in variety and excellence, for Trinity Church. [225, p.38]

The New-England Magazine was only partly correct. The Trinity Church organ was built by the famous London builder Abraham Jordan (the builder credited with introducing the swell to English organs in 1712). It arrived in Boston on November 1, 1744, along with directions for setting it up and a letter revealing that Handel had tried the organ and had given it his approval. Trinity's new two-manual organ, complete with a swell enclosure, had a Trumpet on each manual, and the Great chorus was topped by a "Sisqualtera & Cornett" [BOC 53, pp. 2–3]. It was used until 1837, when a three-manual organ by the English builder Gray was installed [BOC 54, p.2].

Edward Broomfield

Edward Broomfield (Bromfield), Jr., constructed the first organ known to have been built by a native-born colonist. The son of a wealthy merchant, Broomfield (1723–1746) graduated from Harvard in 1742, and took a second degree from Harvard in 1745. He was evidently an ingenious young man, having studied mathematics, theology, and natural sciences. The Reverend Thomas Prince, minister of the Old South Church, said of Broomfield:

> As he was well skilled in Music, he for exercise and recreation, with his own hands, has made a most accurate Organ, with two rows of keys and many hundred pipes, his intention being twelve hundred, but died before he completed it. The workmanship of the keys and pipes [was] surprisingly nice and curious, exceeding anything of the kind that ever came here from England. And what is surprising was that he had but a few times looked into the inside work of two or three organs which came from England. [Cited in 29, p.32.]

This organ was located in the South Church, Boston, but during the siege of Boston, it was removed to a store for safety, where it was later destroyed by fire.

Boston's First Professional Organ Builder

Professional organ building in Boston had its beginning with Thomas Johnston (1708–1767). Although Johnston also engaged in several other crafts (he was an engraver and an ornamental painter), he is credited with building at least three organs between 1752 and 1763. He was active as a musician and was employed as a singer in King's Chapel. His salary there in 1754 was thirteen pounds and five shillings per quarter.

Johnston had been engaged several times to repair the Claggett organ in Old North Church. Finally, on April 15, 1752, evidently impatient with the difficulties of the old organ (although it had been used for only sixteen years), the vestry voted:

> That Mr. Johnson [sic] have Thirty pounds Old Tenour paid him for Taking down the *Old Organ* and putting it up again pr agreement

provided that said Johnson is willing to allow the £30 again out of the cost of a *New Organ* the church is now about agreeing with him for without taking any further advantage of the Church therein.

[Cited in 14, p.130.]

During the time that the old organ was disassembled, Johnston placed an organ of his own in the church, and he received ten pounds Old Tenour for its use. It is not certain that he had built this instrument, but if so, it brings the total of known Johnston organs to four.

When the new organ was officially ordered on August 11, 1752, we have a hint that the organ in Trinity Church may have stimulated interest in acquiring a fine, new organ:

> VOTED That Mr Johnson make for the church called Christ Church a New Organ with the Echo equall to that of Trinity Church of this Town, and that he be paid for it two hundred Pounds Lawful Money to be done according to the Terms already mentioned & also that Mr Johnson if he pleases make a Double Diapason in the Trebble.
>
> [Cited in 14, pp.132–33.]

When Boston was evacuated by the British troops, Old North Church was closed, and the pipes were taken out of the organ and stored. After the war, when the church was again opened, the pipes were replaced, but some were missing. In 1834, an unidentified writer gave this second-hand account of the specification:

> A person, now living, who was well acquainted with this organ thirty or forty years ago, states, that the great organ contained seven stops, viz. stopt diapason, open diapason, principal, twelfth, fifteenth, sesquialter of three ranks, flute, and trumpet; and that the swell, or echo, contained four stops, viz. stopt diapason, principal, flute, and trumpet. The three first stops of the swell were carried through in the bass, outside of the swell box, and thus formed a choir-organ and swell combined. [400, p.206]

The organ remained in use until 1821, when it was replaced by William Goodrich. The case was retained and enlarged, and still forms the central portion of the case in use today.

In 1754 Johnston built an organ for St. Peter's Church, Salem, Massachusetts.[12] It was a one-manual organ with six stops and the following specification:

Open Diapason Treble	8′	Flute	4′
Stopt Diapason	8′	Twelfth	2⅔′
Principal	4′	Fifteenth	2′

[116, p.166]

The Johnston organs for Christ Church (Old North) and St. Peter's Church represent no deviation from the standard practice of the day, although the inclusion of two reeds in the Christ Church organ gave it greater resources than many of its contemporaries had.

On June 27, 1763, the *Boston Gazette* carried the following advertisement:

> Lewis Deblois . . . has for Sale, an Organ, made by Mr. *Thomas Johnston* of this Town, formerly made Use of in Concert-Hall, and can be recommended.—An abatement of Ten Guineas will be made, (from the real Value of said Instrument) if bought and made Use of for any Congregation in this Town. [Cited in 47, p.298.]

Gilbert and Lewis Deblois had owned the Boston Concert Hall, but in 1754 they sold it to their father, Stephen. Stephen later negotiated a loan from Lewis (who had by then moved to London) so that King's Church in Providence, Rhode Island, might purchase the Johnston organ. Their interest in this particular church stemmed from the fact that members of the Deblois family had pews there [361, p.1]. That a new organ, imported from London, had been installed in the Boston Music Hall and that in several years' time no buyer had been found for the Johnston organ may also have been influential.

Finally, in a diary entry for December 12, 1771, Dr. Ezra Stiles wrote:

> An organ is lately erected in the Episcopal called Kings Chh in Providence; and 10th Inst. at a church Assembly, notified by printed Hand Bills, it was first played on in divine Service, Rev. Jn° Graves the Minister preaching a Sermon, and after that, a Contribution for the Expences. This I suppose was *Consecration* of the Organ. This Organ was taken from Concert-hall in Boston—from being improved in promoting Festivity, Merriment, Effeminacy, Luxury & Midnight Revellings—to be used in the Worship of God. [149, p.192]

In 1791 Gilbert Deblois's agents reminded the church that the loan from Lewis had not been repaid. Perhaps with the difficulties of the Revolution and the ensuing depression, the church was unable to meet this obligation. In any event, the account was finally settled for $500 less than the full amount [363, p.77]. The organ was used for many years, and accounts show that it was repaired on several occasions, as late as 1849. It was finally replaced by a three-manual E. & G. G. Hook organ in 1851 [361, p.8].

Probably the most interesting account of work done on the organ is found in the ledger entries of 1811. The church had moved into a new building, and the organ, which had been in storage, was installed in time for consecration on St. Barnabas's Day, June 11, 1811.

April 18	pd Bolston for 1 sheep & 5 squirrel skins for repairing the Organ	$ 1.12½
April 30	pd blowing bellows 1 day—tuning the Organ	.25
	pd a boy . . . Organ Blowing	.56
May 7	pd Young Hay for blowing the Organ Bellows 3 days	.75
May 11	Pd Dan Thompson pr. do for setting up, repairing and tuning the Organ	$56.37½
May 14	pd Saml E. Hamlin pr Bill & rct for a copper glue-kittle &c for repairing the Organ	3.54
May 28	pd Saml E. Hamlin for Lead and casting Ornaments to cover the tops of the two new front Pipes of the Organ	.45
June 4	pd Dan Thompson per Do for repairing an organ pipe which had been stolen and injured; and for returning some other pipes, displaced by the Painter	1.50
June 10	pd Aaron Man for 2 pr. of Butts, Screws & Brass Screw-knobs for the Organ loft doors	.64

[361, pp.1, 8]

Pachelbel and an English Organ

In the vestry records for Trinity Church, Newport, Rhode Island, February 25, 1733, the following action was noted:

> VOTED: that the Church Wardens write to Mr. Charles Theodore Perchival, in Boston, to acquaint him that the organ is arrived for the Church, and that he is desired to come up here and assist us with his advice, in putting the same up, and that he shall be satisfied for his assistance in the affair. [Cited in 435, p.33.]

Thus it was that Karl Theodor Pachelbel, son of the famous German organist and composer, traveled to Newport to assist in the installation of an organ made in England by Richard Bridge.

Pachelbel had arrived in Boston in 1732 or 1733. Some time after his trip to Newport, he went to New York, where a concert including vocal and instrumental music, with Pachelbel playing the harpsichord, was given for his benefit on January 21, 1736. Later he went to Charleston, where he served as organist at St. Philip's Church from 1740 until his death in 1750.

The organ that prompted Pachelbel's trip to Newport was one of the largest imported in America in the early eighteenth century. It was the gift of Bishop Berkeley to the town of Berkeley, Massachusetts, which was named after him. However, considering the organ to be an instrument of the Devil, the town asked Berkeley to take it away. He then gave it to Trinity Church, where, evidently, a more liberal view of instrumental music was held.

Twenty-two years after the installation of the organ, a letter sent to Mr. Bridge from the church shows the original specification[13] and illustrates some of the difficulties and frustrations encountered by early organ owners:

> In the year 1733, you made an organ for the Rev. Doctor Berkeley, late Bishop of Cloyne, in which were the following whole stops (which he presented to Trinity Church): stop diapason, principal, flute, 15th, and human voice. ½ stops: cornet (treble), trumpet (treble), open diapason (treble), echo trumpet, stop diapason, open diapason,—all half stops.
>
> We have sent a box to the care of Mr. Richard Mollineau, Iron Monger, in London, all the box H pipes, which were never of any use here, as no organist could ever make some of them speak, and others when tuned would not stand half an hour. Now, Sir, what we desire is that if you can so alter them as to make them answer their design, pray do; if not, we are of the opinion that if we had a trumpet bass and the treble vox humane, it would be a good addition to the loudness of our organ. We waited so long in hopes an organ builder might accidentally come here, but as there is no one expected now, we hope for the credit of your organ, you'll repair this to your satisfaction, as well as to that of Sir ———.
>
> P.S.—If neither of those ways above mentioned can be made use of, if you think proper, make a 12th in lieu thereof, and Mr. R. M. will pay you. [Cited in 267, p.248.]

There is no record of Bridge's response, if any. But there was evidently still a stop missing in 1769, as noted in the vestry records of June 12 of that year:

> At a meeting of the congregation, voted: that the Rev. Mr. Browne and John Mawdsley, Esq., be requested to procure in London a new stop for the organ, in the room of that which is wanting; either the vox humane or any other stop that may be thought most suitable, and the congregation will pay the expense of the same.
>
> [Cited in 267, p.249.]

A year later they were still trying, with no recorded success. In 1770 Edward Evans was elected organist with a yearly salary of thirty pounds, his duties to begin on his return from London. Evans was supposed to bring a new organ stop back from London, but he did not return [267, p.249].

The contents of "box H" remain a mystery. Dean surmises that the pipes returned to Bridge may have been the cornet (treble) [42, p.37]. However, in view of the difficulties encountered in making the pipes speak properly and stay in tune, it seems more likely that "box H" is a misquotation or misreading of "vox H," and that the pipes were the original Vox Humana. This theory is further substantiated in the continued request of the church authorities for a Vox Humana.

Other Organs in New England

According to Maurer, an English-made organ was installed in Christ Church, Middletown, Connecticut. Richard Alsop imported this instrument and gave it to the parish after the church was completed in 1755 [366, p.24]. In Stratford, Connecticut, Christ Church hailed the arrival of its organ in April 1756 [42, p.214].

New York

The Garden Street Church Organ

New York's first organ made its appearance in 1720 or 1727, when Governor Burnet imported an organ from Europe as a gift for the Dutch Reformed Church. The Garden Street Church, also called The South Church, had been dedicated in 1693, and no pains had been spared in its decoration:

> The windows were long and narrow and fitted with small panes of glass set in lead, on which were burned the coats-of-arms of the principal parishoners [sic]. The bell, pulpit and furniture of the old church were transferred to the new, and many escutcheons of leading families hung against the walls. For plate, the people contributed silverware and money, which was sent over to the silver workers of Amsterdam, who hammered out for them a communion set and a large baptismal basin. [27, p.20]

That Governor Burnet's interest in the Dutch Church was not entirely musical has been explained by Charles E. Corwin:

> He [Burnet] had come to New York a youthful widower, soon to become very popular with the ladies, and he had chosen as the companion of his heart the most beautiful Dutch heiress in town, Anna Maria Van Horne. Wishing to show a favor to the people of his bride, he had ordered as a present for the Dutch Church an organ

from Europe. How proud of their English governor's gift must the happy congregation that assembled in the quaint Dutch Church on Garden street have been! How secretly jealous must have been their Anglican neighbors, whose more pretentious church building was still awaiting its "set of organs." [263, p.12]

Many years later, in 1770, the Reverend Ezra Stiles recalled seeing this organ: "In the year 1754 I saw in the *Dutch calvinist* Chh. at New York a small Organ, which was the first there & had been there I doubt not many years" [149, p.58].The organ was used for about fifty years, but came to an unhappy end during the Revolution. The British troops had appropriated various churches for use as hospitals, riding schools, and prisons. Garden Street Church for some reason escaped this use and the accompanying ruin, suffering "no loss but that of its organ" [126, p.23].

Trinity Parish: The Klemm Organ

The vestry records of Trinity Parish, New York, reveal that a committee was appointed in 1703 to confer with "Mr. Henry Neering, Organ-maker, about making and Erecting an Organ in Trinity Church in New York . . ." [104, p.290]. Nothing came of this action, and no further information has been located about Neering. Since Trinity Parish had been established only six years earlier, it may have had more pressing problems at the time, but in 1709 the Rector, the Reverend Mr. Vesey, wrote to the Archbishop of Canterbury about the need for an organ. Again there was no result.

More than a decade after the arrival of Governor Burnet's organ for the Dutch Reformed Church, Trinity Parish made a new—and this time successful—attempt to procure an organ. This instrument was the one John Klemm was commissioned to build in 1739 and which was completed in 1741. It had twenty-six stops on three manuals.

In January 1744 an agreement between Klemm and the vestry included "that he will change three Treble Stops that are now in wood for Pewter if Required for the sum of fifteen pounds; and will also change the Trumpet stops for a Double Cornett for the sum of fifteen pounds and will make a Pedell compleat for the organ for the sum of twelve pounds if Required." In November of the same year, Klemm replaced the Trumpet with a "Double Cornet Stop in Pewter," installed some new bellows, and made other repairs. Again in 1751 the vestry sent for Klemm to clean and repair the organ, and also "to compleat the Cornet and Sesqui alto stops formerly made by him" [cited in 104, pp.291–92]. Evidently pedals were never added.

Trinity's music historian, Messiter, questions the quality of this instrument, which served the church only twenty years: "it is tolerably evident that the materials were bad: the wood probably not enough seasoned, the leather not properly prepared, and the 'pewter' little better than lead" [104, p.292]. The vestry took steps to buy a new organ in 1761, placing the negotiations in the hands of the organist, Mr. Harison. The next year *The New-York Gazette* (November 15, 1762) carried the following advertisement (and, incidentally, our best description of the Klemm organ):

> Organ in Trinity Church.—To be Sold by the Church-Wardens, the Organ in Trinity-Church. The Instrument is large, consisting of 26 Stops, 10 in the Great Organ, 10 in the Choir Organ and 6 in the Swell, three Sets of Keys; with a Frontispiece of gilt Pipes, and otherwise neatly adorned. It may be inspected; will be sold cheap, and the Purchaser may remove it immediately, (another being expected from England next Spring) but if not disposed of, is, on the Arrival of the new Organ, intended to be shipt to England.

Characteristically, the new organ was a year late in arriving, and Trinity Church had to wait until April 1764 to install the instrument made by the English builder John Snetzler.

Other Organs in New York

In 1756 an organ was set up in City Hall. It was the product of Gilbert Ash, a craftsman who also manufactured soap, candles, and furniture. The announcement of the opening program appeared in *The New-York Mercury* of March 15:

> For the Benefit of a Poor Widow. On Thursday the 18th Instant, will be open'd, at the City Hall, in the City of New-York, a New Organ, made by Gilbert Ash, where will be performed, A Concert of Vocal and Instrumental Musick . . . Tickets, at Five Shillings each, to be had at Mr. Cobham's in Hanover-Square, at the Gentleman's Coffee House, at the King's Arms, at the Province Arms, at the Bible & Crown in Queen-street, and at Mr. Ash's joining Mr. Willet's in Wall-street; who continues the Business of Organ Building, by whom Gentlemen and Ladies, may be furnished with noble Instrument, in a convenient Time after it is bespoke. [Cited in 63, p.109.]

The dedication took place on March 16; an organ concerto by G. A. Hasse was included in the program.

The only other New York organ that comes to our attention during this early period is a chamber organ, advertised for sale in *The New-York Mercury* on December 4, 1758. It had three stops, and was to be sold for forty pounds, one shilling [63, p.371].

The South

Organs in South Carolina

In 1728 St. Philip's Church in Charleston, South Carolina, imported its first organ. Frederick Dalco's 1820 account stated: "The Organ was imported from England, and had been used at the Coronation of George II" [40, p.121]. It must have been a satisfactory instrument, for it apparently was used for 95 years. That it survived at all is surprising, for twice in the year 1744 the organ was struck by lightning. The *South-Carolina Gazette* for Monday, April 30, carried the following account:

> On Thursday we had a violent Storm of Lightning, Thunder and Rain, here.—The Lightning has done considerable Damage to *St Philip*'s Church, the Steeple, and Organ, and kill'd Mr. *Anth Furnis* who was [at] work in the said Church, hanging one of the Bells; Mr. *Isaiah Brunett* (*Furnis*'s Partner) was knock'd down and senless [senseless?] about half an Hour, but recover'd soon after; one *Wilson* was also wounded in the Knee. The Top of the Steeple is much shatter'd, but where the Lightning entered on the North side of the Church, the Holes are not above an Inch and half in Diameter—A Sailor was about the same Time kill'd by the Lightning.

Less than two months later, lightning defied the old superstition and struck again. According to the same paper, on June 11, 1744:

> In the Storm we had last Wednesday se'nnight, the Lightning has again much shatter'd *St. Philip*'s-Church Steeple, and struck the Organ in the same Spot as when *Mr. Furnis* was kill'd; it has likewise hurted the Dissenters Meeting House Steeple, and struck several Houses in different Parts of this Town, yet did no Damage to any Person.

An account written in the 1760s described the St. Philip's organ as having sixteen stops in the Great organ and eight in the Choir. It was said to be a "good" organ and "well ornamented." St. Philip's organist was John Salter, who has a special claim to fame for having given one of the first concerts in the colonies [142, p.11]. Salter remained at St. Philip's until his death in 1740, when he was succeeded in the post of organist by Karl Theodor Pachelbel.

According to Williams, another organ was imported from England in 1755 for a rural Anglican parish in South Carolina. It was placed in St. Andrew's Church, not far from Charleston [514, p.36].

Organs in Virginia

Three churches in Virginia boasted English organs during this time: Hungar's Church, Northampton County; the Petsworth Church, Gloucester County; and Bruton Parish Church, Williamsburg. Hungar's Church, built in 1691, was said to have had exceptionally fine interior furnishings, most of which were gifts of Queen Anne. After the Revolution, however, the church was pillaged, and among the things destroyed was the "large pipe organ." Metal from the organ, according to tradition, was used by fishermen in the area as sinkers for their nets [130, p. 9]. The Petsworth Church organ dated from 1735. No details of its construction are known.[14]

As early as 1744 the vestry records of Bruton Parish showed that there was interest in securing an organ. Evidently no immediate action was taken toward a permanent installation, but a chamber organ may have been in use for several years. Dean has shown from a contemporary diary source that Peter Pelham was organist of the Bruton Church by January, 1751[15] [42, p.75].

In any event, the purchase of an organ not to exceed two hundred pounds was authorized in 1752, with this amount to be paid from public funds. Colonel Landon Carter, wealthy son of Robert "King" Carter, was then a member of the House of Burgesses. In a journal he kept privately of the actions of the House, the following account of the authorization of the organ purchase is recorded:

April 1752

1. Wednesday
   Several other bills brought in, one for an Addition to this Church and an Organ. I opposed it and so did some Others, but it was Carryed for a 2d reading.

14. Tuesday
    In the house nothing but form in Passing bills excepting in the bill for Repairing the Wmsburg Church, which went as for engrossing, Orgain and all.

15. Wednesday
    The bill for repairing the Church passed with its orgain. Some Mountaineers thought an organ was some strange instrument or Rather Monster and so voted only to have an opportunity of seeing one. The repair is to cost £300 and the Organ £200 Sterling, and, when it is got, who is to play upon it? Not in the bill at present. The Gentlemen intend to find one and all other Charges, but I humbly conceive these are but promises and at a future day the money will be askt of us. Yet our fools could not believe this, although I told them the Whole in a long speach. Besides experience had informed us that these instruments could not stand long in this Country. Dust, Spiders, and dirt daubers would Stop up all the Pipes, and when it should be out of Repair what artificer had we to mend it. [31, I, pp.91, 101, 103]

One can only imagine Carter's reaction when he learned that the cost of the organ finally came to between 360 and 420 pounds, and that the additional amount had to be procured partly from the Assembly and partly from private subscription.

The organ may have been sold in 1834 [42, p.79], or it may have been given away in 1835 [292, p.10]. Shortly after that its place was taken by an organ built by Henry Erben. The old organ now in the Bruton Church has no connection with the original instrument. It was imported from England in 1938, and was probably built by Samuel Green.

Organs in Maryland

By the middle of the eighteenth century, interest in organs was growing. Baltimore, for example, became a beehive of activity. The Reverend Thomas Chase, who was at St. Paul's Church from 1748 to 1753, "started his Maryland tenure by ordering a bell and organ, convinced that 'those tended in their own way to advance the general interest in the church.'" An English organ was purchased by subscription and installed by Adam Lynne [90, p.8].

Between 1754 and 1759 a subscription was promoted for an organ at St. Anne's Church, and the new organ for the Reformed Town Clock Church was installed in 1754. Other churches joined the trend, stimulated by the visit of Philip Feyring, a Philadelphia organ builder who gained considerable renown for his instruments, particularly those built during the 1760s.

According to Wolverton, an organ builder named Richard Parker was active in Annapolis around 1760 [168, p.132]. This information is the only evidence we have that Maryland might have had locally built as well as imported organs at this early date.

PART TWO

Organs in a Rural Society
1760–1810

III

SOME GENERAL OBSERVATIONS

The Colonies, 1760–1775

THERE was no thought of revolt against England in 1760, no general discontent with English management of colonial affairs, and no movement toward unity among the American colonies. Quite the contrary, the successful conclusion of the French and Indian War (Seven Years' War)[1] resulted in renewed loyalty to England and the king. Causes for dissatisfaction were not excessive or persistent, and the balance of power between English control and colonial self-government was generally well adjusted.

About one and a half million people inhabited the settled area of the colonies, in farms and communities scattered along some two thousand miles of the Atlantic coast. Forests still covered most of the land, separating plantations and farms except in the more thickly settled areas.

Communication and travel were difficult; the trip from Philadelphia to New York was an ordeal of two or three days, even under the most favorable weather conditions. While there was coastal trading among the colonies, the commerce between the individual colonies and England was far more important.

Under these conditions, the relative isolation of distant colonies from each other strengthened regional distinctions, and what similarities did appear were largely the indirect reflection of their common relationship with England. New England remained essentially democratic, with its wealthy class consisting of particularly successful merchants. Almost all adult men were eligible to vote. In contrast, there was virtually no middle class in Virginia. The First Families of Virginia formed an aristocracy, separated by property, education, and social custom from frontiersmen. The plantation system discouraged the formation of a middle class of small, independent landholders. The differences between northern and southern colonies touched practically every aspect of life, from attitudes toward slavery to differences in speech and manners. In addition to the general North-South distinctions, there were characteristics in forms of government, religion, and the cultural background of the colonists that tended to isolate even some neighboring colonies.

An early attempt at union within the colonial system for common defense against the French and the Indians, initiated by the so-called Albany Congress in 1754, was a dismal failure. Not one colony would agree to the plan. Finally, when Parliament levied a direct internal tax on the colonies in 1765, a common cause brought leaders of nine colonies together. The success of this concerted effort to win repeal of the Stamp Act was an impressive example of the power unity could exert. Even after that time, there was no general animosity toward England, and only the radical Sons of Liberty moved consistently against English authority.

Not until Parliament passed the Coercive Acts in 1774 was public opinion and indignation aroused sufficiently to propel the colonists to decisive, unified action. The Coercive Acts were retaliatory measures for the Boston Tea Party of December 1773, and the response of the colonists was the formation of the First Continental Congress. From that time, relationships between the colonies and England deteriorated, in spite of the efforts of peacemakers on both sides, and the hot war began in 1775.

Music in the Colonies

A wide variety of musical experiences were available to the colonists in the prerevolutionary period, ranging from folk songs to the concerts of the fashionable St. Cecilia Society, established in Charleston in 1762. Performance on the violin, flute, hautboy, or clavier was a hobby cultivated by many a gentleman. Francis Hopkinson (1737–1791), for example, is remembered first as a statesman, but he was also an organist and one of our first native composers. His enthusiasm for music was shared by such prominent contemporaries as Thomas Jefferson and Benjamin Franklin.

For professional musicians, America had to rely for the most part on European- or English-trained immigrants. The English organist William Tuckey (1708–1781) arrived in New York about 1753. He organized the choir at Trinity Church, where a performance of parts of Handel's *Messiah* in 1770 was a landmark in the American colonies. Tuckey's counterpart in Boston was William Selby (1738–1798), the distinguished organist of King's Chapel and a leader in Boston's musical development. The rare example of a native-born professional musician is found in William Billings. Virtually self-educated, Billings composed, taught, conducted, and published music.

The most remarkable musical developments of the time were found in the Moravian communities. In both Bethlehem, Pennsylvania, and Salem, North Carolina, orchestras, quartets, and other performing groups were formed. Contemporary works from Europe were an important part of the repertoire, and original composition was encouraged. Describing musical life in Bethlehem, Rufus Grider wrote:

> As constant accessions were made to the colony from Europe, the same statement is true as to compositions; no opportunity was neglected to obtain all the newest music which their Brethren in Europe possessed. It is know [sic] that the Rev. Emanuel Nitschman, when he came from Europe, brought the first copies of Haydn's Quartettes and Symphonies. It is said that Joseph Haydn, if not directly, was at least indirectly, in communication with the musicians of this place.
>
> [70, p.5]

Prewar Organs and Church Music

Organ building before the Revolution centers singularly on the career of David Tannenberg, a Pennsylvania Moravian. No other builder approached his record of thirteen organs in the decade between 1765 and 1774, although Philip Feyring also deserves recognition for building three organs for Philadelphia churches in the 1760s. Outside Pennsylvania the colonists tended to rely on English organs. The importation of instruments in the 1760s from one of that country's leading builders, John Snetzler, was facilitated by the lively trade relationship and the habitual inclination of colonists to look to the mother country for cultural leadership.

Aside from chamber instruments for home use, the demand for organs came almost exclusively from the German and Anglican churches. Many dissenting churches held firmly to the belief that organs were evil and were inappropriate for use in the church.[2] Ezra Stiles recorded the first use of an organ in a dissenting church in his *Diary*, July 10, 1770:

> Last month an Organ of 200 Pipes was set up in the Meeting-house of the first Congregational Chh. in Providence: and for the first time it was played upon in divine Service last Ldsday, as Mr. Rowland the pastor tells me. This is the first organ in a dissenting presb. Chh. in America except Jersey College [Princeton]—or Great Britain.
>
> [149, pp.57–58]

Stiles further commented that after the organ was set up reports reached the church that a gentleman in England had left a will bequeathing five hundred pounds to the first dissenting congregation to install an organ. There is no record that the Providence church collected this money. Preparations for the organ were evidently made in secret, and a Mr. West "exercised himself upon it a month learning to play" before the organ was first used. Stiles does not describe the reaction of the congregation, but the organ did "give great offense" to the Episcopalians in Providence, who soon after set about the business of acquiring an organ.

We are indebted to Stiles for an account of the order of service, showing the limited use that was made of the organ and giving us an interesting picture of a church service in 1770:

> The course of divine Service in the Congreg^a Chh. at Providence under Rev. Mr. Rowland is this.—The Congregation rise & the Minister asks a Blessing on the Word & the divine presence in the Solemnities of public Worship—then the people sit, & the Minister reads a Chapter in the Bible—then the bills asking prayers &c are read by the Minister—then the Assembly rise & the Minister prays for a quarter & half an hour—then sing Watts Version of Psalms the people striking in with the Organ, & many sing standing, perhaps half the Congregation—then Minister takes a Text of Scripture, expounds it & preaches—the people sitting—Sermon being ended, the people rise & the Minister prays a short prayer—then singing & the Organ—then Minister pronounces the Blessing & dismisses the Congregation. But the Organ does not then play. This is the Forenoon Service. The Afternoon the same, only in addition, between the last prayer & singing is the Contribution—& the last singing always concludes with the Xtian Doxology, & when it comes to the Doxology the whole Congregation rise & stand with great Solemnity. And after the Blessing is given, the Minister publishes the Banns of Marriage. The organ is a Chamber Organ, as large as a Desk & Book Case, containing about 220 pipes. . . . [149, p.60]

Effects of the War

The Revolution dealt a serious blow to interest in organs and organ building. Churches were faced with more immediate problems than organ contracts. Many Anglican churches were closed, and some of the clergymen, loyal to the Crown, fled to England. Churches commandeered for military use were often badly damaged and desecrated. Organs, too, were destroyed or damaged "as a consequence of behavior on the part of the soldiery of both sides quite as barbarous as that of Cromwell's troops in England a century before." According to Owen, the organ in King's Chapel was "probably the only one in greater Boston which survived intact" [117, p.8]. In the South the British raid in

1779 and two years of plundering after the British occupied Charleston in 1780 resulted in damage to many churches [46, p.89].

Important for the history of the organ is the fact that the Moravians, like other groups of pacifists in Pennsylvania, would not permit members of their sect to participate in military combat. Moreover, they wanted to remain as remote as possible from worldly influences, and they were greatly disturbed when buildings in Lititz and Bethlehem were taken over by the colonial army for use as hospitals [6, p.36]. One cannot say that the Moravians remained unaffected by the Revolution, but they did manage to remain out of the mainstream of current events, and they continued their normal pursuits with less distraction than would otherwise have been possible. These circumstances fostered the continuous growth of Moravian musical activities and opened the way for the golden age of Moravian organ building. Between the years 1790 and 1804 the master craftsman David Tannenberg completed eighteen organs.

Postwar Problems

Economic recovery after the war came more quickly in the South than in the North. The southern agricultural exports were important to England, and a prewar level of trade was soon reestablished. Shipbuilding, fishing, and foreign trade, the backbones of northern income, suffered greater setbacks, and readjustment was difficult. For example, before the war many of the ships produced in the northern colonies had been built for English owners. The privileged position for this market no longer existed, and new industries and trade relationships had to be developed to balance the losses. When that was accomplished, the North was in a much stronger economic condition than the South and was much better prepared to profit from the increasing importance of manufacturing and industry in American society.

Meanwhile, Congress was struggling with the problem of keeping the new nation afloat. Without authority to regulate customs or collect taxes, Congress had to meet its crises without power and without money. When the Constitution was ratified (1787–89) and Washington elected (1789) the problems were only beginning. France declared war on England in 1793, and neutral trade was menaced by both sides. Washington, Adams, and Jefferson, in their successive administrations, walked a complicated tightrope between the two powerful nations, but aggressions against American shipping and the impressment of American sailors finally resulted in the Embargo Act (December 1807), prohibiting all exports from the United States and restricting some British imports. Although this act was repealed in 1809, subsequent restrictions halted English-American trade except for a few months in 1810.

The prospective organ customer must have noted the uncertainties of trans-Atlantic trade with concern. Even so, organs by various English builders were installed during the decades after the Revolution. The alternatives were limited. David Tannenberg's reputation was both regional and denominational; most of his organs were for Moravian or Lutheran churches in Pennsylvania and neighboring states. Elsewhere there was little to encourage organ building and much to discourage it. For example, there was no money; there was not even a bank in America until 1781. Tory sympathizers had included a large proportion of wealthy people, and many of them had either left the country or lost much of their property. They were the very people who might have wanted a chamber organ or might have donated a church organ in quieter times.

The churches, too, were faced with problems of reorganizing, repairing, and rebuilding. During the 1780s the Presbyterian Church in America was organized, the Methodists separated from the Anglican church and organized the Methodist Episcopal Church in the United States, Dutch and German sects became independent of European control, and the Roman Catholics were separated from London jurisdiction.

The Church of England was faced with particular hardships in states that had recognized it as the established church in colonial days. No longer was it tax supported after the disestablishment; until the reorganization as the Protestant Episcopal Church of the United States in 1786, there was no leadership; the shortage of clergymen, always a problem, was intensified by the number who had left their posts and gone to England; congregations were greatly disturbed by changes in the liturgy and the omission of prayers for the king; and some of the churches had been damaged beyond repair, while others were allowed to fall into decay. In the North, never having enjoyed state support, the Anglican church had grown on a much firmer basis. As a result, readjustment after the war was much less disastrous there than in the South.

Congregational churches and other denominations that were locally controlled did not have the great reorganization problem that faced the Episcopal church. Of course, churches of all denominations were affected in one way or another by the destructive forces of the war.

Chuch Music at the Turn of the Century

The growing interest in organ building at the beginning of the nineteenth century coincided with the gradual resolution of some of the organizational problems in the government and in the churches, with a growing interest in improving church music, and with the trade restrictions that increasingly hampered the importation of organs. With reluctance, a few more dissenting churches considered installing organs. Their acceptance has usually been ascribed to a more liberal attitude, but actually, the deplorable state to which congregational singing had fallen prompted some of this liberality. In his diary entry for March 28, 1807, the Reverend William Bentley observed: "Singing is with difficulty maintained. We have neither teachers nor scholars. Very few are decent in this quarter in any kind of music" [19, III, p.278]. On January 10, 1808 Bentley commented again on the difficulties of trying to improve congregational singing: "Dr. Barnard's North Meeting are tired of the attempts & have purchased a very expensive organ which is every day expected from Philadelphia" [19, III, p.338].

In an Episcopal church one might hear a broader spectrum of organ music, and we are indebted to Francis Hopkinson for a contemporary viewpoint. In 1786, he wrote a letter to the Rector of Christ Church, Philadelphia, ". . . on the Conduct of a Church Organ." Here he described the proper goals of the organist:

> The excellence of an organist consists in his making the instrument subservient and conducive to the purposes of devotion. None but a master can do this. [81, p.121]

He also discussed specific uses of the organ in the service, which included a voluntary (not over five minutes long) before the reading of the lessons, a prelude "after the psalm is given out" to introduce the psalm tune to be sung, interludes between the verses of the psalm (not longer than sixteen bars triple time, or ten to twelve bars common time), and a voluntary after the service.

In each case, Hopkinson stressed the importance of coordinating the mood of the music with the meaning of spoken and sung words. This sensitivity to the tenor of the service extended through the postlude.

> The voluntary after the service was never intended to eradicate every serious idea which the sermon may have inculcated. It should rather be expressive of that chearful [*sic*] satisfaction which a good heart feels under the sense of a duty performed. [81, p.125; for the entire text of Hopkinson's letter see the Appendix.]

Musical activities continued to flourish in the Moravian communities, reaching a high point of development from about 1790 to 1810. The *Collegium musicum* organized in Salem in 1786 had a repertoire of almost five hundred works. "The preferred composers," according to McCorkle, "were evidently Abel, Haydn, Mozart, and Pleyel. The greater part of the music (which, by the way, was acquired almost as

soon as it was published) was early-classic, i.e., from c.1760 to c.1780"
[376, p.485].

There was no lack of capable organists in the early Moravian communities. Bethlehem's historian, Grider, explained:

> About the year 1800, the town contained about 500 inhabitants, yet
> that small number furnished six persons as *organists*, who were able
> to serve the congregation, and did so, without recompense. Such organists were required to know about 400 church tunes, and be able to
> play them in any key the officiating minister might start them. (The
> officiating minister generally commenced the singing of the hymn,
> without announcing the words, the organist and congregation joined
> in as soon as they could catch the words and the tune.) They were
> required to perform concerted music at sight. Now the congregation
> is about three times greater, and but three persons are found able
> to do so.
>
> It was customary for each organist to serve one week. The key to
> the organ had a small green board attached to it; on this was inscribed
> "Organ Key," and the names of the players. Each organist, at the close
> of his week's service, transferred the key to his successor. Each one of
> them thus serving once in six weeks. It was deemed not only an honor
> to be able to do so, but a great privilege to be serving the congregation
> in that manner. [70, p.10]

Unfortunately, the remarkably musical Moravians had little or no
interest in organ literature. Organ pieces (voluntaries) were evidently
tolerated on occasion, but the words of Christian Ignatius Latrobe imply that the Moravians did not really desire or appreciate them:

> To be able to play a voluntary is by no means an essential part of
> the qualifications of an organist among the Brethren. The congregation will often prefer hearing Hymn-Tunes in its stead; which, besides affording a great variety, produces a pleasing and edifying effect.
> If a voluntary is played, all incongruities should be avoided, and the
> audience, not even undesignedly, be led from the aim of their meeting,
> to attend either with admiration or displeasure to the dexterity of the
> organist's fingers, or rather to the levity of his mind.
>
> [Cited in 377, p.147.]

Characteristics of the Organs

Throughout the period from 1760 to 1810, specifications of American organs exhibited rather consistent characteristics. Even though
there are some interesting differences between the instruments made by
New York and New England builders and those built in Pennsylvania,
the basic choruses of open 8', 4', 2⅔', and 2' plus a stopped 8' are the

same. Thus the specifications of many chamber organs are identical.

To this scheme the Pennsylvania builder would characteristically add a Mixture, while the English-influenced builder would add a Sesquialtera. Although Tannenberg also occasionally used a Sesquialtera or Tierce in this way, the unison-and-fifth-sounding Mixture was more common.

New England and New York organs used more reeds (Trumpet was most common, with an Oboe on the Swell in a two-manual organ). Tannenberg used very few, partly because many of his organs were placed in isolated locations and reed stops require a greater amount of service.

Divided stops, a Swell division with a compass extending only from tenor g, the English GG compass on the Great manual, and the omission of a Pedal division were all characteristics of instruments built in New York and New England as well as of organs imported from England. In Pennsylvania organs divided stops were employed infrequently; the second manual used the same compass as the Great, extending up from C; and pedals were often included. Some stops used by Tannenberg are not found in New England and New York specifications, for example: Quintaden, Salicional, Flauto Amabile, Gemshorn, and 4′ Salicat.

IV

PENNSYLVANIA

Introduction

Colony of Contrasts

LATE eighteenth-century Pennsylvania was almost equally divided between people of English and German backgrounds. They were neighbors geographically, but culturally their differences remained distinct. English-speaking Philadelphia had been caught up in the momentous events and objectives of the Revolution. It was the world of Washington, Jefferson, and Franklin. The largest city and temporary capital of the new postwar nation, Philadelphia attracted not only statesmen but also leaders in cultural pursuits. By 1790, with a population of over 40,000, Philadelphia had two libraries, a theater, and the American Philosophical Society, then in its forty-seventh year [168, p.282].

The growing tensions between the colonies and England before the Revolution had little meaning for the German immigrants. Most of them were farmers and were not immediately affected by the tax, trade, and embargo regulations that were a source of such irritation to the colonists engaged in commerce and industry. Having endured much more personal persecution in Germany, many of them were probably eager to avoid any further conflicts. One can imagine also that the German speakers felt an isolation from the English-speaking colonists, and a consequent isolation from the issues of the Revolution, which were reinforced by the closed communities in which some of them lived and their adherence to ideals of nonviolence.

Organ Builders

At this time most of the organ builders in Pennsylvania were German; Philip Feyring, David Tannenberg, and Johann Philip Bachmann

48

were all immigrants. Near the end of the eighteenth century two families of German background began long and interesting histories as organ builders. The Dieffenbachs and Krausses, working independently in rural Pennsylvania communities, produced organs of high quality. For them, organ building was usually a part-time occupation, and their instruments were made for churches and residences in neighboring areas. Although they never achieved widespread fame, the Dieffenbach and Krauss organ builders made a significant contribution to the music history of Pennsylvania.

Philip Feyring

Contemporary Critiques

The New Organ, which is putting up in St. Paul's Church in this City, will be in such Forwardness as to be used in Divine Service on Christmas Day: It is of a new Construction, and made by Mr. PHILIP FYRING [*sic*], Musical Instrument-maker, in this City, who may, with Justice, be said to be the best Hand at that ingenious Business on the Continent. [Cited in 42, p.159.]

So read the patrons of Benjamin Franklin's *Pennsylvania Gazette* on December 23, 1762.

The success of the new organ and the Christmas Day service inspired a long poem, which appeared in the *Gazette* on December 30, 1762. It concluded with a tribute in the typical style of the day:

> Whilst Organ's dulcet Notes the Breast inspire
> With true Devotion, and a sacred Fire;
> Thy name, O FYRING, thy deserving Name
> Shall shine conspicuous in the Roll of Fame:
> Ages to come, and Men in future Days
> Shall grateful pay their Tribute to thy Praise.
>
> [Cited in 42, p.160.]

Organs by Feyring

Feyring, a German Lutheran, was born at Arfeld, Germany, on September 5, 1730. Few details of his life are known other than that he came to America as a youth and soon established his reputation in Philadelphia as a builder of spinets and harpsichords. He was engaged to rebuild or repair organs in 1755 and 1767 (German Reformed Church, Philadelphia) and in 1763 (Market Square Church, Germantown). The Market Square Church was originally a High Dutch Reformed church but later became Presbyterian. The old church was replaced in 1838 by

A case by Philip Feyring, 1766. Christ Church, Philadelphia. *Photo courtesy Essex Institute, Salem, Massachusetts.*

a brick building, and an account of 1882 tells us "The old Dutch organ disappeared when the church did, in 1838, and nothing is left of it but the 'Trumpet angels in their golden glory,' which the simple-minded children thought, made the music that filled the church [494, pp. 277–78].

Feyring's fame as an organ builder rests primarily on the three instruments he constructed for Episcopal churches in Philadelphia. In addition to the one for St. Paul's Church mentioned above, he built organs for St. Peter's in 1763 or 1764 and for Christ Church in 1766.

Although the vestry at St. Peter's had agreed to the erection of an organ in 1763, by February 1764 the subscriptions were still not sufficient for completing the design [143, p.91]. The organ was finally installed in the north gallery. Displeased, however, that only half the gallery could then be let out for pews, the vestry recommended in 1774 that the organ be removed and sold, subject to the consent of the subscribers. Evidently no immediate action was taken, because it was not until 1789 that the vestry ordered a new gallery to be placed over the chancel for the organ and six gallery pews to be made for the location where the organ then stood. For some reason, the same organ was not reinstalled in the new gallery, but rather the 1762 organ from St. Paul's Church. The case is still to be seen, but what finally became of the original organ is not known. In 1815 a new organ by an unknown builder was installed in the Feyring case [378, pp.10–11]. Later organs in this church included those by Henry Corrie (1829) and Standbridge (1857).

In 1763 members of Christ Church subscribed five hundred pounds for an organ.[1] A committee was appointed, and Feyring was engaged as the builder. Completed in September 1766, this organ was used until 1836, when it was replaced by Erben, but the old case (still extant) was retained. The Feyring organ was reported to have 1,607 pipes, three manuals, and a two-octave pedal ranging up from 16' C. The twenty-seven stops were distributed as follows: Great, twelve; Swell, seven; Choir, five; Pedal, three [36, III, part II, p.226]. The Choir and Pedal were probably later additions. In 1767, a year after completing the Christ Church organ, Feyring died of consumption at the age of thirty-seven [6, p.28].

David Tannenberg

Tannenberg's Career

David Tannenberg's brilliant career as an organ builder in Pennsylvania spans roughly the last half of the eighteenth century—from 1758 to 1804. During this time he built four or five organs with Klemm (see p.468 n.6) and at least forty-one organs after Klemm's death.

Tannenberg was born on March 21, 1728 at Berthelsdorf, Saxony, on the estates of Count Zinzendorf, the patron of the *Unitas Fratrum*, or Moravians. His parents had left Moravia the year before to escape religious persecution. From 1738 to 1742 young David attended various Moravian schools, and also made a trip to Geneva in the company of Count Zinzendorf and about fifty other Moravians [6, p.7]. He was apparently an eighteenth-century school dropout from 1742 to 1746, but may have returned for some additional education between 1746 and 1748. On September 23, 1748 Tannenberg began his journey to Zeist, Holland. From there he went to England, and then to America, arriving in Bethlehem, Pennsylvania, on May 21, 1749.

Soon after arriving, Tannenberg was married to Anna Rosina Kern, who had traveled to America on the same ship. They had five children: three girls and two boys. Tannenberg had entered the Bethlehem community as a joiner, and one may assume that there was no lack of employment for anyone in this trade in the growing Pennsylvania communities. For a short time the Tannenbergs lived in Nazareth, but they returned to Bethlehem in 1754.

Here, in 1757, Tannenberg began working for the organ builder Johann Gottlob Klemm. The four or five organs produced by these two men before Klemm's death in 1762 constituted Tannenberg's apprenticeship. In 1765 Tannenberg moved to Lititz, remaining there the rest of his life and producing "an average of an organ each year" [6, p.26]. He was assisted by his son David, Jr., until 1781, and by his youngest child, Samuel, until the latter's sudden death in 1788. A joiner, Johannes Schnell, worked in Tannenberg's shop for several years beginning in 1786, and again from 1795 until 1804. In 1793 Johann Philip Bachmann arrived from Herrnhut to work for Tannenberg. Bachmann married Tannenberg's youngest daughter, and in spite of quarrels between father-in-law and son-in-law, Bachmann's assistance was necessary to meet the increasing orders for organs, particularly when old age prevented Tannenberg himself from making some of the more difficult trips to install them.

In addition to his profession, Tannenberg participated in other aspects of life in the Moravian community, some of which have been described by Armstrong:

> Tannenberg contributed to the musical life of Lititz also as a vocalist. He and Brother Andreas Albrecht, the village gunsmith, were the church's *cantores* and, as such, sang at least for the church's festive occasions. One of several of these occasions recorded was in 1771. Brother Gregor had prepared a psalm for the annual festival of the Single Brethren's Choir. It was distributed to those present, and then Albrecht and Tannenberg sang it while Brother Grube accompanied them at the organ.
>
> But Tannenberg's participation in the life of the community was not limited to its music. He was also a participant and leader in both the religious and secular life of the village. In 1768 he was admitted as an acolyte—presumably an assistant in the worship services. He was frequently chosen as one of the foot washers during Holy Week services, and also participated in the "Hourly Intercession," the round-the-clock prayer groups which were organized on behalf of Moravian missions.
>
> More important was his contribution to the secular affairs of Lititz. Tannenberg held many offices in the village over the years, most of them having to do with business and financial affairs. He is mentioned as collector or treasurer for various funds, and also served a term as township assessor. He served for many years on the Church Council, the Committee of Oversight, and at times on the Helpers'

Conference and the Greater Helpers' Conference, the latter two being advisory groups to the central management of the Moravian communities. [6, p.24]

On May 17, 1804 Tannenberg fell from a scaffold while he was tuning the new organ being installed in the Lutheran Church, York, Pennsylvania. The accident was not thought to be serious, but the seventy-six-year-old Tannenberg died two days later.

Contemporary Critiques

Tannenberg's instruments received considerable attention and favorable comment during his lifetime. An account of the dedication of the 1770 Lancaster organ in *The Pennsylvania Gazette* for January 10, 1771 found this organ superior to Feyring's:

> Yesterday we had the pleasure of hearing for the first time the new organ of the High Dutch Reformed Church, of this place, accompanied with a variety of vocal music composed for the occasion, which I may venture to say, not only proved by my own experience, but by the approbation of all present was never equaled in any place of worship in the province or perhaps on the continent. The organ was made by David Tannenberger of Lititz—a Moravian town nearby —and I dare venture to assert, is much superior in workmanship and sweetness of sound to any made by the late celebrated Mr. Feyering [*sic*], who is so generally taken notice of for his ingenuity. It does great honor to the maker and is worth the attention and notice of the curious who may happen to pass this way. It will doubtless recommend him to all who are desirous of having work of that nature.
> [Cited in 42, p.120.]

Four years after the installation of the 1774 Lancaster organ, it was described by an enthusiastic, if inaccurate, traveler and army officer, Thomas Anburey.

> The town of Lancaster has no building of any consequence, except the Lutheran church, which is only built of brick, the inside has a most magnificent appearance; the large galleries on each side, the spacious organ-loft, supported by Corinthian pillars, are exceedingly beautiful, and there are pillars of the Ionic order from the galleries to the roof. The altarpiece is very elegantly ornamented; the whole of the church, as well as the organ, painted white with gilt decorations, which has a very neat appearance; it greatly reminded me of the chapel at Greenwich Hospital; the organ is reckoned the largest and best in America, it was built by a German, who resides about seventeen miles from Lancaster, he made every individual part of it with his

own hands; it was near seven years in compleating; the organ has not only every pipe and stop that is in most others, but it has many other pipes to swell the bass, which are of amazing circumference, and these are played upon by the feet, there being a row of wooden keys that the performer treads on. I do not recollect ever seeing an organ of this construction, except those of the Savoy Chapel and St. Paul's; in the latter they are shut up as the vibration of sound was found too powerful for the dome; but then they had only four or five of these wooden keys, whereas this organ has a dozen; the man who shewed the instrument played on it, and the effect of these keys was astonishing, it absolutely made the very building shake. It is the largest, and I think the finest I ever saw, without exception; and when you examine it, you wonder it did not take up the man's whole life in constructing; to estimate its goodness and value, I shall only tell you it cost two thousand five hundred pounds sterling. . . . [3, II, pp.303–305]

When the new organ for Zion Church (St. Michael's and Zion German Evangelical Lutheran Church), Philadelphia, was completed in 1790, an elaborate dedication ceremony was held. On Friday, September 3, a special program was given for President Washington and his aides. Later, on September 24, Governor Mifflin and his officials attended a similar event. Finally, four public services of dedication were held on October 10 and 11. *The Neue Philadelphische Correspondenz* reviewed the proceedings on the following day:

> I believe that Zion Church of the German Evangelical Lutheran Congregation in this city is the most beautiful building in all Philadelphia, and if I err in this judgment, then at least anyone who has seen it will admit that it is one of the most magnificent buildings in all America, and that none which are dedicated to the worship of God approach it in size, proportion, and decoration. An entirely new organ has now been placed in this splendid church, an organ which surpasses everything that one has seen of organs in Philadelphia, and which those who have traveled throughout America profess to be the most magnificent and largest in this part of the world.
>
> Many of the most populous cities in Europe do not yet have such an organ, and it must be a special joy for Americans that this lovely and beautiful instrument is the work of Mr. David Tannenberg, from Lititz, in Lancaster County, who on his own initiative first began organ building here in America, but through reading, thought, and untiring diligence has so perfected his craft that even if the most skillful organ builder from Europe should come here and should test this work of his, according to the judgment of connoiseurs he would have to bestow only praise upon him and appreciate his work.
>
> This beautiful and large organ was played for the very first time on Sunday, the 10th instant at 10 o'clock in the morning, and dedicated

with a solemn address by the Rev. Dr. C. H. Helmuth, senior pastor of
the Evangelical Lutheran congregation in this city.

[Translated in 519, p.4.]

Characteristics of the Organs

Tannenberg's organs ranged in size from one manual with three
registers to three manuals, thirty-four registers, but most of them were
one-manual instruments (see the summary of his organs, pp.58–62).
He built only one three-manual organ—for Zion Lutheran Church,
Philadelphia, 1790. The two-manual organs include the 1770 instrument for the German Reformed Church, Lancaster, Pennsylvania, and
the 1800 organ for the Moravian Church, Salem, North Carolina. In
addition, we may suppose that an organ built in 1774 for the Lutheran
Church of the Holy Trinity, Lancaster, with twenty stops and pedal also
had two manuals. The prices paid for three additional organs might
place them in the two-manual category. Toward the end of his life,
Tannenberg signed a contract with the Moravian Church in Bethlehem
for a two-manual organ, but he died before the organ was built. Eleven
organs were known to be one-manual instruments. Judging from the
information that is available concerning prices and numbers of stops, an
additional eleven were probably also of one manual. The size of twelve
organs remains a mystery. Pedals were included in all of Tannenberg's
larger plans, and are also found in some of the one-manual specifications.

The basic manual scheme of Tannenberg's organs consisted of
principals at 8′, 4′, and 2′, and flutes at 8′ and 4′ pitches. Two 4′ stops
appear with great consistency regardless of the size of the organ or of
the division. To this scheme was often added an 8′ Gamba, Quintaden,
or Salicional, and a Twelfth. A Mixture might next be added, or an
additional 8′ voice. Reeds were comparatively rare. In the fifteen surviving specifications of Tannenberg organs, the only occurrences of
reeds were in the 1770 two-manual organ for the Lancaster, Pennsylvania, German Reformed Church (a divided 8′ Hautboy on the second
manual), and four reeds on Tannenberg's largest organ, built in 1790
for Zion Lutheran Church, Philadelphia (Hauptwerk 8′ Trumpete,
Oberwerk 8′ Vox Humana, Echo 8′ Hautbois, and Pedal 16′ Posaune).
The 1804 York organ (now in the York Historical Society) contained an
8′ Trumpet, but the pipes now used in that stop are not the original
ones. The scheme proposed shortly before Tannenberg's death for a
two-manual organ for the Bethlehem Moravian Church listed two
reeds: an 8′ Oboe on the Hauptwerk and a 16′ Posaunen Bass in the
Pedal.

The standard Tannenberg Pedal division was 16′ Subbass and 8′

Octave,[2] and the manual(s) could be coupled to the Pedal. Again, the notable exception is the 1790 Zion Lutheran specification, which contained the largest Pedal division in America: 16′ Principal Bass, 16′ Subbass, 8′ Octav Bass, 6′ Quinta, 4′ Octave, and 16′ Posaune [6, p.101].

Manual keyboards were usually of fifty-four notes, C to f[3], although the 1791 Spring City organ has a compass of only fifty-one notes, C to d[3]. A twenty-five-note pedal compass seems to have been usual. Tannenberg did not use a pedal that merely pulled keys down from the manual and had no independent stops.

Among the documents preserved in the Moravian Music Foundation archives and evidently used by Tannenberg is a 1764 German treatise on organ building by Georg Andreas Sorge. It contains information on pipe scales, pipe metal, and winding the organ. In preparing to restore the one-manual Tannenberg organ at Old Salem, North Carolina, Charles McManis found that the pipe scales in the treatise had been followed "fairly consistently" [385, p.18]. He also described the pipework in Tannenberg's 1802 organ at Hebron Evangelical Lutheran Church, Madison, Virginia:

> The Madison organ is lightly nicked in the manner of Gottfried Silbermann. . . . Case pipes have slightly heavier (though not by 'Romantic' standards) nicks spaced from one-eighth to ³⁄₁₆″ apart, with light nicks between them. Metal pipes inside the case are nicked lightly, fewer nicks being used in the treble as would be expected. Volume in most instances seems to have been controlled at the mouth, with an occasional pipe having required slight toe coning for better speech and volume control. [385, p.19]

According to Dean, this organ is on wind pressure of slightly less than two inches [42, p.146].

Tonally, the Tannenberg organs closely resemble German Baroque characteristics. The sound is transparent and bright, and the stops are generally balanced with each other in loudness. There is a genuine ensemble sound when 8′ and 4′ principals are drawn, and the 2′ adds a top of well-developed harmonics.

The 8′ and 4′ foundation in the little four-stop organ at Lititz is voiced quite gently, and the bright 2′ is necessary to form an ensemble sufficient for congregational singing. The organs at York, Pennsylvania, Spring City, Pennsylvania, and Madison, Virginia, have 8′ and 4′ principals that are more assertive and are closer to the harmonic development of the 2′. One has the impression that the organ now in Lititz, Pennsylvania, represents Tannenberg's chamber-organ concept, while the other three organs are suitable for somewhat larger rooms or larger congregations.

In adding successively the stops of the principal family, including mixture and mutation stops, one notes that each stop contributes an equal amount, but differing characteristics, to the harmonic development of the ensemble. Particularly interesting is the effect of the Terz that Tannenberg sometimes included in the specification to add a reedy quality to the ensemble. Examples of it may be heard today in the York organ, which includes a two-rank Sesquialtera, and in the Madison, Virginia, organ, which has a Terzian 1⅗', breaking back to 3⅕' at middle C. In his restoration of the organ now at Old Salem (Winston-Salem), McManis also included a 1⅗' Terzian. That these are ensemble stops is evident from their inclusion as undivided stops on one-manual instruments.

Little can be ascertained concerning the tonal characteristics of Tannenberg's Pedal divisions. The only one that is presently playable is at York. Here the two stops follow the style of the manual in clarity. To achieve a balance with larger manual combinations, the coupler must be used.

Two of Tannenberg's organs contained enclosed divisions: the two-manual organ built in 1800 for the Moravian Church in Salem and the Zion Lutheran organ of 1790 (the third division, or "Echo" was enclosed).[3]

The cases of the larger Tannenberg organs characteristically have a large center tower and smaller end towers separated from the center by flats. Various arrangements of elongated feet, with both graduated and horizontal pipe mouths, may be observed. Examples of the typical case arrangement are found in the following organs: 1770 Zion Lutheran (Moselem), 1791 Zion Lutheran (Spring City), 1800 Home Moravian Church (Salem, North Carolina), and 1804 Christ Lutheran (York). It was also used in the 1770 and 1774 organs for Lancaster. Although both of the Lancaster cases have been enlarged by the addition of flats and towers on the sides, the original plan may still be seen. The smaller instruments were placed either in rectangular cases (as was the 1798 Salem organ) or in a Chippendale-style case topped by a broken pediment (as may be seen in the 1793 organ now in Lititz). Again, various plans were used in the treatment of pipe feet and mouths.

The reversed console arrangement, occasionally used by Tannenberg throughout his career, was employed in the 1759 Klemm-Tannenberg organ in Bethlehem, and in the instruments for Lititz (1787), Nazareth (1793), and Salem (1798 and 1800). The usual plan, however, placed the keyboards in the front of the organ case.

Foot levers were introduced in some of the organs, to add or withdraw one or more stops mechanically. The Spring City organ contains two foot-operated controls: an on-off control for the 4' Octave, and one for the 4' Octave and Fifteenth.

Wind supply for the smaller organs could be furnished either by an

David Tannenberg's last organ, 1804. Built for Christ Lutheran Church, York, Pennsylvania. Now in the Museum of the Historical Society of York County. *Photo collection of the author.*

assistant, using hand-operated bellows, or by the organist, using foot power.

It is a sorry comment on the way our national organ history has developed that only eight of Tannenberg's organs are preserved today, and only six of them are playable in more or less their original condition. In addition to these eight instruments, the cases of three more are extant.

The Organs of David Tannenberg

1765   Moravian Chapel, Lancaster, Pa.
        Cost: £ 50.
1765–68 Moravian Chapel, York, Pa.
        Organ of 3 stops.
1766   Residence, Philadelphia, Pa.
1767   Albany, N.Y.
1768   Lutheran Church, Maxatawny, Pa.
1769   German Reformed Church, New Goshenhoppen, Pa.

1770 Zion Lutheran Church, Moselem, Pa.
One manual, 6 stops. Extant, restored in 1974.

1770 German Reformed Church, Frederick, Md.
Cost: $193.37. May have been made by another builder, and repaired or installed by Tannenberg.

1770 German Reformed Church, Lancaster, Pa.
Two manuals and pedal, 15 stops. Cost: £ 250.
Case (enlarged) is extant.

1771 Trinity Lutheran Church, Reading, Pa.
One manual and pedal, 11 stops. Cost: £ 230.

1772 Unknown.

1773 Hebron Moravian Chapel, Lebanon, Pa.
Cost: £ 45.

1774 Holy Trinity Lutheran Church, Lancaster, Pa.
Probably two manuals. Known to have had pedals and 20 stops.
Case (enlarged) is extant.

1775 St. Mary's Roman Catholic Church, Lancaster, Pa.

1775 Evangelical Lutheran Church, Frederick, Md.
Cost: £ 400.

1776 Lutheran and Reformed Church, Easton, Pa.
One manual, 8 stops.

1776 Single Brethren's House, Bethlehem, Pa.
Cost: £ 60.

1777 Single Brethren's House, Lititz, Pa.
Cost: £ 50.

1780 Mr. Fischer, York, Pa.

1782 Moravian Chapel, Hope, N.J.

1783 Hagerstown, Md.

1784 German Reformed Church, York, Pa.

1786 Lutheran and Reformed Church, Egypt, Pa.
Cost: £ 145.

1787 Moravian Church, Lititz, Pa.
One manual and pedal, 9 stops. Cost: £ 200.
Extant. Stored in Lititz.

1790 Zion Lutheran Church, Philadelphia, Pa.
Three manuals and pedal, 34 stops. Cost: £ 1,500.

1791 Zion Lutheran Church, Spring City, Pa.
One manual, 6 stops. Cost: £ 150. Extant and playable.

1793 Moravian Church, Graceham, Md.
One manual, 4 stops. Cost: £65 or £70. Extant, playable.
Now in Lititz, Pa.

1793 Moravian Chapel, Nazareth, Pa.
One manual and pedal, 9 stops. Cost: £274. Case is extant.

1795   German Reformed Church, Philadelphia, Pa.
1795   St. John's German Reformed Church (Hain's), Berks Co., Pa.
Eight stops.
1795   "Guts'town"
May have been an installation of some previous organ.
1796   Zion Lutheran Church, Baltimore, Md.
Cost: £ 375.
1797   Ziegel Union Church, Macungie, Lehigh Co., Pa.
Cost: £ 400.
1798   Lutheran and Reformed Church, Tohickon, Pa.
Cost: £ 200.
1798   Moravian Chapel, Salem, N.C.
One manual, 5 stops. Cost: £ 150. Extant, playable.
Now in Chapel of Single Brethren's House, Old Salem.
1798   Single Sisters' House, Lititz, Pa.
Cost: £ 50.
1799   Moravian Church, Lancaster, Pa.
Cost: £ 260.
1799   St. John's Lutheran Church, Montgomery Co., Pa.
Cost: £ 200.
1800   Moravian Church, Salem, N.C.
Two manuals and pedal, 16 stops. Cost: over £400.
Now in storage in Old Salem.
Only extant 2-manual Tannenberg.
1801   St. Stephen German Reformed Church, New Holland, Pa.
One manual, 10 stops. Cost: £ 200.
1802   Hebron Evangelical Lutheran Church, Madison, Va.
One manual, 8 stops. Cost: £200. Extant and playable.
1804   Christ Lutheran Church, York, Pa.
One manual and pedal (25 notes), 11 stops. Cost: £355.
Extant, playable. Now in Historical Society, York, Pa.

Representative Specifications of Tannenberg Organs

I. A one-manual organ built in 1791 for Zion Lutheran Church, Spring City, Pennsylvania.

Manual: 51 notes, C–d³

Principal	8′
Gedakt	8′
Dulciana	8′
Octav	4′
Hohl Flote	4′
Super Octav	2′

[6, p.102]

II. A one-manual organ built in 1802 for Hebron Evangelical Lutheran Church, Madison, Virginia.

Manual: 54 notes, C–f³

Dullcis	8′
Gedackt	8′
Principal	4′
Flute	4′
Quinta	3′
Fifteenth	2′
Terzian	(1–24) 1⅗′
	(25–54) 3⅕′
Mixtur	II

Mixtur Composition

C-b	19–22
c¹–f³	8–12

[*OHS 1964 Convention Program*]

III. A two-manual organ built in 1770 for the German Reformed Church, Lancaster, Pennsylvania.

Upper keyboard

Principal, of metal	4′ tone
Flauto Traversa (metal through half the manual)	8′
Quinta Tona	8′
Hautboy (divided)	8′
Floet duo [douce], of wood	4′

Lower keyboard or manual

Principal	of metal	8′
Octave	ditto	4′

Lower keyboard (continued)

Supper Octave	of metal	2′
Quinta	ditto	6′
Viol de Gambe	ditto	8′
Mixtur	ditto	IV
Grob Gedackt	ditto	8′
Klein Gedackt	ditto	4′

Pedal

Supbass	of wood	16′
Violon	ditto	4′

[From the original contract, cited in 6, pp.65–66.]

IV. A three-manual organ built in 1790 for Zion Lutheran Church, Philadelphia, Pennsylvania.

Main Manual

1. Principal	8′
2. Quintaden	16′
3. Gambe	8′
4. Gemshorn	8′
5. Gedackt	8′
6. Trompete	8′
7. Octave	4′
8. Quinte	3′
9. Octave	2′
10. Flöte	4′
11. Mixture	IV–VI

Upper work

1. Princip. dulc.	8′
2. Quinta dena	8′
3. Vox Humana	8′
4. Flöte amab.	8′
5. Gedackt	8′
6. Nachthorn	4′
7. Solicet	4′
8. Hohlflöte	2′
9. Cimbel	IV
10. Fistel quint	3′

Echo—to Tenor F		*Pedal*	
1. Dulcian	8′	1. Principal Bass	16′
2. Flöt Traver	8′	2. Posaune	16′
3. Rohr Flöt	8′	3. Quinta	6′
4. Hautbois	8′	4. Subbass	16′
5. Fistula oct.	4′	5. Octav Bass	8′
6. Nachthorn	4′	6. Octave	4′
7. Echo Bass	8′		

Cimbel Stern, Sperr Ventill, two Couplers, Tremolo

[6, p.101]

The enclosed Echo had a nagshead swell, which McManis cites as "evidence of English influence in this obviously German style organ at Zion Church" [385, p.16].

Johann Philip Bachmann

Bachmann's Career

Johann Philip Bachmann was born in Kreuzberg, Thuringia, Germany, on April 22, 1762. As a boy he learned carpentry from his father. After leaving home at the age of sixteen, he became interested in the Moravians, and lived in several of their communities, ultimately at Herrnhut. There he learned to make musical instruments.

Meanwhile, David Tannenberg, concerned that he had no apt apprentice and no one to carry on his work, got permission from the elders at Lititz to send to Herrnhut for help. Bachmann arrived in Pennsylvania on February 17, 1793, and in April of that year he married Tannenberg's daughter Anna Maria.

By this time, Tannenberg had already built twenty-six organs, in addition to those he had built with Klemm. Bachmann assisted Tannenberg with organs until 1800, at times having complete charge of the installations. In that year, however, disagreements between the two men came to a head, aggravated, no doubt, by the suicide of Anna Maria in 1799. The disagreements were resolved sufficiently that Bachmann later installed the Tannenberg organ in Madison, Virginia, and in 1803, when Bachmann built his first organ, the metal pipes were supplied by Tannenberg. Bachmann continued to build organs until 1821.[4] After that he turned to building pianos and to cabinet work. He died in 1837 [6, pp.48–53].

Organs by Bachmann

After Bachmann left Tannenberg's shop he built seven organs and also contracted to complete an organ for St. John's Lutheran Church,

Philadelphia. This instrument was begun in 1818 by Matthias Schneider, but Schneider either could not or would not fulfill his contract. After many delays and difficulties, the church finally dismissed Schneider and negotiated with Bachmann to complete the organ. In a letter to an official of St. John's Church, Bachmann revealed an understanding of the function of upper partials worthy of his German background:

> it is a pity that your fine organ has not got a better disposition and mensuration, and also that there is no couple from the pedal to the great organ as the pedal itself is not very good. In the first place there are too many 16 feet pipes and nothing to give them animation, because a 16 foot C will have no strength without there is an 8 foot C along with it. In that case the 8 foot C will set the 16 foot C in motion.
> [384, I, p.12]

A one-manual organ for Friedens Lutheran Church, Myerstown, shows the typical complete principal chorus on the manual.

Friedens Lutheran Church, Myerstown, Pennsylvania
JOHANN PHILIP BACHMANN, 1819

Manual: 54 notes		*Manual (continued)*	
Diapason	8′	Fifteenth	2′
Stopped Diapason	8′	Mixture	III
Quintadena	8′		
Octave	4′	*Pedal:* 18 notes	
Harmonic Flute	4′	Bourdon	16′
Twelfth	2⅔′		

[6, p.116]

This organ was moved to Tacoma, Washington, in 1904, and was used in the Luther Memorial Church there until 1933.

The Dieffenbach Family

Family Background

> Four generations of the Dieffenbachs built pipe organs in Millersburg, Bethel Township, from 1776 to 1900. I know of no other organ-building concern in this country which has operated under the same name for so long. [382, p.6]

This remarkable succession had its beginnings with John Jacob Dieffenbach (1744–1803) and was continued by his son Christian (1769–1829), his grandson David (1798–1872), and finally by his great-grandson Thomas (1821–1900). In the small town of Millersburg, now named Bethel, these Pennsylvania Dutch builders supplied many of the small churches in their area with organs made by time-honored methods, and in comparative isolation.

Like so many other craftsmen in the early history of the organ, the Dieffenbachs were part-time organ builders, engaging also in cabinet-making and other occupations. Their production was neither large nor continuous; most of the known instruments can be traced to either Christian or Thomas (who also rebuilt some of the earlier Dieffenbach organs). But the workmanship, particularly in the early Dieffenbach organ cases, merits a place of distinction in American organ history.

John Jacob Dieffenbach's grandparents were Germans from the lower valley of the Rhine. In 1709, with other members of the Reformed Church, they left their home to find religious freedom. By way of England they journeyed to America, only to meet with frustrations and more intolerance imposed by the British in New York. Many of the group finally moved to Pennsylvania, and thus in 1723 the Dieffenbach family settled on Tulpehocken Creek on the Berks-Lebanon county line [44, p.2].

John Jacob, the First Dieffenbach Organ Builder

John Adam Dieffenbach was probably born in the New York settlement and made the trip to Pennsylvania with his parents as a young boy. Here he grew up, worked as a miller, and raised his family. One of his seven children was John Jacob, who learned carpentry and cabinet-making. He married Sabina Schmeltzer, and the couple moved to a large farm near Bethel [44, p.3].

Just what prompted John Jacob, in his thirtieth year, to become obsessed with the idea of building an organ is a mystery. Perhaps he had read about organs or had been told about them by older members of the settlement. The family historian, Victor C. Dieffenbach, relates:

> There was at that time no organ in the entire settlement, log buildings had been erected for holding religious services. The early pioneers were a pious folk. But when they sang the hymns of their forefathers they missed the music of the organ. Singing without instrumental accompaniment was similar to mortar minus hair—it didn't hang together. [44, pp.4–5]

This attitude is a striking contrast to the opposition instrumental music encountered so frequently in our early history.

Whatever John Jacob Dieffenbach's previous musical experience might have been, the report that there was an imported pipe organ in Philadelphia seems to have stimulated him to action about 1774. The story of his visit to this organ is most colorfully told by Victor Dieffenbach:

So one day J. J. D. told his family: I am going to Philly to see that organ; and when I come back I am going to build one myself! So said, so done. One morning he filled his pockets with fried sausage, dried beef, bread wrapped in muslin—eatables that would keep for several days, his stout oaken cane, and set out for the city of Brotherly love. Arriving at his destination the church having the organ, the sexton showed him the organ. J. J. D. now took from an inner pocket a small notebook, a footrule and pencil. He measured the height of the organ and put it down in his book, so many feet so many inches from front to back, so many doors, pipes etc. etc., all this he had down in black and white in his little notebook. The caretaker questioned him as to where he lived, how he came, what was his occupation? After telling the man he was a farmer and had walked. The caretaker then asked the young rustic. "Why do you measure the organ all over?" "I'm going to build one when I get home!" Well the caretaker said—"I have some errands that need my attention—you just go ahead with your measuring. I'll be back later." (He well knew that the dumb farmer would not take the organ on his back and run off with it.) Then he went to several members of church Council and told them, "there's a lunatic in the church" and told what J. J. D. had told him. The Council rushed to the church, questioned this uncouth farmer in cow-hide boots and barn-fall trousers; they soon found out that he was far from a lunatic. Arriving home J. J. D. proceeded to make the case of the organ out of previously cut and well dried native black walnut lumber. He made the plans or working drawings from his notes and built a case approximately two thirds the size of the organ he had measured in Phila. Once the shell was finished, he started on the pipes, some of these were of wood and square in shape; these he easily made. Soldering the Zinc pipes, there J. J. D. was up against it—he couldn't solder—he didn't know how. Discouraged he stored the entire project in the loft of the pigsty—a log building with a forebay like a barn. My great grandfather showed me the place when I was a lad of ten and told me that under the roof the organ had lain for a year. Along came a tramp—a German "rumlayfer" or traveling journeyman. He stayed there as long as it took to solder the pipes. J. J. D. then constructed a niche in the wall of his dwelling, also lifted the ceiling to set up the organ in his house and play it. [44, pp.5–6]

Organs by John Jacob and Christian Dieffenbach

Dieffenbach Opus 1 is now in the Museum of the Historical Society of Berks County, Reading, Pennsylvania. The imported Philadelphia organ that served as Dieffenbach's model has not been identified. It could have been the organ built by Johann Adam Schmahl and brought to this country from Germany in 1750 for installation in St. Michael's Church. Feyring's organs in St. Paul's, St. Peter's, and Christ Church had attracted considerable attention in the 1760s, and could have been seen by Dieffenbach, even though they do not qualify as imported. Tannenberg's two Philadelphia church organs had not yet been installed.

The case of Dieffenbach's organ, while differing in detail, has the characteristic structure used in Tannenberg's larger organs, with a large center tower flanked by a pair of flats, and smaller end towers. The case pipes are painted blue with gold trim. The bellows are operated by foot.

Twenty years later, in 1796, the next known Dieffenbach organ was placed in the Bernville Church. It is a curious fact that our present list of known Dieffenbach organs contains one entry every four years from 1796 to 1816:

1796   Bernville Church
1800   New Hanover
1804   St. Joseph's (Hill) Lutheran, Pike Township
1808   Zion Lutheran, Orwigsburg, Schuylkill County
1812   St. John's Reformed Church, Host
1816   Altalaha Lutheran, Rehrersburg

All of these locations are in Pennsylvania, within a limited distance from the organ shop in Bethel.

John Jacob died in 1803, so the organs after that date on the above list were definitely the work of Christian Dieffenbach, perhaps assisted by his son David in the 1812 and 1816 installations. The New Hanover organ survived until the church was renovated in 1903, when a new instrument was installed by Bates and Culley, retaining some parts of the old organ. An old picture of the church, evidently taken just before the renovation, shows that the Dieffenbach case was in the German style, with three rounded towers and two flats. Twelve stops are visible in the picture [159, p.25]. The Hill Lutheran organ was dedicated on May 8, 1804, and was evidently used for more than a hundred years; the church's next organ was built by Edwin Krauss in 1916. The Orwigsburg organ was rebuilt in 1884 by Thomas Dieffenbach and is now installed in a private residence in Ellicott City, Maryland.

Although Christian Dieffenbach's last two instruments belong to a later chapter chronologically, they are included here for the sake of continuity. Little is known of the organ for the Reformed Church in Host, Pennsylvania. A history of the church merely states that the organ was built in 1812 by Christian Dieffenbach and "was remodeled in 1885 by Thomas Diffenbach [sic], a grandson of the original builder. The cost of remodeling was $300.00" [77, p.41].

The last of the known Christian Dieffenbach organs, and certainly the most impressive, is the 1816 organ for the Altalaha Lutheran Church, Rehrersburg, Pennsylvania. It has a manual compass of fifty-one notes and a seventeen-note pedal. The specification is:

Manual		*Manual (continued)*	
Open Diapason	8′	Stop Diapason	4′
Stop Diapason	8′	Flute	4′
Violin Principal	8′	Nighthorn	4′
Flute	8′	Salicional	4′
Dulciana	8′	Quint	3′
Principal	4′	Fifteenth	2′

The case, in typical early Dieffenbach style, is particularly noteworthy. Eugene McCracken has described it well:

> Many persons think its case is the most beautiful of all those built by the Dieffenbachs. It is patterned after the German baroque style. A carved capital surmounts each of the three towers. Wood filigree crowns the flat section separating the towers.
> . . . The pipes of this organ present a rainbow of white, red, yellow, orange, and blue. [382, p.7]

In 1886 Thomas Dieffenbach installed a reversed console and added a 16′ Pedal stop to this organ. They were removed, and the original recessed console replaced, in a 1973 restoration by Thomas Eader.

The Krauss Family

Family Background

It was in September 1733 that Klemm arrived in Pennsylvania with a group of Schwenkfelders. This same migration brought to Pennsylvania another family important to the history of organs: the Krauss family, consisting then of Anna Krauss and her four children.[5]

The Schwenkfelders, like the Moravians, were forced to find new homes because of religious persecution. They came mainly from villages in Silesia. In 1726 they fled to Saxony seeking the protection of Zinzendorf in Herrnhut. When they were again compelled to flee (1732–34), they migrated to Pennsylvania. Having had to leave virtually all their possessions behind in Silesia, the Schwenkfelders had worked in Saxony as farmers and craftsmen. By the time of their eventual arrival in Pennsylvania, they were for the most part destitute. However, their frugality and industry, aided, no doubt, by their closely-knit community, made it possible for them to establish themselves as people of property and means. They were self-sufficient, having in their number carpenters, weavers, farmers, spinners, and other craftsmen. Self-sufficiency, of course, was absolutely necessary, and no doubt when another craft was needed, someone set about learning it. The Schwenkfelders held education in high regard, and in 1764 they established a public school system. Classes were conducted in private homes for about twenty-five years, but the teachers were appointed and salaried.

It was in this atmosphere that John and Andrew Krauss, great-grandsons of Anna Krauss, established a tradition of organ building that was to endure for three generations. But organ building was only one of the accomplishments of this remarkable family. Some members distinguished themselves in the production of farm machinery, milling, and other industrial pursuits.

Members of the Krauss family who engaged in organ building were the brothers John (1770–1819) and Andrew (1771–1841); three sons of Andrew—Joel (1801–1852), George (1803–1880), and Samuel (1807–1904); and George's son Edwin B. Krauss (1838–1929). As in the case of the Dieffenbach builders, the organ-building activity of the Krauss family extends much beyond the scope of the present chapter, and only part of the work of the first generation will be considered at this time.

Unlike the Moravians and the Lutherans, the Schwenkfelders were opposed to the use of musical instruments in church. As with many other religious groups that came to America in the early days, congregational singing was unaccompanied, and a tuning fork was used to give the pitch. The first organ (probably a reed organ) was not used until the new meetinghouse was built in Worcester in 1882 [304, p.12]. Under these circumstances, it is all the more surprising that the Krausses should have become interested in organ building. Tradition tells us that their activity in this field was so frowned upon by the Schwenkfelders that some members of the family eventually left that faith.

John and Andrew Krauss

To recite the beginnings of Krauss organ building, we must go back to one of Anna Krauss's children, Balthasar (1706–1774), who was twenty-seven years old upon arrival in Pennsylvania and who settled in what later was known as Kraussdale. A tuning fork, which may have been the family's only musical instrument, was said to be among the possessions he brought to the new world [463, p.21]. One of his sons, also named Balthasar (1743–1805), was the father of the organ builders John and Andrew. Along with their father and brother, George (1783–1844), John and Andrew are said to have built an organ in 1790—the first in their section of the country—using only Grandfather Krauss's tuning fork as a guide. This story is recounted in several articles, but without any verification or source [304, p.12; 463, p.27; 60, p.152].

While it is hard to imagine that the Krausses might have planned and built an organ with no background or visual model, it is not so hard to believe that they might have become interested in the instrument by seeing an organ or organs in their area. It may have been more than coincidence that the traditional date for the first Krauss organ corresponds with the date of installation of the Tannenberg organ in Zion Lutheran Church, Philadelphia. Significantly, a copy of the consecration service of the Tannenberg organ is preserved among the Krauss papers at the Schwenkfelder Library, Pennsburg, Pennsylvania. By this time Tannenberg had completed some twenty-five organs, in addition to those he had built with Klemm.

John Krauss probably attended the public schools, but had no further opportunity for formal education until 1790, when the Hosensack Academy was opened. Then a young man of twenty, he enrolled and concentrated on the study of languages. After two years he entered the school at Chestnut Hill, near Philadelphia, where he studied mathematics, surveying, astronomy, and navigation. He spent a year at Chestnut Hill, and then in 1794 and 1795 served as a teacher at the Hosensack School [463, pp.22–23]. From 1796 to the year of his death, 1819, John kept diaries, which form a valuable source of information about the early Krauss organs (see Appendix).

Details of Andrew's education are not known. From 1796 to 1812, he and John worked together building organs. Their younger brother, George, became a farmer and stayed at the old homestead. In 1812 John left the organ business and went into the manufacturing of wool carding machines and surveying. Andrew continued building organs, and is said to have built forty-eight organs in his lifetime [304, p.17].

Krauss Organs

Krauss organs of this period include the following:

1790   Home organ, built by John, Andrew, George, and father, Balthasar.
1796   Wentz's Reformed Church, Worcester, Pennsylvania.
1797   Small organ for George Smith.
1797–8 Long Swamp Church, Pennsylvania.
1797–9 Roman Catholic Church, Goshenhoppen (now called Bally), Pennsylvania.
1802   Organ for Mr. Dobit.
1802–3 Pottstown, Pennsylvania (probably for Old Brick Church, later called Zion's Reformed).
1806   Allentown, Pennsylvania.
1806–7 St. Paul's Lutheran Church, Red Hill, Pennsylvania.
1808   Chamber organ.

In 1798, David Tannenberg's son Johann David was employed by John and Andrew Krauss for a period of sixteen months. He assisted them with building organs for the Long Swamp Church and for the Roman Catholic Church at Goshenhoppen [6, p.49]. Johann may have supplied the Krausses with some valuable information from his father's files. Among the Krauss papers preserved in the Schwenkfelder Library in Pennsburg is a copy of the Sorge treatise of organ building—the same one that was available to David Tannenberg. According to the title page, the treatise was copied by John Krauss in 1798.

The Church of the Most Blessed Sacrament at Goshenhoppen (now called Bally), Pennsylvania, possesses the oldest Krauss organ still in use. As completed in 1799, it contained one manual, ten stops, and a thirteen-note pedal. This scheme was enlarged to two manuals, sixteen stops by Edwin B. Krauss in 1864. At that time the pedal compass was increased to eighteen notes. In 1962 the organ was restored by Hartman & Beaty.

Other Builders in Pennsylvania

John Lowe

The monopoly that German organ builders held in Pennsylvania was seldom interrupted. An exception was John Lowe (or Loewe), an apprentice of Robert Gray in London, who arrived in Philadelphia about 1795. His list of accomplishments is neither long nor impressive, and virtually nothing is known of the quality of his work.

In 1804 he built an organ for Peale's Museum in Philadelphia's old State House (Independence Hall) [383, p.4], but the most colorful story of his career is in regard to the organ he built for St. John's Chapel, New York (St. John's dates from 1807). All went well, apparently, until Lowe sent the finished instrument on its way to New York by ship. En route it was captured by a British frigate and held for a ransom of $2,000. The money was paid, the organ recovered, and in 1813 it was finally installed by Thomas Hall.

The organ had been in use for twenty-six years when unusual circumstances again occurred. Trinity Church, New York, found itself in the embarrassing position of having a new organ and no place to put it. A contract had been awarded to Firth & Hall, but before the organ arrived the Trinity Vestry decided that Trinity needed a new church building. So the Firth & Hall organ was placed in St. John's in 1839, and the Lowe organ was "packed away in a tower" [104, p.295]. Finally, it was given to St. Clement's Church in 1845. No more is heard of this organ, and we may imagine that it finally expired from natural causes.

Lowe also built an organ for Zion Lutheran Church, Philadelphia.

After the Tannenberg organ in this church was almost entirely destroyed in a fire, the church rented an organ from Charles Taws, which was used until January 1804 (see p.81). Finally John Lowe was selected to "rebuild" the old organ. The result was practically a new organ, since only some pipes were saved from the Tannenberg instrument. Lowe finished it in 1811, and left Philadelphia a few years later [383, p.4].

Joseph Downer

The first organ built in western Pennsylvania was the product of Joseph Downer. He was born in Brookline, Massachusetts, on January 28, 1765, the son of Dr. Eliphalet Downer. Before he was twenty, young Downer decided to move to what was then considered the West. He started for Ohio but settled on a tributary of the Monongahela in Pennsylvania. Here, near Fayette City, he put up a gristmill and sawmill, and "later added machinery for spinning cotton and weaving jeans" [318].

Soon after arriving in this location, Downer began building organs, and is said to have completed three [42, p.163]. One of them was eventually acquired by the Carnegie Museum.[6] The stop names and most of the pipes are missing from this one-manual, six-stop organ. It is in a white case, ornamented in relief and with gilded display pipes. The keyboard has a compass of forty-nine notes, G to g³.

One can imagine the excitement that this organ caused in the frontier society. An amusing story about it is related by W. J. Holland:

> At the time the instrument was being built the infant settlement was filled with wonder and people came from far and near to observe, and, when it was completed, to hear it played. The story is told that on one occasion a party came twenty miles for the purpose of hearing the organ and on entering the house, one of the company, seeing an old-fashioned warming-pan hanging on the wall, asked "Is that the organ?"
>
> "Well," said Mr. Downer, "I am somewhat bashful about playing an organ before people, but I will go into the next room and play it for you." Whereupon he took down the warming-pan, and such delightful music came from the next room that the strangers were filled with amazement, but finally were disillusioned amid much laughter. [318]

Other organ builders in Pennsylvania during this period were Peter Kurtz, John Schermer, and E. W. (or E. N.) Scherr in Philadelphia; Alexander Schlottmann in Oley Furnace; and Conrad Doll in Lancaster.

V

BUILDERS IN OTHER LOCATIONS

AND IMPORTED ORGANS

Introduction

WITH the notable exception of Pennsylvania, organ building in this country was virtually at a standstill during the last four decades of the eighteenth century. In New England, Josiah Leavitt built his first organ in 1786, marking the tentative beginning of a new era, and Henry Pratt began building small organs in 1792, but the long, continuous, and impressive history of New England organ building actually stems from the opening of William Goodrich's shop in 1804.

Similarly, in New York the first organ builder whose work assumed significant proportions was John Geib, who did not arrive there until about 1798. The handful of small organs constructed in the Carolinas, important as they were in the musical life of their communities, had little relationship with the overall history of the organ. Only the two organs Tannenberg built for Salem bore the mark of a master craftsman.

In spite of the lack of activity in organ building, organs continued to appear in new locations. The first church organ in Georgia was presented to Christ Church, Savannah, by Colonel Barnard of Augusta in 1766. If it was still in the church in 1796, it was probably destroyed in the fire that burned Christ Church to the ground in that year[1] [101, p.36]. Two small organs were used in St. Michael's Church, Charleston, South Carolina, before the arrival of an English organ in 1768. One of them was rented in 1761, and the second was loaned to the church in 1762.[2] In Fredericksburg, Virginia, a lottery was conducted in 1768 to raise money for a new church and an organ to go in it [168, pp.138–39], and in the same year the *Virginia Gazette* (June 23) carried the notice: "On Sunday the 12th instance, the Organ just erected in Stratton Major Church [Williamsburg] was used in Divine service for the first time ..." [168, p.141]. Five years later St. Mary's Parish, Caroline County, Virginia, was advertising for an organist [168, p.139].

Organs appeared not only in new geographical locations but also in new situations. The diary of Ezra Stiles (entry for July 10, 1770) gives an unenthusiastic account of the organ installed in Princeton University about 1760:[3]

> Perhaps about ten years ago there was an Organ erected in Nassau Hall for the use of the Scholars at public prayers—on Ldsdays the college attend pub. Worship in the Meet[g] h. of the Town of Prince-town. I then thought it an Innovation of ill consequence, & that the Trustees were too easily practiced upon. They were a little sick of it. The organ had been disused for sundry years, & never was much used.
>
> [149, p.58]

Social events and public entertainments occasionally included the use of an organ. In Richmond, Virginia, for example, one could hear organ music at the Hay Market Garden (a resort and ballroom) in 1802; at showings of collections of wax figures at Mr. Hallam's Washington Tavern in 1804, and at the Bell Tavern in 1810; or at the opening of the Virginia Museum in 1817 [149a, p.94].

With the exception of Pennsylvania, Americans depended largely on English builders to supply their organs, a condition that endured until the War of 1812. While this situation may have delayed progress in American organ building, the result was not entirely negative; organs of England's most noted builders graced American churches, serving as models for local craftsmen.

New England

Leavitt and Bruce

Organ building, as we have seen, was usually a part-time activity for men otherwise engaged in a variety of crafts. Joiners, clockmakers, and metal craftsmen found it an engaging way to 'moonlight," using their skill with tools and mechanical knowledge. Organ building also held attractions for professional people. Josiah Leavitt (1744–1804) was a practicing physician in Sterling, Massachusetts, when he built his first organ in 1786. Leavitt had had an interest in organ construction since he was a young man, and it is said that he frequented the workshop of Thomas Johnston. At the age of forty-two, he decided to build a small organ of four stops. He was assisted by a young man from Templeton, Massachusetts, Eli Bruce.

Bruce (1767–1839) was a skilled mechanic. Adept in many of the practical arts, he was a cooper, mason, clockmaker, and inventor of several machines [236, p.165]. Bruce later (1790) completed a four-stop organ of his own, consisting of a Stopt Diapason, Principal, Twelfth, and Fifteenth. Probably Leavitt's organ contained a similar specification.

Dr. Leavitt lived in Maine for several years and then moved to Boston, where he continued to build organs. He also completed a combination organ-harpsichord that was praised by the well-known organist Selby [42, p.203]. The instruments could be used either separately or together. A reflection of Leavitt's approach to organ building is seen in an advertisement that appeared in the *Oracle of the Day* (a Portsmouth, New Hampshire, publication) on Christmas Day, 1793:

> Josiah Leavitt, Organ-Builder, Boston, Having a Church-Organ nearly completed, . . . (except the Case and Pipes)—and whereas the price of said Organ when finished, will be greater, or less, in proportion to the number of pipes, and elegance of the case, which shall be made for the same, he begs leave to inform any Church or Society, that may wish to contract with him for the said Organ, that it shall be finished, in the above respect, as may be most agreeable, provided timely application be made.
>
> He likewise informs the public, that he has completed and for sale, an elegant House-Organ, with a Mahogany case, and which might be sufficient for a small Church or Society; which should it be purchased, and sound not large enough to answer their expectation, will be received by him, at any time within the course of one year from the delivery, in part pay for one of a larger size.
>
> [Cited in 123, pp.22–23.]

A one-manual Leavitt organ, purchased in 1793 by the First Universalist Church of Boston, shows a typical eighteenth-century style:

Open Diapason	8′	Fifteenth	2′
Stopt Diapason	8′	Sesquialter	
Principal	4′	Trumpet	8′
Twelfth	2⅔′		

[236, p.165]

Other churches that installed Leavitt organs included an Episcopal Church in Dedham, Massachusetts, Worthington Parish, Hartford, Connecticut, and the First Congregational Church of Newburyport, Massachusetts. It was a particular accomplishment that Josiah Leavitt, a Congregationalist, was able to place instruments in dissenting churches. Many of these churches were still violently opposed to the use of the organ, an attitude that some of them retained through much of the next century.

William Goodrich

While Eli Bruce was building his organ in Templeton, Massachusetts, he was often visited by a thirteen-year-old boy who was no doubt fascinated by the intricacies of organ construction. William Marcellus Goodrich (1777–1833) had early exhibited a mechanical aptitude and an inventive nature. Without formal education, Goodrich had learned to repair and clean watches and clocks and to use the tools of the joiner. He also had a knowledge of music, and was said to possess a "fine musical ear" [225, p.26]. It is interesting to see how Goodrich gradually acquired the other skills he would need to become one of the most respected of America's early organ builders.

In 1798 he went to work for Henry Pratt, an organ builder in Winchester, New Hampshire. Here he may have learned to make and voice wooden pipes. Pratt's knowledge, however, was limited, and Goodrich stayed only a few months. He then went to Boston, where he became acquainted with Captain Joshua Witherle. Captain Witherle had a large chamber organ that had been built by a Mr. Jenneys, an engraver, and he was interested in making some improvements in it. Thus it was that Goodrich was invited to stay in the Witherle home. This situation was particularly fortunate for Goodrich because Witherle was a pewterer, and from him one could learn to cast and solder pewter and brass. Together they made a Twelfth, a Fifteenth, and a Trumpet for the organ. Goodrich also worked occasionally for Witherle's son, a brass founder; this additional experience in metal-craft was to be of great value to Goodrich in his career as an organ builder [225, p.27].

Goodrich remained in the Witherle home for four or five years, except for some months he spent away from Boston. The variety of Goodrich's activities during this period were described by a biographer in 1834:

> He was, for a number of weeks, with Mr. John Mycall, at Newbury-port, repairing and tuning his organ. He taught singing-schools in Harvard, Groton, and other towns. He constructed, in conjunction with Mr. Baldwin, a fire-engine, at Groton. He was, at one period, probably in 1803, in the employment of Mr. Benjamin Dearborn, the maker and inventor of the patent balance, who was then engaged in perfecting a new gold balance for the banks. [225, p.27]

For a while Goodrich resided with Mr. Mallet, a piano tuner and organist of Dr. Kirkland's church, and "organized a piano-forte" belonging to Mr. Mallet [225, p.28]. An organized piano-forte was a piano with a set of organ pipes attached, an instrument that had a short-lived popularity during this time.

The Goodrich Brothers and Thomas Appleton

In 1804 Goodrich entered into a partnership with Benjamin Crehore of Milton, a piano maker. Goodrich's brother Ebenezer also joined the firm. However, the partnership was dissolved after a few months, and the Goodriches opened a shop in Boston. Ebenezer Goodrich (1782–1841) worked with his brother until 1807, when he opened his own shop. He built two chamber organs in Boston, and then moved to Cambridgeport, where he built seven more chamber organs between 1808 and 1810. When he returned to Boston in 1811, he continued to specialize in building small instruments [400, p.211].

In 1806 William Goodrich became acquainted with one of Boston's future leaders in organ building, Thomas Appleton (1785–1872). Appleton's introduction to the Goodrich shop is described in the biography of Goodrich:

> He [Appleton] was then about one-and-twenty, having served an apprenticeship with a cabinet-maker. Intending to set up this business, he had imported a lathe from England; but his ill health preventing his beginning immediately, he sold the lathe to Mr. Goodrich. This produced an acquaintance between them; and Mr. Appleton, being at leisure, was very frequently in Mr. Goodrich's shop. On the restoration of his health, some time in the year 1807, Mr. Appleton became a regular workman and companion with Mr. Goodrich, both in the shop and the family. This arrangement continued uninterrupted till September, 1811. During this time, Mr. Appleton married the sister of Mr. Goodrich, which rendered the connexion between Goodrich and Appleton still more intimate. [225, p.29]

Between 1804 and 1811, six organs were built by William Goodrich, assisted by his brother during the first three years and by Appleton during the later years:

1804   Parlor organ (the Goodriches also built an "organized piano-forte" in this year).

1805–6   Organ for the Catholic Church (now Holy Cross Cathedral), Boston.

1806–7   Organ for the Unitarian Church, Cambridgeport.

1807   Organ for Mr. Samuel Cabot, Jr.

1807   Organ for a church in Walpole, New Hampshire.

1810–11 Organ for the Presbyterian Church in Federal Street, Boston.

The Cambridgeport organ deserves special comment in that it was a divided instrument placed on the two sides of a gallery. This may have been the first time this type of installation was attempted in America. Goodrich was never pleased with the result, and when he received this organ in part payment for a new one in 1828, he "entirely destroyed" the old organ [225, p.29].

In June 1811 a curious instrument called a Pan Harmonicon was brought to Boston. It was invented by Maelzel, whose name is usually linked with the Metronome. William Goodrich was employed to set up and exhibit the Pan Harmonicon in New York and other cities. He left his shop and his tools in Appleton's care and traveled with the instrument from September 1811 until June 1812. Events following Goodrich's return will be considered in chapter 7.

Henry Pratt

Henry Pratt's activity as an organ builder began late in the eighteenth century and extended well into the nineteenth. Pratt (1771–1841), like Leavitt, was a Congregationalist, and with this background he seemed to concentrate on organs suitable for the churches in which musical instruments were just beginning to find acceptance. He built twenty-three church organs and nineteen chamber organs, all one-manual instruments [400, p.210]. The church organs had from four to six stops, and the chamber organs were even smaller.

Pratt was born in Wrentham, Massachusetts, and moved to Winchester, New Hampshire, in 1792. He followed his father's trade as a house joiner, but was also skilled in various other fields. He spent his leisure "constructing wooden clocks, repairing guns, watches, &c. making fifes, violins, and other simple instruments, and in fabricating surgeon's instruments, tools for his own use, and other articles of a like nature" [400, p.209]. He is said to have built a small organ in 1792, evidently with what knowledge he had been able to gain from a Dictionary of Arts and Sciences [400, p.209].

In 1798 he was engaged to build an organ for a Samuel Smith, Esq., of Winchester. Never having seen an organ, unless he actually had fabricated one in 1792, Pratt examined the instrument then in the Episcopal Church at Claremont, New Hampshire. The name of Eli Bruce reappears at this time, for it was Bruce who furnished Pratt with pipe scales. Armed with this information, Pratt proceeded to construct an organ. It is said that Smith, in order to encourage Pratt in this endeavor, gave him a bushel of rye each day that the organ was under construction and a bonus of $300 when it was completed [42, p.218]. It has been in the Winchester public library since 1903, and is probably the oldest extant organ made in New England. It contains the following whole stops: Open Diapason, Stopt Diapason, Principal, Twelfth, and Fifteenth [400, p.210].

Pratt's work covered an unusually wide area for this early period. An incomplete list includes organs that were installed in churches in the Massachusetts towns of Middleborough, Sutton, Oxford, New Braintree, Wrentham, Monson, Westborough, Great Barrington, Leicester, West Brookfield, Rowe, and Fitchburg. He also built organs for the New Hampshire towns of Fitzwilliam, Keene, and New Ipswich; for Albany and Hudson in New York; for Bellows Falls, Vermont; and for Ellington, Connecticut.

Today, the best publicized of Pratt's organs is one that has been in the Storrowton Village of West Springfield, Massachusetts, since 1933. Built in 1821 or 1824, it lay forgotten for many years in the attic of Pratt's granddaughter Mrs. Maria Pratt Smith. It was discovered there by J. W. Morrison, who restored it in 1932. A more recent restoration (1972) was the work of Richard C. Hamar.

The Organ-Building Hobby

As early as the eighteenth century, organ hobbyists found that they could assemble an organ from parts they had purchased if they lacked the skill or inclination to make all the parts themselves. The diary of the Reverend William Bentley is our source of information about two such enthusiasts in Salem, Massachusetts. Bentley's entry of December 18, 1798 notes that Mr. Pickering Dodge had built an organ, having imported the stops [19, Vol. II, p.292]. Bentley returned to the subject of organs again on April 22, 1802, when he recorded:

> Had the Pleasure of seeing & hearing Dr. Oliver's Organ. It is the first ever built in this Town. The pipes were imported from London in separate stops. The frame is handsome, exhibiting a front of 5 by 8 feet probably, with pedals, exhibiting the pipes in a central Oval, & with two towers on each side, surmounted with some instruments of music in high relief with good effect. The wood work was finished by that ingenious mechanic Mr. Macintire. The Dulciana stop was fine, & worthy of any instrument. When this is pronounced to be the first it must be understood, completed. A Mr. Pickering Dodge, had begun one upon a smaller scale, & with fewer steps [stops], importing the pipes, & finishing it at his leisure. Dr. Oliver has made provision for several stops which he has not yet received, & so has Mr. Dodge, but Mr. Dodge has not proceeded so far as the Doctor.
> [19, II, p.427]

In a later entry (May 7, 1818) Bentley gives us an interesting glance at the man, Dr. Benjamin Lynde Oliver, and the later location of his organ:

As a dilettante in music he practiced much on keyed instruments without a voice for singing & at length he provided an organ, built under his own directions, which has been since disposed of to St. Peter's Church. He seemed to have practiced much till some German introduced a different style, which he neither studied nor practiced & therefore neglected his amusement. [19, IV, p.517]

Among the other New England organ builders of this period were George Whitefield Adams (Medfield, Massachusetts), Joel Allen (Middlefield, Connecticut), George Catlin (Hartford, Connecticut), John Meacham (Hartford, Connecticut), Dr. Israel Newton (Norwich, Vermont), and Streit (Winchester, Vermont). Little is known of the work of these men. Catlin built an organ for Christ Church, Hartford, about 1800. Meacham built an organ in 1808. Newton was the builder of an organ that Henry Pratt inspected in the Episcopal Church, Claremont, New Hampshire, in 1798.

New York

Organs for Sale

Although there was not the activity in organ building in New York that could be found in Pennsylvania during the years preceeding and following the Revolution, small organs were no doubt in use in greater numbers than have actually come to light. Advertisements of organs and organ builders appeared in the newspapers frequently enough to hint at a more extensive use of the organ than can be verified.

One such advertisement, in the *Royal Gazette* of July 19, 1780, gives a rather complete description of the organ for sale:

> To be sold . . . a complete Chamber Organ consisting of the following stops, a Principal throughout, a do. fifteenth, do. Stop Diapason, an open Diapason treble, and two Row Sequialtra Bats, all its stops draw by halves, so that the bass or treble may be strengthened at pleasure; it has a Forte Piano, and may be blowed by the Performer in front, or by an indifferent person at one end.
>
> The lowest price is One Hundred Guineas, the seller putting it up and tuning it. For further particulars enquire of the printer.
>
> [Cited in 64, p.373.]

Transcribed to the sterile form of a modern stop list, the organ contained

Open Diapason	8′	(treble only)
Stop Diapason	8′	(divided, treble and bass)
Principal	4′	(divided, treble and bass)

Fifteenth	2′	(divided, treble and bass)
Sesquialtra	II	(treble?)

The reader will have to draw his own conclusions about the "indifferent person" working the bellows.

The term "chamber organ" sometimes denoted a barrel organ. On October 20, 1785, the *New-York Packet* announced such an instrument, to be sold at a bargain price:

> For Sale, a Beautiful, well-toned Chamber-Organ, plays an oratorio by the celebrated Handel, and forty of the most favorite tunes. Originally cost Fifty Guineas, and will be sold for Thirty.
>
> [Cited in 64, p.373.]

One of the organ builders who availed himself of the classified section in 1772 was John Sheiuble. He made and repaired "all kinds of Organs, Harpsichords, Spinnets, and Piano, in the best manner, and with the greatest Dispatch." Mr. Sheiuble had recently come to New York from Philadelphia, and invited customers to see him "at Mr. Samuel Prince's Cabinet Maker, at the Sign of the Chest of Drawers" [63, p.366].

Although we know nothing of Sheiuble's work, he apparently remained in business, for he again advertised two years later in *The New-York Gazette and the Weekly Mercury* of October 10, 1774. He had "now ready for sale, one neat chamber organ, one hammer spinnet, one common spinnet" [cited in 63, p.366]. By this date he had changed the spelling of his name to Sheybli.

Thomas Dobbs and Charles Tawes (Tawse, Taws) were two builders who came to New York from England in the 1780s. According to the *Independent Journal: or, the General Advertiser* for August 13, 1785, Dobbs had just arrived "in the last ship from London," and was ready to build organs, harpsichords, and pianos for "Ladies and Gentlemen, who may have occasion for the above-mentioned Instruments" [cited in 64, p.360].

Tawes arrived a year later, and *The Daily Advertiser* of May 23, 1786 carried the announcement:

> Charles Tawse, Organ Builder, lately arrived in this City from Britain, builds and repairs finger and barrel organs. He also repairs and tunes spinnets, harpsichords, piano fortes and guitars.
>
> [Cited in 64, pp.363–64.]

In 1788 Tawes moved to Philadelphia, and was associated in business there with his two sons [84, IV, p.316]. One of his instruments was a three-manual organ built about 1800 for St. Augustine's Church,

Philadelphia. After fire destroyed the Tannenberg organ in Zion Lutheran Church, an organ was rented from Tawes and was used until 1804 (see p.71).

Other early builders whose names reach us through advertisements were Frederick Hayer, Peter Velat, and Monniot, Peloubet & Co. Apparently most of these instrument makers either turned to other employment or left New York. Of the organ builders mentioned above, only Thomas Dodds is listed in Redway's *Music Directory of Early New York City*[4] (assuming that Dobbs and Dodds are one and the same). Dodds appears in the *Directory* from its earliest year (1786) until the time of his death (1799), with the exception of the years 1788, 1796, and 1798. His name appears as an organ builder, and later as "musical instrument-maker." From 1791 to 1793 he evidently had a partner, as the listing is "Dodds & Claus."

John Geib

The first organ builder in New York to make a significant contribution to our history was a German, John Geib (1744–1819). Geib & Co. or John Geib & Co., as the factory name was sometimes given, had manufactured pianos and organs in London before coming to this country. There the firm built 4,910 pianos, 400 "organized" pianos, and "church and chamber organs in proportion" [65, p.328]. At least one of Geib's organized pianos later made its way to New York, as J. & M. Paff, musical instrument dealers advertised for sale in *The Daily Advertiser* of January 2, 1800: "An elegant organ piano forte, made by the celebrated Geib and Co. organ builders in London . . ." [cited in 65, p.334].

By 1800, however, Geib had been established in New York for at least two years, and had built at least two organs.[5] A visit Geib made to Baltimore in 1803 is also credited with stimulating greater concern about organs there [90, p.62n]. Organs built by Geib include:

1798–99 German Lutheran Church (Christ Lutheran, later known as St. Matthew's), New York.
1798 North Reformed Church, William and Fulton Streets, New York (information of uncertain reliability).
1800–2 Christ's Church, Ann Street, New York.
1802–3 St. George's Chapel, Beekman Street, New York.
1803–4 First Congregational Church, Providence, Rhode Island.
1806 Central Moravian Church, Bethlehem, Pennsylvania.
1808 North Church, Salem, Massachusetts.
1810 Grace Church, New York.

The opening of Geib's organ for the German Lutheran Church, an instrument of 800 pipes, was announced in *Argus. Greenleaf's Daily Advertiser* of January 8, 1799:

> John Geib, most respectfully informs the amateurs of music . . . the Organ built for the Lutheran Church, in William and corner of Frankfort street will be exhibited to view from 12 o'clock in the afternoon till 3; and the two eminent men, Mr. Rausch, and Mr. Moller will perform for the time; when also a few anthems will be sung by eminent singers. . . . [Cited in 64, pp.362–63.]

The specification of this organ, as it appeared in a letter Geib wrote, was:

1. OpDiapasson throughaute from treble [double?] GG. to F in alt—
2. Stopdiapason   do —do —do
3. Principal—   do —do —do
4. 12th   do &c
5. 15th   do &c
6. Tiers   do &c
7. Cornet   treble)
8. Sesq.   Bass) 3 rankes
9. Trumpet—throughaute as befor

Swell from Fidle G

1. opd or Dulciana
2. Stopd
3. Principal
4. Hautbois

Two pair of bellowes, an ellegant best mahogany case, gild front and ornaments—9½ by 15 feet. Duble && in front, and a set of keys in great organ, and one set from fidle G in Swell—a trimland—the cost 1000 in this place. [Cited in 364, p.2.]

While no details are available about the North Reformed Church organ (there may be some doubt that Geib built an organ for this church), the one in the Ann Street Church (Christ's) is well documented. This instrument replaced a London-made organ previously used in the church. While Geib's two-manual organ was still in use, it was described in an 1824 issue of *The Lyre*:

> This organ was built by the late Mr. John Geib, of this city; several of the stops are remarkably fine, and, upon the whole, the instrument is a good one, giving very general satisfaction.
>
> The *exact* dimensions we are not acquainted with, but presume it is about 17 feet high, 11 feet wide, and 7 deep. The compass is from GG to F in alt. The stops are as follow, viz.

Great Organ	Swell and Choir
Open Diapason,	Stop Diapason, treble,
Stop Diapason,	Stop Diapason, bass,
Principal,	Dulceana, treble,
Twelfth,	Principal, treble,
Fifteenth,	Hautboy, treble,
Tierce,	Flute, treble and bass,
Cornet, treble, 3 ranks.	Fifteenth treble and bass.
Sesquialtrra [*sic*] bass, 2 ranks,	Trimland.
Trumpet.	

The stop Diapason, Dulceana, Principal, Hautboy, and Trimland are in the swell; the other stops on the same sounding-board, but out of the swell.

There is a coupling stop to unite the two rows of keys, and a shifting movement to take off the loud stops in the great organ. There is also one octave and half of pedals for the feet, which communicate with the bass of the great organ.

The present organist of the church, is Mr. Wm. Blondel, a young man of fine talents, who promises fair to become a first-rate organist, and an ornament to the profession. [402]

In 1823, Christ's Church moved into a new building on Anthony Street, but part of the congregation continued to hold services in the Ann Street building. However, they finally disbanded in 1825, and a year later the building was sold to a Roman Catholic church, also named Christ's Church. The Geib organ remained intact until the church burned in 1834. The organ in St. George's Chapel probably met a similar fate when that church burned in 1814.

When the First Congregational Church in Providence decided to buy an organ, the church committee was advised against giving the contract to Geib because his organs were said to cost more than those imported from London. David Vinton, chairman of the organ committee, investigated the new English organ built by Avery for the First Church, Salem, Massachusetts, and also corresponded with Geib. Geib's reply of June 6, 1802 to the question of comparative costs has a style all its own:

Mr. Vinton had also the goodness to observe to me, whate he seen at Salem—and that the Organ cost only 341 pounds Sterling, with a deal case; painted, no annulet; and add the Expenses of Paking; fright; insurence; Duty; and till it is put up, will cost from 2000 dollars—and upwards, and then run the Risk, if a good one—well if not —no indepenting on my good work—and flater myselfes, that I thinke to be capable of building an organ with Mr. Avery of London, or a Monser Clico of Paris, and a few more in Europe, and beside responsible for every thing build or manufactured by me.—Considring all advantages—the building an Organ consisting in such a number of different articules, in the country where it is to stand, and to be used, must certainly have the perseverance in durability, and a few dollar connot been a opject to a Society of gentlemen,—a friend of mine seen the Organ at Salem and speak but slightly about it—and I think, I could build one for the same whate that Cost, an the same plane—Sin hier follow a description of the organs I have build for this City, which will be a quiet to the gentlemen to fram the Contract.

[364, p.2]

The letter continued, giving the specifications for the German Lutheran Church and Christ Church organs, and citing the costs as $1,000 and $1,200. Whoever advised the Providence church that Geib's price would be high was quite right: the church agreed on a price of $2,500 for an instrument similar to the Christ Church organ!

Geib had difficulty in getting the Providence church to meet the terms of their agreement. Payments were supposed to begin the month of the contract but they were delayed. Meanwhile, Geib was in financial trouble, and had to transfer his company to his son's name to protect it from seizure. In the *American Citizen and General Advertiser* for October 2, 1802, the following notice appeared:

A Commission of Bankruptcy has been issued by the Judge of the District Court of the United States for the New-York District, against John Geib of the city of New-York, Organ-builder and Trader. . . .

[Cited in 65, p.331.]

Geib finally had to send an agent to Providence to collect, and the organ was delivered on December 5, 1803.

In June 1814 a fire destroyed the church. Some of the pipes from the organ were saved, however, and the Goodrich company of Boston was selected to build an organ using the Geib pipes. That instrument was in turn replaced by one built by E. & G. G. Hook in 1846 [362, pp.6–9].

The 1806 organ for Bethlehem, Pennsylvania, was used in the Central Moravian Church until it was replaced by a Jardine organ in 1873. It was then moved to the Moravian Parochial School, where it remained for many years. Unfortunately, vandals stole some of the pipes, and when the theft was discovered, the church authorities had the rest of the organ, including the case, chopped up and thrown away. The organ had two manuals, pedals, and a reversed console. Some of its characteristics were described by Dr. T. Edgar Shields in 1943:

I recall that the tone was rather shrill, especially when the 2′ was drawn. Also that it had a pretty good 8′ tone on the Great, consisting of a large-scale Diapason, which they called a Principal, an open flute of the Melodia type, a 4' Principal, and a Fifteenth. I think there was a 4' flute, but cannot be sure. Then there was a Gamba of a rather peculiar quality, and a raucous Trumpet that was able to wake the dead. The Pedal was very good; that there were two and possibly three 16' stops I am sure, and the Violone was particularly fine. The pedalboard extended to the B before middle-C. The upper manual was of the Choir type. There was a stop of the Dulciana class on one of the manuals, I cannot recall on which. There was no swell pedal nor any combination pedals; the stops were drawn out several inches, and change of registration was difficult. In many respects the tone was somewhat crude. [Cited in 349, p.180.]

Geib's Salem organ was described by Henry K. Oliver, who had played it:

This organ had two full manuals, from GG to F, omitting GG sharp; but the bass of the upper manual (swell) was fixed, the keys being immovable, and with [without?] pipes, so that the bass of the Great Organ had to serve the swell also. Originally it had no pedal bass. The stops were, in Great Organ (56 notes),—Open and Stopped Diapason, Principal, 12th, 15th, Sesquialtera, Dulciana, Trumpet, and blank Viol di Gamba; in Swell (extending from tenor G upwards, 38 notes), Open and Stopped Diapason, Principal and Cremona. Its touch was exceedingly hard, even affecting skill in fingering.
[Cited in 42, p.208.]

Grace Church, New York, organized in 1805, received a gift of $5,000 from Trinity Church for the purchase of an organ. Unfortunately, the instrument was destroyed by fire in 1813. In addition to his own organs, Geib is credited with building the case for the 1802 Pike England organ in St. Paul's Chapel, New York [495, p.27].

The South

North Carolina

Closely connected with the Pennsylvania builders is the story of early organs in North Carolina. In 1752, twelve years after the founding of Bethlehem, Pennsylvania, the Moravians decided to establish a settlement in North Carolina. The following year, on October 7, settlers left Bethlehem for the new area, called Wachovia, and formed the village of Bethabara. A second village, Bethania, was settled in 1759, and in 1766 work was begun on a new town, Salem,[6] which was to be the central town of the settlement.

On April 20, 1762 a party of sixteen Moravians left Bethlehem to join the settlers in Wachovia. They took a riverboat down the Delaware from Easton, Pennsylvania, and then traveled down the coast to Wilmington, North Carolina, on the sloop *Elizabeth*. Riverboats carried them up the Cape Fear River to a place south of Fayetteville, North Carolina, and the final part of the trip was made by wagon. They arrived in Bethabara on June 8 [167, p.12].

In spite of difficulties that would leave a modern traveler gasping, the Moravians transported an organ to their new home, demonstrating again the importance that was attached to this instrument. The little one-rank organ was in the care of Pastor Johann Michael Graff, and he had it ready to play a month after arrival. An entry for July 8, 1762 in the Diary of Bethabara and Bethania records:

> Reaping continued. Br. Graff set up in our Saal the organ he brought from Bethlehem; and during the Singstunde in the evening we heard an organ playing for the first time in Carolina and were very happy and thankful that it had reached us safely. [160, p.3]

The origin of this organ is not known; Armstrong opines that it may have been the work of Klemm and Tannenberg, since Graff had been living in the Bethlehem-Nazareth area (see p.17).[7] The organ was moved from Bethabara to the Single Brethren's House in Salem in 1798. From 1824 to 1900 it was in the Moravian Church in Friedberg, North Carolina [6, pp.87–88].

An oft-related story of this organ is that it was played for some Cherokee Indians who had stopped in Bethabara in 1774. They were amazed by the remarkable instrument and thought that its music must be made by singing children hidden inside it. The Moravians then opened the organ case to show them that the mechanism contained no children [160, p.6].

When the decision was made to install an organ in Salem in 1772, the contract was given to Brother Joseph Ferdinand Bulitschek, a cabinetmaker and millwright, who had moved to Wachovia in 1771. His many abilities have been described by Vardell:

> He repaired the saw-mill at Bethabara; he made coffins for the deceased Brethren; he built cabinets to house and preserve the precious archives of the community; he understood the mysteries of flour-mill machinery, and could and did construct a bolting chest for making flour of fine quality which could be sold to outsiders for profit; for Brother Herbst, master of tannery, he constructed a small bark and fulling mill, carefully measuring the fall of the run and contriving a dam and an overshot wheel to furnish the power. He was a slow workman, and in the eyes of the careful Brethren the charges for his

professional services were high. And if the expenses of his projects exceeded his first calculation he did not hesitate to ask for more money. Such was the man who built the first Salem organ. [160, p.7]

Bulitschek did indeed ask for more money. The organ was to cost thirty-two pounds, but before it was finished he asked for (and received) an additional ten pounds, since he was making the organ with two stops instead of one [167, p.16].

The organ was placed in the back of the Gemein Saal at Salem, and was so constructed that the organist could see the minister and congregation through a small window in the organ. By 1781 some of the Salem musicians were dissatisfied with the tone of the organ, which "shrieks aloud when facing a congregation" [167, p.18]. For this reason the side toward the front was boxed up, and a top that could be opened or closed was made. Although the tone was reported to be much improved, the next complaint was that the creaking of the pedal controlling the enclosure, i.e., the swell pedal, disturbed the devotions of the congregation.

In 1798 this instrument was replaced by a Tannenberg organ, and Johann Philip Bachmann journeyed to Salem to install it.[8] This was an organ-moving year in Wachovia, for Bulitschek's Opus 1 was moved to Bethabara, replacing the old organ from Pennsylvania, and the latter went to the Single Brethren's House in Salem.

In 1773 Joseph Bulitschek built an organ for Bethania. It was used for more than 170 years and was finally destroyed by fire on November 3, 1942 [167, p.19]. While it was still in use, in 1934, it was described by the Reverend Herbert Spaugh:

> The organ has only one manual, which is built into the case. Above this is a small window, so arranged that the organist may keep the minister in view during the service. There are three stops of four octaves. Two of these stops include eight bass, or pedal, notes. The third has sixteen bass notes. There is no pedal keyboard.
>
> Originally the volume of tone was controlled by means of a rolling canvas shade covering the top of the instrument. This was operated by a strap running over a pulley at the top down to a pedal. At present this is not in use. [474]

Spaugh also notes that two foot pumps resembling stirrups operated the bellows until an electric blower was installed in 1931. The key depression was only about one-eighth inch, and the drawing of stops was "somewhat difficult" [474].

Another Moravian organ builder in North Carolina was Johann Jacob Loesch (1760–1821). A locksmith, clockmaker, and gunsmith, Loesch also began an English school for boys in 1789. Records for the

Elders Conference in Salem, August 2, 1797 stated: "Br. Jac. Loesch is going to come to Salem this week and start the tuning of our organ" [39, p.26]. A letter of April 16, 1804, from C. L. Benzien to the Unity Elders Conference, Salem, mentions an organ that Loesch had built:

> Br. Jacob Loesch, of Bethania, and his son Heinrich Jacob, left today with an organ which Br. Loesch has made. It has been bought by Pastor Storch, and will be set up in his house near Salisbury.
>
> [39, p.26]

There was at least one eighteenth-century Lutheran church in North Carolina that boasted an organ. "Organ Church" is a name found occasionally in rural areas where organs were scarce, and the possession of one was a mark of distinction. Several Organ churches are found in the Pennsylvania Dutch country. Rowan County, North Carolina, also gave this name to one of its early churches. Zion Lutheran, as it is more officially designated, was built of stone in 1791, "and an organ of excellent quality was built by Mr. Steigerwalt [Stirewalt], one of the members of the church" [133, p.281]. The organ was placed in the gallery, and was evidently used for many years. Eighty years later Gotthardt Bernheim mournfully recorded its silent presence:

> The old organ—a relic of the past—is still there, but its voice is no longer heard in the worship of the congregation; like the voices of its contemporaries, who are now mouldering in the adjoining graveyard, its spirit of music is fled, and the external remains, encompassing a number of broken and disarranged pipes, are all that is left to remind us of a former age, a former congregation, and of a master whom it once honored. [20, p.243]

Stirewalt was probably also the builder of a small chamber organ at Mill Hill Plantation, North Carolina.

South Carolina

The only organ builder known to have been in Charleston, South Carolina, in the eighteenth century was John Speissegger (sometimes spelled Spiceacre). The extent of Speissegger's activity remains ill-defined. There is a quotation in Bernheim's *History of the German Settlements* . . . that refers to a Speissegger organ: "In 1769 the officers [of St. John's Lutheran Church, Charleston] made a contract with Mr. Speisseggir for a new organ, but no statement is given as to its cost" [20, p.212]. The source of the quotation is vague, but it seems to have been taken from the journal of Reverend H. M.

Muhlenberg, D. D., written during his visit to the South in 1774.[9]

Speissegger is chiefly remembered for his connection with the installations of organs for St. Michael's, Charleston. He was a pewholder at St. Michael's, and his name has also been important in the musical history of that church during the twentieth century. From 1910 to 1918 a descendent of John Speissegger six generations removed, Arthur Speissegger, held the post of organist of St. Michael's [91, p.49]. When Mr. Sampson Neyle loaned an organ to the church in 1762, John Speissegger was employed to install it and keep it in repair [165, p.218]. Later, when the vestry was ready to purchase a new organ from England, whatever ability Speissegger may have had as an organ builder remained unrecognized by his fellow churchmen. A letter of May 7, 1766 to Charles Crockatt in London in regard to procuring an organ for the church contained the request:

> We must also intreat you to Engage with some proper person to come out with the Organ as we have no One here capable of putting it up, and you may depend we will pay him according to your agreement. . . .
> [165, p.220].

When the new organ built by John Snetzler finally arrived in August 1768, an accompanying letter from the London merchant who handled the transaction stated:

> I consulted Mr. Snetzler about sending out a Person to fix it up, & he recommends Mr. Speisegger now in Charles Town, as a person very able and equal to the Undertaking, and at the same Time assuring me, he could not send a better & fitter Person to do it.
> [165, p.223].

Accordingly, Speissegger installed the organ, and was given 120 pounds per year to tune the organ once every fortnight. In addition, he made repairs in 1786, 1792, and 1800.[10]

Imported Organs

John Snetzler

Noel P. Mander, the English organ builder wrote, "it is the writer's contention that the King of all 18th century organ builders was John Snetzler, the Swiss who came to England about 1750 and carried on the tradition of Bernard Schmidt and Renatus Harris" [360, p.342].

John Snetzler was born in 1710. He evidently had considerable experience before he moved to England (probably earlier than Mander's date of 1750). He was working with Müller when the latter built the famous organ in St. Bavo Church Haarlem. In England, Snetzler was on "intimate terms" with King George III, and was his official organ builder. His organs were noted for the brilliance of their choruses, their purity of tone, and the fine quality of their reeds. However, Samuel Green, who later surpassed the old builder in popularity, referred to Snetzler's organs as "snarling and raucous" [360, p.342].

Several Snetzler organs reached the colonies before the Revolution. A chamber organ, built in 1761, was imported before the Revolution, but was not unpacked until after the war. In 1784 it was given by Dr. Samuel Bard (founder of Bellevue Hospital and physician to George Washington) to his twelve-year-old daughter, Susannah, who is said to have played it for Washington [408].

In 1968 this organ was acquired by the Smithsonian Institution, and restoration followed. Chests, action, case, and all but sixteen pipes are original, making it a particularly interesting example of Snetzler's work. It contains five voices: Stopped Diapason (8′), Open Diapason (8′, treble only, from c¹), Flute (4′), Fifteenth (2′), and a divided Sesquialter (bass)–Cornet (treble) II. The compass is fifty-four notes, GG to e³ (lacking GG♯, AA♯, BB, C♯) [472, p.13].

Through the interest of the Lord Mayor of London, Christ Church, Cambridge, Massachusetts, acquired an organ built by Snetzler in 1761 or 1764. George Washington attended a service at Christ Church on New Year's Day, 1776, but since some of the pipes had been melted to make bullets, the organ could not be used, and the congregational singing was led by a bass viol and a clarinet [50, pp.57–58]. After the Revolution, what was left of the organ was restored and used until 1845. Contrary to popular reports, none of the pipes from this organ are to be found at Christ Church now.[11]

The Congregational Church in South Dennis, Massachusetts, has a 1762 Snetzler organ that is still in use. The early history of this instrument is not known. It was acquired by the South Dennis church in 1858. Later, some tonal changes were made, and in 1959 it was restored by the Andover Organ Company of Methuen. The recessed console has a compass of fifty-seven notes, extending from GG to e³ (lacking GG♯). The pedal has thirteen keys, permanently coupled to the bottom thirteen of the manual. There are no pedal registers. The original specification, derived from old handwriting on the toeboards and pipe racks, was probably:

Open Diapason	8′	Twelfth	2⅔′
Stopped Diapason	8′	Fifteenth	2′
Dulciana	8′	Sesquialtera	III
Principal	4′	Clarion	4′ (bass)
Flute	4′	Trumpet	8′ (treble)

[395, p.12]

An organ by John Snetzler, 1762, Now in the Congregational Church, South Dennis, Massachusetts. *Photos courtesy Thomas Murray.*

According to Fesperman, the organ for the Concert Hall, Boston, was a Snetzler instrument [53, p.27]. It was inaugurated in a concert on May 31, 1763, and was described as "a delicate and melodious new organ, made by the first hand and lately imported from London in Capt. Burges" [142, p.259].

In 1764 or 1765 the Klemm organ in Trinity Church, New York, was replaced by a Snetzler organ that cost about seven hundred pounds. It was destroyed in 1776 by a fire that also leveled the church and much of the lower part of the city. Because of the war, the church was not rebuilt until 1788 [147, p.55]. Trinity's Snetzler contained six reeds and four compound stops.

Trinity Church, New York, New York
JOHN SNETZLER, 1764 or 1765

Great		Swell (treble, from tenor g)	
Open Metal Diapason	57	Open Metal Diapason	34
Open Metal Diapason		Stopped Metal Diapason	34
(smaller scale)	57	Principal	34
Stopped Diapason	57	Cornet III	102
Principal	57	Trompette	34
Twelfth	57	Hautboy	34
Fifteenth	57		
Tierce	57	*Choir*	
Sesquialtera IV	228	Open Metal Diapason	57
Cornet V (treble)	145	Stopped Diapason	57
Fourniture III	171	Principal	57
Trompette	57	Flute	57
Clarion	57	Fifteenth	57
		Cromorne	57
		Vox Humana	57

[503, I, p.16]

Snetzler built an organ for St. Michael's, Charleston, South Carolina, in 1767, and it was installed the following year.[12] The vestry had corresponded with two London merchants, a Mr. Crockatt and John Nutt, to procure an organ. Meanwhile, the organist at St. Michael's, Benjamin Yarnold, wrote to Dr. William Boyce, then organist of St. Michael's, Cornhill (London), asking his assistance in this matter. The organ finally arrived on August 17, 1768, and was installed by Speissegger. The cost of the organ, including freight and installation, was 568 pounds [79, p.15]. In the late nineteenth century, George S. Holmes wrote:

> there is a tradition that it was first played at the coronation of George III in Westmin[s]ter Abbey, but there seems no foundation for this;

yet curiously enough, we find the vestry thanking Chas. Brockett [Crockatt?], Esq., for "enquiring about the Coronation Organ," but declining it as too costly; and this gives a hint of how the story arose.

[79, p.15]

The original specification of this organ is not known. It was repaired and altered by various builders. In 1894 the vestry consulted a former organist of the church. Mr. R. I. Middleton, regarding proposed repairs. His report gives us at least a general idea of the tonal characteristics:

> I think you possess something of far greater value, than the mere mechanical improvements which constitute the main features of so many modern Organs. Whatever changes, in the course of time may again be necessary, I would retain the original pipes as long as possible. It is further true that they are not *voiced* to sound as loud as is now the fashion, consequently the contrasts between loud and soft, especially in the swell, are not so striking; nevertheless, you have a sweetness all round, and an underlying *stratum* of soft but penetrating tone, which is all the more valuable as it becomes more rare.
>
> [165, p.229]

The organ was again in need of renovation in 1904. The Reverend John Kershaw recorded the difficulties experienced by the vestry in trying to preserve the old organ:

> We had the opinions of probably not fewer than ten to twelve representatives of organ manufacturers, and whilst every one of them recommended a new organ, not one of them would agree to undertake and guarantee a renovation of the old instrument . . . at last, with the greatest reluctance, and only under the pressure of stern necessity, our Vestry took steps to have erected a new organ, combining with it as many as possible of the old pipes, and preserving the old case, with such additions only as might be required to accomodate the new instrument, so that there might be left some reminders of our "Old World organ". . . . [91, pp.53–54]

The contract was awarded to the Austin Organ Company, and the new organ was installed in 1911. Wings with dummy pipes were added to the sides of the old case, and some of the pipes were retained. The front of the Snetzler case may still be seen as the central part of the present facade.

Another Snetzler organ came to this country in more recent times— a 1742 chamber organ purchased from a Dublin collection in 1913 or 1914. It is now in the Belle Skinner collection of Yale University. A chamber organ now in Wren Chapel of the College of William and Mary has been attributed to Snetzler, but details of its construction suggest that it was originally the work of another builder. This instrument was built for Lord Kimberley, Norfolk, England. It was acquired by Colonial Williamsburg, Inc. in 1954[13] [53, p.29].

Henry Holland

The English builder Henry Holland supplied two organs for the New World in the postrevolutionary period. One was for Trinity Church, New Haven (1784). The other, which is much more famous, was for Trinity Church, New York (1791), whose building and Snetzler organ had been destroyed by fire in 1776. Because of the unsettled conditions, rebuilding was delayed, but finally the new church was completed in 1788, and the Holland organ was ready three years later.

Messiter, whose kindest word for this organ was "an indifferent instrument," says "the tone was miserably weak and thin, the pipe scales being very small, especially in the bass." Trinity's eminent organist, Dr. Hodges, found it to be an "exceedingly poor affair" [104, pp.293–94]. The reviewer of *The Lyre,* writing in 1824, found, however, that this organ "in point of tone ranks very high" [407]. The Holland organ served Trinity Church for over forty-five years, after which it was set up in the German Reformed Church, Norfolk Street, New York.

Trinity Church, New York, New York
HENRY HOLLAND, 1791

Great Organ	Swell Organ (continued)
Open Diapason	Cornet
Open Diapason to gamut G	Trumpet
Night Horn	Hautboy
Fifteenth	
Sesquialtra, 3 ranks	
Cornet, 4 ranks	*Choir Organ,* in conjunction
Trumpet	with Great Organ
	Stop Diapason
Swell Organ	Dulceano
Open Diapason	Principal
Stop Diapason	Flute
Principal	Cremona

[407][14]

The organ had three manuals, without pedals. The Swell extended only thirty-five notes from tenor g. The Great and the Choir were both of fifty-eight notes, GG to f^3 (lacking GG$\sharp$), and were permanently coupled. This arrangement was described in *The Lyre*:

This organ is curiously constructed, the choir organ being made in part to serve for the fundamental parts of the great organ, by means of a communication between the two rows of keys: the great organ pressing down the keys of the choir, and the choir left to act for itself. [407]

Samuel Green

At least one organ built by Samuel Green came to America in the eighteenth century. Green (1740–1796) was in partnership with John Byfield, Jr., during the years 1770 to 1772. He then went in business for himself. In all, Green built or rebuilt over sixty organs.

Having refused the organ willed to the church by Mr. Brattle, the congregation of the Brattle Street Church, Boston, began to take a different view of church music and the use of the organ. Finally, in 1790 an organ was ordered from London. Not all the members agreed with such a move, for we find

one of the leading members of the Brattle Street Church offering not only to reimburse the church for the organ's purchase but also to contribute a sum of money to the poor, provided the "unhallowed instrument" were thrown into Boston Harbor. [320, p.294]

The organ cost four hundred pounds.[15]

Sir John Sutton, writing in the middle of the nineteenth century, described Green's organs as having Diapasons of a sweet but thin quality and ensembles lacking in fullness and brilliance. His Choir organs were "pretty toned, and would make nice chamber organs, but they want firmness" [cited in 151, p.173]. Of course, this criticism must be evaluated in relation to Sutton's mid-nineteenth-century viewpoint, but we may nevertheless judge from it that the Green organs were of a delicate design. Noel P. Mander has said that "Green's organs were just as good as Snetzler's but entirely different in character and much more orthodox in layout" [360, p.342].

In the Bruton Parish Church, Williamsburg, Virginia, there is an organ built by Samuel Green. However, it was not imported to this country until 1938. The October 1957 issue of *The Tracker* (p.7) reported that another organ built by Samuel Green is in the Kent-Delord House Museum in Plattsburgh, New York.

Astor & Company

A small organ built by Astor & Co., London, is in the Old State House, Boston. Dating from about 1788, it has a manual compass of fifty-three notes (lacking low C#), and tonal resources of 8′ Open

Diapason, 8′ Stopped Diapason (divided), and 4′ Principal. This little organ is interesting chiefly because it belonged to Oliver Holden, and he is said to have used it in composing many of his hymn tunes, including "Coronation." The organ was given to the Bostonian Society in 1898 by Holden's granddaughter Mrs. Nancy Tyler [357].

John Avery

The Reverend William Bentley, pastor of the East Church, Salem, Massachusetts, viewed with interest the growing number of organs in his denomination. On February 28, 1798 his diary entry noted:

> Seriously engaged in the First Church upon the subject of an Organ. Subscriptions have already amounted to one thousand dollars. The absolute want of vocal musick is a plea which they can advance with justice. The first Organs were at Old Church in Boston, Dr. Clarke's, then at Brattle Street, Dr. Thacher's, then at the New South, Mr. Kirkland, tho' one was provided soon at the Bennet Street by the Universalists. A few years since one was purchased for the old Church in Newbury Port. I have heard of no other Congregational Churches. The old Church in Salem has now made a subscription & an Organ will probably be obtained. There is a small one in the Cong. Church at Charlestown. [19, II, p.259]

On August 10, 1800, he recorded the arrival of the First Church organ: "The Organ for the Salem First Church has arrived at Boston. It was procured by Consul Williams who generously gave his services" [19, II, p.346]. The next month (September 15) Bentley wrote: "A Concert is determined for Friday, at the Old Church upon the New Organ" [19, II, p.349].

This organ was the product of the English builder Avery. It was also the subject of some correspondence between John Geib and the First Congregational Church of Providence, Rhode Island (see p.83). In 1892 Sumner Salter noted its presence in Salem, and later commented: "Avery was even more celebrated than Green. The dates of his organs range between 1775 and 1808" [454, II, p.58].

George Pike England

When Edward Hodges came to America and became organist of Trinity Church, New York, he was accompanied by his eldest son, George F. Handel Hodges. G. F. H. Hodges, also a musician, played the organ at St. Paul's while that church was without a regular organist. He wrote less than enthusiastic reports of the George Pike England organ in St. Paul's in two letters to his sisters in London. On May 7,

1840 he commented: "It is not by any means a fine organ, except as regards the tone of some of the stops. There are no Pedal pipes." His letter of June 21 of the same year reveals:

> The organ is no great shakes, though I make some great shakes upon it occasionally. It is an old one built by G. P. England, London. There are no pedals, and each rank of keys is separate and distinct from the other, and incapable of coupling or combining. [78, p.117]

George Pike England came from a family of organ builders. He was active from about 1788 to 1814, and died in 1816. His three-manual instrument built in 1802 for St. Paul's Chapel was installed in a case made by John Geib [495]. It was finally sold to the Immaculate Conception Church in Port Jarvis in 1870, when an Odell organ was installed in St. Paul's [503, I].

An interesting description of the St. Paul's organ appeared in *The Lyre,* twenty-two years after its installation:

> This instrument is certainly one of the finest in this country; the tones are particularly sweet and mellow, and the touch very pleasant. It was built by the late Mr. England, of London, who was considered inferior to none in that metropolis. The height of the organ is 22 feet, width 14 feet, and depth 8 feet. Compass, from GG to F in alt. The stops are as follow, viz.

Great Organ	*Swell Organ to Fed. G*
Open Diapason	Open Diapason
Stop Diapason	Stop Diapason
Principal	Principal
Twelfth	Hautboy
Fifteenth	Trumpet
Tierce	
Sesquialtra, 3 ranks	*Choir Organ*
Cornet, 5 ranks mounted	Stop Diapason
Trumpet	Dulceana
	Principal
	Flute
	Vox Humana

> The Trimland in this organ affects the whole instrument, but is seldom used.
>
> We would suggest that one or two stops of pedal pipes would very materially improve the organ, and give the organist much better opportunity of displaying its powers and fine tones. [406]

Two organs built by England were sent to Baltimore in 1804: one for St. Paul's Cathedral, the other for Christ Church. One of them is now located in St. Joseph's Roman Catholic Church, Taneytown, Maryland. It was rebuilt in 1875 by Henry Niemann.

Other Imported Organs

One of the most widely discussed English organs of this period was the 1771 instrument installed by George and Thomas Catlett in Mount Church, St. Mary's Parish, near Port Royal, Virginia. An organ in the Smithsonian collection was at one time thought to be this instrument, but that has been disproved beyond any doubt [292, p.2]. Another English organ was in Christ Church, New York, until it was replaced in 1800 by an instrument built by Geib. There was also an 1809 Elliot organ in St. John's Church, Portsmouth, New Hampshire.

Advertisements of small imported organs continued to appear in newspapers. Some were said to be suitable for churches, but many of them were clearly intended for home use. One such instrument was the bureau organ advertised in *The New-York Journal or General Advertiser* on November 13, 1766, to be sold by James Fuller "for the want of Money." It was described as

> A Very good and handsome Chamber Organ, which, with a few Minutes Instruction, any Person may play on: It has 6 Stops, 15 Mute Gilt Pipes in the Front, and a Set of Drawers at the Bottom; and will be sold cheap. [Cited in 63, p.371.]

A home organ of particular historic interest belonged to Robert Carter (1728–1804),[16] wealthy grandson of Robert "King" Carter and owner of the plantation Nomini Hall. He also maintained a house in Williamsburg, where he had a London-made organ. When Thomas Jefferson heard the organ, he was so impressed that he later tried unsuccessfully to buy it [168, p.136].

PART THREE

Organs in an Expanding Society
1810 – 1860

VI

SOME GENERAL OBSERVATIONS

Industrial Growth

THE Embargo Act of 1807, followed by the War of 1812, brought commerce between the United States and foreign countries to a halt, and by the time the peace treaty was signed in December 1814, some significant changes had begun to shape the American future. With foreign goods no longer available, domestic industry was called on to provide much more than ever before. As a result there was an unprecedented growth in manufacturing. When normal trade was eventually resumed, although it hurt the new industries, the dependence of the United States on the importation of foreign manufactured goods had been broken, and the move toward an industrial economy was begun.

Both the embargo and the War of 1812 were unpopular, particularly in New England and New York. These areas experienced the greatest industrial expansion, but they also suffered the most serious loss to their foreign commerce and shipping enterprises. New Yorkers spoke of "Mr. Madison's war," and Governor Strong of Massachusetts declared a public fast protesting the war "against the nation from which we are descended" [108, pp.141–43].

These conditions were of great importance to the organ profession. No longer was it possible to send to England for a new organ, nor would the latest fads and fancies of foreign builders be an ever-present criterion for evaluating an instrument.[1] The stage was set for the expansion of the organ industry, freed for the moment from stylistic domination, and yet following a course that derived its direction from the organs imported from England in earlier times. One wonders what the result would have been if the American organ had maintained its autonomy from that time, or if the organs of Pennsylvania's Tannenberg, instead of English organs, had been the models for future builders. With the importation of organs virtually at an end, organ building was further stimulated by domestic conditions that tended to increase the demand for new organs. Briefly stated, they were the westward expansion and the increase in population, particularly in urban areas.

Westward Expansion and Population Growth

The half-century before the Civil War was an exciting and adventurous age. Although it included two major business depressions, there was always more land in the West, and the West became much larger and more accessible during this time. By 1821 four thousand miles of the Cumberland Road had been completed, and six hundred more were authorized: a *paved highway* from Cumberland, Maryland, with Vandalia, Illinois, as its projected terminus. In 1825 the Erie Canal was opened, connecting the Hudson River with Lake Erie and providing an inland waterway from the Atlantic to Toledo and Cleveland. Steamboats were plying the Mississippi, and were so successful that by 1830 the passenger fares had dropped to $25 for the trip from New Orleans to Louisville [108, p.444]. The United States could boast of 3,328 miles of railroad by 1840, and an additional 28,000 miles were completed by 1860.

Even though transportation was making giant advances, moving organs was sometimes very difficult. Lahee has described the journey of the new organ for Pittsburgh's Trinity Church in 1835:

> It was transported over the mountains on the famous Portage road that operated by a series of inclined planes, on which cars were hoisted by steam power. The cars formed the top part of the canal-boats on the canal from Hollidaysburg to Pittsburg, and were run off the boats into the incline flat cars or trucks. The freight charges in those days were enormous, as compared with the small ones now. To bring such a bulky thing as an organ from Philadelphia here was an immense undertaking. [97, pp.280–81]

The big migration to the Pacific Northwest over the Oregon Trail had its beginnings in 1842 and 1843. Only a few years later, in 1847, the Mormons founded Salt Lake City. But the greatest inducement to western settlement regardless of transportation, comfort, or convenience came with the discovery of gold in California on January 24, 1848. Meanwhile, much remained throughout the country for a later generation to accomplish. In 1841 Bishop Polk, the first Episcopal bishop of Louisiana, wrote:

> There is no portion of the whole country so destitute, I presume as Louisiana. She has not, so far as I know a single church west of the

Mississippi river; and I find a few or no Presbyterians, and only now and then a wandering Methodist. [30, p.55]

The spectacular movement to the West was matched by the population growth in the East and the development of big cities. Large numbers of impoverished Irish immigrants flocked to the United States; this migration reached its peak with the entrance of more than 200,000 Irish in 1851. Even larger, and certainly more significant for the history of music, were the waves of German immigrants, driven to the United States by poor farming conditions in the 1840s and as political refugees from the Revolution of 1848. In a peak two-year period, 1853–54, 356,955 Germans arrived, but later waves almost equaled this migration in 1873 and surpassed it in 1882.

The population of the United States in 1810 was 7,239,000. By 1860 it was 31,443,000 [108, p.468]. All the large cities were growing, but the change in New York from 123,700 in 1820 to 1,080,330 in 1860 was most phenomenal. Larger cities meant not only more churches but also bigger churches, as congregations outgrew their old buildings. Some of the changes that took place in organ building during this time were natural outgrowths of the conditions these circumstances imposed.

Organ Factories

Coincident with the new urbanism, the spotlight of organ history turned from the rural areas of Pennsylvania, after Tannenberg's remarkable career, to developments in Boston and New York. Here the traditional organ shop began to experience some changes. Near the beginning of this period, Boston's leading builder, William Goodrich, spent his lifetime making a total of forty-nine organs, eleven of them chamber organs; by the 1850s the E. & G. G. Hook Co. was producing that number of organs in about three years' time. Although there remained a large number of individual craftsmen working in the old-fashioned ways, the trend was toward factories and the application of factory methods to organ building. In addition to the E. & G.G. Hook Co. in Boston, Henry Erben and George Jardine, both of New York, established organ firms that were large according to the standards of the day. Size became important, both in the number of organs produced and the size of the instruments, and the 1850s saw the erection of two four-manual organs: one by John C. B. Standbridge, the other by the Hook firm. Both were inaugurated in 1854.

Characteristics of the Organs

As more emphasis was placed on size, more importance was also placed on loudness, and by the end of this period one had to admit that the popularity of loud organs was increasing. In 1853 Nathaniel

Gould deplored the loss of the gentle, singing style of the early nine-teenth-century organs, in his book on American church music. He de-scribed the organs of the 1820s and '30s as "small organs, and those played lightly, just to accompany the voices, never to be made con-spicuous, but moving gently along, bearing up and sustaining the vocal parts" [66, p.179]. By the 1850s the stylistic changes that were taking place prompted Gould to continue:

> But this manner of suppressing, or keeping back, the tones and power of the organ, could not long satisfy the taste and ambition of organists; and those who had advocated the doctrine of soft playing were observed, either by accident or design, gradually to mark their performance with crescendo, from Sabbath to Sabbath. By and by all restraint was thrown aside, and the struggle was for the organ of the greatest power. The small organs were set aside to make room for thunder tones, still more and more powerful, till an organ was *worthless* that would not make the granite walls of a church tremble, at times, when used in full strength. And many times now, when the doxology is sung, at the close of worship, we hear such a crash of sound on the organ, that, the choir and the whole congregation joining, could no more make words intelligible, than would be the words of a public speaker in the midst of roaring artillery.
>
> [66, p.179]

Gould was writing from an 1853 perspective, and the modern reader must realize that such loudness as builders achieved at that time was no match for the high-pressure sound of sixty or seventy years hence. Wind pressures were light, and the organ ensemble remained bright and well developed throughout the period.

The compass of manuals and pedals achieved no standardization. All areas dominated by the English style produced organs with the old GG compass until about the 1840s. That is, the lower termination of the manuals was GG. The Swell, regarded as a solo manual, was "short," with its stops terminating at about g. The classic exception was the stopped 8′ on the Swell manual, which was usually extended the full compass, with the bass range on a separate stop.

Sometimes two or three of the other Swell stops were given "bass" stops, which might appear as a group, called swell bass or choir bass. In the latter case the Choir was not a separate division, but rather the lower range of the Swell. Regardless of the name given the bass range, it was left unenclosed, while the treble stops were enclosed. By the end of this period the GG compass was a thing of the past, but ghosts of the old short Swell continued to haunt the specifications of builders in New England and New York, particularly in the frequency that divided stops were used on this manual.

Craftsmanship was at a high level during this period, and generally speaking, refinement in the construction of both the tonal and the mechanical parts of the organs was characteristic. Just as today, builders became known for their specialties. In 1851 Zundel wrote: "Every body speaks . . . of Hook's *reed* stops. Appleton's *diapasons* are very well spoken of, and the *brilliancy* of Erben's organs has secured to him the never-failing patronage of the Roman Catholic and Episcopal churches" [524, p.150].

Occasionally builders experimented with new stops, especially toward the middle of the century, and some of Simmons's organs are notably interesting in this respect (see pp.135–39). However, specifications generally show a consistent style, which was gradually modified rather than drastically changed from 1810 to 1860. An 1845 organ instruction book by Thomas Loud, a Philadelphia organist, gives a list of organ stops along with the manuals on which they usually appeared. While some other stop names are found, and the manual location is subject to some variation, this list gives a good index of normal usage:

Stops of the Great Organ

Open Diapason
Stop'd Diapason
Violoncello
Principal
Night Horn
Flute
Twelfth
Fifteenth
Tierce
Cornet
Sesquialtera
Mixture
Trumpet
Clarion

Stops of the Swell Organ

Open Diapason
Stop'd Diapason
Viol da Gamba
Principal
Flute
Fifteenth

Stops of the Swell Organ (continued)

Cornet
Trumpet
Hautboy
Clarionet

Stops of the Choir Organ

Open Diapason
Stop'd Diapason
Dulciana
Principal
Violano
Flute
Fifteenth
Cremona
Bassoon

Stops of the Pedals

Double open Diapason
Sub Bass
Violoncello
Principal or Octave

[100, p.2]

As in the eighteenth century, the pitch at which stops sounded was not usually indicated because each stop was associated with a particular pitch. In the above list, the first two Pedal stops would be of 16′ pitch. Eight-foot stops would be Open Diapason, Stop'd Diapason, Violoncello, Dulciana, and Viol da Gamba. The Principal, Night Horn, Flute, and Violano would be 4′ stops, except for the Principal in the Pedal (an 8′ stop). All the reeds listed were characteristically used at 8′ pitch except the Clarion, which appeared at 4′. The Bassoon, however, was not a complete rank, but rather the bass of a divided 8′ reed stop. It might appear on either the Swell or the Choir. The pitch of other flue stops is self-explanatory, except for the compound stops, which were subject to a variety of treatments, and whose pitch level varied, just as it does today.

Registration Practices

Some concepts of organ registration in the early nineteenth century need clarification. We frequently find references to "the Diapasons," meaning the Open and Stopped Diapasons, which were regarded as similar in function, often being used together. An 1824 article explains:

> The *Diapason* is the foundation of the organ, it being the true pitch, without which no other stop could have a good effect; it binds, in fact, the whole together, in one true body of tone. There are however *two* distinct names for a Diapason, the one denominated the *Stop*, and the other the *Open Diapason*. [487, p.43]

The same source suggests:

> When the performer sits down to the organ, let him draw out the Diapasons on each set of keys, by which means he is sure of a foundation; and indeed this is absolutely necessary, because no stop ought to be used without one, or both of these stops, except the Flute and Dulceana. [487, pp.44–45]

Thomas Loud confirms this usage:

> The proper stops to be used for the accompaniment of voices, are first the two diapasons, if both are too powerful, one may be used; the stopt diapason is the softest—the dulciana and viol da gamba, are unison stops with the diapasons, and may be substituted or added if wished.

A footnote explains:

> It may be proper to remark, that the Diapasons are the ground work of the Organ, and as a general rule, they form the basis of all combinations of stops for accompanying the voices and for other purposes, particular effects in voluntary playing alone excepted.
>
> [100, p.14]

Loud suggests increasing the chorus in the following way:

If more strength is wanted add the principal, making the diapasons and principal, or if wished, the flute or night horn may be used, as they are also unison stops with the principal, but of a different character and power.

If still more strength is wished, add the twelfth and fifteenth: this is what is called a Positive Organ, and consists of the two diapasons, principal, twelfth and fifteenth. It should however be observed, that although the fifteenth may be added without the twelfth, yet the twelfth cannot be used without the fifteenth; the twelfth pipes speaking a fifth above the principal, its effect when it becomes the highest pipes is unbearable; when however the fifteenth is with it, which is an octave above the principal, the ear is not offended, and it adds a richness to the effect.

To the combination of the Positive Organ, when more force is desired, may be added the trumpet or sesquialtera, or both; these combined on a good instrument, are sufficient to accompany the most powerful chorus. [100, p.14]

Loud lists the Clarabella, Dulciana, Viol de Gamba, Stop'd Diapason, Open Diapason, Violina, Flute, and Night Horn as stops that can be used alone as solo stops. For special effects, one can add the Principal and Fifteenth to this list. However, when reed stops are used, one should always draw one of the Diapasons also. The Stop'd Diapason is used with the Hautboy, Clarionet, and Cremona, while the Open Diapason is used with the Trumpet or Clarion, "and in case there are two Open Diapasons in the same set of keys containing the Trumpet, the largest Open Diapason should always be selected for the accompaniement [sic] of the Trumpet." This usage may have been prompted by unreliable or infrequently serviced reeds, for Loud adds: "When the Hautboy is very perfect (which was formerly rare); it may be used without the Stop'd Diapason occasionally" [100, p.74].

The Use of the Organ in the Service

Some congregations were still reluctant to install organs in their churches. For example, the Beneficent Congregational Church, Providence, Rhode Island, held out against instrumental music of any kind until 1816, and it was not until eight years later that a subscription was raised for an organ. In the summer of 1825 an organ built by Thomas Appleton was finally installed.

Meanwhile, Stephen S. Wardell, son of Deacon Wardell of the church, evidently thinking the chances of acquiring an organ were slight, decided in 1822 to learn to play the bass viol to accompany the singing. When his father succeeded singlehandedly in raising the money for the organ by the fall of 1824, Stephen, then twenty-three years old, switched to piano in order to prepare for the forthcoming keyboard instrument. Less than a year later, he played his first church service, and his diary strikes a responsive note in the experiences of many an organist:

> Lord's Day, July 10, 1825. This forenoon I played on the Organ for the 1st time in publick worship in service time. Lord help my weakness and grant me skill to play to divine acceptance & the edification of the congregation. [Cited in 274, p.115.]

Stephen Wardell subsequently presided as organist for a term of eighteen years.

While the church organist's primary duty was still the accompaniment of congregational singing, the voluntaries that had occasionally found a place in the pre-1810 worship service now became more common. The *Musical Magazine,* a New York publication, struck out against abuses in the playing of voluntaries in its July 1835 issue, giving us some clues about church music in that city. One can only imagine what the village organists were playing for voluntaries.

> Every real proficient on the organ, knows that voluntaries upon that noble instrument, ought to consist of broken passages, scattered chords, &c., &c., which will not seize upon the attention of the listener but rather soothe his mind, into calm collected meditation. Any thing like a regular air would here be out of place. Even the learned harmonies of the Germans, impressive and beautiful as they are, prove for the most part too spirit-stirring, in their influence, for American voluntaries. Some of our organists, however, have but little invention, and others but little taste. So when they should either be silent or be endeavoring merely to soothe the worshipers into devout meditation, they rouse them by a march, an overture, a sonata, or a thundering chorus. This is bad enough: but a friend of ours not long since, heard in some neighboring city, for a Sunday voluntary, the ballad, 'Hope told a flatt'ring tale,' when the fair, blooming executant, no doubt assumed a fine languishing appearance to the edification of many a youthful admirer!
>
> Such abuses if tolerated, will bring voluntaries into disrepute; if not lead to the expulsion of the organ from our churches. The rule of playing voluntaries is plain: and the reason for it, is equally obvious. Not a key of the instrument should be touched, on the principles of display or irrelevant sentimentality.
>
> A pious organist of our acquaintance, was once sitting at the keyboard while the remains of a beloved pastor were brought into the church and placed beneath the pulpit in sight of a crowded congregation. It was a trying moment for the performer: but when a few

gentle touches, slow, soft, almost monotonous, upon the deeper notes of the instrument, were given, the audience melted into tears, as if the sound of the 'clods of the valley' was already issuing from the beloved pastor's grave. [409]

The extemporized voluntaries and hymn preludes included certain mannerisms that were considered to be in good taste. One writer suggests that a bass note be sustained while stop changes are being made:

Suppose then that the first movement of a performer be a Diapason; and if it be succeeded by that of a Cornet, let him, at the conclusion of the Diapason piece, hold down with his left hand, the last note in the bass, while with his right-hand, he draws out the cornet on the great organ and swell. When he has finished this movement, his fancy may lead him to try the effects of the swell; and in this case let him not likewise quit the last note in the bass, until he has pulled out the full number of stops in the swell, and put in the cornet in the great organ; after this he may with the right hand, begin on the swell. This will prevent a long interval, which has a bad effect in any performance.

[487, p.45]

Another mannerism was that of arpeggiating the entrance of notes in a chord, rather than striking them together. It was characteristically done at the beginning of a hymn. After the tune had been "given out" and it was time for the congregation to sing, the organist would roll the first chord up from the bottom, sustaining each note as it entered. When the full chord had been sounded, the congregation would begin singing. The chord was broken not only at the beginning of every stanza but also at the beginning of each line of the hymn. Similarly, it was considered good practice to leave the upper notes first in a final chord. Another way to bring the voices in on a hymn was by playing a trill, or shake, on the note above or the note below the first note to be sung [100, p.14]. The shake was often accompanied by a dominant chord when it was used at the beginning of a hymn or chant.

Loud's instruction book contains a "Model Service for the Episcopal Church," which further explains some of the performance practices. All the music needed for the service is included: three voluntaries, two hymns, and accompaniments for the chants. The voluntaries are little pieces of one to one and a half pages, to be used at the beginning of the service, during the collection, and at the end of the service. The second voluntary is in the key of the second hymn, and serves as an introduction to it. The hymn is then "given out," using one setting of the tune. A fuller harmonization is used for the accompaniment of the congregation. Interludes are provided, to be played between the verses. The first hymn is given an Introductory Prelude of eight measures, based on the hymn tune. As in the other hymn, it is then played through before the congregation joins. The organist is instructed to use the Swell for these two sections, moving to the Great for the first verse. Three different interludes are given for use between the verses: one of four measures and two of eight measures [100, pp.15–22].

Repertoire

The best-known organists in the country rarely entered the realm of organ literature. Of Boston's John Henry Willcox it was said: "For a long time his organ repertoire consisted of five or six overtures, and these were produced upon every occasion, until habitual listeners began to descant upon the apparent improvement since the last performance" [97, p.263]. While Dr. Willcox was not regarded by his contemporaries as an exceptionally able performer, he was quite popular and was particularly successful at demonstrating new organs.

But if standards of repertoire were questionable in organ performances, they were at least as low in other media and in other countries. This was the age that saw P. T. Barnum bring Jenny Lind to the United States for a guarantee of $150,000 plus expenses. Jenny Lind conquered wherever she sang, but she did nothing to raise the standards of music. Mendelssohn, praising her voice and her artistry, conceded: "She sings bad music the best" [82, p.203].

Foreign Influences

The early nineteenth century presents a strange paradox in American music. Chase has said: "Most of the nineteenth century is merely an extended parenthesis in the history of American art music" [34, p.325]. While the American organ builder achieved a new independence with the cessation of importation and reached a high point in art and craftsmanship, there was no cessation of importation of the arbiters of church music. Here the apron strings of England remained firmly tied, and many of the organists and directors who were not born in England aped those who were. When the Englishman Edward Hodges became organist of New York's Trinity Church in 1839, he "immediately took steps to bring Trinity's music as near as possible to the standards of the English cathedral service" [50, p.77]. Leonard Ellinwood has noted that many of our leading church musicians in both the eighteenth and nineteenth centuries were Englishmen who had already established careers in their native land. He continues:

It would be interesting but difficult to explore the social and economic considerations which prompted these moves. One factor is well recognized—the snobbishness of fashionable churches which many times hired an inferior English organist in preference to a native musician.

[50, p.106]

Meanwhile, the German migrations beginning in the 1840s included a substantial number of musicians. An entire orchestra of professional musicians, the Germania Society, arrived in 1848 to make America their home. They and other performers brought with them a background that did much to shape American concert life. Here were musicians for orchestras, members for musical societies, and music teachers. Their repertoires and tastes were not entirely discriminating, but did include masterworks of European composition.

One can see in these English and German influences the stylistic separation between "church music" and "concert music" that has plagued American music ever since. One has only to compare English musical history with that of Germany for the first half of the nineteenth century to understand the depth of the separation.

Both styles were superimposed on American culture, providing scant basis for native development, and the original creative talent that did exist was largely ignored. When American composers finally began to gain stature, they still looked to the European Continent for models, while church music persisted in walking in the English shadow. This situation can be blamed for much of the lack of interest and understanding America's leading composers have shown for church music in general and organ music in particular. Few are the composers who have successfully bridged the stylistic difference. English cathedral music, after all, was oriented toward choral music, and provided little encouragement for the organist. No wonder Dr. Willcox played orchestral transcriptions; the early nineteenth-century American organ was an instrument without a repertoire!

And what of the German organ builders who immigrated at this time? They came from a Germany that was ignoring its own heritage in organ building and organ music. George Joseph Vogler (the "Abbé") (1749–1814) had set German builders on a path toward "the 'symphonic' organ, the orchestral arrangements and the third-rate descriptive organ fantasia" [151, p.218]. This style had nothing positive to offer the American organ, but the influx of German builders did result in the establishment of a number of organ factories and the addition of skilled workmen to existing shops. These builders were not responsible for the late nineteenth-century trend toward orchestral organs in America; they merely reinforced a direction already established in the performance field.

Reed Organs

A new factor to influence the organ industry during this time was the appearance of melodeons and harmoniums. These so-called reed organs gained such great popularity both for home use and in country churches that the building of small pipe organs was practically brought to a halt by mid-century. Melodeons were inexpensive, easy to move, and required a minimum of upkeep. These features were so attractive that by 1840 there were forty melodeon builders in the United States, with an annual product of $646,975, but reports listed only twenty pipe organ builders, with an annual product of $324,750 [13, p.132]. While we know of more than twenty pipe organ builders active at this time, many of them were in remote locations untapped by statisticians, and the same was undoubtedly true of melodeon builders. The comparison is significant in that melodeon building was only beginning its ascent in popularity.

Improvements in construction and voicing methods in the 1840s and '50s were necessary preparations for the fantastic growth the industry would soon experience. A significant landmark in the history of this instrument was the formation of a partnership in 1855 between Emmons Hamlin and Henry Mason. Hamlin had pioneered a method of voicing reeds that enabled him to imitate various tone qualities. The Mason & Hamlin partnership was only one of a number of reed organ firms active just before the Civil War. The Estey Co. also had its beginnings at this time; its history goes back to the 1846 company of Jones, Woodbury, and Burdett. By 1853 the firm name was Estey & Green, and later J. Estey & Co. The Estey Co. continued to manufacture reed organs into the middle of the 1950s [276, p.25].

These companies gave their instruments extensive promotion, advertising in music magazines, employing expert salesmen, and publishing periodicals. The *New-York Musical Review and Gazette,* for example, was published by Mason Brothers, and its pages were high in praise of the Mason & Hamlin Organ-Harmonium. The June 11, 1859 issue asserted: "Fortunately we have now a really satisfactory substitute for these small [pipe] organs in the Organ-Harmonium—and enlargement of and improvement upon the melodeon, introduced a few years since by Mason and Hamlin, of Boston." Costing $200 to $500, these instruments were said to be "free from that liability to get out of order," and were "greatly preferable to small organs, as well as cheaper." Unrestrained by government controls on false advertising, promoters sometimes used a curious mixture of fact and fiction. The latter was in the ascendancy as this publication explained the superiority of the Organ-Harmonium:

In these instruments the tones are produced by reeds made of metal instead of wood, as in the pipe-organ. The swelling and shrinking to which wooden reeds are subject, a prolific cause of trouble in small organs, are thus avoided.

VII

NEW ENGLAND

Introduction

New Frontiers in New England

JUST as the settlers were pushing westward into new territory, New Englanders were demonstrating that there were other new frontiers east of the Mississippi. Eclipsing population growth and industrial and commercial development, great creative adventures and literary achievements made Boston the intellectual capital of the United States until after the Civil War.

The "Unitarian Controversy," coming to a climax in 1815, challenged orthodox Congregationalism and implanted a new liberal attitude in New England. The next generation, finding that Unitarianism in its turn had acquired too many of the garments of orthodoxy, broke through even more barriers of dogma and tradition by expounding a philosophy of Transcendentalism. With Ralph Waldo Emerson as its eloquent spokesman, Transcendentalism had its time of ascendancy from 1836 to about 1850.

Closely related to the new freedom in philosophy were the accomplishments of New England's brilliant pre-Civil War writers. Just a few of the literary landmarks of this time were Emerson's *Nature* (1836) and *Essays* (1841, 1844), Henry David Thoreau's *Walden* (1854), Nathaniel Hawthorne's *Twice-Told Tales* (1837) and *The Scarlet Letter* (1850), and Oliver Wendell Holmes's *The Autocrat of the Breakfast Table* (1858).

Meanwhile, the Boston Philharmonic Society was founded in 1810 by Gottlieb Graupner. Graupner was also one of the founders of the distinguished Handel and Haydn Society in 1815. Both societies served as models and led to the establishment of similar organizations in other cities. It was during this period, too, that Lowell Mason pioneered in establishing music instruction in the public schools. Even in progressive Boston it was no easy task to convince the authorities that this innovation was a move in the right direction.[1]

Organs and Organ Builders

It is no accident that Boston, where arts and ideas were considered the vital issues of the day, became a focal point in organ building in the early nineteenth century. By 1846 *The Musical Gazette* (February 16) could boast:

> If Boston deserves credit for nothing else it certainly does for good church organs. With the exception of three or four churches in which there is no room conveniently to place one, every church in the city is supplied with one of these truly ecclesiastical instruments. The following have organs of the largest size, i. e. with three banks of keys; viz.
>
> Salem-st. Church, Second Church, Bowdoin Square Church, Bowdoin-st. Church, New Jerusalem Church, Park-st. Church, Kings Chapel, Old South Church, Franklin st. Church, (cath.) Tremont Temple, Central Church, Trinity Church, Odeon, Berry-st. Church, New South Church, First Church, Melodeon, Harvard st. Church, St. Augustine's Church.

The largest of these organs was the three-manual, thirty-four register instrument installed in 1846 in Tremont Temple by E. & G. G. Hook. It was Boston's first "concert organ," and when it was destroyed by fire, its 1853 replacement was Boston's first four-manual organ, also built by E. & G. G. Hook.

The father of the long and important succession of organ builders who worked in and around Boston was William Goodrich. Not only were his organs of fine quality but also his shop was the training ground for the leaders to follow. In the 1830s Goodrich's mantle fell to Thomas Appleton, whose organs are particularly admired today for their refinement and excellent workmanship. Although Appleton continued to build organs, E. & G. G. Hook moved to a position of leadership during the 1840s, a position they retained for half a century.

The fame of the Hook company tends to obscure the work of contemporaries, but William B. D. Simmons had a share of important contracts beginning in the 1850s, and William A. Johnson, whose greatest period of activity was yet to come, completed almost a hundred organs before 1860 in his shop at Westfield, Massachusetts. Of lesser fame, but still deserving of mention, are George and William Stevens. Their instruments of small and medium size never attracted the attention accorded large installations in famous churches, but their quality was nevertheless high.

The Goodrich Brothers

William Goodrich's Career after 1812

William Goodrich, who had been away from Boston since September 1811 exhibiting Maelzel's Pan Harmonicon (see p.77), returned the following June to find that Thomas Appleton had meanwhile entered into the partnership of Hayts, Babcock & Appleton. Goodrich worked for this company during 1812 and again in 1815, having a small shop of his own during the years 1813–14. In 1815 Hayts, Babcock & Appleton failed, and the company was taken over by Mackay & Co. Goodrich became a partner in this concern, remaining with it until it was dissolved in 1820. From 1821 until the time of his death in 1833 Goodrich worked independently.

During his lifetime Goodrich completed thirty-eight church and eleven chamber organs, and also repaired and rebuilt a number of other organs. He maintained a close friendship with Appleton, and in 1824 he voiced and tuned an organ Appleton had built. It was Appleton, in return, who completed an organ Goodrich was working on at the time of his death.[2]

Goodrich's career was focused on church organs, most of which were intended for churches in New England. Two notable exceptions were three-manual organs for churches in Savannah, Georgia, and New Orleans, Louisiana, built while Goodrich was still with Mackay & Co. The Savannah instrument was installed in the Independent Presbyterian Church in 1820 at a cost of $3,500. Lowell Mason was engaged as organist at a salary of $300 a year, and he remained there until 1827 [76, p.33]. The New Orleans organ may have been built for Christ Church, Episcopal, where an organ was installed between 1816 and 1819, or it may have been the three-manual organ installed in the First Presbyterian Church some time before 1825.

William Goodrich's influence extended long beyond his own time: builders who had had their training in the Goodrich shop dominated New England organ building for years to come. In addition to Appleton, they included Elias and George Hook, George and William Stevens, and William Gayetty. When Goodrich died in 1833, he was succeeded by George Stevens and William Gayetty.

Characteristics of the Organs

Goodrich's smaller two-manual organs had the typical short Swell keyboard. In larger instruments he provided a bass for the Swell, and added a Sesquialter and a Trumpet or Cremona to the basic Great chorus. The larger schemes included a standard Pedal division of one 16′ stop.

In regard to his largest organ, built in 1826–27 for St. Paul's Church, Boston, Goodrich's biographer wrote: "Mr. Goodrich spared no pains to render this organ as good and as perfect as possible, and he was always proud of it" [225, p.33]. The specification was given in an 1834 source.

St. Paul's Church, Boston, Massachusetts
WILLIAM GOODRICH, 1826–27

Great-organ		*Swell*	
First Open Diapason	*8′	Open Diapason	8′
Second Open Diapason	8′	Stopt Diapason	8′
Stopt Diapason	8′	Principal	4′
First Principal	4′	Cornet III	
Second Principal	4′	Trumpet	8′
Twelfth	2⅔′	Hautboy	8′
Fifteenth	2′		
Tierce	1⅗′	*Choir-organ*	
Cornet V		Open Diapason	8′
Sesquialter III		Stopt Diapason	8′
First Trumpet	8′	Dulciana	8′
Second trumpet	8′	Principal	4′
		Flute	4′
		Twelfth	2⅔′
		Fifteenth	2′

Pedals

Open Double-Diapason Bass, seventeen large wooden pipes, extending from B, down to C below the manual keys.

[400, p.211]

* Pitch indications are not given in the original.

Some notable features of this specification are the completeness of the chorus scheme, the appearance of a second Diapason chorus on the Great, and the liberal use of the Tierce. The Pedal compass is evidently incorrect, or the number of pipes in the Pedal stop is wrong.[3] We may assume that the manual compass used the GG termination typical of this period. Unfortunately the specification does not give the compass of the Swell division.

Although sources of information for the early nineteenth-century organ builder were limited, Goodrich managed to acquire a copy of the famous French treatise on organ building, *L'Art du Facteur d'Orgues* by D. Bedos de Celles (published in 1766). He also had a collection of

An organ by William Goodrich, 1831. Unitarian Church (formerly Second Congregational Church), Nantucket, Massachusetts. *Photo courtesy Thomas Murray.*

pipe scales, not only of his own organs but also of those imported from England that he had examined [225, pp.40–41].

He was not reluctant to experiment with ways to improve his instruments, and introduced "the little bellows-like appendage, sometimes called a *winker*, by which the action of the wind upon the pipes is rendered more regular and steady" [225, p.41]. One of Goodrich's interesting, if unsuccessful, experiments was described:

> In the Park-street organ, he introduced a supposed improvement in the double-diapason bass, suggested by an English publication, by which one pipe, by means of ventages and stops or keys, produced two or three notes. There were some disadvantages or inconveniences in this plan, which rendered it afterwards necessary to remove these pipes, and to substitute others after the old mode. [225, p.41]

In 1831, in a one-manual organ he built for the Episcopal Church in Pittsfield, Goodrich enclosed the treble in a swell box. This innovation proved to be unsatisfactory "as he found it impossible to voice the pipes so as to give them, at the same time, a good tone and sufficient power" [225, p.34]. Thus Goodrich learned a lesson builders have been slow to relearn, and he never again used this plan.

Ebenezer Goodrich

After Ebenezer Goodrich opened his own shop in 1807 (see p.76), he concentrated on small organs, and by 1834 he had built and sold 107 organs. An article written in that year reported:

> he has ten others now in progress, in his shop. Of those which have been completed, only six had two rows of keys. Twenty others were put up in churches, but had only one row of keys. Eighty-one were chamber-organs, twenty-six of which had a reed-stop; but the greater part of the rest had probably only two or three stops. [225, p.39]

One of Eben Goodrich's organs is in the Smithsonian collection. Another, originally owned by the Reverend Abiel Abbot of Beverly, Massachusetts, is now in the Salem Towne House, Old Sturbridge Village. Built in 1817, it has a compass of fifty-four notes, C-f^3, and the following specification:

Dulceana (c^1)	8'	30	pipes
Stop Diapason Bass	8'	24	
Stop Diapason Treble (c^1)	8'	30	
Principal	4'	54	

In addition to building organs, Ebenezer Goodrich taught music, and until about 1822 he also made pianos [412, p.5]. He is credited with the invention of a type of reed that became important in the manufacture of reed organs.

Thomas Appleton

Appleton's Career after 1806

From the time Thomas Appleton met Goodrich in 1806 until the Mackay firm dissolved in 1820, Appleton's work paralleled that of Goodrich, and he contributed to the building of many of the organs attributed to Goodrich during that time. Like Goodrich, Appleton went into business for himself after the Mackay company closed. He evidently had some doubts in the early period about his ability as a voicer, for his first three organs were voiced by Eben Goodrich, and the fourth by William Goodrich. From 1824 to 1828 he employed Henry Corrie (see pp.172, 173), an Englishman, as a voicer, but after that he did his own voicing [412, p.5].

An organ by Thomas Appleton, 1831. Centre Street Methodist Church Nantucket, Massachusetts. Oldest extant church organ by Appleton. *Photo courtesy Thomas Murray.*

From 1847 to 1850, Appleton had a partnership with Thomas D. Warren. In 1850 he moved to a new factory his son had built for him in Reading, Massachusetts. From that time on his business diminished, although the quality of his work remained superior [116, pp.68–69]. Appleton's last organ was built in 1869 for the Warren Street Baptist Church. William Horatio Clarke wrote:

> During the later years he took much interest in musical matters, and often visited the factories of other builders, and frequently was seen at the exhibition of new instruments, when every good point presented would be quickly and generously recognized. [251, p.30]

The exact number of organs Appleton built is not known. From 1820 to 1833 he had completed or contracted for forty organs, including four three-manual organs, sixteen two-manual, sixteen one-manual, and four additional organs that were probably one-manual instruments. A newspaper article of 1853 noted: "Mr. Appleton has manufactured thirty-six organs for the city of Boston alone, at a cost, in the aggregate, of $96,000" [BOC 89, p.10]. He built only a few chamber organs, most of his instruments being intended for churches.[4]

Characteristics of the Organs

Appleton's 1831 organ for the Bowdoin Street Church, Boston,[5] attracted considerable attention, and is mentioned in several nineteenth-century sources as an outstanding instrument. Appleton himself considered it particularly successful. James Loring's 1834 publication, *The Musical Cyclopedia*, stated:

> In this country, the art of organ building has made great improvements. That recently built by Mr. Thomas Appleton of Boston, for the Bowdoin Street church, is probably not inferior to any in the country, and will well compare with the best imported organs in power and effect. Its sub-base is peculiarly grand and solemn. The largest pipe is 24 feet in length, and its pitch is G, two octaves lower than the G string of the violincello. Its cost was $4000. [Cited in 431, p.11.]

The New-England Magazine of March 1834 gave the specification of this organ, which was similar in many respects to Goodrich's organ of 1826–27 (see p.117).

Bowdoin Street Church, Boston, Massachusetts
Thomas Appleton, 1831

Great		Swell (continued)	
First Open Diapason	*8′	Principal	4′
Second Open Diapason	8′	Cornet III	
First Stopt Diapason	8′	Hautboy	8′
Second Stopt Diapason (treble)	8′	Cremona	8′
Principal	4′		
Twelfth	2⅔′	Choir	
Fifteenth	2′	Open Diapason	8′
Tierce	1⅗′	Stopt Diapason	8′
Sesquialter III		Dulciana	8′
Trumpet	8′	Principal	4′
Clarion	4′	Flute	4′
		Cremona	8′
Swell			
		Pedals	
Open Diapason	8′		
Stopt Diapason	8′	Double Diapason†	16′
Dulciana	8′	Sub-bass**	8′

** The sub-bass consists of seventeen large open wooden pipes, from G up to C, in *unison* with the lower pipes of the diapasons.

† The double diapason consists, also, of seventeen large open wooden pipes, from G up to C, an *octave below* these, the former being a kind of double principal to the latter.

[400, p.213]

* Pitch indications are not given in the original.

Ten years after the Bowdoin Street organ, an organ for the Unitarian Church, New Bedford, Massachusetts, showed that Appleton maintained a consistent concept in design during this time. The Choir divisions contained identical registers. In the Swell, the replacement of the Cornet III by a Flute 4′ was a significant change. In the Great, the Second Stopt Diapason, Tierce, and Clarion were omitted, and a Mixture III was added. The pedal (one 16′ stop) terminated on C, while the manuals were of GG compass.[6] The Swell contained a typical thirty-seven-note range, f-f³.

The little 1839 Appleton organ in St. Philip's Chapel, Charleston, South Carolina, illustrates the kind of chorus balance that, together with unforced voicing, gives organs of this period their silvery quality. Registers on this one-manual organ are Open Diapason 8′, Stopped Diapason (divided) 8′, Dulciana (tenor g) 8′, Principal 4′, Flute 4′, Twelfth 2⅔′ and Fifteenth 2′. The Open Diapason and the Principal are almost the same in volume. The Twelfth is a little softer than the Principal, but about the same as the Fifteenth. Although the Twelfth in similar organs is often slightly softer than the Fifteenth, this one is particularly effective in the ensemble, adding a somewhat reedy quality. The manual has a compass of fifty-eight notes, GG to f³, omitting GG♯. The eighteen pedals may have been a later addition. Two foot levers add and retire the Principal, Twelfth, and Fifteenth.

Elias and George Hook

The Hook Firm, 1827–1860

When Elias (1805–1881) and George Hook (1807–1880) went to work for Goodrich as apprentices in 1824, they began careers that would lead to the establishment of one of the most successful and important organ companies in the nineteenth century. Sons of a cabinetmaker in Salem, Massachusetts, the young organ builders returned to their hometown in 1827 and opened their shop. There they built nineteen organs: fourteen chamber organs and five small church organs [236, p.168]. (These instruments are not included in the opus list of Hook organs.)

The little organ c.1827 now in the Essex Institute at Salem is said to be their first. An account of this instrument in *The Salem Evening News* for August 12, 1933 states that it "was in constant use in Boston churches for nearly fifty years and then was returned to the maker in exchange for a new one." It remained in the Hook family until it was finally given to the Essex Institute in 1933.

The Hook brothers moved their shop to Boston in 1831 and began their business there on a modest scale, producing an average of about

The first Hook organ, *c.*1827. Now in the Essex Institute, Salem, Massachusetts. Keyboard has GG compass. *Photos courtesy Thomas Murray.*

four organs a year during the first ten years. Three instruments during this decade contained three manuals; the rest were one- and two-manual organs.

Surveying the first hundred organs on the Hook opus list, dating from 1829 to 1849, one finds that most of the organs were constructed for churches in or near Massachusetts. The farthest afield was Opus 62, a one-manual, four-stop organ built in 1845 for Christ Episcopal Church, Macon, Georgia. It was also the Hooks' smallest organ of the period; the list includes a total of thirty-one one-manual, fifty-seven two-manual, and twelve three-manual organs. The largest was Opus 64 (1845), built for Tremont Temple, Boston. A three-manual organ of thirty-four registers, it was "for several years afterward the largest organ in Boston" [116, p.67]. (It should be noted that there were some organs built by the Hooks during this period also that are not included in the opus list.)

The next hundred organs (dated 1849 to 1856) include nine three-manual organs, and for the first time, a four-manual organ, Opus 149. This fifty-four register instrument was completed in 1854 for Tremont Temple, the 1845 organ having been destroyed by fire. Meanwhile, a few more Hook organs found their way beyond the northeastern states, including three for Alabama, one for Tennessee, and one for Ohio. In the 1850s production increased, and a new E. & G. G. Hook factory built in 1853 was said to be the largest organ factory in the country at the time. By the end of 1859 Opus 261 had been completed, with production averaging sixteen organs a year during that decade.

In the management of the factory, Elias Hook headed the business office while George was head voicer and tonal director. One of the important additions to the firm was the employment of Frank Hastings in 1855. Hastings (1836–1916), working in the design department, soon proved to be a valuable asset to the company, and he was later taken into partnership.

E. & G. G. Hook competed successfully with other noted builders of the period. When the First Presbyterian Church of Philadelphia decided to install its first organ in 1846, the contract was given to the Hook firm, even though lower bids for organs with more than four hundred additional pipes had been submitted by both Thomas Appleton of Boston and Henry Erben of New York [61, p.94].

Contemporary Critiques

Some of the contemporary accounts were high in their praise of Hook organs. The December 29, 1849 issue of *Saroni's Musical Times* carried a description of Opus 96 (1849) in Christ Church, Episcopal, Hartford, by an unidentified reviewer:

As I played—changed from register to register—it seemed to me that I never tried or heard an instrument that would surpass it in its easy action and smoothness of tone. The voicing of the pipes, and particularly the two Diapasons (Great Organ), and the Open Diapason (Pedals), deserve particular mentioning. The Reed stops are, as usual, in Messrs. Hook's best manner. I am told that they keep in very good tune. The Swell Organ is beautiful, and strong enough to be almost called Great Organ, and is enclosed in a very light double box. Various new improvements have been introduced, for example, the Melodia (Open Diapason), a wood pipe; and also the Great Organ Separation, by which an organist playing on the Great organ can shut off the great organ and use the full swell without changing hands.

On March 30 of the next year, the same publication contained a a description of the Hook organ in St. Paul's Church, New Haven, Connecticut (Opus 97, 1849). The action, console arrangement, reeds, and diapasons were all mentioned for their excellence, and the reviewer also seized the opportunity to chastise some of the New York builders:

Our New-York organists, who are kept in continual awe by some tyrannical organ-builder, should come here to learn what good stops are. Our church committees, who, for fear of getting cheated by the organ-builder, trust to their own sagacity and get a worse organ for it, should learn at New-Haven what they want. Without the roughness and harshness of our New-York organs, it possesses all their power.

However, when *Dwight's Journal of Music* (July 12, 1856) compared the large four-manual Hook in Tremont Temple (Opus 149, 1853–54) with foreign instruments, the result was considerably less than a glowing report. After some complimentary remarks, the reviewer observed:

yet we cannot say with truth that it compares favorably in many important features with instruments of the same size and general character abroad. All the speaking stops on the four manuals are voiced on too light a wind for an organ designed to fill a hall of such capacity as the Tremont Temple; and, moreover, it is quite apparent that the pipes are not voiced up to the extent of their scales. The diapasons, especially those belonging to the great manual, are of too light volume and too reedy in their character for so large an organ, and they are sensibly deficient in that round, bold and lusty character which distinguishes this stop in the best English and German instruments. Another defect in this organ is the want of sufficient wind. There are but three bellows, one supplying the Great, Choir and Swell Organs, one the Pedal organ, and the smallest of the three the Solo

Organ. A fourth bellows of the same dimensions and capacity as the two largest (12 feet by 6) is absolutely required to give the proper force and steadiness of tone expected from an organ of such pretension and capacity.

When all the stops and couplers are drawn, and the fullest chords played on either the organ at Tremont Temple or St. Paul's, we shall find more or less unsteadiness of tone perceivable at the very moment the bellows feeders commence and complete their work, besides considerable noise in the blowing action, both of which are serious defects, and ought to have been avoided in organs of such pretensions.

Characteristics of the Organs

The old GG compass was used by the Hooks in earlier organs. By the end of the 1840s, however, the change to the C compass had been made, with a range of either fifty-four or fifty-six notes (C to f^3 or g^3). The latter became more common after the 1840s, except in small organs. Pedal compasses varied, as in the organs of other builders, but the Hooks showed a preference for the twenty-five-note pedal in moderate- and large-sized organs. An interesting exception was the twenty-nine-note pedal in Opus 211 (1857), the organ for the Beneficent Congregational Society, Providence, Rhode Island. *Dwight's Journal of Music* (October 24, 1857) also credited this organ with having America's first concave and radiating pedal board:

> The pedals are radiating, so as to converge to a point behind the performer, and they are concave both lengthwise and transversely. This arrangement is exactly conformable to the movements of the feet, and brings the pedals under their control, without forcing the point and heel into awkward and painful contortions; and as the short keys are beveled, all chromatic passages may be played with great facility and smoothness: it is, we believe, an improvement of Dr. Wesley's, and was first used in England, at his suggestion, in the immense organ built by Mr. Willis for St. George's Hall, Liverpool.

The short Swell compass persisted throughout this period in small organs, with all stops except the Stopped Diapason terminating at tenor c or f. The Stopped Diapason was a divided stop, providing the only full range for Swell divisions on many small organs. Occasionally, however, even two-manual organs contained bass stops for several registers. For example, the two-manual organ for Christ Church, Hartford, Connecticut (Opus 96, 1849), contained nine registers in the Swell, and the Swell Bass contained three stops, providing the low octave for the Dulciana 8′, Stopd. Diapason 8′, and Principal 4′.

The short Swell was sometimes used in three-manual organs. The 1859 organ in the First Baptist Church, Jamaica Plain, Massachusetts (Opus 253), has a Swell division terminating at tenor c, and only the Std. Diapason Bass completes the range of fifty-six notes. Some organs of comparable size and age extended almost all the Swell stops the entire range. For example, all the Swell ranks of the three-manual Opus 254 (All Saints Lutheran Church, Boston) have a range of fifty-six notes except for a forty-four-note Hautboy. While Opus 253 represents an unusually late appearance of a short Swell in a larger instrument, this characteristic was found in small organs through the 1880s, and divided stops were used considerably later than that.

In the other divisions, the Choir Clarionet and the Great 16' were characteristically terminated at tenor c. The Great Trumpet was often divided, and a divided Stopped Diapason was frequently found on both the Great and Choir divisions.

The selection of couplers on organs of this period frequently omitted the Choir to Great 8', substituting for it a Choir to Great 16'. The lack of a Swell to Pedal coupler can be noted in organs containing a short Swell. Swell to Great 4' couplers made occasional appearances, while the Pedal octave coupler on Opus 97 was exceptional. Larger organs usually had composition pedals to assist with registration changes on the Swell and Great. Two for the Swell and two or three for the Great were normal. Controls for the Swell enclosure were of the hook-down type.

In their tonal schemes, the early Hook organs followed closely the examples of Goodrich and Appleton. The 1833 three-manual instrument for the First Baptist Church, Providence, Rhode Island (Opus 11), was said to be "nearly similar" to Appleton's Bowdoin Street Church organ. "It will contain about twenty-five stops, and will have, connected with the pedals, an open double-diapason bass, extending down to double-double G, an entire octave below the manual keys" [400, p.213].

The 1849 organ for St. Paul's Church, New Haven, Connecticut (Opus 97), reveals that the style of design remained fairly constant even two decades after Goodrich built the organ for St. Paul's Church, Boston. An interesting detail of construction in the Hooks' Opus 97 was noted in *Saroni's Musical Times* of April 6, 1850: "The Swell is constructed after a plan of Dr. Edward Hodges of New-York, and consists of three boxes one within the other, and three sets of shades."

By the time Opus 171 was installed in the Jamaica Plain, Massachusetts, Unitarian Church in 1854, some trends that continued into the following decades can be noticed. The Tierce as an independent stop on the Great disappeared, although it was still included in the Sesquialtera.[7] The Fifteenth was gone from the Choir, and while Opus 171

E. & G. G. Hook, Opus 11, 1833. First Baptist Church, Providence,
Rhode Island. A modern organ is housed in the original Hook case.
Four additional pipes have been added on either side. *Photo courtesy
Thomas Murray.*

still contained a 4′ Principal, this stop was soon to give way to a 4′
Celestina or Fugara. The Open Diapason, omitted from this organ, continued to appear in the Choir division in most of the larger instruments,
and the Choir Viol d'Amour was standard equipment. The octave-
and-fifth-sounding Mixture on the Swell of Opus 171 was not typical;
preference was usually given to a nonbreaking Dulciana Cornet
throughout the 1850s.[8] This organ lacks a Swell Fifteenth, but this
stop was frequently included in organs of the 1850s and '60s, finally
giving way to a 2′ Flautino. The Pedal division is unusually large. Most
organs of similar size omitted the reed or the Double Dulciana or both.

Typical of the period, Opus 171 has a Great ensemble that builds
up brightly and clearly from the 8′ Open Diapason. The latter has none
of the overpowering quality that one finds in the Romantic period, nor
is it comparable to the assertive character of many modern 8′ Principals,
modeled on the German Baroque style. It has, rather, a mellow character that is both refined and distinctive. The 4′ Principal and higher-
pitched stops are brighter than the 8′, and each contributes significantly
to form an exciting and satisfying ensemble, rich in harmonic develop-

ment. The Great reeds added to the diapason chorus give a new dimension to the ensemble without dominating the timbre.

First Church, Unitarian, Jamaica Plain, Massachusetts
E. & G. G. Hook, Opus 171, 1854

Great			Swell (continued)		
Grand Open Diapason			Principal	4'	56
(T.C.)	16'	44	Mixture	II	112
Open Diapason	8'	56	Vox Humana**	8'	56
Stop'd Diapason Bass	8'	12	Trumpet	8'	56
Melodia Treble (T.C.)	8'	44	Hautboy (T.E.)	8'	40
Gamba (T.C.)*	8'	44	Tremulant		
Principal	4'	56			
Twelfth	2⅔'	56	Choir†		
Fifteenth	2'	56	Dulciana	8'	56
Sesquialtra	III	168	Viol d'Amour (T.C.)	8'	44
Mixture	II	112	Clarabella (44 notes, lowest		
Trumpet Bass	8'	12	5 from Std. Diap.)	8'	39
Trumpet Treble (T.C.)	8'	44	Std. Diapason Bass	8'	12
Clarion	4'	56	Std. Diapason Treble		
			(T.C.)	8'	44
Swell			Principal	4'	56
			Flute	4'	56
Bourdon Bass	16'	12	Clarionet (to G)	8'	49
Bourdon Treble (T.C.)	16'	44			
Open Diapason (56 notes,			Pedal‡		
lowest 7 from Std. Diap.)	8'	49	D'ble Op. Diapason	16'	27
Viol di Gamba (T.C.)	8'	44	Bourdon (from Swell)	16'	—
Stop'd Diapason Bass	8'	12	D'ble Dulciana	16'	27
Stop'd Diapason Treble			Violoncello	8'	27
(T.C.)	8'	44	Possaune	16'	27

Couplers
Swell to Great, Swell to Choir, Choir to Great Sub 8ves, Swell to Pedal, Choir to Pedal, Great to Pedal.

* Probably installed by Hutchings at a later date.
** The Vox Humana is a later installation.
†The Choir division was reportedly "prepared for" in 1854, and was actually installed in 1860.
‡ The original pedal was probably 17 notes.

The Swell and Choir divisions create diminutive, chamber organ impressions when compared with the Great ensemble. The 8' Open Diapason on the Swell could, in fact, be mistaken for a Dulciana (the early nineteenth-century Dulciana had a more robust timbre than its diluted offspring of a century later, however). Except for the decided difference in loudness, the secondary manuals follow the Great in the individuality of the voices and the clarity of the ensembles. The most distinctive voice on the Pedal is the Possaune, and it adds an effective 16′ line to support the Great ensemble.

George and William Stevens

The Stevens Brothers and Their Associates

Several years before the Hook brothers began their apprenticeship with William Goodrich, George (1803–1894) and William Stevens (1808–1896) journeyed from Maine to work in his shop. When Goodrich died in 1833, his successors were George Stevens and William Gayetty. The *New-England Magazine* of March 1834 related:

> They have taken the specious building at East-Cambridge, (Lechmere Point,) lately occupied by him, and are now engaged in the construction of two church-organs. One is to have two rows of keys; the other

Console of an organ by George Stevens, *c.*1852. Now in Lasalette Shrine, Ipswich, Massachusetts. *Photo courtesy Thomas Murray*.

will have one row only. Mr. Stevens was, for a considerable time, in the employment of Mr. Goodrich, immediately antecedent to his death. Mr. Gayetty served a regular apprenticeship with Mr. Goodrich, and had been with him from childhood. They are both excellent workmen, and will, no doubt, succeed in the business which they have undertaken to continue.

The George Stevens–Gayetty partnership lasted until about 1835. In 1853 William Stevens was associated with Horatio Davies and James Jewett, and again with Jewett in 1860. Jewett was also a partner of George Stevens's from about 1855 to 1856, but for the greater part of this period George and William Stevens each maintained independent shops, building one- and two-manual organs for small churches.

George Stevens took an active part in civic affairs, and was an alderman of Cambridge, Massachusetts, for several years. From 1851 to 1853 he served as mayor.

Characteristics of George Stevens's Organs

Although the Stevens brothers' instruments never attained the popularity accorded Appleton and the Hooks, surviving organs attest to

An organ by Stevens & Jewett, *c.*1855. Orthodox Congregational Church, Lanesville, Massachusetts. *Photo courtesy Thomas Murray.*

the quality of their workmanship. An interesting example of George Stevens's work was installed in the First Universalist Church, Dover New Hampshire, in 1852. The manual compass is fifty-nine notes, GG to f³, and the pedal has twelve pipes and eighteen keys, with the top six keys repeating the lower range (the pedal also has a GG termination).

First Universalist Church, Dover, New Hampshire
GEORGE STEVENS, 1852

Great			Swell (continued)		
Op. Diapason	8'	59	St. Diapason	8'	37
Dulciana (TG)	8'	35	Swell Base	8'	22
Clarabella (TG)	8'	35	Principal	4'	37
St. Diapason Treble (TG)	8'	35	Hautboy	8'	37
St. Diapason Base	8'	24	Tremolo (replaced Bellows		
Principal	4'	59	Single or Pedal Check)		
Flute (G)	4'	47			
Twelfth	2⅔'	59	Pedal		
Fifteenth	2'	59	Sub Base	16'	12
Swell ("Base" unenclosed)			Couple Sw. and Gr.		
Op. Diapason	8'	37	Couple Pedals and Keys		
Viola da Gamba	8'	37	Two Great combination pedals		

[BOC 24, p.2]

The use of the old GG compass that had been abandoned by Hook in the previous decade shows a certain conservative tendency that is also reflected in various other ways in the organs by Stevens and other small builders. Doubtless a conservative style was preferred by some of their clients, particularly those in locations removed from the mainstream of musical developments.

In his choice of stops Stevens sometimes appears old-fashioned, but one must consider that the builder of small organs seldom had the opportunity to demonstrate stylistic tendencies and at the same time include the most essential stops for the ensemble. As a result, there is considerable similarity to be found in the small organs of all builders of a given period. For example, the specification of the 1852 George Stevens organ given above is almost the same as that of a small organ built by E. & G. G. Hook for the Unitarian Church of Mount Pleasant, Roxbury, Massachusetts, in 1844 (Opus 59). Hook placed a Cremona in the Great instead of the Clarabella, and omitted the Viol da Gamba from the Swell, but the stop lists are otherwise identical.

A somewhat larger George Stevens organ of 1848 in the First Church in Belfast, Maine, has the same stops as the 1852 organ, but adds a

Sesquialtera (originally three ranks, 12–15–17, but the tierce has been removed) to the Great, a Double Stop Diapason 16' to the Swell, and a Cornet III (12–15–17; 8–12–15) to the Swell [cited in *OHS 1963 Convention Program*].

William Allen Johnson

William Allen Johnson (1816–1901) was twenty-seven years old and was well established in his trade as a mason and contractor before he took his first tentative steps in organ building, and four more years elapsed before he gave it his full attention. He was born in Nassau, New York, and moved with his family to Hawley, and then to Westfield, Massachusetts, where his father worked as a contractor. After attending school in Westfield until he was thirteen, William went to work on a farm. He later worked in a glue factory and a buggy whip factory, finally becoming an apprentice to a mason in 1834.

In 1843 William Johnson assisted in installing a Hook organ in the Methodist Church at Westfield and became interested in the instrument that was to shape his future. The next winter, when bad weather halted his masonry work, he constructed a small organ. In the next three winters he produced five or six more organs, all parlor instruments with one manual.

Finally, in the fall of 1847, he began building organs full time, establishing a firm that would last until 1898 and produce a total of 860 organs. The first ninety-three fall into the pre-1860 period. Johnson's first church organ was Opus 9 (1848), a one-manual, six- register organ for Grace Episcopal Church, Chicopee, Massachusetts. His first two-manual was built in 1849 for the Congregational Church at Westfield, and the first three-manual was installed five years later in the South Congregational Church, Hartford, Connecticut.

The Johnson shop was the training ground for several builders who later established their own companies. Among them were John Steer and George Turner, who opened their shop in 1867. Edwin Hedges, who learned pipe-making from Johnson, became well known in this craft, and opened an organ pipe factory in 1866. Hedges was in charge of all metal and reed pipe-making for Johnson from 1855 on [466, I, p.11].

According to Simmons, the early Johnson organs used a C manual compass of fifty-six notes [466, II, p.4]. However, Johnson is known to have used a GG compass as late as 1859 (Opus 92).[9] The pedal range varied, smaller organs often having only an octave of pedal pipes. The number of keys on the pedal board sometimes exceeded the number of pipes, with the upper keys repeating part of the lower octave. Simmons's description of the Johnson pedal clavier is: "The pedals were narrow, short and close together. The chromatic pedals were of a semi-circular nature. There was also a board mounted above the pedal board which seems to have served as a foot rest" [466, II, p.4].

In their tonal design, the small Johnson organs of this period followed a typical conservative pattern. The 1855 organ for White Church, West Springfield Massachusetts [466, II, p.6], for example, bears a striking resemblance to George Stevens's 1852 organ cited above (see p.132). A larger two-manual organ of 1858 (Opus 76) shows that Johnson still retained a full complement of Swell chorus stops to 2′ pitch. The 1⅗′ appears as an independent stop on the Great in this organ, while the Mixture contains fifths and octaves. Opus 76 was built for the Baptist Church, Shelburne Falls, Massachusetts, and was moved from there to the Baptist Church, North Springfield, Vermont, in 1959 [513]. It is one of the best-known examples of Johnson's earlier organs and is highly regarded for its tonal excellence.

Baptist Church, Shelburne Falls, Massachusetts
WILLIAM JOHNSON, Opus 76, 1858

Great			*Swell (continued)*		
Open Diapason	8′	56	St. Dulciana	8′	18
St. Diapason Bass	8′	18	Principal	4′	38
St. Diapason Treble	8′	38	Celestina	4′	18
Clarabella	8′	38	Twelfth	2⅔′	38
Viola d'Amore	8′	44	Fifteenth	2′	38
Octave	4′	56	Oboe	8′	44
Waldfloete	4′	44	Tremulant		
Twelfth	2⅔′	56			
Fifteenth	2′	56	*Pedal*		
Seventeenth	1⅗′	56	Diapason	16′	17
Mixture	III	168			
Trumpet	8′	44	*Couplers*		
			Great to Pedal		
Swell			Swell to Pedal		
Bourdon	16′	38	Swell to Great		
Diapason	8′	38			
St. Diapason Bass	8′	18	Swell enclosed—hook-down swell		
Viola da Gamba	8′	38	pedal.		

[466, II, p.6][10]

A different plan for the upperwork can be found in a two-manual organ of 1859 (Opus 88). Here Johnson installed a Sesquialtera (17–19–22) on the Great instead of the Mixture and independent Tierce. A variation in the Swell pattern was the inclusion of a Cornet III instead of the Twelfth and Fifteenth[11] [283, II, p.190].

William B. D. Simmons

While some of the New England organ builders were following closely the established formulas of the past, William Benjamin Dearborne Simmons (1823–1876) was busily searching for new directions in both the mechanical and the tonal design of organs. Perhaps his success in winning contracts was due in part to his daring and imagination, for by the 1850s he was building organs of substantial size, not only for prominent New England locations but also for other parts of the country. In 1860 alone his organs included three-manual organs for St. Paul's Cathedral, Louisville, Kentucky, and St. Ignatius' Church, Baltimore, Maryland, as well as the extensive rebuilding of the old Richard Bridge organ in historic King's Chapel, Boston [13, p.159].

Simmons had worked in the Appleton shop before going into business in 1845 with Thomas McIntyre. This partnership, which lasted until 1851, was the first of three such associations for Simmons, the others being with George Fisher (1856–57) and John Henry Willcox (1858–60). During the intervening years, and from 1860 on, the name of the firm was W. B. D. Simmons & Co.

Characteristics of the Organs

Simmons's most common manual range was fifty-six notes. The size of his pedal clavier tended to be greater than that of many builders of the period. His larger organs contained twenty-five or twenty-seven-note pedal compasses; medium-sized organs, twenty to twenty-five notes; while some of the small organs contained as many as twenty-five pedal keys acting on only an octave of pipes. The abbreviated Swell is found in smaller organs, as in the case of other builders, but Simmons tended to extend the Swell stops to the full compass on three-manual organs.

Simmons's interest in unique design is seen in the specification for the c.1855 organ for the First Congregational Church, Montpelier, Vermont (this instrument is now in the Methodist Church, Northfield, Vermont). The upperwork on the Great, including a full set of non-breaking independent stops through 1′ pitch, is most remarkable (p.138).

During the time that Simmons was associated with Willcox (1858–60) his specifications showed a marked German influence. John Henry Willcox[12] was one of the leading organists in the Boston area, and he was involved in organ design as well as performance. It may have been Willcox who brought the German influence to Simmons, for it was only during their partnership that this characteristic appeared in Simmons's organs.

The organ built for Appleton Chapel, Harvard University, in 1859 well illustrates the Simmons-Willcox innovations. In addition to the use of some German stop names, one might note the scope of the seven-stop pedal, the eight reed stops, and the early use of pneumatics (p.139).

Simmons's organ for St. Joseph's Church, R. C., Albany, New York (1859), employed the use of the Barker lever for Great, Swell, Pedal, and coupler action. This large (3–50) organ had a Pedal division of ten stops, and the manual keyboards were extended to fifty-eight notes.

The innovations Simmons used, important as they are in indicating something of the emphasis of his work, did not color all of his production, and many organs, particularly smaller installations, followed standard patterns for the day. Such an instrument was the one installed in St. Jude's Episcopal Church, Philadelphia, in 1856 or 1857. If it varied from the norm it was in matters of voicing and tonal balance rather than in its specification. Walter Lindsay, who had become acquainted with this organ many years before, wrote an interesting description of it in 1926:

There were two manuals, and no overhang to the keys, so that the swell keys were quite far away, and, in fact, they were set well into the body of the case. The white keys were covered with ivory—pretty yellow by my time—and the black keys were very sharp on the edges and extremely narrow—designed, apparently, to be hard to hit. The stop-knobs were in vertical rows, two rows on each side; the knobs were small and flat, the rods thick and cut perfectly square. The names of the stops were engraved in script, those of the great organ on white ivory plates and those of the swell on dark red ivory, almost black, so that they were practically illegible; the mechanical stops had bright yellow knobs, with scarlet wooden plates.

The pedals were very narrow, not wider than your finger, and very close together—so much so that an organ builder who was there once, superintending some repairs, and who had rather large feet, was quite unable to put down less than two pedals at a time. The sharp pedal keys had no defined front end at all, but sloped down imperceptibly between the naturals; consequently, if you pedaled on a natural and got a little too far forward, as the natural key went down your foot would carry down the sharp key also.

The swell pedal was at the extreme right and was of the hitch-down variety; but as the swell-box was quite thin there was really not a great deal of difference in effect whether the pedal was down or up.

[348]

Lindsay described the two composition pedals as "big iron things, almost the size of a soup ladle. . . ." His impression of the Great 8′

Open Diapason and the Pedal stop are surprising; one would not expect a degree of loudness in an organ of this time that would impress anyone accustomed to 1926 organs.[13] None the less, the "foundation was, of course, the big fat open diapason," and the single stop on the Pedal was "a vast wooden 16-foot open diapason that fairly shook the earth when it was going." The Great contained a diapason chorus of 16′, 8′, 4′, 2⅔′, 2′, and a Sesquialtera V. There was also a Clarabella treble to go with a Stopped Diapason bass, a Gamba, 4′ Flute, and a divided Trumpet.

The Swell was short, terminating at tenor c. It contained an 8′ Open Diapason, 8′ Stopped Diapason, 4′ Octave, 2⅔′ Twelfth, 2′ Flageolet, 8′Viol da Gamba, 16′ Bourdon, 8′ Hautboy, 8′ Trumpet, 16′ Tenoroon Trumpet, and 4′ Clarion. The C-c octave on the 16′ Bourdon, 8′ Open Diapason, and 8′ Stopped Diapason were provided on separate stops (the low octave of the Open Diapason was named Violoncello). On this division, the Viol da Gamba was "really a very delicate string-toned aeoline. It was about the softest stop I have ever heard; even close by the organ the sound of ordinary conversation rendered it entirely inaudible."

Lindsay gave a particularly clear account of the use that could be made of the divided stops to achieve variety. While the present-day organist may object that these practices have limited use in playing the literature of the organ, that was not the chief concern of either organists or organ builders in the 1850s.

Now see how this worked out. For manual playing on the swell alone a fair to middling bass could be provided by drawing one or more of the bass stops. But suppose we wanted a solo on the hautboy, with accompaniment on the great and a soft pedal. The big pedal diapason was out of the question. But on investigating the couplers we would find that the swell to great and the swell to pedal both stopped work at tenor C, as the swell manual did; and there were two supplementary couplers, swell bass to great and swell bass to pedal, which acted only on the lowest octave of the swell keys. So for our effect mentioned above we would draw, say, the clarabella and stopped diapason on the great, for the accompaniment, and hautboy on the swell for the solo. The lowest octave of the swell not possessing any hautboy pipes, and thus remaining silent, we would draw on that the swell bass bourdon and swell bass stopped diapason, and couple the swell bass to pedal. Then, by keeping the solo above tenor C, and the pedal part below it, we would have the swell organ supplying both the solo and the pedal parts, the former on an 8-foot reed tone, the latter on a soft 16 and 8-foot flute tone, while the accompanimental chords appeared in a soft 8-foot flute tone on the great.

Or suppose we wished to play alternately loud and soft on the great. We would draw a loud combination and use the pedal open diapason and the great to pedal. Then we would draw the swell bass bourdon and the coupler swell bass to great. We would play the loud passages on the loud great, using the pedals. Then for the soft passages we would cut down the great and instead of using the pedals we would keep the left hand below tenor C; the bass part, being coupled to the soft 16-foot of the bass octave of the swell organ, would give the general effect of a soft 16-foot pedal. You will notice that we have not drawn anything on the swell except this one 16-foot stop in the bass octave; we might therefore arrange a third effect on the upper octaves of the swell organ—say some brilliant reed combination—and by keeping the left hand above tenor C we would produce a tone color in decided contrast to both of the other two. [348]

First Congregational Church, Montpelier, Vermont
WILLIAM B. D. SIMMONS, c.1855

Great

Eolina	(TC)	16′	44
1st Open Diapason		8′	56
2d Open Diapason		8′	56
Viol de Gamba	(TC)	8′	44
Dulciana		8′	56
Clarabell Treble	(MC)	8′	32
St. Diap. Bass		8′	24
Principal		4′	56*
Celestina		4′	56*
Wald Flute		4′	56
Twelfth		2⅔′	56
Fifteenth		2′	56
Teirce [sic]		1⅗′	56
Larigot		1⅓′	56
Twenty Second		1′	56
Trumpet Treble	(TF)	8′	39
Trumpet Bass		8′	17

Swell (enclosed from Tenor C)

Bourdon	(TC)	16′	44
Open Diapason	(TC)	8′	44
Open Diapason Sw. Bass		8′	12
Dulciana	(TC)	8′	44
Dulciana Sw. Bass		8′	12
St. Diapason	(TC)	8′	44
St. Diapason Sw. Bass		8′	12

* Denotes missing stop label.

Swell (continued)

Principal	(TC)	4′	44
Principal Sw. Bass		4′	12
Night Horn	(TC)	4′	44
Nassard [sic]	(TC)	2⅔′	44
Fifteenth	(TC)	2′	44
Trumpet	(TC)	8′	44
Hautboy	(TC)	8′	44
Tremblant			

Pedal

Doub. Open Diapason	16′	25
Double Dulciana	16′	25

Couplers

Gr. & Sw. Unison
Gr. & Sw. Super Octave
Pedals to Great
Pedals to Sw. Bass
Pedal Check
Bellows Signal
Two Great combination pedals
The hitch-down Swell pedal has been replaced by a crude "balanced" pedal.

Manual compass: CC-g³, 56 notes
Pedal compass: CCC-C, 25 notes

[BOC 38, p.2]

Appleton Chapel, Harvard University
Simmons & Willcox, 1859

Great	
Bourdon	16'
Principal	8'
Rohr Flöte	8'
Hohl Flöte	8'
Viola di Gamb	8'
Octave	4'
Spitzflöte	4'
Flute Octaviante	4'
Mixture (12-15)	II
Mixture	III
Symbal	II
Trumpet	8'

Swell	
Bourdon	16'
Principal	8'
Bourdon	8'
Keraulophon	8'
Vox Angelica	8'
Octave	4'
Mixture	(III) 2'
Fagott (tc)	16'
Cornopean	8'
Oboe	8'
Clarion	4'

Choir	
Æolina	16'
Dulciana	8'
Viola d'Amore	8'

Choir (continued)	
Bourdon	8'
Gemshorn	4'
Flute a Cheminee	4'
Flageolette	2'
Corno di Bassetto	8'
Vox Humana	8'

Pedal	
Contra Bass (stopped)	32'
Open Bass	16'
Bourdon Bass	16'
Violoncello	8'
Quint	5⅓'
Octave	4'
Posaune	16'

Couplers

Swell-Great
Swell-Choir
Great-Pedal
Swell-Pedal
Choir-Pedal

Accessories

Two composition pedals
Full Swell (pneumatic)
Great Organ Tacit (pneumatic)
Great Organ, MF
Improved Tremulant
Bellows Signal

The manual compass was 56 notes, the pedal 27 notes, and all stops were full compass save for the Swell 16' reed. The windchests were not of the usual slider and pallet type used by the Boston builders, but were of German spring-valve construction. The organ also had three different wind pressures, pneumatic register movements (ventils), and a crescendo pedal, termed 'a Swiss invention.' [415, pp.4–5]

Other New England Builders
Parlor Organs

The organ-building activity of Eben Goodrich and Henry Pratt extended well into the nineteenth century and represented the continuing tradition of small organ building (see pp.77, 119). There remained a demand for small organs for both home and church use until the middle of the century, when the popularity of the reed organ practically brought that demand to a halt. Owen explains that these small organs were called "chamber organs" in the city and "parlor organs" in the country [116, p.55]. Although organs that fit into this category were also produced by major builders, many of them were made by independent craftsmen working alone, or in small shops.

As we have seen, William Johnson's career started as a typical parlor organ builder. Beginning with a casual acquaintance with the organ, he produced one or two one-manual instruments a year, and meanwhile continued his trade as a mason. While Johnson's shop outgrew the small-builder category and eventually gained a far-reaching reputation, that of Josiah Ware (b.1797) and his partner, George Handel Holbrook (1798–1875), remained forever small. Holbrook, a cousin of Ware's, is remembered chiefly as a bell founder. Ware had served an apprenticeship in 1831 with William Goodrich before returning home to East Medway, Massachusetts, to build organs. His partnership with Holbrook dates from 1837, and they continued in business until 1850. At that time the firm was taken over by Holbrook's son Edwin (1824–1904), who built organs until the 1890s.

New Hampshire was especially blessed with parlor organ builders. In Mont Vernon there was a closely knit group of craftsmen who produced organs of one to four ranks. Simple in design, their work showed some features in their pipe construction that are found only in eighteenth-century Pennsylvania German organs and in "European and English organs of an even older date" [116, p.58]. These builders were all active from about 1830 to 1845, and included Samuel Forrest, William Crowell, J. D. and Benjamin Nutter, and Kittredge. In Keene, New Hampshire, another group, including Joseph Foster, Albert Thayer, and Ephraim Foster, produced organs that resembled more closely the Boston style of building. The Keene builders turned their attention for the most part to reed organs after they became popular.

Experimental Organs: Alley and Poole

Among the smaller builders in New England, Joseph Alley (1804–1880) is remembered today chiefly for his fine organ of 1834, still used by the First Religious Society (Unitarian) of Newburyport, Massachusetts,[14] and for his experimental instruments built to overcome the disadvantages of tempered tuning.

Alley had long been dissatisfied with tempered tuning when he met Henry Ward Poole in about 1848. Poole (b.1825) was a scientist and at various times held positions as geologist, mining engineer, and astronomer. He, too, was interested in intonation and had made some experiments with a monochord. Poole had devised a plan for a key-

An organ by Joseph Alley, 1834. First Religious Society Church, Newburyport, Massachusetts. *Photo courtesy Jim Lewis.*

board instrument that would make possible the use of pure intonation
in any key. Since he did not have the skill to build such an instrument, it
remained for Alley to bring the plan to fulfillment.

The resulting instrument, which Poole and Alley called the Euharmonic Organ, had one manual, five registers. It had a normal keyboard
of twelve notes to the octave, which gave it an advantage, so far as
performance was concerned, over experimental keyboards with added
keys. The temperament was adjusted by a series of foot controls, one
for each key up to and including five sharps and five flats. Separate pipes
were provided for enharmonic notes, thus making the distinction between, for example, C-sharp and D-flat. The organist would press the
appropriate pedal to bring into play the pipes forming the natural
scale for the key in which he wanted to play. Chromatics and altered
chords necessitated a change of pedals, which could be done with one
motion, since pressing one pedal would automatically release the one
previously in use.

It is easy to see that use of this organ demanded a knowledge of harmony and key relationships beyond the scope of many organists. Poole recognized that, as he asserted:

> That many who now assume to play the organ in our churches, would find difficulty in playing their music and making the requisite changes with the pedals, we have not the shadow of a doubt. To such we would recommend a course of study, on the scientific principles of music. . . . [125, p.31]

Poole evidently suspected some limitations inherent in his plan, for he proposed that his organ be used for singable music, in order to avoid some of the more remote chromaticism that was gaining in popularity:

> Although we have not intended the organ for any music except such as *can be sung*, yet, if any one should write music very difficult, on account of its abrupt transitions from key to key, as for instance, from the key of C to four sharps, thence, straightway into four flats, &c., the music nevertheless can be played if the organist understands it. But probably no singers could sing such a composition without a guide, and any such music, (if any such there be) which cannot be played on the euharmonic organ, is certainly very far beyond the ability of singers to sing. [125, p.34]

G. L. Howe recalled playing this organ, and although he recognized that music was not to be confined to the stricter tonalities that made such an instrument practical, he found its effect "extremely delightful" [83, p.346]. The Euharmonic Organ was exhibited in Boston and had a brief moment of glory in the interest it stimulated. Poole and Alley collaborated in the building of a second organ of this type by 1853. They later went their separate ways, but each continued to experiment with keyboard instruments and temperament. Sometime after his association with Alley, Poole joined an exploration party in Mexico, settling there, at least for a time.

Henry Pilcher

From about 1838 until the early 1840s, New Haven, Connecticut, was the home of Henry Pilcher, who later founded the well-known midwestern organ firm. Pilcher had arrived in New York from England some six years before. The first Pilcher organ of which we have any record was built in 1839 for St. Stephen's Church, East Haddam, Connecticut, for $630. In New Haven, the *Chronicle of the Church* carried Henry Pilcher's advertisement of "organs and pianos of every description," with the attraction of "liberal and accommodating terms" [350, p.89]. In addition to building organs, he served as organist at Trinity Church, New Haven, during 1840 and 1841. A short time later the Pilchers returned to New York City (see p.167).

Other Builders in New England

Other builders in New England during this period included the following:

Connecticut: Arvid Dayton (Daytonville), J. Dayton (Wolcottville), Erastus S. McCollum (Hartford), Barzillai Treat (Bristol), Franklin S. Whiting (New Haven).

Maine: Calvin Edwards (Gorham Village), Dr. Joshua Furbush (Wells), Rufus Johnson (Westbrook), John K. H. Paine (Portland), W. Harrison Parlin (Winthrop), Stephen Sewell (Winthrop), William Small & Knight (Portland), Thomas J. Sparrow (Portland).

Massachusetts: George Whitefield Adams (Medfield), John Baker (Boston), David Cannon (Mattapoisett), Edwin H. Clark (Stockbridge), Fisher & Hodges (Taunton), Albert Gemuender & Brother (Springfield), N. B. Jewett (Boston), Jones & Budlong (Boston), Josh Kent (West Newton), Richard Pike Morss (Newburyport), M. O. Nichols (Boston), Parkinson & Greenwood (Boston), Job Plimpton (Boston), Hiram Pratt (Montague), Joseph Richards (West Bridgewater), F. Sieberlich (Boston), Jonas Prescott Whitney and sons Josiah and Jonas (Ashby and Fitchburg).

New Hampshire: Almon Baily (Jaffrey), Hunting (Manchester), Nichols (Manchester), Stephen Rice (Claremont), Josiah Sturtevant (Meredith), William Wilson (Keene).

Rhode Island: Henry E. Barney, Massa Basset, Oliver Kendall, Jr., Samuel Laforest, Franklin Smith, Samuel R. Warren (all of Providence).

Vermont: Ira Bassett (Barre), Lemuel Hedge (Windsor), Robert McIndoe (Wells River), William Nutting (Randolph Center and Bellows Falls), Park & Paddock (St. Johnsbury), Phelps (Brookfield), William Wells (Brookfield), D. A. Wilcox.

VIII

NEW YORK

Introduction

CONCOMITANT with its growth in population, New York City gained preeminence in many other fields. The completion of the Erie Canal (1825), extending from Buffalo to the Hudson River, brought the market of the Great Lakes region to New York. That city became the nation's leading port for imports, while first place in exports was shared by New York and New Orleans. By the 1820s the New York Stock Exchange passed the Philadelphia exchange in volume of trading, and New York also led in the commercial credit field, becoming the financial capital of the United States.

Although the cultural spotlight was on Boston, New York still had much to offer the devotee of the arts. Its writers included the colorful Knickerbocker School, most particularly Washington Irving (*A History of New York . . . by Diedrich Knickerbocker*, 1809; *The Sketch Book*, 1819–20). James Fenimore Cooper (*Leather-stocking Tales*, 1823–41) pursued his literary career in both New York City and Cooperstown. During the 1840s and '50s Walt Whitman (*Leaves of Grass*, 1855) was associated with various New York and Brooklyn newspapers and magazines.

The New York Philharmonic Society was not founded until 1842, but New York had other musical societies and concert series earlier than that. They included a New York Sacred Music Society, which presented the *Messiah* in 1831 and Mendelssohn's *St. Paul* in 1838, just two years after it was written [82, p.151].

Organ building orbited around Henry Erben, whose prima-donna antics can only be excused by the excellence of his instruments. Thomas Hall, John Labagh, and Richard Ferris are other builders whose work figured prominently in New York City, but it was only in the growing popularity of George Jardine that Erben faced any serious competition.

Elsewhere in the state, the firms established by Alvinza Andrews and John Marklove in Utica and Garret House in Buffalo produced instruments worthy of particular note.

Thomas Hall, Hall & Erben, Hall & Labagh

Organs by Thomas Hall

When Thomas Hall (1791–c.1875) opened an organ shop about 1817, it marked neither the beginning of his career nor his introduction to New York. He had been working in Philadelphia since about 1812, and it was he who journeyed to New York in 1812–13 to install the organ Lowe had built for St. John's Chapel (see p.70). Hall's reputation was well established, and after he moved to New York he continued to build organs for locations south of that city. At least three Hall organs were installed in Baltimore: in the First Unitarian Church, Baltimore Cathedral, and St. Paul's Church.

The First Unitarian organ, built in 1818, had 1,400 pipes, and was described as "the finest, richest, most complete in the City" [90, p.62]. Still larger and more elaborate was Hall's organ for the Baltimore Cathedral, installed sometime between 1818 and 1822. A New York magazine reported: "This Organ is the largest in the United States, and in point of tone is very excellent, certainly doing great credit to the builder, Mr. Thomas Hall, of this city" [216, p.5]. Indeed, it was the largest, as its nearest rival, Tannenberg's Zion Lutheran organ (only one stop smaller) had been destroyed by fire in 1794 (see p.61), and when Hall's New England contemporary William Goodrich produced his largest organ in 1826–27, it was considerably smaller than the Baltimore organ (see p.117).

Cathedral, Baltimore, Maryland
THOMAS HALL, c.1820

Great

Double Open Diapason
Open Diapason
Stop'd Diapason
German Flute
Night Horn
Principal
Twelfth
Fifteenth
Tierce
Sesquialtra, 4 ranks
Mixture, 3 ranks
Cornet, 5 ranks

Great (continued)

Trumpet
Clarion, or Octave Trumpet

Swell

Double Stop'd Diapason
Open Diapason
Stop'd Diapason
Dulceano
Principal
Fifteenth
Cornet, 4 ranks
Trumpet

Cathedral, Baltimore, Maryland
THOMAS HALL, c.1820

Swell (continued)

Hautboy
Trimland

Choir

Open Diapason
Dulceano
Viol di Gamba
Stop'd Diapason
Principal
Flute

Choir (continued)

Fifteenth
Vox Humana

Pedal (2 octaves from CC)

Sub-bass, largest pipe 32 feet
Double Open Diapason, largest
 pipe 16 ft.
Double stop'd Diapason, 16 ft.
Open Diapason, 8 ft.

Height of the organ, 33 feet; width, 20 feet; depth, 13 feet; from f in alt. to gg.

The largest pipe is 32 feet long, the organ contains 36 stops, and 2213 pipes. The situation in which the instrument is placed is rather unfavourable to its general effect, but we are confident that in a proper situation, the effect of such a combination of stops must be truly grand. [216, pp.5–6]

The only evidence that Hall may have felt the influence of the German style while he was in Philadelphia is the German Flute in the Great. The Pedal division of four stops may also owe something of its size to this influence (Tannenberg's Zion organ had six pedal stops). In other respects the specification shows its English background. Here one notes the familiar GG compass and the emphasis on third-sounding ranks. Some features of particular interest are the two 16′ manual stops, the 32′ pedal, and the abundance of compound stops and reeds. The use of a C compass in the pedal is a characteristic previously noted in some of the New England organs of this period.

A smaller organ by Hall, installed in Christ Church, Norfolk, Virginia, illustrates a design that differs somewhat from New England specifications. This two-manual organ had a compass of GG to f³, with the Swell terminating at tenor g. There was no Pedal division.

The divided Sesquialtra is a somewhat unusual feature for an organ of this size, since it was generally regarded as an ensemble mixture. The so-called Choir Organ was actually the low octave of five of the Swell stops, playable from the Swell manual. Some builders would have called it Swell Bass. Its distinguishing characteristic is not in its name, but rather in the fact that five Swell stops were provided with a bass octave. In New England there were usually one to three Swell bass stops in an organ of this size.

In New York, Hall's installations included an 1821 organ for Christ Church, Poughkeepsie, an 1820–22 organ for St. George's Church,

Christ Church, Norfolk, Virginia
THOMAS HALL, 1822

Great Organ

Open Diapason
Stop Diapason
Principal
Twelfth
Fifteenth
Tierce
Sesquialtra, treble, 3 ranks
Sesquialtra bass
Cornet, 5 ranks, mounted
Trumpet
Clarion

Swell to Fiddle G

Dulceano
Stop Diapason

Swell (continued)

Principal
Flute
Fifteenth
Cornet, 3 ranks
Hautboy
Trimland

Choir Organ, Bass

Dulceano
Stop Diapason
Principal
Flute
Fifteenth

There is a coupling stop which unites the two rows of keys, ad libitum, and a shifting movement, which takes off the Principal, Fifteenth, and Cornet, of the Swell and Choir. [404, p.110]

New York City (three manuals, twenty-one stops), an 1821 organ for Zion Church, New York City, and an organ for St. Mark's in-the-Bouwerie, New York City.

Hall & Erben

There is a story that twelve-year-old Henry Erben helped Thomas Hall with the installation of the Lowe organ in St. John's Chapel, and if it is true, perhaps that marked the beginning of their friendship. Henry Erben (1800–1884) served an apprenticeship with Hall, beginning about the time Hall moved permanently to New York (1817). That was not the only connection Hall had with the Erben family, for he married Henry Erben's sister Maria [86, p.5].

In 1821 or 1822 the name of the organ shop was changed to Hall & Erben, a partnership that continued until 1835, although Erben also built some organs under his own name during this time [86, p.6]. The greatest period of activity for the Hall & Erben firm was in 1824 and 1825.

Hall & Labagh

After the partnership of Hall & Erben dissolved, there was a lapse of about a decade before we again hear of Thomas Hall. In 1846 he formed a partnership with John Labagh (1810–1892). Organs for St. James Episcopal Church, Philadelphia (1853–54), Fourteenth Street Presbyterian Church, New York (1851), St. Thomas Episcopal Church, New York (c.1852), and a Chancel organ in Trinity Church, New York (1864), resulted from this partnership. Their work was said to be mediocre. James Kemp became a partner in the early 1870s, and the firm "did a large trade" until Hall's death in 1875 or 1877[1] [433, p.166].

A comparison of the Fourteenth Street Presbyterian Church specification of 1851 with those of Hall's earlier organs shows a definite change of style. Gone are the Mixtures, Tierce, and the brilliant reeds from the Great. A Sesquialtra and Trumpet appear instead on the Swell where, with its short compass, they would be used as solo stops instead of in the ensemble. The "Choir Base" is the lower register of three of the Swell stops. An account of 1851 records: "The Sesquialta contains the flat twenty-first, giving the minor seventh with the common chord, a peculiarity never before introduced in this country, and but recently in Europe." A further innovation was that the Swell was placed in a double box, "giving an unusual crescendo and diminuendo." The same source asserts that Thomas Hall "prefers smoothness of tone and adaptedness to church use, before mere power and screaming noise" [490].

Fourteenth Street Presbyterian Church, New York, New York
HALL & LABAGH, 1851

Great Organ

Open Diapason
Stop Diapason
Dulciana
Principal
Twelfth
Fifteenth
Night horn
Cremona

Swell Organ

Open Diapason
Stop Diapason
Viol da Gamba
Principal
Twelfth
Fifteenth
Sesquialta

Swell (continued)

Bourdon
Trumpet
Hautboy

Choir Base [sic]

Open Diapason
Stop Diapason
Principal

Pedals

Open Diapason to C, 16 feet

Couplers

Great and Swell
Pedals and Great
Pedals and Choir

[Pedals:] two Octaves; two rows of keys; twenty-seven registers. [490]

Firth & Hall and Thomas Robjohn
The Firth & Hall–Robjohn Organ

When Trinity Church decided to replace its old 1791 organ in the 1830s, the contract went to Firth & Hall. John Firth and James Hall (not to be confused with the organ builder Thomas Hall) had a music-publishing house in New York, and they also subcontracted for the building of organs. They first engaged Henry Crab (or Crabbe), "an English workman of ability who had then just arrived in this country," [115] to construct the organ.[2] But there was some disagreement, and before the organ was finished Crab left the firm. It was left to another Englishman, Thomas Robjohn, to complete the instrument.

Meanwhile, having decided to build a new edifice, Trinity Church had no place to install the new organ (see p.70). Trinity had also recently engaged an organist who had ideas of his own about the kind of organ the church should have. He was Dr. Edward Hodges, an Englishman who had attained some renown as organist of St. James' Church, Bristol. As a result of these circumstances, the Firth & Hall–Robjohn organ was installed in St. John's Chapel. In his position as organist of Trinity Church, Hodges also had charge of music in St. John's Chapel, and when the organ was finished in 1840, Hodges was at the console for its opening.

Edward Hodges had arrived in New York only the year before, accompanied by his son, George F. Handel Hodges. Young George F. was quite enthusiastic about the new organ, and reported its progress in letters to his sister. On May 5, 1840 he wrote: "Our new organ at St. John's Church is almost finished, and the people are much pleased, delighted, charmed and edified with it. . . ." Two days later his comment was: "It is certainly a very fine instrument, and will be the best in the city, probably in the country" [78, pp.116–17].

Finally, after the opening, George F. wrote a most engaging account of the event in a letter of December 1, 1840, giving us a little taste of the excitement it caused:

> Last Friday evening, we had virtually, a sacred Concert; though nominally, an Exhibition of the new Organ at St. John's Chapel, where Papa is organist.
> I went round to the church a little before half-past five and found everything right, a man lighting the lamps, and another putting the Programmes in the pews. I took about six or eight of these to Mr. Delafield's, to show and give them to Mr. and Mrs. D., as I expected the church would be crowded and they would hardly have a chance to get any. Mr. D. told me he was going to send his coachman to secure

his pew for him so that they might be sure of a good seat, his being in a very central position. I then went home to tea, and went to the church again at 7 o'clock.

It was then almost full, and the people were pouring in from the North and from the South, from the East and from the West.

I ran home for a lady who had volunteered her services to help on this occasion. I seated her comfortably in the organ gallery and left her peeping through the curtain at some gentlemen, to go on my voyage of discovery through the church. I found Mr. and Mrs. D. in a strange pew, for although they had sent their coachman an hour and a half before the time, yet their pew was filled, and as the church was open to all, every pew was free. I had a small conversation with them and also with Harriot D., who was some pews behind them. I thought I would go up the middle aisle to see the organ and how it looked, and was in danger of being left there, for I could, with difficulty, get to the door as the people were pouring in so fast; this was about twenty minutes before the time. While engaged in the charitable work of trying to get seats for some pretty girls and an old gentleman, the clock struck seven. I hurried to get back again, but the people,—who were now so thick that I could have walked on their heads all over the church—kept crowding and pushing so that it took me several minutes of hard work to get back to the organ gallery. I was almost going to give it up as a bad job, but persevered till I gained my end.

[78, pp.118–19]

Characteristics of the Organ

Every division on St. John's organ had a different compass. The Great was GG to f^3 (omitting GG♯); the Choir was C to f^3; the Swell, tenor f to f^3; and the Pedal, C to c^1, twenty-five notes. Probably the most interesting detail of construction was the placement of the Choir division in a separate case that was "perched upon the front of the gallery." St. John's then, had a "rück-choir" long before the present trend in organ placement. This novelty won the flattery of imitation, because when Erben's famous organ was installed in Trinity Church six years later, it too had the Choir division on the gallery rail.[3]

The man actually responsible for St. John's organ, Thomas Robjohn, had been with the firm of Gray & Davison in England, where his brother William also worked. After he came to this country, Thomas Robjohn's organs included three-manual instruments for the South Dutch Church, New York, Wesleyan M. E. Church, Troy, New York, and Rutgers Street Presbyterian Church, New York. According to Radzinsky, the organ in the South Dutch Church was "the first organ in America to have an independent pedal organ of seven stops, and the first to have a pneumatic action."[4] Thomas and William Robjohn later became voicers in the Odell company [433, p.166].

Henry Erben

Erben's Career to 1860

"Erben, during his career, from 1824 to his death in 1884, was undoubtedly the most eminent organ builder in America" [433, p.166]. Henry Erben was the son of a music teacher, organist, and builder of organs and pianos, Peter Erben (1771–1863), who held the distinguished post of organist at Trinity Church, New York, until he was nearly seventy years old.

Thus, young Henry grew up in a musical home. Whether he had any formal education is not known, but when he was about seventeen his apprenticeship with Thomas Hall began, leading to the partnership of Hall & Erben (c.1821–1835). Henry Erben married and had three children, and one of them, Charles, entered the organ business with his father. Erben also took an interest in civic affairs, and in 1836 became an alderman of the Sixth Ward [86, p.12].

His displays of artistic temperament have been the subject of many stories. F. E. Morton wrote:

> Committees calling upon Mr. Erben stated their needs and financial limitations and he specified the organ. If a committee attempted to urge upon him plans inconsistent with his own, it was dismissed with denunciations emphasized by words from his private vocabulary, expressive if not elegant, his walking-stick frequently assisting both emphasis and exit. [374, p.1]

In 1843 Erben was engaged to build an organ for Trinity Church, New York, and by 1846, when the organ was nearing completion, he had quarreled with the organist, Dr. Hodges, as well as with the church authorities. George Templeton Strong, who knew Erben well, recorded in his diary on September 28, 1846:

> Talking of Trinity Church, the old feud between Erben and Hodges has ripened into a row which resulted in Hodges being tossed *vi et armis* out of the organ loft and left sitting on his hinder end in the lobby calling for the sexton and the rector. Erben wants to have an "exhibition" of that instrument (which is finished at last), but the spiritual authorities won't allow it. Erben appealed to the precedent of the exhibition of St. John's organ, and when Berrian gently insinuated that "we'd improved in churchmanship since then," he pointed to the Eagle Lectern and ejaculated, "I suppose you call that turkey buzzard an improvement in churchmanship!"
>
> [150, I, pp.283–84]

The Henry Erben console for the organ in Trinity Church, New York, 1846. The ranges of the manual keyboards are unique. The fourth manual and the white-faced stop-knobs are later additions. Note inkwell and rack of pens. *Photo from the Everett Truette scrapbooks, Boston Public Library.*

Erben had his way, and on October 7 and 8, twenty-one organists took turns at the console. The utter chaos of this exhibition was described in the New York *Express* the next day:

> Two days are named when this church shall be opened, and this organ shall be played, and all these organists shall play it, and such a continuous procession down Broadway, and such a suffocating jam at the gates of the church, and such a rush, when they are opened, into the body of the church, and such a buzz and a chatter, and a running about, up the pulpit stairs, into the vestry, and over the barriers of the chancel, were never seen before . . . while, upon the glorious organ, that sublime achievement of genius . . . have been performed arias from "Robert le Diable," marches from the military bands, and waltzes from the ballroom. These were interspersed with chromatic improvisations, and complicated fantasias, and voluntary variations on popular airs, or perhaps, here and there, a Kyrie from a Mass or a fugue from an opera. [104, pp.300–301]

In all, 17,939 people attended the two-day marathon; the notable exception was Dr. Hodges, who had not been invited to play.

An 1845 list shows that Erben had completed 153 church organs by that date, and by the time of his death he is said to have installed 146 organs in New York City churches alone[5] [433, p.165]. The 1845 list is interesting in that it is an index not only of the scope of Erben's work but also of the effects of the westward expansion as the market for organs began to grow in the midwestern states. Erben's work had the following distribution:

New York	63	Mississippi	3
Connecticut	10	District of Columbia	2
Virginia	8	Florida	2
South Carolina	6	Kentucky	2
Georgia	5	Louisiana	2
North Carolina	5	Maryland	2
Ohio	5	Massachusetts	2
Rhode Island	5	Maine	1
Vermont	5	Michigan	1
Alabama	4	Missouri	1
New Jersey	4	Tennessee	1
Pennsylvania	4	Wisconsin	1
Illinois	3		

In addition, Erben organs had gone to six churches outside the United States [86, pp.69–70]

Business Methods

Erben's productivity can be ascribed to his use of factory methods. When the *New York Observer* reported on October 16, 1841, that a fire had destroyed the "organ manufactory," it noted that there were "upwards of thirty persons employed in the establishment," that it was "one of the largest manufacturing establishments in the city," and that thirteen finished instruments had been destroyed, including a three-manual organ. From 1847 to 1863 Erben also had a branch factory in Baltimore, a convenient link with the large market for organs that developed in the South before the Civil War [413, p.6].

By the 1840s Erben had published a catalogue containing sample specifications and model numbers for organs of various sizes. One of these catalogues was used as a guide by the organ committee of Grace Church, Charleston, South Carolina. After meeting with Erben, the committee recommended to the vestry on February 18, 1848 that Erben be engaged to build an organ "in most respects such as is described in his printed circular and numbered 1 (one), varying only in the case, which must be of Gothic architecture instead of Grecian"

[163, p.139]. The organ was to cost $1,200, and Erben stipulated that he would take it back in trade with a deduction of not more than $50 if the church decided to buy a new or larger organ from him within two years.

Erben's success in dealing with church committees is reflected in the fact that three days later the committee contracted with him for a larger organ: "such a one as would permanently suit; abandoning the opinion of the necessity of any future change." This instrument was to cost $2,000, but "from this sum Mr. Erben has kindly consented to deduct four hundred dollars, as a donation from himself to the Church" [163, p.140].

One of Erben's most successful methods for advertising his organs was by holding exhibitions of important instruments. The notorious example of the Trinity Church exhibition has already been described. Demonstrations of instruments that were to go to other cities were sometimes held in the factory. For example, on June 10, 1848 *The American Musical Times* reported the opening of a new organ for the Cathedral of Detroit:

> On Friday evening, June 2nd, we were present at a grand Organ performance, at the manufactory of Mr. Henry Erben in Centre street. The vast room, in which the Organ was built, was densely crowded by members of the Profession and connoisseurs, attracted by the high reputation of the performers and the rumored excellence of Organ.
> [489]

Critiques

The reviewer who attended the exhibition of the Detroit instrument provided his readers with a description of the organ and an evaluation of its outstanding features:

> The Organ is unquestionably a very fine instrument—among the very best Organs that Mr. Erben has built for years. . . .
> It has three banks of keys, two octaves of Pedals, and 38 stops. —The case is in the Corinthian style 28 feet front and 37 feet high and 15 feet deep. There are but few larger Organs in the United States. It is a very powerful instrument—It has three double Diapasons—also a double Trumpet or Trombone in the Pedals. It has 7 reed stops, viz:— Trumpet and Clarion in the great organ—Bassoon and Clarionet in the choir—Hautboy and Trumpet in the swell, and a Trombone in the Pedals—It has fine coupling stops, and over 2000 pipes in all.
> There are many splendid points in the organ—the Diapasons are full, pure and sweet, and the Reed stops are admirable. All the pipes speak with remarkable rapidity, and the pedals are singularly prompt.
> [489]

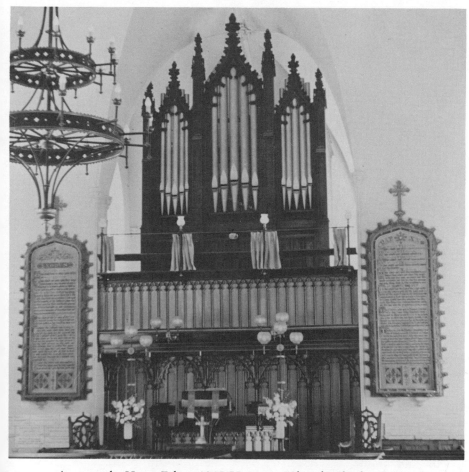

An organ by Henry Erben, 1845. Huguenot Church, Charleston, South Carolina. *Photo courtesy Thomas Murray.*

The renown of Erben's instruments rests solidly upon the quality of his workmanship. Even before its recent restoration, the action of the organ at the Huguenot Church, Charleston, South Carolina, was responsive and a delight to play. When the 1839 organ in the Mercer Street Presbyterian Church, New York, was being rebuilt, Edwin Groll recorded:

> Thorough examination disclosed that the chest work was in perfect condition. The chests, including the Swell, Great, and 2 Pedals, are constructed of 1⅛″ pine and tables and slides of chests being ⁵⁄₁₆″ mahogany; after 84 years use not a split on any of the tables is to be found, no loose divisions in chests. . . . [306, p.300]

Erben was given two awards for his organs: a gold medal from the American Institute after the Trinity organ was completed, and a silver one from the city of Baltimore in 1851 [86, pp. 29–30].

Characteristics of the Organs

Like his New England contemporaries, Erben exhibited a wide variety of manual and pedal compasses. In the organs of about 1845 and earlier, the most usual manual compass was from GG to f³. Just when Erben changed to the C compass is difficult to determine. Extant organs from the 1845–60 period in more or less original condition are rare, and may not give a representative picture. A one-manual organ of 1848 in Turner, Maine, has a compass of sixty-one notes, GG to g³, with a pedal of thirteen notes, GG to G,⁶ which a one-manual organ of 1845 (Specification I, below) is said to have a manual compass of fifty-four notes, C-f³ [368]. The famous Trinity Church, New York, organ of 1846 had unusual compasses, but they were specified by Dr. Hodges. Pedal compasses pose much the same problem. Small organs often had an octave of pedals pulling down from the manuals, while larger instruments had various compasses, including nineteen, twenty, and twenty-five notes. Erben's Swell compasses were short, with a bass range provided for some of the stops, following the prevailing practice of the day.

The following specifications show one-, two-, and three-manual organs of this period. One can readily see that the similarities with the work of other builders of this time far outnumber the differences. One Erben characteristic already seen in an organ by Thomas Hall is the tendency to provide basses for more of the Swell stops than was common among the New England builders. The Huguenot Church organ is an illustration of this practice, with the extension of three of its five Swell stops (Specification II, below). In New England an organ of this size would probably have had a bass for only the Stop'd Diapason in the Swell. A Principal bass in addition would not be a surprise, but a bass for the reed would be most unusual in an organ of such modest proportions.

The Philadelphia organ shows a specification in which practically all the stops extend the full length of the division (Specification III, below). Even the short Swell has been extended to tenor c, and draws its final octave from the Choir division. The New England builder would have divided at least the Stop'd Diapasons in the Great and Choir, and probably would have terminated the Swell on tenor f. However, we must also observe that stop 10 is the bass for stop 11. Here is a reappearance of the divided Sesquialtra Hall had used in his 1822 organ in Norfolk, Virginia.

An interesting feature of this specification is the inclusion in each manual division of one stopped and two open 8′ flue stops, two 4′ stops, a Fifteenth, and at least one reed. The emphasis on the fifth partial, which appears both as a separate stop and in the compound stop is, as we have seen, characteristic of this period. Johnson summarized that not only Erben's Cornets and Sesquialteras but also his stops named Mixture included third-sounding ranks, and that exceptions to this arrangement are rare [86, p.41].

Generally speaking, Erben's organs were voiced in a gentle and refined manner. In the organ of the Huguenot Church, Charleston (Specification II, below), the Great Principal 4′, Twelfth, and Fifteenth are almost equal in intensity. The 8′ Open Diapason is a little stronger, but is not by any means overpowering.

Opinions about Erben's reeds are inconsistent. Strong wrote "I never heard a trumpet stop from Erben yet that didn't sound like a tin horn" [150, I, p.133]. However, the report of a committee of five musicians who examined the Trinity organ for the American Institute said the reed stops "reflect great credit on the maker" [86, p.71]. It is difficult today to judge the quality of Erben's reeds; many have deteriorated or have been replaced. In 1962 Jesse Mercer described playing an original trumpet in the little 1845 Erben organ of only four registers (Specification I, below):

> The trumpet is small and bright, without any hint of shrillness, and is one of the most delightful stops of its type that I have ever had the pleasure to hear. Fortunately, the voicing has never been altered in any way. [368, p.2]

Representative Specifications of Erben Organs

I. One-manual organ built in 1845 for Christ Church, Elizabeth City, North Carolina.

Manual: 54 notes, C to f³

Stop'd Diapason Bass	8′	17 wood pipes
Stop'd Diapason Treble	8′	37 wood pipes
Principal Bass	4′	17 wood pipes
Principal	4′	37 pipes
Fifteenth	2′	54 pipes
Trumpet (tenor f)	8′	37 pipes

[368, p.2]

II. Two-manual organ in the Huguenot Church of Charleston, South Carolina. This organ was installed in 1845. Some changes have been made in the organ, but they are not included in the specification given here.

Great Manual: 58 notes, GG to f³
  (lacking low GG#)

Swell (continued)

Open Diapason	8'	58	Principal	4'	37
Stop'd Diapason Treble	8'	37	Flute	4'	37
Stop'd Diapason Bass	8'	21	Hautboy	8'	37
Principal	4'	58			
Twelfth (from C)	2⅔'	54	*Choir:* Bass stops		
Fifteenth (from C)	2'	54	Stop Diapason	8'	21
Trumpet (from tenor c)	8'	42	Principal	4'	21
			Bassoon	8'	21

Swell and Choir Bass Manual:
  58 notes

Pedal

Swell: Treble stops from tenor f

Twenty notes pulling down from
  Great.

Stop'd Diapason	8'	37
Dulciana	8'	37

GG compass. (The 16' Bourdon is a
  later addition.)

III. Three-manual organ built in 1837 for Christ Church, Philadelphia.
The following description was written by J. C. B. Standbridge, who
was organist of Christ Church.

Great Organ

1. Double Stop'd Diapason	58
2. Large Open Diapason, metal throughout	58
3. 2nd Open Diapason	58
4. Stop'd Diapason	58
5. Principal	58
6. Nighthorn	58
7. Twelfth	58
8. Fifteenth	58
9. Seventeenth	58
10. Sesquialtra, fr. lowest G to middle B inclusive	
28 notes of 4 ranks each	112
11. Mounted Cornet, fr. Middle C to F in Alt., incl.	
30 notes of 5 ranks each	150
12. Trumpet	58
13. Clarion	58
Total Great	900

Compass of Great Organ, GG to FF, or 58 notes [GG
  to f³].

Choir Organ

14. Dulciana	58
15. Open Diapason to Gamut G. remaining 11 pipes,	
stp'd dia.	58
16. Stop'd Diapason	58
17. Principal	58
18. Flute	58

19. Fifteenth   58
20. Cremona down to C., second space in Bass, incl.   42

    Total Choir   390

Compass same as Great.

Swell Organ

21. Open Diapason   42
22. Viol da Gamba   42
23. Stop'd Diapason   42
24. Principal   42
25. Flute   42
26. Fifteenth   42
27. Cornet, 3 ranks   126
28. Trumpet   42
29. Oboe   42

    Tremulant
    Total Swell   462

Compass from C, second space in Bass to F in
    Alt., incl. 42 notes.
The Swell keys are continued down to GG, or 16
    notes, and take down the action of the Choir
    Organ with those 16 notes.

Pedal Organ

30. Double Open Diapason, largest pipe 10 feet long   19
    by about 19 by 22 inches square outside, this
    note speaks G an octave below the lowest G of
    the pianoforte
31. Open Diapason   19
32. Principal, of metal   19

    Total Pedal   57

Compass from GGG to DD or 19 notes

    Total pipes in organ   1809

Couplers

33. Pedals to Great Organ
34. Great Organ to Choir
35. Great Organ to Swell

A Pedal to draw out at once in the Great Organ the
    Nighthorn, 12th, 15th, 17th, Sesquialtra and Cornet.

A Pedal to push in at once, all the above stops.

    Total—32 stops, 3 couplers

[Cited in 387, p.12.]

Erben's most famous organ of this time was the one he completed in
1846 for Trinity Church, New York. The specification was the work of
Dr. Hodges and contained features that were characteristic neither of

Erben nor of American organs in general. Some of the most obvious departures are the compasses of the divisions (note the relationships of the compasses of the stops to the compasses of the keyboards), the four octave couplers, three reeds on the Swell (to say nothing of the Serpent in the Swell bass), and the single 32′ pedal stop. The large- and small-scaled Open Diapasons and Principals on the Great, while not unique, were infrequently found in early nineteenth-century organs.[7]

Dr. Edward Hodges's Specification for the Erben Organ Completed in 1846 for Trinity Church, New York

Great Organ

Open Diapason, large scale
Open Diapason, smaller scale
Stopped Diapason
Flute
Principal, large scale
Principal, smaller scale
Twelfth
Fifteenth
Sesquialtera, 3 ranks
Mixture, 3 ranks
Trumpet
Clarion
Compass: CCC to F, 5½ octaves

Swell Organ

Stopped Double Diapason
Open Diapason
Stopped Diapason
Dulciana
Principal
Cornet, 5 ranks
Hautboy
Trumpet
Clarion
Compass: (Manual) CCC to F in altissimo, 6½ octaves
Compass: (Stops) Tenor C to F in altissimo, 4½ octaves

Swell Bass (outside of Swell box)

Dulciana
Serpent
Compass: CCC to Tenor C, 2 octaves (25 pipes), the upper C connected with Pedals only

Choir Organ

Dulciana
Stopped Diapason

Choir organ (continued)

Principal
Flute
Fifteenth
Clarinet and Bassoon
Compass: (Manual) CCC to F, 5½ octaves
Compass: (Stops) CC to F, 4½ octaves

The lowest octave of keys connected with Swell Bass.

Pedal

Open Diapason, 32 feet, wood, 3 octaves
Compass: (of Pedal-board) CCC to C, 2 octaves

Couplers

Great to pedal, unison
Great to pedal, octave
Swell to pedal
Choir to pedal
Swell to great, unison
Swell to great, octave
Choir to great
Swell to choir, unison
Swell to choir, octave
Pedal, unison
Pedal, octaves

Number of pipes

Great organ	1056
Swell organ	702
Swell bass	50
Choir organ	324
Pedal	37
	2169

[Cited in 104, pp.296–97.]

George Jardine

George Jardine's Career to 1860

George Jardine (1801–1883) was almost an exact contemporary of Henry Erben. A native of Dartford, England, Jardine was apprenticed with Flight & Robson, worked for a time for Joseph W. Walker of London, and also studied architecture. In 1837 he came to America with his wife, five children, and his nephew F. W. Jardine. After serving an apprenticeship with his uncle, F. W. Jardine returned to England.

A clipping from an unidentified issue of *Music Trades* in Everett Truette's scrapbooks reports that George Jardine came to this country to make the barrel organs that were sometimes used in small churches to accompany the congregational singing. However, he found that there was little demand for them, so he turned to building organs with keyboards. The reliability of this source might be questioned, because it continued: "Among other innovations he introduced open diapasons, which have been a specialty with this house ever since" [157].

A barrel organ built by Jardine in 1842 can still be seen and heard in the Zion Episcopal Church, Pierrepont Manor, New York. It is thought to be the only church barrel organ extant in the United States. This little organ has two barrels, each with eleven tunes. Its stops are 8′ St. Diapason (divided, eighteen bass and thirty-five treble pipes), 8′ Dulciana (thirty-five pipes), and 4′ Principal (fifty-three pipes) [*OHS 1970 Convention Program*].

By the time Jardine arrived in New York, Erben was already established in business and was well known in the profession. One can imagine that it was difficult for the newcomer to gain a foothold against such a thriving competitor. Consequently little is heard of Jardine's work during his first decades in New York; the large instruments that were to contribute the most to his fame were built after the Civil War. What may have been the first review of a Jardine organ appeared in *The Musical Review* of September 15, 1838:

> We have been highly gratified in examining a Chamber Organ, made for G. B. Smith, Esq., President of the Butchers' and Drovers' Bank, by Mr. George Jardine, 459 Broadway. The exterior is such as to please the *eye* of the most fastidious; the mechanism throughout well contrived and skillfully executed; and the tone and general effect upon the *ear*, (save a little imperfection in the *tuning*, which, when we heard it, was not completed,) we think, decidedly *good*.

From one source we learn that Jardine's first American organ was a small instrument built for St. James' Church, New York [88, p.79], and in another we read that his first order was for a two-manual organ

A Jardine circus organ of the 1850s. *Photo from a circus poster, courtesy Barbara Owen.*

for the First Reformed Dutch Church of Jersey City, an organ that was awarded a gold medal by the American Institute [115].

George Jardine's four sons—Edward G., Joseph, Frederick, and Dudley—were brought up in the family business and became members of the firm. Edward G. assumed a position of leadership and eventually succeeded his father as the senior member of the company. Two of George's grandsons also became organ builders: Joseph's son Edward D. and Frederick's son Charles. The latter was the senior partner in the last years of the Jardine organ history.

A catalogue of 1869 shows that the Jardine company had completed 370 organs by that date—an average of about twelve a year from the time the family arrived in New York. Their work "was not of the highest price or grade, and yet had a large circulation" [433, p.166].

An Early Jardine Organ

One of Jardine's most impressive pre-Civil War instruments was the organ for the Cathedral of the Immaculate Conception (R. C.), Mobile, Alabama. It contained three manuals, thirty-three registers, and two octaves of pedals.

Cathedral of the Immaculate Conception, Mobile, Alabama
GEORGE JARDINE, 1858

Great Organ

Double open Diapason
Open Diapason
Stopped Diapason
Principal
Night Horn
Twelfth
Fifteenth
Sesquialtera
Mixture
Trumpet
Clarion

Swell Organ

Bourdon
Open Diapason
Viol d'Amour
Stopped Diapason
Principal
Fifteenth
Cornet
Cornopean
Hautbois
Voix Celeste

Choir Organ

Open Diapason

Choir Organ (continued)

Dulciana
Stopped Diapason base [*sic*]
Stopped Diapason treble
Clariana
Hohl Flute
Principal
Cremona
Flageolet

Pedal Organ

Double open Diapason
Double stopped do.
Violoncello
Clarabella

Couplers

Great and Swell
Great and Choir
Choir and Swell
Pedal and Great
Pedal and Choir

Bellows
Pedal Lock
Pedal Octaves

Total, forty-two stops.

[*New-York Musical Review and Gazette*, Jan. 1859][8]

Jardine's interest in unusual colors and unusual stop names makes its appearance in the Swell Voix Celeste and the Choir Clariana. He claimed to have introduced both of these stops into the American organ [43, p.5]. The tendency to experiment with tonal design is a characteristic that continued through the entire history of the Jardine company, giving something of a hollow sound to the words of third-generation Edward D. Jardine:

> True, new and startling names have appeared among organ stops —already a rich and varied field for investigation by the antiquary and the linguist—but unadorned descriptions of these alleged new organ tones, reveal only slight differences in shades and tints of the same old tone-colors. [337]

Richard M. Ferris

Ferris's Career

Richard M. Ferris (1818–1858) is remembered today primarily as the builder of the organ now in the auditorium at Round Lake, New York. This organ has particular historical significance in that it is probably the oldest organ of its size to have survived more or less intact to the present day.

Ferris learned organ building as an apprentice with Hall and Erben. About 1840 he established his own shop, and for the first two years he supplemented organ building by making pipes for other builders. Ferris is said to have built about sixty organs during his lifetime, including twenty-three two-manual, three three-manual, and the rest one-manual organs [245, p.2]. One of the three-manual instruments was not actually Ferris's, but was the completion of Robjohn's organ in the South Dutch Reformed Church, New York. The other two were an 1847 organ for Calvary Episcopal Church and an 1856 instrument for All Souls' Unitarian Church, both in New York.

In 1857 Ferris's half brother, Levi U. Stuart, joined him in business, and for a brief time the firm name was Richard M. Ferris & Co. Ferris died a year later, and Stuart succeeded him in business. For about two years after that Ferris & Stuart was the company name, but the organs with this designation were actually Stuart's work.

The Round Lake Organ

The Calvary Church organ was "the largest and best of Mr. Ferris' productions, and made for him considerable reputation" [245, p.2]. In 1887 the church sold the organ, and it was acquired the next year by the Round Lake Association (a Methodist summer camp) for its present location in the auditorium. The original specification is given below.

Calvary Episcopal Church, New York, New York
RICHARD M. FERRIS, 1847

Great Organ		Great Organ (continued)	
First Open Diapason	8′	Mixture	III
Second Open Diapason	8′	Trumpet	8′
Stopped Diapason	8′	Clarion	4′
First Principal	4′		
Second Principal	4′	*Swell Organ*	
Night Horn (tc)	4′	Bourdon	16′
Twelfth	2⅔′	Open Diapason	8′
Fifteenth	2′	Dulciana	8′
Sesquialtera	III	Stopped Diapason	8′

Calvary Episcopal Church, New York, New York
RICHARD M. FERRIS, 1847

Swell Organ (continued)

Principal	4′
Sesquialtera	III
Cornet	II
Trumpet	8′
Hautboy	8′
Clarion	4′

Choir Organ

Open Diapason (G)	8′
Dulciana	8′
Stopped Diapason	8′
Principal	4′
Flute	4′
Picolo (tc)	2′
Furniture (G)	II
Cremona (C)	8′

Pedal Organ

Twenty-four foot stop	16′
Twelve-foot stop	8′

Couplers

Great and Swell
Great and Choir
Choir and Swell
Pedals and Great
Pedals and Choir
Great and Swell 8va.

2 Great combination knobs

The manual compass was originally GG-f^3 (fifty-nine notes) and the pedal compass GG-c (eighteen notes). The Swell extended down to tenor c, and its lower range was permanently coupled to the Choir. The unusual designations for the Pedal stops result from the GG compass. These stops have been changed, but presumably they originally sounded at 16′ and 8′ pitch, using modern terminology. The composition of the compound stops was given in the *OHS 1967 Convention Program:*

Great	Sesquialtera:	17–19–22, 12–15–17, 8–12–15
	Mixture:	15–17–19, 12–15–17
Swell	Sesquialtera:	17–19–22, 12–15–17
	Cornet:	12–15 throughout
Choir	Furniture:	12–15 throughout

Some alterations in the organ were made by Levi Stuart in 1868, others by Giles Beach at the time the organ was moved to Round Lake. They included changes in compass, changes in the Pedal stops, replacement of the Great Second Principal by a Viol, and replacement of much of the action.

There is a striking similarity between Ferris's choice of stops and the specification of Erben's organ for Trinity Church, New York, installed just the year before. The Great divisions are identical. In the Swell, Ferris chose to use two compound stops, one with two and one with three ranks. The Erben organ had one stop of five ranks instead.

Ferris omitted the two Swell bass stops and added two stops to the Choir. In the Pedal he substituted two stops for Erben's single 32′ stop.

Critiques

Whatever may have prompted Ferris to follow the Trinity organ scheme so faithfully, his organ was well received in its own right. In August 1852 *The Musical World* stated:

> The organ is the best we have heard for some time. The Diapasons are remarkably full, and are not overpowered by the Sequialtera [*sic*], Mixture and Fifteenth, as is the case in many organs in this city. The Solo stops are all carefully voiced; the Hautboy is very even and clear. The touch is also well-regulated and easy.
>
> [Cited in 287, p.1.]

A similar view was given by Clara Beames in 1869:

> One cannot hear some of the larger instruments constructed by Mr. Ferris without according a high rank among New York organ builders. His instruments are especially noticeable for good diapason or foundation work, and for some good solo stops. The Calvary organ ranks among the best in the city; and that in All Souls' Church is also a highly creditable work.

Beames continues with some comments about Ferris himself:

> Mr. Ferris was very nervous, precise and exceedingly irritable. If a piece of work did not exactly suit him, he would destroy it. He had an excellent tenor voice, and was a good church singer. His ear was very acute, and in tuning an organ, he could scarcely satisfy himself, especially during the last year or two of his attendance to business, as the influence of his illness, which was at times of a neuralgic description, increased his sensitiveness and irascibility. In finishing the organ in All Souls' Church—which was one of his last efforts—he was so over-particular about the tuning, being several months about it, that it was thought he would never get through. [245, p.13]

Other Builders in New York City

The Pilcher Family

Two families of organ builders that later became famous in the central states made New York their first American home. Henry Pilcher (1798–1880), an Englishman, arrived there in 1832 with his wife and five children. He had been taught organ and piano building by an older brother, and had served an apprenticeship in London [498]. In 1820 he established his business in Dover, England.

After a brief stay in New York, the Pilchers moved to Newark, New Jersey, and Henry advertised himself as a teacher and organ builder. They next moved to New Haven, Connecticut, about 1838, but by 1844 they were again living in New York. For a time Henry was organist of the Seaman's Institute. There are no records that he built organs independently, but it was probably during this period that he worked for Henry Erben. The years 1848 to 1851 found Pilcher again in Newark, where he was building organs and pianos.

According to Lippencott, it was in 1852 that Henry Pilcher moved to St. Louis. By this time his sons Henry, Jr. (1828–1890), and William (1830–1912) were in business with him, in the firm of Henry Pilcher and Sons [350, pp.90–91]. The business thrived, and by 1857 the Pilchers had both a store and a factory. They sold music, pianos, and other instruments, and also published music. The factory was devoted entirely to the manufacture of organs, but it is not known how extensive its work was. When Henry retired in 1858, the firm was directed by his sons, and later his grandsons, under the name Henry Pilcher's Sons.[9]

The Kilgen Family

About the time the Pilchers moved to the Midwest, the story of Kilgen organs in the United States had its beginning in New York. In 1851 George Kilgen (d.1902) opened an organ shop in New York. He had immigrated from Europe only a year or two before, and had worked for a time in the Jardine factory [204]. According to tradition, Kilgen organ history actually extends back to the middle of the seventeenth century. Sebastian Kilgen, a French Huguenot who was wounded in France and fled to Germany, took refuge in a monastery near Durlach. While he was recovering from his wounds, he learned organ building from the monks [138, p.4]. He is said to have built his first organ in 1640.

Succeeding generations of Kilgens built organs in Durlach. Their family trade and tradition were finally carried to America two centuries later. In 1873 the Kilgens, like the Pilchers, moved to St. Louis, establishing a business that flourished well into the twentieth century. George Kilgen was joined in business by his son Charles (1859–1932) in 1886, and the firm name became Geo. Kilgen & Son. Charles later succeeded his father as the head of the company, and guided it during its most productive years.

Other Contemporary Builders

Many other names appear in connection with the organ industry in New York during this period. A few were men who, like William H. Davis, produced a fair number of instruments, and would have been accorded more attention had their work not been overshadowed by the achievements of such famous builders as Erben and Jardine. Some were known to be employees in the larger shops, perhaps building a few organs of their own. Others were part-time organ builders who also built pianos, taught music, or served as church organists when business was slow. About others we have no knowledge; they are merely names listed as "organ builders" in city business directories.

The builders are listed chronologically, according to the approximate date they became active in the organ industry:

1810–19   William Redstone, Thomas Wester & Son, Robert Sprawll (Sproull), James Buchan (Bucken), Thomas Redstone, Joseph Knapp (Napp), Maurice Mownihan (Moynehan, and other spellings).

1820–29   John Hubie (Huber), Robert Dent, James Knapp, Peek & Burns, Robert Dean, John Fawcett, James Jackson, John Wale, Jr., Elisha Brotherton.

1830–39   Alexander Fowler, N. P. Holt, Thomas Wagstaff, Charles Heckert, William F. Berry, James Heath, Jacob Hyne, Henry Leaman, John H. Enstine.

1840–49   William H. Davis, Thomas Raven.

1850–59   Alexander Mills, F. X. Engelfried, William Pye, James Blake. The work of these builders belongs for the most part in the post-1860 period.

Builders in Other Parts of New York State

By the 1840s organ builders were scattered along the main east-west route through New York (what is now the New York State Thruway) from Albany to Buffalo. Some of their shops reached substantial size, with the greatest period of activity falling in the last half of the century.

In 1834 Alvinza Andrews founded a business for manufacturing "Pipe and Parlour Organs" in Waterville, New York. His son George Norton Andrews (1832–1904) grew up in the business, and in 1854 father and son moved their factory to Utica. After a few years Alvinza retired, but George and his son Charles Backus Andrews (b.1858) continued building organs in Utica until they moved their shop to California in 1886 [4, p.1].

A list of Andrews organs compiled by Alvinza's great-granddaughter is quite incomplete for the pre-1860 period, but it does give an indication that the Andrews factory had already gained a reputation beyond its home territory, and had installed organs as far away as Pau Pau, Michigan, and Washington, D. C.

About the time Alvinza Andrews moved his factory to Utica, a young Englishman who had learned organ building from Gray & Davison came to work for him. John Gale Marklove (1827–1891) had worked in New York City for two or three years before coming to Utica. He remained in the Andrews shop until Alvinza retired in about 1857, and then went into business for himself. In a brief evaluation of Marklove, Robert Reich has said:

> His work was of almost uniformly fine quality until his death in 1892. His influence is thought to be the reason why Morey, his successor, continued to build tracker organs until about 1930 and why some Morey organs are far superior tonally to most instruments of their period.[10] [437, p.3]

Thus, from the opening of the Andrews shop in Waterville, and continuing in Utica, one can trace a succession of organ builders maintaining a traditional craft over a hundred-year period, in spite of the drastic changes taking place in the rest of the organ world during that time.

The leading organ builder in western New York was Garret House (1810–1900). A native of Johnstown, New York, House established his business in Buffalo about 1845. For a time he made both organs and pianos, but soon devoted himself entirely to organs. While most of his organs were placed in neighboring areas of New York and Pennsylvania, a liberal number were also built for midwestern states, including Illinois, Michigan, Ohio, and Wisconsin [373, pp.4–5]. House's best-known work was done between 1860 and 1898.

Among the other builders in New York State were Elsworth Phelps (Guilford), Augustus Backus (Troy), John Meads (Albany), and Giles Beach (Gloversville).[11]

IX

PENNSYLVANIA

Introduction

Pennsylvania's Traditional Contrasts

PENNSYLVANIA was a state of sharply drawn contrasts during the early nineteenth century, contrasts that had existed since early colonial days. On the one hand there was the cosmopolitan atmosphere of Philadelphia, and on the other the little rural communities of German settlers. These differences became more marked with the growth of the city.

Philadelphia was the largest city in America during the last third of the eighteenth century, even though its population in 1790 was only 42,444. By 1820, although outstripped in population by New York, Philadelphia had almost tripled, and in 1860 its population reached 565,529 [108, p.467]. In another forty years this figure was to double. The great leveling sweep of urban developments and factory methods soon obscured the nonconformist, non-Anglicized communities as well as the slowly fashioned products of the handcraftsmen. Large cities are subjected to various forces that change them in ways usually termed "progress." And change they must if they are to maintain their position of leadership and attract their share of population and industry. Thus big cities copy each others' improvements and tend to become ever more alike—a tendency greatly facilitated in the early nineteenth century by the construction of railroad lines between major cities.

In the rural German communities of Pennsylvania these forces for change were slower to arrive, and even slower to take effect. Indeed, some of the groups that had recently endured considerable hardship for the privilege of maintaining particular identities tended to draw their members even closer together when outside influences threatened to destroy or dilute such identity.

Resistance to change in rural communities is not peculiar to Pennsylvania, but it had particular significance there. In New England, for instance, the average farmer and the city dweller were both of English background, drawing on more or less the same traditions and speaking the same language. In Pennsylvania, the average farmer or small-townsman was a German, he spoke German, and he held a strong connection with a German religious group, be it Lutheran, Moravian, Reformed, or Schwenkfelder. The larger, the more cosmopolitan, and the more of a melting pot Philadelphia became, and the more connection it had with the rest of the United States, the less affinity there was between the city and much of the rest of the state.

Two Trends in Organ Design

The cultural differences that existed are strikingly epitomized in Pennsylvania organ history during the early nineteenth century. The German tradition in organ building, so well expressed in the works of Tannenberg, was carried into the 1810–1860 period by his son-in-law Johann Philip Bachmann, the Krausses, and the Dieffenbachs. Bachmann's last six organs, previously discussed, actually fall into this period, as do the last two of Christian Dieffenbach (see pp.62, 64). Andrew Krauss and his sons continued to build organs in their shop in Kraussdale, and brought the organ-building activity of this family to its highest development. Other small shops following much the same patterns were opened in and near Reading by Frederick Obenhauser and by the Bohlers (Daniel, John, and Samuel). From 1855 to 1861 Henry F. Berger, formerly in Baltimore, Maryland, built organs in Jefferson and York. Another contemporary builder was Charles Hanzleman of Allentown.

Meanwhile, something quite different was happening in Philadelphia. From June to the end of October 1854, the *New-York Musical Review and Gazette* carried a series of letters describing church music in Philadelphia, and listing the organs then in use:

Old St. Peter's: c.1829 Henry Corrie organ.

Old Swedes' Church: 1829 A. G. Hunter organ. A small organ.

Grace Church (P. E.): c.1835 Henry Erben organ. Three manuals and pedal, and over thirty stops.

Second Presbyterian Church: 1837 organ. Builder not identified. Three manuals and pedal, thirty-six stops. Described as "exceedingly defective."

Christ Church: c.1838 Henry Erben organ. Three manuals and pedal, thirty-two speaking stops.

St. Paul's: c.1850 Simmons & McIntyre organ. Three manuals and
   pedal and about forty registers.
Arch Street Presbyterian Church: 1851 or 1852 J. C. Standbridge organ.
   Three manuals and pedal.
St. James Episcopal Church: 1853–54 Hall & Labagh. Two manuals
   and pedal and about twenty-six stops.
First Reformed Presbyterian Church: "Neither organ nor choir are
   tolerated by the congregation. . . ."
Tenth Presbyterian Church: Had no organ.

   Three of the builders listed, Corrie, Hunter, and Standbridge, had
their shops in Philadelphia. The organs of Henry John Corrie (1786–
1859) and of Albert G. Hunter (d.1869) cited above were early examples
of the work of these two builders. The *Review and Gazette* gave Corrie's
organ the brief comment: "Externally, it is a tolerable specimen of a
European cathedral instrument, but it is now becoming quite inferior
from use and age, and needs being removed, to give place to something
better." The organ of John C. Standbridge (1800–1871) was described
as an "excellent instrument." Another of the builders represented,
Thomas Hall, had lived in Philadelphia and had built organs there
from 1812 to 1817, when he moved to New York. His partnership
with Labagh dated from 1846 (see p.145). An organ by Thomas Hall
built during his Philadelphia period had served St. James Episcopal
Church for about forty years before the installation of the Hall &
Labagh organ.
   The list given above, concentrating on Episcopal and Presbyterian
churches, does not give the whole picture. Two omissions, for example, were Johann Philip Bachmann's organ in St. John's Lutheran
Church (see p.62) and the organ in the First Moravian Church. The
latter was built by E. N. Scherr of Philadelphia, and was said to be
"very heavy" in sound [61, pp.93–95].
   In spite of its omissions, the *Review and Gazette* showed that in
addition to organs by local builders, leading churches in Philadelphia
contained organs from New York (Erben and Hall & Labagh) and
Boston (Simmons & McIntyre). The New York and Boston organs
followed the English tradition, and even more important, so did
Philadelphia's two leading builders, Corrie and Standbridge. Both men
were born in England, and Corrie had a thorough grounding in organ
building before coming to the United States.
   Whatever attraction the English style may have had for Philadelphia
was lost on the German part of Pennsylvania. Only Pittsburgh, where
the early establishment of Presbyterian and Episcopal churches fostered a similar attitude, followed Philadelphia's footsteps.

Philadelphia and Pittsburgh

Corrie, Standbridge, and Their Contemporaries in Philadelphia

Henry John Corrie (James Henry Corrie, d.1858) was born in London. He worked for Thomas Elliot there, and came to America in 1822 to install one of Elliot's organs in the Old South Church, Boston. He decided to stay in Boston and went to work for Thomas Appleton. By 1828 Corrie was in Philadelphia and was the leading organ builder there during the late 1820s and the '30s. He was assisted by his sons George J. (b.1816) and William A. (d.1896). From 1831 to 1837 he had as a partner John Huber, or Hubie, who had previously worked in New York.

After his father's death in 1858, William Corrie continued in the business with a brother-in-law, John Wright. Corrie joined the Union Army in 1861, and although he returned to organ building after the war, ill health prevented his doing much work.

Most of Henry Corrie's organs were installed in Episcopal and Roman Catholic churches. Their locations included such distant cities as Cincinnati, Louisville, and Nashville, as well as Philadelphia, Pittsburgh, and Baltimore [380, p.2]. The only work of Corrie's known to survive until recent times was the organ of St. Joseph's Church, Willings Alley, Philadelphia.

John C. B. Standbridge, like Corrie, was English-born, but his family moved to Philadelphia by 1807, when John was seven years old. As a young man he helped his father in the chinaware, cotton-spinning, and wholesale-drug businesses, and in 1822 or 1823 he received a degree from the University of Pennsylvania School of Medicine. Although he continued working in the family business, John Standbridge turned an increasing amount of his attention to music. In the 1830s he became organist at Christ Church, Philadelphia, a position he held when Henry Erben's organ was installed there in 1837 (see pp.158–59).

Standbridge built his first organ, a small one, in 1840, with the help of William Darley and a Mr. Jones [381, p.7]. It was placed in the Unitarian Church. In 1850 he built another organ for this church, an instrument that was described as the "most magnificent in the United States" [cited in 381, p.7]. In the early 1850s Standbridge went into organ building on a full-time basis. In 1851 or 1852 he built a three-manual organ for the West Arch Street Presbyterian Church, Philadelphia; in 1854 he completed Philadelphia's first four-manual organ for the Harmonia Sacred Society Concert Hall (see p.103); and in 1855 he built an organ for St. Bridget's Roman Catholic Church, New York. St. Peter's Episcopal Church and the First Moravian Church, both in Philadelphia, acquired new two-manual Standbridge organs in 1856. A three-manual organ for the Cathedral of St. Peter and St. Paul, R. C., and a two-manual for the Green Street Reformed Church date from about 1860, and other Standbridge organs were installed in Calvary Presbyterian Church, Church of the Epiphany, and Central Presbyterian, all of Philadelphia [381, p.7].

Although we have little to judge from today, the Standbridge organs were evidently successful tonally. McCracken has said, "All of the write-ups I have read of Standbridge organs commend them for their sweetness of tone" [381, p.7]. As to the casework, McCracken continues: "I think it would be safe to reflect that the Standbridges, unlike the Hooks, were not master cabinetmakers. Available photographs show some rather bizzare and frequently unsightly cases" [381, p.8].

Other builders who were active in Philadelphia during the period 1810–1860 included Joseph Buffington, D. B. Grover, James Hall, Wilfred Hall, Christopher Knauer, Henry Knauff, Peter LaGrassa, and Peter Schenkel.[1]

Organs and Builders in Pittsburgh

In western Pennsylvania, Pittsburgh was feeling the effects of the population expansion and was beginning to assume the appearance of a city. According to Packer, "by March 1843, out of twenty-five congregations in Pittsburgh, only ten or twelve had no choir, and six churches had organs" [118, p.4].

The Presbyterian church was the first one established in Pittsburgh (1758). The First Presbyterian Church allowed no musical instruments until about 1823, when a bass viol was introduced to accompany the singing. An organ was finally installed in 1863. The East Liberty Presbyterian Church, founded in 1828, permitted only a tuning fork until 1856. Then a melodeon was introduced, causing several families to resign [118, p.7]. Seventeen years later this church had its first organ. Other Presbyterian congregations installed organs in 1850 (Third Presbyterian) and in 1875 (Shadyside Presbyterian).

Trinity Episcopal Church installed what was probably Pittsburgh's first church organ in 1808. By 1819 this church also had an organ in its chapel, and in 1823 a new organ was installed in the church[2] [118].

St. Paul's Roman Catholic Church had a small organ in 1834, but it was destroyed by fire in 1851 (this instrument may have been built by Henry Corrie). The next organ for this church was an 1870 four-manual Jardine of forty-five stops that attracted considerable attention [118, p.6].

Joseph Harvey, who had come to this country sometime before 1823, was an organ builder living in Pittsburgh during this period. An

1838 organ of his is still in use in St. John's (Burry's) Church, Zelienople, Pennsylvania [282]. Another builder, Samuel Arlidge, moved to Allegheny City (now a part of Pittsburgh) in the 1840s.

Pennsylvania's German Tradition

Rural Organs

The organs produced in the rural parts of Pennsylvania, like the parlor organs of New England, seem insignificant in comparison with the large instruments of the famous Hook and Erben factories. Yet size and quantity are not all-important. Even coupled with evaluations of quality, these factors tell only a part of the story.

In spite of the advances made in manufacturing and the growth of cities, America was still an agricultural country. By 1860 only about sixteen percent of the population lived in cities of eight thousand or more inhabitants. If the other eighty-four percent of the population heard an organ at all, it was probably in some relatively obscure rural church or in some well-to-do farmer's parlor.

While these instruments had no widespread influence and established no stylistic trends, there is an intrinsic importance in the fact that they existed, that local craftsmen thought it worth the time and effort to build them, and that churches thought it worthwhile to buy them. The small-town organ was not yet the mass-produced product of a large company or the reed organ substitute.

The installation of a new organ was an important event in rural Pennsylvania. Dedication ceremonies attracted people from towns and villages for miles around. Interest and enthusiasm ran high when the Bohler organ shop of Reading completed an organ for St. Paul's Lutheran and Reformed Church, Fleetwood:

Said organ was dedicated in the summer of 1859 about the time that the East Penn Railroad was completed to Allentown. They ran excursion trains from Reading and from the other end as far as Millerstown as the road was not fully completed to Allentown. There was such an immense number of people coming from both ends of the road that they had to run extra trains from each direction, and Fleetwood (formerly Coxtown until the rail road was built) was unable to accommodate all the people with eatables. Some went out to the farmers, trying to get something to eat. Fleetwood was completely eaten up, and might say, "Drank Dry." It was the greatest crowd of people Fleetwood ever had, before or since. The Ringgold Band of Reading furnished music. Prior to the year 1859 no musical instrument was used in the Church. [33, p.9]

The Krauss Family

Craftsmanship in the small Pennsylvania organ shops was well represented by the Krauss organs. John and Andrew Krauss shared the work in their organ shop until the early nineteenth century. Then John became interested in other pursuits, and organ building was left to Andrew, who was largely responsible for the Krauss organs built between 1812 and the time of his death in 1841. Andrew had five sons. Of them, Joel (1801–1852), George (1803–1880), and to some extent Samuel (1807–1904) worked in the organ factory. After Joel's death in 1852, the organ business was continued by George, and then by George's son Edwin B. Krauss (1838–1929).

An 1868 organ for Zion Evangelical Lutheran Church, Long Valley, New Jersey, marked the end of an era for the Krausses. George was sixty-five years old, and probably by this time much of the work was being done by his son Edwin. In later years Edwin was sometimes called on to rebuild the earlier Krauss organs, and he did build some new organs, but the most productive years of this family were past. Edwin remained in the business for about twenty-five years after his father's death, and thus the Krauss organ history came to an end about 1905, after more than one hundred years of activity[3] [304, pp.17–18].

Some of the Krauss contracts for organs are preserved in the Schwenkfelder Library at Pennsburg, Pennsylvania, and furnish a good source for specifications. Contracts for five organs dated between 1814 and 1820 show that Andrew Krauss used the following stops:

Manual stop		Frequency used in 5 organs
Principal	8′	5
Gross Gedackt	8′	5
Quint Dinne	8′	1
Flöt	8′	5
Violdegamba	8′	5
Solicional	8′	1
Principal	4′	5
Klein Gedackt	4′	4
Gems Horn	4′	1
Quinte	3′	5
Sub Octav	2′	1
Mixtur	III	1
Cornet	II	4
Pedal stop		
Subbass	16′	4
Octav Bass	8′	4

(One instrument did not have pedal.)

After 1820 the Principal, Gedackt, and Viol de Gamba remained the important 8′ stops; the Principal 4′ was a part of every specification; the Quinte and the Cornet lost in popularity, while the previously neglected 2′ made a more frequent appearance; and pedals were less frequently included.

An interesting Krauss organ in more or less original condition is the 1850 instrument now in Old Norriton Presbyterian Church. The manual compass is fifty-three notes, C to e³. The thirteen pedal keys are very short: the naturals are about six inches long and the sharps only about two and a half inches long. They are very inconvenient to play, and could only serve for an occasional cadence or pedal point. The stops are placed in a vertical line at the left of the keyboard, and pull out toward the center of the keyboard. The case displays sixteen small dummy pipes in addition to fifteen speaking pipes of the 4′ Principal. Hinged doors cover the keyboard when the organ is not in use. The stops, as they are arranged on the organ, are:

> Principal 4′ (full stop, with 5 stopped basses)
> Viola de Gamba 8′ (treble)
> 15th 2′ (treble)
> Bass 8′ (C to b)
> Gedact 8′ (treble)
> Coppel Pedal
> Subbass 16′ (pedal stop)

The Bass and the Gedact are colorless, as is the Viola. However, they are light and fairly clear. The Principal 4′ is bright, and the 2′ is interesting and sprightly. The pedal stop seems too light to balance the ensemble, but that may be the fault of poor regulation. Voiced on 1½ inches wind pressure, this little organ is entirely adequate for the small church in which it stands.

The Dieffenbach Family

The period in which the Krauss family reached its zenith in organ building was one of comparative inactivity for the Dieffenbachs. David Dieffenbach (1798–1872), Christian Dieffenbach's son, evidently did not inherit his father's interest in organ building. He was a wheelwright at Frystown, near Bethel, and "he came to the shop at Bethel only when there was an order for an organ to be built" [382, p.7]. Apparently there were few orders, and although there may have been organs built of which we have no record, there is a gap in Dieffenbach organ history extending from Christian's 1816 organ (see p.67) to the 1850s. By that time the contracts were probably being filled by David's son Thomas

(1821–1900), the fourth and final generation of Dieffenbach organ builders. In addition to Christian Dieffenbach's last instruments, two organs fall into the period of time presently being considered: an 1854 organ for Zoar Lutheran Church, Mt. Zion, and an organ of about 1859 for Goshert's Union Church, both in Lebanon, Pennsylvania.[4]

The Organ-Building Hobby

Organ building as a hobby found its place in Pennsylvania as well as in New England. In this classification, the instruments by John Ziegler (1795–1852), farmer, carpenter, cabinetmaker, and organ hobbiest of Montgomery County, Pennsylvania, probably hold some kind of record for survival. Of the four organs he built, three are now located in museums.[5] Ziegler's organs are chamber instruments of three registers. The first was built in 1830, and Opus 4 was not finished at the time of Ziegler's death. The Ziegler organs exhibit fine cabinet work and a light, pleasing tone, and, altogether, would enhance any parlor.

Opus 1, built for Henry Kolb, Ziegler's cousin, contains a stopped 8′ (wood), open 4′ (wood, with 12 stopped basses), and an open 2′ (metal). The manual has fifty-four notes, C to f[3], and the bellows are fed by a foot lever. In his second and fourth organs, Ziegler divided the 8′ stop, but they are otherwise similar to Opus 1. Opus 3 is missing.

X

ORGANS AND BUILDERS
IN OTHER STATES

Maryland and Washington, D.C.
Baltimore

WHILE Boston and New York were the unchallenged leaders in organ manufacturing, history depends on pioneers as well as titans, and trends in creative fields depend on scores of competent people doing their work with more concern for artistic merit than for innovation or quantity. We have seen some of these artists of lesser fame producing organs in the smaller shops, both in rural communities and in leading cities of New York, New England, and Pennsylvania. Few other eastern locations proved to be attractive to organ builders, but in the early nineteenth century Baltimore was an exception. Not only were there resident builders but Henry Erben chose this city for his branch factory, which was in operation from 1852 to 1863.

Going back to the beginning of this period, James Stewart was an organ builder in Baltimore in the first decades of the century. By the 1830s and '40s, with the opening of shops by John Barnhart, Henry Judge, and Norris G. Hales, Baltimore organ building gathered momentum. In 1845 James Hall opened an organ shop, and was active intermittently until his death in 1888. Hall may also have been employed in the Baltimore branch of the Erben factory.

In 1849 Henry F. Berger came to the United States, settled in Baltimore, and began building organs and other musical instruments. Berger (1819–1864) was born in Germany and learned organ building from his father, who was a Frenchman. Berger stayed in Baltimore until 1855, then moved to Jefferson, Pennsylvania, and in 1859 to York, Pennsylvania. His factory there prospered, but in 1861 it was completely destroyed by fire, along with three completed instruments that were in the building. Berger suffered a great financial loss, since his insurance did not begin to cover the extent of the destruction. In 1862 he moved to Tiffin, Ohio, to build an organ for a Roman Catholic church there. He died two years later [291, pp.2, 4]. A little one-manual organ built by Berger in 1855 is located in the Old Fork Church (P. E.), Hanover County, Virginia.

About 1850 a factory was established in Baltimore by August Pomplitz (d.1877) and Henry Rodewald. Instruments by this firm included: St. Mary's Church, Leonardtown; Catholic Church, Catonsville; Catholic Allegheny Church, Pittsburgh; St. Dominic's Church, Washington; St. Barnabas' Church, Upper Marlboro, Maryland; and Kreutz Presbyterian Church, near York, Pennsylvania [277, I, pp.4–5]. Pomplitz became Baltimore's leading organ builder, a reputation that rests largely on his post–Civil War achievements.

Washington, D.C.: Hilbus

Jacob Hilbus (1787–1858) a native of Westphalia, Germany, came to America in 1808 and made his home in Washington, D.C. He apparently built only a few organs, but his name is better known than that of most part-time organ builders through a case of mistaken identity. In 1811 or 1812 Hilbus built an organ for Christ Church, Alexandria, Virginia. After it was removed from Christ Church, its history is a little hazy. A possibility is that it went to the Episcopal Church in Shepherdstown, West Virginia, about 1840, and to St. Thomas's Church, Hancock, Maryland, in 1863. It was presented to the Smithsonian Institution by the vestry of St. Thomas's Church in 1903. There it rested for many years, identified as the Port Royal organ, which was supposed to have been imported in the late eighteenth century. In 1967 it was restored by the C. B. Fisk Company, and research during the restoration disclosed that it was the work of the Washington organ builder Hilbus. This famous little one-manual organ has the unusual compass of FF to f³ and seven registers: Open Diapason 8′, Stopped Diapason 8′ (divided), Dulciana 8′ (treble), Principal 4′ (divided), Flute 4′, Twelfth 2⅔′, and Fifteenth 2′. In addition, it has an Echo Treble (with a guillotine swell) consisting of Open Diapason 8′ and Principal 4′.

Hilbus was probably also the builder of an 1817 organ for the Old Presbyterian Meeting House, Alexandria, Virginia. This organ was destroyed by fire in 1835. Two residence instruments still exist: an 1819 organ now in St. John's Church, Broad Creek, Maryland, and an 1841 organ that is privately owned. The 1819 organ has a more usual compass than the Smithsonian example: GG to f³, fifty-nine notes, and its seven registers are Diapason 8′ (stopped wood, divided at middle C), Dulciana 8′ (treble, middle C), Principal 4′, Flute 4′, Fifteenth 2′, Cornet, and Sesquialtera (treble, tenor C).

South Carolina, Virginia, Georgia, and Louisiana
Charleston

The South depended largely on northern factories to supply organs as well as other manufactured goods. Although no major organ factories were ever built in Charleston, South Carolina, that city had a long and important history of church music stretching back to the installation in 1728 of an organ in St. Philip's Church, where Karl Theodor Pachelbel later served as organist (see p.33), and including the famous Snetzler organ installed in St. Michael's Church in 1767 (see p.92). But by the turn of the century, Charleston's importance in organ history had only begun. That city would soon furnish the South with its most elaborate collection of organ installations. By 1845 Henry Erben of New York had installed organs in five Charleston churches, the largest number of his instruments to go to any city outside of New York. Eventually, seventeen Charleston churches had Erben organs.

With this setting, and with Charleston's acknowledged tradition of liberalism, it is not surprising that one of Erben's organs was installed in Synagogue Beth Elohim, nor that this organ was the first in an American synagogue. Its installation was accompanied by some of the same cries of dismay that greeted the introduction of organs in orthodox Congregational and Presbyterian churches in the North. But in this case the dismay was intensified into a lawsuit, and the organ became the symbol of the controversy between the liberal and traditional factions of the Jewish community in Charleston.

Liberalism was in the air, and we have already noted some of the effects it had on the creative activity of New England (see p.114). Jewish reform movements had begun early in the nineteenth century in Europe, and by 1825 Charleston had already experienced agitation for changes in the services. Some members "were seized with the spirit of innovation" [38, p.2], and they abandoned the synagogue to form the Reformed Society of Israelites. However, this attempt languished and finally died, with some of the "reformers" returning to the congregation.

In 1836 the office of *hazan,* or cantor, became vacant. A candidate was then engaged who was regarded as sympathetic with Orthodox usage. He was to fulfill a two-year trial period before being elected for life, but he so pleased the congregation that the trial period was shortened.

In April 1838 the synagogue was destroyed by fire. A new one was completed in 1840, and while the trustees were deliberating the form of dedication for the new building, it became apparent that the *hazan* approved of "innovation," for he favored the introduction of instrumental music. Moreover, an organ was actually erected and in use during the summer of 1840, much against the wishes of those who wanted to retain their traditional forms of worship. This innovation was only the first of many that led to such disputes as who should have the right to be interred in the burial ground of the congregation, on the use of English in the services, on the observance of holy days, and so on. Although the congregation struggled to resolve its dilemma, the matter finally entered the civil courts in 1843. According to the defendants (the Orthodox members), "they discovered that their first error commenced with the Organ innovation . . ." [38, p.19].

A lower court ruled in favor of the reformers, and the ruling was upheld by the Court of Appeals. Judge A. P. Butler's historic decision in January, 1846 concluded:

> The objection is to the mere form in which music is used and practiced in this Congregation. I suppose it might be admitted, that in its origin, such a ritual was practiced without the aid of instrumental accompaniment—but to suppose that the exact kind of music that was to be used in all future time, had been fixed and agreed upon by the Jewish worshippers who obtained this charter, would be to attribute to them an impracticable undertaking.
>
> That such music was not used, is certain; but that it might not, in the progress of human events, be adopted, would be an attempt to anticipate the decisions of posterity, on matters that must be affected by the progress of art, and the general tone of society—which could not be controlled by arbitrary limitations. [Cited in 219, p.46.]

The significance of Judge Butler's decision was evaluated by Herman Berlinski:

> This remarkable document reveals deeply the evolution of liberal thought in our country, and as such is quite distinguished from court decisions made in Europe in similar cases. In monarchistic Europe such cases were almost without exception decided in favor of the Traditionalists and the organ was permitted only when the Traditionalists themselves desisted from court action against their co-religionists of reform persuasion. Thus the Charleston Organ Case opened the doors of many Synagogues in America to the organ.
>
> [219, pp.46–47]

Other Organs in the South

Elsewhere in the South, local histories contain frequent references to organ installations in the prewar decades. As early as 1820 Frederick

Dalcho could report new organs in the South Carolina Episcopal churches of Prince George, Winyaw (Georgetown); St. Helena's Parish, Beaufort; Claremont, Stateburgh; and Trinity Church, Columbia [40].

In Richmond, Virginia, an organ by a New York builder was installed in St. John's Church (Episcopal) in 1816, Monumental Church (Episcopal) imported an instrument from London between 1817 and 1824 (see chap. 6, n. 1), St. Peter's Church (R. C.) had an organ by 1835, and an organ of 33 stops was in use in St. Paul's Church (Episcopal) by 1845 [149a].

Savannah, Georgia, had an organ in 1766, but after that there is no further mention of organs until the Goodrich instrument was installed in 1820 in the Independent Presbyterian Church.

By 1840 New Orleans was the largest city in the South, but if there were organ builders there they have not yet been discovered. Christ Church (P. E.) installed an organ between 1816 and 1819, and replaced it with a new organ soon after 1837. The First Presbyterian Church had an organ by 1825, and another in 1856. A new organ for St. Patrick's Church arrived from New York in 1843, and the organ for St. Mary's Assumption Church was installed between 1844 and 1874.

New Orleans's oldest church, St. Louis Cathedral, is supposed to have had an organ from its early days. The case still in the rear gallery of the church has been attributed to Cavaillé-Coll, but the reliability of this information is questionable.[1]

Ohio, Missouri, and Illinois

Cincinnati

West of Pennsylvania, settlers relied on rivers for shipping and trade. Thus the nineteenth-century population movement focused on areas that had easy access to rivers, and by 1810 the population of the Ohio and Mississippi valleys had grown to one million [108, p.515]. Cincinnati, founded in 1788, became a principal shipping point, and by 1818 had a population of 10,000. With such a favorable location, Cincinnati attracted large numbers of Germans who immigrated to the United States during the nineteenth century. Among them were several organ builders who were responsible for one of the earliest organ factories in "the West" to operate continuously for a number of decades and to produce a substantial number of organs.

In November 1844 *The World of Music,* Chester, Vermont, contained the following account:

> They have an Organ Manufactory in Cincinnati. An enthusiastic German of Cincinnati, is one of the most successful manufacturers of the Organ in the Western country. He has, says the Gazette, within

ten years, built 37 Organs, mostly for cities in the Western States, and is at this time engaged upon an Organ that will doubtless equal any in the United States. One which he built for the Catholic Church, at Detroit, had 22 stops, and another for St. Louis had 29; and one recently finished for a German Catholic Church, in Baltimore, contained 45 draw stops, 33 of them being full speaking registers.—The largest pipe is the pedal CCC, which is 32 feet in length. The Organ on which he is now engaged, is designed for the new Catholic Cathedral, in Cincinnati, and is to be 28 feet in length, and 25 in breadth. It is to contain 2717 pipes, arranged into 43 stops, among which are three full mixture stops. The smallest pipe is about three quarters of an inch long—the largest 32 feet. It is to be furnished with three banks of keys, five octaves each, besides two octaves of pedals.

[Cited in BOC 39, p. 5.]

Although the organ builder is not identified by name, it seems likely that the article refers to Mathias Schwab (d.1864).[2]

Mathias Schwab was not the first organ builder in Cincinnati; that distinction belongs to the Reverend Adam Hurdus, the "first Swedenborgian preacher west of the Alleghenies, coming to Cincinnati in 1806" [270]. But it was left to Schwab to found Cincinnati's most important nineteenth-century organ firm.

Schwab opened his factory about 1831. In 1839 he employed Johann Heinrich Koehnken,[3] a cabinetmaker who had worked at this trade for two years in Germany and for two more in Wheeling before moving to Cincinnati [418, p.6]. In 1853, Gallus Grimm (1827–1897) arrived and also began work in the Schwab shop. Grimm, like Koehnken, had been apprenticed as a cabinetmaker, but he had the added experience of having worked for four years with the German organ builder Martin Braun. In 1860 Schwab retired, and the firm name became Koehnken & Co.

One of Schwab's instruments was described in detail in the St. Louis *Missouri Republican* on September 20, 1838. Here the builders are identified as "Messrs. Mathias Schwab & Himmel, of Cincinnati, Ohio." The organ, which cost about $4,000, was for the Cathedral of St. Louis (R. C.), and was to be consecrated on the next Sunday,

when its fine powers will be displayed by Mr. Marallano [then organist of the Cathedral], who will be the principal performer on it. On the same occasion Mr. Carrieres, formerly the principal performer on the flute in the Conservatory of Paris, will also unite in the ceremonies of the day. On that occasion's feast may be expected such as has never been realized in the west before.

The *Missouri Republican*'s description of the organ, given below, contains some obvious errors: the second and third stops on the Great should be an Open Diapason and a Stopped Diapason, respectively. The length of the pedal pipes is also curious.[4] It is interesting to note that Schwab's Great division was quite similar to those of the New York and New England organs of this period, while the Swell was considerably different, with its five 8′ stops and full compass for all stops.

The upper row of keys directs the smaller organ, which consists of nine full stops, viz:

1st	An open Diapason,	
2d	A stopped do	
3d	" Principal,	
4th	" Flute,	
5th	" Twelfth,	Each stop having 58 pipes.
6th	" Fifteenth,	
7th	" Oboe,	
8th	" Dulciana	
9th	" Viola	

By an ingenious piece of mechanism, though very simple in its construction, and which is put into operation by means of a pedal, the unappreciable advantage of a *Swell,* or the means of procuring a *Crescendo* and *Diminuendo* are obtained. This is an invention of recent date, and one which was long sought for in former times but without success.

The "Main" organ consists of 14 stops, viz:

1st	A Double open Diapason,	
2d	" " stopped do	
3d	" " do do	Each with 58 pipes.
4th	" Principal,	
5th	" Flute,	
6th	" Fifteenth,	
7th	" double Twelfth, with 37 pipes.	
8th	" Twelfth, with 58 pipes.	
9th	" Cornet, with 4 pipes to each key, making in all 232 pipes.	
10th	A Sesquialter, with 3 pipes to each key, making in all 174 pipes.	
11th	A Tierce,	
12th	" Trumpet,	Each with 58 pipes.
13th	" Horn, with 37 pipes,	
14th	" Clarionet with 58 pipes.	

The lower keys or main organ can be played either with or without the upper one, at the will of the performer, or both may be played conjointly.

In addition to these keys there are 21 *Pedals* for the fundamental *Base,* with four stops, viz:—The double open diapason with a pipe 22 feet long; the double stopped diapason with a pipe of equal length.

The Trombone and the Cymbals form the harmony and each have pipes of 22 feet, equal to 44 feet of pipe. These pedals may be used either separately with either organ or jointly with both, as the performer may desire. The base is superior to any thing we ever heard in music, as in fact is the music of the whole instrument, but this will especially strike the ear of any amateur of music as surpassingly fine.

Johann Koehnken, successor to Schwab, continued to build organs for several years under his own name. He was then joined in partnership by his coworker Gallus Grimm. Humphreys has described the success of this company:

Beginning about 1865 and for 27 years thereafter, the organ in every Catholic church in the Covington, Kentucky diocese was built and installed by Koehnken and Grimm. (Koehnken, incidentally, was a Protestant.) The firm's fame had spread by this time; one year Koehnken loaded a large flatboat with pipes and chests and went downriver with his cargo to St. Louis where he spent seven months installing four organs.

Additional orders soon came from as far away as Memphis and New Orleans. In each case, pipes and chests were shipped by flatboat. [332, p.23]

Other organ builders active in Cincinnati included Alfred Mathers & Co. (from about 1847) and Closs & Hallenkamp (from about 1856).

Cleveland

Communities located on the Great Lakes tended to develop more slowly than the river cities. Such was the case with Cleveland, founded only six years after Cincinnati. The first pipe organ on record there was built by Henry Erben and installed in Old Stone Church (First Presbyterian) in 1838. Trinity Episcopal Church may have had an earlier organ but no records of it exist [26, p.26].

Breitmayer mentions an organist–composer–organ builder named Charles Koebler, who came to Cleveland about 1850 and was organist in a Cleveland church [26, p.30]. George F. Votteler is listed as an organ builder in Cleveland city directories as early as 1856, and his later association with Holtkamp and Sparling formed the beginnings of the present Holtkamp firm [26, p.31].

St. Louis

St. Louis had some of Cincinnati's advantages, with its location on the Mississippi River providing a waterway to New Orleans. This venerable city was founded by French traders in 1764. While its population was a mere 4,000 in 1823 and remained much smaller than that of Cincinnati, one must consider that Missouri was then on the western edge of the settled part of the United States. It was part of the Louisiana Purchase in 1803 and did not achieve statehood until 1820.

As a result of the French origin of St. Louis, the Roman Catholic church had an early start, and erected a building in 1770. By 1818, the old structure, built of logs, was falling apart, and work was commenced on St. Louis Cathedral. Because of financial difficulties, this brick building was never actually finished on the inside. However, it was reputed to have had particularly fine furnishings, including paintings, vases, and ornaments [132, I, p.273]. Unfortunately, no mention of an organ has been located. Meanwhile, the first Protestant church in St. Louis, the Baptist church, was established and had a short-lived existence from 1818 to 1832.

Christ Church, Episcopal (now Christ Church Cathedral) was founded in 1819, and ten years later its first building was finished. Rodgers says that "A small organ was installed in the gallery, but neither the specifications of the instrument nor the name of the builder is known" [449, p.255]. Although the congregation moved into a new building in 1838, the first organ may still have been used until early in 1840, when a new organ built by Henry Erben arrived.

By this time St. Louis Cathedral (R.C.) did have an organ. The new building (its third) was opened in 1834, and Josef Marallano was appointed organist [95, p.7]. Four years later the organ built by Schwab of Cincinnati was installed.

Another early organ in St. Louis was one that Trinity Lutheran Church imported from Germany in 1839, along with four church bells and cloth for vestments [481, p.3].

St. Louis, soon to become the home of several organ builders of national reputation, also had one early builder, but nothing is known of his activity or if he remained in St. Louis. On January 16, 1818 *The Missouri Gazette* noted the arrival of A. C. Van Hirtum, formerly from Amsterdam, an "Organ Factor and Professor of Music on the Pianoforte." Another organ builder in St. Louis from about 1859 to 1861 was William Metz. For about ten years, from 1852 to 1862, the Pilcher family made St. Louis its home. Henry Pilcher and Sons sold pianos and music, published some music, and had an organ factory. One of the Pilcher organs of this period was a two-manual, twenty-eight register instrument installed in Trinity Church (Episcopal), St. Louis, in 1861 [18, p.424]. The Pilchers moved to Chicago in 1862.

Chicago

Chicago is a city of more recent origin. Established at Fort Dear-

born, the village was organized in the early 1830s and was incorpo-
rated as a city in 1837. Only one year later an organ built by Henry
Erben was installed in St. James' Episcopal Church. After the Civil War
Chicago churches installed a large number of organs by the Johnson
firm of Westfield, Massachusetts, but earlier they showed a preference
for New York builders. Following the example of St. James' Episcopal
Church, St. Paul's Universalist Church installed an Erben organ in 1855;
Jardine organs went to the First Unitarian Church in 1850 and to the
Third Presbyterian Church in 1858; Hall & Labagh organs were in
the First Presbyterian Church in 1854[5] and in St. James' Episcopal in
1857 (replacing the Erben organ); and Andrews & Son of Utica installed an organ in the Second Presbyterian Church about 1854. One
Johnson organ (Opus 75) did make an appearance; it was installed in
the Wabash Avenue Methodist Church in 1858 [496, I, p.11]. Chicago
seems to have been content to rely on eastern builders, for it was not
until 1857 that the names of some local organ builders appeared.
Wolfram & Haeckel were active there from 1857 until about 1867.

Texas, California, and Utah

By the middle of the century organs were beginning to appear in
the Southwest and the West. The Republic of Texas was established in
1836, and two years later the capital, Houston, could boast monthly
concerts. Organs were not at that time matters of deep concern to the
Texans, however, and it was not until 1848 (three years after Texas
became a state) that an organ was "shipped from New Orleans by
order of Bishop Odin and installed in the Catholic church in Galveston,
at the cost of $2,000" [144, p.29].

A population explosion in the vicinity of San Francisco accompanied the discovery of gold in California. Five new churches were
erected in the Golden Gate City in 1849, including its first Protestant
house of worship, the Baptist Church. Life in the Far West bore little
resemblance to traditional patterns of frontier life as they had previously
appeared and as they continued to appear in other parts of the country.
A conservative attitude had little place in this environment and, indeed,
was seldom found. When the First Presbyterian Church in San Francisco
decided in 1849 to erect a church building, one was purchased in New
York, dismantled, and shipped by way of the Horn. The dedication
was a remarkable occasion in that thirty-two ladies attended, "the
largest assembly to date of that sex" [98, p.55].

Church music was informal and at first consisted only of unison
congregational singing. But it was not long before choirs began to make
an appearance. That was made possible by the influx of musicians to

California; entertainers in all fields became aware of the lavish sums that were paid there. In contrast to the Puritan attitude that made a place for instruments in the church with reluctance, and then only to accompany congregational singing, instrumental solos were regarded as special attractions in the West. Musicians were often invited to play solos in the services, and one of the favorites was Mr. Lapfgeer, "whose French horn solos were enjoyed by many congregations" [98, p.58].

According to Louis J. Schoenstein, the two-manual W. B. D. Simmons organ in the Howard Presbyterian Church, San Francisco, was installed in the original building of that church in 1852 [465]. By about 1856 the "largest and best" organ on the Pacific Coast was a forty-six-stop instrument built by Henry Erben, said to have cost $8,000 [98, p.175]. About the same time St. Mary's used "a small, plain organ evidently not intended for the finished church," and the Methodist church had only a melodeon [98, p.59].

Organ builders contributed their share to the growth of San Francisco, and before 1860 several had made an appearance, including Joseph Mayer, B. Shellard, Robert Farran, and John McCraith. Mayer, a native of Germany, arrived in California in 1856. He was later succeeded by Felix Schoenstein, founder of San Francisco's veteran firm of organ builders.

While the first organ builders were finding their way to San Francisco on the heels of the gold rush, southern California also had at least a fleeting glance at an organ. This little instrument may hold the claim of being the only Australian-made organ ever imported to this country. In 1857 it was taken to San Bernardino and from there to Salt Lake City [152, p.57].

The seven-stop organ had been built by Joseph Ridges, who was born in Ealing, near Southampton, England, on April 17, 1826. There was an organ factory near his home, and being a young organ enthusiast, he frequented the shop. Ridges was also adventurous, and at the age of twenty-three he went to Australia to look for gold, but he was not successful. He earned his living by working in the mining camps as a carpenter and cabinetmaker for a time, and then went to Sydney. Here he continued working in his trade, but spent his spare time constructing the small organ that was to come to western United States. The organ attracted considerable attention, and Ridges, a convert to the Mormon faith, was persuaded to donate it to the church [110, pp.6–7].

Ridges and the organ sailed for California. At San Pedro they were met by twelve wagons hauled by fourteen-mule teams. After a brief stop at San Bernardino, the wagon train crossed the desert to Salt Lake City. There the organ was set up in the old Tabernacle and was used for the first time in a service on October 11, 1857. It continued in use until the old Tabernacle was finally torn down. According to McDonald, the records of the Mormon Church show only that the instrument was then moved "south," presumably to a Mormon settlement in southern Utah or to the one in San Bernardino, California [110, p.8]. There is also a possibility that it was incorporated in the organ for the new Tabernacle [18, p.82].

PART FOUR

Organs in an Industrial Society
1860 – 1900

XI

SOME GENERAL OBSERVATIONS

Domestic Conditions

Effects of the Civil War

CHURCHES and organs in the Northeast had suffered considerably in the American Revolution, but the damage in the South resulting from the Civil War was even more disastrous. Not only were many important instruments destroyed but the economic ruin left in the wake of the war made replacement impractical or impossible.

Some organs were dismantled and taken to locations considered safe. The controversial organ in Congregation Beth Elohim, Charleston, South Carolina, was taken to Columbia for safety and was lost, along with the Scrolls of the Law and other valuables, when that city was burned by General Sherman in 1865 [129a, p.162]. Countless stories relate the destruction of other instruments. On one occasion in 1864 when the Union army had suffered a defeat in Louisiana, the retreating soldiers set fire to Alexandria, destroying more than twenty blocks, including St. James' Church. Years later, when the church made an unsuccessful claim to the government for damages, a witness, Mrs. Mary J. Smith, stated:

> A Commissioned Officer came to the shop of Mr. Dammon, which was one block in front of St. James' Episcopal Church, and demanded to go into the paint shop for the purpose of getting a tin can which he got and went off in the direction of the Episcopal Church and he said that they intended to blow up the Episcopal Church.
>
> A short time afterwards I saw the fire in that direction and the church was on fire and burned. The houses in a great many places

in the town were fired at the same time and all the houses were burned
for twenty-odd blocks. The soldiers left that same day, as they were
on the retreat. The church was a large and elegantly finished church
and had only been built a short time. It had a large Organ inside,
was well carpeted and handsomely furnished in every particular.
The Episcopal Church with all its contents was entirely destroyed
in that fire with the exception of the Communion Service which was
saved by Mrs. Davidson. [30, p.145]

Mrs. Davidson had saved the Communion Service by hiding it in the
underground cistern at her home.

Members of the 47th New York Regiment testified that in 1863 the
Presbyterian Church of Edisto Island, South Carolina, was robbed of
all its furniture, and the organ was packed to be taken north [28, p.11].
In Charleston, the steeples of St. Philip's and St. Michael's were landmarks that served as targets when the city was bombarded. St. Philip's
suffered particularly, and both the chancel and the organ were destroyed
[109, p.43]. St. Michael's closed after a Thanksgiving service on November 19, 1863 that was "punctuated by the explosion of falling shells"
[91, p.53]. The Snetzler organ was stored in the Sunday School building of St. Paul's, Radcliffeboro, and was reinstalled when the church was
again opened for services two years later. The Henry Erben organ still
in the Huguenot Church in Charleston narrowly escaped a trip back
to New York. William Way has related the story of this organ and a
resolute organist:

> This organ attracted the attention of certain members of the Un-
> ion Army, who determined to send it to New York. The organ was
> taken apart, and more than half of the parts were removed from the
> Huguenot Church and placed on a boat for shipment, when Mr.
> T. P. O'Neale, organist of the Huguenot Church, with influential
> friends, persuaded the soldiers not to take the organ away from
> Charleston. The organ was then brought to Grace Church, where it
> was used until the spring of 1866, when it was returned to the Hugue-
> not Church. Mr. O'Neale served as organist while the organ remained
> in Grace Church. He then returned to the Huguenot Church with
> the organ.[1] [164, pp.71–72]

In addition to the physical damage, the economic results of the
Civil War had a far-reaching effect on organ history. Industry was concentrated even more firmly in the North, and the large organ factories
in New York and Boston gained the lion's share of the contracts. With
the expansion of the organ industry new factories were located in the
Midwest and the West Coast, rather than in the South.

Trends in Population and Industry

Aside from the Civil War and its aftermath, there were several other major factors that affected practically every development in the United States during the final decades of the nineteenth century: a growing and shifting population, industrialization, and technological progress.

The immigration trends and the westward expansion of the early and middle nineteenth century have been noted above (see pp.102–103). Foreign immigration tapered off during the war years, but reached high peaks in 1873 and 1882. In the latter year, the United States received 788,992 immigrants, 250,000 of them German. The overall population increase in the last forty years of the nineteenth century was roughly forty-five million, which represented a considerably higher rate of growth than was the case in the first half of the century.

The westward migration within the United States reached new heights, and during the 1880s more than four million people moved west of the Mississippi. This shift of population created new metropolitan areas, and by 1900 the five leading cities in the United States were:

New York	3,437,202
Chicago	1,698,575
Philadelphia	1,293,697
St. Louis	575,238
Boston	560,892

[108, p.468]

The growth of Chicago, founded barely seventy years earlier, is most remarkable, and the list actually includes a city west of the Mississippi.

Moving even farther west, the Pony Express riders started their fantastic rides from St. Joseph, Missouri, to the Pacific in 1860, but like modern freeways, this enterprise was outmoded almost as soon as it was started. By 1861 a telegraph line to the West Coast was completed, and the junction of the Union Pacific and the Central Pacific railroad lines in 1869 initiated rail service to the West.

This era saw the growth of big industries, notably steel and petroleum; it saw the concentration of economic power in trusts and holding companies; it also saw labor agitation protesting the abuses that accompanied industrialization. Big plants and technological progress were so interdependent that, like the chicken and the egg, it is hard to guess which fostered which. Experimentation and invention were the spirit of the day, and many of the developments had far-reaching consequences. The Niagara Falls plant, opened in 1894, ushered in the age of hydroelectric power. Closer to the layman's heart are Alexander Graham Bell's telephone (1876), Edison's development of a practical incandescent bulb (1879), and that memorable year the Duryea Motor Wagon Co. produced the first automobile made for sale (1895).

Philanthropy: The Carnegie Organs

One of the by-products of big business was philanthropy, and whatever social ills may have accompanied late nineteenth-century empire building, there was also initiated a period of patronage for arts and letters that we are still enjoying. Andrew Carnegie was responsible for one of the biggest giveaway programs the world had ever seen when he offered in 1881 to donate library buildings to cities and towns that would establish and support them by tax appropriations. In 1873 Carnegie began giving away organs, and 8,182 churches, schools, and civic institutions installed organs paid for, in whole or part, by Carnegie [121, p.95]. The first Carnegie organ was installed in the Swedenborgian Church in Allegheny City (now part of Pittsburgh) [223]. In 1890, the opening of the Carnegie-donated organ built by Frank Roosevelt for Carnegie Hall, Allegheny City, was an event of particular significance. First, it established a recital series that was unique in its longevity (terminated in 1972, after eighty-two years), serving as a model for the many series of organ recitals that were begun in the early twentieth century. Secondly, this installation led to the creation of the post of city organist, a feature that was also imitated in many cities when the fad of municipal organs was at its height. The original Roosevelt installation was replaced in 1924 by an E. M. Skinner instrument, the last organ to be given by the Carnegie Corporation [343].

Professional Music

A new note of professionalism entered the American music scene during the late nineteenth century. Both an indication and a source of this new aspect is found in the establishment of music schools: first the Oberlin Conservatory (1865), and soon afterward the Boston, New England, and Cincinnati conservatories, and the Chicago Academy of Music (all in 1867). The 1870s saw the establishment of the Illinois Conservatory of Music, Jacksonville (1871), Northwestern University School of Music (1873), and the Cincinnati College of Music (1878). The number of these schools in the central states reflects the population trends.

Other fields of music were experiencing similar expansion. Theodore Thomas established his orchestra in 1862, a positive force in bringing higher standards in repertoire and performance to that field. One of Thomas's important accomplishments was that he made twenty-two annual tours across the country, giving concerts in many locations where there were no other opportunities to hear orchestral music. Thomas also served as conductor of the Brooklyn Philharmonic Society, the New York Philharmonic, and, during the last fourteen years of his life, the Chicago Symphony. Other important orchestras founded during this time included the Boston Symphony (1881), the Chicago Symphony (1886), the Pittsburgh Symphony (1893), and the Cincinnati Orchestra (1895). Serious musical development beat the railroad to the West, where San Francisco was carving out her own future direction. Twenty-four operas were performed there in 1865. Many of these undertakings were made possible by the immigration of trained musicians, who filled the ranks of the orchestras, choruses, and casts.

Organ Repertoire

One might expect such musical activity to have some kind of effect on organ performance. Actually, it did, but the results were slow to emerge, and they were not always positive. Nothing did more to stimulate interest in orchestral music than the growth of a few proficient orchestras. The orchestral transcription was to remain firmly fixed in organ programs for some time to come, and its popularity was reflected in contemporary trends of organ design. The notorious "storm" scenes continued to receive enthusiastic responses, and Lahee tells of storm scenes "so vivid that people involuntarily reached for their umbrellas. On one occasion an old woman rushed out of the church in great excitement, saying she had left the front door open, and she was afraid her best carpet would get wet" [97, p.279].

On the more sedate side, there was an increase in the number of organ recitals in the late nineteenth century, and more frequently the program was given over entirely to organ performance, though not exclusively to organ music. This was a big step from the early organ dedications that had included a couple of organ voluntaries, with the rest of the program devoted to vocal solos. Even a few works of Bach appeared, and in this respect the opening program of the Boston Music Hall organ was outstanding:

I

Ode in honor of the occasion, recited by Miss Charlotte Cushman.
Opening of the organ by Herr Friedrich Walcker (son of the builder).

Grand Toccata in F   —Bach
Trio Sonata in E flat   —Bach
   played by John K. Paine
   (Professor of Music at Harvard University)

Grand Fugue in G   —Bach
   played by W. Eugene Thayer
   (of Worcester)

II

Grand Double Chorus "He led them through the deep" and
"But the waters overwhelmed their enemies," from Israel in Egypt
                                                —Handel
   played by George W. Morgan (of Grace Church, New York)

Grand Sonata in A, No. 3   —Mendelssohn
   played by B. J. Lang
   (organist of Old South Church
   and of the Handel and Haydn Society)

Lamentatio in Parasceve and Kyrie and Sanctus from a mass
                                              —Palestrina
Movement from the anthem "O give thanks"   —Purcell
   played by Dr. S. P. Tuckerman
   (organist at St. Paul's Church)

Offertorium in G   —Lefebure-Wely
   played by John H. Willcox
   (organist at the Church of the Immaculate Conception)
Hallelujah Chorus   —Handel
   played by G. W. Morgan

By the last decade of the nineteenth century some organists were making strides toward recitals of organ music, and those of William C. Carl were especially notable. In May 1898 a reviewer for *The Pianist and Organist* criticized Harry Rowe Shelley severely for his choice of repertoire in three recitals played on the new Hutchings organ at Fifth Avenue Baptist Church, New York. Shelley had played three Bach chorale preludes, a prelude and fugue, and one other organ composition on each program. The remainder of the programs had been orchestral transcriptions. The reviewer scolded:

> This strong orchestral character of Mr. Shelley's programs together with his orchestral treatment of the instrument in registration is not altogether calculated to exalt the position of the organ and magnify its importance as a musical instrument, unapproachable in its character and artistic value by any other one instrument or number of instruments.
>
> The use of the organ as an imitative instrument tends rather to lower it in the estimation of the public than otherwise.

Mr. Shelley might well have been surprised that he was not praised for including such an unusually large number of works by Bach on his programs. The review seems prophetic when viewed from our own perspective; in the late nineteenth century it represented a small, not very popular, but very important minority opinion.

Foreign Influences

Sources of Foreign Influence

We have previously noted some of the foreign influences present in American music of the early nineteenth century. These factors became even more important during the period 1860–1900, as the successive waves of immigrants brought with them the idea of the superiority of European music and musicians. Visiting artists and Americans who traveled abroad also did much to encourage such an attitude.

Many music students added to their prestige, as well as their knowledge, by studying abroad. Among them were some of the leading organists of the late nineteenth century: James Cutler Parker, Horatio Palmer, B. J. Lang, John Knowles Paine, Dudley Buck, Fenelon Rice, George E. Whiting, Homer Bartlett, E. M. Bowman, Frank Gleason, Clarence Eddy, A. A. Stanley, George W. Chadwick, R. Huntingdon Woodman, and Horatio Parker.

Since few organs had been imported after 1810, organ builders had remained relatively independent of foreign influence for half a century. Their time of stylistic freedom was drawing to an end, however, and hints of the future were already present in the tentative experiments with tone colors and in the bolder, more assertive voicing of the mid-century organ.

The Boston Music Hall Organ

The much-publicized installation of a large German organ in the Boston Music Hall heralded the beginning of the end for the autonomous American organ. An eyewitness account recorded the first hearing of this famous instrument:

> About one thousand gentlemen were present, consisting of stockholders and subscribers and members of the city government. A few gentlemen, comprising the Committee, the builder's son Mr. Heinrich Walcker, and the master workmen, occupied seats on the platform. At eight o'clock, strains of music were for the first time heard from the great organ, which was completely hidden by a green curtain extending from the floor to the ceiling. So thoroughly rapt were the audience in the rich, swelling tones of the organ that they hardly noticed the dimness of the light which seemed to throw a veil of solemnity over the entire scene. For nearly twenty minutes, the audi-

ence sat thus, and the music ceased. Suddenly the gaslight flashed forth in all its brilliance, as the huge curtain began slowly to descend. Not a whisper broke the charmed spell. All eyes were riveted upon the opening space, until the full breadth of the wondrous instrument burst upon their view. The audience rose to their feet, and cheer upon cheer marked the auspicious moment. [Cited in 331, pp.6–7.]

On that evening of October 31, 1863 the opening of the great Boston Music Hall organ was looked upon as the beginning of a new era in organ history. Few present on that occasion would have believed that in little more than twenty years, this monument to America's cultural inferiority complex would be sold, dismantled, and removed from the Music Hall.

The Boston Music Hall was built in 1852. Dr. Jabez B. Upham, president of the Boston Music Hall Association, was an organ enthusiast, and envisioned for the Hall an organ "of the first magnitude." Even before financial backing for such an instrument was secured, he had visited important organs abroad, and had procured specifications from eminent builders [369, I, p.11].

In 1856, with the necessary funds subscribed, Dr. Upham went again to England and the Continent, inspecting many famous instruments and meeting organists and builders. He finally chose Eberhard Frederick Walcker (1794-1872) of Ludwigsburg, Germany, as the builder, "with the proviso that Herr Walcker himself should meet me in Paris, and go thence with me to London, in order to learn and engraft upon his schedule such improvements as the best works of the French and English makers might suggest." The two men spent several days in Paris, and then proceeded to London. Finally, on February 20, 1857, the contract of "forty closely written pages in English and German" was pronounced complete [369, I, p.14].

After five years, the organ was finished and set up in the factory, where it won the approval of an international group of organists before being dismantled and shipped to the United States. Three months were required for the stormy Atlantic crossing, and Bostonians hailed the arrival of the organ in February 1863, relieved that the organ had not fallen into Confederate hands or into the ocean.

The awe-inspiring appearance of the organ, then as well as today, is due in large measure to the elaborately carved case of American walnut. It was not imported, but was designed by Hammett Billings and made by the Herter Brothers Furniture Co. of New York. However regrettable it was that Dr. Upham chose not to give serious consideration to an American builder for the organ itself, his choice was not without impact on the American scene. The interest the organ created and the opportunities for performance it occasioned, particularly during the early years of its installation, were certainly valuable for the organ profession. Some of its characteristics have often been cited as important influences on American builders: the full-compass Swell stops, the large Pedal division, the pedal compass of thirty notes, the balanced swell pedal, the crescendo pedal, and the use of free reeds and other unusual stops. Writing in 1889, G. L. Howe observed:

> The first builders to feel the new impulse were the Hooks, both from their chagrin at having been passed over when the order was placed abroad, and because they lived in Boston where, through the stratagem of employing the workman sent over by Walcker & Son to keep the Music Hall organ in order, they obtained early access to the interior of the instrument, and were able to duplicate its scales or proportions of pipes. The German action was what is known as the poppet valve action, which no American would care to duplicate. In tone quality the Hooks soon surpassed their German masters, except in the string color, where the high price of metal in America rendered the German method of making these pipes of solid tin too expensive.
> [83, p.334]

Some of the stops that subsequently appeared in American specifications were obvious copies, for example, the Physharmonica in Hutchings's New York Avenue Methodist Church organ. The presence of the German organ may also have inspired the use of German stop names found occasionally in New England organs of the 1870s.[2] One characteristic of the Music Hall organ that received the most severe criticism was its slow action and speech. B. J. Lang reportedly said that when he was to play the Boston Music Hall organ, he always felt he should arrive half an hour early if the pipes were to speak in time for the audience to hear them [331, pp.11–12].

Boston Music Hall, Boston, Massachusetts
WALCKER, 1863

Great (First Manual)			*Great (continued)*		
Principal	16′	58	Octav	4′	58
Tibia Major (t.c.)	16′	46	Fugara	4′	58
Viola Major	16′	58	Hohlflöte	4′	58
Basson [*sic*]	16′⎫	58	Flute d'Amour	4′	58
Ophycleide	8′⎭		Clairon [*sic*]	4′	70
Principal	8′	58	Waldflöte	2′	58
Flöte	8′	58	Quint	5⅓′	58
Gemshorn	8′	58	Tertz	3⅕′	58
Viola di Gamba	8′	58	Quint	2⅔′	58
Gedekt	8′	58	Octave	2′	58
Trombone	8′⎫	58	Cornett	(5⅓′) V	190
Trompete	4′⎭		(harmonics of the 16′ series)		

Boston Music Hall, Boston, Massachusetts
WALCKER, 1863

Great (continued)

Mixtur	(2⅔')	VI	348
(harmonics of the 8' series)			
Scharff	(1⅓')	IV	232
(harmonics of the 4' series)			

Swell (Second Manual)

Bourdon	16'	58
Principal	8'	58
Salicional	8'	58
Dolce	8'	58
Quintatoen	8'	58
Gedekt	8'	58
Trombone Bass	8'⎱	58
Trombone Discant	4'⎰	
Basson Bass	8'⎱	58
Hautbois Discant	4'⎰	
Principal Octav	4'	58
Rohrflöte	4'	58
Traversflöte	4'	58
Cornettino	4'	70
Quintflöte	5⅓'	58
Nasard	2⅔'	58
Octav	2'	58
Mixture (2')	V	290

Choir (Third Manual)

Gedekt		16'	58
Principal Flöte		8'	58
Spitzflöte		8'	58
Bifra	(8' & 4')	II	116
Gedekt		8'	58
Clarin Bass		8'⎱	58
Clarin Discant		4'⎰	
Viola		8'	58
Physharmonica		8'	58
Hohlpfeife		4'	58
Principal Flute		4'	58
Dolce		4'	58
Flautino		2'	58

Choir (continued)

Super-Octav		1'	58
Sesquialtera			
(2⅔' & 1⅗'		II	116

Solo (Fourth Manual)

Bourdon		16'	58
Geigen Principal		8'	58
Aeoline		8'	58
Conzert Flöte		8'	58
Corno-Bassetto		8'	58
Vox Humana	(8')	II	116
Gemshorn		4'	58
Piffaro	(4' & 2')	II	116
Vox Angelica		4'	58
Quint		2⅔'	58
Piccolo		2'	58

Pedal

Forte Division:

Principal Bass		32'	30
Grand Bourdon	(32')	V	120
Bombardon		32'	30
Octav Bass		16'	30
Sub Bass		16'	30
Trombone		16'	30
Contra-Violon		16'	30
Octave Bass		8'	30
Hohlflöte-Bass		8'	30
Violoncell [sic]		8'	30
Trompete		8'	30
Corno-Basso		4'	30
Octave		4'	30
Cornettino		2'	30

Piano Division:

Bourdon	16'	30
Viola	8'	30
Flöte	8'	30
Flöte	4'	30
Waldflöte	2'	30
Basson	16'	30

Accessories

4 Manual couplers

13 Combination pedals (all double acting)

Zungenwerke: draws all the reed stops.

Fortissimo, First Manual: draws all stops of Great Manual except the reeds,
and Cornett and Scharff.

Accessories (continued)

Forte, First Manual: draws the 8', 4', and one 16' stop in the Great Manual.
Piano, First Manual: draws the 8' stops in the Great Manual.
Solo, Fourth Manual: draws the Corno-Bassetto stop in the Solo.
Volleswerk: draws the full organ, except the Vox Humana and Physhar-
   monica stops.
Copula, Fourth Manual to Pedal. ⎫
Copula, Third Manual to Pedal.   ⎬ Manual to Pedal Couplers.
Copula, Second Manual to Pedal. ⎪
Copula, First Manual to Pedal.   ⎭
Copula, First, Second, Third, Fourth Manuals to Pedal.
Copula zum forte Pedal: couples the Forte pedal division to the pedal, with-
   out which none of those stops will sound.
(no designation): draws the full Swell Organ.
Register crescendo
Hydraulic Blower

[67]

One of the interesting features of this organ was the use of free reeds: stops 4 and 5 on the Great, 9 and 10 on the Swell, 9 on the Solo, and 3 and 20 on the Pedal. Some of the stops given two pitch designations (e.g., 4 and 5 on the Great) were actually divided stops. One would expect only the larger pitch designation to be used. Numbers 4 and 5 on the Great together formed one 16' reed rank. The Bifra 8' and 4' on the Choir, on the other hand, was "of pure tin, with two pipes to each key; the larger one stopped at the top, the other very slender, and giving an octave higher tone; a *tremolo* is adapted specially for this stop . . ." [67, p.50]. It was, in other words, an 8' metal gedeckt and a 4' string. The Piffaro 4' and 2' on the Solo was composed in the same way as the Bifra, but an octave higher [331, p.9].

The mixtures "comprised, for the most part, octaves of the unison and 10ths and 17ths. We might infer that the apparent reluctance to include quints was due to the presence in the organ of an unusual number of separately drawn stops speaking at $2\frac{2}{3}'$ and $5\frac{1}{3}'$ pitch" [331, p.9].

The two-rank Vox Humana (stop 6 in the Solo) was described: "A reed stop. Has a special *swell* and *tremolo*. Two sets of pipes; one of metal, rather slender; the other of wood, of a most singular shape, the mouths resembling somewhat the human mouth . . ." [67, p.53].

Stop 2 on the Pedal actually consisted of four ranks of its own, the fifth rank being the 16' Sub Bass. The four ranks sounded harmonics of the 32' series, giving a 32' resultant. Howes gives the pitches as $10\frac{2}{3}'$, 8', $6\frac{2}{5}'$, 4' [331, p.11].

The Choir Physharmonica 8′ was an unusual stop:

> It has simply reeds, without pipes, the whole being contained in a box about two feet long and six inches square. It can be used so as to commence with the merest breath of tone, increasing to quite a volume, then diminishing until the tone literally dies away to perfect silence. [67, p.51]

The divided Pedal gave the organist an expressive Pedal division. The Piano Division was placed in the swell enclosure.

The crescendo control was located in front of the expression pedals, and moved from side to side on a track. A dial over the manuals indicated the number of stops activated.

In regard to the voicing, Howes has said:

> Whether it was due to the original voicing or to some revoicing that may have been done in 1909 is not clear, but the fundamental tone at 16′ and 8′ pitch was unusually heavy and would not adhere to the tone of the rest of the organ. Even the use of all mutations and the highest-pitched mixtures could not disguise its thickness. Many of the 8′ and 16′ stops were of unusually large scale and had high mouths and arched upper lips, all of which tended to produce heavy flutey tone. [331, p.9]

Originally the pitch of the organ was a half tone higher than the present standard. That was changed when the organ was later set up in Methuen, Massachusetts, by adding new pipes for the lowest note of each flue rank and by retuning the reeds. In all, the famous organ contained eighty-four registers and ninety-six draw-stops.

Agitation for the removal of the organ began in 1881 when the Boston Symphony Orchestra was founded; the space occupied by the organ was coveted by a too-crowded orchestra. In spite of all Dr. Upham could do, the $60,000 organ was sold in 1884 to W. B. Grover for $5,000. Grover had hoped to have it installed in the New England Conservatory, but he died shortly afterwards and the organ was placed in a storage building of the conservatory. Twelve years later the storage building was to be removed to make room for tennis courts, and the organ was sold at auction.

The May 13, 1897 issue of the *Boston Daily Globe* carried a report of that auction, which was attended by about seventy-five people, many of them students. J. M. Ingraham of the Methuen Organ Co. bid $1,500, and as there were no other bids, the famous organ was sold for this incredible sum. It was later learned that Ingraham represented Edward F. Searles of Methuen, Massachusetts. Searles, for whom money was no object, had a special hall erected in Methuen for the organ, and it was rebuilt and installed in its present location under the direction of James E. Treat. It was first heard there in concert on December 9, 1909.

After Searles's death in 1920 the organ had only limited use. Ernest M. Skinner bought it in the early 1930s, but it was not until 1946 that public interest in the organ revived. At that time a group of citizens in and around Methuen formed a corporation to maintain the hall and the organ as a civic center. A specification was drawn up by Arthur Howes, Carl Weinrich, Ernest White, and G. Donald Harrison, and the organ was rebuilt by Harrison, with considerable tonal alteration. Of the resulting 112 ranks, almost half were entirely new, and many of the remaining ranks were changed. William King Covell commented:

> Tonally, the changes were considerable. Much of the essence of the original organ remained, but the new emphasis on mixture work, the removal of all the original manual reeds and their replacement by reeds of quite a different quality, and the enlargement and completion of the Pedal section together gave both full organ and the color of the individual divisions quite a new character: related to the old, related also to Mr. Harrison's own contemporary work, and yet akin closely to neither. Of course, low pressure (3½″) throughout, almost complete non-enclosure, and the lack of any kind of extension or borrowing—together with the very favorable acoustics of the hall— has given the organ, original and rebuilt alike, a character which is hardly to be found elsewhere in the country.
>
> That this is an unique organ is certain. That it is one of the best in America today, in spite of the many and fundamental improvements in organ building in this country during the last generation, seems equally certain. We may only expect that, a century hence, this particular organ will still be regarded as one of our finest: one to be compared not unfavorably to the best production of the 21st century.[3] [369, II, p.14]

French and English Influence

Not all trans-Atlantic trends were represented by the German-built Boston Music Hall organ; leading American builders were also following developments in other countries. Hilborne Roosevelt and George Jardine were two builders who traveled abroad to gather firsthand information about foreign trends in organ building. Reeds made by Cavaillé-Coll were imported by both Frank Roosevelt and the Hooks for use in some of their organs in the 1870s and '80s, while other colorful voices of European builders found their imitators in America.

The influence of England, overwhelming as it was during the eighteenth century, seemed to reach organ builders more indirectly during the greater part of the nineteenth century, usually as the result of the continuing British domination of the fields of organ performance and church music. One can easily understand that the prominent positions held by English organists were helpful in maintaining a close relationship between the American organ and English ideals. One of the best-known English organists to come to America in the second half of the nineteenth century was George Washbourne Morgan (1822–1892). He arrived in New York in 1853, and held positions in St. Thomas' Church, Grace Church, St. Anne's Church (R.C.), the Broadway Tabernacle, and the Dutch Reformed Church. He has been called the "first outstanding concert organist in this country," and has been credited with the first public performances in the United States of organ works of Bach and Mendelssohn [50, p.124].

The formation of the American Guild of Organists in the late nineteenth century was an outgrowth and a further indication of English influence. Gerrit Smith (1859–1912), a professor of music at Union Theological Seminary and organist at the South Reformed Church, New York, was largely responsible for the meeting in February 1896 that marked the founding of the organization. Twenty-three organists were present. During a summer in England Smith had developed the idea of forming a professional organization in the United States, similar to the Royal College of Organists [15, pp.15–21].

The Organ Industry and Its Products
Major Organ Firms

Organ building paralleled other industries in some respects. The large companies tended to become more powerful and the small builders more obscure. This situation was particularly true in the Northeast, where the established companies were located and commanded the spotlight.

The nineteenth century was size-conscious; the size of the organ factories and the emphasis placed on large organs were concomitant. Organs of seventy, eighty, or one hundred stops required large factories, and these giants, in return, brought their builders the publicity and fame that foster large companies. As this period opened, E. & G. G. Hook in Boston and Henry Erben in New York were the leading builders. The growth of George Jardine's company, the opening of the Odell shop, and, more important, the opening of the famous Roosevelt factory, gradually changed the picture in New York. In Boston the Hutchings company became a major competitor of the Hook firm. The importance of Johnson's factory in Westfield, Massachusetts, must also be acknowledged.

When the New York Avenue Methodist Church, Brooklyn, New York, began plans for an organ in 1889, officials of the church wrote to eighty prominent organists and received replies from nearly seventy. They asked how many manuals and speaking stops an adequate instrument should contain, and who the two best American builders were. All but five of the replies recommended a three-manual organ. There was wide variation in the recommended number of stops, but the average was thirty-six. These organists rated the best American builders in the following order: Roosevelt, Hutchings, Hook & Hastings, Odell, and Jardine. Eight other builders were also mentioned. The church submitted a specification to each of the five builders listed and asked for their prices. Hutchings and Odell quoted the same price; Roosevelt was 28½ percent higher; Jardine was 4 percent higher; and the Hook and Hastings company was 10 percent lower. The contract was awarded to Hutchings [*BOC* 31, p.3].

Action and Wind Supply

The late nineteenth century was the end of the "first tracker period" in American history. True, there is no definite dividing line, and some companies built tracker organs well into the twentieth century, but they were not in the mainstream of organ building. Similarly, it is important to remember that the innovations that appeared with such frequency during the late nineteenth century were exceptions and were only gradually incorporated into organ construction, even where the instruments of the innovators were concerned.

Both structural and tonal changes marked the late-nineteenth-century organ. Indeed, these are false classifications, in that they were interdependent, and together were responsible for the style of the period. The structural changes were largely made possible by the technological developments that played such an important part in ushering in the age of the twentieth century. Machines, electricity, push-button controls, and the end of some forms of manual labor were hailed enthusiastically as signs of progress.

Organists were not the last to taste some of the labor-saving delights, and one can only imagine the joy of the organist who, for the first time, could play the organ without waiting for the arrival of the pumper. Webber has credited William A. Johnson with the installation of the first water motor.[4] Hydraulic motors depended on a water supply of sufficient pressure and reliability, and where that was available, these motors proved quite satisfactory. After a few experimental installations in the 1860s, their use increased, and many were retained long after practical electric motors were available.

Among the experiments of greatest consequence for the future of the organ were those dealing with organ action. English and European builders were the leaders, with their application of a pneumatic lever to organ action in the early nineteenth century. The form known as the Barker lever (named for Charles S. Barker) was adopted by the Frenchman Cavaillé-Coll in 1839, while he was in England. Henry Willis's use of a pneumatic lever dated from 1851. The first American use of pneumatic action is said to have been in the South Dutch Church, New York (see p.150 and chap. 8, n.4). By the mid-1860s several American companies were using pneumatic levers in their larger instruments.

Tubular-pneumatic action had its beginning in French experiments between 1835 and 1845. Ayars credits the first American use of tubular-pneumatic action to the Hooks in 1866 [213, IV]. Odell patented tubular-pneumatic actions in 1872 and 1898. Several other companies used this type of action in the 1890s and the early twentieth century, but it was never a very satisfactory system.

European experiments with electropneumatic action were initiated by Dr. Albert Peschard, and an action of this type was built by Barker in 1861 [151, p.341]. In America, electric action dated from Standbridge's 1868 organ and Hilborne Roosevelt's 1868–69 organs (see pp.265–66).

The use of electricity brought with it the possibility of many other innovations in controls and gadgets on the console, the location of the console in relationship to the pipes, the separation of the divisions of the organ in various parts of the building, and the use of almost unlimited wind pressure. Early electric actions, using batteries for power, posed some problems in reliability, and the exploitation of some of the possibilities electricity offered had to wait until the new century. Meanwhile, hints of things to come were gradually revealed, particularly in the organs of the Roosevelt firm. By the 1890s most of the leading companies were experimenting with electropneumatic action and were applying it to some of their new organs. The December 1892 issue of *The Organ* stated:

> The rapid strides which have been made in electric action (even for small organs) during the past few years, are but the beginning of the "electric era" for the organ. But a few years ago electricity was considered an expensive and unreliable luxury, applied only when the funds were unlimited. But to-day the results of the simplifying process are most promising, and electric action is becoming fully as reliable, and not much more expensive, than direct action.[5]

The Console

The console, as well as the action, was in for a face-lifting during the late nineteenth century. Balanced swell pedals began to replace the old hook-down variety; the compasses of both manual and pedal claviers continued their gradual, inconsistent ascent to modern standards; and the search for a practical combination action was under way. As early as 1847 Henry Willis had replaced the old composition pedals with pistons located in the key-slips between the manuals [151, p.360]. In America, the Odells patented the Odell pneumatic composition knobs in 1866, which were also located in the key-slips, and took the place of the composition pedals. Hilborne Roosevelt's combination action in the Philadelphia Centennial organ of 1876 was the first system that the organist could adjust at the console (see p.267).

The great importance that was attached to the console controls is well illustrated by an editorial that appeared in the November 1897 issue of *The Pianist and Organist:*

> It has been usually a difficult matter to convince organ-building committees of churches, of the comparatively high importance of mechanical devices for the control of an instrument. What they usually are after in purchasing an organ is power and volume of sound, or variety of tone-color. They know, of course, that stops are intended to be combined, and that combinations are more or less effective means of varying the tonal effects of the instrument; but the idea that facilities of getting every resource in the organ under the easy, accurate and quick control of the organist are worth more, relatively, than a large number of stops, is not readily grasped, although it seems evident enough when clearly understood.

Tonal Characteristics

The tendency toward louder organs in the early nineteenth century has been noted (see p.103). This path was followed with increasing enthusiasm through the first quarter of the twentieth century. By 1860 the clear, gentle sound of the earlier organs was a style of the past. One must not think, however, that the excesses of the later Romantic style were to be found. The extant organs of the 1860s and '70s are clear and assertive, and the principal ensemble on the Great presents an exciting chorus. The bold, bright color is quite satisfying to the modern ear, and does not ordinarily seem excessively loud. Wind pressure was generally about 3 or 3½ inches, which in itself prohibited some of the characteristics of a later period.

During the last two decades of the century, the 8′ pitch began to dominate the ensemble with a thicker, heavier sound. Builders tried also to produce more pronounced contrasts between soft and loud stops, and greater dynamic control of the enclosed division. Roosevelt pioneered in enclosing more than one division.

The account in *The News and Courier,* Charleston, South Carolina of January 12, 1896 of the new Hook & Hastings organ in St. Mary's Church, describes some of the tonal ideals of the period:

> Attention is called to the number of 16-foot and 8-foot stops, forming a musical foundation of extra solidity, and giving that impressive and dignified body of tone which is the noblest feature of the "king of instruments." The open and stopped diapasons are full, rich in qual-, ity, and with the bourdons, form an important characteristic of this organ. The balance of the flute, string and reed stops is admirable, both in the great and in the swell organ. The solo stops include, beside those usually found in larger organs, several not generally included, notably the cornets and the aeoline, the latter a stop of such delicacy as to be scarcely audible at the keyboard, though of charming distinct- ness at some distance, when its tones have diffused themselves in space. The reeds possess the delicacy, refinement, and the orchestral quality that are peculiar to this noted American firm of organ builders.

The idea of a large body of sound, described variously as "digni- fied," "majestic," or "grand" was closely related to the accepted musical style of the late nineteenth century. One has only to remember that Wagner's Beyreuth performances began in 1876, that the Brahms sym- phonies were written between 1876 and 1886, and that Liszt died in 1886 to see a connection between the prevailing tonal ideal and organ design. To the extent that builders reflected this ideal in their organs they were children of their age. But not everyone was able to produce an artistic reflection, turning instead to the excesses that prompted Edward Jardine's 1896 remark: "To overblow a sheet-iron cylindrical pipe by 100 inches wind pressure only makes it less diapason and more steam- whistle, for all we may call it Tibia Sonora" [337].

Cases and Placement

Along with the tonal changes, the organ began to assume a new appearance. Cases were gradually abandoned in favor of an open style. In 1883 Hilborne Roosevelt's brochure stated:

> We strongly advocate simplicity of design in case work rather than the expenditure of available funds on a portion of the instru- ment that merely appeals to the eye. For this reason the majority of organ cases are now made with little or no wood-work above the feet of the front pipes. [74, p.9]

As the case disappeared, a screen of pipes, sometimes called a pipe fence, was formed to conceal the interior of the organ. Some of the pipes were functional, others mere decoration.

Now another condition was developing that would cause further changes in the organ's appearance (or more accurately, its disappearance). When Dr. Henry S. Cutler became organist at Trinity Church, New York, in 1858, he quickly made some important changes. Women were no longer used in the choir (a situation that endured until 1968), the choir was provided with vestments, and it was moved from the gallery to the chancel [505, pp.26–27]. This move was prophetic. While many churches had neither reason to ban women from the choir nor adequate substitutes for them, the vestments and the chancel location were very appealing. The choir processional to the front of the church made an impressive ceremony, and its effectiveness at the beginning of a worship service can hardly be denied, even by those who favor the gallery location.

Trinity, and other churches that moved the choir to the front, found that there are certain disadvantages in having the organ at one end of the church and the choir at the other. Trinity's solution was to install in the chancel a small organ (2–15) built by Hall & Labagh in 1864. By the end of the century, electric action had given other churches a new solution to this problem. An organ could be built for the chancel area with a console that would control both the new organ and the organ already located in the gallery. The pioneer model of this type of installation was built in Grace Church, New York, in 1878 by Hilborne Roosevelt (see p.267).

Even if the trend away from the traditional organ case had not already begun, the chancel location would have imposed modifications on the physical characteristics of the organ. Particularly in churches with divided chancel arrangements, space for the organ became a problem that seldom was solved in a satisfactory manner. Stuffing the organ out of sight in chambers became the usual practice, but one that was more frequent in the next historical period.

Exposition Organs

The postwar decades afforded organ builders some notable showcases for displaying their instruments to the public. Visitors to the 1876 Centennial Exposition in Philadelphia could hear recitals on two large organs: a four-manual E. & G. G. Hook & Hastings in the Main Hall and a three-manual Roosevelt in the New York section of the main building. Both instruments incorporated significant departures from traditional practice. Particularly exciting was Roosevelt's use of two remote divisions: an Electric Suspended Organ and an Electric Echo Organ, which used battery-powered electric action and wind supplies furnished by electric motors [314, p.20].

The 1884 Cotton Centennial Exposition in New Orleans featured a Pilcher organ that was later installed in the Church of the Immaculate Conception. Although the main Pilcher factory was located in Louisville, Kentucky, this organ was reportedly built by William Pilcher and Sons of New Orleans [21, p.18]. William Pilcher remained in New Orleans until about 1900, and gained a considerable reputation in musical circles there as an organist and composer[6] [340, p.141].

The marvels of all previous exhibitions were eclipsed in 1893 by the gigantic Columbian Exposition in Chicago, a belated celebration of the four-hundredth anniversary of the discovery of America. Not the least of the attractions was the Egyptian dancer who demonstrated the terpsichorean technique that later became known as the hootchy-kootchy dance [59, p.761]. Other spectaculars included the two-hundred-foot Ferris wheel, waterways with Venetian gondola transportation, and life-size reproductions of Columbus's ships floating in Lake Michigan. Exhibition halls gleamed with recent inventions, and a new era of electrical gadgetry was heralded by demonstrations of fans, dishwashers, and stoves. Indeed, most of the machinery at the fair was powered by electricity.

Three organs were exhibited: a two-manual Farrand & Votey instrument in the Michigan Building, a three-manual Henry Pilcher's Sons organ in the Manufacturers' Building, and the large four-manual Farrand & Votey organ in Festival Hall. A four-manual instrument by the Carl Barckhoff Church Organ Co. of Salem, Ohio, was to have been placed in the Music Hall, but architectural changes in the structure of the building made installation impossible. Although the Barckhoff firm was paid $10,000 by the Exposition authorities, this sum seemingly was not enough to sooth ruffled feelings, and a public letter by H. N. Higinbotham, president of the World's Columbian Exposition, was soon forthcoming, explaining the "non-installation and non-exhibition of said organ as contemplated" [157].

The tubular-pneumatic Pilcher organ had, as one of its advertised features, an advanced design in adjustable combination action. Farrand & Votey had recently acquired the patents from the Roosevelt firm and had employed some of the former Roosevelt workmen, factors that influenced substantially their organs for the Exposition. Both the Farrand & Votey and Pilcher firms made use of tilting tablets. In the large Festival Hall organ they were used for couplers, while the stops were controlled by conventional draw-knobs. Pilcher's stops were described in the August 1893 issue of *The Organ* (p.89):

> The stops are domino-shaped tablets placed over the swell keyboard,
> a slight touch on either the bottom or top of the tablet throws the

stop on or off as desired. Many organists seem to think that this system of stops will soon supersede the old-fashioned draw-stop system,
as this new system is quicker and easier manipulated than the old.

This description set off a small international reaction, and the December
issue of the same publication (p.187) contained the following letter:

Birkenhead, Eng., Oct. 2, 1893.

To the Editor of The Organ:

Dear Sir,—As an interested reader of your paper, I have not failed
to notice that the Hope-Jones Stop Keys (patent applied for in 1891)
have been appropriated and fitted by certain builders to organs in the
States, notably to one of the instruments exhibited at the World's
Fair, and that the words describing the same, published in my pamphlet of December, 1890, have also been adopted.

I am, dear sir,

Yours faithfully,
Robt. Hope-Jones, M.I.E.E.

Reed Organs

During this period the reed organ reached the height of its popularity. So many of them were sold that they became known abroad as
"American organs." While it is not the concern of this book to give a
detailed account of the reed organ, its influence on organ building cannot be denied. These instruments filled a need previously met by small
pipe organs, and were readily accepted for use in homes and small
churches. They were less expensive than either a piano or an organ,
were available in a variety of sizes, were easy to move, and required
little care. Where cost and convenience were a concern and critical
judgment of musical quality was not too severe, the reed organ found a
welcome. It brought the manufacture of small pipe organs for homes
practically to a standstill, and made great inroads on the demand for
small church organs. Many of the smaller organ shops turned exclusively to reed organ building, and it was not unusual for an organ
company to have both reed and pipe organ departments. The popularity of the reed organ declined shortly after the beginning of the
twentieth century, partly because of saturation of the market and the
increased popularity of the piano and partly because of such new
devices for making music in the home as the player piano and the
phonograph.

The statistics on reed organs are amazing. According to Duga, 247
manufacturers of reed organs in the United States and Canada have been
identified [276, p.24]. An advertising circular printed by the Estey

Organ Company in the early 1880s claimed: "About five hundred people are employed the year around in this 'bee-hive of industry,' and the actual production sometimes exceeds sixty Organs per day, or one Organ every ten working minutes." The circular contained a picture of an ornate reed organ (one manual, about eighteen stops) that Estey proclaimed to be "the most elegant Organ of which we have any knowledge. It was brought out in the year 1880, to mark the completion of the 100,000th Estey Organ in process of consecutive numbering."[7]

The W. W. Kimball Company of Chicago was one of the leading reed organ builders of the Midwest. Depending on a small profit margin and large sales volume, Kimball developed an efficient sales organization to distribute his instruments in the sparsely populated central states. The first Kimball reed organs ranged in price from $175 for nine stops to $435 for the Cymbella Organ King with thirteen stops. The latter had "a magnificent chime of bells and useful book closets, together with many other valuable improvements." The music desk also formed a writing desk. Kimball continued building reed organs until 1922, producing a total of 403,390 of these instruments [25, pp.37–38].

XII

NEW ENGLAND

Introduction

Romanticism in Boston

THE erection of the German-built Boston Music Hall organ symbolized the mainstream of musical taste in New England during the last four decades of the nineteenth century. Whatever influence, direct or indirect, this instrument had on organ builders was liberally reinforced by New England's organists, composers, and teachers. Brahms was their ideal, and Germany was Mecca.

The example of John Knowles Paine (1839–1906), organist, composer, and teacher, was closely followed by a younger generation of musicians. Paine, grandson of the organ builder (see p.143), spent four years studying with Haupt and Wieprecht in Berlin, and playing numerous organ recitals in Germany. He returned to America in 1861 and the next year assumed a post on the faculty of Harvard College. George W. Chadwick (1854–1931) and Horatio Parker (1863–1919) both studied in Germany, while Arthur Foote (1853–1937) acquired his German style as a pupil of Paine's.

These men were among the foremost composers of their time.[1] Moreover, they were all organists and teachers in positions to influence opinions regarding ideals of organ design. Chadwick was at the New England Conservatory from 1882 to 1931, and was its director for thirty-four years. Parker was head of the Music Department at Yale University from 1894 to 1919. Foote maintained a private studio. His numerous compositions include some thirty works for organ.

Gilbert Chase has said that the adjectives "noble," "pure," "refined," "dignified," "earnest," and "agreeable" seemed to "epitomize an era and an aspiration that converged in Boston of the *fin de siècle*" [34, p.368]. The Bostonians were well aware of their great heritage and mission, as a light in what they considered to be the vast cultural darkness of America. In 1901 Parker said:

> New England is the centre from which has radiated thus far a great part of all progress in Art, Literature, and other intellectual pursuits in America, and it seems perfectly fair to say that an History of Music in New England would practically cover the subject of the History of Music in America. [410, p.27]

Such a rarefied atmosphere demands occasional relief. That was provided most sensationally by an Irish band director, Patrick Gilmore (1829–1894), who organized a National Peace Jubilee in Boston in 1869 and a World Peace Jubilee in 1872. His first production featured a chorus of ten thousand voices and an orchestra of a thousand. At the 1869 celebration electrically fired cannon and a hundred firemen in red shirts pounding anvils for the "Anvil Chorus" added immeasurably to the Jubilee, if not to the peace. The 1872 Jubilee was even more ambitious, with the sizes of the chorus and the orchestra doubled and participation by international stars (including Johann Strauss, who conducted the *Blue Danube*) [82, p.297].

The casual observer might find little relationship between Gilmore's extravaganzas and the erudite Boston composers. Yet historic perspective shows these two extremes to be manifestations of the Romantic movement, albeit in an excessive form in Gilmore's case and a very conservative form in the work of Boston's Brahmsites.

Organ Style and Organ Builders

The full force of the Romantic trend did not immediately envelope the style of organs in New England; church music has always been the last stronghold of a fading style. Organs of the 1860s and early '70s produced the "last resurgence of the bold and bright tone" characteristic of New England organs [120, p.121]. During the last quarter of the century the new style of larger, louder, more orchestral organs found ready advocates in New England, as elsewhere. Experiments with action and console controls increased as upperwork decreased.

Although it had been temporarily overshadowed by German ideas, ideals, and methods, the still-present English influence began to assert itself more vigorously with the arrival, toward the end of the century, of the Woodberrys, John T. Austin, and Carlton Michell, all from England. To that may be added the enthusiasm some of New England's native builders and organists maintained for the English style.

The bridge from the mid-nineteenth century to the twentieth was spanned by two noted New England companies: E. & G. G. Hook in

Boston and William A. Johnson in Westfield, Massachusetts. The Hooks began building organs in 1827, Johnson in 1844. By 1860 both shops were well established, and the Hooks' factory was said to be the largest in the country. The leadership of both companies later fell to a younger generation of builders, as Frank Hastings was left in command of the old Hook company in 1881, and William H. Johnson had charge of Johnson & Son from 1890. Both firms reached their peak in production before the last decade of the century. The Johnson firm ceased building organs in 1898, and although Hook & Hastings continued well into the twentieth century, the spotlight was swinging in other directions by then. Both companies were important not only for their fine instruments but also for the training a new generation of builders received in their shops.

While the Johnson and Hook companies give us a continuous thread of development through the entire 1860–1900 period, it was a time of change for organ firms as well as for the style of the instrument. Thomas Appleton had moved his factory to Reading, Massachusetts, in 1850, and in 1869 he built his last organ; William Stevens retired from organ building in 1872; William B. D. Simmons died in 1876; George Stevens retired in 1892. Meanwhile, a few of the builders who entered the picture were John Steer and George Turner, J. H. Willcox, George Hutchings, George Ryder, James Treat, James and Jesse Woodberry, and John Turnell Austin.

Nowhere was the end of the century more decidedly the end of an era than in New England, where the nineteenth-century organ had had its most abundant development and many of its most distinguished builders. Although leading organ factories continued to operate in New England, the old regional distinctions were gone or fast disappearing. New pigeonholes must be found to classify the organs of the twentieth century.

The Hooks and Frank Hastings
The Hook Firm, 1860–1900

About twenty organs a year were being built by the E. & G. G. Hook factory as this period opened. This pace was interrupted in 1861, possibly because of the Civil War, but in 1864 production assumed its former level.

Frank Hastings became a partner in 1870, and the name of the firm was changed to E. & G. G. Hook & Hastings. As Elias and George Hook became older, Hastings assumed more and more control of factory policy. George Hook died in 1880, and in the following year Elias died, leaving the factory completely in Hastings's hands. It was at this time that the name of the firm was changed to Hook & Hastings.

E. & G. G. Hook, Opus 322, 1863. Church of the Immaculate Conception, Boston. *Photo courtesy Thomas Murray.*

The Hook factory reached its production peak during the 1870s
and '80s, averaging forty-six organs a year. After that there was a
gradual decline, and by the first decade of the twentieth century, the firm
was building about thirty-seven organs a year. The company was
capable of producing not only a large number of instruments but also
a number of large instruments. The publicity value of the big organs
is a factor that cannot be ignored, and the Hooks' success in coping
with the problem of large installations certainly contributed greatly
to their fame.

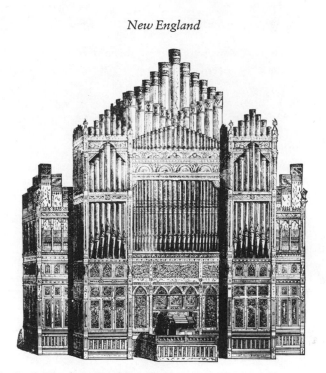

E. & G. G. Hook & Hastings, Opus 869, 1877. Built for the Cincinnati Music Hall. *Photo courtesy Barbara Owen.*

In the 1860s the Hooks built four-manual organs for Mechanics' Hall, Worcester, Massachusetts (Opus 334, 1864), and Plymouth Church, Brooklyn, New York (Opus 360, 1865). One of the best-known organs of this decade is the 1863 instrument in the Church of the Immaculate Conception, Boston. It is the largest surviving E. & G. G. Hook organ, and certainly one of the finest examples of nineteenth-century organ building. In 1902 the original three-manual scheme was enlarged to four manuals, the action was electrified, pedal and manual compasses were extended, and some minor tonal alterations were made. No further changes have been made in the organ since that time.

Some of the large and notable Hook organs of the following decades were:

Opus 801, 1875	Boston, Holy Cross Cathedral, three-manual.
Opus 828, 1876	Philadelphia Centennial Organ, four-manual.
Opus 869, 1877	Cincinnati Music Hall, four-manual.
Opus 975, 1880	Boston, Tremont Temple, four-manual.
Opus 1022, 1881	New York, St. Francis Xavier Church, four-manual.
Opus 1045, 1881	Milwaukee Industrial Exposition, four-manual.

At the time it was constructed, the three-manual Holy Cross Cathedral organ, with its seventy speaking registers, was the largest ever built by an American builder. However, the Hook firm was soon to set a new record with its monumental Cincinnati Music Hall organ with four manuals and eighty-one speaking registers.[2] Sandwiched between them was the 1876 organ built for the Philadelphia Centennial (now in St. Joseph's Old Cathedral, Buffalo), pronounced by the judges as the "highest rank in its class." Although it is a four-manual instrument, the Solo division contains only two stops, and the total number of independent speaking stops is forty-one. During the twenty-four years from the death of the Hooks to 1905 there were no new Hook four-manual organs. However, some of the three-manual organs were quite large and prominent.

While much of the Hook company's fame derived from its large instruments, the firm was not insensitive to the market for small organs. An advertising brochure from about 1876 describes little organs, called the "Choral" organs, ranging in price from $500 to $1,200. The smallest consisted of a single fifty-eight-pipe Open Diapason. The brochure, meeting a serious competitor, noted that this organ was "far superior to any *reed* organ in every respect, especially in dignity and pervading characteristics of tone, and in durability." An inventory of Choral organs and a slightly more elaborate series, the Chapel models, was kept on hand, and the instruments were available on short notice.

Another pamphlet, from the early 1880s, shows that the Hooks then had six models of small organs that were ready-made, while larger models were built to order. Standard specifications and prices were given, but variation from the suggested specifications was possible in the custom-built organs.

Like Erben, the Hooks sometimes won a contract by "donating" a part of the contracted amount to the church. In letters between the company and the First Congregational Church, North Brookfield, Massachusetts, we read that on June 6, 1874 the Hooks stated a price of $3,200 for an organ. By June 11 they had reconsidered, and the price was lowered to $3,100. On June 18 their letter to a representative of the church contained the paragraph:

> We would here allude to our reduction of fifty dollars from our price making it actually $3050., *which should be known only to ourselves.* We have in the contract specified it in full—$3100.—upon payment of which we agree to refund $50. [Cited in *BOC* 34, p.9.]

Critiques

The tone of the Hook organs was generally highly regarded by contemporary critics. Eugene Thayer's *Quarterly* said of the 1865 Hook in Plymouth Church, Brooklyn:

> This work has been in constant use for nearly or quite ten years, and is now in as fine condition as when first erected. Its soft registers are many of them very beautiful; and the reed registers are of great power. The chief characteristic of the work is brilliancy. It has much power, although we think it lacks in solidity for a work of this size.
> [429, p.8]

However, when the same organ was rededicated in 1892 after an overhauling, a New York reviewer wrote unenthusiastically:

> I do not think that the *voicing* was ever equal to some specimens of Erben, of which there are still two or three doing good service in this city . . . I must say that the unwieldy nature of the organ does not lend itself to that class of compositions which requires most artistic and smooth stops, such as Widor has in his organ in St. Sulpice.
> [295]

The organ in Holy Cross Cathedral, Boston, was designed to fill that large edifice, whose nave is 300 feet long and 120 feet high. S. Harrison Lovewell wrote of the Hook organ:

> This great instrument teaches many lessons in nobility and solidity of tone. It has always been noted for its magnificent volume devoid of shrillness. . . .
> . . . A person attending a service at the cathedral during the period when the music was at its zenith could never make sure when the full organ was reached. There seemed always to be more, and heavier, registers in reserve. [355, pp.40–41]

Some of the characteristics of the 1880 Hook in Tremont Temple, Boston, were evaluated at the time that organ was destroyed by fire. Its drawbacks were enumerated:

> The absence of any stop softer than the Salicional in the swell; the Dulciana in the choir being too soft to accompany almost every solo stop or combination in the swell; the ponderous weight necessary to depress the swell-pedal; the unheard of location of the two reversible pedals which worked the Gt. to Ped. coupler; the extreme power necessary to depress some of the combination pedals, and the comparative uselessness of a full-organ pedal which always draws the over-powering Tuba. [488, p.281]

The reviewer notes that efforts were made to get the Tuba removed from the full-organ control in order to increase its effectiveness and utility:

> The superintendent of the Temple sent an order to the builders to make the alteration, but they flatly and positively refused to comply, their only excuse being that "it would seriously disarrange the internal construction of the instrument." No less than a half-dozen of the workmen who have taken care of this instrument, and who are probably as familiar with its "internal construction" as the builders themselves, acknowledged that a pocket-knife in the hands of any one of ordinary sense, who was familiar with organ construction, would make the change in a short space of time, without "disarranging the internal construction" of the instrument. From that very date the decline in popularity of this organ for concert purposes began, till they could be counted each year on the sore fingers of a small boy's left hand. [488, p.282]

As strong points of the organ, the reviewer commended its action, the convenient spacing of the manuals, and the voicing of many of the stops, mentioning particularly the Stentorphon in the Solo, Gemshorn, Doppel-flöte, and Flûte Harmonique in the Great, and the English Diapason, Flûte d'Amour, and Vox Angelica in the Choir.

The speech of the Cincinnati Music Hall organ was less than successful. Parvin Titus observed:

> The organ was tonally superb, though so slow of speech that the performer was required to anticipate the conductor's beat by nearly a bar in rapid tempi. Considerable physical strength was necessary to manipulate the pedal levers controlling the stop combinations, which were set at the time of the installation and were not adjustable by the performer. [486, p.10]

Characteristics of the Organs

The standard compass of manuals in Hook organs during the early part of this period was increased to fifty-eight notes, although a few small instruments were built with the fifty-six-note range of the firm's earlier organs. The final leap to the sixty-one-note manual appeared as early as 1873, in the organ for First Baptist Church, Boston, but this range did not come into frequent use until the turn of the century. In reviewing the installation of a Hook organ in St. Mary's Church, the Charleston, South Carolina, News and Courier noted on January 12, 1896:

> The new organ is a two manual instrument, with full pedal scales, and fifty-eight notes on the key-board. Three small pipes are some-

times added to the upper end, making the compass sixty-one notes. But these three are rarely of any use, add very little to the value and nothing to the cost of the organ, and have not been introduced here.

The usual pedal compass in the 1860s was twenty-seven notes, and the thirty-note compass of the Worcester Mechanics' Hall organ was exceptional. By the next decade, large organs usually had thirty pedal notes, while smaller instruments continued to exhibit a twenty-seven-note range for the rest of the nineteenth century.

Late-nineteenth-century Hook organs generally used moderate wind pressures of about 3 to 3½ inches. Occasionally, higher pressures were used for one division. In the Brooklyn Plymouth Church, for example, pressure for the Tubas was 8 inches, while the rest of the organ was on 3- and 3½-inch pressure. Similarly, the Cincinnati Music Hall organ used pressures of 8 inches for the Solo, 4 inches for the Great and part of the Pedal, and 3 inches for the rest of the organ. This instrument was built for an auditorium with a seating capacity of 4,428.

The pioneer use of tubular pneumatic action by the Hooks has been mentioned (see p.208). By the early 1890s Frank Hastings was experimenting with electric action, and a Hook & Hastings promotion book of 1927 could boast: "The first organ in which we installed such action was built in 1895 and is doing excellent service today" [124, p.19].

The specification of a generously proportioned two-manual organ given as Size No. 14 in an E. & G. G. Hook & Hastings brochure of about 1880 well illustrates normal practice in tonal design, not only of this company, but also of many other late-nineteenth-century organ firms. Some obvious changes from pre-1860 specifications can be noted in the disappearance of the Sesquialtera from the Great[3] and the 4′ Principal from the Swell. Gone also are the short compass and divided stops of the Swell.

A smaller two-manual model, Size No. 8, contained the stops marked with an asterisk in the specification for Size No. 14. The Great of Size No. 8 had three 8′ colors and a diapason chorus from 8′ to 2′. The Swell is left with a basic scheme of Viola, Stopped Diapason, Flauto Traverso 4′, and an Oboe-Bassoon. A normal four-stop Swell division of earlier Hooks would have been Open Diapason 8′, Principal 4′, Stopped Diapason 8′, and Hautboy 8′. Here one can see the shift in emphasis from a diapason-oriented Swell to a flute-oriented Swell. Size 14 shows the further development of the flute family as the Swell characteristic.

One must not assume that the changes in stop names from one

E. & G. G. HOOK & HASTINGS
Size No. 14. Price $5,000.

Great

1.	Open Diapason	metal	16′	58 pipes
2.*	Open Diapason	metal	8′	58
3.*	Dulciana	metal	8′	58
4.	Salicional (Viola da Gamba)	metal	8′	58
5.*	Melodia (Stopped Bass)	wood	8′	58
6.*	Octave	metal	4′	58
7.	Flaute d'Amour	wood and metal	4′	58
8.*	Twelfth	metal	3′	58
9.*	Fifteenth	metal	2′	58
10.	Mixture	metal	III	174
11.	Trumpet	metal	8′	58

Compass C$_0$ to a^3.

Swell

12.	Bourdon	wood	16′	58
13.	Open Diapason	wood and metal	8′	58
14.*	Viola (Keraulophon)	metal	8′	58
15.*	Stopped Diapason	wood	8′	58
16.	Quintadena	metal	8′	58
17.*	Flauto Traverso	wood	4′	58
18.	Violina	metal	4′	58
19.	Flautino	metal	2′	58
20.	Dolce Cornet	metal	III	174
21.	Cornopæan	metal	8′	58
22.*	Oboe	metal	8′	} 58
23.*	Bassoon	metal	8′	

Compass C$_0$ to a^3.

Pedal

24.	Open Diapason	wood	16′	27
25.*	Bourdon	wood	16′	27
26.	Violoncello	metal	8′	27

Compass C$_1$ to d^0.

Mechanical Registers

27.* Swell to Great Coupler
28.* Great to Pedal Coupler
29.* Swell to Pedal Coupler
30.* Tremolo
31.* Bellows Signal

Pedal Movements

1.* Forte, Combination, Great Organ
2.* Piano, Combination, Great Organ
3. Reversible Pedal to operate no. 28
4.* Balanced Swell Pedal

* Indicates the stops of Size No. 8, a smaller, two-manual model, priced at $2,000.

organ to another are indicative of changes in character. A Swell 4′ Fugara might well bear a suspicious similarity to the Swell 4′ Principal of an earlier opus. However, in minimal specifications it becomes apparent just what the builder thought the essential ingredients of an organ were. No longer was 8′ Open Diapason and 4′ Principal the basic design on which the Swell division depended. Although the Swell had characteristically had a diminutive sound in comparison with the Great, the concept of the diapason ensemble as a necessary part of this division is obvious in earlier specifications. The forces that weakened the diapason ensemble on the Swell soon began chopping away at the Great ensemble, beginning, of course, with the higher-pitched stops.

One of the most famous of the large organs built by the Hook company is the four-manual instrument installed in Mechanics' Hall, Worcester, Massachusetts, in 1864. The contract for this organ was signed on August 31, 1863. The price was to be $8,170, but when the final specification had been decided, the price was brought to $9,040. Beasley observes that this organ was a remarkable bargain: "Just a year and one-half following the installation of the Worcester instrument, the large Hook for Plymouth Church in Brooklyn, of the same number of tonal registers, was priced at $20,000 . . ." [18, p.327].

A public inaugural recital was given on November 10, 1864, with three organists participating. The program was:

I

| Grand Hallelujah Chorus | Handel |
| Adagio and Rondo from Concerto | Rinck |

B. D. Allen, organist

II

| Grand Toccata in F | Bach |
| Offertory for Vox Humana | Batiste |

W. Eugene Thayer, organist

III

Offertoire in G	Lefebure-Wely
Improvisation introducing the Vox Humana	
Grand Hallelujah Chorus (Mount of Olives)	Beethoven

J. H. Willcox, organist

[397, p.26]

With a few exceptions, this organ illustrates typical characteristics of three- and four-manual Hook organs during the late nineteenth century. On the Great, a Doppel Flote was more common than the Claribella, and the Stopped Diapason was old-fashioned; 16′ and 4′ reeds would be omitted on a smaller scheme. On the Swell, the 16′ and 4′ reeds were luxuries. By substituting a few stop names (Salicional for Viol d'Amour, Flauto Traverso for Flute Octaviante, Flautino for

Fifteenth, Dolce Cornet for Mixture), we see a typical Swell division. With the exception of the Keraulophon and Mixture, the Choir division corresponds to standard practice. In the Pedal, the 8′ Flute is unusual. Solo divisions defy generalization. For example, the 1881–82 organ for St. Francis Xavier's Church, New York, contained a Solo division of Stentorphon 8′, Viola 8′, Philomelo 8′, Octave Viola 4′, Flauto Traverso 4′, and Tuba Mirabilis 8′ [231, p.4].

Mechanics' Hall, Worcester, Massachusetts
E. & G. G. Hook, Opus 334, 1864

Great

Open Diapason	16′	58
Open Diapason	8′	58
Viola Da Gamba	8′	58
Stopped Diapason	8′	58
Claribella	8′	58
Principal	4′	58
Flute Harmonique	4′	58
Twelfth	2⅔′	58
Fifteenth	2′	58
Mixture	III	174
Mixture	V	290
Trumpet	16′	58
Trumpet	8′	58
Clarion	4′	58

Swell

Bourdon	16′	58
Open Diapason	8′	58
Stopped Diapason	8′	58
Viol d'Amour	8′	58
Principal	4′	58
Flute Octaviante	4′	58
Violin	4′	58
Twelfth	2⅔′	58
Fifteenth	2′	58
Mixture	V	290
Trumpet	16′	46
Cornopean	8′	58
Oboe	8′	58
Clarion	4′	58
Vox Humana	8′	58

Choir

Æolina & Bourdon	16′	58
Open Diapason	8′	58
Melodia	8′	58
Dulciana	8′	58
Keraulophon	8′	58

Choir (continued)

Flauto Traverso	4′	58
Violin	4′	58
Picolo	2′	58
Mixture	III	174
Clarinet	8′	58

Solo

Philomela	8′	58
Salicional	8′	58
Hohl Pfeife	4′	58
Picolo	2′	58
Tuba	8′	58
Corno Inglese	8′	58

Pedale

Open Diapason	16′	30
Violone	16′	30
Bourdon	16′	30
Violoncello	8′	30
Quinte	10¾′[sic]	30
Flute	8′	30
Posaune	16′	30

Mechanical Registers

Swell to Great Coupler
Swell to Choir Coupler
Choir to Great Coupler
Solo to Great Coupler
Choir to Solo Coupler
Great to Pedale Coupler
Choir to Pedale Coupler
Choir to Pedale Coupler (super octaves)
Swell to Pedale Coupler
Solo to Pedale Coupler
Tremulant ("swell")
Bellows signal
Pedale Check

Mechanics' Hall, Worcester, Massachusetts
E. & G. G. HOOK, Opus 344, 1864

Mechanical Registers (continued)

Ventil (for Open Diapason in Pedale)
Ventil (for Quinte, Flute, and Posaune in Pedale)

Combination Pedals

Great Manual Forte
Great Manual Piano
Swell Manual Forte
Swell Manual Piano
Choir Manual Forte

Combination Pedals (continued)

Choir Manual Piano
(Pedale) operates on Open Diapason, Quinte, Flute, and Posaune, and with the aid of Ventils, allows of various combinations.
Couplers Forte
Couplers Piano
Operates on "Great Pedale" Coupler
Balanced Swell Pedal, with double action

[*BOC* 35, pp.2–4.]

Some of the large Hook organs had extraordinary features. The 1875 organ for the Cathedral of the Holy Cross, Boston, for example, was given a fourteen-stop Pedal division, containing a Contra Bourdon 32′, Open Diapason 16′, Violone 16′, Dulciana 16′, Bourdon 16′, Quint Flöte 12′, Bell Gamba 8′, Violoncello 8′, Octave 8′, Flöte 8′, Super Octave 4′, Cornet V, Trombone 16′, and Posaune 8′. This seventy-stop specification also includes three Great mixtures with a total of thirteen ranks, as well as an unusual accessory, a crescendo pedal.

The 1876 organ for the Philadelphia Centennial was given an early example of an augmented Pedal. Each of the five speaking stops was extended, and the ranks Bourdon 32′, Open Diapason 16′, Violone 16′, Trombone 16′, and Bell Gamba 8′ yielded an additional six stops: Bourdon 16′, Quint 12′, Violoncello 8′ Octave 8′, Trumpet 8′, and Super Octave 4′.

William A. and William H. Johnson
The Johnson Firm, 1860–1970

William A. Johnson, like the Hooks, felt the effects of the Civil War, and its concomitant shortage of materials and economic instability. Annual production dropped from eighteen organs in 1860 to fourteen in 1861 and ten in 1862. From this low point there was a rapid increase to the peak years of Johnson history, 1868 through 1870. One hundred organs were built during these three years.

Most of the 248 organs constructed between 1860 and 1870 were one- and two-manual instruments. Of the sixteen three-manual organs, three were installed in Chicago.[4] Johnson was particularly successful in following the westward expansion of the organ market, and in addi-

William A. Johnson, Opus 134, 1862. Old St. Luke's Episcopal Church, Lanesboro, Massachusetts. *Photo courtesy Thomas Murray.*

tion to the three-manual organs, fifteen more Johnson organs went to locations in Illinois. His list of organs during this time also included twelve in Ohio, seven in Iowa, five in Michigan, four in Wisconsin, three in Indiana, two each in Tennessee and West Virginia, and one each in Georgia, Kansas, and Nebraska.

The Nebraska organ, built in 1869, was installed in St. Philomena's Church (R.C.), Omaha, and was Omaha's first organ. It was sent as far as St. Joseph, Missouri, by train; there it was reloaded on a Missouri River steamboat for the trip to Omaha. The specification was similar to that of Opus 76 (see p.134) [420, p.6].

Johnson also placed early organs in California. He built two-manual instruments for St. John's Episcopal Church, Stockton (Opus 105, 1860), Presbyterian Church, Stockton (Opus 161, 1864), St. John's Church, Oakland (Opus 255, 1868), and St. James' Episcopal Church, San Francisco (Opus 302, 1869).

Johnson & Son, 1871–1898

In 1871 a new period began for the Johnson shop. William H. Johnson, son of the founder, was taken into the firm, and four years later the company name became Johnson & Son. Another telling event in 1871 was the destruction of the factory and three completed organs by fire. This setback seemed to cost Johnson the momentum of the peak years. Never again did the company complete more than twenty-eight organs in a year, and eighteen or twenty was a more usual number.

William A. Johnson, Opus 183, 1865. Built for the Congregational
Church, Stockbridge, Massachusetts. *Photo from the Elsworth collection, courtesy Barbara Owen.*

Although the large majority of Johnson organs were naturally
located in the Northeast, the trail of contracts westward continued to
grow after 1870. Installations in Illinois and Ohio were especially
numerous, and Chicago, in particular, was blessed with a large supply
of fine Johnson instruments. Others went to Minnesota, Kentucky,
Texas, Missouri, and the Dakotas. A few more made the long trip to
the Pacific coast, and the first Johnson organs in Southern California
were installed in First Congregational Church, National City (Opus
671, 1887), and First Congregational Church, Pasadena (Opus 740,
1890).

William A. Johnson's health began to fail, and in 1890 William H.
became head of the firm. He continued building organs until 1898,
and after that the company supplied pipes for other builders until

about 1907. William A. Johnson died in 1901, his son in 1921. In all, the firm produced 860 organs.

Characteristics of the Organs

While various types of electric action were coming into use in the late nineteenth century, the Johnson firm continued to use tracker action to the end of its existence. Pneumatic levers were employed in its larger organs from about 1872, and the way this mechanism lightened the touch when manuals were coupled has been described by Simmons:

> The pneumatic principle was used by Johnson and Son to put a pneumatic relay between the keys of the Great organ and the tracker levers to the rest of the organ. This was actually a tracker organ with a pneumatic jack behind the console which affected the Great manual keys only. All the coupling, of the other manuals to the Great was accomplished through this mechanism. These couplers were in the form of "off-on" pistons of modern organs and were placed beneath the Great manual. The coupling accomplished was Swell to Great, Solo (or Choir) to Great, and Great organ separation (which was similar to modern Unison Off). Some organs also had the Swell to Solo arranged to work through the pneumatic system, but not always, as in some cases this was an ordinary tracker coupler. [466, III, p.6]

Johnson is said to have built one tubular pneumatic organ, but found it unsatisfactory. Possibly one of the reasons William H. Johnson left organ building was his refusal, or inability, to convert his action to either tubular pneumatic or some form of electric action at a time when the major builders were moving very rapidly in that direction.

In addition to the use of pneumatic levers, a number of other changes appeared in Johnson organs in the late 1860s and early '70s. Consoles were separated from organ cases, the manual compass was increased from fifty-six to fifty-eight or sixty-one notes, the pedal compass became twenty-seven or thirty notes, divided stops were used less frequently, new stop names appeared in the specifications, a balanced swell replaced the old hook-down swell control, and water motors made an appearance. In other words, the Johnson firm followed most of the tendencies associated with this period of organ building with the exception of experiments with electric action. One finds, however, that the Johnsons did not apply their innovations with unrelenting consistency, and it is not unusual to find one or more of the early characteristics in a late specification.

Typical manual choruses on small instruments carried the diapason family to 2' on the Great. Often, however, only an 8' represented this family on the Swell, with a Fugara 4' taking the place of the traditional

Principal 4'. As in early Johnson organs, the 8' Diapason on the Great was louder than the upperwork. The typical reeds were a Trumpet on the Great (sometimes replaced by a Clarinet) and an Oboe on the Swell. Blanchard has summarized Johnson's choice of flutes in small organs:

> The standard combination [in the Great] then becomes melodia, 8 ft., and flute d'amour, 4 ft. It should be noticed that wherever possible Johnson pairs off an open flute, 8 ft., and a half-covered flute, 4 ft., on the great in contrast to an 8-ft. stopped flute and an open, usually harmonic, metal flute, 4 ft., on the swell. Non-harmonic metal flutes, 4 ft., are relatively rare in all Johnson work, although they do occur (Op. 458, 485). [228, I, p.20]

Small organs often still relied on a single 16' Pedal stop with an octave of pipes. Somewhat larger instruments might contain Pedal divisions of Open Diapason 16', Bourdon 16', and Violoncello 8'.

Two specifications serve to illustrate the larger Johnson organs: The earlier instrument, Opus 410, was installed in the Second Presbyterian Church, Chicago, in 1873. Opus 860, installed in St. Paul's Lutheran Church, Chicago, in 1898, was perhaps the last organ built by the Johnson firm. Although these two organs represent a time span of a quarter of a century, one finds surprising similarities in the stop lists. There is no radical experimentation in the 1898 organ, yet some significant differences do appear. The large Pedal division in Opus 410 must be regarded as an unusual feature; that of Opus 860 is more typical for the period.

Second Presbyterian Church *Chicago, Illinois* JOHNSON ORGAN COMPANY, Opus 410, 1873		*St. Paul's Lutheran Church* *Chicago, Illinois* JOHNSON & SON, Opus 860, 1898	
Great		*Great*	
Open Diapason	16'	Double Open Diapason	16'
Quintatoen	16'	Open Diapason	8'
Open Diapason	8'	Viola Da Gamba	8'
Viola Da Gamba	8'	Dolce	8'
Spitz Floete	8'	Spitz Flote	8'
Doppel Floete	8'	Doppel Flote	8'
Quint	5⅓'	Octave	4'
Octave	4'	Flauto Traverso	4'
Flute Harmonique	4'	Twelfth	2⅔'
Twelfth	2⅔'	Fifteenth	2'
Fifteenth	2'	Mixture	IV
Mixture	III	Trumpet	8'
Scharf	IV	Clarion	4'

Second Presbyterian Church Chicago, Illinois JOHNSON ORGAN COMPANY, Opus 410, 1873		St. Paul's Lutheran Church Chicago, Illinois JOHNSON & SON, Opus 860, 1898	

Great (continued)

Trumpet	8′		
Clarion	4′		

Swell   *Swell*

Bourdon	16′	Bourdon treble	16′
Open Diapason	8′	Bourdon bass	16′
Salicional	8′	Open Diapason	8′
Dolcissimo	8′	Salicional	8′
Stopped Diapason	8′	Aeoline	8′
Quintadena	8′	Voix Celeste	8′
Octave	4′	Stopped Diapason	8′
Fugara	4′	Quintadena	8′
Flauto Traverso	4′	Violin	4′
Piccolo	2′	Flute Harmonique	4′
Mixture	III	Gemshorn	4′
Contra Fagotto	16′	Flautino	2′
Cornopean	8′	Dolce Cornet	III
Oboe and Bassoon	8′	Contra Fagotto	16′
Vox Humana	8′	Cornopean	8′
Tremulant		Oboe and Bassoon	8′
		Vox Humana	8′
		Tremulant	

Solo   *Choir*

Still Gedackt	16′	Geigen Principal	8′
Open Diapason	8′	Dulciana	8′
Geigen Diapason	8′	Melodia	8′
Dulciana	8′	Fugara	4′
Melodia	8′	Flute d'Amour	4′
Violin	4′	Piccolo	2′
Flute d'Amour	4′	Clarinet	8′
Flautino	2′		
Clarionet	8′		

Pedal   *Pedal*

Contra Bourdon	32′	Double Open Diapason	16′
Open Diapason	16′	Double Dulciana	16′
Contrebasse	16′	Bourdon	16′
Bourdon	16′	Quint	10⅔′
Quint Floete	10⅔′	Violoncello	8′
Violoncello	8′	Flote	8′
Floete	8′	Trombone	16′
Super Octave	4′		
Trombone	16′		
Tromba	8′		

[466, III, p.6]	[496, I, p.13]

J. H. Willcox & Co., Hutchings, Plaisted & Co., George S. Hutchings Co.

George Hutchings and His Associates

George Sherburn Hutchings (1835–1913) was a native of Salem, Massachusetts, and was educated in the Salem public schools. Having lost his parents while he was still a boy, he went to work at an early age. After two years of working in a store, he became an apprentice to his brother, a carpenter and builder. It was then that his aptitude and skill in cabinetmaking impressed William Hook, furniture maker in Salem, and father of Elias and George Hook.

Through this connection Hutchings went to work in the Hook organ factory in Boston in 1857. Only a short time later he was made foreman of the case makers, continuing in that capacity until 1861. In that year he enlisted in the Thirteenth Regiment of Massachusetts Volunteers. Two years in the army and a subsequent illness interrupted Hutching's career, but he later returned to the Hook factory, where he rose to the position of factory superintendent.

In 1869, Hutchings together with Dr. J. H. Willcox, M. H. Plaisted, and G. V. Nordstrom formed the company of J. H. Willcox & Co. The history of Hutchings organs, then, actually begins under the Willcox name. Willcox's connection with William Simmons has already been noted (see pp.135–36, 139). About 1860 that partnership dissolved, and Willcox, a capable recitalist, worked with the Hook company, drawing up some of their specifications and playing inaugural recitals on a number of their instruments.

Changes in J. H. Willcox & Co. were soon to come. In 1872 Willcox left the firm, and three years later he died, at the age of forty-eight. Nordstrom's interests were purchased by Hutchings and Plaisted, and the company name became Hutchings, Plaisted, & Co.[5] In 1884 Plaisted sold his interest to Hutchings and moved to California. The firm name was then changed to George S. Hutchings Co., which it remained until a merger was effected with the Votey Company in 1901. It then became the Hutchings-Votey Organ Co.

J. H. Willcox & Co. produced about thirty organs, including three forty-stop instruments. Ayars has said,

> Dr. Willcox' aim was to produce an instrument of moderate size, which, within its limits as to power and technical resources, was to be a perfectly complete organ, not an isolated section of a larger instrument.
>
> In the period about 1870 this company probably did the finest work in America. [13, pp.160–61].

About one hundred organs were built during the Hutchings-Plaisted period (1872–84). This production is comparatively small, but the company managed to attract some contracts of considerable size. The largest organ of this partnership was the sixty-four-stop organ for the New Old South Church, Boston.

The late 1880s and the '90s was a time of great expansion for the George S. Hutchings Co., and during the '90s production averaged close to thirty organs a year. The 1890 organ for New York Avenue Methodist Church, Brooklyn, was Hutchings's largest organ at the time of its installation and for some years to come. It boasted sixty-eight stops. An 1894 magazine stated:

> Since the construction of the organ in the New York Ave. M. E.
> Church, Brooklyn, Mr. Hutchings's business has more than doubled;
> and he has been compelled to considerably enlarge his factory. . . .
> This factory is now one of the largest and best equipped in the world.
> [302, p.222].

Hutchings and E. M. Skinner

In 1889 or 1890 Hutchings hired a young man who was to exert a powerful and lasting influence on the American organ. Ernest M. Skinner (1866–1960), with four years' experience working for George H. Ryder, entered the Hutchings factory as a tuner. He left Hutchings for a brief time to work for Jesse Woodberry, but returned as a voicer, and was soon transferred to draftsman. He later became factory superintendent, and was vice president at the time of the merger with Votey in 1901. Skinner described his association with Hutchings as "most pleasant," and recalled: "About the year 1901, to my great regret and through no act of Mr. Hutchings or myself, I left my old friend and partner and hung my shingle out on a shack in South Boston" [469, p.18]. After a two-year partnership with James Cole (Skinner & Cole Organ Company), Skinner established his own firm in 1903.

While he was working for Hutchings, Skinner had the good fortune to tune and regulate the residence organ of Montgomery Sears. Sears was so pleased with the results that he sent Skinner to Europe to study organs. The first stop was London, and Skinner later recalled hearing Dr. Peace play the organ in St. George's Hall:

> Dr. Peace played operatic airs on a big Vox Humana to a crowd that
> filled the hall. After each number there was clapping and yelling and
> a spontaneous expression of enthusiasm in full keeping with what
> we hear in these United States at a ball game. There was no doubt
> whatever that Dr. Peace played to that crowd just what would please
> them most and that they thoroughly enjoyed it. I then and there

acquired an overwhelming sympathy with the idea of music for the common public as well as for the musician. [237, p.176]

Skinner was greatly impressed by English reeds, a factor that influenced his later work, both in the Hutchings factory and still later in his own shop. He remarked: "I had read of the Willis Tuba on 22" wind in St. George's Hall. When I heard it I was wild with enthusiasm. It was so incredibly fine and superior to anything I had ever heard. I owe everything I know of the trumpet family to Henry Willis, Senior and Junior" [237, p.177].

He found the action of British organs antiquated, and the organs of Holland bad both tonally and in action. He thought French building methods and action were inferior, but admired the sound that French organs had in their advantageous acoustical situations [237].

Hutchings's English Voicer

Skinner was not alone in bringing English ideas to the Hutchings factory. The English organ builder Carlton C. Michell arrived in the United States in the mid-1880s. He built a few organs, did some voicing for Hutchings, worked with several other builders, including Cole & Woodberry, and then returned to England.[6] He was responsible for voicing the much-admired organ in the New York Avenue Methodist Church, Brooklyn.

Michell was sharply critical of American organs. After hearing Guilmant play at the New Old South Church (Hutchings-Plaisted, 1876), he wrote:

> All the organs in this country are built as psalm-tune organs,— as such many are, in detail, musical, as this particular instrument certainly is; beyond this point of requirement they will not bear testing. They behave remarkably well so long as the player keeps to the jog-trot, London cab-horse pace, but beyond that you cannot go without developing asthmatic symptoms,—the panting and gasping for breath of an instrument inadequately winded.
>
> Witness, for instance, the effect of the last movement of Mendelssohn's First Organ Sonata under the fingers of Mons. Guilmant— not half the notes sounded which were touched, and in every rapid passage the effect was as if the full organ had been suddenly shut off and brought on again with each chord. . . .
>
> I am not finding fault with this particular instrument. I am speaking in general terms in saying that the accepted model of the day is on similar lines of construction entirely defective,—primitive to a degree; for we find better method adopted as early as 1559 in the celebrated organ in Lubeck. [370, p.186]

George S. Hutchings, Opus 410, 1896. Our Lady of Perpetual Help Church, Roxbury, Massachusetts. *Photo courtesy Jim Lewis.*

Characteristics of the Organs

The specifications of Hutchings's organs were usually quite similar to those of Hook & Hastings. Occasionally an exotic stop was included, e.g., the Physharmonica 8′ on the Choir of the New Old South Church organ or the Saxophone 4′ on the Swell divisions of the organs in New York Avenue Methodist Church, Brooklyn, and Church of Our Lady of Perpetual Help, Roxbury, Massachusetts. In details of construction, Hutchings tended to accept experimental ideas more quickly than did his New England contemporaries. He favored the sixty-one-note manual range, although his pedals were given the customary twenty-seven- or thirty-note range.

As early as 1874 Hutchings, Plaisted & Co. had used a system of borrowing stops. In Eugene Thayer's Studio organ the Pedal contains a Bourdon 16′ borrowed from the Swell by means of an extra set of trackers and pallets. Boadway has described the mechanism as follows:

> The "soft" Pedale stop borrowed from the Swell seems too complicated a system but it works well. Vertical trackers run from the Pedale action below the chest to 27 additional pallets at the rear of the Swell chest. The 16′ rank is on two sliders and the channels are partitioned off at the rear; in the toeboard are leather flap-valves that close when the stop is drawn in the Pedale so that the rank will not sound in the Swell, and the reverse occurs when the stop is used in the Swell alone. [BOC 40, p.6]

In November 1892 Hutchings exhibited a two-manual organ at the Mechanics' Fair, Boston, "to exhibit the tubular pneumatic action and changeable combination pistons which this firm have just perfected and which are being patented" [393, p.215]. The combination system is one that is occasionally found in modern organs of modest size. Small push-knobs corresponding to the stops of the organ were placed above the Swell manual. They came in pairs: an *on* and an *off*. The combination was set by pushing the *on* push-knobs for the required stops. Then when the combination piston was pushed, only these selected stops would sound, but without disturbing the location of stops drawn by hand. The Hutchings organ had enough sets of push-knobs to have three combination pistons for each manual. The pistons were duplicated by pedal controls. Another innovation on this organ was a Prolongment Harmonique, "for the purpose of *sustaining* one or more notes on the great after the hands are removed from the keys" [393, p.215]. Such a device had previously been used by Cavaillé-Coll.

Ernest M. Skinner claimed credit for developing the electric action that appeared with increasing frequency in Hutchings's larger organs in the mid- and late 1890s. With the use of electricity came many other possibilities. For example, the large Hutchings organ for the South Congregational Church, New Britain, Connecticut (c.1896), contained an augmented Solo division (three stops, one rank) and an augmented Pedal (sixteen stops, seven ranks). The 1897 electropneumatic organ for Our Lady of Perpetual Help, Roxbury, was given a movable console, twelve couplers, eighteen pedal movements, and twenty-one adjustable pistons.

Further steps toward the Romantic style are noted in the enclosure of the Choir division of the New York Avenue Methodist Church, Brooklyn, in an expression chamber. One of the large Hutchings installations was the Chancel organ for St. Bartholomew's Church, New York

George S. Hutchings, Opus 431, 1897, console. Built for the Church of the Divine Paternity, New York. The stops of this electric-action console are mounted on hinged wings, shown in a position suitable for performance. *Photo from the Everett Truette scapbooks, Boston Public Library.*

(1893 or 1894). This organ was connected with the old organ in the gallery, and the action was "tubular electric."[7] Four stops of the chancel organ Choir division were enclosed, as well as both Swell divisions and the gallery Solo division. The specification included a variety of sub- and supercouplers as well as 8′ couplers. There were fifteen combination pistons, fifteen combination pedals, a crescendo pedal, and a pedal for coupling all swells.

An interesting and unusual Hutchings organ was a huge one-manual instrument built for the Boston Music Hall. After the removal of the big Walcker organ, there was no instrument to use in oratorio performances, and "the directors felt that it was necessary to do something to prevent the Handel and Haydn Society from leaving the hall which had so long been its home . . ." [224]. The new organ was completed in December 1884 and was first used in a performance of Handel's *Messiah.* With nineteen manual voices and nine pedal voices, this instrument was surely a giant among one-manual schemes. Six of the manual stops were enclosed in a swell box. The action was mechanical, "without any pneumatic appliances."

New York Avenue Methodist Church, Brooklyn, New York
GEORGE S. HUTCHINGS, Opus 200, 1890

Great			Great (continued)		
Double Open Diapason	16′	61	Open Diapason		
Open Diapason (large			(medium scale)	8′	61
scale)	8′	61	Viola di Gamba	8′	61

New York Avenue Methodist Church, Brooklyn, New York
GEORGE S. HUTCHINGS, Opus 200, 1890

Great (continued)

Viola d'Amour	8'	61
Clarabella	8'	61
Doppel Flöte	8'	61
Flute Harmonique	4'	61
Octave	4'	61
Gambette	4'	61
Octave Quint	2⅔'	61
Super Octave	2'	61
Mixture	V	305
Scharff	III	183
Double Trumpet	16'	61
Trumpet	8'	61
Clarion	4'	61

Swell

Bourdon Bass	16'	12
Bourdon Treble	16'	49
Open Diapason	8'	61
Gemshorn	8'	61
Hohl Flöte	8'	61
Salicional	8'	61
Vox Celestis (t.c.)	8'	49
Æoline	8'	61
Stopped Diapason	8'	61
Quintadena	8'	61
Octave	4'	61
Fugara	4'	61
Flauto Traverso	4'	61
Flautino	2'	61
Dolce Cornet	V	305
Contra Fagotto	16'	61
Cornopean	8'	61
Oboe	8'	61
Vox Humana	8'	61
Saxophone	4'	61

Choir

Lieblich Gedackt	16'	61
Open Diapason	8'	61
Geigen Principal	8'	61
Spitz Flöte	8'	61
Concert Flute	8'	61
Dolcissimo	8'	61
Gedackt	8'	61
Octave	4'	61
Violina	4'	61

Choir (continued)

Flute d'Amour	4'	61
Piccolo Harmonique	2'	61
Orchestral Oboe	8'	61
Clarinet	8'	61

Pedal

Contra Bourdon	32'	30
Open Diapason	16'	30
Violone	16'	30
Dulciana	16'	30
Bourdon	16'	30
Quint	10⅔'	30
Octave	8'	30
Violoncello	8'	30
Flute	8'	30
Trombone	16'	30
Tromba	8'	30

Couplers

Swell to Great ⎫
Choir to Great ⎬ Operated by Piston Knobs between keyboards
Swell to Choir ⎬
Great to Pneumatics ⎭

Great to Pedal
Swell to Pedal
Choir to Pedal

Swell Tremolo
Choir Tremolo
Wind Indicator

Pedal Movements

1– 5. G & P adjustable combination pedals
6–10. S & P adj. comb. ped.
11–14. C & P adj. comb. ped.
15–18. P adj. comb. ped.
19. Full Organ.
20. All Couplers.
21. S-G and Swell on itself.
22. G-G Sub-octaves.
23. Reversible G-P.
24. Balanced Swell Pedal.
25. Balanced Choir Pedal.
26. Grand Crescendo affecting full organ except Sw. Vox Humana and Ch. Clarinet.

[Adapted from *BOC* 31, p.6]

Music Hall, Boston, Massachusetts
GEORGE S. HUTCHINGS, Opus 138, 1884

Manual: Compass C to C⁴   *Pedal:* Compass C to D

Double open diapason	16′	Contra bourdon	32′
Dulciana	16′	Double open diapason	16′
Open diapason	8′	Bourdon	16′
Open diapason	8′	Violone	16′
Doppel flote	8′	Quinte	10⅔′
Viola da Gamba	8′	Flote	8′
Stopped diapason	8′	Violoncello	8′
Dulciana	8′	Octave	4′
Octave	4′	Trombone	16′
Flute harmonique	4′		
Twelfth	2⅔′	*Mechanicals*	
Fifteenth	2′	Manuale to pedal couples	
Mixture	IV	Blower's signal	
Mixture	III		
Mixture	III		
Dolce Cornet	IV		
Trumpet	8′		
Trumpet (T.C.)	16′		
Clarion	4′		

Pedal Movements

Forte combination, with appropriate pedal combination
Mezzo combination, with appropriate pedal combination
Piano combination, with appropriate pedal combination
Chorus organ separation
Octave coupler manuale
Octave coupler pedals
Balanced swell pedals
Nos. 2, 4, 7, 8, 10, and 16 [of the manual stops] are enclosed in a swell box.

[224]

Steere & Turner, J. W. Steere & Sons
Steere and His Associates

In 1867 two former employees of the Johnson company opened their own firm in Westfield, Massachusetts. John Wesley Steer (1824–1900), a native of Southwick, Massachusetts, had built at least one organ under his own name before he was joined by George William Turner (1829–1908). The firm suffered severe losses from both fires and flood, and by 1877 it was also in financial difficulties. The factory was moved to Springfield in 1879, and about 1890 Steer began spelling his name "Steere." Turner left the firm in 1891, and its name was revised from Steere & Turner to J. W. Steere & Sons. In 1894 it became J. W. Steere & Son. Later changes were: 1901–19, J. W. Steere & Son Organ Company; 1919–20, The Steere Organ Co.

Pullman Methodist Church, Chicago, Illinois
STEERE & TURNER, Opus 170, 1882

Great			Swell		
Bourdon Bass	16′	17	Open Diapason	8′	58
Bourdon	16′	41	Stopped Diapason	8′	58
Open Diapason	8′	58	Salicional	8′	58
Melodia	8′	58	Aeoline	8′	58
Dulciana	8′	58	Flute Harmonic	4′	58
Octave	4′	58	Violina	4′	58
Flute d'Amour	4′	58	Flautino	2′	58
Twelfth	2⅔′	58	Bassoon	8′	12
Fifteenth	2′	58	Oboe	8′	46
Mixture	III	174	Tremolo		
Trumpet	8′	58			
Clarionet (t.c.)	8′	46	*Pedal*		
			Open Diapason	16′	27
			Bourdon	16″	27

8′ Couplers

Great-Pedal rev. foot lever
Great forte: all stops except Trumpet
Great mezzo: Bourdon Bass, and 8′ flues, 4′ flute
Great Piano: cancels all stops except Melodia and Dulciana
Swell forte: all stops
Swell piano: cancels all stops except Stop'd Diapason, Salicional, and Aeoline
Water motor

Mixture Composition

C-b	2′–2′–1⅓′–1′
c¹-b¹	2⅔′–2′–1⅓′
c²-a³	4′–2⅔′–2′

[522, I, p.30]

In 1920 the factory burned. In the next year E. M. Skinner acquired the Steere business and consolidated it with his own. Meanwhile, George Turner was in partnership for a short time (1893–94) with one of Steere's sons, John S., and they built organs using the old name of Steere & Turner. Turner later moved to Buffalo, where he was associated with Emmons Howard.

J. W. Steere and his associates operated a shop of moderate size, with an overall average production of fourteen organs annually from 1867 to 1900. In 1871 the factory employed twenty-eight workmen. The organs were mostly of one and two manuals, with an occasional three-manual installation. While Steere organs were occasionally located in the Central states, few reached the West, and it was not until 1901 that a Steere organ was installed in California (a tubular pneumatic three-manual organ for First Methodist Church, Pasadena).

In spite of natural disasters and monetary troubles, Steere & Turner produced organs of notable quality in workmanship, and their early instruments were especially fine tonally. Later Steere organs followed the trends of the day, and have less appeal for the modern listener.

Characteristics of the Organs

J. W. Steere & Sons began using tubular pneumatic action in 1897, although the firm continued building tracker action as well. It was still using the old fifty-eight, twenty-seven compasses at the close of the century, and was still dividing the Swell reed (Oboe-Bassoon). The 16′ manual Bourdon was usually divided, and the Great Melodia-Stop'd Diapason Bass combination remained frequent until after 1880. Some of these old-fashioned characteristics are attributable to the moderate size of most of the organs. Even less conservative companies exhibited these characteristics in the specifications for their smaller instruments.

In the selection of stops, the Steere & Turner organs generally bore a close resemblance to Johnson organs of the same size and period. The 1882 organ built for the Pullman Palace Car Co. Church, Pullman, Illinois (now Pullman Methodist Church, Chicago), illustrates typical Steere & Turner characteristics. An interesting feature common to many Steere & Turner organs is the inclusion of the Great reeds in the Swell enclosure.

James Treat and the Methuen Organ Company

James Treat (1837–1915) was a native of New Haven Connecticut. He learned organ building in the Johnson shop, worked for a couple of years (1860–62) with Erben in New York, and then moved to Boston, where he was engaged in various occupations before going to work for Hutchings, Plaisted & Co. in 1876.

Treat's major contribution to organ history resulted from his association with the wealthy architect Edward F. Searles. An organ fancier, Searles hired Treat in 1886 to build an organ for his home. After the death of his wife two years later, Searles gave more and more time to his hobbies, and the collaboration of his interest and money with Treat's ability as an organ builder resulted in some fine organs. Searles established an organ factory for Treat at Methuen, Massachusetts, and here, with cost as no object, only the best materials were used and the employees were the most competent workmen available. Organs were built under the names James E. Treat & Co. and later (from about 1898 to about 1911) Methuen Organ Co. Treat is best known today for the renovation and installation of the Walcker Boston Music Hall organ in Methuen, completed in 1909 (see pp.204–205).

An organ of the 1880s by James Treat (Methuen Organ Company). Now in St. George's Primitive Methodist Church, Methuen, Massachusetts. The organ is shown as it appeared on exhibition in Old South Church, Boston, in 1889. *Photo from the Everett Truette scrapbooks, Boston Public Library.*

Treat's organ cases, using burnished tin and elaborate wood carving, were among the most opulent produced in this country. There are three surviving examples in Methuen: in the Searles estate, the First Congregational Church, and St. George's Primitive Methodist Church. The organ in St. George's was exhibited in Old South Church, Boston, during the winter of 1889–90, after which it was used as an exhibition organ in the factory. In 1904 Searles gave this organ—and a church building to place it in—to St. George's Primitive Methodist Church. It was rebuilt by Skinner and was later restored by the Andover Organ Co.

An organ of the 1890s by James Treat (Methuen Organ Company).
Now in First Congregational Church, Methuen, Massachusetts. The
organ is shown as it appeared at the Searles estate, Great Barrington,
Massachusetts. *Photo courtesy Jim Lewis.*

An important Treat organ of the 1890s was built for Grace Church
(later Grace Cathedral), San Francisco. It was a gift to the church from
Searles in memory of his wife. Before it was sent to San Francisco, the

organ was exhibited in the factory. In March 1894, *The Organ* (p.246) reported:

The construction of this organ has been something unique in the history of organ building in this country. Nothing that money and skilled workmen could accomplish has been omitted, and the result is an instrument which is a credit to any builder in the world.

Grace Episcopal Church, San Francisco, California
JAMES E. TREAT & CO., 1894

Great

Open Diapason	16'	61
Open Diapason, 1st	8'	61
Open Diapason, 2nd	8'	61
Gemshorn	8'	61
Viola di Gamba	8'	61
Doppel Flöte	8'	61
Octave	4'	61
Flûte Harmonique	4'	61
Twelfth	2⅔'	61
Fifteenth	2'	61
Mixture	III	183
Trumpet	8'	61

Swell

Bourdon Treble ⎱ Bourdon Bass ⎰	16'	61
Open Diapason	8'	61
Flûte Harmonique	8'	61
Salicional	8'	61
Dolcissimo	8'	61
Stopped Diapason	8'	61
Octave	4'	61
Hohl Flöte	4'	61
Gambette	4'	61
Flautino	2'	61
Mixture	IV	244
Trumpet	16'	61
Cornopean	8'	61
Oboe and Bassoon	8'	61
Vox Humana	8'	61
Clarion	4'	61

Choir

Lieblich Gedeckt	16'	61
Open Diapason	8'	61
Viola Dolce	8'	61
Dulciana	8'	61
Melodia	8'	61
Quintadena	8'	61

Choir (continued)

Violin	4'	61
Flûte d'Amour	4'	61
Piccolo Harmonique	2'	61
Contra Fagotto	16'	61
Clarionet	8'	61

Pedal

Grand Bourdon	32'	30
Double Open Diapason	16'	30
Double Gamba	16'	30
Double Dulciana	16'	30
Bourdon	16'	30
Flute	8'	30
Violoncello	8'	30
Trombone	16'	30

Couplers

Great to Pneumatic
Swell to Great
Choir to Great
Swell to Choir
Great to Pedal
Swell to Pedal
Choir to Pedal

Accessories

14 Combination Pistons
10 Combination Pedals
7 Mechanical Movements
   Great to Pedal Reversible
   All Couplers
   Swell Tremolo Reversible
   Balanced Swell Pedal
   Crescendo and Diminuendo
   Crescendo Indicator
   Wind Indicator
Swell Tremolo
Choir Tremolo
Blowers' Signal

The organ was inaugurated on June 22 and 23, 1894; the performers were Henry H. Bosworth, organist of Grace Church, and Everett E. Truette of Boston.

The organ was placed in a richly detailed Gothic case designed by Henry Vaughan of Boston. The three-manual instrument had no adjustable combinations, but there were twenty-four pre-set combinations, including ten double-acting pedals that did not affect the draw-stops and fourteen pistons that did. The organ was destroyed in the 1906 earthquake and fire.

> The Key Desk is of improved construction. A system is introduced by which the registers most used are placed nearest the performer. The Pneumatic Motor is applied to the Great and its couplers, and to the lower octave of the Swell, Choir, and Pedal organs. The Register action is Tubular Pneumatic. There are three wind reservoirs, aggregate capacity 135 square ft. All the manual chests are on a level, insuring equal temperature. The Swell Box is 12 × 12 ft. 6 in., and 10 ft. high, with double louvers. A separate box with adjustable front is located in the rear, within, for the Vox Humana. The Organ is blown by a powerful hydraulic engine, operating duplex feeders underneath, throwing 50 cubic feet of compressed air drawn from the interior of the organ exclusively at each movement of its piston. There are two distinct systems of combination movement,—by pistons under their manual, affecting the drawstops, throwing on the combination and taking off all others; and by the usual double acting pedals not affecting them, making in all 24 fixed combinations, each different from the other. These systems can be used jointly or severally, the changes made with the greatest speed and ease.
>
> All the Stops are full compass of the keyboard. The Reed 16 ft. octaves are full length. The pitch is 435 A. . . .
>
> It has been the fixed intention of the builders, by the elimination of sensational features and a careful attention to details, to construct an instrument eminently fitted for use in divine service; to make it a memorial in fact as well as name, and they submit it as an absolute art production. [*The Organ,* March 1894, pp. 251–52.]

Some English Immigrants

The Woodberrys and Their Associates

Jesse Woodberry (1841–1922) and James Woodberry learned organ building in England, and came to America with Carlton Michell. For a time they worked for Hook and Hastings. Then in 1886 they formed a partnership with James Cole. Two years later, Jesse left the firm and became a partner of Charles T. Harris. From 1888 to 1893 both Cole & Woodberry and Woodberry & Harris were active. In 1893 the Woodberry-Harris partnership split, and Jesse Woodberry continued building organs independently until his retirement in 1910. Meanwhile, Harris went to work for E. W. Lane as a voicer. The Woodberry-Cole partnership remained in business until 1899, and after that Cole continued to build organs until about the time of World War I (see p.234). He died in 1934.

The three-manual Woodberry & Harris organ built in 1892 for St. Mary's Church (R.C.), Charlestown, Massachusetts, shows a conserva-

St. Luke's Church, Germantown, Pennsylvania
COLE & WOODBERRY AND MICHELL, 1894

Great

First Division	
Bourdon	16'
Principal Diapason	8'
Small Diapason	8'
Flûte Harmonique	4'
Octave	4'
Octave Quinte	2⅔'
Super Octave	2'

Second Division, Trumpet Organ	
Trombone	16'
Tromba (Harmonic)	8'
Clarion	4'
Mixture (15, 19, 22, 26, 29)	V

Third Division, Echo Organ	
Echo Salicional	8'
Quintadena	8'
Flute Octaviente	4'
Clarinet	8'
Tremulant	

Swell

Geigen Diapason	8'
Viole d'Orchestre	8'
Viole Céleste	8'
Rohr-flöte	8'
Octave	4'
Mixture (15, 19, 22)	III
Contra Posaune	16'
Cornopean	8'
Oboe	8'
Voix Humaine	8'
Unison	
Octave (on itself)	
Tremulant (light wind)	
Tremulant (heavy wind)	

Choir

Viola	8'
Echo Viole	8'
Flûte Traversière	8'
Salicet	4'
Flûte d'Orchestre	4'
Piccolo Harmonique	2'
Orchestral Oboe	8'
Sw. to Choir	
Sub. Octave (in itself)	
Tremulant	

Pedal

North Side	
Great Bass	32'
Open Bass	16'
Great Flute	8'
Bombard	16'

South Side	
Sub. Bass	16'
Flûte d'Amour	8'

Mechanical

Ch. to Gt. Sub. Octave
Sw. to Gt. Unison
Sw. to Gt. Octave
7 Combination Pistons
7 Special Pedals

The organ is divided into two-parts (fifty feet apart).

A Ross water motor operates the four square feeders in the basement.

The action is Tubular pneumatic.

[*The Organ*, March 1894, p.267.]

tive specification; indeed, in many respects it resembles Johnson's Opus 410, built almost twenty years earlier (see p.231). In contrast, one may find a Cole & Woodberry organ with radical departures from traditional organ design. Such an instrument was the one built in 1894 "in conjunction with Mr. Carlton C. Michell" for St. Luke's Church, Germantown, Pennsylvania. The organ was tubular pneumatic and was divided into two parts, fifty feet apart. Michell was probably responsible for the design of this organ, and he has sometimes been credited with building it. It "introduced many features which have been copied by leading American organ builders" [61, p.317], including heavy pressure reeds, harmonic reeds, new string timbres, and heavy swell shutters.

John and Basil Austin

John Turnell Austin (1869–1948) was born near Bedfordshire, England. His father is credited with building six organs for neighboring churches, and John Turnell had his early experience in organ building assisting his father.

At the age of twenty he came to America and went to work for Farrand & Votey in Detroit. Three years later he was joined by his brother Basil G. Austin (1874–1958). Dissatisfied with the unsteady wind in Farrand & Votey organs and the concomitant difficulties of keeping the organs tuned and regulated, young John Austin set about designing a new type of chest. The Universal Air Chest, completed and patented in 1893, not only provided an unshakable quantity of wind but also had the advantage of a completely accessible bottom surface.

Farrand & Votey, having recently purchased the Roosevelt Organ Co. of New York, was much more interested in using the Roosevelt patents and characteristics than in the Austin invention. However, the Clough & Warren Co. (also in Detroit) agreed to manufacture organs under Austin's patent, and both John and Basil joined this firm. The first organ using the Austin chest was installed in the Central Christian Church, Detroit, in 1893. This 2–16 organ had a movable console and an electropneumatic action that used batteries for current. It was later destroyed in a fire.

While they were installing Opus 22 in Hartford, Connecticut, the Austins learned that fire had destroyed the Clough & Warren Co., with all its equipment and records. This misfortune was ultimately good fortune for the Austins, for it resulted in the establishment of their own factory in Hartford. By late 1899 the new shop was ready for business.

Expansions of the original facilities were soon necessary, and by 1914 the factory had its own power plant, central heating, two organ studios, and seven voicing rooms.[8]

Heaton has described the heavy construction of the early Austin organs:

> Originally the plan was for the manual chests to contain rows of pipes extending from the back to the front of the chest, with the largest pipes in the back. Consequently many of these old chests were constructed with a standard depth of twelve feet; this being the depth necessary for planting a rank of sixty-one pipes of sizeable scale in a single row. Very large scale ranks were planted in two rows with alternate notes "staggered." The finished lumber used in these massive chests was from two and one quarter to two and one half inches thick. This heavy type of construction was continued for many years, even though they later changed the plantation of pipes to the crosswise method used almost universally today. In later days higher shipping costs and the much higher cost of lumber necessitated a careful conservation of wood, so the company gradually devised satisfactory means of bracing its chests so that thinner lumber could be used.
>
> [73, pp.6–7]

Other Builders in New England

Thomas Appleton, whose career as an organ builder began in 1807, was now the elder statesman of New England organ builders. Although his major contribution was made in the first half of the nineteenth century, he continued to build organs until the late 1860s.

Among his younger contemporaries whose work also bridged the Civil War period were W. B. D. Simmons and the Stevens brothers. In 1860 the partnership of William B. D. Simmons and John H. Willcox was drawing to a close—a partnership that had resulted in some notable instruments (see pp.135–36). Simmons continued building organs until his death in 1876 at the age of fifty-three. The stop lists of Simmons's later organs do not exhibit the daring and experimentation of some of his earlier work, but they show the concern for the ensemble that still characterized New England organs in the 1870s.

George and William Stevens were both building organs in the 1860s. William dropped out of organ building about 1872, but George continued in business until 1892. The June 1892 issue of *The Organ* reported that: "Mr. George Stevens, who for over fifty years manufactured organs in East Cambridge, Mass., has retired from business, being over ninety years old. Messrs. Gilbert and Butler will continue the business." Butler and Gilbert, former Stevens employees, remained in business for ten years.

Both Stevens brothers remained essentially builders of small organs, with George's output including a few three-manual instruments. Their specifications tended to be conservative, including more divided and short-compass stops than might be considered normal for the period. Although George Stevens was still building organs at a time when many builders were experimenting with other forms of action, he remained a builder of tracker organs.[9]

Meanwhile, several builders whose works deserve more than a casual mention had established shops in New England. Samuel S. Hamill (1830–1904) had worked for Erben in New York City before establishing a shop in East Cambridge, Massachusetts, in the early 1860s. His organs date from about 1863 to the 1900s. In the 1870s and '80s he was building about fourteen or fifteen organs a year. They were small instruments, and he is not known to have built any three-manual organs. A fine example of Hamill's work is the twenty-one-rank organ in Notre Dame Church, Ogdensburg, New York. It has exceptional clarity for an instrument of its vintage (1891), and a very favorable acoustical environment further enhances the effect of this modest-sized instrument.[10]

George H. Ryder (1838–1922), a performer as well as builder, held several organ positions in Boston churches. He learned organ building in the Hook factory, and for about a year (1871–72) he was in partnership with Joel Butler, but after that he continued building independently. A printed catalogue lists 185 organs built by the Ryder firm from 1871 to 1896. Most of them were two-manual instruments, but there are some one-manual and a few three-manual organs.

A former Johnson employee, Emmons Howard (1845–1931), opened his own shop in Westfield, Massachusetts, in 1883, and built organs from then until the 1920s. His factory was small, employing about a dozen workers in the late 1890s.

Howard's most famous organ was built for the 1901 Pan-American Exposition in Buffalo. It was installed in the Temple of Music and was given the fair's highest award, a gold medal. It was in this same Temple of Music that Leon Czolgosz assassinated President McKinley on September 6, 1901. Simmons asserts that there is no indication that the organ was used on that fateful day [467, p.8]. However, an article from *Music Trades,* dated Buffalo, Nov. 11, 1901, relates:

> Aside from the value of the organ from a musical standpoint, it will always have a historical interest, because of the fact that it was this instrument upon which Organist William J. Gomph was playing when Czolgosz fired the shot that killed President McKinley. A Bach sonata was the selection, and probably never was a recital so tragically interrupted. [157]

The four-manual organ had many "modern" features, including

tubular pneumatic action, an enclosed Choir division, adjustable combination action, crescendo pedal, and sforzando pedal [467, p.8]. After the exposition, the organ was purchased from the builder by a local businessman, J. N. Adams, who gave it to the city of Buffalo. He reportedly paid $10,000 for the organ, although its stated price was $18,000. This reduction was made because Howard wanted to move his factory to Buffalo, and thus was interested in having the organ remain in that city.[11]

Branch Street Tabernacle, Lowell, Massachusetts
EMORY LANE, 1906

Great: 61 notes

Untersatz	32'
Sub Gedeckt	16'
Principal Diapason	8'
Viola Dolce	8'
Flauto Dolce	8'
Claribel-Flöte	8'
Octav Principal	4'
Lieblich-Flöte	4'
Quinta Octava	2⅔'
Octavin Acuta	2'
Tromba	8'

Swell: 61 notes

Sub Gedeckt	16'
Principal	8'
Æola	8'
Viola di Concerto	8'
Viola Celesta	8'
Viola Angelica	8'
Still Gedeckt	8'
Flauto Pleno	8'
Violina Dolce	4'
Flauto Harmonico	4'
Quint-Flöte	2⅔'
Flageolet	2'

Swell (continued)

Terzetto	1⅗'
Vox Humana	8'
Wald Horn	8'
(Derived solo-compounds, first use.)	
Violi Tutti	8'
Glocken-Pfeife	8'
Quintadena	8'
Sarussophone	8'
Corno Francese	8'
Euphonium	8'

Pedal: 30 notes

Principal Untersatz	32'
Lieblich Untersatz	32'
Sub Quint	21⅗'
Principal	16'
Quintatön (II R.)	16'
Bordone	16'
Lieblich Gedeckt	16'
Terz	12⅘'
Octav Principal	8'
Flauto Bass	8'
Lieblich-Flöte	8'
Quint	5⅓'
Octavino	4'

[Couplers included a selection of sub- and super-couplers as well as the usual 8' couplers. There were 15 pedal movements and two swell tremulants. The organ used electric key action, and tubular-pneumatic stop action.][12]

Emory W. Lane (1862–1935) worked for a time in the Hook and Hastings office, but went into business for himself about 1890, using the firm name Waltham Church Organ Factory. In 1908 this concern was taken over by the Hutchings company, and Lane was made business manager. In 1911 Hutchings moved to other quarters, while Lane remained where he was, resuming the original name of his firm. In

1920 or 1921 he went out of business and became the eastern agent for W. W. Kimball Organ Co., Chicago. He retired about 1930.

Lane built mostly small organs, including several practice organs for the New England Conservatory of Music. An organ he built in 1906 for the Branch Street Tabernacle, Lowell, Massachusetts, was probably his most unusual instrument, and its interesting specification deserves inclusion. However, it should not be considered characteristic of Lane's work: it was designed by W. G. Goodwin of Lowell, an organ consultant with very original ideas about organ style.

Some of the other New England organ builders of this period were Welcome K. Adams and his son C. W. Adams in Providence, Moritz Baumgarten and Harry Hall in New Haven, Joel Butler in Boston, Harry L. Hall in Portland, and Reuben Reed and his son George Warren Reed in West Boylston, Massachusetts.

XIII

NEW YORK

Introduction

Music in New York City

NEW YORK CITY, with its million inhabitants, was struggling to reach a position of artistic development worthy of the nation's largest city. The only more or less permanent orchestra in the city had been the New York Philharmonic (established in 1842), but the scope of New York's orchestral offerings was considerably enlarged by an orchestra organized and conducted by Theodore Thomas, which gave its first concert in 1862. Four years later Thomas initiated a series of summer-night concerts at Terrace Gardens, at which he tried to increase gradually the substance of his programs and the appreciation of serious music, without forfeiting popular appeal.

In 1878 the Symphony Society of New York was organized in competition with both the Philharmonic Society and Thomas's orchestra. Leopold Damrosch was the first conductor, and when he died in 1885, he was succeeded by his son Walter. By that time momentum of New York's musical development was increasing. The Metropolitan Opera House had opened in 1883, and when it was destroyed by fire nine years later, no time was lost in drawing up plans for a new building, which opened the next year. A professorship of music was finally created at Columbia University in 1896, and Edward MacDowell (1861–1908) was appointed to the position. He filled it with distinction until 1904, when he resigned in a much-publicized dispute over policy [34, pp.352–53].

In the last year of the century, America's oldest school devoted exclusively to the training of organist-directors for Protestant churches was founded. Under the directorship of William C. Carl, the Guilmant

Organ School "was in a large measure the result of a renewed interest in organ and church music, caused by a visit, in 1898, to this country by the great French organist of that day—Alexandre Guilmant" [135, p.1]. A two-year diploma course was offered, and about forty students were enrolled for the initial session.

New York, no less than Boston, looked across the Atlantic for its musical leadership. Theodore Thomas and the Damrosches were all natives of Germany. MacDowell went abroad when he was fifteen, and his two years of study in Paris were followed by a ten-year residence in Germany. Nor was foreign influence lacking among organists. In addition to Guilmant's French ideas, one could find imported models from both England and Germany. The English George Washbourne Morgan was organist at Grace Church in 1860. One of America's most famous church musicians, Dudley Buck, arrived in New York in 1875. He was organist at St. Ann's Church for a short time, and then assumed a similar post at Holy Trinity Church, Brooklyn. Buck had a well-established reputation by that time, and had held positions in Hartford, Chicago, and Boston. A native American, Buck qualified for success by studying for three years in Germany, followed by a year in Paris.

The awakening to professional standards in performance had its effect on church music and on church budgets. An 1876 periodical revealed that the total amount paid by 350 New York City churches for their choirs was "not less than half a million dollars a year" and reported the salaries in some of the larger churches:

The organist of Trinity Church receives a salary of $3,500; the choir boys' salaries range from $50 upward, and the total appropriation for music, including $2,000 paid to an associate organist, is not far from $15,000. The choir consists of 13 treble, 4 alto, 5 tenor, and 6 bass singers. There are five singers in the Church of St. Bartholomew who receive salaries ranging from $1,000 to $1,500 apiece, and the same may be said of at least half the other churches in the city. The highest paid singer is Miss Thursby, of Dr. Chapin's church, who receives $1,500 for singing three hymns, an opening anthem, and a voluntary during a service. Contrary to the general belief, the music in Roman Catholic churches costs less than that furnished by the Protestant choirs, notwithstanding the fact that in the former a higher degree of artistic excellence generally is required and obtained. The average cost of their music is about $3,000, and none of them pay over $4,000. Going over to Brooklyn, Plymouth Church is at the head of the list, having the largest volunteer chorus ever assembled for regular service in this country. The entire charge of the organization is in the hands of Mr. Henry Camp, who receives $2,500 for his services; the organist gets $1,500, the soprano $1,300, and the tenor $1,250. [264]

Organs and Organ Builders

The American Music Directory, published in 1861 by Thomas Hutchinson, listed more than a hundred churches in New York City that had organs. The oldest instrument was the 1807 England organ in St. Paul's Episcopal Church. Except for this old imported organ and three E. & G. G. Hook organs, all the instruments were products of New York builders. They ranged in size from one manual, ten stops to the three-manual, forty-eight-stop T. Robjohn organ in the South Dutch Reformed Church. In addition, forty-eight organs were located in Brooklyn and fourteen in Albany. Congregationalists in Brooklyn showed a marked preference for New England organs, but organs by New York builders were in a large majority of the other churches. West of New York City, one could find a variety of both New York and New England builders represented [2].

The leading names among New York City organ builders during this period were Erben, Jardine, Roosevelt, and Odell. Builders in other parts of New York could not compete with these firms in quantity, but their work was nonetheless important in proportion to its quality. No doubt many a local congregation felt that Garret House in Buffalo, William King in Elmira, or Andrews or Marklove in Utica would give more personal attention and tender loving care to an organ for a nearby church than could be expected from a famous builder in the big city.

Henry Erben

Erben's Career from 1860 to 1884

In the last quarter-century of his life, Henry Erben continued to hold a position of influence among organ builders in New York, although other names were now beginning to supersede that of the old builder. He had reached a peak of productivity in the decade preceding the Civil War, but the Baltimore branch he had opened in 1847 closed in 1863. Erben had been very popular in the South, and no doubt the Civil War had more effect on his business than on some of the New England builders. Nevertheless, Erben was still a monumental figure in the organ world, and one of his most important organs was built when he was sixty-eight years old. Completed in 1868 for Old St. Patrick's Cathedral, New York, it has been in service for over a century, and is the only extant three-manual Erben organ.

A year later, another three-manual organ, virtually a twin to the St. Patrick's organ, was installed in the Cathedral of the Immaculate Conception, Portland, Maine, at a cost of $15,000. This organ was "very likely the largest Erben in northern New England" [*BOC* 25, p.6]. When he was seventy-four, Erben was still installing important organs, and in that year, one went to St. John's Chapel, Varick Street, New York. In all, Erben has been credited with building 1,734 organs[1] [86, p.10].

Late in life Erben took William M. Wilson into partnership, but at Erben's death in 1884, the business was taken over by Lewis C. Harrison, who had been superintendent of the factory [433, p.166]. Of the workmen in Erben's factory who later built organs independently, the one who became best known was Henry Pilcher.

Characteristics of the Organs

Erben turned to the C compass in his later organs, using a range of fifty-six or fifty-eight notes, which gave an upward extension to g^3 or a^3. Pedal ranges varied from twenty to thirty notes. The 1868 St. Patrick's organ and the 1869 Immaculate Conception, Portland, organ both had thirty-note pedal boards. The lack of standardization is reflected in the fact that a twenty-five-note pedal was assigned to the two-manual organ in St. John's Church, Baltimore, while a later, one-manual organ of 1872 had only twenty pedal keys.

In the specification of the St. Patrick's organ, some of the changes that took place in Erben's style are evident. Compared with the 1837 organ for Christ Church, Philadelphia (an organ of thirty-two speaking stops; see pp.158–59), one notices first the enlarged Pedal division, which is much more complete than the Pedal of many larger organs. The inclusion of the 4' stop is particularly interesting. The independent Seventeenth and the treble Mounted Cornet are no longer found on the Great, but the Tierce is still included in the Sesquialtera. The old short-length Swell of the Christ Church organ had largely given way to full-compass stops. There is a reflection of the old style in the derivation of the bass octave for the Swell Viol d'Amour and two of the Choir stops. However, in the organ for the Cathedral of the Immaculate Conception these registers had fifty-eight pipes.

The specification for St. Patrick's was conservative for its time: conservative in choice of stops and conservative in size. One can compare it, for example, with the 1864 Hook & Hastings organ in Mechanics' Hall, Worchester, Massachusetts, or the Johnson organ for Second Presbyterian Church, Chicago (see pp.226, 231). The conservative aspects of Erben's style are even more distinct when compared with the experiments and innovations of his New York contemporaries in the Jardine shop, and one can only imagine what the crusty old builder had to say about the radical ideas young Hilborne Roosevelt demonstrated in the late 1870s.

Old St. Patrick's Cathedral, New York
HENRY ERBEN, 1868

Great

Grand Open Diapason	16'	58
Open Diapason	8'	58
Gamba	8'	58*
Melodia	8'	58
Stop^d. Diapason	8'	58
Principal	4'	58
Wald Flute	4'	58
Twelfth	2⅔'	58
Fifteenth	2'	58
Mixture	III	174**
Sesquialtera	III	174
Trumpet	8'	58
Clarion	4'	58

Swell

Bourdon	16'	58
Open Diapason	8'	58
Stop. Diapason	8'	58
Dulciana	8'	58
Viol d'Amour (bass from Dulciana)	8'	46
Principal	4'	58
Flute Harmonique	4'	58
Piccolo	2'	58
Cornet	III	174
Cornopean	8'	58
Oboe	8'	58

Choir

Pyramid Diapason (bass from Melodia)	8'	46
Dolce	8'	58
Keraulophon (bass from Dolce)	8'	46

Choir (continued)

Stop. Diapason	8'	58
Melodia	8'	58
Principal	4'	58†
Flauto Traverso	4'	58
Flageolet	2'	58
Cremona (t.c.)	8'	46‡
Bassoon (bass)	8'	12
Tremulant††		

Pedal

Double Open Diapason	16'	30
Bourdon	16'	30
Contra Gamba	16'	30
Violon Cello	8'	30
Claribel Flute	4'	30
Trombone	16'	30

Pedal Accessories

Swell Piano
Swell Forte
Great Piano
Grear Mezzo
Great Forte
Great to Pedal Reversible
Swell Crescendo Lever

Couplers

Grcat to Pedal
Swell to Pedal
Choir to Pedal
Pedal to Pedal 8^ves
Swell to Great
Choir to Great
Swell to Choir

* Modern replacement
** Replaced 1878 by 4' Flute
† Knob marked "Flautina"
‡ Knob marked "Clarinet"
†† Not original

[*OHS 1969 Convention Program*, p.17.]

In the smaller schemes of Erben's later organs one sees increasingly the inclusion of a rank or two of Pedal pipes instead of the earlier reliance on a pull-down pedal. A specification of 1880 shows a Pedal of 16' Double Open Diapason and 16' Bourdon in a two-manual organ [86, p.89], while one of 1863 included an 8' Violoncello instead of the

16' Bourdon. Divided stops continued to play an important part, and frequently a twelve-note Stopped Diapason Bass served as the bottom octave for two or more stops.

The 1863 Erben organ in the Church of St. John the Evangelist, Baltimore, a two-manual organ of twenty-one registers, shows a manual diapason chorus similar to Erben's earlier organs. The tone of this organ has been described as "quite rich, not too bright, but very pleasing" [230]. By contrast, a two-manual, seventeen-register scheme in an Erben catalogue of 1880, offered the buyer the alternative of a diluted chorus. One could substitute a Violana 4' for the Principal, a Flageolet for the Fifteenth, and a Gamba for the Trumpet in the Great division. A Swell Violana 4' took the place formerly assigned to a Principal [86, p.89].

Throughout his life Erben continued to rely on the fine materials and expert craftsmanship that had established his reputation. In 1920 Gustav Dohring evaluated the construction of an 1867 Erben organ: "As to the fundamental structural qualities and materials used therein, none better were ever employed in the building of an organ" [275, p.65].

George Jardine, George Jardine & Son
The Jardine Firm, 1860–1899

During the last four decades of the century, most of the leadership of the Jardine company fell to George's son Edward, and in 1871 the name of the firm was changed to George Jardine & Son. Edward G. Jardine was a competent performer and held the post of organist at St. James' Episcopal Church, New York. He was also a frequent recitalist for the inaugural programs of new Jardine organs. His "Representation of a Thunder Storm" was evidently an effective piece for that sort of occasion. It so impressed the audience of the Church of St. Mary the Virgin in 1886 that he was asked to repeat it when the church dedicated its second Jardine installation in 1896. Jardine's "Storm" was a piece in three movements, bearing a program remarkably similar to that of Beethoven's Sixth Symphony.

After the death of Edward Jardine, the business was carried on by his nephews Edward D. and Charles Jardine. Further changes were indicated by the announcement in the September 1897 issue of *The Pianist and Organist* that the firm had "concluded arrangements whereby the interests of Mr. Carlton Michell, the noted English organ builder, will become amalgamated with their own. . . ." Michell had by this time amalgamated his interests with several builders, including Hutchings in 1890 and Cole & Woodberry in 1894. The Jardine firm was dissolved in 1899[2] [433, p.166].

Jardine organs followed the expanding market, and by 1869 the company catalogue could list thirty states in which installations had been made. In contrast to Erben, the Jardines built a number of four-manual organs, and although that may be explained in part by the fact that the Jardine firm continued in business fifteen years after Erben's death (a period that showed a growing delight in large instruments), a number of the large Jardine organs were built in the 1860s and '70s, e.g., the organs for St. George's, New York (1867–69) and the Pittsburgh Cathedral (1870). The St. George's organ included:

Great	13 stops	1,037 pipes
Swell	14	947
Choir	9	549
Clavier de Bombardes	7	336
Pedal	7	210
	50	3,079

[22, p.349]

Characteristics of the Organs

The Jardines were innovators, and as early as 1868 *Watson's Art Journal* (September 5) could describe a combination action and a crescendo pedal in the new organ for the Catholic Church of the Redeemer, Augusta, Georgia:

> The organ under notice contains many new effects and ingenious mechanical arrangements, facilitating the labor of the organist,— among which are knobs within reach of the fingers while playing, by which instant change can be made. Also, a crescendo pedal, by which a gradual transition from the softest stop to the full power, and *vice versa,* can be effected. [Cited in 43, p.17.]

After describing the action of the Barker pneumatic lever used by Jardine, the *Descriptive Circular* of 1869 listed some of the "firsts" this builder claimed:

> Mr. Jardine was the first to bring out in America the combination movements, reversible pedals and couplers, his own invented pneumatic and vacuum pallets—now generally used by the London organ builders, and accredited to him as one of the best improvements, (see "Hopkins & Rimbault's work on the organ") published in London— also vertical swell blinds, rendering a single set more effective than the double blinds as usually made. He was the first to make, several years ago, projecting or over-hanging keys, now universally adopted, with diagonal draw-stops, and also arranged in steps; radiating and

curved pedals, also the grand improvement of reversed bellows ribs, which entirely remedies the variableness of the wind caused by unsteady blowing. [43, pp.4–5]

The *Circular* then credits Jardine with the introduction in America of the Vox Celeste, Clariana, Flute harmonique, Viol de Gamba, and several other stops, as well as equal temperament tuning.

Even if these claims were overstatements, it is clear that Jardine was no traditionalist. Both George Jardine and his son Edward traveled frequently to Europe to keep informed on the latest "improvements" being made in organ building there [88, p.80], and although quick to accept new ideas, in 1896 Edward D. Jardine could still state: "The old tracker action continues to be the cheapest and most simple for an organ of ordinary size and straight-forward construction" [337].

The Jardines were noted for the appearances of their organs, and Radzinsky called their case designs "probably the best and most elaborate in America" [433, p.166]. The famous organ for St. George's Church was a veritable encyclopedia of pipe decoration, climaxed by a centerpiece of radiating Tubas. A more fabulous and daring display never entered American organ history [see 22, Fig. 400].

Jardine was one of the builders to exploit some of the placement innovations made possible by electric action. The Church of St. Mary the Virgin moved into a new building in 1895, and the next year the new organ was ready (replacing an 1886 Jardine). The description that appeared in the inaugural program noted:

It is equipped with two consoles or key boards, both being movable, and enabling the Organist to play from either end of the church. Each console is provided with three manuals and pedals, with over fifty speaking stops, and accessories. The main part of the instrument, consisting of the Great, Swell and part of the Pedal Organ, is located in the Gallery, over the entrance. The other division, consisting of the Choir Organ, is located at the Chancel end of the Church, a distance of 150 ft. from the main instrument, as is also the 16 ft. Bourdon of the Pedal Organ, all enclosed in an effective Swell Box, operated by electric action. The console in the Chancel is on the ground floor, and connected with the organs by a cable, capable of moving 50 ft., in any direction. The other console is located in the Gallery, and likewise connected with a cable to the organ, and can be moved to any position. The entire instrument can be played from either point, and every part is available through the medium of the accessories, unison, octave and sub-octave, couplers and combination pedals, all actuated by electro-pneumatic action, so easy of operation, that the performer can make all the various changes of tonal effect, while playing, with the greatest facility. The whole action is constructed on the most improved electro-pneumatic system, which has been introduced by Mr. Jardine for several years in some of his finest instruments, that have stood the test of several years' use, with the greatest success, showing that this system is so far perfected as to be past the experimental stage. [Cited in 154, pp.25–26.]

As one might expect, Jardine organs often deviated from the usual specification patterns. For example, a small organ with only one reed might have the Trumpet located on the Swell, and its bass octave might be called Bassoon, thus giving the Trumpet the Oboe's traditional home. Fanciful names, such as Boehm Flute, appeared along with the Jardine-originated Clariana. But one might also find occasional old-fashioned characteristics, e.g., the fifty-six-note manual compass in the three-manual 1890 organ at St. Patrick's Church, R.C., Watervliet, New York. This organ contains a Sesquialtra as the Great compound stop—a stop that had long been gone from the menu of many builders.[3] However, when mixtures began to lose favor as an essential part of the ensemble, they disappeared from Jardine's small- and medium-sized two-manual organs more rapidly than from most contemporary organs. Thus one finds in Jardine specifications a degree of inconsistency, showing now an innovative and now a conservative trait.

A very interesting specification is that of the 1893 organ built for St. Michael's Church, P.E., New York. Here one sees as the organ's unusual feature a Pedal disposition consisting of Contra Diapason 32', Double Open Diapason 16', Violon 16', Bourdon 16', Violoncello 8', Principal 4', Octave 2', Cimbale III, and Euphone 16' [390].

One of the last Jardine organs was Opus 1257, built in 1899 for Saint Thomas' Episcopal Church, Taunton, Massachusetts. The three-manual organ, thirty-five ranks, extended the Great chorus from 16' to 2', with no mixture. The Swell contains a Viole Celeste and the Choir an Unda Maris, in addition to their chorus stops. The Pedal has three 16' stops that are extended to produce a 10⅔' and three 8' stops.[4]

Jardine built a four-manual organ for the Brooklyn Tabernacle Presbyterian Church in 1873. It was destroyed by fire in 1889, and the next year the specification for a new four-manual organ for this church appeared in *The Organist's Journal* (September 1890, p. 7). It illustrates well Jardine's approach to a large scheme:

Brooklyn Tabernacle Presbyterian Church, Brooklyn, New York
GEORGE JARDINE & SON, 1890

Great		Great (continued)	
Double Open Diapason	16'	German Gamba	8'
Open Diapason	8'	Gemshorn	8'
Second Open Diap.	8'	Open Flute	8'

Brooklyn Tabernacle Presbyterian Church, Brooklyn, New York
GEORGE JARDINE & SON, 1890

Great (continued)		Choir (continued)	
Dopple Flute	8′	Gedacht	8′
Quint	6′	Melodia	8′
Principal	4′	Wald Flute	4′
Gambetta	4′	Salicet	4′
Flute Harmonic	4′	Flageolet	2′
Nasard	3′	Dolce Cornet . . .	
Acuta	2′	Clarionet	8′
1st Sexquialtra [sic]	III	Vox Angelica	8′
2nd Mixture	V		
Double Trumpet	16′	Solo	
Trumpet	8′	Double Melodia	16′
Octave Trumpet	4′	Cathedral Diapason	8′
		Bell Gamba	8′
Swell		Flute à Pavillion	8′
Bourdon	16′	Concert Flute	4′
Open Diapason	8′	Fife Harmonic	2′
Second Open Diap.	8′	Bombard	16′
Stopped Diapason	8′	Song Trumpet	8′
Viol d'Amour	8′		
Aeolina	8′	Pedal	
Quintadena	8′	Double Open Diap.	32′
Vox Celestes	8′	Open Diapason	16′
Principal	4′	Contra Gamba	16′
Violin	4′	Bourdon	16′
Flauto Traverso	4′	Violoncello	8′
Piccolo	2′	Bass Flute	8′
Cornet . . .		Night Horn	4′
Contra Fagotto	16′	Trombone	16′
Cornopean	8′	Tromba	8′
Oboe and Bassoon	8′	Bassoon	8′
Vox Humana	8′		
Clarion	4′	Accessories	
		10 Couplers	
Choir (enclosed in a separate Swell Box)		11 Mechanical movements	
		6 "Pneumatic Great Organ,	
Lieblich Gedacht	16′	Piston Knobs"	
Violin Diapason	8′	11 Combination Pedals	
Keraulophon	8′	6 Pedal Movements	
Dulciana	8′		

Manuals: 61 notes; Pedal: 30 notes

Hilborne and Frank Roosevelt
The Roosevelt Firm, 1872–1893

No builder did more than Hilborne Roosevelt (1849–1886) to cata-
pult organ design toward the style we associate with the early twentieth

century, and one may say that the Roosevelt organs actually marked the beginning of a new era in organ history. Hilborne Roosevelt, first cousin of President Theodore Roosevelt, exemplified the person born at the right time and under the right circumstances for success. In addition to intelligence and ambition, he had other advantages, not the least of which was money.

As a young boy, Hilborne showed interest in science, invention, and particularly in electricity. One of his early encounters with the organ took place at the Church of the Holy Communion in New York. Hilborne and a young friend stepped into the church while the tuners were at work on the 1846 Hall & Labagh organ, and they had an opportunity to explore its interior [504, I, p.9]. Roosevelt later became an apprentice in the Hall & Labagh factory. Webber relates that setting out for the organ factory at daybreak in overalls, lunch pail in hand, was not exactly the image the illustrious Roosevelt family had envisioned for this young man. When he succeeded in constructing an organ that won a gold medal at a New York industrial fair in 1869, however, opposition to nineteen-year-old Hilborne's choice of occupation ceased [504, I, p.9].

In 1872 Roosevelt traveled to England and the Continent, meeting organ builders and studying styles of design and methods of construction. After his return to New York, he employed a staff of experienced organ builders and opened his own organ factory, the Roosevelt Organ Works. In his diary, Hilborne Roosevelt recorded: "My first payday was Dec. 2, 1872. Number of men 8, amount paid $88.78. On Jan. 13, 1873, 19 men, $366.16. March 24, 1873, 24 men, $676.24" [450, V, p.261]. Opus I was a new organ for the Church of the Holy Communion, where Hilborne had had his introduction to organ construction. The organ was completed in September 1873, and the January 1874 *New-York Musical Gazette* observed that Roosevelt

> has recently returned from Europe, where he has spent some time in carefully studying the characteristics and improvements of the best organ builders, and this is the first large organ built by him since his return. It is one of the best and most evenly balanced instruments we ever saw. The foundation stops especially are remarkable for a round, full quality of tone, which is particularly satisfactory in the heavier combinations, and the action is as light and elastic as that of a pianoforte.

Roosevelt's reputation mushroomed with the installation of two important three-manual organs in 1876: Opus 15 for the Centennial Exhibition in Philadelphia and Opus 25 for Chickering Hall, New York. Only ten years later, at the age of thirty-seven, Hilborne Roosevelt died. He was succeeded in business by his brother Frank (1861–1894), who

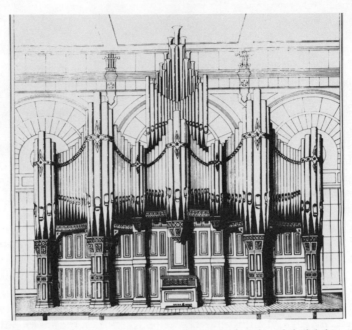

Hilborne Roosevelt, Opus 15, 1876. Built for the Philadelphia Centennial. *Photo courtesy Jim Lewis.*

continued building organs for another six years. In the January 1893 issue of *The Organ,* an open letter from Frank Roosevelt appeared:

> I have the honor to announce my intention to close the Roosevelt Organ Works, and retire from the business of manufacturing organs. The work now on hand will be completed about January 1, 1893, and after that time no organs will be built under the name of Roosevelt.
>
> It is my pleasure to further announce that I have completed negotiations with the Farrand & Votey Organ Company of Detroit, whereby the exclusive right to the use of all the patents and systems controlled by me passes to them. It is their intention to incorporate their various specialties with my own, and as they have also secured the services of a number of my department foremen, and other leading men, they should be now in a position to produce instruments of great perfection.

Within the comparatively short span of two decades the Roosevelt company had reached a position of prestige recognized throughout the organ world. A letter written by James Treat to Edward Searles contained a revealing evaluation of the end of this important company.

> An item of interest and regret is the closing of the Roosevelt Organ Works. Mr. Frank Roosevelt believing that the good name of Roosevelt could not be preserved by any other arrangement, i.e., no one

could build first class organs and at a profit, and he would not prostitute it for that. He is worthy of esteem if this is true. I looked upon the business as practically closed when Hilborn [*sic*] L. died as Frank is a business man. Although the organs were not of our standard, it was high, and as such the closing is a loss to the country. The building of fine organs in America is a charity. I understand that with the finishing of contracts already on hand the business will be closed out. Some of the employees are already gone. There is an extensive plant —to [*sic*] expensive for anyone to handle—which I suppose will be bought up by one or another and scattered. Too bad, but the inevitable. [Cited in *BOC* 28, pp.2–3.]

Hilborne Roosevelt built 358 organs, an average of more than twenty-five a year, including two four-manual organs (one for the Cathedral of the Incarnation, Garden City, New York, and the other an enlargement and rebuilding of the organ in St. Thomas Church, New York),[5] fifty-two three-manual organs, ninety-eight two-manual, and the rest one-manual organs. Many of the one-manual instruments were of a type called the Roosevelt Portable Pipe Organ. They were mass-produced, twenty or twenty-five at a time, and more than 140 of them were built between about 1884 and 1886. Branch factories established in Philadelphia and Baltimore remained in operation until 1891.

Under Frank Roosevelt's leadership, production rose to close to thirty organs a year, with a total of 178 organs from January 1887 to January 1893. The proportion of one-manual organs decreased in favor of more two- and three-manual organs, and the four-manual instruments included organs for Trinity M.E. Church, Denver (Opus 380, 68 stops) and the Chicago Auditorium (Opus 400, 109 stops).

Characteristics of the Organs

From the very beginning of his career, Hilborne Roosevelt was concerned with adapting new methods and materials to organ construction.[6] He also experimented with tonal design, and these experiments were quite often related to innovations in other aspects of organ structure. For example, his use of electric action made possible experiments in the placement of the tonal divisions of the organ.

The organ Roosevelt exhibited in New York in 1869 has often been hailed as the first organ in the United States with electric action. However, in an 1868 enlargement of an H. F. Berger organ, John C. B. Standbridge added a Solo division that used electric action [381, p.8]. It is anybody's guess which action was really completed first. An entry in Hilborne Roosevelt's diary implies that an organ he built before the exhibition organ also used electric action. He noted that Barker (the

Frank Roosevelt, Opus 382, 1888, console. Built for St. Paul's M. E. Church, Denver. Now in First Methodist Church, Boulder, Colorado. *Photo courtesy Thomas Murray.*

inventor of the Barker pneumatic lever) had patented an electric action in January 1868, only a few months before his own patent:

> I filed a caveat in October '68 and obtained my patent in April 1869. The first organ was erected in the factory of Messrs. Hall-Labagh Co., New York. The next was exhibited at the Fair of the American Institute, Sept. '69—and received the First Medal & Diploma. (This was the first Medal given for an electric organ in any country.) [450, II, p.163]

Roosevelt remarked that his experiments with electric action had been made without knowledge that it had been tried in Europe.

When Roosevelt opened his factory, a subdivision in the Great of his first organ (Church of the Holy Communion, 1872) demonstrated his inventiveness. It was an experimental Electro-Melody Organ of five stops, a device "especially useful in leading congregational singing, as the melody of the upper note is heard above the rest of the harmony" [371, p.367].

The Philadelphia Centennial Exposition and the New York Chickering Hall organs (both of 1876) made sensational use of electricity. The Centennial organ had an Electric Suspended Organ and an Electric Echo Organ. The Echo division was situated in a tower, and the suspended organ was hung directly in front of the gallery. The Chickering Hall organ also had an Echo organ located above the ceiling, with the rest of the organ divided on either side of the stage.

Such disbursement of the divisions of the organ had never before been possible. The builder was freed from the limitations mechanical action had imposed on the relative placement of console and chests. Roosevelt exploited this new freedom further in his 1878 three-manual organ for Grace Church, New York. The new organ was placed near the chancel, and the console (placed in the chancel) was connected to both the new organ and an 1830 Erben organ of three manuals, twenty-six stops, which was already in the gallery. Roosevelt promotion material boasted: "We believe that this is the first case on record where two distinct instruments, widely separated from each other, have been placed under the control of one performer by means of but one set of keyboards" [74, p.105].

The flexibility in placement that electricity afforded continued to excite experimentation under Frank Roosevelt's leadership, and even at the end of the factory's history *The Organ* of December 1892 reported:

> The final shots which Roosevelt's factory will fire into the world before bowing their *adieu,* will be models of the perfection of electric action. The organ for the Mendelssohn Glee Club of New York will have electro-pneumatic action throughout. The console will be connected with the organ only by an inch-and-a-half cable, and will be movable. For organ concerts the console can be placed in the centre of the stage, facing the instrument. For concerts when the organ is used with chorus and orchestra, the console can be placed wherever desired, facing the conductor. For miscellaneous concerts the console can be wheeled into the ante-room, and used for a lunch-table if necessary.

Even as early as the Centennial organ (1876) Roosevelt was using an adjustable combination action that allowed the performer to reset combinations at the console. Subjected to later experimentation and improvement, the Roosevelt combination action in its pioneer form relied on setter-knobs, and was operated by combination pedals. The Centennial organ brochure described it:

> Directly over the draw-stops in the key box, are six rows or sets of small knobs, one above the other. Each row or set, representing all

the stops of the organ. The lowest row belongs to pedal no. 1, the next above to pedal no. 2, and so on. To set a combination, say on no. 1, it is only necessary to push in the knobs representing the stops you wish drawn; then when no. 1 pedal is pressed down, it will bring on those stops. The pedals do not throw out the registers, but are hooked down when on, and released when off. Therefore, the registers may be drawn and will not be interfered with by the Combination Pedals or Knobs. The combinations on the knobs are set in the same way. Each pedal has an indicator placed directly above the swell keys, showing when it is on or off. [Cited in 314, p.19.]

The Roosevelts used every available type of action. In the huge 1879–83 Garden City, Long Island, Cathedral organ the Great, Swell, and Choir of the Chancel division used tracker action; Pedal key action and all drawstop action of the Chancel division was tubular pneumatic; and the entire action of the Tower, Chapel, and Echo divisions was electric. The organ in First Congregational Church, Great Barrington, Massachusetts (1883), was one of the first organs to have a completely electric action [102, p.14]. It is also "the only really large Hilborne L. Roosevelt that has survived with relatively little change" [BOC 86, p.3]. In general, the Roosevelts preferred tracker action for small organs and reserved electric action for situations in which the distance involved required its use.

Roosevelt's 1883 promotion brochure advocated the use of water motors to furnish the wind supply. He found them superior in reliability, safety, and ease of control [74]. Here, again, Roosevelt's versatility is apparent. As early as the 1876 organs for Chickering Hall and the Philadelphia Centennial, we find him using electric motors to furnish the wind for divisions in remote locations. In the Centennial organ the wind was furnished for the Electric Suspended Organ and the Electric Echo Organ by electric motors, each operated by a LeClanche battery. Wind for the other divisions was furnished by hydraulic motors. In 1889, when the Chicago Auditorium organ was installed, Frank Roosevelt used electric motors to supply the wind for the entire instrument [345].

Despite all his spectacular innovations, what contributed most to Hilborne Roosevelt's fame was the fact that he built the world's largest organ. It took him from 1879 to 1883 to complete the mammoth instrument for the Cathedral of the Incarnation, Garden City, Long Island. The four-manual instrument contained 115 speaking stops, 18 mechanical stops, 21 pedal movements, and a total of 7,253 pipes. While the giant Walcker & Son organ for the Riga Cathedral in Russia, completed the same year, had 124 speaking stops, it contained only 6,828 pipes. The Garden City organ had divisions placed in various parts of the building. The Chancel division was actually a complete instrument of Great, Swell, Choir, and Pedal. The Tower division was also a complete organ, but of different design, containing Great, Swell, Solo, and Pedal. Another division, called the Chapel division, was located in the chapel beneath the cathedral. It was playable either from the Choir manual of the main console or from a separate console in the chapel, where it was used as an independent instrument for chapel services. Here its thirteen manual stops and two pedal stops were distributed on two manuals. Finally, the Echo Organ located between the ceiling and roof, consisted of seven manual stops and one pedal stop.

In spite of its size, the Garden City organ was not very loud. Senator Emerson Richards recalled:

> Since both the Great and the Swell were obstructed by a great mass of action parts and Pedal pipes, and the Choir restricted to an absurdly small opening, the ensemble was disappointingly soft and retiring. . . . The organ therefore was not big in tone but very polished and refined and, in a large measure, reflected its blue-blood ancestry. [444, p.416]

Richards further commented that an embezzlement of the organ fund by the treasurer prevented the completion of the organ, and the pipes for the Solo were never installed.

Cathedral of the Incarnation, Garden City, Long Island
HILBORNE ROOSEVELT, Opus 66–70, 1879–83

Great

Great (continued)

Chancel Division		Tower Division	
Double Open Diapason	16′	Contra Gamba	16′
Bourdon	16′	Double Melodia	16′
Open Diapason	8′	Open Diapason	8′
Gemshorn	8′	Dolcan	8′
Viola di Gamba	8′	Viol d'Amour	8′
Principal Flöte	8′	Clarabella	8′
Doppel Flöte	8′	Rohr Flöte	8′
Quint	5⅓′	Principal	4′
Octave	4′	Flute Octaviante	4′
Gambette	4′	Twelfth	2⅔′
Wald Flöte	4′	Fifteenth	2′
Octave Quint	2⅔′	Acuta	IV
Super Octave	2′	Horn	8′
Mixture	IV-VI		
Scharff	III-IV		
Ophecleide	16′		
Trumpet	8′		
Clarion	4′		

Cathedral of the Incarnation, Garden City, Long Island
HILBORNE ROOSEVELT, Opus 66–70, 1879–83

Swell

Chancel Division
Bourdon	16'
Open Diapason	8'
Salicional	8'
Dolce	8'
Stopped Diapason	8'
Quintadena	8'
Principal	4'
Flute Harmonique	4'
Flageolet	2'
Cornet	III-V
Contra Fagotto	16'
Cornopean	8'
Oboe	8'
Vox Humana	8'

Tower Division
Quintatön	16'
Open Diapason	8'
Spitz Flöte	8'
Harmonica	8'
Clarinet Flute	8'
Violina	4'
Hohl Flöte	4'
Doublette	2'
Cymbal	III-IV
Contra Bassoon	16'
Trompette Harmonique	8'
Bassoon	8'
Vox Humana	8'

Choir

Chancel Division
Lieblich Gedeckt	16'
Violin Diapason	8'
Dulciana	8'
Flute Harmonique	8'
Principal	4'
Flute à Chiminèe	4'
Nazard	2⅔'
Piccolo Harmonique	2'
Euphone	16'
Clarinet	8'

Choir (continued)

Chapel Division
Bourdon	16'
Open Diapason	8'
Geigen Principal	8'
Salicional	8'
Dolcissimo	8'
Doppel Flöte	8'
Stopped Diapason	8'
Octave	4'
Flauto Traverso	4'
Fifteenth	2'
Cornet	III
Oboe	8'
Vox Humana	8'

Solo (Pipes in tower)
Stentorphone	8'
Horn Diapason	8'
Concert Flute	8'
Prestant	4'
Hohl Pfeife	4'
Tuba Mirabilis	8'
Baritone	8'

Echo (Pipes between ceiling and roof)
Keraulophone	8'
Dolce	8'
Unda Maris	8'
Stopped Diapason	8'
Principal	4'
Flute Harmonique	4'
Vox Humana	8'

Pedal

Chancel Division
Double Open Diapason	32'
Contra Dulciana (Resultant)	32'
Open Diapason	16'
Dulciana	16'
Sub Bass	16'
Octave	8'
Violoncello	8'

Cathedral of the Incarnation, Garden City, Long Island
HILBORNE ROOSEVELT, Opus 66–70, 1879–83

Pedal (continued)		Pedal (continued)	
Chancel (continued)		Chapel Division	
Super Octave	4'	Bourdon	16'
Mixture	III	Principal	8'
Contra Bombard	32'	Bourdon (Pipes above ceiling)	16'
Trombone	16'		
Tromba	8'	*Couplers*	
Tower Division		Swell to Great 8', 4'	
Contra Bass (Resultant)	32'	Choir to Great 8'	
Open Diapason	16'	Solo to Great 8'	
Violone	16'	Swell to Choir 8'	
Flute	8'	Solo to Pedal 8'	
Serpent	16'	Swell to Pedal 8'	
		Great to Pedal 8'	
		Choir to Pedal 8'	

Accessories

Mechanical Accessories:
Tremulants for Chancel Swell, Tower Swell, Choir, Echo. Ventils for Tower Great, Tower Swell, Tower Pedal, and Chapel.
Eclipse Wind Indicators for Chancel and Tower.
Chime Action Switch (connecting Chime Pneumatic Action with Solo Keys)

Adjustable Combination Pedals:
6 for Chancel Division
Chancel Piano Pedal—to release the above
3 for Tower Division
Tower Piano Pedal—to release the above

Ventil Pedals:
Chancel Division, Chancel Great, Chancel Swell, Chancel Choir, Chancel Pedal, Tower Division, Tower Great, Tower Swell, Tower Pedal

Miscellaneous Pedals:
Great to Pedal Reversible Coupler
Balanced Swell controlling Chancel and Chapel Swell-boxes
Balanced Swell controlling Tower and Echo Swell-boxes

Miscellaneous Details of Construction
Great and Pedal reeds and mixtures enclosed in swell box.
Steam power used to furnish wind.
Action: Great, Swell, and Choir of Chancel Division—tracker; Pedal key action and all drawstop action of the Chancel—tubular; entire action of Tower, Chapel, and Echo Divisions—electric.
Solo and Echo play from the same keyboard.

[74, pp.85–87]

Frank Roosevelt, Opus 408, 1890. Schermerhorn Street Evangelical Church, Brooklyn, New York. *Photo courtesy Thomas Murray.*

While the Garden City organ was soon to be outstripped as the world's largest, it did not represent the only Roosevelt adventure with giant schemes. When Opus 400 was installed in the Chicago Auditorium in 1889, it ranked as the fifth largest in the world, but in the United States it was second only to the Garden City organ in size. The Chicago organ was much less complex in its design, consisting of Great, Swell, Choir, Echo, Solo, Stage, and Pedal organs. The Echo and Stage organs were playable from the Solo manual, and the Stage organ had a separate console on the stage.

Standard manual range on Roosevelt organs was fifty-eight notes, C-a^3. On a few large organs it was extended to sixty-one notes. Very small organs were given a one-octave pedal. Pedal ranges of twenty-seven or twenty-nine notes were used in most organs of medium size, but larger organs were given a thirty-note pedal, and some medium-sized organs also had this range.

In matters pertaining directly to the tonal character of organs, the Roosevelts anticipated the style of the twentieth century most effectively through the use of enclosures, voicing techniques, choice of stops, and the overall concept of the function of the divisions. Their ideas and methods resembled closely those of George Ashdown Audsley.

Hilborne Roosevelt's use of enclosures prompted Howe to write in 1889:

> No other builder in the world has gone so far as he has in making the whole organ capable of crescendo and diminuendo of volume of tone. This he accomplishes by means of several swells. Not alone the swell organ proper is inclosed in a box with swell blinds adapted for opening to let out more tone, or shutting to suppress the volume, but the choir and the solo organ, and part of the great organ, are also inclosed in swell boxes. In his ordinary two-manual organ, for church use, he incloses all the pipes of both manuals in a swell box, except the diapasons of the great. This great innovation is bitterly inveighed against by many builders, but the advantages of it are so great upon the side of expression that it is more likely to become general than to be given up. [83, pp.335–36]

In the 1876 Philadelphia Centennial organ, Roosevelt enclosed the Mixture, Fifteenth, and reeds of the Great in the swell box. In Frank Roosevelt's Opus 528 (Temple Kenesth Israel, Philadelphia, 1892), the Great and Choir divisions were placed in one enclosure and the Swell was given another, but the Great 16′ Double Open Diapason and the 8′ First and Second Open Diapasons were left unenclosed. The big Chicago Auditorium organ had three expression pedals: Swell, Great and Choir, and Solo and Echo. Everything was enclosed except the Pedal stops and seven Great stops.

The Roosevelts patterned themselves after European builders in striving for orchestral effects, particularly in the voicing of reeds. One of Hilborne Roosevelt's most publicized stops was the Vox Humana in the 1876 Chickering Hall organ. According to *The Roosevelt Organ Journal* of July 1876, this stop was supposed to be an exact copy of "the celebrated one at Freiberg of which he [Roosevelt] made drawings and measurements." It was placed in the Echo organ in the ceiling, and the *Journal* compared it to "the voices of a male choir chanting in the remote distance." The New York correspondent for *The Musician & Artist* wrote somewhat more prosaically in March 1876:

> The critics and organists here are all crazy over the vox humana in this organ, and I think it is a fine one,—the best, in fact, that I have heard; Roosevelt claims that it is the exact counterpart of that much-famed one in Freiburg Cathedral: but I never could like a vox humana; the only human voice it resembles is that of a ninety-year-old French tenor, with a very bad cold. It is nasal, it is shaky (being always used with tremulant), and the only enjoyment it affords me is the strictly negative one of being glad when it is over.

The same critic, however, was quite favorably impressed with the quality of the organ:

> The instrument is an unusually fine one, and possesses more variety than any organ of its size with which I have met, while the *ensemble* is exceedingly rich and satisfactory.

No one denied the quality of the Roosevelt workmanship, but the tonal style was sometimes questioned. At the time the factory closed, a reviewer for *The Organ* (December 1892) opined:

> Mr. Roosevelt created a decided revolution in organ-building by his close attention to the finish of many minor details which had been up to that time neglected. He used to make periodical visits to Europe, and, being possessed of ample means, he could secure there all the latest improvements of the best English, French, and German builders, which are not a few, and promptly applied them in his productions. As a result, we have to-day very many specimens of remarkable work-manship, which will last for many years to come as monuments to his industry and love of his work. . . .
>
> Whilst it is undeniable that the Roosevelt work as far as action and finish, from the key-board to the last pallet and screw, has been almost beyond criticism, still I cannot say that I have ever been very enthusiastic over their peculiar style of voicing. There are a great many organists who like it, and again others who do not. It has always seemed to me as if their voicing has been characteristic of the French; that is, with the string and reed qualities predominating, which makes them more of a colossal harmonium, and lacks the full, round, and pervading organ tone.

A distinction between the "concert organ" and the "church organ," to say nothing of the "chapel organ" and the "chamber organ," a feature in Audsley's concept of the organ, is one that the Roosevelt factory followed rather faithfully. *The Roosevelt Organ Journal* of July 1876 described the character of the Chickering Hall organ:

> The solemnity, heaviness, and grandeur which we expect in the foun-dation stops of a large church organ, are not needed here; instead of them we find a remarkable variety of brilliant and carefully voiced solo stops, a close imitation of orchestral effects, and withal a solid and clear bass. The clearness of all the stops indeed is one of the marked merits of the instrument. The reeds, for which Mr. Roose-velt's organs have always been noted, are of the finished French-school.

In contrast to the Chickering Hall organ, a brochure said of the "church organ" in First Congregational Church, Great Barrington,

Massachusetts: "The amount of 8 feet flue work is also in excess of that usually met with, and is thus increased in order to form a foundation of extra solidity . . ." [74, p.97]. The same source gives sample specifications of differing sizes and styles of organs, and shows clearly the distinction between church and chamber organs. In the latter, the ensemble stops are forfeited in favor of solo stops. For example, a Great Mixture would be replaced by a 4' Flute, and the Clarinet substituted for the Trumpet.

The Roosevelt specifications did not always differ radically from those of their contemporaries. They often *seem* quite exceptional because the most famous are those organs that contained extraordinary features, such as an Echo division or unusual size. But the Roosevelts built hundreds of organs with more or less normal specifications, differing tonally from those of other builders chiefly in voicing and in the proportion of the instrument enclosed. Medium- and large-sized organs usually contained fully developed choruses, including compound stops, throughout Roosevelt history.

Actually, it is in very small instruments that one can often see most clearly the builder's concept of design. In these organs he is limited to the stops he considers most essential. Most builders of the 1880s and '90s were increasing the proportion of 8' tone in their organs, at the expense of the chorus development. In this development, Frank Roosevelt was years ahead of many of his contemporaries. His typical small organ of this period contained 8' Open Diapason, 8' Salicional, 8' Doppel Flöte, and 4' Gemshorn on the Great; 8' Violin Diapason, 8' Dolce, 8' Stopped Diapason, and 4' Flute Harmonique on the Swell; 16' Bourdon in the Pedal; and 8' couplers, plus Swell to Great 4'.

J. H. and C. S. Odell

John H. Odell (1830–1899) and his brother, Caleb S. Odell (1827–1892) had both worked for Ferris & Stuart before opening their own business in 1859. In spite of the competition from the larger, well-established builders in New York, the Odells earned a reputation for fine workmanship, and were soon producing eight to ten organs a year.

In 1909 Charles Radzinsky wrote:

During a long and honorable career, from 1859 to 1909, the firm has built over 200 church organs for New York City alone, and over 500 for other places, all of the highest type of excellence, mechanically and tonally. The most notable examples of their work are the organs in Temple Emmanu El (4 mans. and 65 stops), Forty-third street and Fifth avenue, New York; Church of St. Nicholas (4 mans. and 50 stops), Forty-eighth street and Fifth avenue; Second Church of Christ,

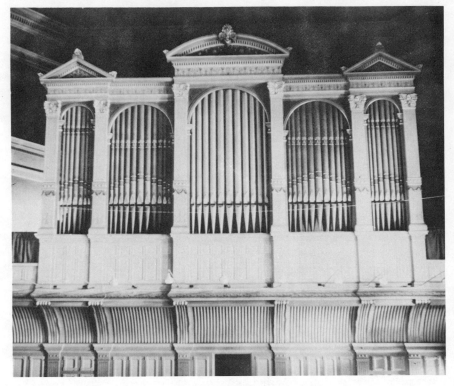

J. H. & C. S. Odell, Opus 190, 1882. Music Hall, Troy, New York.
Photo courtesy Thomas Murray.

Sixty-eighth street and Eighth avenue (4 mans. and 46 stops), Fifth
Avenue Presbyterian Church, Dr. Hall's (3 mans. and 46 stops), and
Peddie Memorial Baptist Church, Newark, N. J. (4 mans. and 55
stops). At the present time (1909) this is the sole firm engaged in the
manufacture of church organs in the old city of New York (Man-
hattan Borough), having survived all others. [433, p.167]

When Caleb S. Odell died in 1892 his son, William H. and John
Odell's son George W. were admitted to partnership. In later years,
members of a third generation who became partners were William H.
Odell's two sons, Caleb H. (1911) and Lewis C. (1925).

The Odells were able to build so many large instruments partly
because of their mechanical skill. In the 1860s they placed combination pistons between the manuals for operating the stops. Known as
the Odell pneumatic composition knobs (patented in 1866), this invention was so successful that it resulted in an enlargement of the factory to accommodate the business. The first patent issued in America

for tubular pneumatic action was granted to John H. Odell in 1872, and an improved Odell tubular pneumatic action was patented in 1898 [468]. Meanwhile the firm was also building tracker-action organs.[7]

While some prospective customers were undoubtedly impressed by the Odell innovations in organ action and controls, it was probably the tonal character of their organs that contributed the most to their success. The Odell style was eminently suited to late-nineteenth-century taste. The foundation was emphasized in generously proportioned 8′ stops, and higher-pitched principals were smaller scaled. The overall effect impresses the present-day listener as "mild," "pleasant," or less sympathetically, as "unexciting" or "undistinguished." Reeds, as well as flues, were given a well-mannered, disciplined character, with a fine tonal quality, if lacking in fire and brilliance.

Church of Saint Charles Borromeo, Brooklyn, New York
J. H. AND C. S. ODELL, Opus 178, 1880

Great

Double Open Diapason	16′	58
Open Diapason	8′	58
Gamba	8′	58
Clarionet Flute	8′	58
Principal	4′	58
Harmonic Flute	4′	58
Twelfth	3′	58
Fifteenth	2′	58
Mixture	III	174
Trumpet	8′	58

Swell

Bourdon	16′	58
Open Diapason	8′	58
Salicional	8′	58
Stopped Diapason	8′	58
Fugara	4′	58
Fluto Traverso	4′	58
Flageolet	2′	58
Cornet	III	174
Cornopean	8′	58
Oboe	8′	58
Tremulant		

Solo (lowest manual)

Open Diapason	8′	58

Solo (continued)

Keraulophon	8′	58
Dulciana	8′	58
Melodia	8′	58
Flute d'Amour	4′	58
Piccolo	2′	58
Tuba Cornet	8′	58
Clarionet (t.c.)	8′	46

Pedal

Open Diapason	16′	30
Bourdon	16′	30
Violoncello	8′	30
Trombone	16′	30

8′ Couplers

Manual Accessory

Swell to Great Reversible piston

Pedal Accessories

Swell Piano
Swell Forte
Great Piano
Great Forte
Great to Pedal Reversible
Swell Crescendo Lever

[221, pp. 7–8]

The largest surviving Odell tracker-action organ still playable in New York City is Opus 178, the three-manual instrument built in 1880 for the Church of Saint Charles Borromeo (R.C.) in Brooklyn. Many typical Odell features are found on this thirty-six-rank organ. Both of the mixtures, for example, have the same composition:

1–25:	17–19–22	31–37:	12–15–17
26–30:	15–17–19	38–58:	8–12–15

[221, p.7]

The use of the Tierce in both mixtures was characteristic. The 8′ Clarionet Flute, a favorite Odell voice, is a stopped wooden flute, with pierced stoppers, except in the bass range.[8] An unusual mechanical feature is a Swell to Great coupler reversible piston located in the Great key slip.

Other Builders in New York City and Brooklyn

Although the organ firms of Levi Stuart in New York and Reuben Midmer in Brooklyn were overshadowed by their famous contemporaries, they can hardly be classed as obscure. Each built a substantial number of organs, and the Midmer name would later attract international attention when Midmer-Losh built the largest organ in the world (see pp.362–63).

Levi U. Stuart was born in New York in 1826, and was apprenticed to his half brother, Richard M. Ferris, at the age of fourteen. In 1857 he became a partner in the business, and he succeeded Ferris when the latter died. Stuart's four brothers were also organ builders: William learned organ building from Henry Erben, and Louis, George, and Henry were apprentices in the Ferris shop. William became principal voicer and also specialized in making reed pipes when he worked in his brother's company. He later had his own business in Albany, New York.

An article in the *New York Weekly Review* of June 1870 credited Stuart with building ninety organs since 1861, forty-six of them two-manual instruments. His three-manual organs were built for the Broadway Tabernacle, New York; St. Mary's Roman Catholic Church, Norfolk, Virginia; and Holy Trinity Episcopal Church, New York. The Broadway Tabernacle organ, built in 1859 and enlarged in 1864 to thirty-four speaking stops, was "his largest and best work and ranks as one of the best in the city" [245, pp.13–14]. A 1910 periodical reported that one of the Stuart brothers and a son still had a small business doing repairs in The Bronx [433, p.167].

Reuben Midmer (1824–1895), a native of Sussex, England, moved to New York when he was about sixteen years old. He served an apprenticeship with Thomas Hall and also worked for Stuart in the old

Ferris & Stuart shop. In 1860 he opened his own shop in Brooklyn, and remained active there until his retirement in 1888.

Midmer's son Reed began working for his father when he was fourteen. He rose to take full charge of the factory, and about 1875 the firm name was changed to Reuben Midmer & Son. When his father died, Reed Midmer bought the factory from the estate, and in 1906 he moved it to Merrick, New York [289].

The first Midmer organ was installed in the Elm Place Congregational Church, Brooklyn. By 1909, 113 Midmer organs had been built for Brooklyn churches alone. Some of the most prominent were for the Church of St. Francis Xavier, St. Luke's Episcopal, Tompkins Avenue Congregational, and St. Anthony's Catholic Church [433, p.168].

Other New York City builders whose activities extended from mid-century were William H. Davis, Alexander Mills, and Hall & Labagh. The latter firm became Hall, Labagh & Kemp in the 1870s, and then Labagh & Kemp. The Labagh & Kemp factory was sold in 1892 to Chapman & Symmes. John Labagh died, on July 13, 1892, at the age of eighty-two (see chap. 8, n.1).

The last four decades of the century saw shops opened (and, for the most part, closed) by George Earle, James Mandeville, William Mandeville, William Schwartz, William B. Williams, Reuben May, and Müller & Abel.[9]

Builders in Other Parts of New York State

Utica, Elmira, and Buffalo form a large triangle in the western arm of New York State. Well separated from each other and from New York City, each of these communities could pride itself on the organs built by local firms. On the eastern point of the triangle, the shops of Andrews and Marklove were already established in Utica as this period opened. Marklove remained in business there until his death in the early 1890s. The fine quality of his work was continued by his successor, Clarence E. Morey.

The small organ firm of George N. Andrews produced about seven or eight organs a year during the late 1860s and early '70s. A bumper crop of twelve organs were on the 1871 production list, most of them of modest size, costing about $1,500. One can estimate the size by the fact that the price was about $85 a rank. The largest (or at least the most expensive) Andrews organ of this period was the 1872 instrument for St. Paul's Church, Oswego, costing $4,700. This price was exceptional and was more than balanced by a number of small instruments in the less-than-$1,000 class.

A decided slump in production from about 1873 on must have

been an important factor in the decision made by George Andrews and his son Charles B. to move their families and business to California. They did so in 1886, and Oakland became the new Andrews home.

The southern point of the triangle, Elmira, is near the Pennsylvania border. Here William King (1836–1923) opened his shop in 1865, having learned organ building in the Robjohn and Erben factories in New York. In 1889 his firm became William King & Son, and it continued in business for about a decade. In addition to organs for locations near Elmira, King's instruments included some organs of three and four manuals for prominent Philadelphia churches, and a few organs for such distant locations as Fargo, North Dakota, and Gainesville, Texas. The one-manual organ in the Baptist Church, Watkins Glen, New York, and the three-manual organ in the North Philadelphia Seventh Day Adventist Church, Philadelphia, are rare examples of King's work that remain in more or less original form [419].

At the western corner of the triangle, Buffalo's best-known organ builder was Garret House, who was in business there from about 1845 until his retirement in 1898. His business was sold the next year to

Chapel of the Sacred Heart, University of Notre Dame
GARRET HOUSE, 1864

Great			Swell (continued)		
Double Open Diapason	16′	44	Picola	2′	44
Open Diapason	8′	56	Cornet	III	132
Dulciana	8′	56	Trumpet	8′	44
Stopped Diapason	8′	56	Hautboy	8′	44
Wald Flute	4′	56			
Principal	4′	56	*Swell Bass*		
Twelfth	3′	56	Bourdon	16′	12
Fifteenth	2′	56	Dulciana	8′	12
Sesquialtera	IV	224	Stopped Diapason	8′	12
Viol d'Amour	8′	56	Principal	4′	12
Trumpet "Treble"	8′	44			
Trumpet "Bass"	8′	12	*Pedal*		
Cremona	8′	44	Double Open Diapason	16′	25
			Double Dulciana	16′	25
Swell (T.C.)			Open Diapason	8′	25
Double Stopped Diapason	16′	44	Tremule, "French Pattern"		
Open Diapason	8′	44			
Clarabella	8′	44	*Mechanical Stops*		
Viol d'Gamba	8′	44	Couple Swell to Great Organ		
Stopped Diapason	8′	44	Couple Great Organ to Pedals		
Principal	4′	44	Couple Swell Organ to Pedals		
Spitz Flute	4′	44	Bellows Alarm		

[351, p.10]

Charles B. Viner & Son. House completed 142 organs in the period from 1860 to 1898 (an average of three or four a year).

The first pipe organ for the University of Notre Dame, South Bend, Indiana, was one of House's instruments. It was constructed in 1864 for the Chapel of the Sacred Heart, at a cost of $3,000 and posed an immediate problem: The organ was too big for the chapel, and an addition had to be made to the building before it could be installed. For the inauguration on August 15, 1864 the Local Council "thought [it] proper to send for an organist from Buffalo at our own expense, which it is presumed, will not amount to $25.00" [166]. After only five years the chapel was found to be inadequate for the growing number of students at the university, and the decision was made to build a new one. House's organ was sold, and A. B. Felgemaker installed an instrument in the new church in 1875 [351, p.10].

The House organ had a very old-fashioned specification, with its Sesquialtera and Cremona on the Great and the tenor c Swell with four bass stops.

There were other organ builders in Buffalo, including Michael Beckel, Christian Dishmer, Wm. J. Davis, William Mohr, Moore & Sherman, and G. A. Prince, but House's best-known contemporaries were Abraham B. Felgemaker (1836–1905) and Silas L. Derrick. Derrick & Felgemaker had their shop in Buffalo from 1865 until the early '70s, when they moved to Erie, Pennsylvania (see pp.287–88).

Other builders in New York State were Giles Beach in Gloversville, Joseph Roegert in Rochester, Philip Schmidt (Schmeitt), in Troy, Frank Beman and N. P. Kraig in Binghamton, C. H. Campbell, J. H. Hidley, and Wm. Jackson & Co. in Albany, Thomas Knollin and W. J. Staub in Syracuse, John Pole in Geneva, and Francis J. N. Tallman in Nyack.

XIV

ORGANS AND BUILDERS

IN OTHER STATES

Eastern States

Two Musical Cities

BOTH Philadelphia and Baltimore had cultural institutions of high standing during the late nineteenth century, and could supply locally the necessary talent for a number of musical organizations. In Philadelphia the Germania Orchestra was a vital part of the city's life from its organization in 1854 until 1900, and the opening of the Academy of Music in 1857 was a milestone of far-reaching effect. In Baltimore George Peabody founded the Peabody Institute in 1857. His objective was a cultural complex including a library, an endowment for lectures, an art gallery, and an academy of music (later named Conservatory of Music). The Institute was the backbone of a number of important developments, including the Peabody Artist Recitals, begun in 1866, and the organization of the Peabody Orchestra in the mid-1870s.

Both cities, situated on the main route from New York to Washington, D.C., were logical stopping places for touring artists. Soloists, opera companies, and orchestras performing in New York found it advantageous to include them in their itineraries. Organists from New York were featured in inaugural recitals in both cities, and George Washbourne Morgan was a favorite. When the new Pomplitz organ for St. James' Roman Catholic Church, Baltimore, was opened, the *New-York Musical Gazette* of May 1873 reported: "Professors Morgan of New-York, J. Linhard and Fred. Eversman, Jr. of our city, presided, and the programme was varied, made up of music of a high order." In addition to

Sonata in F by Mendelssohn, Fugue in D by Bach, and Sonata no. 10 by Corelli, the program offered some of the inevitable overtures (*Occasional* by Handel and *Zampa* by Herold) and a new "overture" which introduced "Home Sweet Home." Lest anyone question too severely the organists' choice, the last-named number was originally written for, and performed by, the New York Philharmonic.

Organs and Builders in Philadelphia

The 1876 Philadelphia Centennial Exposition offered a wide variety of musical treats, not the least of which was the salute of a hundred cannon during the closing measures of a performance of Handel's "Hallelujah Chorus." Philadelphians were also treated to the sight and sound of some of America's most exciting new organs at the exposition. Hook & Hastings, Roosevelt, and other builders vied with one another for honors. It is significant that the famous organs at the Centennial were products of Boston and New York builders. Philadelphia could in no respect compete with those cities in the size and renown of their organ industries. Yet Pennsylvania, as a whole, retained at least a suggestion of the fascinating contrasts that give the state a unique place in American organ history: There was still the English-born Standbridge in Philadelphia, a few small shops representing the old Pennsylvania Dutch tradition, and, in addition, Pennsylvania's share of the nineteenth-century German immigration, bringing with it more recent European trends in organ building.

After the Civil War, John C. B. Standbridge continued to hold a leading position in Philadelphia's organ world. He was now joined in business by his two sons, George O. and John C., and the firm name became J. C. B. Standbridge & Sons. Some of their organs for Philadelphia churches were: St. Augustine's Roman Catholic Church (four manuals, 1868), Zion Lutheran Church (three manuals, 1870), and Arch St. Methodist Church (three manuals, 1870). In 1868 J. C. B. Standbridge made a pioneer experiment with electric action, one of the first, and possibly *the* first, use of electricity in organ construction in America (see p.265).

McCracken credits the 1870 three-manual organ for Temple Rodeph Shalom to Standbridge's sons [381, p.7]. After the death of their father in 1871, they continued in business as Standbridge Brothers until the firm dissolved in 1880. Their three-manual organ built in 1876 for Third Presbyterian Church, Philadelphia, was considered to be the last Standbridge organ existing in its original form until its destruction in 1969. McCracken praised the tone of this organ, which still reflected refined voicing "in a day when higher wind pressures and more blatant voicing were becoming common"; but of the exterior he

commented: "The Standbridge Brother's [*sic*] organ in Third Presbyterian Church will never take a prize for the quality of its casework,
for although seemingly built of durable material, the quality of the work
borders more on orange-crate construction" [381, p.8]. It had thirty-
three speaking stops, and the Great chorus was topped by a three-rank
Sesquialtera [448, pp.1–2].

McCracken has summarized late-nineteenth-century organ building
and the end of an era in Philadelphia:

> The German influence was again revived during the seventies by such
> men as: J. C. Burner [Durner?], Cornelius Bachman, Felix Barckoff,
> and Bernard Mudler, but it was not the same influence that pervaded
> Tannenberg's day.
>
> The Roosevelt branch, and later C. S. Haskell, represented the last
> concentrated efforts in Philadelphia at artistic organ building. Roose-
> velt's Philadelphia plant was the training ground for such later firms
> as C. S. Haskell . . . Bates and Culley, Beaufort Anchor, and Bar-
> tholomay. Philadelphia ceased to be an organ-building city in 1954,
> when Frederick Bartholomay (the son) closed his doors in favor of
> retirement. [383, p.4]

Pennsylvania's Old German Tradition

At a time in our history when large factories claim the greater part
of our attention, it is both interesting and important to note that some
old traditions continued. There was still the solitary craftsman, turning
out a few instruments, working at other crafts, and in general following
a pattern that dated back to the earliest organs built in the colonies.

Such a man was Thomas Dieffenbach, the fourth-generation organ
builder of his family. His shop adjoined his house at the corner of the
village square in Bethel, Pennsylvania. There he worked as a cabinetmaker, undertaker, and organ builder. He made over a thousand coffins by hand and had charge of some twelve hundred funerals.

Some of his methods and equipment were described by the family
historian, Victor Dieffenbach:

> Well do I remember when he would have a finished pipe organ in
> the display room (an extra building,) sandwiched in between the
> dwelling-house and the shop proper. It had an extra high ceiling, for
> some of those instruments were 14 feet tall. At the same time he had a
> second organ ready for assembly, and a third well on the way of con-
> struction. Making the case or shell as it is sometimes called was
> childs play compared to the forming of all the pipes, be they wood or
> metal. A tiny splinter or an air leak in the soldering may put the whole
> assembly out of tune. Worst of all Tom could never play any of the
> instruments he built. So, when it was fully assembled, his son John

Adam (Punch) would then tune it; although he was almost blind, he had the finest ear to hear "sour notes" as he called them.

Thomas D. shop was never modernized, as much as I recollect he never had a power tool except a ratchet screwdriver and a breast-drill all of the dozens of mortises and tenons were made by hand up to the hair and they just HAD to fit. [44, pp.10, 12]

Thomas Dieffenbach's organs (all in Pennsylvania) included:

1865	St. Paul's Union Church, Hamlin.
1872	Salem Church, Bethel.
1874	Zion (Reed's) Church, Stouchsburg.
1876	Epler's Union Church, Leesport.
1876	Pine Grove.
1878	St. John's German Reformed Church, Lower Heidelberg Township, Berks County (Tannenberg organ remodelled by T. Dieffenbach).
1885–90	Frieden's Union Church, Shartlesville.
	Zion Lutheran Church, Straustown.
	Alleghenyville.

Thomas Dieffenbach also rebuilt some of the earlier Dieffenbach organs. Two organs that were in his shop when he died went to Pine Grove and Perkasie, Pennsylvania [252, p.20]. The organ in Epler's Church is his only known two-manual instrument.

Epler's Union Church, Leesport, Pennsylvania
THOMAS DIEFFENBACH, 1876

Manual: 54 notes; Pedal: 18 notes

Great (unenclosed)

Open Diapason	8'	
Stop Diapason	8'	
Flute	8'	
Dulciana	8'	
Principal	4'	
Stop Diapason	4'	
Quint	3'	
Fifteenth	2'	

Swell

Stop Diapason	8'
Clarab. Flute	8'

Swell (continued)

Salicional	4'
Gamba	4'
Tube Flute (Chimney)	4'
Flute	4'

Pedal

Sub Bass	16'
Octave Bass	8'

Manual Coupler
Pedal Coupler (Great only)

[Cited in *OHS 1960 Convention Program*.]

The organs in Salem Church and Frieden's Union Church are one-manual and pedal instruments, nearly identical to the Great and Pedal divisions of the Epler's Church organ. In the Salem organ a Flute 4′ is substituted for the Quint 3′, and the Pedal 8′ is a Violincello. The Frieden's organ has a 2′ Flauto instead of the Fifteenth, and the 8′ pedal is called Violin Bass.

Contemporaries of Thomas Dieffenbach in the predominantly German parts of Pennsylvania were Samuel Bohler and his successor, Elmer E. Palm, in Reading, and A. B. Miller of Lebanon.[1] An outstanding organ built by Miller was installed in 1888 and is still in the Old Salem Lutheran Church, Lebanon. It is a three-manual instrument with twenty-seven speaking stops. Its Great chorus, extending from 16′ to a three-rank Mixture, is exceptionally clear and satisfying to the modern listener. Both the Swell and the Choir have good secondary choruses, greatly enhanced by the brightness of the 4′ and 2′ lines.

A New Arrival from Germany

Standbridge and Thomas Dieffenbach represent two extremes of Pennsylvania's old traditions of organ building. In between were a number of builders whose production certainly exceeded that of Dieffenbach yet they never produced instruments of a size and sophistication comparable to Standbridge's.

One such builder was Charles Friedrick Durner (1838–1914), born in Wurtemburg, Germany. He came from a family of organ builders and learned his craft in his father's shop. When Durner arrived in America in 1859, he settled near Quakertown, where his parents already lived, and began building organs. Two years later he opened his own shop in Quakertown. Here he built organs for Philadelphia churches, as well as for locations in rural areas and small towns. One of his instruments was exhibited in the 1876 Philadelphia Centennial, and for a time during the 1880s his brother J. Christian had a Philadelphia sales office for the firm.

Durner built a number of little one-manual parlor organs with two to four stops. His church organs were usually small two-manual organs with one Pedal stop (Bourdon 16′). The Great chorus was complete to the 2′ on the earlier organs, but by 1880 the Twelfth was omitted, and in the 1890s the Fifteenth was also often absent. In spite of that, the organs maintained a degree of clarity, and as McCracken stated:

> Even with the lack of upper work, Durner organs never fell to the dismal tonal standards of the Hope-Jones inspired instruments of a few years later. Always, the Durners gave an essence of lightness and cheeriness to the voicing. In so far as I was able to see, the quality of the workmanship never did waver. [379, p.13]

A typical Durner instrument is the ten-stop organ in Keelor's Union Church, Obelisk, Pennsylvania, built about 1895. It contains 8′ Open Diapason, Melodia, and Dulciana; 4′ Principal; and 2′ Fifteenth on the Great. The Swell has four stops: 8′ St. Diapason, Viola, and Oboe Gamba; and 4′ Flute Harmonique. The Pedal has the characteristic 16′ Bourdon. There are the usual 8′ couplers, a Great to Pedal reversible, and two combination pedals. The manuals have fifty-eight notes, the pedal twenty-seven. The Oboe Gamba was Durner's usual substitution for a reed, although he occasionally did install an Oboe [510]. When C. F. Durner died in 1914, he was succeeded by his son Charles Edward Durner (1863–1932).

Erie: Derrick & Felgemaker

When Abraham B. Felgemaker and Silas L. Derrick moved their firm from Buffalo, New York, to Erie, Pennsylvania, in the early 1870s, northwestern Pennsylvania acquired its first large organ company.[2] Derrick & Felgemaker (the company name later became A. B. Felgemaker) completed some seven hundred organs by the year 1900, and remained in business until 1918. Its interests and unfinished contracts were then taken over by the Tellers Organ Company, and the factory was sold to a firm engaged in making coffins.

Felgemaker's location on Lake Erie, not far from the Ohio border, gave him an advantage over the builders farther east in capturing a generous share of the midwestern market. He capitalized on this advantage by specializing in small instruments, easily transported and easily installed, featuring excellent workmanship. As a result, Felgemaker organs were scattered throughout the Midwest, as well as in Pennsylvania and New York. The first 418 organs produced by this company included 350 Felgemaker Patent Portable Pipe Organs. These little one-manual organs were mass-produced, as many as forty-eight in a series.

From the first, Felgemaker seems to have favored a sixty-one-note manual range, although the pedal range varied from seventeen to thirty notes. His organs maintained a complete chorus on the Great (8′ to 2′, plus a Mixture in larger instruments) at least until the mid 1880s. After that, the upperwork was decreased in some organs and eliminated in others. In this characteristic, however, Felgemaker was not as consistent as some of his contemporaries.

A large two-manual Derrick & Felgemaker organ was installed in the Church of Our Lady of the Sacred Heart, University of Notre Dame, Indiana, in 1875. Its specification is an interesting example of this company's early work.[3]

Church of Our Lady of the Sacred Heart, University of Notre Dame
DERRICK & FELGEMAKER, Opus 256, 1875

Great			Swell (continued)		
Double Open Diapason	16′	61	Still Gedackt	8′	61
Bourdon (t.c.)	16′	49	Flauto Traverso	4′	61
Open Diapason	8′	61	Fugara	4′	61
Geigen Principal	4′	61	Flute Angelique	2′	61
Melodia	8′	61	Dolce Cornet	III	183
Dulciana	8′	61	Oboe with Bassoon Bass	8′	61
Choral Flute	4′	61	Octave Horn	4′	61
Principal	4′	61			
Twelfth	2⅔′	61	Pedal		
Fifteenth	2′	61	Double Open Diapason	16′	30
Mixture	III	183	Double-Stopped Diapason	16′	30
Doublette	II	122	Floete	8′	30
Trumpet	8′	61	Violoncello	8′	30
Clarion	4′	61	Trombone	16′	30

Swell			Mechanical Registers	
Bourdon	16′	61	Couple Swell to Pedals	
Open Diapason	8′	61	Couple Great to Pedals	
Salicional	8′	61	Couple Swell to Great	
Double-toned Diapason	8′	61	Tremulant	
Zephyr Gamba	8′	61	Bellows	

Pneumatic Combinations
Full great manuals; solo great manuals; full to 4 ft. great; Reversible Great to Pedals; balance swell pedal; pneumatic key action in bass.

Mixture III: C: 17—19—22   Doublette II: C: 15—22
           c^1:   15—17—19 $c\sharp^3$:   8—15
           c^2:   12—15—17
           $g\sharp^2$:   10—12—15   Dolce Cornet III: 12—15—17

Wind Pressure: 2¾″

[351, p.11]

Mathias Möller in Pennsylvania and Maryland

Shortly after Derrick and Felgemaker moved their plant to Erie, Pennsylvania, they hired a young Dane who would later become one of America's most famous builders. Mathias Peter Möller (1854–1937) was born on a farm on the eastern coast of the Isle of Bornholm. When he was six months old, his family moved to Dalegaard, and it was there that he spent his childhood.

When he was about fourteen years old, Mathias went to Ronne, where he became an apprentice to a carriage maker. After three years of learning the use of tools and woodworking, he came to America along with his sister and her husband. He went first to stay with a half brother, George Möller, in Warren, Pennsylvania, and worked at his trade there for a short time. Not particularly satisfied with cabinet-making, he found a woodworking job in Erie, Pennsylvania, with Derrick & Felgemaker.

Mathias Möller had much to learn. He had no musical background, no knowledge of organ construction, and, to add to the confusion, he had to cope with a new language. But by the end of 1874, he had designed a new wind-chest and had developed so many other ideas about organ construction that he decided to go into business for himself. In January 1875 he returned to Warren and built his first organ, using his brother's parlor as a shop. It was a two-manual instrument, and was purchased by the Swedish Lutheran Church in Warren after its completion in September.

Encouraged by his success, Möller went to Philadelphia with the idea of building an organ for the Centennial. Since he had to interrupt his work on the organ frequently to earn his living, it was not completed in time. When it was finally finished, he sold it to the St. George Society of Philadelphia, and it was praised by some of the city's leading organists. In 1877 Möller moved to Greencastle, lured by the promise of a partnership that would give him the capital he needed for materials. However, it seems that his would-be partner had no funds, and Möller was forced to continue on his own. He built and sold several organs during this period.

About 1881 civic leaders in Hagerstown, Maryland, eager to develop the commercial and industrial potential of their town of 6,000, invited Möller to establish a factory there. Here the long, continuous history of the Möller company really begins. Möller was given financial assistance in building a factory, and by April 1881 his two-story shop was ready. Five additions were made to the factory in the next eleven years—evidence of its growth [111, p.11].

By the early 1890s the Möller company was producing about twenty organs a year, and the future seemed secure. However, in 1895, while Mathias was out of town, the factory burned, and with it, six completed organs ready for delivery. Only a fraction of the loss was covered by insurance. Although Möller received some offers of partnerships elsewhere after this disaster, he was determined to stay in business in Hagerstown, and by January 1896 his new factory, farther out of town, was ready for use. Here business grew phenomenally, and with almost a hundred employees, the output reached an organ a week.

The early Möller organs included some for distant locations, as well as many installed in the East. Opus 79, for example, went to the Mt. Auburn M.E. Church, St. Louis (1896), and Opus 128 was installed in the First Methodist Church, Pueblo, Colorado (1896). Both were two-manual organs.

Möller built tracker-action organs until the early part of the twentieth century. His tubular-pneumatic organs date from about 1902 to 1918, although some trackers were built during the early part of this period. By 1919 the standard Möller action was electropneumatic. At first Möller depended on outside sources for metal organ pipes, but in 1894 he began making his own zinc pipes, and by 1896 all metal pipes were made in the factory.

Möller specifications followed closely the trends of the time. Opus 346, completed for the Charleston, South Carolina, Exposition of 1901, was one of Möller's largest three-manual tracker organs, and it has been described by Richard Peek:

> Tonally, this instrument possessed many beautiful features. The entire Great Diapason Chorus was mild, of moderate scale and without a heavy 8′ unduly dominating the ensemble. The Great Trumpet was particularly noteworthy, having an even timbre and a brilliance not often found on instruments of this vintage. The flute chorus of the choir was also pleasing, providing a light, bright contrast to the Great without the dull quality so often found in a chorus built upon a Melodia. The swell strings were of good quality, though unfortunately the soft metal has not withstood the test of time as well as the other ranks. Particularly pleasing was the extremely small scale 16′ swell Bourdon which was also playable from the Pedal by transmission. All in all this instrument was a fine example of an early 20th century concert instrument which was particularly well suited to the music of Franck and other Romantic masters. [421]

Organ Builders in Baltimore

Two important builders in Baltimore were August Pomplitz and Henry Niemann. The firm of August Pomplitz and Henry Rodewald had been building organs since 1850 (see p.180). In the early 1860s Rodewald left, but Pomplitz continued in business. He was known for his fine workmanship, and when the organ for Trinity M.E. Church, Lafayette, Indiana, was completed, a reviewer for the *New-York Musical Gazette* (April 1873) gave his praise, if not unqualified, to the $4,300 two-manual organ:

> The action is excellent, and the tone clear, strong, and church-like. I like particularly the balance of tone, which seems to me more church-like than we often hear. The mixtures did not appear to me to be quite as *ringing* as they might have been, principally, I think, from the undue presence of the 17th in them. I hear that this builder is now building a fine organ worth $40,000, for Mr. Thomas Winans, of Baltimore.

The Pomplitz organs of the 1870s have stood well the test of time, and when Thomas Eader reviewed the 1875 organ in St. Gregory's R.C. Church, Baltimore, in 1958, he could say:

> The full tone of either of the manuals is not a big sound but is rather brilliant and has excellent blend. Most of the stops are of the same power, making the possible number of combinations almost limitless. Each and every pipe is beautifully voiced and regulated, as in all Pomplitz organs, and the diapasons are worthy of special mention, having an exceptionally rich sound which is best described as being distinctly Pomplitz. [277, II, p.4]

This organ, one of the last built by August Pomplitz, was given the rather unusual luxury of two reeds on each manual (Great Trumpet and Clarionett, Swell Trumpet and Oboe). In other respects its twenty-six speaking stops follow a normal pattern for organs of this time.

St. Gregory's R.C. Church, Baltimore, Maryland
AUGUST POMPLITZ, 1875

Manuals: 58 notes; Pedal: 27 notes

Great		*Swell (continued)*	
Bourdon	16′	Violin	8′
Open Diapason	8′	Stopd Diapason	8′
Melodia	8′	Aeoline	8′
Stopd. Diapason	8′	Principal	4′
Salicional	8′	Flute (label missing)	4′
Dulciana	8′	Waldflute	2′
Principal	4′	Cornett	III
Rohrflute	4′	Trumpet (t.c.)	8′
Twelfth	2⅔′	Oboe	8′
Fifteenth	2′		
Mixtur	IV		
Trumpet	8′	*Pedal*	
Clarionett (t.c.)	8′	Double Open	16′
		Bourdon	16′
Swell		Violincello	8′
Bourdon	16′		
Open Diapason	8′	8′ couplers	

[277, II, p.4]

August Pomplitz's two sons, Herman and Louisa, also became organ builders. Louisa, with John W. Otto as his partner, succeeded his father in the factory, which in 1876 was known as the Pomplitz Church Organ Co. Otto later continued in business under his own name, after the Pomplitz firm ended its history in the late 1880s. The later organs of the Pomplitz factory, while retaining some of the old distinctive voicing, followed the trend toward the emphasis on the 8′ stops and the accompanying loss of brilliance [277, II, p.4].

Henry Niemann (1838–1899), a German by birth, was a builder of extraordinary background, who began working in Baltimore in 1872. He had been apprenticed as a cabinetmaker, worked for John Closs in Cincinnati from 1857 to 1859, went to London to work for Barker until 1862, worked for Cavaillé-Coll for five years, built organs in both France and Germany, studied the methods of the major European builders, and then returned to the United States to open his factory in Baltimore.

His output included about forty organs for Baltimore, in addition to those for other locations. His 1897 organ for the Otterbein Memorial Church, Baltimore, has been described by Eader as "very full, though not overbearing. It is brighter than most classic style organs of today, but the tone is balanced well from treble to bass" [277, III, p.3]. Even at this late date, Niemann gave the little thirteen-stop organ a complete diapason chorus from 8′ to 2′ on the Great.

Other builders in Baltimore from 1860 to 1900 included James Hall, Bernard Tully, Leon P. Beaulieu, C. Louis Miller, George E. Barker, George A. Schumacher, and Adam Stein.

The Southeast

After the disastrous years of war and so-called reconstruction, the Southeast offered little attraction to organ builders. The instruments that were installed in the last decades of the century were almost all from northern factories. Even so, there were repairs to be done, installations to be made, and perhaps a few small contracts for a local builder.

The Charleston, South Carolina, city directories list the organ builders John Baker from the years 1867 to 1878, J. C. Olerich from 1872 to 1881, and James S. Baker, who advertised himself as "Organ Builder/Organs and Melodeons Tuned and Repaired" from 1885 to 1898.

Central States
New Factories and New Challenges

The Civil War hastened the industrialization of the North Central states, and along the shores of the Great Lakes, manufacturers found excellent locations for their factories. Chicago, in particular, attracted not only factories but also farmers, and the farm market became one of its most important industries. Surrounded by rich, cultivated lands and connected to the East by rail, Chicago became the marketing hub for much of the Midwest. Chicago was eager to take the farmer's products, supply his needs, and share his profits. Montgomery Ward & Co. of

Chicago solved the problem of reaching the isolated farmhouse in 1872 by opening the first mail-order house.

Organ builders, too, found that they must adjust their methods if the rural midwestern churches were to have organs. Distances were greater, farms were larger, and towns were more scattered than in the East. Repair service for ailing instruments was nonexistent. Some builders avoided or ignored the issue, building organs for their immediate locales. Other enterprising organ men looked for new ways to build organs that were compact, easily transported, easily installed, and cheap enough to meet the reed-organ competition.

Musical Developments in the Midwest

The great influx to the Midwest of German and Swedish immigrants had an unmistakable effect on musical life. Every large city had its singing society, some had professional music schools, and performances of the *Messiah* and *Elijah* could be heard even in remote towns. A visitor to central Kansas found that the little town of Lindsborg had had performances of the *Messiah* each year since 1887:

> in this little town of less than fifteen hundred inhabitants Handel's oratorio, "The Messiah," was sung by a chorus of three hundred, two nights of this week in the auditorium of Bethany College. A pipe organ that cost five thousand dollars and an orchestra of thirty-four pieces furnished the instrumental music. The solos were by teachers and graduates of the college. The audience of seven thousand people came from the surrounding country and from towns up and down the Smoky and Solomon Valleys, and some across the Arkansas away to the South. Distance does not count for much in Central Kansas. . . . The history of Lindsborg, a settlement of music loving Swedish-Americans, its colleges and its great annual oratorio festival is the history of a struggle for higher education, and yet this great love for music is no uncommon phase in Kansas prairie life.
>
> [Cited in 84, VIII, p.225.]

Cincinnati had long been a center of musical activity, and when Beethoven's Ninth Symphony was performed there in 1869, the enthusiasm was frightening.

> The hall was packed far beyond its capacity. Panic seemed imminent, and the story goes that Reuben R. Springer, a devout Catholic, prayed to his Madonna and made a vow that if she helped these people to safety, he would build a hall in her honor. The fulfillment was Music Hall, for years the home of May Festivals and the Cincinnati Symphony concerts. [48, p.121]

The Cincinnati Music Hall was also the home of the famous E. & G. G. Hook and Hastings organ (see pp.222, 223).

The popularity of orchestral music was fast gaining momentum. While Theodore Thomas dominated the national scene, he was not working alone in this field. From 1860 to 1866 the St. Louis Philharmonic Society was conducted by the distinguished Edward de Sobolew, who was a friend of Mendelssohn's and a pupil of Carl Maria von Weber's [48, p.141].

Chicago had more large and important organs by eastern builders than did any other city in the Midwest. Many of them were destroyed when the city burned in 1871, but replacements were soon under way. Johnson organs were particular favorites, and sixty or more organs by this builder were installed there, some before and some after the fire [496, I, p.11]. The later ones included three-manual organs for the Second Presbyterian Church, Third Presbyterian Church, Central Music Hall, and Hershey Hall.

An interesting organ of 1870, spared by the fire, was the three-manual instrument built for the Holy Family Roman Catholic Church by Louis Mitchell, a Canadian. Its more than sixty speaking stops included twelve for the pedal [115, p.1]. A still larger milestone in Chicago organ history was the installation of Frank Roosevelt's giant 109-stop organ in the Auditorium in 1890.

One of Chicago's most famous organists of this time was Clarence Eddy. He was born in Greenfield, Massachusetts, in 1851, and studied organ in America with Dudley Buck and in Germany with August Haupt. He concertized extensively in Europe, and then went to Chicago to become organist of the First Congregational Church, later moving to the First Presbyterian Church. Lahee noted: "He has undoubtedly dedicated more organs in this country than any other organist; among them may be mentioned the great Auditorium organ in Chicago and the noted organ in Trinity Church, Denver" [97, p.283].

Dudley Buck became organist at St. James' Church in 1869, but when the church burned (and along with it a number of Buck's manuscripts) in the 1871 fire, he moved to Boston. Other noted Chicago organists in the late nineteenth century included Harrison M. Wild and Wilhelm Middleschulte. The Chicago Exposition in 1893 had a star-studded series of sixty-two organ recitals. Clarence Eddy played twenty-one of them, and Alexandre Guilmant was brought from Paris for four concerts. Nineteen leading organists from various parts of the country divided the remaining recitals.

Some of the Midwest's organ builders of this time were German-born, some were English, and a few were even native Americans. They represented a varied cross section in their styles. There were a few of the more radically modern builders, some firmly rooted traditionalists, and an assortment of degrees between the extremes. By the end of the century the interesting little traits in nomenclature carried over by some of the German builders from the "old country" had, along with regional differences, been dissolved in the cultural melting pot.

Detroit: Farrand & Votey

Farrand & Votey of Detroit had a relatively short existence, but nevertheless managed to rise to a place of importance in the organ world. Quick to seize the new inventions and the latest style, the firm aligned itself with the "modern" school of organ building.

William R. Farrand (1854–1930) was a member of a Detroit family that bought out the Whitney Organ Company in the mid-1880s. He was joined by Edwin Scott Votey (1856–1931), who had had his training with the Estey Organ Company of Brattleboro, Vermont. They bought the business of Granville Wood and his son William D. Wood in 1890 [520], but more important was their acquisition of the Roosevelt patents and business in 1893. Several workmen from the famous Roosevelt shop also made a valuable addition to the Detroit firm.

Large Farrand & Votey organs included the one built for the Chicago Exposition of 1893 (see p.212), a four-manual instrument with sixty-five stops for the Carnegie Library in Pittsburgh, a four-manual organ of eighty-five speaking stops for St. Ignatius Church, San Francisco, and a four-manual organ of sixty stops for the Pabst Theater, Milwaukee. Opus 748, built in 1895 for the First Church of Christ, Scientist in Boston, incorporated many features of the Farrand & Votey style. It was a three-manual organ with thirty-four speaking stops, sixty-one-note manuals, and a thirty-note pedal. It used the Roosevelt Patent Windchests, the Roosevelt Patent Automatic Adjustable Combination Pedals, and the Farrand & Votey Patent Electric Action. There were two swell enclosures: one for the Swell and another that contained all Great and Choir stops except the Great 16' and 8' Open Diapasons. The only compound stop was a Cornet III in the Swell (there was no Great Mixture). Couplers included Swell to Swell 4', Swell to Great 4', Swell to Great 16', and Choir to Great 16'. The blower was electric.[4]

Farrand & Votey began building organs for the Aeolian Company of New York in the early 1890s. The first was completed in 1893 and was installed in Aeolian Hall. In 1895 Edwin S. Votey invented the Pianola. This instrument, along with his development of the Duo Art Organ and Duo Art Piano, placed the Aeolian Company in the forefront of manufacturers of player instruments. It also placed Votey firmly on the board of directors of the Aeolian Company (he became first vice-president in 1916).

Farrand & Votey remained in business until 1897. After that the Farrand Organ Co. made reed organs, while the Votey Organ Co. made pipe organs. In 1899 the Votey company merged with the Aeolian company, and the factory was located in Garwood, New Jersey. Here the Pianola and other Aeolian instruments were manufactured in quantity [281]. Aeolian factories were also opened in France, England, and Germany to meet the demand. While the Aeolian firm continued in this line of activity, the Votey Organ Company was purchased in 1901 by Hutchings, forming the Hutchings-Votey Organ Co., with George S. Hutchings as president and Ernest M. Skinner as vice president (see p.234).

Cincinnati: Koehnken & Grimm

Cincinnati's old, established organ firm was Koehnken & Co. (see p.184). Gallus Grimm became Johann H. Koehnken's partner in 1875, and for twenty-one years the company did business under the name of Koehnken & Grimm. In 1896 Koehnken retired, and the firm became G. Grimm & Son. Both Koehnken and Grimm died the next year, leaving Grimm's son Edward in charge of the business. There were several changes of leadership after 1900, and the business was finally acquired in 1908 by Alfred Mathers [418, p.6].

While later organs conformed closely to the prevailing style of American instruments, specifications until at least the mid-1870s reveal quite a different concept. The 1866 Koehnken & Co. organ in the Isaac M. Wise Temple, Cincinnati, is unusual in many respects, with its use of the 16′ series Tierce in the two Cornets, the location of the Oboe and Clarionet, and its spectacular Pedal division.

Isaac M. Wise Temple, Cincinnati, Ohio
KOEHNKEN & CO., 1866

Great			Great (continued)		
Principal	16′	54	Sesqualtera	III	162
Principal	8′	54	Cornet (c♯¹)	V	145
Melodia	8′	38*	Trompete	8′	54
Gedackt	8′	54	*Swell*		
Flauto	8′	54			
Viola di Gamba	8′	42**	Bourdon	16′	54
Quinte	5⅓′	54	Principal	8′	54
Octav	4′	54	Gedackt	8′	54
Nachthorn	4′	54	Violine	8′	54
Quinte	2⅔′	54	Salicional	8′	41†
Wald Floete	2′	54	Octav	4′	54

Isaac M. Wise Temple, Cincinnati, Ohio
KOEHNKEN & CO., 1866

Swell (continued)			Pedal		
Rohrfloete	4'	54	Subbass	16'	25
Piccalo	2'	54	Bourdon	16'	25
Cornet (t.c.)	III	126	Violoncello	8'	25
Clarionet	8'	42	Octav	4'	25
Tremulant‡			Posaune	16'	25
			Trompete	8'	25
Choir			Bassethorn	4'	25
Hohlfloete (c#¹)	16'	29			
Principal	8'	54	*Couplers*		
Fugara	8'	42††	Swell to Great		
Gedackt	8'	54	Choir to Great		
Octav	4'	54	Great to Pedal		
Flauto	4'	54			
Oboe	8'	42	Hitch-down swell pedal		

Great Sesqualtera:	1–24	17–19–22	Great Cornet: 26–54: 5–8–10–12–15
	25–30:	15–17–19	
	31–37:	12–15–17	Swell Cornet: 13–48: 8–10–12
	38–54:	10–12–15	49–54: 5–8–10

* Common bass with Gedackt
** Common bass with Flauto
† Common bass with Violine
‡ May not be original
†† Common bass with Principal

[OHS 1965 Convention Program]

Pallage cites the specification of an 1875 Koehnken & Grimm organ of similar size in Covington, Kentucky, with a Pedal division of 16' Principal, 16' Subbass, 10⅔ Quint, 8' Octave, 8' Violoncello, 16' Posaune, and 4' Posaune. In this organ there is one Cornet (on the Great), and the Swell and Choir reeds are in their normal locations. There are four 16' manual stops: Great Principal and Bourdon, Swell Bourdon, and Choir Principal [418, p.7].

Orrville: The Schantz Company

Almost all the organ firms established in the Midwest in the post-Civil War period went out of business years ago. A notable exception is the Schantz Organ Co. of Orrville, Ohio. A. J. Schantz (d.1921) served the traditional apprenticeship as a cabinetmaker in Orrville. He began building reed organs in 1873, and, according to John Schantz, his tracker organs dated from 1885 to 1908[5] [459, p.9]. A. J. Schantz's three sons all worked in the shop while they were attending high school, and they assumed full control of the business when their father retired in 1913 [206]. Today, another generation of Schantz organ builders directs this firm.

Indianapolis: William Horatio Clarke

William Horatio Clarke had one of the most remarkable careers of any nineteenth-century American organ builder. Clarke was born in Newton, Massachusetts, in 1840. Among other accomplishments, he was superintendent of music instruction in the Dayton, Ohio, public schools; professor of music in a Toronto college; organist at several large churches, including Tremont Temple, Boston; author of several books and methods, including a book on organ construction [37]; compiler of organ and choir collections; composer of anthems and organ pieces; recitalist; organ builder; and consultant. Clarke was also interested in optics, and was elected a member of the Society of Arts of M.I.T. on the basis of his lecture on the properties of reflected light [241].

Under such dynamic leadership, one could not expect the Wm. H. Clarke & Co. organ firm of Indianapolis to content itself with the little organs that furnished the bread and butter of most small shops. During the 1870s Clarke's organs included:

1874   First Presbyterian Church, Dayton, Ohio, thirty stops.
1875   First Baptist Church, Indianapolis, Indiana, three manuals, fifty-two stops.
1876   Calvary Church (Episcopal), Louisville, Kentucky, two manuals, forty stops.
1876   Roberts Park Methodist Church, Indianapolis, Indiana, three manuals, sixty stops.

Clarke finally settled in Woburn, Massachusetts, in 1890. Two years later he suffered a paralytic stroke, which brought to an end his career as an organist, but he continued to work as a writer, editor, and organ consultant. He died in 1914.

St. Louis: George Kilgen & Son

St. Louis's largest and best known organ firm at the turn of the century was George Kilgen & Son. George Kilgen had been building organs in New York since 1851 (see p.167), but with the increasing westward population movement, he saw St. Louis as an ideal, centrally located city with many opportunities for development, large supplies of raw materials, and good transportation. Accordingly, he moved his factory there in 1873. His son Charles C. (1859–1932) became a partner in 1885, and the firm became George Kilgen & Son. Charles Kilgen was responsible for adding the old Pfeffer Organ Co. of St. Louis to the Kilgen assets in 1909 [284].

The Kilgen firm remained in business until labor trouble and financial difficulties closed its doors in 1960. Some large and notable organs were built by this company, particularly in the early decades of the twentieth century, and by 1924 over four thousand Kilgen organs had been installed [204].

Kilgen's success in the late nineteenth century was based on the production of small, well-built tracker-action organs, most of them with two manuals and a rather predictable specification. A typical Great contained 8' Open Diapason, Dulciana, and Melodia; 4' Octave; and 2' Fifteenth. The Swell would then have 8' Violin Diapason, Salicional, and Stop Diapason; and 4' Flute Harmonique and Violina. The Pedal was usually no more than a 16' Bourdon. The manuals had sixty-one notes, the pedals twenty-seven or thirty. A slightly larger organ might add an Oboe or an Oboe-Gamba to the Swell and a second Pedal stop (perhaps Lieblich Gedackt 16' or Violincello 8'). Countless churches in small midwestern towns installed Kilgen organs of this general design, give or take a few stops, and one does not have to look far in Missouri to find one in good condition, still serving its intended purpose.

Mail-Order Organs from Central Illinois: John Hinners

> John L. Hinners had never been to Europe to see a Schnitger and knew only the American organs, builders, and organists of the day; however, he did have a great deal of common sense and could readily distinguish a useless fad from a sound musical idea. [316, p.3]

John Hinners (1846–1906), the son of German Pietists who had come to this country in 1836, was born in Wheeling, Ohio. He attended school in Chicago, served in the Civil War, and then went to work as an apprentice in the reed organ department of Mason & Hamlin. In 1879 he moved to Pekin, Illinois, and after working two years for a reed organ builder there, he opened his own business. For a time he was in partnership with J. J. Fink, but in 1885 U. J. Albertsen bought Fink's interest, and the company became Hinners & Albertsen.

Aware of the large number of churches in the Midwest that could use small, inexpensive organs of reliable quality, Hinners & Albertsen began building pipe organs in 1890. John Hinners put his experience in reed organ manufacturing to work, designing small organs that could be built along standardized patterns, thus reducing the cost. Such mass production led Coleberd to remark:

> The instrument built by Hinners was indeed as much an innova-
> tion in pipe organ building as the Model T produced by Henry Ford
> was to the automobile industry. Ford brought the passenger car to the
> common man while Hinners brought the pipe organ to the small
> church. [255, p.4]

Actually, other builders also engaged in this sort of production, e.g.,
Felgemaker and Roosevelt, but there were still over three thousand
customers waiting for Hinners's organs.

The catalogue was especially important to this company, relying
as it did on direct-mail orders to the factory (no salesmen were employed). The 1890 Hinners catalogue was printed in both German and
English, and offered one-manual organs with three to six ranks. Descriptions of two-manual organs were available upon request [316,
pp.2–3]. One model was a one-manual instrument with four divided
manual stops and a fifteen-note Pedal Bourdon:

> For only $485.00 we deliver this organ, securely packed in boxes
> and crates, on board cars or steamboat in Pekin. Added to this is
> merely the nominal expense of freight on the organ and the fare for
> the round trip for one of our men to go and set up, regulate and tune
> the organ. We make no charge for the time required to do the work
> —only the traveling expense. We can not, in any case, nor under any
> consideration, deviate from this rule, because the price named is the
> very lowest for which we can build this organ. . . . [470]

The company's location in central Illinois was advantageous for
reaching the numerous German communities that developed in the
Midwest during the late nineteenth century. Many of these communities maintained German schools and continued to hold church services
in German until the time of World War I. One such church was the
German Methodist Church (later Trinity Methodist) in St. Joseph,
Missouri. Its larger-than-average 1895 Hinners & Albertsen organ,
free-standing in the front of the church, boasted two manuals and
thirteen stops. It gave sturdy, reliable support to the congregation's
singing and remained a source of pride for nearly sixty years, until the
congregation moved to a different location, forming the Ashland United
Methodist Church. For eighteen years the congregation regretted leaving the old organ behind, and it was finally reacquired in 1973 for installation in the Ashland church.

In 1902 Albertsen retired, and the firm was incorporated as Hinners
Organ Company. When John L. Hinners died in 1906, his son Arthur
W. (1873–1955) succeeded him as president of the company. Under his
leadership the firm had its peak year in 1921, when ninety-seven em-

Hinners & Albertsen, 1895. Built for the German Methodist Church, St. Joseph, Missouri. Now in Ashland United Methodist Church, St. Joseph. *Photo courtesy Ashland United Methodist Church.*

ployees were busy in the factory. However, in the 1930s the company was a victim of the depression, and finally went out of business in 1936. Arthur W. Hinners went to work for the Wicks Organ Co. as a salesman. The reed organ department, which had produced close to 20,000 instruments, was continued as a separate business by Louis C. Moschel until 1940.

In regard to twentieth-century developments, John R. Hinners, a descendant of the builder, wrote:

> The first radical departures from the past came in 1910 when the Hinners company made its first tubular-pneumatic action, and in 1916

when the first electro-pneumatic organ was built. The first tubular organ must not have been an overwhelming success as the second was not constructed until two years later. Of the more than three thousand pipe organs built by the Hinners firm, only 223 were tubular-pneumatic and 280 were electro-pneumatic. Trackers were the mainstay of the company nearly to the bitter end. The first theater organ (curiously enough, a five rank tracker) was sold in 1911; and, in all, twenty of these were made, some quite large. [316, p.4]

Before 1920 all metal pipes in Hinners organs were products of Anton Gottfried in Erie, Pennsylvania.

Chicago: Kimball and Pilcher

Chicago's most successful organ builder, Wallace W. Kimball (1828–1904), presents an unusual figure among nineteenth-century American builders. He was not a musician, nor had he been apprenticed as a carpenter, cabinetmaker, or organ builder. He was, rather, an astute salesman and businessman. A native of Rumford, Maine, Kimball had lived in Boston and Decorah, Iowa, before finally moving to Chicago in 1857. He began buying and selling pianos, and added to his sales by offering an installment plan, an unusual method of payment at that time. In 1880 he opened a reed organ factory (he built a total of 403,390 reed organs from 1880 to 1922), and eight years later he began manufacturing pianos.

The same year that John Hinners began building pipe organs, 1890, a young Englishman joined Kimball's staff. Frederic W. Hedgeland had been repairing organs in St. Paul, Minnesota, for several years, and had made plans for a portable pipe organ, small enough to be boxed and shipped anywhere, and presenting no installation problems. Kimball, like Hinners, understood the need for such an instrument in the Midwest's rural churches and small towns. While Hinners developed his solution to this problem along traditional lines, Kimball's instrument portrayed a new approach to the compact organ.

The Organ described some of the details of Kimball's Portable Pipe Organ:

> The Portable Pipe Organ of the W. W. Kimball Company is one of the most remarkable instruments now before the public. It is a real pipe organ, having six stops in the manuals and two in the pedal, as follows:

Great Organ:	Open Diapason, metal (lower 12 wood)	61
	Dulciana, metal	46
	Cornopean (impinging reeds)	46

Swell Organ:	Viola di Gamba, metal	46
	Stopped Diapason, wood	61
	Flute, wood (4 feet)	61
Pedal Organ:	Bourdon, 16 feet (reeds with qualifying tubes)	31
	Open Diapason, 16 feet (reeds with tubes)	31
Couplers:	Great to Pedal,	
	Swell to Great,	
	Swell to Pedal,	
	Octaves	

. . . The vibrators in the pedal stops are free reeds, blown by pressure, exhausting into qualifying tubes, which impart the soft, distant, and pervading effect proper to a pedal, without leaving anything perceptible of the flabby tone usual to pedal reeds. . . . All the action, draw-stop and key, is pneumatic. Every key has its valve or little pneumatic bellows. These operate upon a new principle, and cannot get out of order or cipher. All the pneumatics are carried by a six-inch wind. The pipes are blown by a three-inch wind.

All of the organ above described is brought within a compass of six feet wide, three feet, six inches deep, and seven feet high. The pedal keys project in front enough to make the total floor space required six feet square. The organ is packed by removing the pedal-board, which requires to turn one button and raise the board off the two dowels which hold it in place, then the entire keyboard and stop action come off by removing four screws. All the action detaches without unfastening anything beyond the button and the four screws above mentioned. The part remaining with the pipes and bellows is then six feet wide, seven feet high, and three feet, six inches deep. It can be boxed in a plain box, laid down upon its side, and even ended upon its head, without loosening or disarranging the pipes or any part of the action. Hence, it will go through any door or window affording a space three feet six, by six feet. It requires no expert to set it up.

. . . Here we have two wind supplies, one of six inches and one of three, all within a compass mentioned above, yet enough to run eight stops, with octave coupler, under all circumstances. This is, perhaps, the greatest marvel of all. It is done by a new system of feeders, and by putting the bellows of the heavy wind inside that for the light wind. The six-inch wind exhausts into the three-inch bellows, and, coming under less pressure, expands, and thus enables the supply to be kept up by feeders which, if operated upon a three-inch pressure, would be wholly incapable of doing the work. [365, pp.90–91]

The Portable Pipe Organ had a pipe clutch and rack holding the pipes in place during shipment, and presumably they were still in tune on arrival, ready to play. All one had to do was hook on the pedal board, attach the blower lever (it could be put on either end of the organ), and start pumping. The Kimball instrument came in several sizes, from one manual without pedal to two manuals and pedal.

With Hedgeland still in charge, Kimball began building "stationary" pipe organs in 1894; the first one was installed in the First Methodist Church, Kewanee, Illinois [25, p.181]. The Kimball firm continued manufacturing organs for nearly half a century, and competed successfully with the large organ firms in the East for a share of important contracts. In 1942, with declining profits in organ building and the war restrictions on materials, the organ factory was closed. The last Kimball organ, #7,326, was installed in the Hope Lutheran Church, Bucyrus, Ohio.

Chicago became the home of the Pilcher organ factory in 1862 or 1863 (see pp.167, 187). By this time Henry Pilcher had retired, and the business was in the hands of his sons, Henry, Jr., William, and Robert. From 1864 to 1866 the Pilchers had a partnership with an organist, W. H. Chant. Their work during this brief time included the rebuilding and enlargement of the organ in the Second Presbyterian Church, where Chant was organist. They also built an organ for the First Universalist Church, Chicago [18, p.425].

The Pilchers apparently thought they would be less affected by the Civil War in Chicago than in their former location in St. Louis. However, Chicago had its own perils, and their factory was destroyed in the 1871 fire. After this disaster, Henry Pilcher's Sons moved to Louisville, Kentucky. In this location their organs gained in popularity, especially in the South Central states. The interests of the Pilcher firm were purchased by M. P. Möller, Inc., in 1944.

Like most of their contemporaries, the Pilchers first built tracker-action organs, converting later to other forms of action. In their organs, too, the conversion was gradual, and tracker organs were still built for a considerable period after tubular-pneumatic action was introduced. As late as 1912, in Pilcher's Opus 744, tracker action was used for the manuals and tubular-pneumatic for the pedals [227]. One of the most famous of the nineteenth-century Pilcher organs was the three-manual tubular-pneumatic instrument exhibited at the Chicago Exposition in 1893 (see p.212–13).

Milwaukee: William Schuelke

William Schuelke was representative of the small builder, working along conservative lines. His shop operated in Milwaukee, Wisconsin, during the last quarter of the nineteenth century. When he died in 1902, the firm was taken over by his son Max. The early Schuelke organs were all tracker action, as were some of the early twentieth-century organs. Tubular-pneumatic action was also used in some of their organs, beginning in the 1890s.

Stop lists of Schuelke organs show more variety than do the rather standardized specifications of some builders, but the ensemble maintained its position of importance longer than it did in the work of most builders. After the turn of the century, the Great on even small organs still had a full Diapason chorus to 2′ pitch.

An organ described as the "oldest of the Schuelke organs still in use" was built in 1891 for a church in Iowa. An unusual feature is the appearance of two 8′ pedal stops.

St. Boniface Catholic Church, New Vienna, Iowa
WILLIAM SCHUELKE, 1891

Manual I		*Manual II (continued)*	
Principal	16′	Aeolian	8′
Melodia	8′	Fugara	4′
Viola da Gamba	8′	Flute Harmonique	4′
Principal	4′	*Pedal*	
Flute d'Amour	4′		
Quinte	2⅔′	Pedal Principal	16′
Octave	2′	Sub Bass	16′
Mixture, 3 fach	2′	Octave Bass	8′
Trompete	8′	Violoncello	8′
Manual II		*Couplers and Mechanical Stops*	
Bourdon	16′	Manual Coppe [Coppel]	
Organ Principal	8′	I Manual-Pedal	
Gedackt	8′	II Manual-Pedal	
Salicional	8′	Calcant	

[460, p.3]

Other Midwestern Builders

While the foregoing describes the work of a cross section of midwestern organ builders of the late nineteenth century, it is by no means a complete picture. Some of the other builders active during this time were:

Cleveland, Ohio: G. F. Votteler.

Cincinnati, Ohio: Closs & Hallenkamp; Joseph Lorenz; Alfred Mathers & Co.; James Schwer.

Salem, Ohio: Carl Barckhoff and Phillip Wirsching were both born in Germany, and both built organs in Salem, Ohio. Barckhoff (1849–1919), whose locations also included Pittsburgh and Latrobe, Pennsylvania, and Pomeroy, Ohio, was credited with building more than three thousand organs by the time of his death. Wirsching (1856–1928) was a good friend of George Ashdown Audsley, and the two men were associated in the building of a number of organs. Although the fine quality of his workmanship was recognized by some leading members of the profession, Wirsching never enjoyed a full measure of success, and the history of his company was broken by periodic financial reverses. The Wirsching Organ Co. closed in 1919.

Detroit, Michigan: A. A. Simmons had a shop in Detroit about 1865. He took James E. Clough into partnership, forming the firm of Simmons, Clough & Co. Later Simmons and his son retired, and the Warren brothers joined Clough, forming Clough & Warren. [520]. Other Detroit builders were Henry F. Hammer; Andrew Moeller; Louis Van Dinter; and William H. Vincent.

Chicago, Illinois: Ira Bassett; Blessing; Burdett; Coburn & Taylor; Davie, Jackson & Co.; A. Fischer & Co.; Lyon & Healy; Nicholson; George Prince; M. Schlaundecker; Tischer; and Wolfram & Haeckel.

Alton, Illinois: Joseph Gratian (1830–1897) learned organ building in England. He opened his shop in Alton, Illinois, in 1858, and most of his instruments were small tracker organs for nearby towns in Missouri and Illinois.

Chester and Jacksonville, Illinois: Jackson Organ Co.

Ripon, Wisconsin: John F. Lancashire was an English organ builder with the Willis firm. He came to Ripon to install a Willis organ, and remained to form the Marshall Brothers Organ Company, in association with four members of the Marshall family. This firm, with subsequent locations in Milwaukee, Moline, Illinois, and Rock Island, Illinois, changed its name many times: Lancashire & Turner, Moline Pipe Organ Co., Lancashire-Marshall Co., Marshall-Bennett Organ Co., Bennett Organ Co. The company built a large number of instruments, and under Lancashire's direction the quality was high. He died at the end of the century, and after that the quality declined rapidly.

Milwaukee, Wisconsin: Philip Odenbrett had been building reed organs and pipe organs in Waupun, Wisconsin. In 1867 he went to work for Marshall Bros. Organ Co. in Ripon, Wisconsin. By 1870 he was in Milwaukee, a partner in Odenbrett, Abler & Co., building parlor organs and melodians. He also built pipe organs independently and in partnership with his son. Other Milwaukee builders were Bernard Schaefer and George Weickhardt.

Watertown, Wisconsin: E. C. Gaebler.

Minneapolis, Minnesota: Bergstrom Organ Manufacturing Co.

St. Louis, Missouri: Bahner & Weber; Brazelton; Faust; Frederick K. Hertel; Jackson & Gallagher; Kunkell Bros.; Lady & Milford; Mayer & Ulbricht; Carl Otto; J. L. Peters; John G. Pfeffer; Sumner; G. Wienrich & Bros.

Louisville, Kentucky: August Prante.

The West

Organs in Texas

Texas ordered most of its post–Civil War organs from eastern builders, although a few were also supplied by Kilgen, Pilcher, and other midwestern organ firms. Texas also had its first local builders as early as 1860, and as one might guess, they were German. Working part-time, they produced only a few organs, in situations that remind one of the earlier builders in rural Pennsylvania. A small settlement of Germans had arrived in Texas in the 1830s. Furnas relates: "In 1870, thanks to persistent emigration from the *Vaterland*, San Antonio had more Germans and Alsatians than Americans, English and Irish combined" [59, p.389].

The first known organ builder was Traugott Wantke, an 1860 settler in the German community of Round Top, Texas. One of his organs, in the Evangelisch-Lutherische Bethlehems Kirche of Round Top, is a one-manual organ with eight stops, and he is known to have built two other small organs [137, pp.65–72].

Edward Pfeifer (1837–1907) worked as an organ builder in Germany. He settled first in New York in 1865, but after a year and a half he moved to Texas. There, nine years of farming ended in failure, and he finally moved to Austin in 1875, where he opened a music store. He also built several organs, making his own wooden pipes but buying the metal ones from a supplier in the East. Schurer lists five organs by Pfeifer: for Baylor University, Waco; the Protestant Church in New Braunfels (1898); Zion Lutheran Church, Walburg (1900); the Wendish community at Serbin (1904); and a two-rank positive organ [137, pp.73–80].

Across the Plains

If one wanted to travel west from Missouri to Denver at the close of the Civil War, it meant five days of punishment in the stagecoach. Samuel Bowles made that trip in 1865, and described the land across the plains from Nebraska:

> The region is substantially uninhabitable; every ten or fifteen miles is a stable of the stage proprietor, and every other ten or fifteen miles an eating-house; perhaps as often a petty ranch or farm-house, whose owner lives by selling hay to the trains of emigrants or freighters; every fifty or one hundred miles you will find a small grocery and blacksmith shop; and about as frequently is a military station with a company or two of United States troops for protection against the Indians. This makes up all the civilization of the Plains. [24, pp.20–21]

The fact that one could reach the West Coast by rail in 1869 was certainly a milestone in history, but equally important was the possibility of reaching all those places between the settled Midwest and the Pacific. That was not accomplished by one line; the Northern Pacific, Southern Pacific, and Santa Fe were all pushing west, and by 1884 all had reached the West Coast. The railroads meant new towns along the way, new markets for the farmers, and incidentally, new churches for the organ builders.

During the last three decades of the nineteenth century, 430 million more acres of land were occupied, and 225 million were placed under cultivation, a case of instant cultivation, perhaps, but not instant culture. While the old frontiers were fast disappearing, the Old West style of law and order was still to be found in the mining camps. Gold fever ran high with the opening of mines in the Snake River Valley of Idaho (1861), Montana (1863), and the Black Hills of South Dakota (1875).

And there were still the Indians, enough of them to give Samuel Bowles and his companions some anxious moments in 1865:

> The distance from Denver to Salt Lake City is six hundred miles; we should have driven it in five days but for the Indians, who broke in upon the line before us and cleaned it out of horses for fifty miles, threw the country into confusion and travel into anxiety, and delayed our progress for two or three days, so that we were in all seven days in the trip. But we just escaped more severe possible disaster; for the "pesky sarpints," as they were not unnaturally reckoned by everybody in the West, hovered close upon both our front and our rear; our escort drove off a band of them who were attacking a train of repentant and returning Mormons, right in our path; and they swooped in upon a stage station the night after we passed it, stole all its horses, killed the two stock-tenders, also three of the five soldiers who were located there as guard, and severely if not mortally wounded the other two. But though our escort was small over this line, never over ten cavalrymen, and sometimes none at all, our coach came through unmolested. [24, pp.67–68]

Although the Indian problem was never solved, the violence was over with the defeat of Chief Crazy Horse of the Sioux (1877) and the Apache Geronimo (1886).

By the time Bowles made his trip through Colorado, he could have seen Denver's first organ, brought from St. Louis in 1862 for St. Mary's Roman Catholic Church[6] [141, p.727]. He could also have met the first organ builder in Colorado, Charles Anderson (1836–1922), a Swedish jeweler who arrived in Colorado in 1862. He lived first in Blackhawk and later moved to Denver. Anderson is known to have built eleven instruments, among them the one-manual organ in Grace Church, Georgetown, the "oldest surviving pipe organ in the state and . . . the second one in the Colorado Territory" [234].

Organs by J. W. Steere & Son, William Schuelke, Farrand & Votey, and Roosevelt appeared in Colorado in the 1880s and '90s. George Ryder's Opus 101 for St. George's Episcopal Church, Leadville, was "brought up over Weston Pass in 1883 in an ox cart with Mr. Ryder in attendance" [234, p.33]. The most famous of Denver's early organs was the Roosevelt Opus 380, installed in 1888 in Trinity Methodist Church. With a case designed by Audsley and electric action, Opus 380 was in the latest style. Bratton notes: "Except for 10 of the 14 sets of reed pipes the organ remains tonally untouched" [234, p.45].

The first organ in the Dakota Territory was Marklove's Opus 146, installed in the Yankton Episcopal Church in 1887. Five years later, *The Organ* of July 1892 announced: "The first organ ever erected in the State of Wyoming has recently been built by Mr. Frank Roosevelt for St. Matthew's Cathedral, Laramie." It had two manuals and twelve voices.

Utah: The Salt Lake City Organ

At the time of its installation, the new organ for the Mormon Tabernacle in Salt Lake City was probably the most important instrument in the West. Even today, few organs in America can match its record for fame outside the circle of the organ profession. Of the original organ, little remains. It was subjected to revisions and enlargements in 1885, 1901, 1916, and 1948. But probably more important than the form of the instrument itself has been its use, its influence, and the interest in organs that it has stimulated. The Tabernacle organ was always used extensively in public performances. Beginning in 1900, biweekly recitals were held. In 1908, daily recitals during the summer months were inaugurated. In 1916, the schedule was increased to include daily recitals throughout the year, with additional evening recitals in the summer. The famed Tabernacle broadcasts began on a national network in 1929, and are believed to be the oldest continuous radio program [462], taking the sound of the Tabernacle choir, the organ and "the spoken word" to all parts of the country every Sunday morning.

The little organ Joseph Ridges built in Australia had been in use in the old Tabernacle since 1857 (see p.189). When plans for the present Tabernacle were being made, Ridges was asked to submit a proposal for a suitable organ, and his ideas were accepted. Preliminary work on the organ began in 1866, and in October of the next year the new organ, with fewer than half its pipes in place, was used for the thirty-seventh Semi-Annual Conference of the Church of Jesus Christ of Latter Day Saints.

Finally in 1869 the organ was almost completed, and the *Deseret News* of July 3 described some of the features of the new instrument:

THE NEW ORGAN

On entering the new Tabernacle today, we were filled with admiration at the beauty and grandeur of the great organ, now that the scaffolding has been removed and the organ case grained and varnished. Its cathedral-like shape, with immense towers and symmetrical proportions now stand out beautifully, and the entire work reflects great credit upon Brother Joseph Ridges, the designer and builder. When completed the organ will compare favorably with any in the world for its beauty of design and purity of tone. Brother Ridges informs us that a large amount of work has yet to be bestowed upon it and that the octave of immense pipes in front, which are now white, will be covered with gold leaf, and that many other smaller ornamental pipes have to be placed where the green drapery is now arranged, together with some beautifully carved panel work for the pedestal portion of the case. We have heard but one expression about the organ from the many visitors who have examined the workmanship and listened to its tones; they think it is a remarkable piece of mechanism to be built in this country, and that it is not inferior, as far as completed, to the Eastern and foreign made articles of its class.

Many stories are told of the work that went into the organ, and it is sometimes difficult to separate enthusiasm from reality. It is certain that Ridges had the help of craftsmen the equal of any in the country. This fact is well verified in the construction of the Tabernacle itself. There seems scant reason to doubt that the action, case, and wooden pipes were Salt Lake City products. Building them would pose no insurmountable obstacles to the industrious and devout Mormons, many of whom had walked hundreds of miles to Salt Lake City from the Midwest, taking their personal belongings with them in small handcarts.

Some of the stories of hauling logs by wagons from southern Utah to build the organ must be placed in the category of folklore, however, since Ridges and his cabinetmakers would hardly use lumber that had not been well seasoned for such an important project. True, the logs may have arrived in the city by that means at some earlier time.

Some parts of the organ, however, were not local products. McDonald tells us:

With $900 from church funds Mr. Ridges went to New York and Boston to purchase those items that could not be manufactured in

Utah. He procured spring wire, thin sheet brass, soft fluff leather for the valves, ivory for the keys, and other items unavailable in the West. These were brought into Salt Lake City by ox team from the nearest railroad. Although the fact cannot be verified, it is believed that these smaller items were purchased from the Simmons Organ Company of Boston and that about a thousand pipes were obtained a little later from the Samuel Pierce Company of that city. It seems feasible also to assume that it was at this time that Mr. Ridges was inspired to model his organfront after the casework of the Boston Music Hall organ. . . .[7]

[110, p.10]

Mormon Tabernacle, Salt Lake City, Utah
JOSEPH RIDGES, 1869

Great		Swell (continued)	
Bourdon	16'	Claribella	8'
Open Diapason	8'	Principal	4'
Stopped Diapason	8'	Stopped Flute	4'
Hohl Flute	8'	Piccolo	2'
Flute a Cheminee	8'	Mixture	II
Dulciana	8'	Hautboy	8'
Principal	4'	Bassoon	8'
Flute Harmonic	4'	Cromorne	8'
Twelfth	2⅔'		
Fifteenth	2'	*Pedal*	
Grave Mixture	III		
		Open Bass	16'
Swell		Dulciana Bass	16'
		Principal Bass	16'
Bourdon	16'	Stopped Bass	8'
Open Diapason	8'	Great Open Bass	32'
Stopped Diapason	8'		

[110, p.12]

McDonald comments on the finished two-manual organ:

> The casework of this organ cannot be considered without mentioning the large, round set of 32' open diapason pipes in the case. They are perhaps the only pipes of their kind in the world, being of a laminated wood construction. It is interesting to note that these pipes were constructed in the very same manner as the pillars supporting the gallery of the Tabernacle. Perhaps one craftsman built both.
>
> [110, p.13]

In 1885 the organ was enlarged by Niels Johnson to three manuals, forty-six speaking stops, with Great, Swell, Choir, and Echo divisions. Subsequent alterations and enlargements were the work of Kimball, Austin, and Aeolian-Skinner. The last named, in a 1948 revision under the direction of G. Donald Harrison, resulted in an instrument of 189 ranks of pipes.

Early Organs in Nevada

Nevada's first settlers were Mormons who arrived in 1847. Other denominations soon made appearances in the communities built by the gold seekers. Methodists were holding services in the late 1850s, the Roman Catholic church dated from 1860, and the next year saw the organization of the first Episcopal church in Nevada. The last two were in Virginia City.

The first organ in Nevada may have been the one installed in the Methodist Church in Austin, where, in 1867, was erected "the finest Methodist Church edifice in the State" [5, p.210]. How the Reverend J. L. Trefren obtained for his parish this building, "a splendid organ," and a parsonage is a story reflecting the business enterprise of the wild West.

As Trefren approached the members of his congregation about financing a church building, he found that nearly every member had mining claims, but money was another matter. They were ready and willing to pledge interest in these claims toward the erection of the church, so Trefren decided to accept their offers and use his ingenuity to turn them into cash.

First he pooled all the claims and organized the Methodist Mining Company. "The church was subsequently built on this magnificent claim, and considerable surplus capital remained with which to carry on operations underground" [5, p.210]. Here is how the Reverend Mr. Trefren got his money:

> He made a journey to the granite hills of New Hampshire, his native soil, and diligently labored with the brethren there. He unloaded on his brother parsons in New England. He pointed out to the faithful the brilliant prospects of his mine in the silver hills of Nevada, and the stock could not be disposed of rapidly enough for the demand. They saw, as though by intuition, how they could at the same time serve the Lord, do good, and make money. [5, p.210]

Trefren realized more than $250,000 from the sale of stock. The church, organ, and parsonage cost $35,000. The stock had been sold on the installment plan, but before the last installments were paid, the wildcat mine collapsed and the church was left with an indebtedness of $6,000. The property was sold to the county for a courthouse, but the Church Extension Society of the Methodist Episcopal Church advanced the money to redeem it. The church finally paid off its debt, and when all was said and done, the church owned property worth $35,000, for which it paid only $6,000.

Among the other early organs in Nevada was one in the Episcopal Church of Virginia City. The $3,000 organ was installed in the gallery in 1874 and was destroyed by fire the next year. In 1876 the church was rebuilt, and another organ installed [5, p.200], a two-manual, eighteen-rank instrument built by Alexander Mills of New York.[8] Another Mills organ was installed in St. George's Church, Austin, in 1878. This $1,000 organ was presented to the church by James S. Porteous [5, pp.202–203].

California: The San Francisco Area

California presented a scene of vivid contrasts. It was the California of Mark Twain's "Celebrated Jumping Frog of Calaveras County" and Bret Harte's "The Luck of Roaring Camp." It was also a California that could prompt Samuel Bowles to observe:

> In costliness of costume, too, there is apparent rivalry among the San Francisco ladies. . . . Perhaps in no other American city would the ladies invoice so high per head as in San Francisco, when they go out to the opera, or to party, or ball. Their point lace is deeper, their moire antique stiffer, their skirts a trifle longer, their corsage an inch lower, their diamonds more brilliant,—and more of them,—than the cosmopolite is likely to find elsewhere. [24, pp.325–26]

San Francisco was the center of trade, banking, and social life. The rough days were over, and the city had emerged. While some of the eastern cities were content to double or triple their populations, San Francisco's population swelled from 800 in 1848 to 56,800 in 1860, and to 298,997 in 1890.

Just when California mining was declining, the first of the rich Comstock silver mines was opened in 1859, the richest mines in the West. Most of the money found its way to San Francisco, creating multimillionaires among the men who financed the development of the mines, to say nothing of the wealth it brought to the firms that supplied everything from machinery to luxuries for the new mining towns.

Visitors from the East to San Francisco's first world's fair, the 1894 California Midwinter Exposition, found more than mining speculation among the city's unique features. There were the cable cars, a familiar sight to San Franciscans since 1873, the remarkable Chinese community, and a climate that had to be experienced to be believed.

The Tivoli Opera House was the center of musical activity. Artists and opera troupes from all parts of America and Europe performed there, and found a warm, western welcome.

> The Tivoli's proudest memory is Tetrazzini. "Doc" Leahy, Tivoli impresario, found her in a troupe stranded in Mexico. He brought her here and her triumph was immediate and prodigious. From San Francisco she moved on to Covent Garden and New York. But she kept returning to San Francisco after the fire. [48, p.168]

When Adelina Patti first appeared in San Francisco in 1884, the house was sold out and scalpers could name their prices for tickets. But the warmest welcome of all was inadvertently given to Caruso, who was in San Francisco for a Metropolitan Opera Company engagement at the Tivoli when the 1906 earthquake and subsequent fire destroyed most of the city.

The leading organist in San Francisco in the late nineteenth century was Humphrey John Stewart. He was born in London in 1856 and was a graduate of Oxford University. After his arrival in San Francisco in 1886, he held positions at the Church of the Advent, Trinity Church, and (after two years in the East) St. Dominic's Church. Stewart moved to San Diego in 1915, when he was invited to be official organist for the Exposition in that city.

Californians continued to send to the East for some of their organs. Typical is the story of the organ William Stevens built in 1863 for Trinity Episcopal Church, San Jose. This two-manual, twenty-four stop organ was transported by boat to the Isthmus of Panama, taken by cart across the isthmus, again loaded on a boat for San Francisco, and finally taken by wagon to the church. The organ cost about $1,200 and the freight added $800. The old organ was given to the St. James' Episcopal Church, Paso Robles, in 1924, where its centennial was observed in 1963 by a recital played by Richard Purvis [523]. Probably the most impressive organs in San Francisco in the last years of the century were the one built by James Treat for Grace Church (a three-manual organ with forty-seven speaking stops, installed in 1894) (see pp.244–46) and California's first four-manual organ, a Farrand & Votey instrument installed in St. Ignatius Church in 1896.

San Francisco's Organ Builders

In 1877 Felix Schoenstein (1849–1936) established a firm in San Francisco that has continued in business to the present time. He was born in Villigen, Baden, Germany, and learned music and organ building from his father, whose principal occupation was clockmaker.

Young Felix arrived in San Francisco in 1868 and became associated with one of the pioneer organ builders there, Joseph Mayer. He lived with the Mayer family, and was Mayer's foreman for about six years.

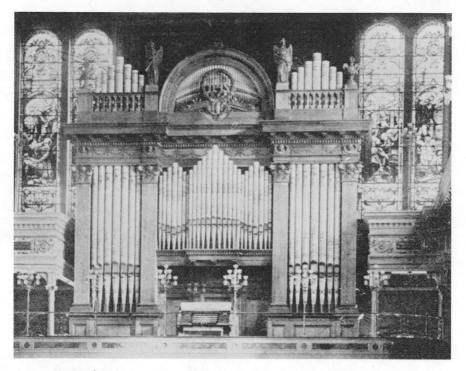

Farrand & Votey, 1896. Built for St. Ignatius Church, San Francisco. California's first four-manual organ. Destroyed in the earthquake and fire of 1906. *Photo courtesy Jim Lewis.*

Their largest organ was a three-manual instrument for Temple Emanuel (destroyed in 1906). When Mayer left organ building to look for gold, Schoenstein succeeded him in business, and among his largest instruments were those for St. Mark's Lutheran Church, San Francisco, and St. Mary's Church, Stockton.

Schoenstein was a skilled voicer, and was capable of making all parts of the organ. He cast his own pipe metal, and is also said to have produced "fine string stops made of wood" [286]. Following the trends of the day, he patented a tubular-pneumatic action in 1890.

Schoenstein continued building organs until the San Francisco earthquake struck in 1906. Forty churches that had organs were destroyed in the quake and the three days of fire that followed it. After that, Schoenstein installed organs for eastern builders and had a maintenance service [461, p.2]. In 1909, his son Louis joined him in business as a partner. Two other sons, Otto and Erwin, joined the partnership about 1929. The business is now under the management of Erwin Schoenstein.[9]

George Andrews and his son Charles were also early California builders. They had been building organs in Utica, New York, but in 1886 they moved to Oakland, believing that opportunities would be greater in the West. Andrews had a brief partnership with Thomas Whalley, but after constructing one instrument they dissolved this association. By 1904, when George Andrews died, he and his son had built twenty-eight organs in the West. Most of them were small- and medium-sized instruments for churches in the San Francisco area (see pp.168, 280).[10] Charles Andrews remained in business for two more years; after the earthquake he moved to Los Gatos, California, and became a rancher.

After his association with Andrews, Thomas Whalley (d.1930) entered into another brief partnership, Whalley & Genung. The company built only a few organs, but Whalley built many more independently. A Whalley & Genung organ of 1889 is still in use in the First Presbyterian Church, Port Townsend, Washington. It is said to be the oldest organ in the state. The manuals have a fifty-eight-note compass, the pedal twenty-seven. The Great contains 8′ Open Diapason, 8′ Dulciana, 8′ Melodia, 4′ Octave, 2⅔′ Twelfth, and 2′ Fifteenth; the Swell: 8′ Open Diapason, 8′ Stopped Diapason, 8′ Viola, divided 8′ Bassoon and Oboe (12–46), and 4′ Flute. The two Pedal stops are 16′ Double Open Diapason and 16′ Bourdon [220].

Other San Francisco builders during this time included Robert Farran, John McCraith, B. Shellard, W. S. Pierce, Woodworth, Allovan & Co., Antisell, Balch, Jno. Bergstrom, and Melville Clark.

Early Organs in Los Angeles

In the mid-1880s, with railroad connections south to Los Angeles established, the population of southern California began to grow. There had been fewer than 15,000 inhabitants in all of Los Angeles County in 1865, but by the end of the century the city alone had about 100,000 people, and 154 churches had been established.

According to Swan, the first organ in Los Angeles was the gift of Jotham Bixby to the Congregational Church in 1872 [152, p.117]. By 1883 the church had a new organ, made by the Bergstrom Company of San Francisco. It was considered the best instrument in town, although the Methodist Church had also installed an organ only the year before. The Congregational Church's third organ was built by Farrand & Votey in 1895.[11] Between 1895 and 1900 organ recitals were held there and at Simpson's Tabernacle, with Skeele's recitals at the Congregational Church outnumbering all others. Two famous visiting organists who gave recitals in Los Angeles during this time were Middelschulte and Eddy [89].

The first organ-building firm in Los Angeles was Fletcher & Harris, established in 1895. Their early organs were tracker-pneumatic, but they soon turned to tubular and electropneumatic actions. Murray M. Harris (d.1922) was the son of a Presbyterian minister, John H. Harris. He had worked for Hutchings, Plaisted & Co. before moving to the West [116, p.139]. Harris evidently had some business proficiency; Hopkins relates that he

> early became identified with the hyper-activity of the financial experts who were busily exploiting Los Angeles climate and land. From his own lips I learned that he was at one time on the Board of Directors in sixteen different promotion enterprises, being President of six.
>
> [329, p.62]

With typical western aplomb, Harris had as his slogan "The Finest Organ in the World." Henry C. Fletcher soon left the partnership and moved to Phoenix. Edward L. Crome was brought into the company at an early date, and he remained "for some years the moving spirit in mechanical matters" [329, p.62].

In 1895 Fletcher & Harris built the first organ constructed in Los Angeles, for the Episcopal Church at Sierra Madre [152, p.174n]. When it was completed, the *Los Angeles Daily Times* of December 3, 1895 announced a demonstration program that included several Los Angeles organists and other soloists:

> The performers at the organ recital at Fletcher & Harris's Hall, Nos. 325–329 New High Street, this evening will be Mr. Dunster, organist of St. Paul's Episcopal Church; Mr. Wyckoff, organist Immanuel Presbyterian Church; Mr. Colby, organist Simpson Tabernacle, and Mr. Fletcher, organist First Universalist Church, Pasadena. The soloists of the evening will be Miss Bernice Holmes and Miss Lulu Baittie. Mr. Harris will play the flute. The recital will be given in commemoration of the completion of the first pipe organ ever constructed in Los Angeles, which has just been built by Messrs. Fletcher & Harris for the Episcopal Church at Sierra Madre.

One of Murray M. Harris's first large instruments was built for the First Methodist Church, Los Angeles. The high point in this period of his career came with the construction of a three-manual, fifty-seven stop organ for Stanford University Memorial Church in 1901.

PART FIVE

Organs in the Twentieth Century

XV

THE ORCHESTRAL ORGAN

Introduction
Progress and Problems

WITH the opening of the new century a new age was at hand. The frontier was gone, and Americans turned their efforts to shrinking still more the distance from the Atlantic to the Pacific. The railroad was the major means of transportation between cities, and many more miles of track were laid. However, the ride of the future was coming into view with the Wright brothers' flight in 1903 and the automobile. There were 8,000 passenger car registrations in 1900, and by 1913 the number had increased to 1,250,000. By 1900 there were over a million telephones in the United States. A New Yorker could place a call to Chicago, but he had to wait until 1911 to reach Denver and until 1915 to call San Francisco. The greater ease of transportation and communication between distant cities, coupled with the ever-increasing consumer market, was a boon to large industries. U.S. Steel (formed in 1901) was the country's first billion-dollar corporation, and the government had its hands full trying to control it and other industrial giants. Antitrust legislation became an urgent issue.

Immigration reached its all-time high during the early twentieth century. Six times between 1905 and 1914 the annual immigration rose to over a million. However, there was a distinct change in the source of this population growth; most of the new arrivals came from eastern and southern Europe, particularly Russia, Italy, and Austria, diluting the effects of the large number of Germans who had arrived in the nineteenth century. The entrance of the United States into World War I further reduced the German influence in American society, and dealt a deathblow to many German societies and schools.

America was fast changing from a rural to an urban society, and keeping them "down on the farm" became ever more difficult. The rush to the urban centers contributed vastly to the problems of the cities, which were ill equipped to cope with such skyrocketing social problems as slums and wretched working conditions. There was an abundance of material to fill the magazine articles and books of the muckrakers who sought to expose the worst of the urban conditions contributing to human suffering. But the cities were not entirely bad, and certainly their growth offered many advantages to the more fortunate segments of society.

Musical Developments

Permanent orchestras were established in many cities during the early decades of the twentieth century. However, public support was not so enthusiastic as to assure the continued existence of orchestras devoted too strictly to the symphonic repertoire. Conductors were under constant pressure to popularize their programs. Even in New York, Gustav Mahler met with strong opposition to the "heavy" programs he performed when the New York Philharmonic was under his baton (1909–11). Musicians like the Kneisel Quartet, who were able to set their standards high and who were financially able to maintain those standards regardless of public support, were indeed rare.

Whatever obstacles were in the path of orchestras, the sound of a large aggregation of musicians had an unmistakable appeal, and for the music lover the symphony orchestra became something of a musical Olympus. While opera also grew in prestige in the largest cities, it was not as easily taken on tour, nor could the smaller cities hope to muster the nucleus of a local opera company.

The European influence maintained its traditional hold on American concert music. The American artist's chances of survival were so small that a talented young Miss Hickenlooper from San Antonio, Texas, was prompted to change her name to Olga Samaroff. The music of Charles Ives, almost all composed before 1921, remained virtually untouched until recent times.

Popular music was another matter. In the early twentieth century ragtime came into its own, Sousa was practically a national hero, and the Irish-born Victor Herbert captured many American hearts with "Kiss Me Again" and "Ah! Sweet Mystery of Life." Popular songs ran the gamut from "Sweet Adeline" to Irving Berlin's "Alexander's Ragtime Band."

World War I actually had more effect on concert music than on popular music, if one discounts the rash of patriotic songs. Fritz

Kreisler, who had been in the Austrian army, retired from the concert stage for the duration. Karl Muck, conductor of the Boston Symphony from 1906 to 1908 and 1912 to 1918, was ignominiously victimized by rumor, riots, imprisonment, and finally deportation. Patriotism extended to banishing German works from the repertoire. Even Beethoven was classed as an enemy alien, and Wagner was banned until late in 1919. Bach's music was so infrequently performed that its elimination caused little excitement.

When business-as-usual was resumed after the war, music in American life was swayed by a new commercialism. The radio and phonograph gave particular rewards to writers of popular songs, the jazz age developed its own set of virtuosi, and the cream of the crop could be heard in one's living room. Concert musicians, too, profited from the stay-at-home audience, and the sale of records of serious music showed a steady increase. The unique figure who managed to bridge the chasm that separated the popular idioms from the concert repertoire was George Gershwin.

Hollywood was the hub of the infant movie industry after 1913. Its dream became reality in the 1920s with the formation of such big companies as Loew's (M.G.M.), Warner Brothers, and Columbia. The silent screen stars became a new breed of national idol, as the whole country ogled the pantomimes of Mary Pickford, Rudolph Valentino, Douglas Fairbanks, and Harold Lloyd. The music accompanying the silent screen was sometimes supplied by an orchestra, but more often by that creative and thoroughly American musician, the theater organist. When the movies became vocal in the late 1920s they opened up new channels for the popular composer, but they switched off many a Mighty Wurlitzer.

During the 1920s many of Europe's finest performers and conductors came to America looking for greener pastures than postwar Europe could provide. They could not have arrived at a better time, for this decade, with its relative affluence, was ready to make music as never before. An unprecedented number of professional orchestras were formed, but at least as important was the grass-roots development that resulted in literally thousands of semiprofessional community orchestras and thousands more school orchestras. The violin was really brought home to the living room.

The old traditional European study for the music student had to come to a sudden halt during the war. Afterwards, with the arrival in America of a generous supply of internationally famous artist-teachers, European training seemed less essential. Professional music study in America was further enhanced by the establishment of the Eastman School of Music (1918), the Juilliard Graduate School (1924), and the

Curtis Institute of Music (1924). Even so, Paris welcomed a parade of budding young composers eager to study with Nadia Boulanger.

Concert Organists

Among the visiting artists who toured America during the first quarter of the century were three distinguished French organists: Alexandre Guilmant had already concertized in the United States, and his return in 1904 was welcomed with enthusiasm; Joseph Bonnet made his first extended tour here in 1917; and Marcel Dupré made his American debut in 1921. American organists had much to learn from the repertoire of these performers. When Bonnet gave two recitals at Emmanuel Church in Boston, the first was devoted to pre-Bach composers and Bach, and the second included organ works of Schumann, Liszt, Guilmant, Franck, Bonnet, Foote, and Widor. Dupré astounded the organ world with his brilliant improvisations in large forms, and his transcontinental tours in the years that followed were received with great enthusiasm. In 1922–23 he played 96 recitals in America. The next season he gave 110, and included the first complete performance in America of Bach's organ works (at the Church of St. Andrew and St. Paul, Montreal) [471, p.27].

But by this time there were also virtuoso performers on this side of the Atlantic. Foremost among them was Lynnwood Farnam, a native of Canada. Farnam became organist of the Emmanuel Church, Boston, in 1914. After serving in the war, he accepted the post as organist at Fifth Avenue Presbyterian Church, New York, and later moved to the Church of the Holy Communion.

The Organ Industry

Focus on Large Companies

Just as big industries in other fields grew at the expense of small businesses, in part because of advances in transportation and communication, the large organ companies also benefited. The advantages that small, local builders had had in proximity to the customer were diminished. Many small builders found themselves unable to meet the competition, and either went out of business or contented themselves with installing the organs of the larger companies and rebuilding and maintaining local organs.

A summary of census reports shows that 94 establishments were building organs in 1904. The number dropped to 85 in 1914 and to 68 in 1919. During the 1920s the number fluctuated between 56 and 63. But in spite of the smaller number of companies, the average annual value of the products produced in the 1920s was approximately twice that of the years 1904 to 1919. In other words, fewer companies were building more organs. The largest drop in the number of organ-building firms occurred between 1914 and 1919; at least part of this slump can be attributed to the war.

The Effects of World War I

By the early part of 1918 the organ industry was beginning to feel the effects of national mobilization, although by no means to the extent that would later result from World War II. The Organ Builders' Association of America, with John T. Austin as president, was formed partly as an outgrowth of the industry's attempt to evaluate what the war effort required of it and what steps should be taken. In May 1918 *The Diapason* announced that Washington had ordered a 30 percent cut in organ construction to conserve fuel, transportation facilities, and raw materials. Manufacturers were being permitted to determine the best method of curtailing their production.

Evidently the results were not extremely damaging to the industry, for in August 1918 *The American Organist* could report:

> Another feature which has been established after careful investigation is that the building world has not been hampered by lack of labor any more than any other industry, and that interference on the part of the Government has been more a myth than a reality. Those builders who have been enterprising and using their usual methods in advancing their work have had plenty of it, and have been permitted to proceed without curtailment other than that which is the natural result of the chaotic conditions of to-day.

The unfortunate war victims in the organ world included some fine old instruments that were "modernized" as a part of the effort to conserve materials. Sad as that was, one may be assured that under normal circumstances many of the old instruments would have been discarded completely. C. S. Losh suggested:

> The tonal material of a dozen of the older builders from Henry Erben down to the end of the past century is of a high order of merit and well worthy of preservation in a new instrument. The range in power and color of tone is of course not comparable with an instrument of the present day but the application of electro-pneumatic devices, especially duplex action, and the inclusion of a few modern stops of larger scale and more pronounced tone color, will produce an instrument that to the taste of many is superior to a simon-pure modern organ. . . .
>
> The old pipes will gain by a limited increase in wind pressure with skillful re-cutting of mouths and re-nicking. Some Diapasons may be

made to sound very modern by leathering the lips. Slide tuners should be applied to the pipes without a tuning slot. . . .

Beautiful Harmonic Flutes have been made from old Mixture and Fifteenth pipes; Gross Flutes of great beauty and effectiveness from old Flute D'Amour sets, and many other radical transformations of tone quality with only slight changes in the structure of the pipe, but it is needless to say that such work can only be undertaken by voicers of great skill and experience. . . .

The most hopeless sounding old reeds are valuable for the bells. With new tongues, eschalots and partly or wholly capped, the most delightful Horns and Oboes are produced. An old wooden Trombone is a magnificent beginning for a fine modern high pressure Tuba. An old Trumpet or Clarion may form the treble of such a stop if used harmonically—that is an octave higher than the old pitch. [353]

Company Representatives

As the larger organ companies widened their horizons and competition got keener, it became the practice for each company to have its own representatives in various parts of the country. Often a local organ firm or a person engaged primarily in organ maintenance would represent a larger company. When an organist served in this capacity, a question of ethics entered the picture, and more than a few members of the profession frowned on such an arrangement. This disapproval had been voiced many times before. In 1877 William H. Clarke wrote:

> Church organ-builders who are known for their honorable transactions and excellency of their work, do not employ agents or pay commissions. Organists and musical people who speak highly of their efforts do so voluntarily from their experience with the intrinsic merits which their instruments possess. [37, p.89]

There was a fine distinction between the representative and the organist who accepted a commission. While the commission might be a just payment, it carried a faint odor of bribery. An editorial in *The Diapason* of January 1913 explained:

> Many builders complain that in places where conditions were favorable to them they find a sudden loss of favor and of the expected contract because a rival has held out a commission to the organist or some member of the committee making the purchase.
>
> This is a hard problem to solve. There is naturally a desire on the part of a builder to recompense an organist who has taken the trouble, probably from honest conviction, to champion his cause, and there it all starts. Often, too, a church—frequently a strange one—asks an organist to give his expert advice and expend his time without

any return in order to assist it. The only way out is to take a commission from the builder. . . .

And as for the churches, which always have expected much for nothing from the organ builders, they should select, for their own good, only capable and conscientious organists as advisers at the time of purchase, and should pay them for their trouble.

Organ Builders

The largest and most influential builders in the eastern part of the country during this time were all comparative newcomers: Möller, Austin, and Skinner. The old, established firms were moving into their twilight years, and one heard less and less of Hook & Hastings and other companies that had been in the foreground of nineteenth-century organ building.

In the Midwest, Kimball and Kilgen continued to be leaders in Chicago and St. Louis, while the Pilcher family ruled the area around Louisville. Organ building went crashing to the ground along with most of the city of San Francisco in 1906. In Los Angeles, organ-building history had just begun with the opening of Murray Harris's shop.

Some of the old-line builders died, and others closed their shops for one reason or another. Whatever the causes, there was considerable turnover in the organ industry from 1900 to 1925. The Carl Barckhoff Co. failed in 1913 after floods in the Ohio River valley caused much damage and destroyed all accounts and records; Francis Hastings died in 1916; Hutchings went out of business in 1917; the A. B. Felgemaker shop was closed the next year; and in 1921 the Steere factory was sold to Skinner.

On the other hand, some of the builders who continued in business during all or part of this time were Odell, Midmer (became Midmer-Losh in 1920), Harry Hall, Schantz, Hinners, Schuelke, Bennett, and Durner. Among the companies entering the field of organ building were Hillgreen-Lane (1898), Wangerin-Weickhart (1903), Wicks (1906), Kimball, Smallman & Frazee (1910), and Reuter-Schwarz (1917). The Estey and Wurlitzer companies had been manufacturing musical instruments in the nineteenth century; their first pipe organs date from 1901 and 1910, respectively.

M. P. Möller was an astute business man, with interests that extended well beyond organ building. When he was first elected president of the National Association of Organ Builders in 1920, he was also president of Crawford Automobile Co., W. H. Reisner Manufacturing Co., New York Central Iron Works, and Home Builders' Building and Loan Association. He held other offices or was on the board of directors of an impressive list of other companies and organizations.

Expansion continued in the Möller plant. By 1920 it had produced more than three thousand instruments, and in May 1921, the company's ad in *The American Organist* claimed:

> Our present capacity of two hundred and fifty organs per year is being increased as rapidly as possible to meet the unprecedented demand and insure early delivery of all orders. Fourteen service stations are maintained in different parts of the country to care for future tuning.

Möller could boast that his plant was the largest in the world devoted exclusively to the manufacture of pipe organs. No area within that field escaped his attention; the company built theater organs and residence organs, as well as instruments for schools, churches, and auditoriums.

When Ernest M. Skinner left the Hutchings factory in 1901, his first organ was built for the Unitarian Church, Ludlow, Vermont. This little two-manual organ had seven stops, three of them duplexed. But by 1925 T. Scott Buhrman could write: "There are about five hundred Skinner Organs in the world today, with perhaps fifty more under contract. California contributed $350,000 in contracts in less than two years. In New York City there are nine Skinner 32′ Diapasons" [237, p.179]. At that time the largest Skinner organ was a five-manual, 160-stop organ in the Cleveland Auditorium.

Skinner had no patience with opposing viewpoints, and throughout his long career the pages of the organ journals were colored by his sharp criticisms and stinging rebuttals. He claimed a number of inventions, many of which were adaptations or improvements of mechanisms already in use. While that in no way detracted from their usefulness, it led to countless letters to editors when the inventions were credited to someone else.

He designed his own electropneumatic action, shutter design and swell action, register crescendo, and combination action. He could well claim to be the originator of some aspects of these designs. His organs had distinctive tonal features, and the voices that Skinner either designed or felt were particularly characteristic of his work were Erzahler, Orchestral Oboe, English Horn, French Horn, Kleine Erzahler, Gross Gedeckt, Corno di Bassetto, Tuba Mirabilis, French Trumpet, Orchestral Bassoon (16′), Gamba Celeste, Bombarde (32′), and Violone (32′) [237, p. 183].

From about 1910 to about 1930 Ernest Skinner was at the peak of his popularity, and his position as one of the leading American builders was well deserved. He was a master craftsman, and his organs were refined expressions of his concept of tonal beauty. Skinner could achieve a remarkable degree of unity and cohesion in his organs, and attempts to "modernize" them seldom leave one in doubt about where Skinner left off and the revisions began.

By 1924 the Austin company had built over 1,300 instruments, including one five-manual organ and 108 four-manual organs. Six of their organs had over one hundred stops [202]. John and Basil Austin developed the typical Austin-type console in the first decades of the century. By eliminating the need for wind in the console and by using stop-tongues rather than draw-knobs, the Austins designed a console that was much smaller than those most builders were using; and their capture-type combination action, perfected in the 1920s, could not be surpassed for reliability. The mechanical excellence of the Austin organs was no small factor contributing to their popularity. Coleberd attributes "no less than forty-eight patents for inventions pertaining to the pipe organ" to John T. Austin [256, p.14]. In 1917 he was awarded the Edward Longstreth Silver Medal by the Franklin Institute of Philadelphia for achievement in invention and improvement of machines and mechanical processes.

The Secular Organ
Municipal Organs

While most builders still relied on churches for the greater part of their business, organs reached an unprecedented popularity as instruments for concerts, entertainment, and education. Larger cities and towns throughout the country began experimenting with municipal music programs during the second decade of the twentieth century. Appropriations ranged from about $5,000 to $30,000 to support such activities as orchestra and band concerts, organ recitals, singing societies, and individual and class instruction in piano and violin. Portland, Maine, claims to have the first municipal organ in America, a gift to the citizens of that city from the Philadelphia publisher Cyrus Curtis. It was built in 1912 by the Austin Organ Co. and installed in the Portland City Hall. Dr. Will C. Macfarlane was the first organist, and he established a series of organ recitals that is still continued. After the first year of recitals on the new organ, *The Diapason* of February 1914 reported that attendance had reached a total of about 225,000.

The opening of a large new municipal organ was an occasion of major importance. When the E. M. Skinner organ in the Cleveland Municipal Auditorium was opened, *The Diapason* of October 1922 reported that more than 20,000 attended and an estimated 5,000 more were turned away. Edwin Arthur Kraft was the recitalist. "Beginning with the national anthem, he gradually built a musical edifice that, crowned with five Wagnerian selections, brought his audience to such a pitch of enthusiasm that even the excessive heat failed to dampen it."

Exhibition Organs

The publicity attached to building a large organ for a fair or exhibition continued to attract organ builders, and competition was keen for contracts to install the instrument in the concert hall of an exhibition of major importance. Competition was equally keen among organists for recital appearances at the fairs.

The organs for the fairs in both San Diego and San Francisco remained in those cities as municipal organs. The Panama-California Exposition in San Diego opened in 1915. Its Austin organ with sixty-one speaking stops was the gift to the city of John D. Spreckels and his brother Adolph. This instrument is still in its original location, in a weatherproof concrete house on the stage of the open-air amphitheater in Balboa Park. Humphrey John Stewart became the exposition's official organist, and he remained in San Diego as the executive head of municipal music. Stewart's official report for 1917 shows the extensive use that was made of this organ:

Organ Recitals given		307
By Dr. Stewart	267	
By visitors	40	
Omitted because of weather		10
Electric current failures		2
Special Concerts		15
Unfavorable weather in five years		28
Compositions played in 1917		2,492
Played by Dr. Stewart		2,170
Played by visitors		322
Composers represented		350

The Panama-Pacific Exposition in San Francisco threw the organ world into turmoil. American organists were incensed when the announcement was made in 1914 that an Englishman, Edwin H. Lemare, had been engaged as the principal organist for the exposition and that he was also to design the console for the 111-voice Austin organ. In spite of the opposition, Lemare not only fulfilled his engagement at the exposition, but stayed on as municipal organist after the organ was moved from the Festival Hall to the Civic Auditorium.

Residence Organs

For some twenty years, until about 1930, the installation of residence organs furnished the elegant music rooms of the wealthy with status symbols and helped to line the pockets of the organ builders. The Aeolian Company specialized in this field, but one could also choose from a wide selection of other builders, among them Skinner, Möller, Austin, and Kimball.

Aeolian had been making automatic player mechanisms for both reed organs and pianos, and the adaptation of a similar device to the organ was largely responsible for the popularity of residence organs. Few who were blessed with the money to buy such organs were able to play them. Organ rolls were either fully automatic or semiautomatic. All aspects of performance were cut into the fully automatic ones, but semiautomatic rolls offered do-it-yourself registration and expression. Skinner advertised:

> With no technical knowledge you can learn to play these beautifully arranged rolls in a few hours with orchestral brilliancy absolute master of the expression, the tempo, the phrasing.

It was natural that the mechanical mind of John Austin would produce a player system. Coleberd has described the computerlike feats the Austin automatic player could perform:

> The Austin self-player mechanism operated three 61-note manual keyboards, the 32-note pedal keyboard, 32 speaking stops, two sets of expression shades, and the crescendo device. The magazine-type Austin player could perform twenty different compositions in any sequence pre-selected by the operator, thereby affording a recital of some two hours' duration. After the last number had been played the entire mechanism, including the organ blower, came to rest automatically.[1] [256, p.16]

In the late 1920s the Möller company introduced an automatic organ called the Artiste (a name applied later to a small standard organ). The process for cutting rolls for this instrument differed from other systems in that the artist had only to determine the rhythm. The notes, cut by a technician, required no actual playing. Using this process, the number of parts that could be reproduced were not limited by practical performance possibilities. Melodies could be given a solo treatment, or a massive harmonic style could be used at will. The Möller Artiste was particularly suited to playing orchestral transcriptions, and most of the rolls cut for this instrument were of that nature [218, p.542]. The Artiste was put on the market too late, however; the depression brought to an end the demand for such luxury items.

One American-built chamber organ with automatic player had a romantic history. In the early 1900s George Ashdown Audsley and J. Burr Tiffany formed the Art Organ Company, a not-too-successful attempt to market chamber organs designed by Audsley. The Wirsching Organ Company (see p.305) was engaged to build the instruments, and one was displayed in Steinway Hall in New York. Robert Coleberd, Jr., has recounted the subsequent events:

> Among those who inspected the demonstration instrument in Steinway Hall was H. P. Gibbs, an engineer with the General Electric Company who was on loan to the province of Mysore, India, and who had seen the organ while on a return trip to America. He described the wondrous instrument to the musically educated Maharajah of Mysore who then contracted with Wirsching to build one for his ornate new palace. This instrument was installed in 1908 by Stanley Williams, an English organ builder . . . who began working for Wirsching in 1906.[2] The local press was much awed by the self-player, commenting that his majesty the Maharajah could now listen to Guilmant's "Grand Chorus," Barnby's "Sweet and Low," or Batiste's "Offertoire" by means of this marvelous mechanism which, it noted in italics, was capable of playing the solo part on one manual and the accompaniment on the other. Western technology had now entered the drawing room of India's upper class. [258, pp.25–26]

Theater Organs

The history of the theater organ generally spanned the same period as that of the residence organ, and these two special types of instruments contributed greatly, if briefly, to the prosperity of the organ industry. Organists, too, shared in that prosperity. In Philadelphia salaries for theater organists ranged from $35 to $60 a week in 1917. At the same time the annual salary for church organists in that city ranged from $50 to $3,000; the average was $600 [61, pp.328–29].

The theater organ, too, had its specialists, and Wurlitzer and Robert Morton were among the best known. However, every major builder acquired some of the contracts that were supplied by this new field. Kimball built more theater organs than church organs during the 1920s, and Möller supplied a large number of organs for the Fox and Loew theaters. The Austin organ for the Eastman Theater in Rochester claimed fame as the world's largest theater organ. Its specification contained 134 ranks plus an assortment of 30 traps.

School Organs

In addition to organs blossoming forth in colleges and universities, some were also installed in high schools. New York City had ten high school organs by 1914. The largest was a four-manual Möller in Washington Irving High School. Its forty-six ranks were augmented to sixty-three stops, but the Pedal was given only one independent rank, a 16' Bourdon.

Möller was particularly successful in obtaining commissions to install organs in New York City schools because of the influence of Caleb Whittier Cameron, organ architect for the New York City Board of Education and director of its high school recitals. In 1919 Cameron left this post to become the Möller representative in the Midwest. Möller's popularity in the New York schools continued; the firm received seven new contracts for three-manual organs in 1925, bringing the number of organs in New York public schools to nineteen, seventeen of them by Möller.

But the largest and most famous high school organ of this time was located in another city, constructed by another firm. The 1924 Atlantic City High School organ was designed by Emerson Richards and built by Midmer-Losh. Its five manuals controlled eighty-six ranks, augmented to 165 stops.

Organs on the Radio

Broadcasting stations were a little slow in exploiting the organ. Studios with organs were rare, and the technical problems of broadcasting from a location removed from the station were not entirely solved. In 1923 Parke Hogan described the initial steps in organ broadcasting:

> Prior to November, 1922, more or less numerous attempts were made to broadcast organ music. These efforts, however, were of a sporadic nature so far as organ music per se was concerned, and most of the organ music broadcast was that incidental to church services.
>
> In November, 1922, the Westinghouse Electric Company, in its quest for an organ which had the tonal requirements, and was compactly built, discovered the residence organ in the studios of the Estey Organ Company. Arrangements were made which were mutually agreeable to the Estey Company and the Westinghouse Company, and a permanent wire was installed between the Estey studio at 11 West Forty-ninth street, New York, and the broadcasting station at Newark, N. J. Nov. 26 the first of a definitely planned series of organ recitals was broadcast. [317]

Foreign Influences

To understand the style of the American organ of the first decades of the new century, one must refer to the ideas proposed to organists and builders by two men from abroad. One was from England and the other from Scotland, and each in his own way won many disciples.

Robert Hope-Jones

The most controversial figure to enter the American organ industry in the early twentieth century was Robert Hope-Jones (1859–1914). An electrical engineer for an English telephone company, Hope-Jones was an enthusiastic, if amateur, church musician. In 1887, with the help of volunteer choir members, he constructed a movable electric console for the church of St. John's, Birkenhead, where he was then serving as organist. He decided to devote his full attention to organ building, and by 1893 Everett Truette's publication, *The Organ,* was carrying a series of articles on "The Hope-Jones System of Electrical Organ Control." In that same year, Hope-Jones's American debut was an electric action and console for the organ in St. Thomas' Episcopal Church, Taunton, Massachusetts.

Such was the fame of Hope-Jones, that when organ builders learned he was coming to America in 1903, they clamored for his services. Robert Pier Elliot (1871–1941) was at that time a member of the Austin firm, and it was evidently his influence that brought Hope-Jones into the Austin fold. This relationship was short-lived, and less than a year later, while Elliot was out of town, Hope-Jones's resignation was effected. Elliot, none too pleased with this turn of events, left Austin soon after. He founded the Kinetic Engineering Company, spent some time mining in Mexico and South America, and returned to become president of the Hope-Jones Organ Company in 1909.

Meanwhile, Robert Hope-Jones became a vice president of the Ernest M. Skinner Co. in 1905, and two years later he formed the Hope-Jones Organ Company at Elmira, New York. The first issue of *The Diapason* (December 1909) reported: "For the last two years the Hope-Jones Organ Company has steadily employed seventy hands and it continues to send out its organs at the rate of about one every three weeks. . . ." But the firm lasted only three years. Mounting financial difficulties faced the company, and in 1910, with about forty organs completed, the Hope-Jones factory was closed. Patents were taken over by the Rudolph Wurlitzer Co., North Tonawanda, New York, and Hope-Jones was placed (at least nominally) in charge of the Wurlitzer organ factory. On September 13, 1914, Hope-Jones took his life; the coroner's verdict was suicide while insane [446].

Hope-Jones had revolutionary ideas about organ design, and the instrument that ultimately resulted from these ideas was appropriately called the Unit Orchestra. It found a home in countless theaters throughout the country as a substitute for an orchestra, providing accompaniment for silent films. His ideas also seeped into the specifications of church organs, and it is here that they became a point of particular contention. Sumner concluded that his influence on organ design, both in England and America, was "entirely unfortunate" [151, p.242].

Hope-Jones's most famous organ was built in 1907 for the Auditorium at Ocean Grove, New Jersey. In 1910 he gave a lecture for the National Association of Organists explaining the design of this organ, its unique features, and something of his philosophy of organ building. He traced the opposition that changes in organ style and mechanism had usually met from experienced organists. Having practiced and studied for years to master the instrument, he said, these men "are not likely now to approve some modification in the organ that will necessitate their unlearning their life acquired methods and beginning the study of the instrument afresh" [80, p.1]. Mixtures were a prime target of Hope-Jones, as he spoke of "the absurd 'mixture work' so vigorously defended by the older school . . ." [80, p.2].

The extraordinary features of the Ocean Grove organ are best described by Hope-Jones himself, in excerpts from his lecture:

Expression: Is it not obvious that every stop and every pipe of every organ should, as a matter of course be enclosed?

. . .

In these organs I build, the swell shutters are located immediately over the open ends of the pipes so that when they are opened the tone passes straight upward into the building without any impediment.

Swell boxes should not be made of wood. . . . By using a cement construction I am able to obtain vastly superior results. A cement box when closed with my patent aluminum vacuum shutters, with sound trap joint, will reduce the power of any stop many thousand percent.

. . .

With sound trap boxes of this kind the costly necessity for putting soft stops in an organ disappears. Every stop may be powerful when its box is open; for we know that closing its shutters reduces the power of the largest open diapason below that of the softest dulciana or aeoline.

. . .

High Pressures: Twenty years ago a pressure sufficient to lift a column of water three or three and a half inches, was practically universal. In this organ before you the pressures employed are ten inches, twenty-five inches and fifty inches.

. . .

The leathered lip for flue pipes and the "pneumatic blow" to strike reed tongues that would otherwise prove too thick to start promptly enable us to secure increased refinement from increased pressure.

. . .

Diaphone (Patent): The basis of this organ we have been examining is the Diaphone. It is the most powerful foundation stop in the instrument. This particular Diaphone resembles a Diapason in tone quality, but many distinct colors of tone can be produced from a Diaphone. This one that I hold in my hand is a diaphonic flute. It consists, as you see, of a small aluminum piston which rapidly and freely vibrates in an enclosing cylinder. Though the whole thing is scarcely larger than my two fists it would (if supplied with air of sufficient pressure) produce a sweet musical note that could be heard twenty miles away.

. . .

Unit Organ (Patent): This Ocean Grove instrument is a "Unit Organ," though from the limitation in funds, necessarily a skeleton one. Months before its completion the "Unit Organ" had developed on the following published lines.

The old departments of Pedal, Great, Swell, Choir, and Solo are abandoned in favor of Foundation, Spring, Woodwind, Brass, and Percussion departments. Each of these latter is enclosed in its own independent cement swell box. The whole organ is treated as a unit. Practically any of the stops may be drawn upon any of the manuals (or on the pedal) at any pitch.

The Foundation department contains the Diaphone, the Tibias, and two or three Diapasons. The Strings department contains a couple of mild and robust Gambas, two or three very keen viol d'orchestres, a Quintaton Flute for furnishing the deep body tone often heard in strings, a Vox Humana Celeste, and perhaps my new Vox Viola—in fact any stops that go to make up a thrilling mass of "live" string tone.

The Wood Wind department contains the Oboe, Orchestral Oboe, Clarinet, Cor Anglais, Kinura, Concert Flutes, etc.

The Bass department contains the Trombones, Trumpets and Tubas.

The Percussion department embraces the Tympani, Drums, Triangle, Glockenspeil [*sic*], Chimes, etc.

A set of stop keys representing all or most of these stops, at various pitches, is provided in connection with the great manual. Another set is provided in connection with the swell; another in connection with the choir, another with the solo, and another with the pedal. By their means any selection of the stops from the various departments may be freely drawn and mixed on any keyboard quite [in]dependently of what may at the same time be in use on the other keyboards.

. . .

Because of limited funds this organ has but 14 stops. It is easily the most powerful instrument in the world, and I fancy it would be difficult to find any fifty stop organ giving equal variety of effect.

. . .

Suitable Bass (Patent): On each keyboard there is provided a double touch tablet or piston labeled "Suitable bass." Upon touching this tablet the pedal stops and couplers instantly so group themselves as to provide a bass that is suitable to the stops at the moment in use upon that particular manual. If the tablet be pressed much more firmly it will become locked down and then the pedal stops and couplers will continue to move automatically so as to keep the bass suited to that particular manual, whatever changes may be made in registration. This locked suitable bass tablet will release itself the moment the performer touches any of the pedal stops or couplers by hand or touches the suitable bass tablet belonging to any other manual.

All the combination pistons in the Unit Organ are provided with double touch. The first touch moves the manual stops only, but a much firmer touch will provide the suitable bass for the particular combination in use.

. . .

Double Touch: In the Unit Organ all keys and pedals are provided with double touch. The first touch is an ordinary or normal one and the key is brought to rest against an apparently solid bottom in the usual way. When, however, great extra pressure is used the key will suddenly give way again about a sixteenth of an inch and a strengthening of tone, either of the same or of another quality, will be brought into play. [80]

In spite of his ridicule of traditionalists and his apparent confidence, Hope-Jones must be credited with understanding better than many of his contemporaries the limitations his instrument had, and he predicted with uncanny foresight the area of its future use. After declaring himself "in favor of the bold introduction of the organ into the secular field," he continued:

We have heard much said against "degrading the organ" and "prostituting our art"—I cannot see the matter in this light. Such remarks are indeed forceful when applied to the Church organ; but I fail to see their applicability to a new instrument avowedly designed for amusing a large section of the public. This public will have light and popular music, and if any of you organists are minded to meet the demand and have an instrument to enable you to do so, I fail to see that you thereby hinder yourselves from performing the highest classical compositions on the Church organ when the proper times and seasons arrive. . . .

"Degrading our art" indeed! Let me tell you that there is scope for the exercise of the highest art any of you can bring to bear, in rendering effectively good popular compositions on the new orchestral organ or "Unit Orchestra" as I prefer to call it. If any of you will successfully study this new art I can promise you will not lack remunerative employment. [80, p.13]

Builders who availed themselves of Hope-Jones's idea of the "unit" organ did not confine themselves to theater and amusement park organs. The world was waiting for a cheap organ, so it seemed. The little portable organs developed by Kimball and other builders and the small designs by Hinners were all attempts to meet this challenge. Now that the power of electricity had been unleashed, why shouldn't small churches have organs with thirty stops instead of ten? Or fifteen instead of four or five? The additional cost would be minimal, and, just as important, little additional space would be needed for the few extra octaves of small pipes.

The new ideas were intoxicating. Science was progress, and surely science applied to the organ console was progress. One can imagine that the fingers of the organists in the National Association of Organists itched to try the double-touch and the elaborate console controls. Certainly it would be impressive to hush the loudest stops to a pianissimo and then let the sound well forth to fill the auditorium, merely by opening the swell box.

Then there was the volume. Hope-Jones claimed that the Ocean Grove instrument was the "most powerful organ in the world." The desirability of loud sounds from an organ was an idea that had been growing in popularity for years. Now here was a builder who could wrest more decibels from a pipe than anyone had thought possible. Church committee members wanting to put a small, inexpensive organ in their sanctuary might well be impressed by the amount of sound they could get per dollar.

Viewed in retrospect, one can see that other Hope-Jones ideas had already made an appearance: higher pressures for reeds, the derivation of more than one stop from a rank of pipes, the decline of upperwork, console gadgetry, and orchestral effects. It would seem that Hope-Jones did not so much alter the course that organ design was taking as to hurry it along its chosen route. He was the supreme spokesman and the extreme exponent of the new style.

His design found expression in its most pure form in the hands of theater organ builders, most particularly the Wurlitzer company. Other builders applied the unit principle, though not exclusively; raised the pressures, though not as high; leathered the lips, though not as many; and tightened up their swell enclosures, without building them of cement.

In 1923 a series of articles appeared in *The American Organist* contrasting the "unit" concept with the "straight" concept in organ design. Opinions were solicited from builders and organists. While the builders tended to be noncommittal, most of the organists favored some kind of compromise. Even the more conservative organists agreed that some unifying added flexibility to straight schemes. Unifying flutes, reeds, and soft stops but not diapasons was a typical compromise.

George Ashdown Audsley

The most severe and persistent critic of the Hope-Jones school was the architect and organ designer George Ashdown Audsley (1838–1925). He was a native of Elgin, Scotland, and had already published thirty articles on organ design in England before coming to America in 1892. A man of scholarship, Audsley wrote books on Oriental art, taste and fashion in color, Christian symbolism, art printing, architecture, and a number of other subjects. His books on organ design, all written in the United States, are *The Art of Organ-Building* (2 vols., 1905), *The Organ of the Twentieth Century* (1919), *Organ-Stops and their Artistic Registration* (1921), and *The Temple of Tone* (1925).

Audsley's mammoth classic, *The Art of Organ-Building* [8], clearly details his early views on design. A formidable opponent of many of the concepts held by Hope-Jones, this dignified intellectual with the impressive list of credentials and publications presented arguments supported by historic reference, logic, and reason for a scientific approach to organ design. In this posture he must have been an attractive leader for those who found Hope-Jones too strong a dose, who were categorically opposed to radical action, who felt that the old organs were really not so bad, given a few improvements, and, of course, for those who thought that anyone who could write two thick volumes (twenty-three pounds of literature) on the organ must surely be the absolute authority.

Audsley differed most strongly from Hope-Jones in regard to mixtures and other upperwork, unification, wind pressure, and the use of enclosures. Throughout his career, he insisted on "harmonic corroborating" stops (i.e., mixtures and other high-pitched stops reinforcing the natural harmonics of the fundamental). At a time when "screaming" modified "mixtures" so often in discussions of organ design that for all practical purposes they became one word, Audsley wrote three sentences that nearly crackled the cover of an issue of *The American Organist:*

> As might be expected, it was an organ-builder, not distinguished for his artistic attainments, who sprung the theory on the organ-building world that the special harmonic-corroborating stops, which ever since the construction of the first important Organ had been found absolutely essential to the production of true and characteristic organ-tones, were altogether unnecessary when certain assertive unison stops were introduced, the tones of which were rich in harmonics. It is quite easy to see that, from a tradesman's standpoint, the wish was father to the thought. This absurd theory—if theory it can be called—was strongly advanced by the late Robert Hope-Jones, doubtless because it favored the pernicious unit system of stop-appointment, which he borrowed from Léonard Dryvers, of Kessel-

Loo-Louvain, Belgium, the inventor of the ridiculous 'Orgue Sim-
plifié'; and which, had it been favored by musicians and adopted by
our prominent organ-builders, would have absolutely destroyed the
art of organ-building, and have ended in perpetuating monstrosities
and unscientific and inartistic blunders, after the fashion of the Hope-
Jones instrument in Ocean Grove, N. J. [211, p.11]

Audsley extended his idea of upperwork to the pedal. He recognized
the inadequacies of this division, and wrote pedal specifications sur-
passing anything that had been attempted in England or America.

From an ideal standpoint, Audsley believed that every stop should
be independent. This view, of course, placed him in direct opposition to
the unit organ concept. From a practical standpoint, he admitted some
borrowing, particularly in the Pedal divisions of medium- and small-
sized organs. Here he recognized that where space and/or money were
limited, it was sometimes better to have a borrowed stop than no stop
at all. Stops of this sort were carefully designated Auxiliary Stops in his
specifications, to distinguish them from the independent stops that
made up the basic design. No specification in *The Temple of Tone* [12]
has more than three auxiliary stops.

The wind pressures Audsley advocated in *The Art of Organ-Building* were lower than the practice of the day. For a medium-sized church
organ he suggested 3½ inches for Pedal and Swell, 3 inches for the
Great, and 2½ inches for the Choir [8,I, p.212]. He recommended
2⅜ inches as a reasonable pressure for an ordinary chamber organ,
with a minimum of 1½ inches and a maximum of 2½ inches for the
manuals [8, I, pp.318–19]. As for concert hall organs, he concluded:
"higher pressures may be consistently adopted for the Concert instrument than for either the Church or Chamber Organ . . ." [8, I, p.266]. In
all cases, he recognized that it might be desirable to place some solo
stops on a higher pressure. Here, too, he deplored the excesses of some
builders. He called the voicing of a Tuba Mirabilis on 100 inches
pressure "the height of absurdity," and said that such a stop should be
called "Tuba Miserabilis" [8, I, p.239].

Audsley objected to the "mile-away sound annihilation, which too
many organ builders seem to think is the acme of perfection in a Swell
Organ" [8, I, p.232]. He did not object to enclosing most of the organ,
but he opposed the Hope-Jones type of swell enclosure.

Up to this point Audsley's views seem amazingly modern. However,
his system of stop-apportionment and enclosures is a matter that must
be considered in the context of his overall concept of organ design, and
it is here that we find a departure from classic principles as they are
interpreted today.

From the first, Audsley made a distinction between the Church

Organ and the Concert-hall Organ. Their functions were different, and therefore their designs should be different. A third classification was the Chamber Organ, similar in its use and concept to the Concert-hall Organ, but much smaller. In later years he added another classification, the Theater Organ, again designed to fit its particular function.

In *The Art of Organ-Building* he advocated enclosing the Swell, the Choir, and part of the Great and Pedal in church organs. The Great and Pedal stops could be included in the Choir enclosure, if separate enclosures were impractical. The distribution of stops on the manuals conformed generally to standard practice. The enclosure of such a large proportion of the stops was designed to give greater flexibility to the instrument in performing its primary function. Audsley interpreted this function to be the accompaniment of choral and congregational singing.

The enclosure of the Choir found general acceptance, and by October 1920, Gordon Balch Nevin could write: "I have collected specifications for over fifteen years and am blest if I can find more than two small and unimportant examples of an unenclosed choir organ out of a collection of nearly 300!" [389]. The enclosure of the Great, or a portion of it, remained a matter of debate.

Audsley felt that on the Concert-hall Organ one should be able to play any piece effectively, whether it was written for organ or orchestra, and that it should be an adequate substitute for the orchestra, or a companion to the orchestra, in accompanying oratorios or other major works. Consequently, he designed the organ along orchestral lines. The first manual, partly enclosed, should be characterized by "grandeur, majesty, sublimity of tone." The second manual, also partly enclosed, should have "subdued dignity, refinement, and liquid brightness of tone." The third would be an orchestral division, with a string section and a woodwind section, all enclosed. The fourth would then have solo voices and brass-wind imitations, enclosed.

Parts of manuals I and II were enclosed together. Manual III, however, would have two enclosures: one for the strings and one for the woodwinds. Manual IV would then have a separate enclosure. Now it becomes apparent that an elaborate selection of couplers is necessary. One might, for example, want to use the strings of the third manual on one keyboard contrasted with the woodwinds on another keyboard. Audsley further increased the number of couplers by his custom of including a selection of sub- and supercouplers. With this array of couplers, more help in the way of combination pistons was necessary. There were also the extra swell pedals to be considered.

Audsley was concerned about the inclusion of a sufficient body of strings. He felt that they should be grouped together and increased in number if they were truly to give the effect of the string section of an orchestra. The usual practice of scattering a few string stops on different manuals he found "insufficient for the demands on the Concert Organ, and for much of the music now rendered thereon" [8, I, p.251].

Thus the Audsley Concert-Hall Organ grew to be an instrument with which the modern organist feels little sympathy. The key to understanding it lies in considering "the music now rendered thereon": the repertoire of Audsley's day.

Audsley later extended his idea of manual subdivisions (with more than one swell enclosure for some manuals) to his Church Organ specifications. These organs, however, remained distinct from concert instruments in their stop selections. One finds new names for the manuals in *The Temple of Tone* [12], but they do not represent a basic change in concept. They simply designate more clearly what Audsley had always considered to be the character of the manuals of a church organ:

> I Grand Organ [Audsley always favored the lowest manual for the "Great" or principal ensemble manual.]
> II Accompanimental Organ
> III Choir Organ [Omitted in three-manual specifications]
> IV Solo Organ

The Concert-room Organ meanwhile had its manuals designated:

> I Grand Organ
> II Accompanimental Organ
> III Wood-wind Organ
> IV Brass-wind Organ
> V Solo Organ

Manuals III and IV were combined as Orchestral Organ in a four-manual plan.

In addition, the organ was provided with one or more Ancillary Organs, floating divisions (having no designated manual home) that could be coupled to any manual. The most important was the Ancillary String Organ. This basic orchestral division was thus available on any manual. Additional Ancillary divisions might be Ancillary Aërial Organ (a quiet division), Ancillary Harmonic Organ (a concentration of mutations and mixtures), Ancillary Fanfare Organ (reeds), and Ancillary Percussion Organ (Carillon, Harp, Celesta, Xylophone—Audsley would not tolerate drums, even in his theater organ specifications). Each one had its own enclosure, and one could couple the swell mechanism of any Ancillary Organ to one's choice of several of the swell pedals. The Ancillary divisions, their expression couplers, and the expressive subdivisions of the several stationary manuals increased the number of couplers to a formidable assortment. In addition, one had to keep track of up to seven swell pedals and an increased number of miscellaneous console controls.

Audsley and his followers were responsible for the design of some large, important instruments. By 1926 Hopkins could write:

> They [Audsley's plans] were not always carried out as he desired, unfortunately. This was not because of the expense involved, however, but in those days the organists and committees usually objected to the enclosure of the Great Organ and could see no value in the Dual System of Tonal Appointment which he advocated. It is interesting to note their change of attitude in these days.[3] [329, p.64]

If Audsley accomplished nothing else, he provided organ designers with a system for planning large organs. What does one add to a hundred-rank organ when money and space are available to double its size? There was no historic precedent to turn to, if, indeed, one had an inclination to honor precedent. But the plan of adding more divisions of specialized tonal character could be extended indefinitely. For this reason, organs of unusual size more often than not paid homage to Audsley, if not in detail, at least in the nature of the "luxury" divisions. The only other plan that presented itself for very large organs was the one that evolved from the chancel location of the choir, that is, the linking of the gallery organ with a new organ in the chancel.

Both the Hope-Jones Unit Orchestra and the Audsley Concert-hall Organ were designed for situations that have all but disappeared and for a repertoire that is no longer played. It is difficult, if not impossible, to view these concepts of organ design objectively today, when one is inclined to dismiss the first quarter of the twentieth century as a period of decadence in organ building. While Hope-Jones and Audsley were not the sole contributors to those characteristics now regarded as decadent, their influence was considerable. The validity of Audsley's views on some aspects of organ construction gained for him the respect of many thoughtful organists, and he has seldom been criticized as severely as Hope-Jones was. Yet his Concert-hall design had as little relationship with organs past or future as did the Hope-Jones Unit Orchestra.

The American Orchestral Style

The Orchestral Ideal

Thankful that the past age of organ building was over and the great time of progress and enlightenment was now at hand, organists and builders alike set themselves to the task of making the most of the opportunities science and invention afforded. In January 1911 the advertisement for Austin Organs in *The Diapason* summarized the new style. With the exception of the Universal Air Chest, the list may be applied to most of the builders of that time:

Old Fashioned Organs Had	Austin Organs Have
Faint Wind Supply	Universal Air Chest
Heavy Key Action	Light, Unvarying Action
Straight Pedal Board	Concave, Radiating Pedal Board
Poverty in Couplers	All Octave Couplers
Few Mechanical Aids	More Mechanicals than Stops
Tracker Action	Electric or Pneumatic Action
Few and Poor Reeds	Eloquent, Colorful Reeds
Inadequate Diapasons	Big Noble Diapasons
Draw Stops at Side	Stop Keys in Line of Vision
Bellows Whining and Grunting	Fan Blowers Noiseless

The new style was, most undisputable of all, orchestral. Here we find the common meeting ground for the followers of both Hope-Jones and Audsley. Every major builder paid homage to the orchestra as a source of inspiration. So unanimous was this trend that Audsley's distinctions between the Church Organ and the Concert-hall Organ became blurred, and the orchestra became the tonal ideal generally applied.

The popularity of the orchestra and the thirst for favorites of the orchestral repertoire were in no small measure responsible for this trend. When an orchestra was not available, the organ was the best substitute. Instant masterworks via radio and phonograph were in their infancy in the 1920s, and until these media improved in quantity and quality the organ transcription remained an important part of the repertoire.

It is hardly surprising that organ builders should seek to provide organists with instruments particularly suited for such a popular purpose. And however much we may question the taste of organists who responded to the demand for orchestral music, there was never a time when organs were received with more enthusiasm by the general public. If the profession did nothing else in the early twentieth century, it sought to be relevant to its age. E. M. Skinner could look back over his first twenty-five years in business and credit his tonal design to his "unbounded belief" in the organ. He claimed to have worked out all the orchestral colors and [to] have included them in the Skinner Organs." Noting that the reception of the orchestral stops met with a variety of attitudes on the part of organists, he said: "Those who are interested in music for music's sake, the orchestra, opera, piano and any good music have welcomed these voices. The Classicist, the Ritualist and the Purist have fought and disapproved them" [237, p.183].

Some disapproval there was, but the vocal majority were of Skinner's opinion. Van Denman Thompson, in comparing Bach's instrument with the organ of 1919, wrote:

> Instead of tonal charm there was little but harshness and stridency; instead of shifting and contrasting tone-colors, only a basic full organ effect, with little chance for variety. In other words, Bach's organ music is written for an instrument not only *inferior* to the present-day instrument, but so markedly *different* in chief characteristics that while these works are playable on the modern organ, they are not in its best or most characteristic idiom; in fact, are not really suited to it. . . . Bach treated the organ, in a large part of his works, as an unwieldy, inflexible, and cumbersome instrument—which is exactly what it was. He did not utilize charming tonal effects, because he had none to utilize and he did not plan his work to that end. [484, pp.485–86]

Electric Action

The improved reliability of electric action in the early twentieth century was real reason to rejoice. George Miller explained some of the problems he had encountered with battery-powered action in his church: "The steady use of the organ for an hour-and-a-half's choir rehearsal would exhaust the batteries. The organ-builder would be notified and on coming next day *would not find anything the matter,* the batteries having recovered themselves in the interim." He noted that many of the electric organs built before 1904 had had to be rebuilt, and he credited Hope-Jones with the development of improved electric action [105, p.85].

Even in 1905 Audsley felt it necessary to recommend: "Never depend upon electricity in organ-building when anything more reliable can be used" [8, I, p.200]. In later years, James Reynolds recalled:

> Few realize what a task it was to build electric action then. Magnets and all other parts had to be made by the builder, and every action was different. There was no such thing as buying on the market, there were no electric supplies, and naturally every builder thought the others were all wrong. The greatest trouble was with the magnets. They were all too large, all consumed too much current, and they did not last long. [441]

But these problems were fast coming to an end; every year saw more advanced solutions. One of the happy results was that the development of satisfactory electropneumatic action hastened the end of tubular-pneumatic action. The latter died a slow, unlamented death during the first quarter of the century. Estey was old-fashioned in the 1923 statement: "We stand firmly as the champion of tubular-pneumatic action when it is possible to use it." The Estey company claimed that superior service and reliability determined this choice [122, p.40]. Even more old-fashioned were those few builders who continued to use tracker action, for example, Hinners and Morey.

Builders using electric action prided themselves on the speed of the key action. When the new Hutchings organ was installed in Hill Auditorium, University of Michigan, *The Diapason* of November 1912 observed:

> While it is probably true that no organist can exceed a repetition of more than fifteen or twenty a second with his hands, it is also true that he can easily feel the difference between an action which is capable of a repetition of fifty a second and one which will repeat 100 times a second, even if the ear fails to hear the repetition. The extreme rapidity of this new simplified action gives the organist, it is claimed, a feeling of absolute control of the organ, which is due entirely to the extreme promptness in response. This is much the same as if he had hold of the valves at the feet of the pipes.

But however fast it was, organists found it difficult to control a key action that was too light. As a result, several builders developed an action with a greater initial resistance. Skinner's key action required a weight of four ounces for the initial depression of the key and one and a half ounces at the bottom of the key fall [140, p.13].

The Console

The pedal, too, had a face-lifting. In the mid-nineteenth century the English builder Henry Willis had developed the radiating and concave pedal board that, with some modification, became the pattern for the standard American pedal board. Its use gained popularity during the early part of the century, and along with it came an extension of the range to thirty-two notes. In July 1906 an irritated organist complained in a letter to the organ editor of *The Musician:*

> It is hard enough to reach the extreme lower or higher notes with the 30 note keyboard, and I do not believe in reducing the space between the naturals in order to insert the extra notes at the top. I do not see any use for these two extra notes at the right, excepting to display pedal melodies by an expert organist on one or two special pieces.

With all the new couplers, combination pistons, and swell controls that seemed to grow in geometric ratio with the size of the instrument, the problem of where on the console all the gadgets should be located and just what form they should have was good for many a discussion. Preference for stop tabs, tilting tablets, and draw-knobs differed from one organist to another and from one builder to another. Console characteristics usually associated with theater organs were also used by some builders for church organs. Horseshoe-shaped consoles, colored stop tabs (a different color for each tonal family), and double-touch all made occasional appearances.

One experiment with stops was the Estey Luminous Stop Console, initiated about 1923. The stops were small buttonlike pistons of a translucent material, on which the names of the stops were engraved and under which electric lights were placed. When the piston was pressed, the light came on and the stop was brought into play. With another press the stop was off and the light went out. The advantages advertised for this plan were: (1) the same motion was used to bring on or to retire the stop; (2) it was compact, and "more than fifty [stops] can be placed in the space covered by one's hand"; (3) the console could be small; (4) the stops were easy to see; and (5) they were within easy reach [122, p.46]. The stops were placed above the top manual on a slanted plane and looked very much like cash register buttons. Using the crescendo pedal or the combination action also brought on the lights of the stops affected. With visible consoles, this electric-light display was interesting to watch, if distracting. It had certain disadvantages that soon led to its unpopularity. Chief among them was the fact that when the light burned out it was impossible to tell if a stop was on or off. Also, if there was a reflection or strong light on the console, the piston lights were difficult to see.

Another experiment was Midmer-Losh's seven-octave keyboard. It made its debut in 1925 as the lower keyboard of a three-manual organ for the Central Christian Church, Miami, Florida. In its defense, C. S. Losh wrote:

> To play a Grossflote at 8′ pitch throughout the manual range and then be obliged to drop to the pedal board for its 16′ octave would make anyone wonder who decreed that the organ, the first instrument to have a keyboard, must have a range of only five octaves while its upstart imitator, the piano, with less musical range, may have more than seven. Yes, and when we want the four-foot register of this same Grossflote we must draw another stop—or more likely a coupler and another stop! Seven octave organs are here to stay! [352, p.415]

Combination actions were the subject for considerable debate. The major question was whether or not the stops should move when one pressed a combination piston, i.e., "dead" combinations as opposed to "visible" combinations. These two systems were also known, respectively, as "dual" and "absolute." Stops did not move for the dead or dual system, but they did move for the visible or absolute system. An important characteristic of the dual system was that the use of a combination piston did not affect stops already drawn by hand.

A console standardization committee appointed by the American Guild of Organists leaned toward the dead combinations. In 1913 its chairman, J. Warren Andrews, observed: "The objection that is so often heard—'I want to see what I have drawn'—is not worthy of consideration. If an organist's ears don't indicate to his inner self what he has on, of what earthly use are his eyes in this regard?" [208]. Foremost among the opponents of dead combinations was Ernest M. Skinner, although he had earlier used this system.

The A.G.O. committee was unsuccessful in establishing a standard for combination actions, and five years later the debate still dragged on. Many of the arguments that appeared in the organ journals sought to prove the superiority of one system over the other by showing that fewer motions would be required to effect a given series of registration changes. The advantages of the absolute system, found on most American organs today, are well understood. The dual system was held by its champions to be more flexible, lending itself better to the orchestral treatment characteristic of the style of the day. T. Scott Buhrman summarized:

> There is little to be added to the argument pro or con. It is self apparent which system gives a stereotyped registration that is for each piston always and invariably the same, until the piston itself is readjusted, and which gives the kaleidoscopic registration that may be distinctly different and colored according to other considerations each of a dozen successive times. Pull the 4′ Flute D'Amour on the swell, push successively the Absolute pistons 1, 2, 3 and 4, and the effects are exactly the same as though the 4′ flute had not been drawn for the past century. But repeat the process on the Dual system and pistons 1, 2, 3 and 4 are all of them colored by the Flute. Do we want stereotyped registration? or kaleidoscopic orchestral colorings?
> [239, p.318]

A further advantage of the dual system that was not generally recognized was that it could be used very much like the ventils on French organs, and would lend itself easily to the registration of much French Romantic organ literature. All arguments to the contrary, however, organists found that it was easier to work with pistons that actually moved the stops, and, in the long run, the flexibility of the system depended for the most part on the ability of the organist.

Placement and Enclosure

Before this time organs had already begun to disappear. With the dismissal of the organ case, the use of pipe fences, and now the fad for having the organ and the choir in the front of the church, chambers became the solution. Some of the chambers were covered by a grill; others used a display of false pipes. E. M. Skinner answered the charge that fake pipes were in poor taste with the blunt and undeniable: "A silent pipe is no more a dummy than the bunch of quartered-oak grapes on the woodwork which supports it" [140, p.41]. In the April 1925 issue of *The American Organist,* the nonappearance of the new Möller organ in Temple Beth-El, New York, was described:

> The organ and choir are located in the front, one floor above the pulpit, behind an imposing row of columns. Just back of the columns have been hung black draperies so that the congregation sees but nothingness behind the pillars, the music coming from sources invisible.

Few organ builders of the early twentieth century would admit defeat in coping with poor placement. With higher pressures and an emphasis on 8' tone, the loss of upper partials and clarity was not held to be the disaster that it is today. One wonders if an organ contract was ever turned down in this period because the organ would have to be placed in an unfortunate location. Skinner remarked: "In some cases a basement offers the only opportunity for an installation. This plan may be developed successfully if provision is made for properly conveying the tone from the organ to the audience room" [140, p.39]. Yet Skinner and most of his contemporaries knew that the less obstruction the sound had and the more direct its entrance into the room the better its effect would be.

Now that the organ was well out of sight, the question of enclosing the Great and the Pedal could be considered. Some followed Audsley in enclosing part of the Great and Pedal, but there were many stout voices favoring the unenclosed Great. For example, Percy Chase Miller wrote:

> There is an aesthetic quality in an unvarying and invariable tone, that can be indefinitely prolonged, at pleasure, without alteration of quality. No other instrument has it, the great organ-music from Bach to Reubke, and from Reubke to Widor and Vierne, is conceived for it; why, then, throw it away simply to substitute the "knee-swell" effect that you can get on the cheapest and nastiest melodion ever built? [372, p.277]

On the other hand, when Clarence Dickinson designed the 1918 organ built by E. M. Skinner for Brick Church, New York, he specified separate enclosures for each manual division (Great, Swell, Choir, Solo, String, and Echo organs). In addition, the entire organ, with the exception of the Echo division, was enclosed in a general swell box. The general swell box, then, included the Pedal, as well as giving the other divisions a double enclosure.

Tonal Characteristics

The importance of dynamic contrast in the design of orchestral organs is revealed in the relative loudness of stops, as well as in the increase of enclosures. A typical concept of stop balance is found in J. B. Jamison's description of an Estey organ built for Claremont College:

> There are two 8′ flutes in the Great. Neither of them can be heard when the Second Diapason is drawn—which is eminently as it should be. There is no logical excuse for Great organ flutes that can be heard in full Great, even slightly. [335, p.599]

The question of mixtures was the subject of much debate. The arguments, particularly those against mixtures, were greatly confused by erroneous historical data. It would be interesting to know who originated the myth that mixtures were added to the organ at some time in the past because the foundation tone was found to be inadequate. A typical statement was that of Clifford Demarest in 1914:

> Previous to the introduction of metrical hymns into the church service, the organs were small and used for the playing of interludes between the verses of the Psalms, and not to accompany the singing at all. With the advent of the Lutheran chorale the whole situation became changed. In trying to accompany and support large bodies of lusty singers it was soon found that the existing organs were inadequate. An attempt to increase the foundation work of the organ was prevented by necessarily larger pallets, causing an additional weight of the touch, which already was so heavy that it took the strength of a blacksmith to depress the keys.
>
> In this emergency it was discovered that, by introducing a few mixture stops, the resulting noise was sufficient to overpower the largest bodies of singers. This soon became a fad and the builders began to exaggerate it to such an extent that many organs of that time contained fifty and more ranks of mixture.
>
> Toward the beginning of the Fourteenth century a crusade against excessive mixture work set in and has continued to the present day. It was not, however, very successful until the pneumatic action was

invented, when it was found that a massive volume of good sustaining foundation tone is far better to support large bodies of singers. Unfortunately many builders of the commercial type are loath to give up in this matter. In estimating the cost of an organ it is much cheaper to increase the number of stops by adding fifteenths, twelfths and mixtures with their small and inexpensive pipes. The result is an organ with more noise than musical foundation tone. Happily the old method of estimating the size of an organ by the number of its pipes is rapidly passing away. [272]

Mixtures were not unanimously dismissed, and Audsley had considerable support in his insistence on their value. Such was the view of Arthur B. Jennings:

> The majority of our organs built in the last ten years by standard firms have a cold and brutal tone in the full organ. This, due in part to heavy wind pressures and excessive use of reeds, would not be so obvious if the insistent stops were properly mollified by being blended with good mixtures. [338]

In general, though, upperwork was included in ever fewer organs. In the fourteen specifications quoted in *The Diapason* in January and February 1917, there appeared one Great Mixture, one Great 2-⅔′, one Swell "Solo Mixture," and one Swell Cornet. Some organists, fond of the sound of the older organs, complained about the lack of upperwork. Frank Adams wrote:

> What is done in the modern organ to reproduce upper partials? All the registers, especially the strings, are made of thin scale. The fancy strings, celestes, and voices like the Orchestral Oboe are put on the Register Crescendo and intended to be used with other registers to give brightness—the brightness of squawking poultry.[200, p.153]

Basil Austin was among those who replied to this attack on the modern organ. With the advent of electric blowers, he explained, voicers were no longer limited in pressure or quantity.

> The result has been that the volume of foundation tone has been increased and other varieties of tone introduced; notably the "string" tone of which the Author spoke. If we analyze this string tone what do we find? A mixture of harmonics, nothing more or less, though differing from a mixture of separate tones in that all the harmonics are perfectly in tune with each other and so finely graduated that they blend together perfectly. The point is, that strings, suitably scaled and voiced, do replace to a large extent the functions of mixtures. Small scale strings are, moreover, beautiful in themselves and give the modern organ coloring which few if any organists would care to lose.
> [212, p.256]

The importance of strings in the design of the orchestral organ can hardly be overestimated. Audsley had pointed that out early in the century, and many heeded his advice. The strings were, after all, the basic voice of the orchestra, and the distinguishing feature of the orchestral organ. There were probably more string stops made between 1910 and 1930 than in the entire history of the organ, before or since. Very well endowed in this respect was the large Möller for Temple Beth-El, New York, which contained nine ranks of strings in the Swell, in addition to a String Ancillary division with thirteen more ranks of strings.

Along with the other inventions of the early twentieth century were some new pipe forms. William E. Haskell patented several varieties of flue pipes designed to imitate orchestral reed instruments. His reedless saxophone, oboe, clarinet, and other orchestral voices would stay in tune with the rest of the flue ranks—a particular advantage for organs in out-of-the-way locations. Among Haskell's other inventions was a short-length pipe that had the tonal character and pitch of an open pipe of twice its length. It was formed by inserting a chamber in the interior of the pipe, dividing it longitudinally into two sections. The advantages of the short-length Diapason (or Haskell bass, as it was sometimes called) for an organ installed in inadequate space are obvious.[4]

First consideration in preparing a specification was given to the representation of the families of organ tones at the 8' pitch level. In a very small organ little else was found unless there was augmentation. The small, straight organ of nine stops built in 1918 by J. W. Steere & Son is an example.

St. John's Congregational Church, Springfield, Massachusetts
J. W. STEERE & SON, 1918

Great			Pedal		
Diapason	8'	61	Bourdon	16'	32
Melodia	8'	61			
Dulciana	8'	61	3 set Pistons (Dual)		
			Sforzando		
Swell			Gt. to Ped. Reversible		
Diapason	8'	73	Swell control		
Gedackt	8'	73			
Salicional	8'	73	*Couplers*		
Harmonic Flute	4'	73	Sw. to Gt.	16', 8', 4'	
Oboe	8'	73	Gt. to Gt.	4'	
			Sw. to Sw.	16', 4'	
			Gt. to Ped.	8'	
			Sw. to Ped.	8'	

[*The American Organist,* May 1918, p.271]

The comparative virtues and vices of unifying were much discussed during the first three decades of the century. Unifying of very small organs was widely practiced. A five-rank specification proposed by Arthur J. Thompson of the Aeolian company illustrates unit organ design.

ARTHUR J. THOMPSON (proposed), 1928

Great			*Swell (continued)*		
Diapason	8′		Rohrflote	8′	
Dulciana	8′		Flauto d'Amore	4′	⎫
Salicional	8′	(Sw.)	Nazard	2⅔′	⎬ Rohrflote
Rohrflote	8′	(Sw.)	Piccolo	2′	⎭
Flauto d'Amore	4′	(Sw.)	Oboe	8′	
Swell			*Pedal*		
Diapason	8′	(Gt.)	Bourdon	16′	(Rohrflote)
Dulciana	8′	(Gt.)	Stille Gedeckt	8′	(Sw.)
Salicional	8′				

[483, p.244]

Theater organs were often (though not always) unit instruments. A specification typical of those used by Möller for theater organs is given below.

Standard Three Manual Duplex Concert Organ
MÖLLER, c.1915

Great (Duplex to Orchestral and at Octaves)		*Orchestral (continued)*	
Viol Diapason (t.c.)	16′	Orchestral Oboe	8′
Open Diapason	8′	Fagotta (t.c.)	16′
Viole D'Orchestre	8′	Clarinet	8′
Doppel Floete	8′	Concert Harp	
Octave	4′	Tremulant	
Zart Flute	· 4′		
Piccolo	2′	*Solo*	
Mixture	III	Gross Flute	8′
French Horn	8′	Concert Flute	8′
Octave Horn	4′	Gemshorn	8′
Bass Clarinet (t.c.)	16′	Violoncello	8′
Cathedral Chimes		Flute Overte (t.g.)	4′
		Gemshorn (t.g.)	4′
Orchestral		Tuba	8′
Violin Diapason	8′	Bass Tuba (t.c.)	16′
Horn Diapason (Synthetic)	8′	Vox Humana	8′
Quintadena	8′	Tremulant	
Viole D'Orchestre	8′		
Viole Celeste (t.c.)	8′		
Flute Harmonic	4′		

Standard Three Manual Duplex Concert Organ
MÖLLER, c.1915

Pedal		*Couplers (continued)*	
Sub Bass	16′	Solo to Solo 16′, 4′	
Gemshorn	16′	Orchestral to Orchestral 16′, 4′	
Lieblich Gedeckt	16′	Great to Pedal 8′	
Violoncello	8′	Solo to Pedal 8′	
Flute	8′	Orchestral to Pedal 8′	
		Great to Pedal 4′	

Couplers

Solo to Great 16′, 8′, 4′
Orchestral to Great 16′, 8′, 4′
Solo to Orchestral 8′
Orchestral to Solo 8′
Great to Great 4′

Adjustable pistons
Great to Pedal Reversible
Orchestral to Pedal Reversible
Solo Expression Pedal
Orchestral Expression Pedal
Crescendo Pedal

Tonal Elements

Sub Bass—Gross Flute	16′	85
Open Diapason—Octave	8′	85
Doppel Floete	8′	73
Violin Diapason—Viol Diapason	8′	73
Concert Flute—Pedal Flute	8′	73
Gemshorn—Pedal and Manual	16′	85
Violoncello—Pedal and Manual	8′	73
Viole D'Orchestre	8′	73
Viole Celeste—Mixture	8′	73
Quintadena—Mixture, Zart Flute	8′	73
Flute Harmonic—Mixture	4′	73
Tuba—Bass Tuba	8′	73
French Horn—Octave Horn	8′	73
Orchestral Oboe—Fagotta	8′	73
Clarinet—Bass Clarinet	8′	73
Vox Humana	8′	61
Concert Harp		
Cathedral Chimes		

[111, pp.43–45]

Unifying one or more soft stops in an otherwise straight specification was a practice defended by many builders and organists who
were opposed to the unit organ in its "pure" form. Augmentation of
the pedal, by extending 16′ stops to play also at 8′, was standard practice in large organs as well as small. In designing the 1925 organ for
the Temple, Cleveland, Carleton Bullis started with a straight scheme
of thirty-three stops and augmented it to one hundred stops on four
manuals [243]. This approach differed from a pure unit scheme in that
the thirty-three original stops formed a rather normal specification for
that time.[5] The Hope-Jones approach, on the other hand, began with

basic tone colors rather than a specification representing not only tone colors but also pitch differences.

E. M. Skinner's 1928 organ for the First Presbyterian Church, Dallas, was given an augmented pedal, and four of the Great stops were borrowed from the Swell. "Judicious" was the favorite adjective for this degree of enlargement of a straight specification, although one might expect a larger organ to be even more judicious in its inclusion of derived stops. When this specification appeared in *The American Organist* (May 1928) it was presented as "a stoplist by Mr. Ernest M. Skinner which represents his own personal ideas in organ planning. . . ."

First Presbyterian Church, Dallas, Texas
ERNEST M. SKINNER, 1928

Great			Swell (continued)		
Bourdon	16'	17 [sic]	Cornopean	8'	73
Diapason	8'	61	Vox Humana	8'	73
Clarabella	8'	61	*Choir*		
Octave	4'	61			
Rohr Flute (Sw.)	8'		Chimney Flute	8'	73
Flute Celeste (Sw.)	8'		Gamba	8'	73
Flute (Sw.)	4'		Dulciana	8'	73
Cornopean (Sw.)	8'		Flute	4'	73
French Horn	8'	73	Clarinet	8'	73
Chimes (20 notes,			Harp	8'⎫	61
in Sw.)	8'		Celesta	4'⎭	
Swell			*Pedal*		
Bourdon	16'	73	Resultant	32'	
Diapason	8'	73	Major Bass	16'	32
Rohr Flute	8'	73	Bourdon	16'	32
Salicional	8'	73	Echo Lieblich (Sw.)	16'	
Voix Celeste	8'	73	Contra Oboe (Sw.)	16'	
Flauto Dolce	8'	73	Octave (Pd.)	8'	12
Flute Celeste	8'	61	Gedeckt (Pd.)	8'	12
Flute Triangulaire	4'	73	Still Gedeckt (Sw.)	8'	
Mixture	III	183	Chimes (Gt.)	8'	
Contra Oboe	16'	73			

Skinner recognized some basic traditions in organ design that saved him from the excesses of his more radical contemporaries and contributed immeasurably to the satisfaction organists found in playing his instruments. He understood that the main divisions of an organ should contain variety in both tone color and pitch. Special divisions, such as the String division in the organ for Woolsey Hall, Yale University, or his occasional 8' Solo divisions, were reserved for large organs.

The Great on the Dallas organ extended only as high as 4', but

Skinner organs of larger size characteristically included a Fifteenth and also a Mixture. The sixty-eight-stop organ for the University of Florida, for example, contained the following Great division: 16′ Double Open Diapason, 8′ First Diapason, 8′ Second Diapason, 8′ Third Diapason, 8′ Claribel Flute, 4′ Flute, 4′ Octave, 2⅔′ Twelfth, 2′ Fifteenth, Mixture III, 16′ Ophicleide, 8′ Tuba, 4′ Clarion, 8′ Tromba, and Chimes. The Ophicleide, Tuba, Clarion, and Chimes were duplicated in the Solo. All the other stops in the Great were independent.

It is significant that the relatively small Dallas organ contained a Swell Mixture. Skinner believed that it was an important ingredient, and that large organs should ideally have two five-rank Swell Mixtures: a Quint Mixture and a Cornet.

Although he prided himself on his development of solo stops that imitated orchestral instruments and although his pitch variety was sometimes minimal, Skinner never really tried to force the organ into an orchestral pattern. Paradoxically, in an age that was intoxicated with the sound of the orchestra, Skinner organs were representative of the highest achievement in American organ building not because of their success as orchestral imitations but because they were still fundamentally traditional organs.

Some Famous Organs

The Wanamaker Organ

One of the most famous of the large early twentieth-century organs symbolized the unity that improved modes of transportation and communication had given the United States. This organ was designed by a man in New York, built by a California firm, exhibited in Missouri, and permanently installed in Pennsylvania. The 1904 Louisiana Purchase Exposition in St. Louis had more to its musical credit than "Meet Me In St. Louie, Louie." Its record music budget of $450,000 topped that of the Chicago Fair by $134,000. By 1902 organ builders were vying with one another for the opportunity to build the principal recital organ. In January 1903 *Music Trades* announced that the Murray M. Harris Organ Company had been selected to build the Kansas City Convention Hall organ, and that the organ would be exhibited first in St. Louis as the Louisiana Purchase Exposition organ.

Newspapers throughout the country noted the progress of the organ, which carried a price tag of $67,000. On November 15, 1903 the Chicago *Chronicle* stated: "It is an instrument capable of producing 17,179,869,183 distinct tonal effects, a continuous performance that would last 32,600 years if a different one of these combinations were drawn every minute in those centuries of time."

Meanwhile, Murray M. Harris had built a new factory in Los Angeles and had employed additional craftsmen to meet the demands of the large contract. William B. Fleming (1849–1940), who had been with George Ryder, Roosevelt, and later with Farrand & Votey, was appointed superintendent and director [294]. Unfortunately, Murray Harris had overextended his financial resources. Hopkins relates the resulting chain of events:

> In order that the work might be completed, outside capital was called upon. Mr. Eben Smith was the financier. Mr. Harris resigned and Mr. Fleming was given control of the new Los Angeles Art Organ Company. Hence it was that Mr. Harris' greatest contract went to the world with no mark upon it of his own part in its manufacture.
>
> [329, p.63]

The Los Angeles Art Organ Company also had financial problems:

> Records show that the factory cost of the St. Louis Organ was $105,000.00! The Company could not stand the strain. In 1905 the name was changed again to the Electrolian Company, and the plant moved bodily to Hoboken, New Jersey. After a year of desultory effort it was closed and the force disbanded. [329, p.64]

The Los Angeles builders had sacrificed their companies to produce the world's largest organ.[6]

In spite of these difficulties, the organ was finally ready for the trip east:

> Ten cars were required to transport from Los Angeles, the place of building, the finished parts which entered into the construction of the organ in Festival Hall. That organ has 140 stops. The largest organ built heretofore has 128 stops. It is in the town hall at Sydney, Australia. There are 10,000 pipes in this new masterpiece. In the construction were utilized 80,000 feet of lumber, chiefly pine from Oregon, 115 miles of wire, 40,000 pounds of zinc and 6,000 pounds of soft metal. Scores of sheep gave up their skins to help make the 271 separate actions possible. [148, p.197]

George Ashdown Audsley designed the tonal resources. He later commented:

> This Organ—the most important Concert-room Organ in existence at the time of its construction—was carried out in accordance with the original tonal scheme, with the exception of the appointment of the Pedal Organ, in which the imparting of flexibility and expression to the Second Subdivision was abandoned, being too great an

innovation to be recognized according to the old-fashioned ideas of its builders. This was much to be regretted on several grounds: one of which was that the Organ, as schemed, presented the first opportunity of placing on record, in the History of the Organ, the imparting of flexibility of tone and expressive powers to the Pedal Organ.

[10, p.508]

Although the fair opened on April 30, 1904, the organ was not ready for its first recital until June 9. After that, daily recitals were given. The official organist was Charles Galloway, a native of St. Louis, but the star guest artist was Alexandre Guilmant, who was to give thirty-six recitals in six weeks. They were so successful that he gave three extra recitals during his last week. The admission fee for most of the recitals preceding the Guilmant series was 10¢. For Guilmant it was raised to 25¢, where it remained for the rest of the time [55, p.195]. The Guilmant recitals deserve special mention because they contained repertoire that few organists knew, and even fewer played. Compositions by Samuel Scheidt, Frescobaldi, Pachelbel, and Titelouze were heard, as well as Bach, Handel, and Franck.

The giant organ never did get to Kansas City, the contract having been voided. It was in storage when John Wanamaker was looking for such an instrument to complete the Grand Court of his new Philadelphia store in 1909. William B. Fleming was engaged to install the instrument, and together with George Till, already on the Wanamaker staff, he opened an organ shop to maintain and enlarge this and other Wanamaker organs.

Additions to the organ began only a few years after its installation in Philadelphia, and its growth to a staggering 469 ranks was traced by *The Diapason* in 1943:

The metamorphosis of the Philadelphia organ until a tripling of its size was attained came about through the addition of 4,000 pipes in 1914, another addition of 4,000 pipes in 1917 and further additions between 1923 and 1930.

A summary of the resources of the instrument shows a total of 469 ranks and 30,067 pipes, distributed over the various divisions as follows:

Orchestral, 38 ranks, 2,774 pipes.
Ethereal, 23 ranks, 1,679 pipes.
Solo, 52 ranks, 3,796 pipes.
String, 88 ranks, 6,424 pipes.
Great, 50 ranks, 3,170 pipes.
Swell, 70 ranks, 5,110 pipes.
Choir, 24 ranks, 1,752 pipes.
Echo, 34 ranks, 2,482 pipes.
Pedal, 90 ranks, 2,880 pipes.

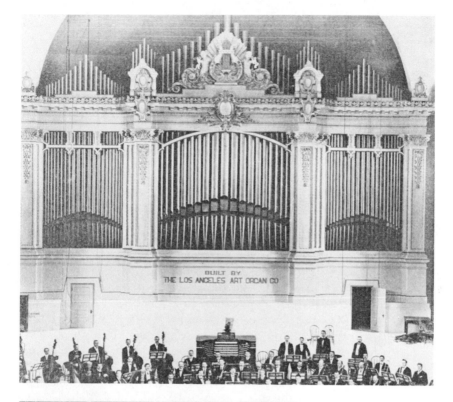

St. Louis Louisiana Purchase Exposition Organ, 1904. Built by the Los Angeles Art Organ Company. Alexandre Guilmant at the console. The organ was later enlarged and installed in the Wanamaker store in Philadelphia. *Photos courtesy Jim Lewis.*

There are ninety-six ranks of mixtures, seventy-six ranks of reeds, thirteen ranks of vox humanas, 139 string ranks, fifty ranks of diapasons and ninety-five ranks of flutes. . . .

The console is a marvel of completeness, beauty and convenience. With its six manuals, 451 stops and 964 controls, nothing is out of the organist's reach. The console's 729 tilting tablets are operated by remote control from the 168 pistons under the manual keys, of which there are forty-six masters and forty-six reversibles. There are also forty-two accessories for the feet. All combination pistons are adjustable at the keyboard and even the beat of the tremolo is adjustable to ten different stages at the will of the organist.[7] [521, pp.1, 4]

The West Point Organ

The organ in the Cadet Chapel, U. S. Military Academy, West Point, New York, had its initial installation in 1911. Its modest three-manual specification with thirty-eight ranks would not be particularly noteworthy had it not grown into 213 ranks. The original Möller organ was purchased with a congressional appropriation. All the additions since that time have been memorial gifts. Frederick Mayer became organist when the organ was installed, and it was under his direction that the numerous additions were made. Mayer was a close friend of George Ashdown Audsley's, and the enlargements to the organ followed closely the Audsley concept of organ design.

A number of small additions were made after 1913, and the first major addition, made in 1923, was a large Orchestral division that included flutes, strings, and solo reeds. Then in 1927 a twelve-rank Viol division was added. The largest addition, the Harmonic Organ, was made in 1930. It included a French Mixture, an English Mixture, and upperwork of gemshorns, dulcianas, flutes, reeds, and a large collection of Pedal harmonics extending to the 1' pitch.

In all, by 1951 the organ included:

Main Divisions	Ranks	Floating Divisions	Ranks
Pedal	28	Harmonic	46
Great	36	Orchestral	23
Choir	15	Viol	12
Swell	16	Reed	5
Solo	15	Vox Humana	4
		Echo	13
			213

[72, p.80]

St. Matthew Lutheran Church Organ

Another famous organ that has gradually been enlarged and revised is the organ in St. Matthew Lutheran Church, Hanover, Pennsylvania. It was built by the Austin Organ Company to specifications planned in cooperation with the organist J. Herbert Springer. When it was originally dedicated in 1925 it contained eighty-seven speaking stops on four manuals.

As concepts of organ design changed, this organ was changed, enlarged, and rebuilt, most recently in 1964. There are now 227 ranks, 239 stops, on four manuals. In addition to Great, Swell, Choir, Solo, and Pedal, its divisions are String Organ, Celestial Organ, and Echo Organ. The String and Celestial Organs, in Audsley style, are floating divisions, available on any manual, while the Echo is playable on the Great and Solo manuals.

An Italian Organ

Probably the most unusual organ installed in the 1920s was placed in St. Vincent Ferrer's Church, New York, where Constantino Yon was organist. His famous brother, Pietro Yon, was responsible for the stop list, and the builder was Natale Balbiani & Co. It was the first Italian organ imported to America.

The organ was divided, with a five-manual console in the chancel and a two-manual console in the gallery. Both chancel and gallery divisions were playable from the chancel console. All stops were straight, with the exception of the Pedal 32′, an extension of the 16′ Contrabasso. There were sixty-seven stops, eighty-seven ranks. The compound stops formed a unique feature of this organ:

	Ranks	Pipes
Chancel Great: Gran Ripieno	VIII	488
Chancel Swell: Ripienino	V	365
Chancel Swell: Concerto Viole	V	365
Chancel Choir: Cornetto	III	183
Gallery Great: Ripieno	VII	511

Balbiani gave his views of the Italian Ripieno, which were as foreign to American thinking at that time as the names on the stop list:

> Three essentials control the success of the Ripieni: Scales, Pressures, and relative Voicings. Pipes of large scale must be excluded, with the Violin Principal making about the correct scale. Wind pressures should vary between 50 and 80 mm. The voicing must be soft and uniform, on the foundation of the basic register. No ranks among the 16′, 8′, and 4′ dare predominate; the fusion of tones must be as perfect as possible. The beauty of the Ripieno is its silvery, clear tone, giving the ensemble a sense of grandeur and nobility. [215, p.144]

St. Patrick's Cathedral Organ

Pietro Yon was also responsible for the inclusion of some Italian Ripieno stops in the large organ built by Kilgen in 1927–28 for St. Patrick's Cathedral, New York. With 118 speaking stops, considerably enlarged by borrowing and extensions, it ranked among the large church organs of the time.

The St. Patrick's organ was another example of a divided organ, this time with the larger part in the gallery. Its divisions included Great, Swell, Choir, Solo, String, and Pedal organs.[8] The chancel organ had three manual divisions and Pedal. In addition, an Echo organ and Echo Pedal were located in the South Gallery. Ripieno mixtures were included on the gallery Great (eight ranks), gallery Swell (five ranks), Echo (five ranks), and chancel Great (five ranks) [394]. The chancel organ was completed first, and when Yon played for its dedication on January 30, 1928, an estimated 5,000 people attended. T. Scott Buhrman reported:

> Before the hour of service began the mobs broke through the police lines at the Fifth Avenue door and it was necessary to take unpleasant steps to restore order in the rear of this great Cathedral. All possible space was taken to the very limit of the Cathedral's capacity. [240, p.90]

The Atlantic City Convention Hall Organ

The "World's Largest Organ in World's Largest Auditorium" is the title of a pamphlet describing the organ in the Atlantic City Convention Hall. Seven and a half pages are required just to list the stops controlled by the seven-manual console. Some of the interesting statistics contained in the pamphlet are:

The total number of pipes is 33,112.
The largest pipe is low C of the 64′ Diaphone Profunda, and it is 64 feet 9 inches long, 10 inches square at the base, and 36 inches square at the top.
It contains the only reeds anywhere on 100″ wind pressure.
There are 1439 stops, 455 ranks of pipes.
Great and choir manuals are 7 octaves long, and the swell is 6 octaves long.
There are 30 tremolos, adjustable to various speeds by the organist.
The organ contains 22 divisions:

Pedal	Wood Wind	Unenclosed Choir
Great	Great Ancillary	Grand Choir
Grand Great	Swell	Swell Ancillary
Solo	Choir	String Organ No. 1

String Organ No. 2	Echo Organ	Diapason Chorus Gallery 3
String Organ No. 3	Reed-Diaphone Gallery 1	Orchestra Reeds Gallery 4
Brass Chorus	Flute Organ Gallery 2	Percussion Division
Fanfare		

This gigantic instrument was designed by Senator Emerson Richards. Bids were out in 1929, and the contract went to Midmer-Losh for $347,200. A subsidiary contract for $100,000 was later added. William H. Barnes, who acted as alternate consultant, recalled:

> The great depression caught up with everybody before the organ was completed. The builder went broke, the Senator went broke, the city went broke, and the bonding company that had guaranteed the completion of the organ went broke, so it was unanimous. [16, p.86]

Finally, on May 11, 1932, the entire organ was given its first public hearing. The times since then when the organ has been used for the performance of serious organ music have been exceedingly rare. Its usual function has been as an accompaniment to ice shows and other entertainments.

During World War II the vast Convention Hall served as headquarters for Army Air Forces Basic Training Center Number 7. For over a year, beginning in the spring of 1943, daily half-hour recitals were given on the organ, as well as a few full-length recitals. They were ended when a hurricane struck Atlantic City in September 1944, causing considerable damage to the blowers and other mechanism. After repairs were made and the armed forces returned the hall to the city, the organ was once more used as before, primarily for the performance of popular music.

XVI

THE AMERICAN CLASSIC ORGAN

Introduction

THE 1920s roared right up to the stockmarket crash in the fall of 1929. Conditions went from bad to worse, and by 1933 there were around fifteen million people unemployed. Although there was a turn for the better after that low point, at the end of the decade there were still about ten million out of work. By 1940, effects of the war in Europe and the accelerated military program in the United States could be seen in American industry. The expansion that would last until the end of the war was well under way. And after that, the demand for civilian products that had been neglected for four years was sufficient to keep manufacturers well occupied for a time. The trends of the economy since then are too recent to require rehearsal, nor is it possible to view them objectively.

People engaged in the arts were hard hit by the depression. Under the Federal Music Project of the W.P.A. (Works Progress Administration) the government spent some $50 million to give employment to fifteen thousand out-of-work musicians between 1935 and 1939. Concerts, research projects, music classes, and lessons were among the activities subsidized by this agency. A particularly beneficial W.P.A. music project was the Composers' Forum-Laboratory. Works of living American composers were performed, and in many instances a composer was given his first opportunity to hear his major works played.

In spite of the dismal state of the economy during the 1930s, there were forces at work that had some profound effects on the American musical climate. They come under the general description of "home entertainment." By 1930, the radio was able to bring into the family living room a variety that was never possible before. Major network broadcasting was established by N.B.C. in 1926, followed the next year by C.B.S. Opera and symphony broadcasts were increasingly available from about 1926 on. Other musical opportunities were soon to follow, for example, the famous "Damrosch Music Appreciation Hour" for school children, which was initiated in 1928. Everyone who had a radio could become acquainted with good music if he wanted to, and many did avail themselves of these opportunities.

Another type of home entertainment was the phonograph. In the mid-1920s recording industry production approached an annual rate of 100 million discs. A near-disastrous slump in the early 1930s brought predictions that the depression and popularity of the radio would soon make the phonograph obsolete. About 1937, however, sales began to climb rapidly, and by 1940 they had surpassed previous figures. Improved recording techniques, the availability of inexpensive phonographs, drastic cuts in record prices, and imaginative marketing all contributed in bringing record collecting to new heights of popularity.

Foreign Influence

Although Americans had always turned to Europe for artistic models and standards, it was not a new idea for Europe's creative talent to seek political asylum in the United States. Once again, this time with Hitler's rise to power, oppression and conflict in Europe prompted many musicians to move to America. Their impact on American concert life and on standards of teaching and scholarship in music schools can hardly be overestimated. Never before had such a glittering array of world-famous conductors, composers, and performers been included among the immigrants. For some, leaving their homes was a question of survival. With the suppression of artistic freedom and the outbreak of World War II, others soon followed. By 1940, Stravinsky had given his famous lectures at Harvard, Schönberg was teaching at U.C.L.A., Hindemith at Yale, and Bartók at Columbia University.

The United States emerged from World War II a dominant power in world politics, able to shape the future of nations. Yet her music emerged even more firmly tied to traditional imported apron strings. The same musicians whose arrival so enhanced American musical life assured the continued influence of European musical patterns.

The Organ Industry

The Depression Years

One can hardly imagine a situation less conducive to organ building than an extended depression followed by war. But these problems were not the only ones adding to the gloom of the organ builder. The situations that had contributed to the enormous popularity of the organ earlier in the century seemed to have turned sour.

With the introduction of sound in movies in the late 1920s, the era of the theater organ was at an end. The availability of symphonic favorites on both radio and phonograph greatly diluted the enthusiasm for these works played as transcriptions on the organ. The radio and phonograph also outmoded player mechanisms and rolls on both pianos and organs.

The depression chopped up or eliminated the municipal music programs that had begun to flourish in previous decades. One by one, the large, expensive municipal organs fell silent. By 1931 organ recitals had been discontinued in the Cleveland Auditorium (five-manual Skinner, 1922), the Detroit Art Museum (four-manual Casavant, 1927), and the Minneapolis Auditorium (five-manual Kimball, 1928), to mention some of the more prominent examples. Church budgets were also drastically reduced. The demand for residence organs for the idle rich had ended; there were plenty of idle, but they were not rich.

With the sources organ builders had tapped so successfully for contracts seriously reduced, organ building was not for the fainthearted. According to census reports, 2,471 organs were built in 1927, but only 479 in 1935. In 1927, 63 organ firms employed 2,770 wage earners; in 1935 there were only 28 firms, employing 614 people. The paucity of new organ specifications in the organ magazines was appalling. The November 1935 issue of *The Diapason* described the rebuilding of an organ by Wicks and a division Holtkamp was adding to an existing organ, but no new organs were reviewed. It was truly a buyer's market. In 1936 the Wicks Pipe Organ Co. advertised "real" organs starting at $775.00, available for only a small down payment and $23 a month for two years.

The War Years and Postwar Expansion

By the late 1930s the picture had brightened. The number of organ firms had increased to 34, employing about a thousand workers. But organ builders had only a few years to recover some of the lost momentum. In 1942 the War Production Board ordered the entire organ industry to convert to defense work, effective July 31 of that year. In the following year, the use of metals for organ pipes, including replacement parts, was banned. For the duration of World War II, organ factories produced plywood glider parts, coffins, and metalwork of various kinds.

In December 1945 the government relaxed the restrictions on the use of tin by the organ industry. Shortly afterward specifications for new organs began to appear in the professional magazines, and a two-decade boom in organ building was on its way. New churches accounted for much of the demand. The *Wall Street Journal* of February 23, 1955 reported:

> Last year religious institutions spent an estimated half-billion dollars on new construction of all kinds—ten times the 1939 total. And the majority of new churches built have gotten new pipe organs.

Further increases in both church building and the demand for organs were predicted. The major organ builders had a comfortable backlog of orders, and customers could expect to wait eighteen months or two years for the delivery of a new instrument. That, said the *Journal*, was the "happy position of the small but super-busy firms in one tiny but ancient industry—pipe organ manufacturing" [253].

Organ Companies

Victims of the depression included the old Hook & Hastings and Hinners companies; both closed their doors in 1936. Some others who weathered the 1930s gave up the struggle in the next decade: Kimball built organs until 1942; two years later Möller purchased Henry Pilcher's Sons; Harry Hall, of New Haven, Connecticut, was active only until 1945. Survivers in the passing parade of organ companies in the late 1930s included A. J. Schantz, Sons, & Co., Hillgreen, Lane & Co., Odell, Estey, Wicks, Reuter, Skinner, Austin, and Möller.

The firm of George Kilgen & Son was liquidated in 1939. The reorganized firm, headed by Eugene R. Kilgen, became The Kilgen Organ Co. of St. Louis. Alfred G. Kilgen moved to the West Coast, and from 1945 to 1958 he maintained his own organ firm, independent of the St. Louis company. The last of the St. Louis Kilgen organs was installed in 1959, in the Cathedral of the Immaculate Conception, R.C., Kansas City, Missouri. On March 29, 1960 the *St. Louis Globe-Democrat* announced that the machinery, dies, and tools of the Kilgen Organ Co. had been sold for $20,000. Labor trouble was blamed for the financial difficulties that resulted in a foreclosure by the Small Business Administration on a $160,586 loan. The Estey Organ Corporation was also having serious financial problems, and by 1959 was operating by court order under the bankruptcy act. Attempts at reorganization were ultimately unsuccessful, and Estey, too, closed in the early 1960s.

Some of the more fortunate companies also experienced changes of leadership or reorganization. The Reuter-Schwarz factory was moved to Lawrence, Kansas, in the 1920s, but before production was begun in the new plant, Schwarz left, and the firm became the Reuter Organ Company. Louis J. Wick (1869–1936) had founded the Wicks

Pipe Organ Co. in 1906. Its growth was modest, but steady, and during the difficult decade 1926–36, nearly 1,000 organs were built. In 1936 the founder died, leaving the leadership of the company to his survivors.

In 1937, when Mathias P. Möller left to his son the presidency of the famous company he had founded, some seven thousand organs had been built in the Möller factory. M. P. Möller, Jr. (1902–1961), followed in his father's footsteps as a successful industrialist, banker, and lay church leader. He was president of the Hagerstown Trust Company, a director of the Potomac Edison Company and of the Remington Book Company, and member of the Board of Foreign Missions of the United Lutheran Church of America and of the Board of the National Council of Churches.

During World War II he steered his company through the conversion to the manufacture of aircraft materials. Wings for Fairchild planes, gun turret training devices for the navy, doors and elevators for Flying Boxcars all paraded off the assembly lines of the Möller factory [111, pp.27–28]. After the war he charted the reconversion course that kept the Möller name prominent among leading builders in America. By the late 1960s the firm had completed well over 10,000 contracts.

The Austin company was in good condition when the depression arrived, but with the pressures of the time, the Austin brothers decided to liquidate and retire. In 1935 the process of closing the business was begun. Concurrently the firm of Austin Organs, Inc., was formed, a company that included many who had been connected with the original business. The leadership fell to Frederick B. Austin (nephew of John and Basil), president, and Basil F. Austin (son of Basil G.), secretary.

The factory, patents, and other assets were sold to the new company in 1937, and the first organ produced under the name Austin Organs, Inc., was Opus 2002, a two-manual instrument for the First Presbyterian Church, Grand Haven, Michigan [73, pp.19–21]. When the company reconverted from making glider wings during the war, the steady demand for Austin organs enabled this firm to maintain its position among the big three of America's established organ builders, along with Möller and Aeolian-Skinner.

The Skinner Organ Company bought the Aeolian company in 1931, and at that time the now-familiar name, Aeolian-Skinner, was adopted. Ernest M. Skinner was not to remain long with the firm he had founded. Growing tension between the famous builder and his associate, G. Donald Harrison, exploded, with the curious result that Skinner left the firm. By 1935 he was reestablished in Methuen, Massachusetts, but his factory was destroyed by fire eight years later. By this time, new tonal ideas were running roughshod over orchestral design, and the old builder, so positive of the validity of the style he had developed, lived to see his achievements pass into obsolescence. Ernest M. Skinner died in 1960 at the age of 94. Meanwhile, Skinner's bitterest rival, the Aeolian-Skinner company, rose to a position of first-rank importance, with its nameplate on some of America's most famous organs of the mid-twentieth century.

Herman Schlicker is the builder who beat the depression. While other companies were closing their shops, Schlicker, in his quiet and unassuming manner, inaugurated his company in the unlikely year of 1932. He had come to America in 1925, and had worked for Tellers and several other builders before launching Opus 1 of the Schlicker Organ Company. His small factory made machine gun cases during World War II, and after reconversion, the rise to prominence was steady, if not spectacular. With his knowledge of European methods and his sympathy with German trends in design, Schlicker emerged as one of the country's most progressive builders.

Votteler, Holtkamp & Sparling was another firm that gained in prestige as the orchestral style waned. Unlike the Schlicker company, it was a long-established firm, dating back to the 1850s. George F. Votteler, its founder, had opened a small shop in Cleveland about 1856, in partnership with Hettche. In 1903 they were joined by Henry H. Holtkamp, and when Allen G. Sparling entered the firm in 1914, the name became Votteler, Holtkamp & Sparling. Walter Holtkamp (1895–1962) became an active partner after World War I, and it was under his guidance that efforts were directed toward the search for a new style. When Henry H. Holtkamp died in 1931, Walter became the head of the company, and after the retirement of A. G. Sparling in 1943, its name became the Holtkamp Organ Company.

The Holtkamp firm shared some of Schlicker's advantages: a company of moderate size and progressive views, a sensitivity to the voices of knowledgeable organists and scholars, and a willingness to take the risks involved in moving ahead of most builders in organ design.

Electronic Instruments

While the organ industry was struggling for existence during the depression, it was brought face to face with a new threat. Electronic substitutes could hardly have appeared at a worse time, but there they were, in the 1930s, appealing to the public for many of the same reasons that had led to the popularity of the reed organ: size, economy, and ease of maintenance.

Experiments in producing sound electrically were in progress even before the end of the nineteenth century. The telharmonium built by Thaddeus Kahill in New York was a pioneer electric instrument. Another, dating from about 1910, was Farrington's invention, the choral-cello. But it was not until 1932 that the possibilities of electronically produced sounds were brought to the attention of organists in a practical form.

Captain Richard H. Ranger described the way sound was produced in his newly developed Rangertone:

> Our first Rangertone consists of small electric generators, motor-driven. Twelve such machines furnish the electric vibrations. One machine takes care of all the Cs, for example, from the very lowest to the very highest in the musical scale. The other machines take care of the other eleven semi-tones of the tempered scale. A tuning fork for each machine keeps each true to pitch.
>
> Then come the vacuum tubes. A very specially designed amplifier works on any note selected to treat that note in exactly the desired manner as determined by stops drawn by the player, in exactly the same manner that stops are drawn to sound specific pipes on the usual organ. Then the amplified tones are delivered to the bank of loudspeakers which turn the electric energy into sound-waves. It has been our experience that a group of such speakers working each lightly gives far greater clarity and fulsomeness to the tones than if one speaker alone were required to handle the entire energy.
>
> The amplifier furnishes an excellent medium for modifying the tone structure at the will of the player. It is here that the harmonics are combined in varying degrees to give the widest possible range of qualities. Also the attack on the tones may be changed from a slow buildup to a very rapid staccato and even percussion attack. Not only may straight harmonics of the fundamental tone be added, but enharmonic combinations may be used for chime and other effects. [434]

Ranger believed that the most immediate and most practical application of his invention was as a supplement to an organ. He cited the advantages in space, economy, and quality in producing a 32′ sound electronically, and announced that a 32′ Rangertone section was to be added to the Kimball organ at Vassar College.

Two years later, *The Diapason* of April 1934 reported on the use of a Rangertone instrument to supplement an orchestra accompanying a performance of the Brahms Requiem in the Barnard College gymnasium, where no organ was available. A one-manual and pedal instrument was used, although the reporter added that a two-manual version with five stops on each manual was available. "This equipment," he noted, "opens up the possibility of extending the field of the organ to places where the occasional requirements would make a permanent installation uneconomical. It is also effective in open-air installations. The volume is flexibly adjusted for any requirements" [473].

The Hammond Organ made its public debut on April 15, 1935. It was developed over a period of years by Laurens Hammond (1895–1973) of the Hammond Clock Company, a Chicago firm. In May, a reviewer for *The Diapason* opined:

> A hearing and trial of the instrument impresses one with the possibilities it contains. As developed thus far its usefulness will be limited to small buildings and rooms that are not very large and its strongest appeal will be where at present there are no organs because of lack of space or money. It would not in its present state be considered as a competitor with large organs from the standpoint of tonal ensemble or power. [310]

Other electronic instruments appeared. One was the Eremeeff electronic organ, which was introduced soon after the Hammond. It was designed by a Russian scientist, Ivan Ivanovitch Eremeeff, who, along with Leopold Stokowski, had set up a laboratory in Philadelphia to study and promote electronic music in America.

The Hammond Case

Promotion of electronically produced music was something the Hammond company managed with unusual skill and success. By late 1935, organists and builders alike had become concerned about Hammond's advertising and the company's claims that its instruments could serve a church as well as a pipe organ that cost much more. The fact that these instruments were called "organs" was also a matter of concern to some, although that objection did not actually become the major issue.

Organ builders fought ads with ads. The 1936 organ journals carried promotions for the "genuine article," countering Hammond's paid announcements of the number of churches in which the Hammond product had been installed since the last issue. By August, Hammond claimed to have placed the $1,250 instruments in 567 churches.

Meanwhile, the Council of the American Guild of Organists took up the matter of the electronic instrument. While the use of the word *organ* was questioned, the Council found more important the claim that these instruments could produce the effects possible on a pipe organ. Complaints were filed with the Federal Trade Commission in 1935, charging the Hammond Clock Co. with unfair competition. No action was taken at that time, but the case was reopened in 1936. The complaint charged the Hammond company with misrepresentation of the tone quality and value of the Hammond instrument. The statement of the Federal Trade Commission explained:

> Among representations allegedly made by the respondent company in its advertising matter are that use of "The Hammond Organ"

means "that real organ music of unbelievably beautiful quality is now possible in any home at an expense no greater than that of a good piano"; that the instrument "produces the entire range of tone coloring necessary for the rendition, without sacrifice, of the great works of classical organ literature," and that many organists agree the instrument is comparable to pipe organs costing $10,000.

[The complaint was that these and similar representations were false; that] with the exception of the flute notes the respondent's instrument is not capable of producing faithfully the musical tones of a pipe organ necessary for the accurate, adequate rendition of the great compositions of organ music; that its tone is not an improvement over that of any modern organ of recognized merit, and that it is not comparable to a $10,000 pipe organ or to any pipe organ. [201]

Hearings began in Chicago in March 1937, and the debates make up one of the liveliest chapters in American organ history, as organists and builders sought to prove what an organ can and should do. Dr. C. P. Boner, professor of physics at Texas University, used a tone analyzer to compare a Hammond instrument with the pipe organ in the home of Dr. William H. Barnes. There were auditory tests, in which "disinterested musicians" were asked to compare the sound of the Aeolian-Skinner organ in the University of Chicago Chapel with that of a Hammond Organ with six power cabinets and twenty-four amplifiers.

Senator Emerson Richards, Arthur Dunham, William Lester, William H. Barnes, Horace Whitehouse, and Barrett Spach were among the organ authorities who testified in the hearings. At one point, Mr. Spach stated that Hammond "falsified the intentions of Bach." Lynn A. Williams, counsel for Hammond, asked, "Did Bach tell you what his intentions were?" to which Mr. Spach retorted, "Did Blackstone tell you what his intentions were?" [315, p.20].

Laurens Hammond was, of course, examined. He revealed that his background was in engineering, science, and mathematics, that he was not qualified to answer musical questions, and that he did not play an instrument. Part of his testimony consisted of demonstrations of the tonal resources of a Hammond instrument that had been set up in the courtroom. Repeated attempts were made by the defense to introduce into the testimony a wave-analyzer test of an alarm clock buzzer, which was supposed to produce pitches up to the fiftieth harmonic. This evidence was not admitted, and the "government counsel declared that the clock was not an organ" [309, p.4].

Hammond testified that his instrument could do the things claimed for it, and, further, that it could do many things that a pipe organ could not do, and in this respect was a "noticeable improvement" on the organ. A member of the Hammond firm "reproduced for the entertainment of the audience the rumblings of the San Francisco earthquake, a guitar solo, a xylophone, a dance orchestra, a calliope at the circus, a whistler and dog, a locomotive whistle and other classics not found on service lists" [309, p.5].

In October 1937 the hearings were reopened in Atlantic City, and were followed by the final hearing in Washington, D. C. Dr. Charles Courboin and T. Scott Buhrman were new witnesses, and there were additional demonstrations, this time using the Atlantic City Convention Hall organ and a Hammond Organ that had been set up in a church.

Dr. Boner again testified in the final hearings. The December issue of *The Diapason* described his experiments since the Chicago hearings. They were made outdoors, "a trumpet pipe being placed in a tower twenty-three feet high and a microphone in another tower of the same height, while a Hammond electronic organ was raised to the top of a pole with block and tackle and the wave analyzer was again brought into use." Boner concluded that a Hammond instrument would have to have thirty to forty drawbars to duplicate organ tones, and, finally, that it could not produce pipe organ music.

The final oral arguments took place in April 1938. Hammond's attorney predicted that pipe organ building would soon be as lively a business as the making of kerosene lamps. However, on July 12 the Federal Trade Commission ordered the Hammond company to cease its claims that its instruments could equal a pipe organ in its range of harmonics, that it could produce the tone colors necessary for proper rendition of the great works of organ literature, or that it was comparable to a $10,000 pipe organ.

After the trial, Laurens Hammond said that the case had cost a considerable sum, but the publicity had been so extensive that resulting extra sales had covered the expense. The silver lining in the electronic cloud was the much-needed advertising revenue it showered on the depression-parched tills of the organ periodicals.

Electronic Competition

In the comparatively affluent period after World War II electronic instruments posed a less serious economic threat to the organ industry as a whole. The headlined hysteria of the Hammond trials faded, and the initiative in efforts to meet or beat electronic competition fell to the local representative of the large companies, the small builders, and organists who found the electronic organs unacceptable on artistic grounds.

Although the firms manufacturing electronic organs have occasionally attracted the attention of the organ profession with the installation of a large "custom" instrument, most of their products have been installed in small churches, places of entertainment, and homes. William Minter's 1960 survey of church music in Baptist churches in the San Francisco Bay area documented the well-recognized popularity of electronic instruments in small churches. He reported that in nineteen churches with a membership of 40 to 297, fourteen used electronic instruments for their worship services. The remaining five used pianos. Seven out of nine churches with a membership of 300 to 600 used electronic instruments, while the other two had pipe organs [106 p.8].

Such figures suggest that pipe organ builders have generally failed to produce and market instruments that would be both attractive and practical for small churches. On the other hand, the immediate availability and small space requirements of electronic organs, along with aggressive advertising, have helped manufacturers of these instruments to gain virtual control over the small-church market. An uneasy peaceful coexistence has prevailed, pierced by occasional wails of anguish from organists harnessed to instruments ill suited to their musical tastes.

Steps toward a New Style

The Historical Model

The bleak years of the 1930s were not without their rewards. Shorn of the excitement and ballyhoo of large organs, deprived of the lucrative theater organ contracts, and then bombarded with competition from the new electronic instruments, performers and builders alike were forced to reevaluate their art. The whole concept of the organ as a one-man orchestra was challenged, and the basis of the challenge was found not in the scientific research advocated by Audsley but in historical research.

It is nothing short of amazing that in a society destined to be dominated increasingly by the cult that worships at the shrine of scientific development, the organ profession could successfully direct its art toward principles based not on so-called scientific progress but rather on historic traditions. And through the decades that followed, the more wedded society became to scientific exploits the more firmly organ building attached itself to examples of the past.

Parodoxically, science aided this transition. Through scientific methods of research, which stress accuracy, thoroughness, and measures of reliability, musicologists began to separate fact from fiction where early music was concerned. As examples of that music began to sift down from the scholarly publications to the organist's music rack, it became increasingly obvious that it was not primitive but was exciting both to play and to hear. Interest in the historic repertoire went hand in hand with problems of performance style, problems we are still trying to unravel. How did the composers intend it to sound? Bach was the subject of particular scrutiny, and it was the interest in hearing his music to the best advantage that provoked searching questions about organ style.

The European Reform

During the years that George A. Audsley was preparing the manuscript of *The Art of Organ-Building,* the roots of an entirely different concept were forming in Europe. In 1906, the year after Audsley's large, impressive volumes were published, a pamphlet by Albert Schweitzer was issued, entitled *The Art of Organ Building and Organ Playing in Germany and France.* Schweitzer had spent a decade studying and evaluating the current trends in organ building in Europe, and his conclusions condemned the so-called scientific approach to organ design, the imitation of orchestral sounds, electric action, high wind pressure, and placement that interfered with the free diffusion of the organ's sound [426, pp.13–14]. Just as the orchestral organ was emerging in America under two such different leaders as Audsley and Hope-Jones, Schweitzer was suggesting that organ building was moving in the wrong direction, and that the new organs were particularly unsuited for performing Bach's music. However, Schweitzer did not suggest a return to the eighteenth-century style of organ; he admired the organs of Cavaillé-Coll and other builders of the post-Baroque and Romantic periods, and found them satisfactory for the performance of Baroque music as well as that of later times.

Schweitzer's dissatisfaction with European organ design gradually gained attention, but it was not until the 1920s that German organ builders began a definite movement to reestablish the tonal characteristics of an earlier style. The departure was actually much more radical than Schweitzer had suggested; rather than returning to the style of Cavaillé-Coll, the German builders found their model in the North German builder Arp Schnitger (1648–1719) [426, p.14]. The application of Schnitger's methods to modern organs was a gradual process, and, of course, some builders were more reluctant than others to join the march back to the late seventeenth century. But the overall trend in German organ building since the 1920s has been in that direction: a trend that has had a most persistent influence on organ style in modern times.

Briefly stated, Schnitger's style depends on choruses of narrow-scale (principal) and wide-scale (flute) stops on each division, with emphasis placed on the inclusion of upperwork rather than on the duplication of 8′ pitch. Reeds add a new timbre, but do not dominate the ensemble.

The divisions are characterized by differences in fundamental Principal pitch and other tonal distinctions, instead of differences in volume. There is also a similarity of intensity between individual stops. The organs are placed in elevated, free-standing positions in the rooms, and the pipes are surrounded on three sides by cases. Within the case, the arrangement is functional, clearly defining the divisions of the organ. All stops are independent, and none are in a swell enclosure. The scaling is variable, pipes are given open-toe voicing on low wind pressure, and nicking is generally avoided. The action is mechanical.

The Influence of Repertoire

Organists in the United States had no such models to turn to, but the more interested they became in playing the masterworks of organ literature the more apparent it was that the orchestral organ was ill suited for that purpose. The visits of Guilmant, Bonnet, and Dupré, Lynnwood Farnam's masterful performances of organ literature, the opportunities for some American organists to study in France with Widor and Guilmant, and the increasing availability of practical editions of early music were some of the counterforces that were at work even while the orchestral organ was at the height of its popularity.

America's political alignment in World War I helped stimulate interest in Paris as a goal for foreign study. The serious organ student had much to gain there. In addition to the works of the French organ symphonists, there were Guilmant's monumental research in early music, recitals without any transcriptions, and the distinctive style of the French organs.

In 1925, after returning home from studies with Vierne, Widor, and Libert, Homer Whitford recorded his impression of French organs:

> Tonally, these organs excel in bright, yet smooth voicing, and satisfying ensemble. Orchestral imitation has been avoided, and there is an absence of highly individualized solo voices; but on the other hand we find foundation registers unrivalled in sonority, rich mixtures, and dominating, though seldom strident reeds. These give a grandeur and thrill to the fuller effects which are often lacking in American instruments. [509, p.51]

The Estey Organ Company did its share to encourage organ students to study in France by establishing a scholarship in 1924 for the Summer Course at the Fontainebleau School of Music. The award went to the person making the highest grade on the written part of the A.G.O. Fellowship examination.

But whether they traveled to Europe or sat at their consoles at home and practiced their Bach, organists became convinced that the design of the organ must relate to the music of the organ. In some ways that was an old idea: The orchestral organ had developed in response to the popularity of orchestral transcriptions. The revolutionary aspect actually lay in the organists' choice of music. Europeans could test that principle for they had the tools at hand to prove that Bach's music fitted Bach's organs. In America there was no precedent. Even the best of the nineteenth-century instruments, beautiful as they were, were not constructed for a classic organ repertoire.

Stylistic Changes in America

The new theory of organ design related to organ music required time for its formulation, and much more time for its acceptance and application. The years of comparative inactivity during the depression acted as a valuable buffer zone and provided the necessary time for discussion and experimentation. The steps that were taken in a new direction could be subjected to further scrutiny when World War II halted all organ building.

Senator Emerson Richards (1884–1963) was among those calling for a change in style. Richards was neither an organist nor a builder by profession, but he had five organs of his own (one at a time) and was the designer of a number of others. A senator in the New Jersey Assembly, Richards was responsible for the large municipal organs (which he designed) in the Atlantic City High School and the Atlantic City Convention Hall (see pp.333, 362–63).

While a cursory view of the specifications for the gigantic Atlantic City Convention Hall organ shows it to be a child of the 1920s, closer examination reveals some features that reached toward the new style. The most obvious is the unenclosed section of the Choir Organ. It is on 3½ inches wind pressure (most of the flues on the organ are on 10 to 20 inches pressure), and contains a Quintatone 16′, Diapason 8′, Holz Flute 8′, Octave 4′, Fifteenth 2′, Rausch Quint (12–15) II, and Scharf (19–22) II.

Richards had traveled to Europe, examined old organs, and seriously studied the trends in both Europe and America. The Choir division was one weakness he saw in American organs. In 1925 he wrote:

> The truth seems to be that the Choir has become a sort of depository for all of the fancy stops and organists' pets that cannot be conveniently distributed to other manuals.
>
> Both builders and organists will tell us that the Choir is an accompanimental organ. Aside from the fact that there is nothing accompanimental about a Clarinet or French Horn or Orchestral Oboe, one finds nothing but the Diapason and an occasional flute that will serve for accompanimental purposes. [443, p.336]

Richards went on to point out that the flaw in current practice lay in the fact that the great organ music was written for a "brilliant and colorful" Choir:

> No wonder that Bach sounds uninteresting and stodgy as played on the average American organ compared with the blaze of color that Bach had at his command two centuries ago! [443, p.337]

The Convention Hall organ was not Richards's first attempt to provide an organ with a Positive-type division. The Atlantic City High School organ included an unenclosed Choir section on 2 inch wind, which may have been America's first modern Positive division. It included Diapason 8′, Holzflute 8′, Octave 4′, Fifteenth 2′, and Fourniture IV.

In other ways, Richards searched for a more satisfactory answer to tonal design. In the Atlantic City High School Organ, both low- and high-pressure diapasons were used. The high-pressure diapasons, on 7½ inches wind, had the high cut-ups, narrow mouths, and leathered lips of the Hope-Jones type. The low-pressure diapasons, on 3¾ inches, with wide mouths and low cut-ups, were copies of those made by a German builder who exerted a considerable influence on the style of English organs, Edmund Schulze (1823–1878). Neither the American organ world, in general, nor Senator Richards, in particular, were ready to give enthusiastic endorsement to Schulze-type diapasons in 1924. The senator concluded:

> It may be said generally however that the Hope-Jones type embodies greater development of the ground tone with a great sense of weight and dignity, undoubtedly of greater carrying power. Considering the small scale, the Shultz [sic] type is nearly as loud when heard close at hand, but is of a very different quality. It inclines more to a silvery ring. . . . Where only one Diapason is to be included, our experience seems to indicate that the Hope-Jones type is to be preferred, to be followed by the low pressure type where the size of the organ admits. [442, p.406]

While some of Richards's experiments were unsatisfactory, and his designs were really modifications of the existing style rather than a break with current practice, his concern was with the new idea—the relationship of style to organ music. The articles he wrote and the encouragement he gave to others who shared this goal were no small contributions to the style of mid-century organs.

Meanwhile, the attitude gaining popularity among organists was phrased typically by Arthur J. Thompson in 1927:

we are just discovering the merits of the Schulze, Cavaillé-Coll and Willis schools of organ building, based on the idea of cohesive ensemble, with clarity and balance on and between all manuals and pedals. [482]

Thompson correctly judged that a "renaissance of the older conception of the organ" was just beginning.

Hand in hand with the interest in the historical organ was the demand of scholars for accuracy. In exploding the widely accepted theory that the Harmonic Flute was a development of Cavaillé-Coll, Caspar Koch (1872–1970) traced this stop back to its description in Michael Praetorius's *Syntagma Musicum*. Koch concluded:

> We should not be so unkind as to expect infallibility on the part of writers of histories and dictionaries of the organ, albeit we look to them for information rather than misinformation. But is it too exacting to expect of them that they acquaint themselves with the most important source of information on all matters pertaining to the organ of the sixteenth century? [342]

Harrison, Holtkamp, and Others

Harrison and Skinner

In 1927 a thirty-eight-year-old organ builder who was to play a major role in forming the new style joined the staff of the Skinner Organ Company. G. Donald Harrison (1889–1956) had been associated with Henry Willis in London. He coupled an appreciation for some of the outstanding European styles with his thorough background in English organ building.

Harrison, however, was not a disciple of the German reform movement that copied the organs of Arp Schnitger. In an evaluation of his style, Lawrence Phelps described the influences that most deeply affected Harrison's work:

> Motivated by strong artistic convictions, he chose to limit his basic tonal concepts to ideals he felt were best set forth in the work of Gottfried Silbermann, who was really the first of the great Romantic builders, and in the work of Cavaillé-Coll, the last and greatest Romantic builder. His goal was to produce an instrument on which all of the organ's literature could be interestingly—and thus for him satisfactorily—performed regardless of the tonal environment of the school that produced it. From his own point of view and in the judgment of his many admirers, Harrison achieved this goal in the few short years between 1932 and 1940. What few people seemed to be aware of at that time was that, his concepts being restricted as they

were to tonal techniques and ideals that were essentially Romantic, his instruments were really only fine Romantic instruments even though the stop lists often indicated more classical aspirations.

[426, p.24]

Ernest M. Skinner had strong artistic convictions of his own, and it was not long before the conflict between Skinner and Harrison began to cause trouble. The result was that Skinner left the company. He acquired the property in Methuen, Massachusetts, on which Searles had built the hall for the old Boston Music Hall organ and the factory run by James Treat (see pp.205, 242). Here he made a new start in 1935, building "authentic" Skinner organs.[1] Meanwhile, in 1931 the Skinner company had merged with the Aeolian company to form the Aeolian-Skinner Organ Company, a name that became identified with the organs of G. Donald Harrison.

Harrison's Organs of the 1930s

Harrison's early organs showed some deviations from the current practice. Pedal choruses became increasingly well developed and independent, and in the 1933 organ for All Saints Church, Worcester, Massachusetts, French reeds were used exclusively for the first time. But it was in the organs for Groton School, Groton, Massachusetts, and the Church of the Advent, Boston, that Harrison's style really asserted itself. Significantly, these instruments were built in 1935, not long after Ernest M. Skinner had left the firm, and it may have been that Harrison, for the first time, felt completely free to follow his own ideas.

In both organs all the major Pedal stops are completely independent, the reeds were originally omitted from the Great, and the specifications included Harrison's first Positive divisions. With these organs Harrison established the pattern for what became known as the American Classic design, a pattern that was accepted with enthusiasm by those organists who had been crying for reform and was despised by those who were wedded to the 8′ orchestral organ. None the less, it gradually gained in popularity, and became the mainstream development in American organ building.

A characteristic of Harrison's organs that is sometimes criticized is the reed-less Great. The necessity of coupling another division to the Great to add reed tone to the ensemble presents difficulties in registration. As organists have become more reluctant to sacrifice the independence of manuals, this difficulty has become more apparent. An 8′ Bombarde was later added to the Great of the Groton organ, and while other examples of Great reeds occasionally appeared in Harrison's organs, they were not typical of his style.

The Groton School and the Church of the Advent organs each had a 16′ principal chorus on the Great, as well as an 8′ chorus. The Groton School Great division originally included:[2]

Sub Principal	16′	Grosse Tierce	3⅕′
Principal	8′	Quint	2⅔′
Diapason	8′	Super Octave	2′
Flûte Harmonique	8′	Tierce	1⅗′
Gemshorn	8′	Full Mixture	IV
Grosse Quint	5⅓′	Fourniture	IV
Octave	4′	Cymbel	III
Principal	4′		

It can be seen that the harmonic series for the 16′ Principal is represented by mutations as well as by 8′ and 4′ Principals. The Diapason 8′ is topped by a 4′ Octave, a 2′ Super Octave, and mutations of the 8′ series. There was no attempt in the original scheme to provide a flute chorus or reeds on the Great.

The Great division of the Advent organ similarly put all its eggs in the principal-diapason basket, leaving an 8′ Flûte Harmonique to fend for itself. In its original form this division consisted of:

Diapason	16′	Octave	4′
Principal	8′	Quint	2⅔′
Diapason	8′	Super Octave	2′
Flûte Harmonique	8′	Fourniture	IV
Grosse Quint	5⅓′	Cymbel	III
Principal	4′	Sesquialtera	IV-V

[491]

The Swell divisions of both organs were topped by six ranks of mixtures (Plein Jeu VI in the Groton organ, Grave Mixture III and Plein Jeu III in the Advent organ). The Swell reeds on both organs were Bombarde 16′, First Trumpet 8′, Second Trumpet 8′, Clarion 4′, and Vox Humana 8′. Harrison used the third manual to accommodate both an enclosed Choir and the unenclosed Positive. The latter provided a meaningful third division, and while Harrison's Positive divisions sound timid by present-day standards, they were a revelation in the 1930s. The Advent and Groton Positives had identical specifications, extending from 8′ to a four-rank compound stop. They had a full series of mutations, and duplicated pitches only at the 4′ level. The more conservative Choir divisions emphasized old-fashioned quiet voices of lower pitch, but unlike most Choirs, they each contained an 8′ Trumpet.

The Groton Pedal marked such a change from traditional practice that it is worth noting in detail. Its fourteen independent stops gave it a size comparable to that of the Great division (fifteen stops), and it is sobering to realize how few organs in the ensuing years have equalled this example.

Contre Basse	32′	12	Quint	5⅓′	32
Principal	16′	32	Super Octave	4′	32
Contre Basse	16′	32	Flûte Harmonique	4′	32
Bourdon	16′	32	Gedeckt (Sw)	4′	
Flûte Conique (Sw)	16′		Mixture (17–19–22)	III	96
Grosse Quint	10⅔′	32	Fourniture (22–26–29)	III	96
Octave	8′	32	English Horn (Ch)	16′	
Contre Basse	8′	12	Bombarde	16′	32
Flûte Ouverte	8′	32	Trompette	8′	32
Gedeckt (Sw)	8′		Clarion	4′	32

While it was one stop smaller than the division cited above, the Pedal of the Advent organ was similar in design and was actually more impressive in relationship to the overall size of the organ. The Groton organ contained 85 ranks, the Advent organ 76.

The Harrison organ for Strong Auditorium, University of Rochester, was installed in 1937. Designed in consultation with Harold Gleason, this organ showed even more clearly the direction of the future. Here the Great flute chorus is developed rather than a 16′ principal series, and the tierce ranks are omitted. While the Rochester organ borrowed one Pedal 16′–8′ combination from each of three manual divisions (more than either of the two earlier organs discussed), the Pedal chorus stops were entirely independent, and a separate Pedal 2′ was included.

Within the framework exemplified by these organs of 1935–37, Harrison defined his style and established his position of leadership among American organ builders. In some ways it was to his advantage that so few organs were actually being built in the mid-1930s, for his organs received more attention and were more widely discussed than would probably have been the case if the organ-building boom of the previous decade were still in progress.

It is also interesting, as scarce as organ contracts were, that Harrison could successfully break with the orchestral tradition and rise to a popularity that overshadowed those working along more established lines. Perhaps that is another indication of how generally the need for change was felt among the leading organists. It is possible, also, to overestimate Harrison's actual popularity in the 1930s because of the acceptance his principles eventually found. It is no problem to find specifications of the orchestral variety during this period, while we view the select few organs that are presently regarded as indicative of Harrison's contribution to American organ building.

Strong Auditorium, University of Rochester, Rochester, New York
AEOLIAN-SKINNER (G. DONALD HARRISON), 1937

Great (Wind pressure 3 inches)

Violone	16'
Principal	8'
Diapason	8'
Hohlflöte	8'
Gemshorn	8'
Octave	4'
Flûte Harmonique	4'
Quint	2⅔'
Super Octave	2'
Blockflöte	2'
Full Mixture	IV
Fourniture	IV
Cymbel	III
Chimes (in Choir box)	

Swell (Wind pressures 3¾ and 6 inches)

Gedeckt	16'
Geigen Principal	8'
Stopped Flute	8'
Viola da Gamba	8'
Viola Celeste	8'
Octave	4'
Flute Triangulaire	4'
Violina	4'
Nazard	2⅔'
Flageolet	2'
Full Mixture	IV
Plein Jeu	IV
Double Trumpet	16'
Trumpet	8'
Clarion	4'
Oboe	8'
Tremolo	

Choir (Wind pressure 3¾ inches)

Dulciana	16'
Viola	8'
Orchestral Flute	8'
Dolcan	8'
Dolcan Celeste	8'
Zauberflöte	4'
Nazard	2⅔'
Piccolo	2'
Tierce	1⅗'
Clarinet	8'
Chimes, 25 tubes	
Tremolo	

Rück-Positiv (Wind pressure 2½ inches)

Koppelflöte	8'
Quintade	8'
Prinzipal	4'
Nachthorn	4'
Nasat	2⅔'
Blockflöte	2'
Terz	1⅗'
Larigot	1⅓'
Sifflöte	1'
Scharf	IV
Zimbel	III
Krummhorn	8'

Solo (Enclosed in Choir box; wind pressure 7 inches)

Orchestral Oboe	8'
Harmonic Trumpet	8'
Clarion	4'
Tremolo	

Pedal (Wind pressure 3¾ and 5 inches)

Principal	16'
Contre Basse	16'
Violone (Great)	16'
Flute Conique	16'
Lieblich Gedeckt (Swell)	16'
Dulciana (Choir)	16'
Octave	8'
Open Flute	8'
Violoncello (Great)	8'
Still Gedeckt (Swell)	8'
Dulciana (Choir)	8'
Super Octave	4'
Nachthorn	4'
Blockflöte	2'
Mixture	III
Fourniture	II
Trombone	16'
Trumpet	8'
Bassoon	8'
Clarion	4'
Chimes (Choir)	

[*The Diapason*, October 1937, pp.1–2]

G. Donald Harrison had arrived in America with certain important built-in advantages. The mere fact that he was a foreigner was one of them. Another was his entrance into one of America's most successful and respected organ firms. The comparatively large and important contracts the Aeolian-Skinner Company was still able to obtain, even during the worst of the depression, provided Harrison with the showcases to establish his reputation. The break with E. M. Skinner placed Harrison on a pedestal as the champion of the anti-orchestral-organ movement.

The diplomatic phrasing of articles Harrison wrote for the professional journals enhanced his image. In pointing out the deficiencies of American organs, he could still mention the "perfection of design, workmanship and long life of the electric action as perfected here" and the "wonderful orchestral imitative stops, to say nothing of the exquisite and colorful soft work as developed by Ernest M. Skinner" [311, p.32]. Or he paid homage to the school of American organists "which, in my opinion, is second to none" [312, p.23].

In the spring of 1937 an organ was opened that added greatly to Harrison's renown. It was installed in the Busch-Reisinger Museum of Germanic Culture at Harvard, and it was the closest to a Baroque organ that any American organ builder had come since Tannenberg. It was entirely unenclosed, free-standing, and used 2½ inches wind pressure.

E. Power Biggs is credited with the idea that the Germanic Museum ought to have an organ that represented Germany's contribution to music. *The Diapason* revealed the subsequent events:

> Failing to arouse any interest among the Harvard authorities, Mr. Biggs mentioned the idea to Mr. Harrison, who became so interested that he recommended to the Aeolian-Skinner firm that they build the organ as an experiment. His ideas for the construction of a classical organ had been accumulating in the course of building organs for Harvard University, the Church of the Advent, Groton School, Wellesley College, St. Mark's in Philadelphia, and Grace Cathedral, San Francisco. The new organ, while not by any means Mr. Harrison's ultimate ideal for a church organ, does express his philosophy of organ building. The instrument is the property of the company, but will remain at the Germanic for at least one year. [262, p.4]

Actually, it remained until 1958, when it was replaced by a Flentrop organ.[3]

The Germanic organ might have been nothing but a museum piece, known by a few and understood by fewer, had it not been for a series of weekly radio broadcasts initiated in 1942 over c.b.s. Biggs and guest performers acquainted countless organists (and, incidentally, other listeners) all over the country with the qualities of this relatively small instrument. Even the more progressive organists were surprised at its possibilities. In a review of its opening, Edward B. Gammons wrote:

> The color and versatility of this little organ of twenty-five stops are beyond conception and withal it is the most satisfying musical medium for the interpretation of classical organ music that the writer had ever hoped to hear. [299]

Busch-Reisinger Museum of Germanic Culture, Harvard University
AEOLIAN-SKINNER (G. DONALD HARRISON), 1937

Hauptwerk			*Pedal*		
Quintade	16'	61	Bourdon	16'	32
Principal	8'	61	Gedeckt Pommer	8'	32
Spitzflöte	8'	61	Principal	8'	32
Principal	4'	61	Nachthorn	4'	32
Rohrflöte	4'	61	Blockflöte	2'	32
Quinte	2⅔'	61	Fourniture	III	96
Super Octave	2'	61	Posaune	16'	32
Fourniture	IV	244	Trompete	8'	12
			Krummhorn (Pos)	4'	
Positiv					
Koppel Flöte	8'	61	*Couplers*		
Nachthorn	4'	61	Positiv to Pedal 8'		
Nasat	2⅔'	61	Hauptwerk to Pedal 8'		
Blockflöte	2'	61	Positiv to Hauptwerk 16', 8'		
Terz	1⅗'	61			
Sifflöte	1'	61	Eight general pistons		
Cymbel	III	183	Crescendo pedal		
Krummhorn	8'	61			

[262, p.1]

The Aeolian-Skinner organs for the Church of St. Mary the Virgin, New York (1933; revised 1942–43), and the Worcester Museum of Art, Worcester, Massachusetts (1942), are among Harrison's other important prewar instruments. In the former, Harrison made his first use of unenclosed, free-standing pipe work in a rear-gallery installation. All divisions on the three-manual Worcester Museum organ are unenclosed (the pipes are located above the court skylight, out of sight). Like the Germanic Museum organ, it was given twenty-three independent voices, and was actually originally planned as a two-manual organ. The opening recital was given by Joseph Bonnet on November 18, 1942.

Walter Holtkamp

During the years that G. Donald Harrison was beginning to demonstrate his tonal ideas, the Cleveland firm of Votteler, Holtkamp &

Sparling was initiating its own reform. Walter Holtkamp (1895–1962), who established the company's policies after 1931, lacked some of Harrison's automatic prestige. A native of St. Mary's Ohio, he was a member of a relatively small and relatively obscure firm. During the depression it struggled along with contracts for rebuilding old organs, plus a few orders for new organs.

Little of Harrison's conciliatory tone can be found in Holtkamp's messages to the organ profession. They were, rather, direct and to the point. When W. W. Kimball made a plea for standardization in the arrangement of couplers, Holtkamp responded:

> Mr. Kimball's plea for uniformity comes at this ideal time, when we are all settling down to serious effort after our long debauch of sensational console gadgets as well as queer organ tone. There now seems to be a genuine desire on the part of serious musicians to reduce the number of console appliances and spend this money on the inside of the organ. This matter of simplifying console equipment directly concerns the couplers. *We have far too many couplers.* If fewer couplers were used the present confusion in coupler arrangements would never have arisen. [327]

In 1936, when the organ industry was in a frenzy over the new rivalry from the Hammond company, Holtkamp suggested that if the electronic manufacturers were willing to spend so much money marketing their instruments it was "just possible" that something might be wrong with the modern organ.

> If the organ had remained true to its heritage and if, whether built for cathedral, arena, chapel or music hall, it had retained its definite artistic characteristics, there would today be no competition from machine-made, scientific substitutes. . . .
> . . . We have been having a grand time in this substitution of dramatic tone for music and of virtuosity for expression, but the orgy is about finished. . . .
> I believe that the organ profession should thank the inventors of the electronic substitutes for the flattery of imitation and then divest their own instrument of the rococo overlay of artificialities which cloaks its naturally serene and grand character. [323]

Such statements, coupled with the style of his instruments, earned for Holtkamp the image of an uncompromising, radical exponent of the Baroque style. Conservative organists who thought Harrison's organs were bad found Holtkamp's impossible. It is probably no exaggeration to say that Holtkamp's reputation as an extremist earned him opponents who had never heard any of his instruments. On the other hand, as the new style gained in popularity, those who found Harrison perhaps too tame rallied around the Holtkamp banner. Actually, as Phelps has pointed out, there was an underlying similarity in objectives that places both Holtkamp and Harrison in the mainstream of the American Classic development.

> If reduced to words, the goal that motivated Holtkamp was quite like that of Harrison—to produce a kind of all-purpose instrument— but Holtkamp was willing to work in a much smaller frame; he was much more selective in what he felt was worthy literature and made no pretense whatever that his instruments were suitable for the larger Romantic works. Thus Holtkamp's instruments rarely had an enclosed Positive or Choir, and rarer still are his instruments with more than three manual divisions. The rather large differences apparent in the sound of their work is due mostly to Harrison's natural English love for breadth of tone and a smooth tonal finish, in contrast with Holtkamp's determination to let his well-designed pipes speak for themselves without any attempt to make them conform to a pre-determined norm. In this respect, at least, Holtkamp's philosophy was closer to that of good classical practice, even if his fundamental voicing technique was not substantially different from that used by Harrison. So far as voicing of the individual pipe was concerned, the difference was one of degree rather than method. Also, Holtkamp's success in obtaining very open positions for most of his organs gave them a presence and spontaneity that won him many friends.
>
> [426, p.24]

Holtkamp's Functional Design

The installation that first attracted widespread attention to Holtkamp was really only a nine-rank division added to the Skinner organ in the Museum of Art, Cleveland, in 1933. It was hailed, somewhat inaccurately, as the first "rückpositiv" in the United States.[4] Melville Smith and Arthur Quimby were consultants, and they initiated the enlarged organ by presenting the organ works of Bach in a series of twenty recitals. After the first recital, reviewer Carleton Bullis registered astonishment: "One was able to listen attentively to a whole program of Bach music without feeling bored, so delightfully sparkling and incisive and alive was the effect of the music" [242].

More free-standing organs and rückpositivs followed in the 1930s, including a rückpositiv for St. Philomena's Church, Cleveland, an organ with rückpositiv for the First Congregational Church, La Salle, Illinois, and Holtkamp's first completely exposed instrument, built for St. John's Church (R.C.), Covington, Kentucky, in 1934. As significant as the rückpositivs and the visible, free-standing pipe work is the fact that some of these organs were rear-gallery installations.

To say that the Covington instrument is completely exposed requires qualification, since there is a Swell division. Holtkamp explained: "The Swell is the only division under the influence of shutters. The shutters are plainly visible and the on-looker is not in doubt as to the function of this apparatus" [325, p.272].

Throughout his career, Holtkamp insisted that design should be functional, and that the appearance of the organ should express its character.

> Too often a lacy or delicate effect is imposed on casework and this is incongruous with organ tone properly conceived. Although delicate tracery may reflect to some degree the softer and more effete tones, where such exist, it is totally incapable of suggesting to the eye the counterpart of the massive and virile effect which the whole ensemble should produce. This is much better achieved by exposing to the eye the pipes massed in strong architectural forms and by reducing the casework to a minimum consistent with good design. The hand of the craftsman should be evident everywhere, as well as in the construction of the pipes and the treatment of the casework. In this connection, grilles are particularly indefinite, weak and purposeless in appearance.
> [325, p.270]

His concern with visible pipes was, of course, related to their sound as well as their appearance. "With the present conditions of organ placement," he said, "the organist is in the unfortunate position of the man who must woo his lady by correspondence" [324, p.356].

Holtkamp maintained that the musical value of any instrument was "in direct proportion to its free-standing position" [324, p.355]. This principle he translated into a simple matter of dollars and cents: a small organ, well placed, is worth more than a much larger instrument, poorly placed. He argued for smaller instruments that could be properly seen and heard: "They are more of a pleasure to build and certainly more of a pleasure to listen to. The mammoth thing may satisfy the ego of the purchaser but it sins against all the dictates of good taste and the laws of musical sound" [321, p.124]. Not all of Holtkamp's locations were ideally situated for open placement, but he did more than any other American builder to get the pipes out of their tombs and at the same time demonstrate the aesthetic value of a beautifully designed arrangement of pipes.

Organs by Holtkamp

Holtkamp's style did not reach its mature form as early as Harrison's did. None of Holtkamp's organs built before World War II can compare with the one in the Church of the Advent or with the other famous Harrison organs, but the three-manual instrument for the First Congregational Church, La Grange, Illinois (1937), was well within the borders of the new style.

Rather than treating the Positiv as a supplement to a Choir division in Harrison's manner, Holtkamp provided a second Swell by enclosing part of the Great. The principal chorus, however, was left unenclosed. Holtkamp did not have the advantage of the open, visible location he preferred for this organ. The Great, Swell, and Pedal were placed in chambers on either side of the chancel. The chambers opened into the nave as well as into the chancel and provided as much freedom of tonal egress as is possible in that situation. The Positiv was placed on the back wall of the chancel, and although entirely unenclosed, it was hidden from the view of the congregation.

First Congregational Church, La Grange, Illinois
Votteler, Holtkamp & Sparling, 1937

Great		Positiv	
Quintaton	16′	Quintaton	8′
Principal	8′	Gemshorn	8′
Salicional	8′	Prestant	4′
Hohlflöte	8′	Rohrflöte	4′
Octave	4′	Nazard	2⅔′
Fugara	4′	Tierce	1⅗′
Doublette	2′	Cymbal	III-IV
Plein Jeu	V	Cromorne	8′
Posaune	16′		
Harp		*Pedal*	
Chimes			
		Contrabass	16′
Swell		Soubasse	16′
		Violoncello	8′
Gamba	8′	Flute	8′
Voix Celeste	8′	Choralbass	4′
Harmonic Flute	8′	Nachthorn	2′
Bourdon	8′	Bombarde	16′
Ludwigtone	8′	Fagotto	8′
Flute Octaviante	4′	Clarion	4′
Piccolo	2′	Posaune (Gt.)	16′
Mixture	IV	Quintaton (Gt.)	16′
Dolce Cornet	III		
Trompette	8′		
Oboe Clarion	4′		
Vox Humana	8′		
Tremolo			

The best-known works of Walter Holtkamp were built after World War II. Many of them were placed in colleges and universities, and in these locations their influence on a younger generation of organists was marked. Webber summarized the postwar Holtkamp achievements:

An organ by Walter Holtkamp, 1958. Alfred Hertz Memorial Hall of Music, University of California, Berkeley. *Photo by Roger Sturtevant.*

Among the many Holtkamps in American colleges and universities are these: Alabama, California at Berkeley, Fish [*sic*], Hollins, Houghton, Kentucky, Maryville, MIT, Oberlin, Trinity, Syracuse, Wooster, Yale, Concordia Seminary, St. Louis, and General Seminary, New York. Several of these have more than one Holtkamp of recital size and practice size instruments are to be found in many other institutions.

Walter Holtkamp provided many organs for churches in the Cleveland area: St. Paul's Evangelical Lutheran, St. Paul's Episcopal, Cleveland Heights, First Congregational Church, Elyria, Epworth Euclid Methodist. Several in churches in various parts of the country have been featured at conventions and conclaves: Corpus Christi, New York City, Trinity Lutheran, Houston, Christ Church, Baltimore. [499, p.29]

Holtkamp followed more closely the paths of the German reform than did Harrison. For example, where size permitted, the traditional 8′ reed was included in the Great division and the Swell became the only enclosed division. The organ in the Alfred Hertz Memorial Hall of Music, University of California, Berkeley, illustrates the Holtkamp design of the 1950s.

Alfred Hertz Memorial Hall of Music
University of California, Berkeley, California
WALTER HOLTKAMP, 1958

Great			Positiv		
Quintadena	16′	61	Copula	8′	56
Principal	8′	61	Praestant	4′	56
Gedackt	8′	61	Rohrflöte	4′	56
Octave	4′	61	Nazard	2⅔′	56
Spitzflöte	4′	61	Octave	2′	56
Doublette	2′	61	Flute	2′	56
Octave Quinte	1⅓′	61	Tierce	1⅗′	56
Plein Jeu	IV	244	Fourniture	III	168
Scharf	III	183	Cromorne	8′	56
Dulzian	16′	61	Glockenzimbel, 12 bells		
Trumpet	8′	61			

Swell			Pedal		
			Principal	16′	32
Flute à Cheminée	8′	61	Subbass	16′	32
Dulciane	8′	61	Quintadena (Gt)	16′	
Gambe	8′	61	Octave	8′	32
Voix Celeste	8′	61	Gedackt	8′	32
Octave Geigen	4′	61	Choralbass	4′	32
Bourdon	4′	61	Hohlflöte	4′	32
Flautino	2′	61	Nachthorn	2′	32
Piccolo	1′	61	Mixture	III	96
Cymbale	III	183	Cornet	V	160
Cornet	V	245	Posaune	16′	32
Basson	16′	61	Dulzian (Gt)	16′	
Fagott	8′	61	Trumpet	8′	12
Clarion	4′	61	Schalmey	4′	32

The console is equipped with 9 couplers, 18 manual pistons (12 of which are duplicated on the pedalboard), 6 pedal pistons, 6 general pistons (duplicated on the pedalboard), sforzando pedal, and crescendo pedal.

An eleven-stop gallery organ was added to this instrument in 1964. It can be played from the Positiv manual of the main organ, or from its own 56-note manual and 13-note pedal.

Möller and Austin

The English influence in American organ building was not isolated in Harrison's work. Both the Austin and Möller firms turned toward tonal ideals inspired to a large extent by precedents established by Willis in London.

Richard O. Whitelegg (1890–1944) entered the Möller company as a voicer in 1930, and he later became a director of the company. Whitelegg had worked for Harrison & Harrison, August Gern, and Willis, as well as several American firms. At the Möller plant he was influential in establishing the trend away from the theater organ influence. Whitelegg's tonal concept was more conservatively English than Harrison's, and in spite of that, or perhaps because of it, the Möller firm remained extraordinarily successful in gaining contracts.

While the Austin company had been among the first to be exposed to the Hope-Jones ideas, wholesale unifying never became a characteristic of Austin organs. A few unit organs were built, but with the exception of some Pedal stops, Austin organs usually relied on independent stops. Their orchestral tendencies in the early part of the century were expressed by oversized scalings for the diapasons and extremely narrow scales for the strings.

When the demand for a brighter, lighter sound with greater independence arose, Austin was in a better position than many companies to make the adjustment. Accordingly, a middle-of-the-road path toward the new style was adopted, and James Jamison is generally credited with initiating "reform" in Austin tonal design. Jamison subscribed to the American Classic ideal, with more emphasis on English traditions than on German and French. In 1939 he wrote:

> I believe the ideal organ of the future will be built around the "international ensemble" idea. . . . We are trying for an organ that will play all types of organ music well, that has the "grand sound" and that fits its church or hall as though it grew out of it. The works of Schulze, Silbermann and Willis, with a touch of Cavaillé-Coll, form our ingredients. [336, p.20]

When the postwar demand for new organs resulted in an expansion of Austin's facilities and personnel, Jamison was sent abroad to look for a voicer. His choice was Richard J. Piper. With thirty years' experience working for Willis, Piper's tonal ideas meshed well with the direction in which Austin had been moving. He joined the Austin organization in 1949, and became tonal director of the company in 1952.

Postwar Patterns

The American Classic Style

When organ building was resumed after the war, the companies that had resisted the reform movement found that a brighter ensemble would be required for survival. Even so, some of the basic necessities recognized by Holtkamp and Harrison more than a decade earlier were slow to find acceptance. The most persistent leftovers from the orchestral organ were Pedal divisions relying heavily on derived stops and Choir divisions of the old accompanimental variety.

The objective of combining the old and new elements into one style had been stated many times: an organ suited for the repertoire of all periods. That remains the goal of many organ builders in this country today, and no small factor contributing to this position is the fact that the eclectic organ is the choice of many organists and church committees looking for new organs.

From the beginning, the advocates of the American Classic style roundly denounced imitation as a basis for developing organ design. In fact, "slavish imitation" became the derogatory cliché that replaced "screaming mixtures." William King Covell's 1943 statement is one of many that expressed this viewpoint:

> there is a possibility of sterility were the attempt made to copy too literally the work of the past. That danger, however, has not yet become real, since in the best work of the present only ideas and principles are taken from older times; there is ample range of adaptation to conditions, acoustical, architectural and musical, of our own times. Such intelligent adaptation is vital, whereas literal copying cannot but be insipid. [265]

Within this framework considerable divergence of practice can be found. The proportion of old ideas used, the original source of those ideas, and the extent of their modifications are ingredients that can be mixed in countless ways. Organs leaning heavily toward French practice, organs more closely related to Schnitger's than to Silbermann's can all be seen as part of the American Classic plan.

As the influence of European practice filtered into American organs, the objective style of Schnitger, so perfectly suited to polyphonic music, began to dominate the specifications of some builders. This development brought warnings that organs so constructed were losing their all-purpose flavor.

In 1962 Robert White compared César Franck's indicated registration in thirteen compositions with eight new three-manual organs by six different builders. He found that only two of these instruments contained the minimum resources necessary for the *fonds de 8* registration required on two divisions by Franck. Also conspicuous by its absence was an 8′ Hautbois. Noting that some enthusiasts for the Baroque style claimed that Franck's music really sounded better when re-registered according to eighteenth-century German practice, White warned:

But this is the very thing we find insulting when it is applied to Bach. Many organists around 1920 thought that Bach sounded better when his climaxes could be driven home by the blast of a high pressure stentorphone and tuba mirabilis. They should serve to warn us that aesthetic judgment does not always resist temporary enthusiasms. ... We need only a tiny backward swing of the pendulum away from the German baroque model, just enough to get an 8 ft. principal on a second manual, an 8 ft. hautbois on a third, and flutes and gambas that are not reduced to a whisper—that is all. It is more reasonable to ask the 18th-century purist to let these stops rest silent, if he must, then to ask an organist of more catholic taste to play on stops that are not there. [506]

Noehren's Design

Robert Noehren, who combines a career as one of America's leading recitalists with organ building, has developed a style of organ using as models the instruments of Arp Schnitger, François-Henri Cliquot, and Aristide Cavaillé-Coll. These builders represent the three great traditions in organ style, which had their fulfillment in the music of Bach and Buxtehude, Couperin, and Franck, respectively. "Here then," according to Noehren, "are perhaps the three most significant traditions from which the organist and organ builder in our day might find inspiration" [396, p.40].

Briefly stated, Noehren's plan incorporates principal and flute ensembles in the Schnitger tradition on two manuals and pedal, the mutations and mounted Cornet necessary for the performance of early French music, and the harmonic flutes and gambas typical of Cavaillé-Coll. The reeds are also of the Cavaillé-Coll type, but modified to make them more suitable for use in music of earlier periods. Further support is given the nineteenth-century French style by additional flute ensembles. In its practical application, Noehren's plan may be seen in the specification for the 1969 organ in the First Presbyterian Church, Buffalo:

First Presbyterian Church, Buffalo, New York
ROBERT NOEHREN, 1969

Great		Great (continued)	
Quintadena	16′	Waldfloete	2′
Principal	8′	Mixture	III-IV
Rohrfloete	8′	Scharf	III
Octave	4′	Cornet (discant)	IV
Spitzfloete	4′	Bombarde	16′
Octave	2′	Trompette	8′

First Presbyterian Church, Buffalo, New York
ROBERT NOEHREN, 1969

Swell

Bourdon	16'
Bourdon	8'
Gambe	8'
Voix Celeste	8'
Unda Maris II	8'
Flute Harmonique	8'
Flute Octaviante	4'
Octavin	2'
Plein Jeu	III-V
Bombarde	16'
Trompette	8'
Hautbois	8'
Clairon	4'
Tremulant	

Positiv

Principal	8'
Gedeckt	8'
Octave	4'
Spielfloete	4'
Octave	2'
Mixture	III-IV
Scharf-Cymbel	III
Sesquialtera (c)	II
Cromhorne	8'

Solo

Contre-Gambe	16'
Bourdon	8'
Gemshorn	8'
Viol d'Gambe	8'
Flute Harmonique	8'
Prestant	4'
Flute	4'
Nasard	2⅔'
Doublette	2'
Tierce	1⅗'
Larigot	1⅓'
Piccolo	2'
Flageolet	1'
Plein Jeu	III-V
Cymbel	III
Trompette	8'
Voix Humaine	8'

Solo (continued)

Clairon	4'
Tremulant	

Bombarde

Trompette	8'
Clairon	4'

Pedal

Subbass	32'
Principal	16'
Subbass	16'
Contre-Gambe	16'
Octave Bass	8'
Gedeckt Bass	8'
Octave	4'
Flute	4'
Octave	2'
Nachthorn	2'
Mixture	V
Harmonics	IV
Contre-Bombarde	32'
Bombarde	16'
Trompette	8'
Clairon	4'

Couplers

Swell to Great
Positiv to Great
Solo to Great
Swell to Positiv
Solo to Positiv
Swell to Solo
Positive to Solo
Great to Pedal
Swell to Pedal
Positiv to Pedal
Solo to Pedal
Solo to Swell
Positiv to Pedal 4'
Solo to Great 16'
Solo 16'

Combinations

Great, 5; Swell, 5; Positiv, 5; Solo, 5;
Pedal, 5; General, 8; Coupler, 1; Master, 1.

Divisional pistons 1 through 4 and general pistons 1 through 8 are adjustable by means of data processing cards. All remaining pistons are capture type.

[*A.G.O. National Convention Book, 1970*]

An organ by Robert Noehren, 1969. First Presbyterian Church, Buffalo, New York. *Photo courtesy Buffalo Evening News.*

Italian and Spanish Influences

Other styles are occasionally represented in the Classic plan. Several organs in the Los Angeles area include divisions in the Italian Renaissance style, which is particularly suited for the music of Frescobaldi and his contemporaries. The 1966 Reuter organ for Calvary Presbyterian Church, South Pasadena, California, is a three-manual organ with Great, Swell, and Italian Positiv as its manual divisions. Subsequent installations of Italian divisions are found in Justin Kramer's 1969 organ for Saint Basil's Church, R.C., Los Angeles, and the Schlicker organ installed the same year in the First Congregational Church, Los Angeles. In the latter, the Italian division consists of:

Principale	8′	Decima Nona	1⅓′
Voce Umana (TC)	8′	Vigesima Seconda	1′
Flauto	8′	Vigesima Sesta	⅔′
Ottava	4′	Vigesima Nona	½′
Flauto in Ottava	4′	Trigesima Terza	⅓′
Quintadecima	2′		

The horizontal reeds typical of early Spanish organs are another source of inspiration. Actually, the prone trumpets that have capped the specifications of some large modern specifications carry only a vague resemblance to their Spanish ancestors. The latter were integral members of the ensemble, while modern versions are usually the whipped-cream topping of an otherwise independent specification. Horizontal reeds made earlier appearances in American organs, for example, in the 1915 Austin organ for the Chapel of the Intercession, New York [22, p.166]. One can see a picture of the Tuba Clarion en Chamade in the Atlantic City Convention Hall organ in *The American Organist* of July 1934 (p.307). This stop was voiced on fifty inches wind pressure.

The horizontal reed, as it has been used most frequently in recent decades, was introduced by the Aeolian-Skinner company in a 1949 organ for the First Presbyterian Church, Kilgore, Texas. Called Trompette-en-Chamade, the stop was mounted under the high chancel window and was "aimed" at the rear of the church. The rest of the organ was installed in chambers on either side of the chancel. Thus the Trompette was separated from the rest of the organ, although it lacked the antiphonal location at the opposite end of the church that similar stops have often been given in subsequent installations. This stop was designed to be a solo voice balanced against the full organ or to add the final climax to the full ensemble. Roy Perry, then organist-choirmaster of the Kilgore church, was enthusiastic:

> The first time I used the stop for a hymn descant I thought for a moment that the people were going to stand up in the pews and cheer. What they did was to sing as they had never sung before. The stop was worth its cost then and there. [391]

Even more spectacular is the antiphonal reed Harrison designed for the Cathedral of St. John the Divine, New York. The famous State Trumpet is mounted horizontally under the rose window in the west end of the cathedral, some five hundred feet from the main organ. It speaks on 50 inches wind pressure. This stop was installed in 1954, when the Aeolian-Skinner company rebuilt and enlarged the 1910 E. M. Skinner organ.

Large Organs

Just as Audsley's Ancillary divisions (see p.342) had provided an outline for the design of organs of great size in the early twentieth century, the American Classic theme was expandable, furnishing the basis for postwar organs built in grand proportions. If a specification includes, with some degree of thoroughness, the tonal contributions of several schools of organ building in one instrument, stop lists of formidable length may result. Indeed, this concept, by its very nature, depends on large size for its fulfillment. In the United States, modern organs in the near-hundred-rank bracket and larger have characteristically been designed to meet the requirements of a representative cross section of organ literature. A detailed description of these large organs installed in the 1950s and '60s would fill a book, but a brief survey of a few illustrates this aspect of modern organ history and the companies that have contributed to it.

The ninety-eight-rank Aeolian-Skinner organ[5] for New York's Lincoln Center was inaugurated in December 1962. A committee of organ consultants was engaged to solve the problems of "the design and construction of a comprehensive pipe organ primarily for use with orchestra" [507, p.10]. Serving on that committee were Robert Baker, Searle Wright, Carlos Moseley, Charlotte Garden, and Joseph Whiteford.

A double organ plan was used by consultants Edward B. Gammons and Paul St. George in preparing the specifications for the 1964 Möller installation in the National Shrine of the Immaculate Conception, Washington, D.C. There is a four-manual Gallery Organ of 119 ranks, and a three-manual Chancel Organ of 48 ranks. Gammons summarized: "Tonally these two organs have been designed to permit the service player and the solo organist every possible use in accompanying choirs and congregations, in playing with orchestra and organ solo performance" [300, p.12]. A more recent large Möller installation is in the Metropolitan United Methodist Church, Detroit, Michigan. This 119-rank organ was dedicated in 1973.[6]

The resources of the 1969 organ built for the First Congregational Church, Los Angeles, by the Schlicker Organ Company were described by the consultant, Clarence Mader:

> First, it must be said that this is a *triple* organ—a 1932 Skinner organ (71 ranks) located on both sides of the choir in chambers behind carved cases; a near-replica of a sixteenth century Italian organ (11 ranks) exposed in an arch above the clergy stalls and below the Skinner; and the Schlicker organ (132 ranks) in the west gallery. [359, p.21]

The Skinner organ was enlarged and tonally revised to provide accompaniment for anthems and oratorios and to augment the Romantic resources available in the Swell division of the gallery organ. Mr. Mader continued:

An organ by the Aeolian-Skinner Organ Company, 1962. Philharmonic Hall, Lincoln Center, New York. *Photo by Sedge LeBlang.*

For the performance of music from the Renaissance through the
Baroque and Classic Periods, all tonal demands are encompassed in
the "Italian" organ, and the Gallery Organ's Great, Rück-Positiv,
and Brustwerk divisions. The Pedal of twenty-one registers plus its
two 32-foot extensions is equal to every nuance of color and balance.[7] [359, pp.21, 23]

Another builder who shared well in the big-organ boom was the
Austin Organ Company. New York City hailed the installation of large
Austin organs in the Fifth Avenue Presbyterian, Brick Presbyterian,
and First Presbyterian churches in the early 1960s. A more recent example of this company's work is seen in the 113-rank organ dedicated in
1969 in the First Presbyterian Church, Tulsa, Oklahoma.[8]

Small Organs

As the size of the organ is reduced, the designer adhering to the
eclectic concept meets his most serious challenge. Compromise is inevitable in instruments of moderate size, and organs of small size cannot
really represent American Classic design.

In 1965 Joseph Whiteford, then tonal director of the Aeolian-
Skinner Organ Company, defined his company's solution for the
design of small church organs, stressing the need for providing stops
suitable for accompanying anthems: "We approach the American two-
manual organ as primarily an accompanimental instrument and not
one destined to perform with any great sense of validity Bach's great
Kyrie or the Widor Toccata" [508, p.35].

A frequent solution to small organs in situations where some stylistic versatility is required is to include a skeletal German principal
chorus based on 8' in the Pedal, 4' on the Great, and 2' on the Swell.
Tapered, stopped, and chimney ranks are used to complete the pitch
spectra and add tonal variety. A Celeste and perhaps a reed on the
secondary manual add further flexibility. Often only the secondary
manual is enclosed, although practice in this regard is inconsistent.

In their efforts to extract maximum versatility from a small scheme,
organists and builders alike often resort to old-fashioned methods. As
recently as 1968, Walter Holtkamp, Jr., could still voice a complaint
that reverberates through half a century of American organ building:

> What frightens this builder is the fact that this practice of maximizing
> ranks of stop tablets while minimizing ranks of pipes is on the in-
> crease. Our musicians not only accept, but rather, demand these
> large stoplists. And our builders acquiesce. Happiness is a big mess
> of draw knobs! [328, p.19]

XVII

THE NEO-BAROQUE ORGAN

Introduction

Toward Stylistic Purity

AUTHENTICITY in performance has been consistently stressed in leading music schools. Generations of students have started Baroque ornaments on the auxiliary note; a whole new industry for the manufacture of harpsichords, recorders, and other early instruments has emerged; and madrigal societies, Renaissance chamber ensembles, and recorder clubs have given amateur performers as well as professional musicians an increased interest in early music. It should not be surprising, then, that organists have frequently expressed dissatisfaction with instruments that allow only partial fulfillment of their desire for stylistic purity.

The postwar trend in organ building in northern Europe was toward an ever more faithful reliance on the Schnitger example in specification, pipe scaling, voicing, the use of cases, and other details. M. A. Vente, a leading Dutch organ authority, explained that it was not a matter of imitating Baroque organs; it is a "comparative incident" that the modern organs in Germany and Holland greatly resemble the old instruments.

> The modern way searches for the essentials of sound and for the way to attain this. It appears that the 17th–18th century organs knew these essentials, whence the resemblance between the modern organs and the former ones: the starting-point is alike; there is no imitation. [492]

Imitation or not, the similarity was obvious, and it did not escape the attention of shiploads of students traveling to Europe after the war, aided by Fulbright grants and a growing assortment of foreign study

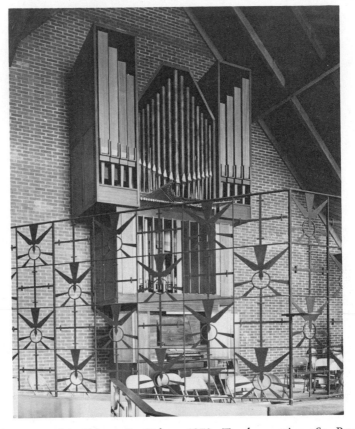

An organ by Abbott & Sieker, 1970. Tracker action. St. Peter's Episcopal Church, San Pedro, California. *Photo courtesy Jim Lewis.*

programs. Countless organists, organ students, and builders took advantage of opportunities to see and hear firsthand not only the new European instruments but also the historic organs that were their models.

Some were convinced that the American Classic concept, in attempting to serve all styles, like the jack-of-all-trades, did justice to none. How, they questioned, can one reconcile French Romantic reeds with a German Baroque flue chorus? If a compromise is made, neither style is given valid representation.

If one is convinced that purity and authenticity of style are important in performance, it is only a short step to conclude that these factors are also important in instruments. If the stylistically valid performance goes beyond merely playing the right notes to include details of tempo, rhythm, phrasing, and ornamentation, then it extends also to all details of the actual sound. When applied to the organ, then, one must be concerned with the acoustical environment, balance of the stops and divisions, voicing, and action, as well as the selection of stops.

Neo-Baroque versus American Classic

No one has denied that it takes more than a Baroque stop list to produce a Baroque organ. Just how far one must go in following the practices of the Baroque builders to produce an instrument equally satisfactory for the performance of Baroque music and other polyphonic styles was a prime stylistic problem of the 1950s and '60s. An even more basic problem is whether or not stylistic purity can be justified if it is accomplished at the expense of other important styles. In other words, which takes precedence: one style represented in the best possible manner, or a cross section of styles represented with acknowledged compromises? This question symbolizes the conflict in philosophy between the advocates of a neo-Baroque style and the American Classic style. Some members of the profession have taken positive positions on one side or the other, and have justified their viewpoints with reasonably convincing arguments. Others contend that the choice must be based on the use to be made of the organ.

A brief, and necessarily incomplete, catalogue of opinions includes the following:

Polyphonic music is the most important body of organ literature, and is most characteristic of the instrument. Therefore, the organ design best suited to this type of music should be given priority in all situations.

All styles of music are enhanced by the clarity of line characteristic of the German Baroque organ.

Organ recital literature is admittedly at its best on a neo-Baroque organ, but such an instrument is ill suited for the variety of styles used in the church.

The neo-Baroque organ is the traditional organ of the church, and while one might want the versatility of an American Classic organ for playing recitals that include the large works of the Romantic period, such an instrument has no liturgical significance or use.

Neo-Baroque organs find their most reasonable home in college and university music departments. Students should have the opportunity to play and hear polyphonic music on an organ ideally suited for it. However, this style is too limited for general use.

The neo-Baroque style is a fad that has no relevance today, in view of the advances that have been made in organ building since the eighteenth century.

Clearly, matters of taste and personal preference in repertoire enter into the formation of such widely differing opinions. The function of the organ in the church service is also a matter of no small influence. Varying as it does from one denomination to another, as well as within denominations, one would hardly expect general agreement regarding the organ design that can best serve the church in the United States.

An organ by John Brombaugh & Company, 1972. Tracker action. Ashland Avenue Baptist Church, Toledo, Ohio. *Photo courtesy John Brombaugh.*

One undeniable fact is that the neo-Baroque organ has steadily gained in popularity since the mid-1950s.

There is no clear-cut dividing line between the American Classic style and the neo-Baroque style. In theory, one may define the former as a style incorporating the characteristics of more than one period of organ building, and the latter as a style oriented specifically to the performance of polyphonic music, drawing its model from one period of organ building. In practice, there are the borderline cases that draw heavily from North European practice, and yet contain some concessions to the Romantic style (e.g., an enclosed division). To set up arbitrary pigeonholes to give definitive classification to all organs is as futile as trying to define how chromatic or subjective a composition must be in order to qualify as Romantic.

We now return to the problem of how faithfully an organ builder must follow the techniques of Arp Schnitger in order to produce an instrument ideally suited to the performance of polyphonic music, thereby qualifying as neo-Baroque. Must it be encased? Must it have mechanical action? In a strict interpretation of the style, the answers are in the affirmative. Other important concerns for the modern builder are voicing techniques, the nature of the wind supply,[1] the relative merits of different systems of tuning, and the possibility of following some of the stylistic characteristics of other early builders (e.g., Cliquot, or Andreas or Gottfried Silbermann).

Imported Organs

Three- and Four-Manual Imported Tracker Organs

A few small European organs began filtering into the United States in the mid-1950s, attracting but little attention from the profession as a whole. When larger imported organs appeared in prominent places, the impact of the European reform began to exert a significant influence.

The earliest one was a mechanical-action organ with four manuals, forty-four stops, and sixty-five ranks built by Rudolf von Beckerath of Hamburg, Germany, installed in 1957 in Trinity Lutheran Church, Cleveland. It was soon followed by a three-manual, twenty-seven-stop, thirty-three-rank organ by D. A. Flentrop, Zaandam, Holland, installed in 1958 in the Busch-Reisinger (Germanic) Museum, Harvard University. While the latter is a comparatively small three-manual instrument, its location had particular significance. Through recordings and broadcasts, the Aeolian-Skinner organ built by G. Donald Harrison in 1937 had become a well-known instrument (see pp.384–85). Now it was replaced by this new Dutch organ with mechanical action and wind pressures of 1-7/16 to 2-1/16 inches. In typical European style, these new organs were provided with cases.

Other impressive installations by these two builders followed in the 1960s. Von Beckerath installed organs in Stetson University, DeLand, Florida (three manuals, thirty-seven stops, 1962), St. Paul's Cathedral, Pittsburgh, Pennsylvania (four manuals, sixty-seven stops, 1962), St. Michael's Church, New York (three manuals, thirty-eight stops, 1967), and Christ Lutheran Church, Washington, D. C. (three manuals, 1969). Flentrop organs went to Reynolda Presbyterian Church, Winston-Salem, North Carolina (three manuals, thirty stops, 1961), and St. Mark's Cathedral, Seattle, Washington (four manuals, fifty five stops, 1965).

The first major United States installation by Rieger Orgelbau of Schwarzach, Austria, was placed in the Unitarian Church of Germantown, Philadelphia, Pennsylvania (three manuals, forty stops, 1964). Other large instruments by this firm are in the Wellesley Congregational Church, Wellesley, Massachusetts (three manuals, forty-three stops, 1968), and All Souls Church (Unitarian), Washington, D. C. (four manuals, sixty stops, 1969).

Werner Bosch of Kassel, Germany, was the builder of the organ in St. Mark's Episcopal Church, Portland, Oregon (three manuals, thirty stops, 1966).

As the decade of the 1970s opened, new three-manual imported organs were installed in Ladue Chapel, St. Louis (Werner Bosch, 1970), Dwight Chapel, Yale University (Rudolf von Beckerath, 1971), First Congregational Church, Berkeley, California (Paul Ott, 1971), First Church, Congregational, Cambridge, Massachusetts (Theodore Frobenius, 1972), First Congregational Church, Columbus, Ohio (Rudolf von Beckerath, 1972), Pomona College, Claremont, California (Rudolf von Beckerath, 1972), First Lutheran Church, Galveston, Texas (Freiburger Orgelbau, 1973), University of Wyoming (E. F. Walcker, 1973), and United Methodist Church, Berea, Ohio (Rudolf Janke, 1974).

These instruments and many smaller ones are important examples of contemporary European organ building. Dispersed about the country, they have given organists and builders in various locations opportunities to study their effectiveness as church and recital instruments and to compare them with organs built in the United States.

Canadian Influence

While the European instruments facilitated experiments in the neo-Baroque style by builders in the United States, recognition must also be given to the leadership exerted by Canada's veteran firm

Casavant Frères Limitée of St. Hyacinthe, Quebec.[2] In 1958 the Casavant company appointed Lawrence Phelps (b.1923) as tonal director. Phelps had been employed by G. Donald Harrison, and then by Walter Holtkamp, as a voicer and tonal finisher. His later activities as an independent organ consultant and his writings on tonal design established Phelps's reputation as an advocate of the European reform. Under his leadership the Casavant firm initiated a department for building mechanical-action organs, and by 1968 Phelps had been responsible for the completion of some 450 Casavant organs, including twenty-five tracker-action instruments. At that time he was named vice president and director of the Casavant company.

In an address delivered at the International Organ Festival at St. Albans, England, in June 1969, Phelps noted the growing demand for organs with mechanical action:

> At Casavant, we recently estimated from information in our files that, even now, we could easily sell about twenty-five good size mechanical-action instruments a year if we were in a position to make them. . . . it is clear that in the foreseeable future, we at Casavant Frères will be producing mechanical-action organs exclusively and at a rate at least equal to our current total production of about 1200 stops per year.
>
> [427, p.39]

Under Phelps's direction, the installation of mechanical-action Casavant organs in the United States included three-manual instruments for the United Lutheran Church, Grand Forks, North Dakota (1964), St. Andrew's Episcopal Church, Wellesley, Massachusetts (1965), Colorado State University, Fort Collins, Colorado (1968), the Choate School, Wallingford, Connecticut (1968), Wheaton College, Norton, Massachusetts (1970), Carnegie-Mellon University, Pittsburgh, Pennsylvania (1970), and the University of Iowa, Iowa City, Iowa (1971). In 1972 Phelps formed his own company, and tonal leadership of the Casavant firm was given to the German organ builder Gerhard Brunzema.

Style Characteristics

Size Reevaluated

The most famous European organs installed in the United States are "large" when mechanical-action organs are considered, but few of them compare in size with the "large" organs built according to American Classic principles. Notable exceptions are the Pittsburgh von Beckerath organ (sixty-seven stops controlling ninety-seven ranks) and the Rieger organ in All Souls Church, Washington, D. C. (sixty stops, ninety-five ranks). Runner-up is the Flentrop organ in Seattle (fifty-five stops, seventy-five ranks).

Size receives a new interpretation when the neo-Baroque style is considered. An oft-declared principle states that an organ should be as small as possible for a given situation. The idea that large size might be a detriment instead of an asset in organ design was revolutionary. For a century American organists had associated size with importance, and dimensions were sometimes simply a matter of prestige. When the builder incorporates the tonal resources of several styles in an American Classic organ, he has a musical justification.

The neo-Baroque organ, on the other hand, concentrates its resources on a single musical style. While there were large organs built in the Baroque period, the actual demands made by the music of Bach, Buxtehude, and their contemporaries can be fulfilled by an instrument of moderate size, and much of the music of that period is appropriately played on organs of very limited means.

That capability has been a factor of great importance; the neo-Baroque style has given the small organ of two manuals, or even one manual, a new significance. While the American Classic style must make more stylistic compromises as the size of the instrument is reduced, the small organ based on Baroque practice retains its stylistic integrity. Even a very small organ of this type is a valid, authentic medium for performing a large body of excellent organ literature. For these reasons, the neo-Baroque style as a solution to the problem of small organ design has found favor with many organists, even among those who prefer the American Classic plan for larger instruments.

The stylistic significance that neo-Baroque design gives to small instruments has brought about some far-reaching changes in the organ industry. The resources of a big factory and elaborate machinery are not needed to produce a small organ. Small shops and individual builders, committed to the principles of the European reform, have been the leaders in producing neo-Baroque organs in the United States. Thus there has been something of a return to the importance of the independent craftsman of earlier periods of American organ history.

Range

The pedal range of thirty-two notes and manual range of sixty-one notes, along with other matters pertaining to console standardization, were officially adopted by the American Guild of Organists in 1933. They had been in general use long before that date, and until recently their acceptance was seemingly unanimous. Most of the recent large, imported organs have a European manual compass of fifty-six notes, but concede to American specifications for a thirty-two-note pedal. Some American organ builders have followed this pattern, occasionally even reducing the manual range to fifty-four notes. The advocates of a thirty-note pedal remain in a minority, although a few new instruments use this compass.

Exposed and Encased Organs

Through the 1950s Holtkamp remained the leading exponent of free-standing, exposed pipe work. When Joseph Blanton's beautifully illustrated book *The Organ in Church Design* [22] was published in 1957, the representation of Holtkamp organs far outnumbered those of any other American builder. Most organs were still being placed in chambers.

Visible pipe displays were not unanimously endorsed, even in the late 1960s. A letter to *The American Organist* (October 1965, p. 3) from the Reverend Gunther J. Stippich touched off a flurry of letters in that publication pro and con exposed pipes. Stippich argued that if organ pipes are really beautiful, we should take the hoods off our automobiles to show the beauty of the engines.

The controversy continued for several months, with some letters calling attention to the tonal advantages of exposed pipes, some referring to the great unenclosed European organs, and some suggesting that consideration be given to organ cases. References were made to pictures of organs in recent magazine issues illustrating the use of exposed pipe work to enhance the architecture. Naturally, less complimentary installations also drew attention. One writer observed: "The cover of one of your recent issues shows a New York church similarly injured by an instrument which resembles a giant porcupine crouching behind the altar" [*The American Organist*, January 1966, p.3].

While the desirability of exposed pipes was contested, cases received less attention, so infrequent was their appearance. In his 1957 book, Blanton could list only four modern organs in the United States that were entirely encased: the von Beckerath organ in Cleveland, a small Flentrop positiv in the University Presbyterian Church, San Antonio, Texas, and two organs built by Otto Hofmann [22, p.80], one of which was installed in the Matthews Memorial Presbyterian Church, Albany, Texas, the other in Zion Lutheran Church, Walburg, Texas. Hofmann's 1956 organ for Matthews Memorial Presbyterian Church was "the first permanent installation of a tracker-action organ in a contemporary case in America" [22, p.423].

In his second book, *The Revival of the Organ Case,* Joseph Blanton could illustrate thirteen encased organs built in the United States between 1960 and 1965. Since the book contains illustrations of 112 organ cases, all products of the 1956–65 decade, the record was not impressive. Blanton traced modern European cases to a 1940 choir organ by Marcussen, and lamented: "It is no exaggeration to say that organ building in the United States is fully twenty years behind that in Europe" [23, p.14]. He attributed the reluctance of the larger American firms to adopt "more progressive and artistic practices" to the economic difficulties of a changeover, rather than ignorance.

Placement

Where church instruments are concerned, these economic difficulties are often complex, and are related to other problems. To place a free-standing, encased organ in a Dutch or North German church, where it is used for a prelude, accompaniment for congregational singing, and occasional recitals, is a comparatively uncomplicated matter. To place the same instrument in an American church, where it is to accompany the vested choir in the chancel, presents difficulties. Not only is a location for the organ often not available but also there are such delicate questions as which visible setting the parishioners will feel is most conducive to worship. Even if these problems are somehow overcome, the chancel area does not often afford the unencumbered, elevated situation best suited for the organ from an acoustical standpoint. For the organ, organist, and choristers to retreat to the rear gallery, whence they came, has been an obvious solution, provided the church has a rear gallery. Frank Cunkle, editor of *The Diapason*, noted a trend in that direction in his March 1958 editorial:

> It is interesting to note that the Joint Commission on Church Music of the denomination which has probably led the trend in this country of divided chancel choirs and *chambered* organs, the Episcopal Church, has recently come forth in a letter to diocesan music commissions with: "To sound at its best the organ pipes should be so placed that their sounds may properly blend and the ensemble tone may travel freely in several directions. A free standing position in a rear gallery is ideal, and in any case an organ should stand as much in the open as possible, rather than recessed in a chamber."
> An ever-increasing number of the specifications published on our pages would indicate a definite turn in this direction. . . . Maybe our forbears knew what they were doing. [269]

Neither a case nor an elevated, free-standing placement will produce a neo-Baroque organ, and it is quite possible to find American Classic organs incorporating these characteristics. Both, however, are considered to be essential to the neo-Baroque style, and the growing agitation during the 1960s for their use must be recognized as a part of the neo-Baroque trend.

Mechanical Action: The First Decade

Walter Holtkamp may be credited with launching America's second tracker period. His little three-stop Portative with mechanical action and slider chest was ready for sale in 1935. One description noted:

> The builders of the Holtkamp Portative feel that a direct physical control of the tone-generating agency is essential in any small intimate musical instrument, regardless of whether that instrument be a violin or an organ, and that adherence to this principle is especially desirable if an instrument is to be played in ensemble with other instruments or voices. [322]

In a small two-manual organ built in 1938 for Emmanuel Lutheran Church, Rochester, New York, Holtkamp again used slider chests. By this time he was convinced that the effect of the key-chambered chest on the blend of the pipes was of primary importance. Early the next year his article "Plea for Reviving the Sliderchest" appeared in *The American Organist*. "A set of pipes," he noted, "voiced on and for a modern individual-valve chest and at low pressure generally improves in speech and tone when placed on a sliderchest" [326, p.13]. Holtkamp further explained:

> As we know, pipes on the same chamber have a tendency to draw together. Since on the key-chamber chest all the pipes corresponding or belonging to a given key are placed on a common chamber and have a common wind-supply, these pipes tend to draw together or blend. [326, p.14]

The most detailed reply to Holtkamp's article was written by Emerson Richards. He maintained that the effects slider chests have on pipe tone are undesirable, and that they are particularly noticeable in the speech initiation:

> there is a period of indecision at the beginning of the speech of the pipe. It is quite true that this period is very short, but it is also true that it is heard and becomes a part of the aural impression of the build-up of the tone. Very frequently this hesitation causes the pipe to be actually off its speech at the beginning of the tone.
>
> [445, pp.120–21]

Richards also discussed the flexibility in placement and arrangement of other types of chests, the difficulty of obtaining proper wood for making slider chests, and other practical considerations.

These articles and shorter opinions that appeared in *The American Organist* were written in a dispassionate, objective manner, and the incendiary nature of the tracker-action and slider-chest question was not yet apparent. But the American organists' Thirty Years' War was soon to erupt, and even if the flames have finally died down, the coals are still warm.

Readers of *The Diapason* could enjoy a lively dialogue in the late 1930s and the early part of 1940 as the pages of that magazine were opened to a debate on organ style. Principals in this discussion were Ernest M. Skinner, William King Covell, and Edward B. Gammons, and the topic was old, familiar ground, with Skinner defending the orchestral design against classic tendencies.

In June 1940 the whole issue took an unexpected turn when Gilman Chase suggested that organ playing would probably be more musical on tracker action than on electric action. Chase apparently had no idea of joining the tonal-style argument; he was rather responding to a letter that had praised electric action. But Chase's letter was all that was needed to switch the direction of the debate from the style of the recent past to the style of the future. Chase's idea was so startling to *The Diapason*'s editor, S. E. Gruenstein, that he wrote an editorial entitled "Advancing Backward," closing with the statement: "Any musician who fails to realize what electricity has done for him lays himself open to the charge of ingratitude" [307].

In July, a letter from Walter Blodgett expressed concern that the organ in recent years had developed "a rather intimate bedside manner," and observed that "perhaps a return to the tracker action and slider chest is not such a silly notion after all." Meanwhile, Ernest Skinner, whose ability with the barbed pen was never to be outdone, queried: "Inasmuch as the diapason is now disappearing from the organ, would it not be a good idea to change the name of your publication to *Sesquialtera* or *The Baroque Times*?" More organists entered the fray, and it seemed that sooner or later every organist of note would take his stand with the new trackerites, the moderates, or the romantics.

Meanwhile, possibilities of practical application and experimentation had been all but eliminated by the shortage of critical materials. With the entrance of the United States in World War II, organ building ceased, and all arguments became purely theoretical. There was an exception, of course. Charles McManis had been inducted into the army in 1942 and was stationed in California. With borrowed tools and a borrowed woodworking shop, he completed one division of a projected two-manual and pedal mechanical-action organ during his spare hours in 1943 and 1944 (his Opus 7). Since no metal was available, all pipes were made of wood [386].

Mechanical Action: Postwar Developments

After the war, tracker action was still far from the minds of most organists, and only a few organ builders were ready to pioneer in this territory. Otto Hofmann of Austin, Texas, rebuilt two old instruments in 1948 and 1952, retaining the mechanical action. In 1955 he constructed a two-manual, ten-stop tracker organ for Beacon Hill Presbyterian Church, San Antonio, Texas. More ambitious was the 1956 organ for the Matthews Memorial Presbyterian Church in Albany, Texas. For this two-manual instrument, Hofmann imported the pipes and the pedal chests from Flentrop in Holland. The Beacon Hill organ had exposed pipes, but the 1956 organ was given a handsome case designed by Joseph Blanton [137, p.115].

By that time, experiments with mechanical action had begun elsewhere. In 1950 Robert Noehren was consultant for the rebuilding by the Schlicker Organ Company of an 1893 Johnson organ. The tracker action was retained, the wind pressure lowered, and the pipe work rescaled and rebuilt with new languids and mouths.

In 1953 Lawrence Phelps could affirm:

> the writer must state here his personal conviction, based upon his present experience, that there is no substitute for the slide chest if tonal matters are the only consideration. All other devices must be considered as compromise measures. [424, II, p.42]

The same year Charles McManis built a four-stop portativ with mechanical action and a "sliderless keychamber chest idea with pneumatic stop-action" [430]. In 1956 the Schlicker Organ Company rebuilt a two-manual Felgemaker organ, retaining the tracker key action, but adding electric stop and combination action.

The Organ Historical Society was organized in 1956. With Barbara Owen as its first president, this organization was formed primarily to collect information about early organs and to prevent further destruction of examples of early American organ building. Having a keen appreciation for the outstanding examples of mechanical action still in use, particularly in New England, the members of the society, both individually and collectively, were quick to encourage the use of mechanical action in new organs.

Still, results were slow to appear, and even slower to gain recognition. An editorial in *The Diapason* of June 1958 stated: "As of this writing, we know of no American builder who is willing or able to produce a modern tracker instrument." A letter from Barbara Owen the next month replied that Charles McManis had completed one the year before, and that the Andover Organ Company was then building two.

Mechanical Action since 1958

Heated debates on the relative merits of mechanical and electro-pneumatic action continued through the late 1950s and early '60s. Much of the evidence on each side could be reduced to matters of personal preference. Some organists enjoyed the flexibility in placement that electropneumatic instruments permitted. Others felt that while tracker action was fine for Baroque music, large tracker organs were impractical, and their limited size as well as their characteristic tone quality made them unsuitable for much of the Romantic organ literature. Some, who had had unfortunate experiences with old tracker organs, warned that the action was heavy, particularly when manuals were coupled, and playing fast passages would be out of the question. Organists accustomed to smooth regulation found the speech initiation of unnicked pipes and the comparatively uneven regulation in some new instruments both annoying and unmusical.

On the other side of the question, convinced trackerites argued that mechanical action and its concomitant tonal character gave a more rhythmical quality to their playing, making it seem more alive. The direct control of the action of the pallet by the finger was a satisfying experience. Opinions differed about the amount of influence the performer could actually exert over the attack of the note, but the psychological effect was one that pro-tracker organists found both pleasing and helpful.

As recently as 1961 Harold Frederic could write:

> It is unlikely that any more organs will be built with tracker action; certainly not on a commercial basis. At the moment most builders are faced with a heavy backlog of work and are unwilling to divert manpower to tinker with old work. Building a slider chest requires the most consummate artistry and any man capable of doing so would be 120 years old, and his efforts with a hammer and chisel would be attended with dire consequences. [296, p.28]

In that year the Andover Organ Company completed a two-manual, thirty-seven-stop tracker organ for the Mount Calvary Church, Baltimore. Planned by Charles Fisk (then president of Andover) in consultation with Arthur Howes (organist of the Mount Calvary Church) and the Dutch builder D. A. Flentrop, the beautifully encased organ was given a rear-gallery installation.

Three years later the *Organ Institute Quarterly* made a survey of modern tracker organs in America. It listed twenty-three builders and 152 organs in the United States. While many of these instruments were imported, the growing list of tracker builders in the United States in-

An organ by the Andover Organ Company, 1968. Tracker action. Lawrenceville School, Lawrenceville, New Jersey. *Photo courtesy Andover Organ Company.*

cluded Andover Organ Co., C. B. Fisk, Otto Hofmann, Charles McManis, Noack Organ Co., and Herman Schlicker. The distribution of these organs is interesting: Massachusetts and Texas were the undisputed leaders, with twenty-eight and twenty-two organs, respectively. New York had thirteen, and Ohio twelve. The rest of the states had fewer than eight new tracker organs, and many had only one or two, if any.

A point of particular significance is that forty-eight of these organs had been installed in educational institutions or their chapels. Here countless students would have firsthand experience with modern tracker action, and one might reasonably expect an organ in such a situation to have far greater influence than if it were used primarily by one organist. The Episcopal and Lutheran churches had been most active in installing tracker organs, but a number of other churches were also represented.

The organs ranged in size from one manual, one stop, to four manuals, sixty-six stops; the most favored size was two manuals with seven to twelve stops. The only new four-manual tracker organs then in the United States were imported from Rudolf von Beckerath: for Trinity Evangelical Lutheran Church, Cleveland, and for St. Paul's Cathedral, Pittsburgh, Pennsylvania.

During the 1960s tracker organs remained to a large extent the domain of the small builder. The number of new tracker builders that appeared each succeeding year in the annual "Two Manual" issue of *The Diapason* was nothing short of amazing. The United States had not had so many active small organ shops since the nineteenth century. The Schlicker Organ Company was the largest American firm committed to slider chests and using mechanical key action when it was possible. In 1959 the M. P. Möller company announced that Dirck Flentrop would supply tracker actions and chests for organs using Möller pipes. Perhaps Möller was too far ahead of the market, or perhaps those who were interested in Flentrop action also wanted Flentrop pipes. In any case, this arrangement aroused little interest.

As the 1960s drew to a close, several of the larger organ firms took steps toward the production of mechanical-action organs. Early in 1969 the Reuter company announced an affiliation with the Emil Hammer Organ Company of Hannover, Germany, to produce Hammer-Reuter tracker organs. About the same time the Aeolian-Skinner company was ready to supply tracker organs built by Robert L. Sipe. Sipe had had his own firm in Dallas for ten years. He joined Aeolian-Skinner as a representative in 1968, and moved to Boston the next year. From mid-1970 until 1972 the technical and artistic direction of that company was under his leadership. "Holtkamp Builds First Tracker for Summit Church" was the inaccurate, but indicative, heading of a *Diapason* story in September 1969 describing an instrument built for St. John's Lutheran Church, Summit, New Jersey. The same issue announced a Möller mechanical-action organ to be built for Nativity Evangelical Lutheran Church, Allison Park, Pennsylvania.

The list of tracker organ builders continued to grow, and many more geographical areas were represented. W. Zimmer & Sons, Inc., formerly of Germany, opened a plant in Charlotte, North Carolina, in 1964. This company builds both tracker and electropneumatic instruments. Abbott and Sieker, of Los Angeles, completed the first modern two-manual tracker organ built in southern California in 1967. The ten-stop, twelve-rank, encased instrument was produced as a shop project. The first mechanical-action organ built in the Louisville area since the last of the Pilcher trackers was a two-manual instrument produced by Steiner Organs, Inc. This rear-gallery-with-rückpositiv installation was dedicated in the Church of Our Lady of Perpetual Help, New Albany, Indiana, in May 1970. The organ installed in the First Evangelical Lutheran Church, Lorain, Ohio, in 1972 by John Brombaugh & Co. contains the first modern American examples of hand-hammered metal pipes. Another interesting feature of this two-manual encased tracker organ is the use of unequal temperament based on the principles of Andreas Werckmeister.

Meanwhile, some of the smaller companies produced instruments of major proportions. The first modern three-manual tracker organ built in the United States was the product of Charles Fisk of Gloucester, Massachusetts, and was installed in King's Chapel, Boston, in 1964. Fisk served his apprenticeship with John C. Swinford and Walter Holtkamp, and later was president of the Andover Organ Company, Methuen, Massachusetts. In 1961 he moved to Gloucester, Massachusetts, changing his company's name to C. B. Fisk, Inc. A new firm, formed in 1961, using the old name of the Andover Organ Company, continued in business in Methuen under the direction of Robert Reich and Leo Constantineau [232, p.27]. When Fisk's four-manual organ for the Memorial Church, Harvard University, was completed in 1967, its forty-eight stops, seventy-five ranks classed it as the largest modern tracker-action organ built in the United States. Even larger is Gilbert F. Adams's four-manual organ for St. Thomas Church, New York (fifty-nine stops, ninety ranks), dedicated late in 1969.

One could feel that the building of mechanical action organs was coming of age as 1968 and 1969 saw the opening of beautifully encased three-manual tracker organs by the Andover Organ Company (Lawrenceville School, Lawrenceville, New Jersey), Schlicker Organ Company (Texas Lutheran College, Seguin, Texas), and Noack Organ Company (Trinity Lutheran Church, Worcester, Massachusetts).

Tonal Design

It is not in the larger tracker organs, however, that one sees most clearly the style characteristics of the neo-Baroque. Three- and four-manual organs tend to wed this style with the objectives of the American Classic. In describing the organ at Memorial Church, Harvard University, Charles Fisk wrote:

> A conscious effort has been made to create within this single instrument the features required for performing all styles of serious organ music. While this is not the first attempt to achieve this goal, the chief difference between the present effort in eclecticism and those

which have preceded it is an emphasis not on choice of stops, but rather on the method of controlling them. [293, p.13]

The organ in St. Thomas Church, New York, built by G. F. Adams –Organ Builders, Inc. has been described:

> This is probably the first organ in this country specifically designed and voiced for the authentic performance of the French classic literature. The design has been expanded to make possible performance of music of all schools. [392]

It is actually in the two-manual organ that the neo-Baroque builder finds his most natural expression and his greatest challenge. Here the problems of balance and the character of the individual stops are the most critical. Each division must contain its own independent ensemble, and the pedal must balance either of the manual divisions. In addition, each division should be as complete as possible. Lawrence Phelps has written:

> Whereas a two-manual is beginning to reach fulfillment with 25 stops, a three-manual scheme cannot boast a comparable completeness until it has acquired more than thirty stops . . . a three-manual instrument of less than 30 stops can seldom be justified. . . . [423, p.9]

The individual stops must be well balanced. For example, a trio registration using an 8′ stop in each division is basic. If one must compensate for an underpowered 8′ on one manual by adding a mutation, then the possibilities of obtaining any variety in trio registration are greatly reduced. An 8′ pedal stop that will balance in a trio registration often remains an unsolved problem.

One of the most striking characteristics of the old European organs is the great beauty of the individual stops. Organists accustomed to the more Romantic varieties of American organs are surprised to hear an 8′ Principal of such rich quality that it could well be used as a solo voice. Each stop is, in itself, a satisfactory musical instrument.

The neo-Baroque builder in America, striving to achieve similar tonal warmth in each stop has a more difficult task than did Arp Schnitger. Seldom does one find an acoustical environment equal to that of European churches, and yet the luster that reverberant rooms add to the sound of the old organs is not the least of their attributes. Compensation for acoustical realities is one of the modern American builder's headaches. The European builder might successfully imitate the Baroque builder in scaling, wind pressure, and other details, since his organs are designed for the same kind of environment. One might expect the same details to produce an emaciated, underscaled effect in an American church, even if the placement is good and the organ is encased.

On the other hand, overcompensation can be disastrous. The Baroque organ is assertive, lively, and perhaps even aggressive, but it is not oppressively loud, nor do its mixtures seem to punch holes in the ceiling. Earlier attempts to clarify the organ's ensemble sometimes erred in this direction. When builders began bringing pipes out of chambers, they had much to learn about the effects of pipes that can be heard clearly. One of the most fundamental ideas was that musical sounds can be exciting without being loud.

In all fairness to organ builders, performers have had to learn some of the same lessons. The organist who has not felt it necessary to reconsider his registration plans for the major works of the Baroque period in the past fifteen or twenty years must certainly have been ahead of his time.

Some Modern Tracker Organs Built in the United States

One Manual and Pedal
Semi-Portable Tracker Organ
SCHLICKER ORGAN CO., 1968

Gedeckt	8'	
Rohrfloete	4'	Treble and Bass
Principal	2'	
Quint	1⅓'	

Pedal

Trompetenregal   16'

[Advertisement in *The American Organist,* December 1968, p.19.]

Community Church, Barrington, Illinois
NOACK ORGAN CO., 1968

Gedackt	8'	Blockfloete	2'
Principal	4'	Mixture	III
Koppelfloete	4'		

Hook-down pedal

[*The Diapason,* October 1968, p.20]

Cleveland State University, Cleveland, Ohio
HOLTKAMP ORGAN COMPANY, 1970

Gedackt	8'	Scharf	III
Rohrflöte	4'	Regal	8'
Principal	2'		

[*The Diapason,* November 1970, p.7]

Mount Calvary Episcopal Church, Baltimore, Maryland
ANDOVER ORGAN COMPANY, 1961

Hoovdwerk		Rugwerk (continued)	
Bourdon	16′	Octaaf	2′
Prestant	8′	Terts	1⅗′
Roerfluit	8′	Quinta	1⅓′
Fluitdous	8′	Siffluit	1′
Octaaf	4′	Scherp	III
Spitsfluit	4′	Krumhoorn	8′
Quint	2⅔′		
Superoctaaf	2′	Pedaal	
Blokfluit	2′	Subbas	16′
Mixtuur	IV	Lieflijk Gedekt	16′
Cymbaal	III	Octaaf	8′
Cornet	III	Gedektpommer	8′
Trompet	8′	Superoctaaf	4′
Zymbelstern		Vlakfluit	4′
		Nachthoorn	2′
Rugwerk		Ruispijp	IV
Holpijp	8′	Mixtuur	IV
Quintadeen	8′	Fagot	16′
Prestant	4′	Trompet	8′
Roerpijp	4′	Schalmei	4′
Nasard	2⅔′		

[*The Tracker,* January 1962, pp.2–3]

St. John's Lutheran Church, Northfield, Minnesota
ANDOVER ORGAN COMPANY, 1965

Great (enclosed)		Rückpositiv (continued)	
Principal	8′	Principal	2′
Gemshorn	8′	Sesquialtera	II
Gemshorn Celeste	8′	Cymbal	II
Octave	4′	Krummhorn	8′
Rohrflöte	4′		
Blockflöte	2′	Pedal (unenclosed)	
Mixture	IV	Sub Bass	16′
Trumpet-en-chamade	8′	Principal	8′
		Bourdon	8′
Rückpositiv (unenclosed)		Principal	4′
Gedeckt	8′	Mixture	IV
Hohlflöte	4′	Posaune-en-chamade	16′

[*The American Organist,* September 1965, p.14]

St. John's Lutheran Church, Summit, New Jersey
HOLTKAMP ORGAN COMPANY, 1969

Great

Quintadena	16'
Principal	8'
Gedackt	8'
Octave	4'
Spitzflöte	4'
Doublette	2'
Mixture	IV
Trumpet	8'

Swell

Gamba	8'
Copula	8'
Principal	4'
Rohrflöte	4'

Swell (continued)

Flute	2'
Cornet	II
Scharf	III
Cromorne	8'

Pedal

Subbass	16'
Quintadena	16'
Octave	8'
Gedackt	8'
Choralbass	4'
Mixture	III
Fagott	16'
Schalmey	4'

[*The Diapason,* September 1969, p.15]

First Evangelical Lutheran Church, Lorain, Ohio
JOHN BROMBAUGH & CO., 1972

Great

Bourdon	16'
Praestant	8'
Rohrflöte	8'
Octave	4'
Spitzflöte	4'
Quinte	2⅔'
Nasard	2⅔'
Octave	2'
Gemshorn	2'
Tierce	1⅗'
Mixture	IV
Scharff	III
Trumpet	8'

Positive

Gedackt	8'
Praestant	4'
Flute	4'

Range: 56/30

Positive (continued)

Octave	2'
Larigot	1⅓'
Sesquialtera	II
Scharff	IV
Dulcian	8'

Pedal

Praestant	16'
Octave	8'
Octave	4'
Nachthorn	2'
Mixture	VI
Posaune	16'
Trumpet	8'

Couplers

Great to Pedal
Positive to Pedal
Positive to Great

[*Music/ A.G.O.,* March 1972, p.32]

Chapel of the Abiding Presence
Texas Lutheran College, Seguin, Texas
SCHLICKER ORGAN CO., 1968

Great		*Rueck-Positiv*	
Quintadena	16′	Gedeckt	8′
Principal	8′	Principal	4′
Spillfloete	8′	Rohrfloete	4′
Octave	4′	Nasat	2⅔′
Hohlfloete	4′	Principal	2′
Octave	2′	Blockfloete	2′
Mixture	V	Terz (Tenor C)	1⅗′
Trumpet	8′	Scharf	III
		Krummhorn	8′
Swell		Tremolo	
Rohrfloete	8′		
Salicional	8′	*Pedal*	
Principal	4′	Principal	16′
Spitzfloete	4′	Subbass	16′
Waldfloete	2′	Octave	8′
Klein-Nasat	1⅓′	Metalgedeckt	8′
Siffloete	1′	Choralbass	4′
Mixture	IV	Nachthorn	2′
Terzzimbel	III	Mixture	III
Dulzian	16′	Fagott	16′
Schalmei	8′	Schalmei	4′
Tremolo			

Memorial Church, Harvard University, Cambridge, Massachusetts
C. B. Fisk, 1967

Great

Bourdon		16'
Prestants	(I-II)	8'
Spitzflute		8'
Octaves	(I-II)	4'
Chimney Flute		4'
Twelfth		2⅔'
Fifteenths	(I-II)	2'
Cornet		II-V
Mixture		IV-V
Sharp		III-IV
Double Trumpet		16'
Trumpet		8'
Clarion		4'

Swell

Spindle Flute	8'
Gamba	8'
Voix Celeste	8'
Gemshorn	4'
Night Horn	2'
Clarion Mixture	V
Bassoon	16'
Trumpet	8'

Positive

Violin Diapason	8'
Chimney Flute	8'
Italian Principal	4'
Nazard	2⅔'
Doublet	2'
Tierce	1⅗'
Mixture	IV
Cymbal	III

Range: 61/32

Positive (continued)

Cremona	8'
English Horn	8'

Choir (in Rückpositiv position)

Stopped Diapason	8'
Prestant	4'
Spire Flute	4'
Fifteenth	2'
Nazard	1⅓'
Mixture	II-III
Regal	8'

Pedal

Prestant	16'
Bourdon	16'
Octave	8'
Rohrpipe	8'
Superoctave	4'
Mixture	V
Contrabassoon	32'
Trombone	16'
Trumpet	8'
Clarion	4'

Couplers

Great to Pedal
Positive to Pedal
Swell to Pedal
Choir to Pedal
Positive to Great
Swell to Great
Choir to Great
Swell to Positive

Trinity Lutheran Church, Worcester, Massachusetts
NOACK ORGAN COMPANY, 1969

Great	
Quintadena	16′
Principal	8′
Spielflöte	8′
Octave	4′
Blockflöte	4′
Nachthorn	2′
Mixture	IV-VI
Cornet	V
Trumpet	8′

Swell	
Chimney Flute	8′
Gemshorn	8′
Celeste	8′
Principal	4′
Koppelflöte	4′
Flachflöte	2′
Larigot	1⅓′
Mixture	III
Cymbal	III
Bassoon	16′
Schalmey	8′
Clarion	4′
Tremolo	

Positiv	
Gedackt	8′
Principal	4′

Positiv (continued)	
Spitzgedackt	4′
Nazard	2⅔′
Octave	2′
Superoctave	1′
Tertian	II
Scharff	V
Krummhorn	8′
Trompette-en-Chamade	8′
Tremolo	

Pedal	
Principal	16′
Bourdon	16′
Octave	8′
Spielflöte	8′
Choral Bass	4′
Rauschpfeife	II
Mixture	IV
Trombone	16′
Trumpet	8′
Trumpet	4′

Couplers

Swell to Great
Positiv to Great
Great to Pedal
Swell to Pedal
Positiv to Pedal

Range: 56/32

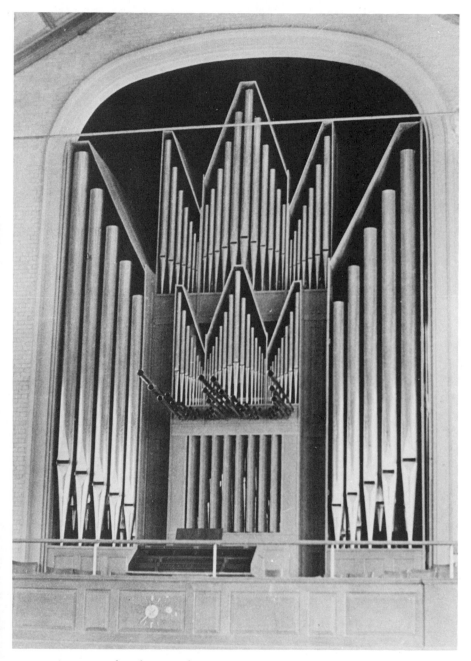

An organ by the Noack Organ Company, 1969. Tracker action. Trinity Lutheran Church, Worcester, Massachusetts. *Photo courtesy Noack Organ Company.*

St. Thomas Church, New York, New York
G. F. ADAMS, 1969

Grand Orgue

Montre	16'
Bourdon	16'
Montre	8'
Bourdon	8'
Prestant	4'
Flute	4'
Grosse Tierce	3⅕'
Nasard	2⅔'
Doublette	2'
Tierce	1⅗'
Plein Jeu	V-IX
Bombarde	16'
Trompette	8'
Clairon	4'
Dessus de Chamade	8'
Grand Cornet	V

Echo

Gambe	8'
Voix céleste	8'
Bourdon	8'
Prestant	4'
Flute	4'
Doublette	2'
Flageolet	1'
Sesquialtera	II
Cymbale	IV
Hautbois	8'
Voix humaine	8'
Clairon	4'
Tremblant	

Positif

Montre	8'
Bourdon	8'

Range: 58/32

Positif (continued)

Dessus de Flute	8'
Prestant	4'
Flute	4'
Nasard	2⅔'
Doublette	2'
Quarte de Nasard	2'
Tierce	1⅗'
Larigot	1⅓'
Fourniture	IV
Cymbale	III
Trompette	8'
Cromorne	8'
Clairon	4'
Tremblant	

Récit

Flute allemande	8'
Cornet	V
Trompette	8'

Pédale

Bourdon (prepared)	32'
Flute en Montre	16'
Bourdon	16'
Flute	8'
Bourdon	8'
Flute	4'
Gros Plein Jeu	VII
Contre Bombarde	32'
Bombarde	16'
Basson	16'
Trompette	8'
Clairon	4'
Chalumeau	4'

[*The Diapason,* December 1969, p.2]

Appendix

A Letter to the Rev. Doctor White, Rector of Christ Church and St. Peter's [Philadelphia] on the Conduct of a Church Organ
BY FRANCIS HOPKINSON, 1786

I am one of those who take great delight in sacred music, and think, with royal David, that heart, voice, and instrument should unite in adoration of the great Supreme.

A soul truly touched with love and gratitude, or under the influence of penitential sorrow, will unavoidably break forth in expressions suited to its feelings. In order that these emanations of the mind may be conducted with uniformity and a becoming propriety, our church hath adopted into her liturgy, the book of psalms, commonly called *David's Psalms*, which contain a great variety of addresses to the Deity, adapted to almost every state and temperature of a devout heart, and expressed in terms always proper, and often sublime.

To give wings, as it were to this holy zeal, and heighten the harmony of the soul, *organs* have been introduced into the churches. The application of instrumental music to the purposes of piety is well known to be of very ancient date. Indeed, originally, it was thought that music ought not to be applied to any other purpose. Modern improvements, however, have discovered, that it may be made expressive of every passion of the mind, and become an incitement to levity as well as sanctity.

Unless the real design for which an organ is placed in a church be constantly kept in view, nothing is more likely to happen than an abuse of this noble instrument, so as to render it rather an obstruction to, than an assistant in, the good purpose for which the hearers have assembled.

Give me leave, sir, to suggest a few rules for the conduct of an organ in a place of worship, according to my ideas of propriety.

1st. The organist should always keep in mind, that neither the time or place is suitable for exhibiting all his powers of execution; and that the congregation have not assembled to be entertained with his performance. The excellence of an organist consists in his making the instrument subservient and conducive to the purposes of devotion. None but a master can do this. An ordinary performer may play surprising tricks, and shew great dexterity in running through difficult passages, which he hath subdued by dint of previous labour and practice. But *he* must have judgement and taste who can call forth the powers of the instrument, and apply them with propriety and effect to the seriousness of the occasion.

2nd. The voluntary, previous to reading the lessons, was probably designed to fill up a solemn pause in the service; during which, the clergyman takes a few minutes respite, in a duty too lengthy, perhaps, to be continued without fatigue, unless some intermission be allowed: there, the organ hath its part alone, and the organist an opportunity of shewing his power over the instrument. This, however, should be done with great discretion and dignity, avoiding every thing light and trivial; but rather endeavouring to compose the minds of the audience, and strengthen the tendency of the heart in those devout exercises, in which, it should be presumed, the congregation are now engaged. All sudden jirks [sic], strong contrasts of *piano* and *forte,* rapid execution, and expressions of tumult, should be avoided. The voluntary should proceed with great chastity and decorum; the organist keeping in mind, that his hearers are now in the midst of divine service. The full organ should seldom be used on this occasion, nor should the voluntary last more than *five minutes* of time. Some relaxation, however, of this rule may be allowed, on festivals and grand occasions.

3d. The *chants* form a pleasing and animating part of the service; but it should be considered, that they are not songs or tunes, but a species of *recitative,* which is no more than speaking musically. Therefore, as melody or song is out of the question, it is necessary that the harmony should be complete, otherwise *chanting,* with all the voices in unison, is too light and thin for the solemnity of the occasion. There should at least be half a dozen voices in the organ gallery to fill the harmony with bass and treble parts, and give a dignity to the performance. Melody may be frivolous; harmony, never.

4th. The prelude which the organ plays immediately after the psalm is given out, was intended to advertise the congregation of the psalm tune which is going to be sung; but some famous organist, in order to shew how much he could make of a little, has introduced the custom of running so many divisions upon the simple melody of a psalm tune, that the original purpose of this prelude is now totally defeated, and the tune so disguised by the fantastical flourishes of the dexterous performer, that not an individual in the congregation can possibly guess the tune intended, until the clerk has sung through the first line of the psalm. And it is constantly observable, that the full congregation never join in the psalm before the second or third line, for want of that information which the organ should have given. The tune should be distinctly given out by the instrument, with only a few chaste and expressive decorations, such as none but a master can give.

5th. The interludes between the verses of the psalm were designed to give the singers a little pause, not only to take breath, but also an opportunity for a short retrospect of the words they have sung, in which the organ ought to assist their reflections. For this purpose the organist should be previously informed by the clerk of the verses to be sung, that he may modulate his interludes according to the subject.

To place this in a strong point of view, no stronger, however, than what I have too frequently observed to happen; suppose the congregation to have sung the first verse of the 33^d psalm.

> "Let all the just to God with joy
> Their chearful voices raise;
> For well the righteous it becomes
> To sing glad songs of praise."

How dissonant would it be for the organist to play a pathetic interlude in a flat third, with the slender and distant tones of the echo organ, or the deep and smothered sounds of a single diapason stop?

Or suppose again, that the words sung have been the 6th verse of the vith psalm.

> "Quite tired with pain, with groaning faint,
> No hope of ease I see,
> The night, that quiets common griefs
> Is spent in tears by me"

How monstrously absurd would it be to hear these words of distress succeeded by an interlude selected from the fag end of some thundering figure on a full organ, and spun out to a most unreasonable length? Or, what is still worse, by some trivial melody with a rhythm so strongly marked, as to set all the congregation to beating time with their feet or heads? Even those who may be impressed with the feelings such words should occasion, or in the least disposed for melancholy, must be shocked at so gross in [an?] impropriety.

The interludes should not be continued above 16 bars in *triple,* or ten or twelve bars in *common* time, and should always be adapted to the verse sung: and herein the organist hath a fine opportunity of shewing his sensibility, and displaying his taste and skill.

6th. The voluntary after service was never intended to eradicate every serious idea which the sermon may have inculcated. It should rather be expressive of that chearful satisfaction which a good heart feels under the sense of a duty performed. It should bear, if possible, some analogy with the discourse delivered from the pulpit; at least, it should not be totally dissonant from it. If the preacher has had for his subject, penitence for sin, the frailty and uncertainty of human life, or the evils incident to mortality, the voluntary may be somewhat more chearful than the tenor of such a sermon might in strictness suggest; but by no means so full and free as a discourse on praise, thanksgiving, and joy, would authorize.

In general, the organ should ever preserve its dignity, and upon no account issue light and pointed movements which may draw the attention of the congregation and induce them to carry home, not the serious sentiments which the service should impress, but some very petty air with which the organist hath been so good as to entertain them. It is as offensive to hear lilts and jiggs from a church organ, as it would be to see a venerable matron frisking through the public street with all the fantastic airs of a *columbine*. [81, pp.119–26]

The Diary of John Krauss:
Entries Pertaining to Organs

John Krauss's diary, now in the Schwenkfelder Library, Pennsburg, Pennsylvania, is an invaluable aid in establishing the dates for the organs built by John and Andrew Krauss. Here, also, are entries for the period when Tannenberg's son Johann David, Jr., worked for the Krauss brothers. John and Andrew divided the expenses and profits from their organ-building enterprises equally, and the diary records the accounts of the two brothers. Entries pertaining to the organ installations are quoted below, with additional information about the organs.

1796

Nov. 2   I went to Worcester for to sett up the new organs in the Calvinist Church [Wentz's Church] and did work until the 12th

Nov. 17   I went the second time to Worcester for finishing our work The consecration of said organ was held on the 26th Sundy of the Holy Trinity by the Rev. Mister Helfenstine, and we received the sum of 54 Pounds being part of 170 Pounds, the half of which   27–0–0

[Wentz's Church was founded in 1762. The Krauss organ is not extant.]

1797

Jan. ?   The first week I was working in the Shop on the small organs for George Smith the Expences for the same   0–4–18

Jan. 23   We finished George Smith's organ

Feb. 2   This week we worked on the L. Sw. [Long Swamp, or Long-swamp] Organs through 7 Days

Mar. 15   Received from LongSwamp from the bearer Phillip Altender-fer, joiner, the sum of 21 pounds, part of 325 pounds for their organs   10–10–0

Apr. 6   Mr. Altenderfer finished his Work in making Case for a pair of Organs for which Labour he asks 20 pounds.
6–2–6 we have already paid unto him.

[The organ in the Longswamp Church was rebuilt several times by members of the Krauss family. The original building in which it was installed was built in 1791. When it was torn down in 1852, the organ was taken to George Krauss's shop for repairs. In 1853 the organ was installed in the new church. It was again repaired in 1902 by Edwin B.

Krauss, and remained in the church until 1944 [358]. It was then replaced by an organ built by F. A. Bartholomay's Sons of Philadelphia, retaining the old case and display pipes. It is not certain that the diary entry for April 6, above, refers to the case of this organ.]

June 5   A bargain was made between me and Andrew and several Members of the Catolic Church to make an Organ in their Church. We agreed to make it for the rate of one hundred & seventyfive Pounds which is to pay into three terms viz Fifty Pounds down & fifty Pounds as soon it is finished and the remaining Part in 12 Months afterwards. And we received at the conclusion of the Bargain thirty pounds, seven shillings & 6 pence = per me   15–3–9

[The Church of the Most Blessed Sacrament at Goshenhoppen (now called Bally), Pennsylvania, possesses the oldest Krauss organ still in use (see p.70).]

Dec. 7   On this Day we begunt again on the Organs.

1798
Feb. 19   I and Andrew and Andrew Yeakle went to the church near Tohickon where we took a view of that organ. Spent 2–9 paid for a cristal in my watch 2–6.   0–5–3

[The entry of February 19 refers to the Tannenberg organ installed for the Lutheran and Reformed congregations. In 1839 Andrew and George Krauss contracted to enlarge this organ [6, p.105].]

Apr. 14   This evening J. D. Danneberg [Johann David Tannenberg] came from Philada.

[Tannenberg worked for the Krausses for sixteen months, until the summer of 1799.]

May 22   To day our organ for Longswamp was examined & found probatum, I sold 1 qt of brandy   0–1–6
May 24   I & Andrew went up to Longswamp to take the other organs down and on the 25 they sent 2 waggons for fetching their organs.
June 4   Did I & Andrew & Danneberg went to Long Swamp for to set up the new organs, spent   0–0–11
June 15   This Day we finished our organ in the church & on the 17th the same was consecrated to the service of God. This day we received for said organ £68 ½ to me   34–0–0
June 17   We Receaved from Joseph Roohr £6 for the organs is to made in the Roman Church   3–0–0
Spent this Day one Dollar   0–7–6
Payd to Altenderfer Carpenter—10–18–7 for making the Shrine of said organ likewise for Paints etc.

Nov. 14   Did I & Al. Schlottman vissit Long Swamb concerning their Organs & I agreed with several of the Church to repair their organs till May the next. Spent   0–0–11

Nov. 21   To Day we get the Bellows done for the Chatty [Catholic?] Organs

1799
Jan. 30   this Day the Roman Catholics fetcht their Organs
Jan. 31   We set up the organ frame
Feb. 4   We went with the slay to the Roman Chappel for to set up the Organs pay to George Krauss 25¢
Feb.14   I went again to the Roman Chappel for tuning the Organs &c.
Feb. 23   I went to Roman Church & on the 24th our Organ was examined by W. Wind   spend 25¢
Mar. 10   The New Organ was consecrated to the service of their Church, payd 12¢
Mar. 27   The Catholic Priest & Simon Adam brought us Monney for their Organs viz £28 being Part of £50 payable at the finishing of their organs, we accepted their organ for the Prise of £15 but we agreed at Last to sell the same for 13. so we have to take now 28– for 30 &c.   my Share comes to $37.33.
May 7   I & Andrew went to the Chatolic Chapple for tuning the Organs   get done on the 9th
May 27   . . . £12–2–6 we reccaved from the Romans for their Organs. The remainig 200 Dollers we have to reccave the next Year.
June 15   We went to Longswamb & settled with them concerning their Organs Etc.
July 6   I was at the Roman Chapple.
Nov. 4   . . . This Day & And went down to worcester Township for tuning the Organs in their Church we went home & get done on Thursday the 7   spent 12¢

1800
Sept. 21 . . . Received $2.50 being payment for tuning the Organ in Worcester vid. Nov. 4th alt. $2.50

1801
May 15   I went to Roman Chaple for setting the new organ
May 20   we begunt to tune the Organ in the Roman Chaple
July 17   I been making Pipes for P. Wind
& 18
July 21   I finisht Mr. Winds pipes & begunt to make for John Seller
July 25   I finish Sellers pipes 26   I sent them of
July 27   I Send Mr. Sellers Pipes over rec. $10 part of 14.

July 31	I brought Phillip Wind his Pipes.
Oct. 19	I rode to Bethlehem for employing a man to tune/ or to help/ the Organ in the Roman Chaple
Oct. 23	I went to Roman Chapple for repairing the Organs
Oct. 29	I fetcht George Weiss from Bethlehem for tuning the Roman Organs spent 29¢ on the 26 we begunt on the 28 we get done spent about 40¢ on the 29th I brought Mr. Weiss again home payd him for helping $6.10 spent 38¢.

1802

Jan. 4	. . . I brought a Stop of Organ Pipes to John Sellors not payd $7
Mar. 1	To Day I begunt to work at the Organ
Mar. 17	. . . Recd. from Mr. Wind for making Organ Pipes July 18 alt. he then payd me in Lime. . . .
May 3	. . . the 5th & 6 I been tuning a little Organ for Ph. Wind payd.
May 24	[Krauss went to Philadelphia and bought and sold various items.] I took a Organ case home
July 19	This Week I worked 4 Days at Mr. Dobs Organ
Oct. 4–7	I workt at Mr. Dobsons Organ
Oct. 10	I & A. been at New hanover by a consecration of a New Organ spent nothing.
Oct. 15–20	I workt at Dobs organ
Dec. 28–30	I workt at the little organ

[The diary skips from the end of 1802 to September 1803, and there appear to be pages missing.]

1803

Sept. 26	We took down the Organ
Oct. 12	Our Organ was fetcht to Pottstown
Oct. 13	We went to Pottstown in order to set up the organs
Oct. 15	We got the Case up and part of it painted
Oct. 16	we went home 17 our Distiller begunt to still
Oct. 18	we went to pottstown again 21 we sat in the first pipes
Oct. 29	we rode over & finisht our work.
Oct. 30	the 30th the Organ was consecrated for holy service & we receivd 200 Dollers I payd to Saml. Shoch as a present $10 & I spent since the time $1.01 & gave 25 to the Organ I got only 36 Dollers

[In 1796 a new brick church was erected by the Lutheran and Reformed congregations in Pottstown. An organ was installed there some time before 1838; it may have been the Krauss installation. In 1891 the old pipe organ was replaced with a "modern two manuel [*sic*] organ" [93, p.43]. There is an interesting story about a miser and the organist of the Pottstown Union Church, which is recorded in the history of the church.

> One day there was to be a funeral in this man's family [the miser's family], and Dubbs as a student was sent by Herman [the Pastor] to conduct the services. It was the custom to give the officiating clergyman several dollars and the organist a smaller sum. On this occasion the miser handed the student fifty cents and the organist twenty-five cents. The former thanked the giver, but the organist, determined to teach the miser a lesson, held up his coin so that all could see, and in a loud voice asked, "What is that for?" "That's your fee," answered the miser. "You miserable skinflint," responded the organist, "do you imagine that I can afford to lose my school, hire a horse, and give you a whole day's service for twenty-five cents? I insist on another dollar." The miser's contortions were very amazing, but at last he finally yielded and paid the dollar. Then, as if struck by conscience, he exclaimed, "The minister deserves a dollar as well as the organist," and insisted on giving him the same amount. [93, p.17]

This incident is supposed to have happened between 1799 and 1838.]

1804

Jan. 6   I prepared some wood for a new Organ

Feb. 23   Henry Weist Michael Kline & G Ewold been here concerning an Organ.

Feb. 25   I & Andw. been in the New Lutherian Church for the above purpose

[This and subsequent references to a Lutheran church are in regard to the organ the Krausses installed in St. Paul's Lutheran Church, Red Hill, Pennsylvania. A new stone church had been erected in 1803, and thus it is that we find members of the church visiting the Krausses early in 1804 to discuss a new organ for their church. When the contract was finally written, it was for an "organ already begun and for sale for the sume of £262–10s.–00 . . ." [304, p. 15]. The Krausses agreed to accept an old organ for the amount of £25. The fate of this organ is not known. The church erected a new building in 1877, but it was destroyed by fire in 1895. If the organ was still in use at that time, it was probably destroyed too.]

June 3   We been in Pottstown received part of our Money viz 100D

1805

Jan. 7–19 I workt at the organ case   I have workd now about 15 days

Jan. 21   . . . This Week I been working at the organ case finishd partly on the 31st.

Feb.	till the 2d I have worked again at the Organ 9ds.
Feb. 16	till this Day I workd again 9½ Days at the Organ
Mar. 1	I work at the Organ got the wind Chest finisht
Mar. 2	till to Day I workt again. 6½
Mar. 6	George Smith payd me 5D. for one octav of wodden pipes.
Mar. 23	. . . this week worked 6 Days at the Organ.
Mar. 30	. . . Work at the Organ 2½ Days
Apr. 6	. . . workt on pipes for P. Wind
Apr. 22	I went with my wife & Polly to Philada. . . . . Lether for the organ my share $2 . . . Ornament for the Organ. my share 50¢
May 1	. . . This week I worked again 3 Days at the Organ.
May 18	. . . worked again 6 Days at the Organ
May 20	I workt at the organ
May 22	I workt at the organ
May 26	I been in the Lutherian Church
May 27	I begunt to make a full Stop of Diapason for G. Smith workt 2½ Days thereon. . . .
May 30 & 31	. . . Red. from Philip Wind for 3 Octaves pipes $10.00
June 9	I finished 4 full Octave Pipes—Diapason 8 Feet for George Smith.
Aug. 12 & 13	I workt at the Pipes abt. 1 D.
Aug. 22	I finished 2 full Stops of Organ Pipes for George Smith
Aug. 24	he fetched them home.
Oct. 5	. . . George Smith paid me for the Pipes the residuary part 13$ I remain due $13.05
Dec. 17	I begunt to work again at the Organ. workt 5 Days
Dec. 24	workt 2 Days at the Organ
Dec. 31	I workt at the organ
1806	
Jan. 1	I workt at the Organ
Jan. 11	. . . Workt again 3½ Day at the Organ
Jan. 20	. . . This week I workt 4 Days at the Organ
Feb. 1	. . . workd again 3 Days at the Organ
Feb. 4	I & Andrew made an Agreement with John Rhoads & John Keiper from Allentown for an Organ of 8 Stops for the Consid^n of 560$ spent 40.
Feb. 5	We made an agreement with Philip Wind for 4 Stops of pewter Pipes at $173.33

Feb. 7	We made an Agreement the Lutherian society for our Organ which is partly finished for 700$
Feb. 8	I finished a full Stop of Pipes being the 5th (Quint) (worked about 5D thereon) This week I worked 3½ Days at the Organ
Feb. 15	. . . This week I workt 3 Days at the organ
Feb. 22	. . . This week I workd 4 D at the Organ
Mar. 22	til then I workd 3 Days at pipes
Apr. 7–12	I workd again 5 Days at the organ
Apr. 26	This Week I workd again 4 D. at the O.
May 1	. . . This Week we took off of our Organ—workd 4+ Days
May 5	The Lutherians fautcht their Organ & we being setting up till the 9th
May 12	We went again to Church & workd till the 16th
May 24	We finished our Organ
May 26	We red. for the said £48 being part of the first payment viz £100—my part is $64. . . . Item we red. on the said 26th Day from the Allentown congregation the first payment for their Organ viz 160$ my part 80. . . .
May 27	. . . This Week 3+ Days at pipes for Philip Wind
June 4	I worked at Winds pipes
June 5 & 6	I begun at the Organ intended for *Allentown*
June 14	. . . This Week I workd 4½ Days at the Organ
July 17 & 18	we workt at the Organ
July 21–25	I been working at the Organ 6 Days I have now workt longer than Andw on this Organ
July 28–31	I worked at the Organ
Aug. 1–2	At noon I workt at the o— again 5½ Days longer than Andw. . . .
Aug. 11–16	we workd at the Organ each 5½ Days
Aug. 18–23	we workt the greatest part on the Organ
Sept. 4	we begunt Sowing til 6th we workd the most part at the Organ.
Sept. 8	this Week I workt a little at the organ
Sept. 22	I went to Allentown made a bargain with Adam Recb [?] & Abrm Neuhard for making the Case to the Organ we agreed for 60$ & 500 feet bords
Sept. 23	I went to Bethlehem to view the new celebrated Organ

[In 1806 a new organ by John Geib of New York City was installed in the Moravian Church in Bethlehem. That is probably the instrument John Krauss saw.]

Sept. —	til 27 I workd at the organ
Oct. 6–11	I workd at the Bellowses
Oct. 19–25	I been working at the Organ
Oct. 28	I been in Allentown brought the Bellowes & to the Church
Nov. 11	I & Andrew brought a part of the Organ to Alln. Andrew begun. to work in the Church
Nov. 13	I went to Allentown for setting up the Organ in the Church at Allentown
Nov. 17	we finished the Organ pipes
Nov. 19	We went to Allentown again & worket til the 25
Dec. 1	I with Andrew went to Allentown in order to finish our Organ we got done the 6th
Dec. 13	We went with the Slay to Allentown on the 14 the New Organ was playd the first Time & Examined on the 15 we received part of the payment of our Organ viz 200$—& we payd 62$ to the joiner for making the Case of sd Organ spent about 75¢. . . . Then we receivd 6– for bringing the Organ to the Church
Dec. 29	. . . Payd him (Andrew Yeakle) bords for the Organs $3
1807	
Jan. 13	. . . further I promised to make a full Stop of 2 ft. tin pipes to Kratz
Feb. 3	I Cast tin for pipes
Feb. 4	workt at pipes
Feb. 9–12	I been working in tin Pipes
Feb. 12	I finished a full Stop of 2 feet Pipes & 1 Octav 2 ft.
Feb.16, 17, 19, 21	I workt at pipes for George Smith
Feb. 21	Red. from Kratz 8$ being part for a Stop of pipes
Feb. 21	Red. from Kratz for pipes 8$ part of 16
Mar. 20–24	at noon I repaird a Chamber Organ for Kratz red. $9.50
May 18	To Day we setled with the Romans concerning their Organ they payd to us £17–9–9 & gave a Note for 10 Pounds from the 17–9–9 I got £3–19–7 = $10.63
May 23	Our Machine for Carting Wooll was finished I gave him an order to receive from the Allentown Organ the residuary Part of my Money viz 100 so I payd for the Machine 100. . . .
Aug. 18	I went to Philad since I was requested concerning a New Organ.

1808
Jan. 11   I begunt at a Chamber Organ
Jan.   til 21 I been working at my Organ about 8 days.
Jan. 26–29   I work at the organ.
Feb. 2   I work at the Organ
Feb. 8 & 9   I been working at my Organ
Feb. 15–17   I workt a litl at my Organ.
Feb. 22   I workt at the Organ
Mar. 2 & 5   I workt at the Organ.
Mar. 7 & 8   I workt a litle at my organ
Mar. 10   workt at the organ.
  & 11
June 12   Recd. of Michael Reiter £20.00.00 being part in payment
                   of the Organ made for His Church = $53.33
July 19   Recd of Wm. Eckhard the sum of 57½ Dollr. part of pay-
                   ment for their Organ & 1.50 as part of intered for Do. = 59

1809
Jan. 30   I was dividing a barrel for a Organ for G Faber
May 30   I recd. of Jacob Kemmerer 80$ as part in paymt of the
                   Lutheran Organ
Nov. 30   . . . Recd of William Ekhard 115$ being the residuary
                   payment with Interest for an Organ.

1810
May 5   . . . recd . . . of George Faber 8$ for dividing two Barrels
                   of a hand Organ.

[From the time that the wool carding machine arrived in 1807, John Krauss's involvement in organ building decreased and he turned his attention to other pursuits. The 1806 contract with the Red Hill Lutheran Church is the last extant contract he signed.]

Cavaillé-Coll Organs for North America

The book *Artistide Cavaillé-Coll* by Cécile and Emmanuel Cavaillé-Coll (Paris: Librairie Fischbacher, 1929) contains a list of Cavaillé-Coll organs, including organs for "Amérique du Nord" on p.160. The fact that an organ for Canada (Montréal) and one for Mexico (Guadalajara) are listed separately seems to suggest that the following instruments were for the United States:

M. Agard de Nard.—Orgue de Choeur.
MM. Alcain et Cie.—Grand Orgue.
MM. Alcain et Cie.—Orgue de Choeur.
M. Aldecoa.—Orgue de Choeur.

M. Bihour.—Orgue de Choeur.
MM. Carton et Cambissa.—Orgue de Choeur.
M. Dupont.—Grand Orgue.
M. l'Abbé Durier.—Orgue de Choeur.
M. Guerrico.—Grand Orgue.
MM. Lefèvre et Amaury.—Orgue de Choeur.
MM. Ed. Lefèvre et Cie.—Orgue de Choeur.
M. Olano.—Orgue de Choeur.
MM. Racine et Perrot.—Orgue de Choeur.
MM. Thirion et Damien.—Orgue de Choeur.
Paincourville (Louisiane).—Orgue de Choeur.

Bibliography

Books, Dissertations, and Pamphlets

1. Allwardt, Anton Paul. "Sacred Music in New York City 1800–1850." Union Theological Seminary dissertation, 1950.
2. *The American Musical Directory.* New York: Thomas Hutchinson, 1861.
3. Anburey, Thomas. *Travels Through the Interior Parts of America in a Series of Letters.* 2 vols. London: William Lane, 1789.
4. Andrews, Alice. "George Norton Andrews and Charles Backus Andrews Organ Builders." Unpublished paper (1964) in Historical Society library, San Francisco.
5. Angel, Myron. *History of Nevada.* Oakland: Thompson & West, 1881.
6. Armstrong, William H. *Organs for America.* Philadelphia: University of Pennsylvania Press, 1967.
7. *Art and Music in the South.* Institute of Southern Culture Lectures at Longwood College. Farmville, Virginia: Longwood College Publication, 1961.
8. Audsley, George Ashdown. *The Art of Organ-Building.* 2 vols. 1905. Reprint. New York: Dover, 1965.
9. ———. Notebooks. 6 vols. Unpublished collection in New York Public Library
10. ———. *The Organ of the Twentieth Century.* New York: Dodd, Mead & Co., 1919.
11. ———. *Organ-Stops and their Artistic Registration.* New York: H. W. Gray Co., 1921.
12. ———. *The Temple of Tone.* New York: J. Fischer & Br., 1925.
13. Ayars, Christine Merrick. *Contributions to the Art of Music in America by the Music Industries of Boston 1640 to 1936.* New York: H. W. Wilson; 1937.
14. Babcock, Mary Kent Davey. *Christ Church Salem Street, Boston, Historical Sketches, Colonial Period, 1723–1775.* Boston: Thomas Todd, 1947.
15. Baldwin, Samuel Atkinson. *The Story of the American Guild of Organists.* New York: H. W. Gray Co., 1946.
16. Barnes, William H., and Edward B. Gammons. *Two Centuries of American Organ Building.* Glen Rock, N. J.: J. Fischer & Bro., 1970.
17. Baudier, Roger. *A Historical Sketch of the St. Louis Cathedral of New Orleans.* New Orleans, 1940.

18. Beasley, William Joseph. "The Organ in America, as Portrayed in Dwight's *Journal of Music*." University of Southern California dissertation, 1971.

19. Bentley, William. *The Diary of William Bentley, D. D.* 4 vols. Salem: The Essex Institute, 1905–1914.

20. Bernheim, Gotthardt D. *History of the German Settlements and of the Lutheran Church in North and South Carolina*. Philadelphia: The Lutheran Book Store, 1872.

21. Biever, Albert. *The Story of the Church of the Immaculate Conception (Jesuits) Baronne Street*. New Orleans, 1928.

22. Blanton, Joseph Edwin. *The Organ in Church Design*. Albany, Tex.: Venture Press, 1957.

23. ———. *The Revival of the Organ Case*. Albany, Tex.: Venture Press, 1965.

24. Bowles, Samuel. *Across the Continent*. Reprint. Ann Arbor: University Microfilms, Inc., 1966.

25. Bradley, Van Allen. *Music for the Millions: the Kimball Piano and Organ Story*. Chicago: Henry Regnery Co., 1957.

26. Breitmayer, Douglas Reece. "Seventy-Five Years of Sacred Music in Cleveland, Ohio 1800–1875." Union Theological Seminary thesis, 1951.

27. *A Brief Account of an Historic Church*. New York: The Consistory, the Reformed Church, c.1899.

28. *A Brief History of the Presbyterian Church of Edisto Island*. Edisto Island, S. C., 1963.

29. Brooks, Henry M. *Olden-Time Music*. Boston: Ticknor & Co., 1888.

30. Carter, Hodding, and Betty Werlein Carter. *So Great a Good*. Sewanee, Tenn.: The University Press, 1955.

31. Carter, Landon. *The Diary of Colonel Landon Carter of Sabine Hall, 1752–1778*. 2 vols. Edited by Jack P. Green. Charlottesville: University Press of Virginia, 1965.

32. *Centennial Anniversary of St. John's Reformed Church of Sinking Springs, Pa*. Sinking Springs, 1894.

33. *The Centennial Celebration Booklet of St. Paul's Reformed Church*. St. Paul's, Fleetwood, Pa., 1941.

34. Chase, Gilbert. *America's Music*. 2d ed. New York: McGraw-Hill Book Co., 1966.

35. ———. *The Music of Spain*. 2d ed. New York: Dover Publications, Inc., 1959.

36. *Church Music and Musical Life in Pennsylvania in the Eighteenth Century*. 3 vols. Prepared by the Committee on Historical Research. Philadelphia: The Pennsylvania Society of the Colonial Dames of America, 1926–47.

37. Clarke, William H. *An Outline of the Structure of the Pipe Organ*. Boston: Oliver Ditson, 1877.

38. *Congregation Beth Elohim—Brief in Organ Controversy*. Charleston, S. C., 1843.

39. Craig, James H. *The Arts and Crafts in North Carolina 1699–1840.* Winston-Salem: Old Salem, Inc., 1965.

40. Dalcho, Frederick. *An Historical Account of the Protestant Episcopal Church, in South-Carolina.* Charleston: E. Thayer, 1820.

41. David, Hans T. *Musical Life in the Pennsylvania Settlements of the Unitas Fratrum.* Winston-Salem: The Moravian Music Foundation, 1959.

42. Dean, Talmage Whitman, "The Organ in Eighteenth Century English Colonial America." University of Southern California dissertation, 1960.

43. *Descriptive Circular and Price List of George Jardine and Son, Organ Builders.* New York: Baker & Godwin, 1869.

44. Dieffenbach, Victor C. *The Dieffenbach Organ Builders.* Printed privately, 1967.

45. Disosway, Gabriel P. *Earliest Churches of New York.* New York: Gregory, 1865.

46. Dorsey, Stephen P. *Early English Churches in America, 1607–1807.* New York: Oxford University Press, 1952.

47. Dow, George Francis. *The Arts and Crafts in New England 1704–1775.* Topsfield, Mass.: The Wayside Press, 1927.

48. Eaton, Quaintance, ed. *Musical U.S.A.* New York: Allen, Towne and Heath, Inc., 1949.

49. Edwards, George Thornton. *Music and Musicians of Maine.* Portland: The Southworth Press, 1928.

50. Ellinwood, Leonard. *The History of American Church Music.* New York: Morehouse-Gorham, 1953.

51. Elson, Louis C. *The National Music of America.* Boston: L. C. Page & Co., 1900.

52. Engelhardt, Charles A. (Fr. Zephyrin). *Mission San Juan Bautista.* Santa Barbara: Mission Santa Barbara, 1931.

53. Fesperman, John T. *A Snetzler Chamber Organ of 1761.* Washington: Smithsonian Institution Press, 1970.

54. Fisher, William Arms. *Notes on Music in Old Boston.* Boston: Oliver Ditson, 1918.

55. Francis, David R. *The Universal Exposition of 1904.* St. Louis: Louisiana Purchase Exposition Co., 1913.

56. Francis, James G. "Changes in the Concepts of Tonal Design in the Small Service Organ Since 1920." Union Theological Seminary thesis, 1956.

57. Freund, John C., ed. *The Piano and Organ Purchaser's Guide for 1903.* New York: The Music Trades Co., 1902.

58. ———, ed. *The Piano and Organ Purchaser's Guide for 1904.* New York: The Music Trades Co., 1903.

59. Furnas, J. C. *The Americans—A Social History of the United States— 1587–1914.* New York: G. P. Putnam's Sons, 1969.

60. *Genealogical Record of the Schwenkfelder Families.* New York: Rand McNally Co., 1923.

61. Gerson, Robert A. *Music in Philadelphia.* Philadelphia: Theodore Presser Co., 1940.

62. Getz, Pierce A. "Organ Mixtures in Contemporary American Practice." Eastman School of Music, University of Rochester, thesis, 1967.

63. Gottesman, Rita Susswein, compiler. *The Arts and Crafts in New York 1726–1776.* New York: The New-York Historical Society, 1938.

64. ———, compiler. *The Arts and Crafts in New York 1777–1799.* New York: The New-York Historical Society, 1954.

65. ———, compiler. *The Arts and Crafts in New York 1800–1804.* New York: The New-York Historical Society, 1965.

66. Gould, Nathaniel D. *Church Music in America.* Boston: A. N. Johnson, 1853.

67. *The Great Organ in the Boston Music Hall.* Boston: Ticknor and Fields, 1865.

68. Green, Joseph. *Diary of Rev. Joseph Green, of Salem Village.* Edited by Samuel P. Fowler. *Essex Institute Historical Collections,* vol. 10, part I. Salem: Essex Institute Press, 1869.

69. Greenleaf, Jonathan. *A History of the Churches of All Denominations in the City of New York.* New York: E. French, 1850.

70. Grider, Rufus A. *Historical Notes on Music in Bethlehem, Pennsylvania.* Philadelphia, 1873. Reprint. Winston-Salem: The Moravian Music Foundation, Inc., 1957.

71. Hackett, Charles Wilson, ed. *Historical Documents Relating to New Mexico, Nueva Vizcaya, and Approaches Thereto, to 1773.* 3 vols. Collected by Adolph F. A. and Fanny R. Bandelier. Washington, D. C.: Carnegie Institution, 1923–37.

72. Harvey, John Wright. "The West Point Organ." Union Theological Seminary thesis, 1952.

73. Heaton, Charles Huddleston. "A History of Austin Organs, Incorporated." Union Theological Seminary thesis, 1952.

74. *Hilborne L. Roosevelt, Manufacturer of Church, Chapel, Concert and Chamber Organs.* Advertising brochure. New York: Hilborne L. Roosevelt, 1883.

75. *Historical Manual of the South Church in Andover, Mass.* Andover: Warren F. Draper, 1859.

76. *History of the Independent Presbyterian Church and Sunday School, Savannah, Ga.* Savannah: Geo. N. Nichols, 1882.

77. *History of the St. John's Reformed Church, Host, Pennsylvania.* 200th Anniversary booklet, 1927.

78. Hodges, Faustina H. *Edward Hodges.* New York: G. P. Putnam's Sons, 1896.

79. Holmes, George S. *A Historic Sketch of the Parish Church of St. Michael, in the Province of South Carolina.* Charleston: Walker, Evans & Cogswell Co., 1887.

80. Hope-Jones, Robert. *Recent Developments of Organ Building.* North Tonawanda, N. Y.: The Rudolph Wurlitzer Co., 1910.

81. Hopkinson, Francis. *The Miscellaneous Essays and Occasional Writings of Francis Hopkinson, Esq.* vol. II. Philadelphia: T. Dobson, 1792.

82. Howard, John Tasker. *Our American Music.* 4th ed. New York: Crowell, 1965.

83. Howe, Glanville L., and William S. B. Mathews, eds. *A Hundred Years of Music in America.* Chicago: G. L. Howe, 1889.

84. Hubbard, W. L., ed. *American History and Encyclopedia of Music,* vols. IV, VII, VIII. New York: Irving Squire, 1908.

85. Jamison, James Blaine. *Organ Design and Appraisal.* New York: H. W. Gray, 1959.

86. Johnson, James. "Henry Erben, American Organ Builder, A Survey of His Life and Work." Yale University thesis, 1968.

87. Jones, A. S. Scrapbooks. Microfilm of unpublished collection in the library of the Berks County Historical Society, Reading, Pa.

88. Jones, F. O., ed. *A Handbook of American Music and Musicians.* Buffalo: C. W. Moulton & Co., 1887.

89. Karson, Burton L. "Music Criticism in Los Angeles, 1895–1910." University of Southern California dissertation, 1964.

90. Keefer, Lubov. *Baltimore's Music.* Baltimore: J. H. Furst, 1962.

91. Kershaw, John. *History of the Parish and Church of Saint Michael, Charleston.* Charleston, 1915.

92. Kieffer, Rev. Henry Martyn, trans. *Some of the First Settlers of "The Forks of the Delaware."* Translated from the record books of the First Reformed Church of Easton, Pa., from 1760 to 1852. Lancaster: New Era Printing, 1902.

93. Kosman, Howard A. *A Brief History of the Old Brick or Union Church now occupied by Zion's Reformed Congregation.* Anniversary booklet. Pottstown, Pa., 1936.

94. Krauss, John. Diary. 2 vols. Unpublished manuscript in the Schwenkfelder Library, Pennsburg, Penn.

95. Krohn, Ernst C. *A Century of Missouri Music.* St. Louis, 1924.

96. Lahee, Henry C. *Annals of Music in America.* Boston: Marshall Jones Co., 1922.

97. Lahee, Henry. *The Organ and Its Masters.* Boston: L. C. Page & Co., 1902.

98. Lengyel, Cornel, ed. "Music of the Gold Rush Era." Vol. I of "History of Music in San Francisco." Mimeographed. W.P.A. publication, 1939.

99. Lopéz, Fray Atanasio. *Relacion historica de la Florida, escrita en el siglo XVII.* Madrid, 1931.

100. Loud, Thomas. *The Organ Study: Being an Introduction to the Practice of the Organ.* . . . Philadelphia: Louds Piano Forte & Music Store, 1845.

101. Malone, Henry Thompson. *The Episcopal Church in Georgia 1733–1957.* Atlanta: The Protestant Episcopal Church in the Diocese of Atlanta, 1960.

102. Marshall, G. Daniel, "Existing Tracker Organs Berkshire County (Massachusetts) and Vicinity." Unpublished compilation, 1967.

103. Meade, Bishop William. *Old Churches, Ministers, and Families of Virginia.* 2 vols. 1857. Reprint. Baltimore: Genealogical Publishing Co., 1966.

104. Messiter, A. H. *A History of the Choir and Music of Trinity Church, New York.* New York: Edwin S. Gorham, 1906.

105. Miller, George L. *The Recent Revolution in Organ Building.* New York: The Charles Francis Press, 1909.

106. Minter, William John. "Church Music in the American Baptist Union of the San Francisco Bay Cities." Union Theological Seminary thesis, 1960.

107. Mittelberger, Gottlieb. *Journey to Pennsylvania.* Reprint. Cambridge: Harvard University Press, 1960.

108. Morris, Richard B., ed. *Encyclopedia of American History.* New York: Harper & Row, 1965.

109. McCrady, Edward. *A Sketch of St. Philip's Church, Charleston, S. C. . . .* Charleston: Lucas & Richardson, 1897.

110. McDonald, Donald Gordon. "The Mormon Tabernacle Organ." Union Theological Seminary thesis, 1952.

111. Newton, Sarah M. "The Story of the M. P. Möller Organ Company." Union Theological Seminary thesis, 1950.

112. Nichols, George Ward, ed. *The Cincinnati Organ.* Cincinnati: Robert Clark & Co., 1878.

113. Ogden, John C. *An Excursion into Bethlehem and Nazareth, in Pennsylvania, in the Year 1799.* Philadelphia: Charles Cist, 1805.

114. *The Old Trappe Church.* Pamphlet issued by Augustus Lutheran Church, Trappe, Penn.

115. Organ Scrapbook. Clippings from unidentified newspapers (1871), in the library of the New-York Historical Society, New York.

116. Owen, Barbara J. "Organ Building in New England in the Eighteenth and Nineteenth Centuries." Boston University thesis, 1962.

117. ————. *The Organs and Music of King's Chapel.* Boston: King's Chapel, 1966.

118. Packer, Mina Belle. "A Brief Survey of Sacred Music in Pittsburgh, Pennsylvania Past and Present." Union Theological Seminary thesis, 1955.

119. Palóu, Fray Francisco, O. F. M. *Historical Memoirs of New California.* 4 vols. Edited by Herbert Eugene Bolton. Berkeley: University of California Press, 1926.

120. Parks, Edna Dorintha. "A History of the Building Techniques and Liturgical Uses of the Organ in the Churches of Boston." Boston University thesis, 1944.

121. Peyser, Ethel. *The House that Music Built.* New York: Robert M. McBride & Co., 1936.

122. *The Philosophy of an Organ Builder.* Estey Organ Co. advertising booklet. Brattleboro, Vt., 1923.

123. Pichierri, Louis. *Music in New Hampshire 1623–1800*. New York: Columbia University Press, 1960.

124. *Pipe Organs*. Hook and Hastings advertising book. Boston, 1927.

125. Poole, Henry Ward. *Essay on Perfect Intonation and the Euharmonic Organ*. New Haven: B. L. Hamlen, 1850.

126. *Proceedings at the Centennial Anniversary of the Dedication of the North Dutch Church*. New York: The Consistory, the Reformed Protestant Dutch Church, 1869.

127. Quade, Robert M. "A History of the Washington Cathedral—Its Structure and Its Music." Union Theological Seminary thesis, 1955.

128. Raisen, Jacob B. *Centennial Booklet Commemorating the Introduction of Reform Judaism in America*. Charleston, 1925.

129. Redway, Virginia Larkin. *Music Directory of Early New York City*. New York: New York Public Library, 1941.

129a. Reznikoff, Charles. *The Jews of Charleston*. Philadelphia: The Jewish Publication Society of America, 1950.

130. Rines, Edward F. *Old Historic Churches of America*. New York: Macmillan Co., 1936.

131. Ritter, Frédéric Louis. *Music in America*. New York: Charles Scribner's Sons, 1890.

132. Rothensteiner, John. *History of the Archdiocese of St. Louis*. 2 vols. St. Louis: Blackwell Wielandy Co., 1928.

133. Rumple, Rev. Jethro. *A History of Rowan County North Carolina*. Salisbury, N. C.: J. J. Bruner, 1881.

134. Sachse, John F. *Justus Falckner, Mystic and Scholar, Devout Pietist in Germany, Hermit on the Wissahickon, Missionary on the Hudson. A Bi-Centennial Memorial*. Philadelphia, 1903.

135. Schanck, Robert E. "A History of the Guilmant Organ School, 1899–1953." Union Theological Seminary thesis, 1953.

136. Schmauk, Theodore E. *Old Salem in Lebanon*. Lebanon: Report Publishing Co., 1898.

137. Schurer, Ernst. "The History of the Tracker Organ With Special Reference to Texas." University of Texas thesis, 1960.

138. *Seven Generations in the Building of Pipe Organs*. St. Louis: The Kilgen Organ Co., 1946.

139. Sewall, Samuel. *Diary of Samuel Sewall*. Vol. II. In *Massachusetts Historical Collections*, 5th Series, VI.

140. Skinner, Ernest M. *The Modern Organ*. 1917. Rev. ed. New York: H. W. Gray, 1945.

141. Smiley, Jerome C. *History of Denver*. Denver: J. H. Williamson & Co., 1903.

142. Sonneck, Oscar G. *Early Concert-Life in America*. New York: Musurgia Publishers, 1949.

143. Sonneck, Oscar G. *Francis Hopkinson, the First American Poet-Composer (1737–1791) and James Lyon, Patriot, Preacher, Psalmodist (1735–1794)*. 1905. Reprint. New York: Da Capo Press, 1967.

144. Spell, Lota M. *Music in Texas*. Austin, 1936.

145. Sterner, Frederick A., ed. *The History of the Reading Classis, Eastern Synod of the Reformed Church in the United States 1895–1940*. (n.p., n.d.)

146. Stevenson, Robert. *Music in Mexico*. New York: Crowell, 1952.

147. ———. *Protestant Church Music in America*. New York: W. W. Norton, 1966.

148. Stevens, Walter B. *The Forest City*. St. Louis: A. D. Thompson Publishing Co., 1904.

149. Stiles, Ezra. *The Literary Diary of Ezra Stiles, D. D., LL. D.*, Vol. I. Edited by Franklin Bowditch Dexter. New York: Charles Scribner's Sons, 1901.

149a. Stoutamire, Albert. *Music of the Old South*. Cranbury, New Jersey: Associated University Presses, 1972.

150. Strong, George Templeton. *The Diary of George Templeton Strong*. 4 vols. Edited by Allan Nevins and Milton Halsey Thomas. New York: The Macmillan Co., 1952.

151. Sumner, William Leslie. *The Organ*. 3d ed. London: Macdonald & Co., 1962.

152. Swan, Howard. *Music in the Southwest—1825–1950*. San Marino, Cal.: The Huntington Library, 1952.

153. Tapley, Harriet Silvester. *St. Peter's Church in Salem, Massachusetts before the Revolution*. Salem: The Essex Institute, 1944.

154. Teichert, Adolph. "Some Notes on the Music at St. Mary-the-Virgin, New York City." Union Theological Seminary thesis, 1953.

155. Trautmann, Jean E. "A History of Music at Saint Bartholomew's Church, New York." Union Theological Seminary thesis, 1951.

156. Trexler, Mark K., ed. *The Lutheran Church in Berks County—1723–1958*. Kutztown, Pa.: The Kutztown Publishing Co., 1959.

157. Truette, Everett. Scrapbooks. 6 vols. Unpublished collection in the Boston Public Library.

158. *The 200th Anniversary of Christ Lutheran Church at Stouchsburg, Berks County, Pennsylvania*. Church Council, 1943.

159. *Two Hundred Fiftieth Anniversary*. New Hanover, Pennsylvania, Sept. 10–17, 1950.

160. Vardell, Charles G. *Organs in the Wilderness*. Winston-Salem: Salem Academy and College, 1944.

161. Ver Steeg, Clarence. *The Formative Years*. New York: Hill and Wang, 1964.

162. Vollstedt, Don A. "A History of the Music at Saint Thomas' Church, New York." Union Theological Seminary thesis, 1955.

163. Way, William. *The History of Grace Church, Charleston, South Carolina*. Charleston: Grace Church, 1948.

164. ———. *Seventy-Fifth Anniversary of the Consecration of Grace Church*. Charleston: Grace Church, 1923.

165. Williams, George W. *St. Michael's, Charleston, 1751–1951.* Columbia: University of South Carolina Press, 1951.

166. Winterton, Harry J. *Noted Organs and Organists.* Unpublished collection in the Library of Congress, Washington, D. C.

167. Wolfe, Lucy Louise. "Moravian Church Music in Wachovia, North Carolina." Union Theological Seminary thesis, 1951.

168. Wolverton, Byron Adams. "Keyboard Music and Musicians in the Colonies and United States of America Before 1830." Indiana University dissertation, 1966.

169. *Year Book—1884 City of Charleston, So. Ca.*

Articles

200. Adams, Frank Stewart. "Self Determination for Small Organs." *The American Organist,* vol. 4, no. 5 (May 1921), pp.152–57.

201. "Allege Unfair Claims to Sell Electronics." *The Diapason,* vol. 27, no. 12 (Nov. 1936), p.1.

202. "American Organ Builders of Today: Austin Organ Company." *The Diapason,* vol. 16, no. 1 (Dec. 1924), p.6.

203. "American Organ Builders of Today: Frazee Organ Company." *The Diapason,* vol. 16, no. 7 (June 1925), p.8.

204. "American Organ Builders of Today: George Kilgen & Son." *The Diapason,* vol. 15, no. 12 (Nov. 1924), p.36.

205. "American Organ Builders of Today: J. H. & C. S. Odell & Co." *The Diapason,* vol. 16, no. 9 (Aug. 1925), p.36.

206. "American Organ Builders of Today: A. J. Schantz, Sons & Co." *The Diapason,* vol. 16, no. 4 (March 1925), p.6.

207. "American Organ Builders of Today: The Rudolph Wurlitzer Manufacturing Company." *The Diapason,* vol. 16, no. 5 (April 1925), p. 8.

208. Andrews, J. Warren. "Dead Combination Stirs Live Debate." *The Diapason,* vol. 4, no. 10 (Sept. 1913), p.5.

209. "Anton Gottfried, Figure in Organ Field, Reaches Four-Score." *The Diapason,* vol. 33, no. 4 (March 1942), p.27.

210. Arnold, Robert A. "The Krauss Organ and Church of The Most Blessed Sacrament." *Historical Review of Berks County,* vol. 33, no. 3 (Summer 1968), pp.98–101.

211. Audsley, George Ashdown. "The All Important Harmonic-Corroborating Stops." *The American Organist,* vol. 4, no. 1 (Jan. 1921), pp.10–15.

212. Austin, Basil G. "The Builder's Viewpoint." *The American Organist,* vol. 4, no. 8 (Aug. 1921), pp.255–58.

213. Ayars, Christine M. "Earliest Beginnings of Organ History in New England Traced." *The Diapason,* I: vol. 27, no. 9 (Aug. 1936), p.21; II: vol. 27, no. 10 (Sept. 1936), p.20; III: vol. 27, no. 11 (Oct. 1936), p.27; IV: vol. 27, no. 12 (Nov. 1936), p.27.

214. Babcock, Mary Kent Davey. "The Organs and Organ Builders of Christ

Church, Boston: 1736–1945." *Historical Magazine of the Protestant Episcopal Church,* vol. 14, no. 3 (Sept. 1945), pp.241–63.

215. "The Balbiani Organ." *The American Organist,* vol. 9, no. 5 (May 1926), pp.143–44.

216. "Baltimore Cathedral Organ." *The Lyre,* vol. 1, no. 1 (June 1, 1824), pp.5–6.

217. Barnes, William H. "Emerson Richards: His Influence on American Organs." *The Diapason,* vol. 55, no. 2 (Jan. 1964), pp.42–43.

218. ———. "Moller's Artiste." *The American Organist,* vol. 13, no. 9 (Sept. 1930), pp.542–43.

219. Berlinski, Herman. "The Organ in the Synagogue." Part III. *Music* (A.G.O.), vol. 2, no. 11 (Nov. 1968), pp.34–37, 46–47.

220. Berry, Beth. "Whalley and Genung Organ Restored." *The Tracker,* vol. 13, no. 4 (Summer 1969), p.17.

221. Berry, Chester H. "Brooklyn's Three-Manual Odell Lives On." *The Tracker,* vol. 13, no. 3 (Spring 1969), pp.7–8.

222. ———. "New York City's Oldest Tracker-Action Odell." *The Tracker,* vol. 13, no. 2 (Winter 1969), pp.3, 7.

223. Bidwell, Marshall. "Pittsburgh Organs Given by Carnegie are Cultural Force." *The Diapason,* vol. 48, no. 5 (April 1957), p.8.

224. "Big News in 1884." *The Tracker,* vol. 5, no. 3 (April 1961), p.5.

225. "Biographical Memoir of William M. Goodrich, Organ-Builder." *The New-England Magazine,* vol. 6 (Jan. 1834) pp.25–44. See also *The Tracker,* vol. 12, no. 1 (Fall 1967), pp.13–18; and vol. 12, no. 2 (Winter 1968), pp.6–8, 15–16.

226. Black, William. "Journal of William Black, 1744." *The Pennsylvania Magazine of History and Biography,* vol. 1, no. 4 (1877), pp.404–19.

227. Blanchard, Homer D. "Henry Pilcher's Sons' Opus 744." *The Tracker,* vol. 3, no. 3 (April 1959), pp.2–3.

228. ———. "Johnson's 860 Organs Present a Challenge to Designers To-day." *The Diapason,* I: vol. 36, no. 5 (April 1945), pp.20–21; II: vol. 36, no. 6 (May 1945), p.14.

229. Boadway, Edgar A. "An Early Studio Organ." *The Tracker,* vol. 2, no. 1 (Oct. 1957), pp.4–5.

230. ———. "The Henry Erben (1863) Organ." *The Tracker,* vol. 3, no. 1 (Oct. 1958), p.5.

231. ———. "One of the Largest Tracker Organs in America." *The Tracker,* vol. 7, no. 1 (Oct. 1962), pp.4, 8.

232. Bozeman, George, Jr. "C. B. Fisk, Inc., of Gloucester, Massachusetts." *Art of the Organ,* vol. 1, no. 1 (March 1971), pp.25–37.

233. "The Brattle Organ Restored." *The Tracker,* vol. 10, no. 2 (Winter 1966), p.5.

234. Bratton, James M. "Pipe Organs Before 1900." *Music* (A.G.O.), vol. 2, no. 5 (May 1968), pp.33, 45.

235. Bressler, Katherine. "Three Early Pennsylvania Trackers." *The Tracker,* vol. 11, no. 3 (Spring 1967), pp.5–6.

236. Bruce, W. J. "A Chapter on Church Organs." *The American Historical Record*, vol. 3, no. 28 (April 1874), pp.161–71.

237. Buhrman, T. Scott. "Ernest M. Skinner: Organ Builder." *The American Organist*, vol. 8, no. 5 (May 1925), p. 173.

238. ———. "Hillgreen, Lane and Company." *The American Organist*, vol. 10, no. 4 (April 1927), pp.84–93.

239. ———. "Piston Definitions." *The American Organist*, vol. 1, no. 6 (June 1918), pp.317–18.

240. ———. "St. Patrick's Cathedral Organs." *The American Organist*, vol. 11, no. 3 (March 1928), pp. 90–93.

241. "Builder-Author's Noted Career Ends." *The Diapason*, vol. 5, no. 2 (Jan. 1914), p.1.

242. Bullis, Carleton H. "New Rueckpositiv on Cleveland Organ is First in America." *The Diapason*, vol. 25, no. 1 (Dec. 1933), p.11.

243. ———. "Unit Principles and Why I Adopted Them." *The American Organist*, vol. 8, no. 11 (Nov. 1925), p.385.

244. Cameron, Peter T. "Business Records of Hall, Labagh & Co." *The Tracker*, I: vol. 14, no. 4 (Summer 1970), pp.5–6; II: vol. 15, no. 1 (Fall 1970), pp.1–3; III: vol. 15, no. 2 (Winter 1971), pp.6–8; IV: vol. 15, no. 3 (Spring 1971), pp.6–10; V: vol. 15, no. 4 (Summer 1971), pp.14–18; VI: vol. 16, no. 1 (Fall 1971), pp.11–15.

245. ———. "A Contemporary Sketch of Richard M. Ferris and Levi U. Stuart." *The Tracker*, vol. 12, no. 2 (Winter 1968), pp.1–2, 13–14.

246. ———. "Third Home for Thomas Robjohn Organ." *The Tracker*, vol. 10, no. 2 (Winter 1966), pp.3–4.

247. Caparn, H. A. "The Decadence of Organ Building." *The Musician*, vol. 11, no. 10 (Oct. 1906), p.501.

248. Carruth, William W. "Ancient Organ Now in California Church Once Used by Handel." *The Diapason*, vol. 32, no. 1 (Dec. 1940), p.23.

249. "Casavant Brothers Complete Century as Organ Builders." *The Diapason*, vol. 28, no. 2 (Feb. 1937), p.8

250. Challis, John. "The Slider-and-Pallet Wind Chest." *Organ Institute Quarterly*, vol. 3, no. 3 (Summer 1953), p.5.

251. Clarke, William Horatio. "Thomas Appleton, an Early New England Organ-Builder." *The Organ*, vol. 1, no. 2 (June 1892), pp.29–30. See also Clarke, William Horatio. "American Pioneer Organ Builders." *The Musician*, vol. 11, no. 2 (Feb. 1906), p.92.

252. Clemens, Gurney W. "The Dieffenbach Organ." *Historical Review of Berks County*, vol. 11, no. 1 (Oct. 1945), pp.18–21.

253. Cole, Richard B. "Pipe Organ Producers Enjoy a Vast, but Relaxed Prosperity." *Wall Street Journal*, vol. 145, no. 37 (Feb. 23, 1955), pp.1, 10.

254. Coleberd, Robert E., Jr. "Built on the Bennett System." *The American Organist*, vol. 51, no. 1 (Jan. 1968), pp.20–25.

255. ———. "John L. Hinners: The Henry Ford of the Pipe Organ." *The Tracker*, vol. 10, no. 3 (Spring 1966), pp.4, 6.

256. ———. "John Turnell Austin: Mechanical Genius of the Pipe Organ." *The American Organist*, vol. 49, no. 9 (Sept. 1966), pp.14–19.

257. ———. "Joseph Gratian—A Pioneer Builder in the West." *The American Organist*, vol. 48, no. 8 (Aug. 1965), pp.20–22.

258. ———. "Philipp Wirsching / the Consummate Builder." *The American Organist*, vol. 51, no. 10 (Oct. 1968), pp.13–15, 24–29.

259. ———. "A Tracker Trek Across Missouri." *The Tracker*, vol. 12, no. 4 (Summer 1968), pp.4–5, 7.

260. ———. "Two Gratians in Illinois." *The Tracker*, vol. 11, no. 1 (Fall 1966), pp.1–2.

261. ———. "Yesterday's Tracker—The Hinners Organ Story." *The American Organist*, vol. 43, no. 9 (Sept. 1960), pp.11–12, 14.

262. "Copy of Bach Organ is Placed at Harvard." *The Diapason*, vol. 28, no. 6 (May 1937), pp.1, 4.

263. Corwin, Charles E. "First Church Organ in New York in 1727; Story of Early Days." *The Diapason*, vol. 23, no. 1 (Dec. 1931), p.12.

264. "Cost of Church Music." *The Musician and Artist*, vol. 1, no. 1 (Jan. 1876), p.31.

265. Covell, William King. "Baroque Movement Seen as the Result of Study of History." *The Diapason*, vol. 34, no. 6 (May 1943), p.7.

266. ———. "Emerson Richards: The Man and his Work." *The Diapason*, vol. 55, no. 2 (Jan. 1964), p.42.

267. ———. "The Organs of Trinity Church, Newport, Rhode Island, U.S.A." *The Organ* (London), vol. 14 (April 1935), pp.245–55.

268. ———. "Senator Emerson Richards." *The American Organist*, vol. 47, no. 1 (Jan. 1964), p.12.

269. Cunkle, Frank. "Back to the Gallery." *The Diapason*, vol. 49, no. 4 (March 1958), p.20.

270. Cunningham, Tom. "Westward Ho!! for the Big Tenth." *The Tracker*, vol. 9, no. 2 (Winter 1965), p.12.

271. Demarest, Clifford. "The Dual Pistons." *The American Organist*, vol. 1, no. 1 (Jan. 1918), pp.16–19.

272. ———. "Tone Colors in the Organ." *The Diapason*, vol. 5, no. 10 (Sept. 1914), p.4.

273. Dinneen, William. "Early Music in Rhode Island Churches. II. Music in The First Baptist Church, Providence, 1775–1834." *Rhode Island History*, vol. 17, no. 2 (April 1958), pp.33–44.

274. ———. "Early Music in Rhode Island Churches. IV. Music in Beneficent Congregational Church and the Richmond Street Congregational Church, 1744–1836." *Rhode Island History*, vol. 17, no. 4 (Oct. 1958), pp.108–18.

275. Dohring, Gustav F. "Concerning An Old Organ." *The American Organist*, vol. 3, no. 2 (Feb. 1920), pp.65–66.

276. Duga, Jules J. "A Short History of the Reed Organ." *The Diapason*, vol. 59, no. 8 (July 1968), pp.24–25.

277. Eader, Thomas S. "The Baltimore Organ Builders." *The Tracker,* I: vol. 2, no. 3 (April 1958), pp.2–5; II: vol. 2, no. 4 (July 1958), pp.3–5; III: vol. 3, no. 1 (Oct. 1958), pp.3–4.

278. Eader, Thomas S. "David Tannenberg's Last Organ." *The Tracker,* vol. 4, no. 3 (April 1960), pp.3–4.

279. "Early History of the Organ in America." *The Organ,* vol. 1, no. 8 (Dec. 1892), pp.174–75.

280. Edmonds, John Henry. "Some Organs and Organists in Colonial Boston." *The Diapason,* vol. 14, no. 9 (Aug. 1923), pp.4, 29.

281. "Edwin S. Votey." *The American Organist,* vol. 14, no. 3 (March 1931), p.152.

282. "1838 Organ in Zelienople, Pa. Church Restored Completely." *The Diapason,* vol. 62, no. 10 (Sept. 1971), p.7.

283. Elsworth, John van Varick. "Johnson Again: No. 5—More of Them." *The American Organist,* I: vol. 32, no. 5 (May 1949), pp.155–56; II: vol. 32, no. 6 (June 1949), pp.189–91.

284. Eversden, Percy. "Charles C. Kilgen Passes." *The American Organist,* vol. 15, no. 6 (June 1932), p.367.

285. "Family of Organ Builders. . . ." *The Diapason,* vol. 4, no. 12 (Nov. 1913), p.13.

286. "Felix F. Schoenstein Had Notable Career." *The Diapason,* vol. 27, no. 7 (June 1936), p.22.

287. "Ferris' 1847 Organ at Round Lake, New York Will be Featured at '67 Convention." *The Tracker,* vol. 11, no. 2 (Winter 1967), pp.1–2.

288. Fesperman, John. "Music and Organs at 'The Old North'—Then and Now." *Organ Institute Quarterly,* vol. 10, no. 3 (Autumn 1963), pp.15–28.

289. "Fifty-seven Years As Organ Builder." *The Diapason,* vol. 9, no. 1 (Dec. 1917), p.3.

290. Finch, Thomas L. "The Hamill at Notre Dame, Ogdensburg." *The Tracker,* vol. 14, no. 2 (Winter 1970), pp.10–11, 19.

291. Fisher, Cleveland. "Henry F. Berger." *The Tracker,* vol. 8, no. 2 (Winter 1964), pp.1, 2, 4.

292. ———. "The Port Royal Confusion—Among Other Things!" *The Tracker,* vol. 12, no. 1 (Fall 1967), pp.1–2, 7–10.

293. Fisk, C. B. "The Fisk Organ in Harvard's Memorial Church." *The American Organist,* vol. 51, no. 12 (Dec. 1968), pp.13, 15.

294. Flint, Edward W. "An Unknown American Organ Builder: William Boone Fleming." *The Diapason,* vol. 62, no. 6 (May 1971), p.18.

294a. ———. "The Works of George Ashdown Audsley." *Art of the Organ,* vol. 2, no. 2 (June 1972), pp.19–31.

295. Frankus, Juxtus. "Organ News in New York." *The Organ,* vol. 1, no. 8 (Dec. 1892), p.186.

296. Frederic, Harold. "All is Vanity, Saith the Preacher." *The Diapason,* vol. 52, no. 8 (July 1961), pp.8–9, 28.

297. Fry, Henry S. "Advance in Mechanical Resources of the Organ." *The Diapason,* vol. 6, no. 1 (Dec. 1914), p.8.

298. Gammons, Edward B. "The Organ in Saint John's Chapel Groton Chapel." *Organ Institute Quarterly,* vol. 7, no. 1 (Spring 1957), pp.21–24.

299. ———. "Recitals on Baroque Organ at Harvard Rouse Enthusiasm." *The Diapason,* vol. 28, no. 6 (May 1937), p.4.

300. ———. Untitled description of organ in National Shrine of the Immaculate Conception, Washington, D. C. *The American Organist,* vol. 48, no. 4 (April 1965), pp.8–12.

301. Gaul, Harvey B. "The First Organ West of the Alleghenies." *Musical America,* vol. 32, no. 8 (June 19, 1920), p.26.

302. "George S. Hutchings." *The Organ,* vol. 2, no. 10 (Feb. 1894), pp.221–22.

303. Gerhard, Elmer Schultz. "Krauss Brothers." *Schwenckfeldiana,* vol. 1, no. 5 (Sept. 1945), pp.5–11.

304. ———. "The Krauss Organ Builders." *Schwenckfeldiana,* vol. 1, no. 5 (Sept. 1945), pp.12–20.

305. Grillo, Joseph, and Robert A. James. "The Organs of St. Bernard's Church." *The Tracker,* vol. 11, no. 4 (Summer 1967), pp.5–6, 9.

306. Groll, Edwin. "New York in 1839." *The American Organist,* vol. 7, no. 5 (May 1924), pp.299–301.

307. Gruenstein, S. E. "Advancing Backward." *The Diapason,* vol. 31, no. 7 (June 1940), p.18.

308. ———. "Let Youth Have Its Fling." *The Diapason,* vol. 31, no. 10 (Sept. 1940), p.12.

309. "Hammond Defense Ends; Order Awaited." *The Diapason,* vol. 28, no. 8 (July 1937), pp.4–5.

310. "Hammond Electric Organ Makes Debut." *The Diapason,* vol. 26, no. 6 (May 1935), p.3.

311. Harrison, G. Donald. "British Builder's Impressions After Two Years in U.S." *The Diapason,* vol. 20, no. 12 (Nov. 1929), pp.32–33.

312. ———. "Present Organ Trend Sound in Principle and Not an Imitation." The Diapason, vol. 24, no. 10 (Sept. 1933), pp.22–23.

313. ———. "Slider Chests?" *Organ Institute Quarterly,* vol. 3, no. 3 (Summer 1953), p.9.

314. Hawke, H. William. "Pages from the Past." Part II. *The American Organist,* vol. 48, no. 1 (Jan. 1965), pp.17–20.

315. "Hearing on Hammond is Hard-Fought Battle." *The Diapason,* vol. 28, no. 5 (April 1937), pp.1, 2, 20–22.

316. Hinners, John R. "Chronicle of The Hinners Organ Company." *The Tracker,* vol. 7, no. 2 (Dec. 1962), pp.1–3.

317. Hogan, Parke V. "Interesting Experiences in Organ Broadcasting." *The Diapason,* vol. 15, no. 1 (Dec. 1923), p.25.

318. Holland, W. J. "The First Pipe Organ Built in the United States West of the Allegheny Mountains." *The Diapason,* vol. 11, no. 5 (April 1920), p.16.

319. Holmes, Charles Nevers. "America's Oldest Organ." *Musical Courier,* vol. 72, no. 11 (March 16, 1916), pp.5–6.

320. ———. "The Oldest Organ in the United States." *The Granite Monthly,* vol. 52, no. 7 (July 1920), pp.293–95.

321. Holtkamp, Walter. "Building the Rückpositiv." *The American Organist,* vol. 17, no. 3 (March 1934), pp.122–24.

322. ———. "The Holtkamp Portative." *The American Organist,* vol. 19, no. 2 (Feb. 1936), p.57.

323. ———."Organ Builder Calls for Introspection by His Profession," *The Diapason,* vol. 27, no. 3 (Feb. 1936), p.24.

324. ———. "Organ Music and Organ Architecture." *Architecture* (June 1934), pp.355–56.

325. ———. "An Organ to See and Hear." *The American Organist,* vol. 18, no. 7 (July 1935), pp. 269–72.

326. ———. "Plea for Reviving the Sliderchest." *The American Organist,* vol. 22, no. 1 (Jan. 1939), pp.13–15.

327. ——— " 'Too Many Couplers,' Says Organ Builder in Discussing Topic." *The Diapason,* vol. 23, no. 5 (April 1932), p.45.

328. Holtkamp, Walter, Jr. "The Two-Manual Limited: An Approach to Integrity of Instrumental Form." *The Diapason,* vol. 59, no. 10 (Sept. 1968), pp.18–19.

329. Hopkins, Edward Cadoret. "Organ Building in the Southwest." *The American Organist,* vol. 9, no. 3 (March 1926), pp.62–67.

330. "How Old Ship Church, Oldest in America, Is Able to Keep Young." *The Diapason,* vol. 25, no. 5 (April 1934), pp.10–11.

331. Howes, Arthur. "The Methuen Organ." *Organ Institute Bulletin* (Summer 1951), pp.5–15.

332. Humphreys, Henry S. "The Koehnken Orgelbau . . . a casualty to progress." *Music* (A.G.O.), vol. 4, no. 9 (Sept. 1970), pp.23–25.

333. James, Robert A. "Brooklyn Had a Famous Hook." *The Tracker,* vol. 12, no. 4 (Summer 1968), p.12.

334. ———. "The Organs of Saint Alphonsus Church." *The Tracker,* vol. 10, no. 2 (Winter 1966), pp.1–2, 15.

335. Jamison, J. B. "An Advance in Organ Design." *The American Organist,* vol. 14, no. 10 (Oct. 1931), pp.597–602.

336. ———. "Principles of Ensemble; A study of the Tonal Architecture of the Organ." *The Diapason,* vol. 30, no. 12 (Nov. 1939), pp.20–21.

337. Jardine, Edward D. "New Ideas in Organs." *The Pianist,* vol. 2, no. 5 (May 1896), p.84.

338. Jennings, Arthur B. "A Plea for Mixtures." *The Diapason,* vol. 6, no. 10 (Sept. 1915), p.13.

339. Jordan, John W. "Early Colonial Organ-Builders of Pennsylvania." *The Pennsylvania Magazine of History and Biography,* vol. 22, no. 2 (1898), pp.231–33.

340. Kendall, John Smith. "New Orleans' Musicians of Long Ago." *The Louisiana Historical Quarterly,* vol. 31, no. 1 (Jan. 1948), pp.130–49.

341. Kistler, Rev. William U. "Early Organ Builders in Northern Montgomery County." *Historical Sketches Vol. IV.* Norristown, Pa.: Historical Society of Montgomery County, 1910, pp.112–17.

342. Koch, Caspar P. "Who Was Inventor of Harmonic Flute? Light on Question." *The Diapason,* vol. 23, no. 3 (Feb. 1932), p.16.

343. Koch, Paul. "3000th Recital Recalls Carnegie's Philanthropy." *The American Organist,* vol. 49, no. 5 (May 1967), p.26.

344. Lahee, Henry C. "Organs and Organ Building in New England." *The New England Magazine,* New Series, vol. 17, no. 4 (Dec. 1897), pp.485–505.

345. "Large Pipe Organs." *The Tracker,* vol. 12, no. 4 (Summer 1968), p.11. Reprinted from *Denver Music and Drama Magazine,* vol 1, no. 29 (July 21, 1891).

346. Laubenstein, Sarah. "An Organ in 16th Century Florida?" *A.G.O. Quarterly,* vol. 12, no. 2 (April 1967), pp.66–67, 78, 90.

347. Lewis, Jim. "A Forgotten Organ in San Francisco." *The Diapason,* vol. 63, no. 7 (June 1972), p.3.

347a. ———— "Hilborne Roosevelt and the St. Thomas Church Organ." *The Diapason,* vol. 64, no. 3 (Feb. 1973), p.19.

347b. ————. "James E. Treat and the Organs for the Searles Estates." *The Diapason,* vol. 64, no. 3 (Feb. 1973), p.1.

347c. ————. "A San Francisco Treat." *The Tracker,* vol. 17, no. 4 (Summer 1973), pp.12–13, 16.

348. Lindsay, Walter. "An 'Early Victorian' Organ." *The Diapason,* vol. 17, no. 9 (Aug. 1926), p.32.

349. ————. "Only a Picture Remains." *The American Organist,* vol. 26, no. 8 (Aug. 1943), p.179.

350. Lippencott, Margaret E. "Henry Pilcher, Organ Builder." *The New-York Historical Society Quarterly Bulletin,* vol. 27, no. 4 (Oct. 1943), pp.87–93.

351. Loris, Michael Anthony. "The Organ at the University of Notre Dame." *The Tracker,* vol. 6, no. 3 (April 1962), pp.10–12.

352. Losh, C. S. "Charging the Windmills." *The American Organist,* vol. 8, no. 12 (Dec. 1925), p.414.

353. ————. "Rebuilding: a War-time Expedient." *The American Organist,* vol. 1, no. 9 (Sept. 1918), pp.473–74.

354. Lovewell, S. Harrison. "Boston's Michell Organ." *The American Organist,* vol. 19, no. 7 (July 1936), pp.230–32.

355. ————. "Cathedral of Holy Cross in Boston and its Historic Organ." *The Diapason,* vol. 21, no. 1 (Dec. 1929), pp.40–41.

356. ————. "New England's Oldest Organ." *The Diapason,* vol. 17, no. 1 (Dec. 1925), p.29.

357. ————. "The Oliver Holden Organ; Where He Wrote 'Coronation.' " *The Diapason,* vol. 16, no. 11 (Oct. 1925), p.32.

358. Lutz, Charles. "Krauss Organs in Pennsylvania." *The American Organist,* vol. 52, no. 1 (Jan. 1969), pp.12–13, 15.

359. Mader, Clarence. "An Important American Organ." *The American Organist,* vol. 53, no. 3 (April 1970), pp.21, 23.

360. Mander, Noel P. "Harpsichord-Organ." *The American Organist,* vol. 42, no. 10 (Oct. 1959), p.342.

361. Mangler, Joyce Ellen. "The Deblois Concert Hall Organ—1763–1851." *The Tracker,* vol. 3, no. 1 (Oct. 1958), pp.1, 8.

362. ———. "Early Music in Rhode Island Churches. I. Music in the First Congregational Church, Providence, 1770–1850." *Rhode Island History,* vol. 17, no. 1 (Jan. 1958), pp.1–9.

363. ———. "Early Music in Rhode Island Churches. III. Music in King's Church (St. John's), Providence, 1722–1850." *Rhode Island History,* vol. 17, no. 3 (July 1958), pp.73–84.

364. ———. "Some Letters From Mr. John Geib of New York." *The Tracker,* vol. 2, no. 2 (Jan. 1958), pp.1–3.

365. Mathews, W. S. B. "Portable Pipe Organ." *The Organ,* vol. 2, no. 4 (Aug. 1893), pp.90–91.

366. Maurer, Maurer. "Colonial Organs and Organists Are Research Subject." *The Diapason,* vol. 48, no. 4 (March 1957), pp.24–25.

367. Mayton, James, and Wallace McClanahan. "Mobile Cathedral Organ." *The American Organist,* vol. 34, no. 6 (June 1951), pp.187–88.

368. Mercer, Jesse B. "Two North Carolina Organs." *The Tracker,* vol. 6, no. 3 (April 1962), p.2.

369. "Methuen." *The American Organist,* I: vol. 45, no. 3 (March 1962), pp.10–14; II: vol. 45, no. 4 (April 1962), pp.14–15; III: vol. 45, no. 5 (May 1962), pp.14–17; IV: vol. 45, no. 6 (June 1962), pp.14–17.

370. Michell, Carlton C. Letter to the editor. *The Organ,* vol 2, no. 8 (Dec. 1893), pp.186–87.

371. Miller, Percy Chase. "Roosevelts in Philadelphia." *The American Organist,* vol. 16, no. 7 (July 1933), pp.366–67.

372. ———. "The Swell Idea." *The American Organist,* vol. 5, no. 7 (July 1922), pp.276–77.

373. Morse, Jack. "Garret House." *The Tracker,* vol. 5, no. 1 (Oct. 1960), pp.3–5.

374. Morton, F. E. "Henry Erben and his Work." *The Diapason,* vol. 1, no. 2 (Jan. 1910), pp.1, 3.

375. Murray, Thomas. "The Hook & Hastings Organ in Holy Cross Cathedral, Boston." *The Diapason,* vol. 63, no. 12 (Nov. 1972), pp.4–6.

375a. ———. "A Victorian Organ." *Music* (A.G.O.), I: vol. 7, no. 7 (July 1973), pp.24–26; II: vol. 8, no. 2 (Feb. 1974), pp.23–26.

376. McCorkle, Donald M. "The Collegium Musicum Salem: Its Music, Musicians, and Importance." *The North Carolina Historical Review,* vol. 33, no. 4 (Oct. 1956), pp.483–98.

377. ———. "Prelude to a History of American Moravian Organs." *American Guild of Organists Quarterly,* vol. 3, no. 4 (Oct. 1958), pp.142–48.

378. McCracken, Eugene M. "Duck Soup." *The Tracker,* vol. 4, no. 1 (Oct. 1959), pp.9–12.

379. ———. "The Durners, C. F., and C. E." *The Tracker,* vol. 8, no. 4 (Summer 1964), pp.11–13.

380. ———. "The Elusive Corries." *The Tracker,* vol. 3, no. 2 (Jan. 1959), pp.1–5.

381. ———. "He Built a Better Pipe Organ." *The Tracker,* vol. 3, no. 4 (July 1959), pp.7–8.

382. ———. "The Organs of Berks County." *Historical Review of Berks County,* vol. 28, no. 1 (Winter 1962–1963), pp.6–10.

383. ———. "Pennsylvania, The Keystone State." *The Tracker,* vol. 4, no. 2 (Jan. 1960), pp.1, 3–4.

384. ———. "The Spirits Cost $0.75." *The Tracker,* I: vol. 5, no. 1 (Oct. 1960), pp.8–12; II: vol. 5, no. 2 (Jan. 1961), pp.6–8.

385. McManis, Charles W. "David Tannenberg and the Old Salem Restoration." *The American Organist,* vol. 48, no. 5 (May 1965), pp.15–20.

386. ———. "An Organbuilder Looks at His Art." *The American Organist,* vol. 27, no. 11 (Nov. 1944), pp.263–65.

387. ———. "Restoration of Tannenberg Organ at Old Salem." *The Diapason,* vol. 57, no. 4 (March 1965), pp.36–37.
vol. 57, no. 4 (March 1965), pp.36–37.

388. McManis, Charles W., and Frank P. Albright. "Tannenberg Restoration." *The Tracker,* vol. 9, no. 2 (Winter 1965), pp.1–2, 7–8.

389. Nevin, Gordon Balch. "Have We Made Tonal Progress?" *The Diapason,* vol. 11, no. 11 (Oct. 1920), p.10.

390. "New Organ in St. Michael's P.E. Church, New York." *The Organ,* vol. 1, no. 12 (March 1893), p.263.

391. "New Tonal Resource and Its Placement Pictured by Builder." *The Diapason,* vol. 41, no. 2 (Jan. 1950), p.34.

392. "New Tracker Instrument in St. Thomas Opened." *The Diapason,* vol. 61, no. 1 (Dec. 1969), p.2.

393. "New Tubular Pneumatic Organ." *The Organ,* vol. 1, no. 9 (Jan. 1893), p.215.

394. "New York Cathedral Scheme Interesting." *The Diapason,* vol. 18, no. 9 (Aug. 1927), p.2.

395. Noack, Fritz. "John Snetzler's 1762 Organ at South Dennis, Mass." Edited by Barbara J. Owen. *The Tracker,* vol. 5, no. 2 (Jan. 1961), p.12.

396. Noehren, Robert. "Schnitger, Cliquot and Cavaillé-Coll: Three Great Traditions and their Meaning to Contemporary Organ Playing." Part I. *The Diapason,* vol. 57, no. 12 (Nov. 1966), pp.40–41.

397. Ogasapian, John Ken. "The Mechanics Hall Organ." *The American Organist,* vol. 43, no. 11 (Nov. 1960), pp.25–26.

398. "Old and New United at Williamsburg, Va." *The Diapason,* vol. 30, no. 11 (Oct. 1939), p.4.

399. Oliver, Henry K. "An Account of the First Organs in America." *The Organist's Quarterly Journal and Review,* vol. 2, no. 1 (April 1875), pp.4–6.

400. "Organ-Building in New England." *The New-England Magazine,* vol. 6 (March 1834), pp.205–15.

401. "Organ Built in 1761 by Snetzler Now in New York Museum." *The Diapason,* vol. 31, no. 10 (Sept. 1940), p.17.

402. "Organ in Christ Church, Ann-Street." *The Lyre,* vol. 1, no. 3 (Aug. 1, 1824), p.36.

403. "Organ in Christ Church, Anthony-Street, New-York." *The Lyre,* vol. 1, no. 5 (Oct. 1824), p.77.

404. "Organ in Christ Church, Norfolk, Virginia." *The Lyre,* vol. 1, no. 7 (Dec. 1, 1824), p. 110.

405. "Organ in St. George's Church, Beekman-street, New-York." *The Lyre,* vol. 1, no. 10 (March 1825), p.160.

406. "Organ in St. Paul's Church." *The Lyre,* vol. 1, no. 3 (Aug. 1824), p.37.

407. "Organ in Trinity Church, New-York." *The Lyre,* vol. 1, no. 5 (Oct. 1, 1824), p.78.

408. "Organ 154 Years Old in Wisconsin." *The Diapason,* vol. 6, no. 5 (April 1915), p.7.

409. "Organ Voluntaries." *The Musical Magazine,* vol. 1, no. 3 (July 1835), pp.77–78.

410. Osborne, William. "Five New England Gentlemen." *Music* (A.G.O.), vol. 3, no. 8 (Aug. 1969), pp.27–29.

411. Owen, Barbara J. "American Organ Music and Playing from 1700." *Organ Institute Quarterly,* vol. 10, no. 3 (Autumn 1963), p.7.

412. ———. "The Goodriches and Thomas Appleton, Founders of the Boston Organ Industry." *The Tracker,* vol. 4, no. 1 (Oct. 1959), pp.2–6.

413. ———. "Henry Erben's Baltimore Branch." *The Tracker,* vol. 1, no. 3 (April 1957), pp.6–7.

414. ———. "The Nineteenth Century Organ." *The American Organist,* vol. 40, no. 5 (May 1957), pp.143–45.

415. ———. "Organs at Harvard." *The Tracker,* vol. 12, no. 2 (Winter 1968), pp.4–5, 14.

416. ———. "Some Early American Organ Oddities." *The American Organist,* vol. 44, no. 1 (Jan. 1961), p.16.

417. ———. "A Tale of Two Organs." *Historic Nantucket,* vol. 10, no. 4 (April 1963), pp.7–14.

418. Pallage, George J. "A Brief Sketch of Cincinnati's Early Major Organ Builders." *The Tracker,* vol. 9, no. 3 (Spring 1965), pp.6–7.

419. Paterson, Donald R. M. "Organs Built by William King." *The Tracker,* vol. 16, no. 4 (Summer 1972), pp.5–10. See also "Watkins Glen and King Organs." *The Tracker,* vol. 14, no. 4 (Summer 1970), pp.12–15; vol. 15, no. 1 (Fall 1970), pp. 12–13; vol. 15, no. 2 (Winter 1971), pp.12–15; vol. 15, no. 3 (Spring 1971), pp.13–17.

420. Payne, Wilfred, and Martin W. Bush. "Omaha's First Organ, Johnson's Opus 293, on Its 75th Birthday." *The Diapason,* vol. 36, no. 1 (Dec. 1944), p.6.

421. Peek, Richard. "Moeller's Opus 346, Exposition Organ." *The Tracker,* vol. 7, no. 3 (March 1963), p.5.

422. Petty, William E. "The Fabulous Quad." *The Diapason,* vol. 60, no. 2 (Jan. 1969), pp.12–14.

423. Phelps, Lawrence I. "Designing a 2 Manual Organ." *The Diapason,* vol. 52, no. 10 (Sept. 1961), pp.8–9, 40–41.

424. ———. "Effects of Wind Chest Design on the Speech of Organ Pipes." *Organ Institute Quarterly,* I: vol. 3, no. 1 (Winter 1953), p.19; II: vol. 3, no. 2 (Spring 1953), pp.38–42.

425. ———. "Perspective." *Organ Institute Quarterly,* vol. 4, no. 1 (Winter 1954), pp.21–33.

426. ———. "A Short History of the Organ Revival." *Church Music,* 1967, no. 1, pp.13–30.

427. ———. "Trends in North American Organ Building." *Music* (A.G.O.), vol. 4, no. 5 (May 1970), pp.36–43.

428. "Pipes of Haskell Patent; III. Short Length Pipes." *The American Organist,* vol. 3, no. 8 (Aug. 1920), pp.282–86.

429. "Plymouth Church Organ, Brooklyn, N.Y." *The Organists' Quarterly Journal and Review,* vol. 1, no. 4 (Jan. 1875), pp.7–8.

430. "A Portativ—in Two Parts." *The American Organist,* vol. 36, no. 10 (Oct. 1953), p.326.

431. Porter, William S. "The Musical Cyclopedia." *The Tracker,* vol. 7, no. 4 (June 1963), pp.9–11.

432. "A Quote of Unusual Interest." *The Tracker,* vol. 9, no. 1 (Fall 1964), p.7.

433. Radzinsky, Charles A. "Organ Builders of New York, 1800 an 1909." *The New Music Review,* vol. 9, no. 99 (Feb. 1910), pp.165–68.

434. Ranger, Richard H. "Electric Music as New Supplement to Tone of Organ Pipes." *The Diapason,* vol. 23, no. 12 (Nov. 1932), p.25.

435. Redway, Virginia Larkin. "Charles Theodore Pachelbell, Musical Emigrant." *Journal of the American Musicological Society,* vol. 5, no. 1 (Spring 1952), pp.32–36.

436. Reich, Robert J. "An Historical Organ at Schuylerville, N.Y." *The Tracker,* vol. 5, no. 2 (Jan. 1961), pp.3–4, 8.

437. Reich, Robert J. "John G. Marklove." *The Tracker,* vol. 1, no. 2 (Jan. 1957), pp.3–6.

438. ———. "The Organ at the First Religious Society, Newburyport." *The Tracker,* vol. 2, no. 1 (Oct. 1957), pp.1–4.

439. ———. "The Story of a Hook and Hastings Renovation." *The Tracker,* vol. 9, no. 1 (Fall 1964), pp.9, 12.

440. Reynolds, James N. "Organ Built in 1820 Is Found in Historic Charleston Church." *The Diapason,* vol. 33, no. 9 (Aug. 1942), p.20.

441. ———. "Organ Development in 45 Years Recalled by James N. Reynolds." *The Diapason,* vol. 35, no. 9 (Aug. 1944), p.4.

442. Richards, Emerson L. "Atlantic City High School Organ." *The American Organist,* vol. 7, no. 7 (July 1924), pp.406–21.

443. ———. "The Choir Organ." *The American Organist,* vol. 8, no. 9 (Sept. 1925), p.334.

444. ———. "Roosevelt's Place in Organ History." *The American Organist,* vol. 33, no. 12 (Dec. 1950), pp.415–16.

445. ———. "The Sliderchest's Many Serious Defects." *The American Organist,* vol. 22, no. 4 (April 1939), pp.119–24.

446. "Robert Hope-Jones Meets Tragic End." *The Diapason,* vol. 5, no. 11 (Oct. 1914), pp.1–2.

447. Robinson, Albert F. "Tracing an Organ's History." *The Tracker,* vol. 5, no. 3 (April 1961), p.7.

448. ———. "The Tragic End of a Standbridge." *The Tracker,* vol. 14, no. 2 (Fall 1969), pp.1–2.

449. Rodgers, Eugene L. "Christ Church Cathedral and Its Music." *Bulletin of the Missouri Historical Society,* vol. 24, no. 3 (April 1968), pp.255–71.

450. Roosevelt, Hilborne L. "The Roosevelt Diary." *The American Organist,* I: vol. 33, no. 4 (April 1950), pp.131–34; II: vol. 33, no. 5 (May 1950), pp.163–66; III: vol. 33, no. 6 (June 1950), pp.195–97; IV: vol. 33, no. 7 (July 1950), pp.227–28; V: vol. 33, no. 8 (Aug. 1950), pp.261–62; VI: vol. 33, no. 9 (Sept. 1950), pp.295–97.

451. Rutledge, Anna Wells. "The Second St. Philip's, Charleston, 1710–1835." *Journal of the Society of Architectural Historians,* vol. 18, no. 3 (Oct. 1959), pp.112–14.

452. "St. John's Evangelical Lutheran Church, Brooklyn." *The Organ,* vol. 1, no. 2 (June 1892), p.43.

453. Salter, Sumner. "Early Organs Heard in America Did Not Find Ready Welcome." *The Diapason,* vol. 28, no. 10 (Sept. 1937), p.20.

454. ———. "An Echo of the Past." *The Organ* (London), I: vol. 7, no. 28 (April 1928), pp.251–52; II: vol. 8, no. 29 (July 1928), pp.55–58.

455. ———. "How Historic Church in New York Bought First Organ in 1887." *The Diapason,* vol. 28, no. 5 (April 1937), p.23.

456. ———. "Long and Interesting Career for America's Second Oldest Organ." *The Diapason,* vol. 28, no. 11 (Oct. 1937), p.28.

457. ———. "Organs of Early Day Built for Historic Churches of Boston." *The Diapason,* vol. 28, no. 12 (Nov. 1937), p.28.

458. Saxton, Stanley E. "The Schuylerville, Organ of 1756. . . . Again?" *The Tracker,* vol. 11, no. 3 (Spring 1967), p.3.

459. Schantz, John A. "Three Schantz Tracker Organs." *The Tracker,* vol. 14, no. 1 (Fall 1969), pp.9, 16.

460. Schmitt, Elizabeth Towne. "William Schuelke Organs in Iowa." *The Tracker,* vol. 11, no. 2 (Winter 1967), pp.3–5.

461. Schoenstein, Louis. "The Autobiography of Louis Schoenstein." *The Tracker,* vol. 14, no. 2 (Winter 1970), pp.1–2, 17.

462. Schreiner, Alexander. "100 Years of Organs in the Mormon Tabernacle." *The Diapason,* vol. 58, no. 12 (Nov. 1967), p.19.

463. Schultz, Selina Gerhard. "John Krauss (1770–1819)." *Schwenckfeldiana,* vol. 1, no. 5 (Sept. 1945), pp.21–33.

464. Shackley, Frederick N. "Organ's History Covers 170 Years." *The Diapason,* vol. 17, no. 5 (April 1926), pp.36–37.

465. "Simmons Built in 1852 Still in Use in San Francisco." *The Diapason,* vol. 61, no. 10 (Sept. 1970), p. 28.

466. Simmons, Kenneth F. "A History of the Johnson Family and Firm." *The Tracker,* I: vol. 7, no. 3 (March 1963), pp.10–12; II: vol. 7, no. 4 (June 1963), pp.4–7; III: vol. 8, no. 1 (Fall 1963), pp.4–6; IV: vol. 8, no. 2 (Winter 1964), pp.6–8; V: vol. 8, no. 3 (Spring 1964), pp.2–5, 11.

467. ———. "The Temple of Music Organ." *The Tracker,* vol. 14, no. 2 (Winter 1970), pp.8–9, 18.

468. "Sixty Years Devoted to Building Organs." *The Diapason,* vol. 11, no. 4 (March 1920), p.3.

469. Skinner, E. M. "Some Reminiscences." *The Diapason,* vol. 14, no. 12 (Nov. 1923), p.18.

470. "A Small, Low-Cost Pipe Organ." *The Tracker,* vol 7, no. 2 (Dec. 1962), p.9.

471. Smith, Rollin. "Dupré in the Twenties." *The Diapason,* vol. 62, no. 7 (June 1971), pp.26–27.

472. "Snetzler Restored At Smithsonian." *The Tracker,* vol. 14, no. 3 (Spring 1970), pp.13, 19.

473. "Solves the Problem of Portable Organ." *The Diapason,* vol. 25, no. 5 (April 1934), p.35.

474. Spaugh, Herbert. "Organ Built in 1773 Serves Historic Fane in South to This Day." *The Diapason,* vol. 25, no. 12 (Nov. 1934), p.22.

475. Spell, Lota M. "Music Teaching in New Mexico in The Seventeenth Century." *The New Mexico Historical Review,* vol. 2, no. 1 (Jan. 1927), pp.27–36.

476. Spiess, Lincoln Bunce. "Benavides and Church Music in New Mexico in the Early 17th Century." *Journal of the American Musicological Society,* vol. 17, no. 2 (Summer 1964), pp.144–56.

477. ———. "Church Music in Seventeenth-Century New Mexico." *The New Mexico Historical Review,* vol. 40, no. 1 (Jan. 1965), pp.5–21.

478. "Tannenberg Organ Restored." *The American Organist,* vol. 43, no. 5 (May 1960), p.28.

479. "Then & Now—a Century Apart: No. 1." *The American Organist,* vol. 29, no. 6 (June 1946), pp.165–68.

480. "Thirty Per Cent Cut in Organ Construction." *The Diapason,* vol. 9, no. 6 (May 1918), p.1.

481. Thomas, Robert I. "1839 German Organ in Venedy, Ill." *The Tracker,* vol. 14, no. 1 (Fall 1969), pp.3, 14.

482. Thompson, Arthur J. "Some Reflections on Organ Ensemble." *The Diapason,* vol. 18, no. 4 (March 1927), p.40.

483. ———. "Two-Manual Organ Schemes." *The American Organist,* vol. 11, no. 7 (July 1928), pp.243–44.

484. Thompson, Van Denman. "The Modern Organ—And Bach." *The American Organist,* vol. 2, no. 12 (Dec. 1919), pp. 484–86.

485. Tilton, Edwin A. "The Brattle Organ." *The Organ,* vol. 1, no. 8 (Dec. 1892), pp.173–74.

486. Titus, Parvin. "Famous Cincinnati Music Hall Organ Has Interesting History." *The Tracker,* vol. 9, no. 3 (Spring 1965), pp.9–12.

487. "A Treatise on the Organ, Explanatory of that Noble Instrument." *The Lyre,* vol. 1, no. 3 (Aug. 1824), pp.42–48.

488. "Tremont Temple (Boston) Organ Destroyed by Fire." *The Organ,* vol. 1, no. 12 (April 1893), pp.281–82.

489. Untitled report of an organ by Henry Erben. *The American Musical Times,* vol. 2, no. 2 (June 10, 1848), p.28.

490. Untitled report of the organ installed in the 14th St. Presbyterian Church, N.Y., July 23, 1851. *The Choral Advocate,* vol. 2, no. 4 (Sept. 1851), p.52.

491. Valentine, Ralph B. "Church of the Advent Organ." *The American Organist,* vol. 49, no. 2 (Feb. 1966), pp.20–22.

492. Vente, M. A. Letter to the editor. *Organ Institute Quarterly,* vol. 3, no. 1 (Winter 1953), p.30.

493. ———. "My View of Organ Building Today." *Organ Institute Quarterly,* vol. 2, no. 3 (Summer 1952), p.5.

494. Ward, Townsend. "The Germantown Road and its Associations." Part VII. *The Pennsylvania Magazine of History and Biography,* vol. 6, no. 3 (1882), pp.257–83.

495. Webber, F. R. "Back to Gallery Editorial Provokes Writer's Comments." *The Diapason,* vol. 49, no. 7 (June 1958), p. 27.

496. ———. "Chicago: A Johnson Town." *The Tracker,* I: vol. 10, no. 2 (Winter 1966), pp.11–13, 15; II: vol. 10, no. 3 (Spring 1966), p.7.

497. ———. "Henry Erben, Organ Builder of Century Ago, and His Work." *The Diapason,* vol. 44, no. 1 (Dec., 1952), p.16.

498. ———. "Henry Pilcher 1798–1880." *The Tracker,* vol. 9, no. 4 (Summer 1965), p.6.

499. ———. "A Holtkamp Story." *The Diapason,* vol. 53, no. 5 (April 1962), pp.28–29.

500. ———. "Nineteenth Century Americana." *The American Organist,* vol. 40, no. 10 (Oct. 1957), pp.328–30.

501. ———. "Organs of Early Day in Chicago Churches When Frontier Town." *The Diapason,* I: vol. 45, no. 1 (Dec. 1953), p.23; II: vol. 45, no. 2 (Jan. 1954), p.23; III: vol. 45, no. 3 (Feb. 1954), p.25.

502. ———. "The St. Louis Exposition Organ." *The Tracker,* vol. 3, no. 3 (April 1959), pp.5–8.

503. ———. "Some Early Organs in New York City Described Vividly." *The Diapason,* I: vol. 48, no. 7 (June 1957), p.16; II: Vol. 48, no. 8 (July 1957), pp.16, 34; III: vol. 48, no. 9 (Aug. 1957), p.8; IV: vol. 48, no. 10, (Sept. 1957), p.30.

504. ———. "Two Roosevelts Build Church Organs." *The Tracker,* I: vol. 10, no. 3 (Spring 1966), pp.9–10; II: vol. 10, no. 4 (Summer 1966), p.7.

505. West, Edward N. "History and Development of Music in the American Church." *Historical Magazine of the Protestant Episcopal Church,* vol. 14, no. 1 (March 1945), pp.15–37.

506. White, Robert W. "Franck and the 8 ft.-less Organ." *The Diapason,* vol. 53, no. 7 (June 1962), pp.8–9.

507. Whiteford, Joseph S. "An Organ for an Orchestra." *The American Organist,* vol. 46, no. 2 (Feb. 1963), pp.10–13.

508. ———. "Two Manual Organs." *The Diapason,* vol. 56, no. 10 (Sept. 1965), pp.34–35.

509. Whitford, Homer P. "France and Its Student Appeal." *The American Organist,* vol. 8, no. 2 (Feb. 1925), p.51.

510. Whiting, Robert Bruce. "Charles F. Durner Organs." *The Tracker,* vol. 10, no. 1 (Fall 1965), pp.1, 9.

511. ———. "John Ziegler." *The Tracker,* vol. 9, no. 3 (Spring 1965), pp.3–4.

512. ———. "Rebuilding a William King and Son Organ." *The Tracker,* vol. 9, no. 2 (Winter 1965), pp.5–6.

513. "William A. Johnson, Opus 76." *The Tracker,* vol. 4, no. 4 (July 1960), p.6.

514. Williams, George W. "Charleston Church Music 1562–1833." *Journal of the American Musicological Society,* vol. 7, no. 1 (Spring 1954), pp.35–40.

515. ———. "Early Organists at St. Philip's, Charleston." *The South Carolina Historical Magazine,* vol. 54, no. 2 (Apr. 1953), pp.83–87.

516. ———. "Eighteenth-Century Organists of St. Michael's, Charleston." *The South Carolina Historical Magazine,* I: vol. 53, no. 3 (July 1952), pp.146–54; II: vol. 53, no. 4 (Oct. 1952), pp.212–22.

517. Wirling, Eliot I. "Pipe Organs of New England." *Old-Time New England,* vol. 45, no. 2 (Fall 1954), pp.37–48.

518. Wolf, Edward C. "The Organs At St. Michael's and Zion Lutheran Churches, Philadelphia." *The Tracker,* vol. 6, no. 3 (April 1962), pp.6–8.

518a. ———. "The Schmahl and Krauss Organs in Old St. Michael's Philadelphia." *The Tracker,* vol. 17, no. 4 (Summer 1973), pp.8–11.

518b. ———. "Sequel to 'Journey to Pennsylvania'" *The Tracker,* vol. 17, no. 3 (Spring 1973), pp.12, 16.

519. ———. "The Tannenberg Organ at Old Zion Church Philadelphia." *Journal of Church Music,* vol. 3, no. 4 (April 1961), pp.2–5.

520. Wood, William D. "Story of Earlier Day in History of Organ is Told by a Veteran." *The Diapason,* vol. 33, no. 10 (Sept. 1942), p.14.

521. "Worldwide Fame Won by Wanamaker Organ." *The Diapason,* vol. 34, no. 2 (Jan. 1943), pp.1, 4–5.

522. Wyly, James. "The Steere & Turner Organ of Pullman Methodist Church, Chicago." *The Diapason,* I: vol. 59, no. 10 (Sept. 1968), pp.30–31; II: vol. 59, no. 11 (Oct. 1968), pp.24–25.

523. Yeats, Jane Luce. "Purvis Recital Observes Organ's 100th Birthday." *The Diapason,* vol. 55, no. 3 (Feb. 1964), p.1.

524. Zundel, John. "The Organ." Part II. *The Choral Advocate and Singing-Class Journal,* vol. 1, no. 10 (March 1851), p.150.

Notes

Part One: Organs in a New Land, 1524–1760

I. The Spanish Missions

1. An article by Sarah Laubenstein ("An Organ in 16th Century Florida?") in *A.G.O. Quarterly,* April 1967, p.66) suggests the possibility of an earlier organ in Florida. The evidence is not conclusive, however, since it relies on a mistranslation of *canto de órgano,* the sixteenth-century Spanish term for polyphony, which does not necessarily imply the use of an organ.

2. The small Spanish organ now in the San Fernando Mission was brought to this country in 1944.

II. The British Colonies

1. Population growth was not limited to the German migration, however, and by the time the first census was taken in 1790, the total population was approaching four million [108, p.468]. A hundred years earlier the population was an estimated 200,000 to 250,000 [161, p.167].

2. A traveler to Pennsylvania in 1750, Gottlieb Mittelberger was so distressed by the miseries his countrymen endured, both in the six-month journey and in the conditions that awaited them on arrival in America, that he wrote a book describing their sufferings in vivid detail. The book was published in 1756 in Germany, and it was Mittelberger's hope that it would dissuade some prospective immigrants from leaving their homes [107].

3. Now in the Metropolitan Museum of Art, New York. This instrument is inscribed "Johannes Clemm fecit Philadelphia 1739."

4. Robert Harttafel, organ builder of Lancaster, Pennsylvania, was born on February 25, 1717, at Leidek, Karmstadt. He came to America and settled first in Warwick township, Lancaster County. He died of apoplexy on November 7, 1782. It is probably the 1751 rebuilding that was mistaken by Rufus A. Grider for a new organ: "The first organ was obtained when the present chapel was built, in 1751." Grider also adds an interesting historical note to this organ: "Benjamin Franklin, in a letter to his wife, in 1756, says, that 'he heard very fine music in the church; that flutes, oboes, French horns, and trumpets, accompanied the organ' " [70, p.4].

5. This organ may have been built by Tannenberg. For more on this subject see 42, pp.106–108.

6.   Klemm Organs

    1739   Trinity Parish, New York
    1746   Klemm-Hesselius organ installed, Bethlehem, Pennsylvania
    1752   Christ Lutheran Church, Berks County, Pennsylvania

1752 One stop added to Trappe Augustus Lutheran Church organ, Montgomery, Pennsylvania

Klemm-Tannenberg Organs

1758 Chapel, Nazareth Hall, Nazareth, Pennsylvania
1758 Nazareth Hall (positive), Nazareth, Pennsylvania
1759 Moravian Chapel, Bethlehem, Pennsylvania
1760 Moravian Chapel, Christian's Spring, Pennsylvania
1762 Bethabara, Forsyth County, North Carolina (may have been built by Klemm and Tannenberg).

7. Dr. Christopher Witt, physician, botanist, astronomer, mechanic, teacher, clockmaker, portrait painter, and amateur musician, was born in Wiltshire, England. He joined the Mystics of the Wissahickon in 1704, and is credited with the translation of a book of hymns written by Kelpius.

8. William Black was "Secretary of the Commissioners appointed by Governor Gooch, of Virginia, to unite with those from the colonies of Pennsylvania and Maryland, to treat with the Iroquois or Six Nations of Indians, in reference to the lands west of the Allegheny Mountains" [226, p.404].

9. "I went to the Funeral of Mrs. Whetcomb's Grand-daughter; who is also Grand-daughter to Col. Townsend. I used to go to the same Room for the Sound of Mr. Brattle's Organs" [139, p.235].

10. Fisher is inaccurate in designating the Brattle organ as "the first pipe organ used in a church in the Colonies. . . ."

11. The remaining parts of the Bridge organ were combined with several additional sets of pipes and a new case to form a two-manual organ for the Congregational Church in Ware, Massachusetts. In 1888 it was moved to the Methodist Episcopal Church of Schuylerville, New York, where it is still in use [436, p.4].

12. This organ was not the first at St. Peter's; eleven years earlier the congregation had purchased an organ by subscription [13, p.142].

13. J. C. Swann, who played the organ from 1840 to 1842, gave the compass of the Great manual as C to d³. He quoted the specification as:

Great		Great (continued)	
Principal	51	Trumpet	38
Stopped diapason	51		
Open diapason	50	*Swell*	
Twelfth	50	Stopped diapason	27
Fifteenth	50	Open diapason	27
Tierce bass	25	Flute	27
Tierce treble	25	Trumpet	27
Flute	50		

[454, II, p.55]

The stop panel and one of the two keyboards, preserved in the Newport Historical Society, bear the inscription "Ricardus Bridge Londini, Fecit. MDCCXXXIII." That there are only twelve stops indicates that Swann may not have quoted the specification accurately. The keyboard has a compass of fifty keys, C-d³, minus low C♯.

An account of 1897 says that this organ was rebuilt in 1848 by Henry Erben, retaining only the case and two stops. The remaining stops, action, and keyboard were placed in Grace Church, Brooklyn, until 1850, when they went to St. Mary's Church, Portsmouth, Rhode Island. In 1880 all of the interior of the Trinity organ was taken to the Kay Chapel in Newport, with only the case remaining in its original location [344, pp.489–90].

An interesting sequel to the story of the Berkeley organ is found in a clipping in the Scrapbook of Everett Truette. It describes Henry Ford's attempt to buy an old organ then stored in the Christian Church at Portsmouth, Rhode Island, and believed to be the Berkeley organ:

> No less notable men than Bishop Darlington of Pennsylvania, John Nicholas Brown and ex-Governor R. Livingston Beeckman of Rhode Island stand between Henry Ford and fulfillment of his desire to buy and add to his historical museum of musical instruments the old organ now at the Christian Church in Portsmouth, R. I. If, as these men believe, this is the old organ the Lord Bishop of Cloyne, George Berkley [*sic*], gave Newport's Trinity Church in 1733 (which was removed from that church some years later to make room for a better organ Trinity was then able to buy, and was given to the Portsmouth church) they assert Mr. Ford, if their influence and mind about it count, cannot have the organ to be removed to Dearborn, Mich. [157]

14. Bishop William Meade gives the following information: "At a vestry-meeting in 1735, it is noted that 'there were great subscriptions made by the present vestry for an organ, to be purchased for the use of the church at Petsworth . . .' " [103, I, p.322].

15. Maurer relates: "Pelham was born in London, but when he was still a very young boy his father brought him to America where he received all of his musical education" [366, p.25].

Although he had been serving as organist of Bruton Parish before, Pelham was not officially appointed to this post until November 1755. He, himself, installed the new organ, completing the work in April 1756. Pelham had evidently met Karl Theodor Pachelbel in Boston, had gone with him to Newport when Pachelbel installed the organ in Newport's Trinity Church, and had later accompanied Pachelbel to other locations, studying with him for about nine years. Pelham returned to Boston, where he remained until 1749. It was then that he moved to Virginia. Held in high regard by his contemporaries, he served as organist at the Bruton Parish Church for more than forty years and gave organ concerts regularly as late as 1795. He is credited with the maintenance of the organ until 1802. At that time his eyesight failed, and he moved to his daughter's house in Richmond. Pelham died in 1805.

Part Two: Organs in a Rural Society, 1760–1810

III. Some General Observations

1. Although the peace treaty was not signed until 1763, hostilities on American soil ended in 1760.

2. Such prejudice was not limited to the New World. Elson recorded: "in Boston, a century ago, one of the Congregational churches appealed to its London benefactor, the wealthy Mr. Hollis, for assistance in establishing an organ in their meeting-house. He promptly responded by sending them five hundred copies of a tract, entitled 'The Christian religion shines brightest in its own dress, and to paint it is but to deform it' " [51, p.59].

IV. Pennsylvania

1. Sonneck points out that minutes of Christ Church for 1763–67 pertaining to the purchase of this organ never refer to it as a "new" organ, placing doubt on the theory that the old Sprogel organ was still in the church at that time [143, p.90].

2. An unusual specification is that of Tannenberg's 1793 organ for the Moravian congregation, Nazareth, Pennsylvania. An original sketch and specification in the library of the Moravian Music Foundation, Winston-Salem, North Carolina, lists the following stops for this one-manual organ: Manual: Principal 4′, Viol da Gamba 8′, Quintatön 8′, Suboctav 2′, Flöt amabile 8′, Flöt douce 4′, Grob gedackt 8′. Pedal: Octav Bass 16′, Sub-Bass 32′. The use of 16′ and 32′ in the pedal is the only recorded Tannenberg pedal specification of this kind.

3. An earlier American-made swell enclosure was that of Klemm's 1739–41 organ for Trinity Church, New York (see p.31).

4. Bachmann Organs

1803 Moravian Congregation, Schoeneck, Pa. (metal pipes made by Tannenberg).

1805 Emmanuel German Reformed Church, Hanover, Pa.

1808 Old Salem Lutheran Church, Lebanon, Pa. On May 11, 1808, the Lebanon newspaper carried the notice:

> On the 12th of June a new organ will be dedicated and consecrated. Lovers of divine service will have opportunity to hear not only the preaching of ministers from abroad, but also a new beautiful organ, and are hereby invited to attend. [Cited in 136, p.162.]

This organ was replaced by the 1888 Miller organ that is still in the Old Salem Church (see p.286).

1810 Zion Lutheran Church, Jonestown, Pa.

1813 St. Michael's Union Church, Hamburg, Pa.

1818 Zion Lutheran Church, Harrisburg, Pa.

1819 Friedens Lutheran Church, Myerstown, Pa.

1821 Contract to complete the organ in St. John's Lutheran Church, Philadelphia, Pa.

5. It is quite possible that there were much closer connections between the early Pennsylvania organ builders than history has recorded for us. The first coincidence is that the Klemms and the Tannenbergs arrived in Herrnhut in the same year, 1726. This was also the year that Anna and Melchior Krauss moved to Herrnhut. Correlating the dates relating to the three families, we find:

1726 Johann Tannenberg, wife, and son arrive at Herrnhut (moving to nearby Berthelsdorf the next year).
Klemm and wife arrive at Herrnhut.
Anna and Melchoir Krauss and four children arrive at Herrnhut.

1728 David Tannenberg born.

1733 The Klemm and Krauss families move to Pennsylvania.

1749 David Tannenberg arrives in Pennsylvania.

1758 David Tannenberg begins working for Klemm.

1760 Johann David Tannenberg born, son of David.

1770 John Krauss born, great-grandson of Anna Krauss.

1771   Andrew Krauss born, great-grandson of Anna Krauss.

6. One of Downer's organs is said to have been used in Trinity Episcopal Church, Pittsburgh, until it was replaced in 1835 [380, p.2].

V. Builders in Other Locations and Imported Organs

1. It is surprising that information has not come to light regarding other early organs in Georgia. A colony of about two hundred Germans settled there, the first ones arriving in 1734. The first building of the Savannah Lutheran Church (founded in 1741) was erected in 1772, and a second one was built in 1792, when the original building was destroyed by fire. In view of the important part German immigrants played in the early history of the organ, it seems strange that no records of early German organs in Georgia have been found.

2. These organs were not the earliest ones in Charleston, however. St. Philip's Church had an organ in 1728 (see p.33).

3. Ezra Stiles (1727–1795) was then pastor of the Second Congregational Church in Newport, Rhode Island. He later became president of Yale College.

4. The *Directory* covers the period 1786–1835, and is compiled from listings in New York City directories [129].

5. The name Geib was connected with musical concerns listed in New York directories from 1798 to at least 1858. The listings cited by Redway [129] show that John Geib and his son Adam were active as organ builders until 1815, as piano builders between 1804 and 1808, and that the music store bearing their names was in business at least by 1816. William Geib was added to the firm, and shortly after John's death in 1819, the music store was known as A. & W. Geib. Later, other partners were also connected with the company. Wolverton has stated that the Geibs were as important as publishers of music as they were in the field of instrument construction. "John, Adam, and William Geib issued music both individually and collectively from 1815 until 1826; and George Geib published some items from a separate firm in 1822" [168, pp.219–20].

6. In 1849 the state legislature purchased land from the Moravian church for a county seat, which was named Winston. It was very close to Salem, and the two towns were legally combined as Winston-Salem in 1913.

7. Johann Michael Graff, originally a Lutheran, was born in Saxony in 1714, and studied keyboard instruments as a boy. He was ordained in the Moravian clergy in 1741. Ten years later he came to America and lived in Bethlehem until 1762.

8. Tannenberg also built an organ for the Moravian Church in Salem in 1800. See p.60.

9. George Williams gives an earlier date for an organ at St. John's in his survey of Charleston's church music: "The German Church was established in 1759 and the church building opened in 1763. An organ was installed promptly, and Frederick Hoff was engaged as organist until 1765" [514, p.37]. This reference could be to an organ preceding Speissegger's. St. John's dedicated a new church building in 1818, and installed a new organ in 1823 [169, p.268].

10. It seems likely that a John Speissegger, Sr., listed in the obituary notices of the Charleston *Gazette* in 1793 (he died on October 2) was the organ builder. If so, the repairs in 1800 may have been made by his son, John Speissegger, Jr.

The name Speissegger also appears in New York's church music history.

John D. Speissegger was appointed organist of St. Mark's In-the-Bouwerie, New York, in 1846 [479, p.168].

11. There are several interesting accounts of this organ's fate during the conflict. Ayars relates that in 1778 a funeral service was being held for a British officer who had been killed through a misunderstanding. Since the church was Anglican, it had been closed, but on this occasion Americans entered the church and destroyed and defaced all they could. In this desecration the bellows and remaining pipes were ruined. [13, p.145]. Another account, of questionable reliability, suggests that parts of the Christ Church organ eventually traveled to the West Coast [248, p.23].

12. This organ was not the first one at St. Michael's—it was preceded by two chamber organs, both temporary installations. The first was rented in 1761 from a Mr. Stroubell. However, in 1762 Mr. Sampson Neyle offered the use of his chamber organ until the arrival of the English organ [91, p.49]. Neyle's organ was installed by John Speissegger, and was said to have had four whole and two half stops [165, p.218].

13. For more on this subject see *The Tracker*, vol. 15, no. 2 (Winter 1971), p.5.

14. Messiter gives a somewhat different specification for this organ: Great: Open Diapason, Open Diapason (from Gamut G), Twelfth, Fifteenth, Sesquialtera, Cornet, mounted (five ranks), and Trumpet; Swell and Choir: same as the specification cited, with the exception of a Night Horn added to the Choir [104, p.293]. See also 503, I, p.16.

15. *The New-England Magazine,* January 1834, contained the following description of the Brattle Street organ: "It has only two rows of keys; but the stops of the swell are carried through, outside of the swell-box, so that the swell is, also, in effect, a choir-organ. This instrument now contains sixteen stops, and about one thousand pipes. A cremona and sub-bass were added to it, by Mr. Appleton, a few years since" [225, p.36].

16. Robert Carter was the nephew of Landon Carter (see p.34).

Part Three: Organs in an Expanding Society, 1810–1860

VI. Some General Observations

1. Among the few English organs imported to the United States after 1810 were:

1822   A three-manual organ built by Thomas Elliot of London was installed in Old South Church, Boston [116, pp.37–38]. This organ was rebuilt by Hook in 1859. In 1876 it was moved to St. Mary's Church, Milford, Massachusetts. It was in regular use there until about 1955, when it was moved to Barre, Massachusetts. Part of it formed an addition to the existing organ in the Congregational Church, and part was installed in a private residence. See *The Tracker*, vol. 13, no. 4, p.8; and vol. 14, no. 2, p.17.

1824   A two-manual organ "built by Mr. Bevington, of London" for the Monumental Church, Richmond, Virginia, is described in *The Lyre*, vol. 1, no. 7 (Dec. 1, 1824), pp. 110–11. The date of the organ is not given.

1837   A three-manual organ by Gray, of London, was installed in Trinity

Church, Boston. This organ was destroyed by fire in 1872 [*BOC* 53, p.2].

? An organ built by George Pike England was installed in Old South Church, Hallowell, Maine, in 1823. This organ was built some years earlier, as England died in 1816. It was destroyed by fire in 1878.

VII. New England

1. So progressive in some respects, Massachusetts lagged behind in important social reforms. For example, the ten-hour day was standard among most skilled workers and common laborers by 1860, and had become law in many states a decade earlier. Massachusetts had no such legislation, and the mills at Lowell and Salem continued to exceed the ten-hour working day [108, p.549].

2. William Goodrich Organs

1812   Finished several organs for Hayts, Babcock & Appleton.
          Chamber organ for Mr. S. Bean.
1813–14   Chamber organ for Hart.
1815–20   Organs built while Goodrich was with Mackay & Co:
          6 chamber organs.
          8 church organs at $1,000 each, for various locations.
          Three-manual organ for Savannah, Georgia.
          Three-manual organ for New Orleans, Louisiana.
          Organ for Church Green, Boston.
          Organ for the Handel and Haydn Society, Boston.
1821   Organ for Christ Church, Boston.
1821–22   Organ for Dr. Channing's Church, Boston.
1822   Temporary organ for St. Paul's Church, Boston.
1824   A "powerful chamber-organ" begun for Dr. G. K. Jackson, but finished after Jackson's death for Mr. John Sowden.
1825   Organ for Universalist Church, Providence, Rhode Island.
1825–26   Organ for Unitarian Church, Portsmouth, New Hampshire.
1826–27   Organ for St. Paul's Church, Boston.
1827   Organ for Congregational Society, Cambridge, Massachusetts.
          Organ for Mr. Gannett's Church, Cambridgeport, Massachusetts.
1828   Organ for Episcopal Church, Lowell, Massachusetts.
1829–30   Organ for Park Street Church, Boston.
1829   Organ for a church in Charlestown, New Hampshire.
          Organ for Orthodox Congregational Society, Dover, New Hampshire.
1830   Organ for Unitarian Church, East Cambridge, Massachusetts.
1831   Organ for Salem Church, Salem, Massachusetts.
          Organ for Congregational Society, Nantucket, Massachusetts.
1831   Organ for Episcopal Church, Pittsfield, Massachusetts.
1832–33   Organ for Congregational Society, Jamaica Plain, Massachusetts.
          Organ for First Baptist Church, Lowell, Massachusetts.
          Organ for Unitarian Society, Templeton, Massachusetts.
          Organ for Unitarian Society, Sudbury, Massachusetts.
1833   Organ for Unitarian Society, Charlestown, Massachusetts.
          Organ for Winthrop Society, Charlestown, Massachusetts (finished by Appleton).

Goodrich may have been the builder of the c.1816 organ in St. John's Lutheran Church, Charleston, South Carolina.

3. The pedal termination was probably GG, although an inconsistency in manual and pedal terminations is also possible. See, for example, p.122. In regard to the Pedal stop in New England organs of the 1820s and '30s, Owen has written:

> If there was a Pedal, it contained but one large-scaled covered wood stop generally called a Sub Bass or Bourdon, but sometimes given labels such as "Double Stopped Diapason," or even "Open Diapason," (which it rarely was, Pedal opens not coming into use until later, and then only in larger organs).
>
> [414, p.144]

4. Appleton's Three-Manual Organs

1827   Mr. Pierpont's Church, Hollis Street, Boston.
1831   Bowdoin Street Church, Boston.
1832   Handel and Haydn Society, Boylston Hall, Boston.
1835   Center Church, Hartford, Connecticut.
1835–36 Lowell Mason's Academy of Music, Boston.
1838   Park Street Church, Boston.
1841   Unitarian Church, New Bedford, Massachusetts.
1849   Independent Congregational Church, Charleston, South Carolina.

An organ Appleton built in 1846 for the Church of the Pilgrims, Brooklyn, was said to contain forty-three stops [412, p.6].

In a letter to the editor of *The Diapason* (May 1945, p.20), Henry H. Marston wrote:

> One of his [Appleton's] largest organs was in the Universalist Church on Columbus Avenue, Boston; it was a three-manual and twenty-seven-note pedal. Some friends of mine bought the pipes and I assisted in their removal. This organ had thirty-six stops and was a very noted organ in its day. It was built in 1848.

According to Owen, this organ was probably an 1872 Hutchings-Plaisted rebuild of a two-manual 1841 Appleton organ.

The earliest extant Appleton organ known is in the Centre Street Methodist Church, Nantucket, Massachusetts [417].

5. Lowell Mason was organist of the Bowdoin Street Church at this time. His connection with one of Goodrich's organs has previously been mentioned (see p.116).

6. The specification of this organ is given in *BOC* 11, p.10. See *BOC* 58, p.7 for a later three-manual Appleton organ.

7. The Sesquialtra on the Great of the Jamaica Plain Unitarian Church organ, Opus 171, has the following composition: C: 17–19–22; c. 12–15–17.

The Hooks used a variety of mixture schemes, and an interesting one is that of the Jamaica Plain First Baptist Church organ (Opus 253, 1859). Here the Tierce appears in the lower range in the Sesquialtera, and in the Mixture from c^1. Boadway gives the following compositions in *BOC* 19, p.6: "The Mixture is pitched at 22–29; 19–22; 17–22; 15–17; 12–15. The Sesquialtera is pitched at 17–19; 15–17; 12–15; 8–12; 1–8, and all breaks in both stops are on the C's."

8. The Swell Mixture in Hook Opus 171 is: C: 19–22; c^1: 15–19; g^1: 12–15; c^3: 8–15.

9. Opus 92 is in the Greenville Baptist Church, Rochdale, Massachusetts.

The specification and some interesting details of construction are given in the *OHS 1968 Convention Program*. According to this source, the manuals originally had the unusual compass of sixty-one notes, GG-g³. The pedals, however, had a C compass of thirteen pipes, seventeen keys, the higher keys repeating the lower pipes. This use of a C pedal compass with a GG manual compass has also been seen in one of Appleton's organs (see p.122).

10. The Mixture in this organ is identified in *The Tracker*, vol. 4, no. 4 as a two-rank rather than a three-rank voice, with the scheme 19–22, 12–15 [513].

11. A three-manual Johnson organ of this period is described in *BOC 55*, pp.4–5. See also *The Tracker*, vol. 14, no. 1 (Fall 1969), p.6. This organ, built in 1855 for the First Presbyterian Church, Syracuse, New York, has a typical mid-nineteenth-century specification.

12. John Henry Willcox (1827–1875) was a native of Savannah, Georgia. He graduated from Trinity College, Hartford, in 1849. Willcox became well known as organist of the Immaculate Conception Church, Boston, where he presided over the famous Hook organ from its installation until July 1874. His Doctor of Music degree was conferred by Georgetown College in 1864. G. L. Howe, writing in 1889 observed:

> Dr. Wilcox [sic] was one of the most pleasing players who ever went out to show off a new organ. He played delicate solos, soft and pleasing effects, and by way of grand finale a transcription of a Handel or Haydn chorus, such as the *Hallelujah* or *The Heavens are Telling*. . . . He was a prominent figure in New England for many years, but he never possessed a complete organ technique of the modern school. [83, p.240]

For a time Willcox was associated with E. & G. G. Hook, and later with Hutchings.

13. The organ committee for the First Congregational Church, Burlington, Vermont, evidently felt it was necessary to bring up the matter of loudness in corresponding with Simmons in 1853:

> We wish to make one suggestion (which has doubtless occur[r]ed to you)— The organ proposed is full as large as it should be for the size of the Church and its principal use will be for choir purposes in the church. In voicing the different stops, therefore, the aim should not be to secure loudness & power of tone, but rather beauty and melody and variety. —We hope you will bear it constantly in mind that we are not seeking and shall not be satisfied with a *noisy & boisterous* instrument. [Cited in *BOC 37*, p.8].

14. For specification and history of this organ see *BOC 13*, pp.2–4.

VIII. New York

1. The dates for the firm Hall, Labagh & Kemp are given by various sources as follows:

> Later on, about 1865, Mr. James Kemp, who had worked for them for many years, was admitted to the firm. . . . [433, p.166]

Hall & Labagh (John)	1846–1870
Hall, Labagh & Kemp	1870–1879
Labagh & Kemp (James)	1879–1885

[Peter Cameron, *OHS 1969 Convention Program*, p.31.]

> a firm founded by Thomas Hall in 1811, renamed Hall & Labagh in 1846, and Labagh & Kemp in 1873. [Edgar Boadway, *BOC 54*, p.3.]

Business records of Hall, Labagh & Co. indicate that Kemp became a partner of the firm by 1868, although the nameplate "Hall, Labagh & Co." was used on an organ built in 1871. These records are found in 244.

2. Crab is also credited with building organs for New York University [1, p.99], Holy Trinity Church, Brooklyn, Christ Church, Bridgeport, and Dutch Reformed Church, Washington Square, New York [503, II, p.16].

3. Other early "rück" divisions were in Ferris's instrument for the Broadway Tabernacle, and the Jardine organ for the First Presbyterian Church, Newburgh, New York.

4. Peter Cameron gives the date of this organ as 1839, and the additional information that Robjohn did not complete it. The church paid Richard M. Ferris $1,200 in about 1850 to complete the organ, and Ferris also repaired it in 1854 [245, p.2]. If Robjohn actually used some form of pneumatic action, it was not only the first in America, it was among the first in the world. Even if this innovation were an addition of Ferris's of 1850 or 1854, it would still be quite early.

5. James Johnson cites the *New York Tribune* of May 9, 1884 as the authority for his statement that at the time of Erben's death "he is recorded as having built some 1,734 organs" [86, p.10]. If this surprisingly high figure is valid, Erben was exceeding E. & G. G. Hook's production from 1845 to 1884 by about ten organs a year. That seems excessive, although with Erben's Baltimore branch in operation for sixteen of those years, such production may have been possible.

6. Specification is in the *OHS 1963 Convention Program*. Note also that this unusual sixty-one-note compass was used by Johnson in his Opus 92, 1859. See chap. 7. n.9.

7. Other examples are found in Goodrich's organ for St. Paul's Church, Boston (see p.117), and Ferris's organ for Calvary Episcopal Church (see p.165). [For further information about the Trinity Church organ see 375a.]

8. For further information about this organ see 367.

9. A different account of the early history of the Pilcher firm is found in *The Diapason*, October 1912, p.2. According to this source, the Pilchers established an organ factory in New York that was continued by the father (Henry) until 1870. During the Civil War William enlisted in the Seventh Missouri, and when he was discharged he went to Chicago and started an organ factory there. It was destroyed in the fire of 1871, and it was *then*, rather than in 1852, that a factory was built in St. Louis. However, when William E. Pilcher died in 1946, *The Diapason* (April 1946, p.1) recorded that he had been born in St. Louis in 1859, and had spent the early years of his life in Chicago. These dates give support to those recorded by Lippencott. [350].

10. The date of Marklove's death is given as 1891 in *BOC* 27, p.6.

11. Beach installed the Ferris organ in the Auditorium at Round Lake (see pp.164–66).

IX. Pennsylvania

1. Also Matthias Schneider, see p.63.

2. McCracken says, however, that Trinity's first organ was built by George Downer (Joseph Downer?, see p.71), that it was replaced in 1835, and another new organ was installed in 1852. One of these instruments was probably an organ by Henry Corrie (see p.173), [380, p.2]. Further confusion in the story of Trinity's organs is found in Lahee's date of 1804 for the first one [97, p.279].

3. Krauss Organs, 1813–1868

1813   Jordan Reformed Church, Whitehall Township, Lehigh County, Pennsylvania.

1814   St. Michael's and Zion Church, Upper Milford Township, Lehigh County, Pennsylvania. St. Michael's and Zion Corporation, Philadelphia, contracted in 1814 with Andrew Krauss for an organ to replace the old Johann Schmahl organ (see p.18). This organ is undoubtedly the one referred to in the 1814 contract in the Schwenkfelder Library, although it specifies a location in Lehigh County. For more on the history of this organ, see 518a and 518b.

1817   Evangelical Reformed and Lutheran Church, Colebrookdale, Upper Milford Township, Lehigh County, Pennsylvania.

1817   Old Mother Church, Philadelphia.

1818   Old Mother Church, Chester County, Pennsylvania.

1818   Upper Milford Township, Pennsylvania.

1819   Lutheran Church, Indianfield, Pennsylvania.

1820   Lutheran and Reformed Church, Hanover Township, Lehigh County, Pennsylvania.

1823   Unidentified. Part of a contract bearing this date exists.

1823   Mertztown, Berks County, Pennsylvania.

1824   Joseph Miller home organ, Lower Milford Township, Bucks County, Pennsylvania.

1827   Mertz Church, Berks County, Pennsylvania.

1830   Salem Reformed Church, Spangsville, Berks County, Pennsylvania.

1832   German Reformed Church, Easton, Northampton County, Pennsylvania.

1833   Stone Church, Allen Township, Northampton County, Pennsylvania.

1837   Sassaman's Church, Douglas Township.

1837   Christ Lutheran Church, Little Tulpehocken, Berks County, Pennsylvania.

1837   Christ Lutheran Church, Stouchsburg, Berks County, Pennsylvania There is possibly a case of mistaken identity here. Our first clue is the fact that this church and the one listed just above have the same name. Secondly, the Stouchsburg church is in the Tulpehocken region, and in earlier years was called Christ Church, Tulpehocken. It is said that Andrew Krauss's name is carved on the wood in the wind chest of the Little Tulpehocken organ [382, p.9]. According to an anniversary booklet of the Stouchsburg church, its organ was built by Joel Krauss [158].

1838   St. Peter's Reformed Church, Richmond, Berks County, Pennsylvania.

1839   Lutheran and Reformed Church, Tohickon, Bedminster Township, Bucks County, Pennsylvania (enlargement of the Tannenberg organ).

c.1840 St. Paul's Anglican Church, Rahns, Pennsylvania. This organ is probably the one recently acquired by the Goshenhoppen Museum of Pennsylvania German history. See *The Tracker*, Fall 1973, p.19.

1846   Zion Union Church, Maxatawnay, Lehigh County, Pennsylvania.

1850   Organ for Mrs. Maria Krause Heebner (now in Old Norriton Presbyterian Church, Fairview Village, Pennsylvania).

1852   Union Church, Huff's Church, Pennsylvania. For further information regarding this organ, see *The Tracker*, Winter 1973, p.9; and Robert Whiting's Letter to the Editor, *The Tracker*, Summer 1973, p.19.

1858   Contract with an unidentified church.

1868   Zion Evangelical Lutheran Church, Long Valley, New Jersey.

Krauss organs were also said to have been built for Kreidersville, Keller's Church, Goshenhoppen, Niantic (1900), Spinnersville, Lower Saucony, Hereford, Plow Church–Robeson. Edwin B. Krauss built an organ in 1916 for St. Joseph's (Hill) Lutheran Church, Pike Township [156, p.176], which was replaced in 1935. One of the last of the E. B. Krauss organs was at one time in the auditorium of Perkiomen School, Pennsburg, but is no longer there.

That this list of Krauss organs is quite incomplete is evident from the fact that Andrew is supposed to have built forty-eight organs (see p.69).

4. A Dieffenbach organ for St. Paul's Union Church, Hamlin, is given the date 1850 in one source [252, p.21], but a history of the church dates it 1865, and the latter seems to be the more direct information.

5. Present location of Ziegler organs: Opus 1: Goschenhoppen Folklife Museum, Pennsylvania; Opus 2: Landis Valley Museum, Lancaster County, Pennsylvania; Opus 3: missing; Opus 4: Museum of the Historical Society of Montgomery County, Norristown, Pennsylvania.

X. Organs and Builders in Other States

1. Cavaillé-Coll has traditionally been given credit for this organ. Blanton, for example, says: "the Cavaillé-Coll organ of 1794 still stands in the rear gallery of St. Louis Cathedral in New Orleans" [22, p.95]. He cites Roger Baudier, *A Historical Sketch of the St. Louis Cathedral of New Orleans* (New Orleans, no date) as the reference for this statement.

The first problem is that Aristide Cavaillé-Coll's dates are 1811 to 1899. Could this instrument have been made by the famous builder's father? Sumner says: "Aristide's father, Dominique Cavaillé-Coll, had some fame as an organ-builder in Languedoc, and his grandfather, Jean-Pierre Cavaillé, had built some large organs in Barcelona" [151, p.221].

Baudier's book gives the following additional information (the copy the writer saw was dated 1940, so it may be a different edition from the one Blanton consulted): "From its early years the Cathedral had an organ and a choir" [17, p.10]. When Major Amos Stoddard visited the city in the first decade of the nineteenth century, he reported that the church had a "large organ" [17, p.16]. In 1881 lightning struck the tower and "damaged the organ." Baudier refers to repairs, but mentions only the services of an architect and a church painter [17, p.20]. "The splendid organ dates back to the last years of the Spanish domination and was blessed by Pere Antoine" [17, p.24].

The list of organs Cavaillé-Coll built for North America is of no help (see Appendix.)

2. The dates for Schwab's retirement and death are cited in 418, p.6. According to Henry Humphreys, however, Schwab died "in 1843, at the age of eighty-three . . ." [332, p.23]. The *OHS 1965 Convention Program* contains a reference to an 1846 organ by Mathias Schwab, built for St. Paul's German Evangelical Congregational Church, Cincinnati. If accurate, this reference supports the later date for Schwab's death. It is possible, of course, that Koehnken continued to build organs under Schwab's name for some time.

3. Koehnken's dates are given as 1819–1897 [418, p.6] and as 1819–1901 [332, p.25].

4. In this regard, the "22 feet" length for the pedal pipes suggests either that the Pedal division did not have a C compass or that the number is an error. In another part of the same article we read: "The whole number of pipes exceeds 1860, the longest being about 32 feet long, which, owing to the want of room, has been curved or turned several times." Thus the number 22

should possibly be 32 for the Double Open Diapason. The length of the other pipes is open to conjecture.

5. The date of this organ is given as 1857 in 501, I.

Part Four: Organs in an Industrial Society, 1860–1900

XI. *Some General Observations*

1. Grace Church also had an Erben organ (1848), but it was sent to Columbia for safekeeping during the war. That explains the fact that Grace Church was without an organ when the Huguenot instrument was temporarily located there. The Grace Church organ was brought back to Charleston in 1866, the year the Huguenot organ was returned to its own church.

2. The Walcker firm also installed some church organs in America in the nineteenth century, e.g., First Church (Unitarian-Universalist), Boston, three-manual, 1869.

3. For a detailed description of the Harrison changes in this organ see 369, II, III, IV.

4. In a letter to Ferris Bradley, F. R. Webber wrote: "I think Dr. Clarence Eddy's studio organ had a ratchet swell pedal. I know Dr. Buck had such a swell pedal on his Hartford Johnson [1867], which had not only the first known example of a 'water engine' in America, but a Clapp Patent Leaf Turner. His Chicago studio organ [1869] had the second water engine, and no doubt a leaf turner." [Cited in *The Tracker* vol. 12, no. 3, Spring 1968, p.15.]

5. "Direct action" refers, of course, to mechanical action, and not to direct electric action.

6. Another member of the Pilcher family in New Orleans was George W. D. Pilcher. He had charge of the Philip Werlein factory there when that firm began building pipe organs in the early years of the twentieth century.

7. The Estey company was founded in 1846 for the manufacture of reed organs. The first Estey pipe organ was built in 1901.

XII. *New England*

1. For a list of published organ compositions by these composers see 410, p.29.

2. Nine builders submitted proposals for the construction of the Cincinnati Music Hall organ. Finally, with the advice of Dudley Buck, the committee awarded a contract to E. & G. G. Hook and Hastings for $26,000 exclusive of the case. Actually, the organ was given an unencased treatment, using a carved wooden screen, with the pipes extending above the screen. The wooden panels of the lower portion of the screen, the braces across the fronts of the pipes, and the console platform were elaborately designed and carved by members of two carving schools in Cincinnati, as a contribution to the city's artistic endeavor. In addition, the pipe decoration was the work of a local artist. "They [the pipes] are radiant with silver and gold, and chastely decorated here and there with bands and borders of rich arabesque ornamentation. This exquisite decoration in gold, silver, and with color is the work of Wm. H. Humphreys, assistant superintendent in the School of Design" [112, p.5]. Everette Truette's publication, *The Organ* (February 1894, p.223), noted: "The organ was paid for by public subscription; and all the carving of panels, mouldings, etc., was

done by residents of Cincinnati, no less than ninety-one ladies and gentlemen contributing one hundred and eighty-two distinct pieces of carving."

The organ was later rebuilt by Austin. It was destroyed in 1971 to make room for operatic productions [*BOC* 67, p.2].

3. The Tierce, however, was sometimes included in a Great "Mixture." See, for example, *BOC* 33, p.5; and *BOC* 93, pp.6–8.

4. Opus 216, First Baptist Church; Opus 294, Dudley Buck's Studio organ; Opus 334, St. James' Episcopal Church.

5. Ayars gives the following modifications that occurred in this title: c.1881, Hutchings & Plaisted Mfg. Co.; 1882, Hutchings & Plaisted; 1883, Hutchings, Plaisted & Co. [13, p.161].

6. For a description of Michell's organ for Church of Our Lady of Pompeii, Boston, see 354. Michell is also credited with the organ for St. Michael's and All Angels' Church, Baltimore.

7. A specification of this instrument is given in *The Organ*, vol. 2, no. 7 (Nov. 1893), p. 165.

8. This information finds confirmation in most Austin sources. A somewhat different version of the founding of the Austin firm is given by Coleberd: "While installing an organ in the Shawmut Congregational Church in Boston he [John T. Austin] received word that fire had swept the Clough and Warren factory in Detroit" [256, p.15]. The Shawmut organ was Opus 30. Coleberd further states:

> Within a year after opening a shop in Boston, Austin received a contract from the Fourth Congregational Church in Hartford. This installation created much interest among several prominent businessmen of the congregation who saw in Austin's system of universal windchests a prospect for profitable investment. [256, p.15]

It was thus, according to Coleberd, that Austin was persuaded to move to Hartford.

9. Specifications of George Stevens's organs of this period may be found in *BOC* 32, p.5; and *BOC* 34, p.14.

10. Specification is in *OHS 1970 Convention Program* [see also 290]. In a letter to the editor of *The Diapason* (May 1945, p.20), Henry H. Marston states that Hamill worked for Appleton before going into business for himself.

11. The following, reprinted from an unidentified source, appeared in *The Tracker*, vol. 14, no. 4 (Summer 1970), p.18:

> When the Pan-American Exposition was over, its organ was presented to the city and installed in the Elmwood Music Hall. Its cost was originally $18,000, by the way.
>
> It gave 37 years of service there until the Hall was demolished in 1938. Herman Schlicker, incidentally, supervised its dismantling and crating.
>
> It was stored in the old city horse barns and for four years rotted away under leaky roofs until in May, 1942, it was sold for scrap. The poor old girl only drew a bid of $165.—less than an old stonecrusher.

See also *BOC* 67, p.4.

12. The specification is adapted from *BOC* 7, pp.9–10, where it is quoted from the program for the opening of the organ. The "Sub Quint 21⅖" is probably a misprint for 21⅓.

XIII. New York

1. Webber records: "At the time of his [Erben's] death the newspapers

stated that he had built 1,734 organs over a period of sixty years and 150 of these for New York City and immediate vicinity" [497]. A catalogue published about 1885 by Erben's successor, L. C. Harrison, states that more than 1,400 organs were produced before 1875 (nine years before Erben's death). However, Harrison was still numbering organs in the 1300s as late as the 1890s [*BOC* 65, p.4].

2. George Jardine's sons were Edward, Joseph, Frederick, and Dudley. All four were brought up in the organ business, but Dudley later resigned his interest. He broke away from his friends and family and lived for years in the Bowery as "William Smith." When he died in 1913 his only friend found the name of Frederick Jardine among his papers. The latter was summoned, and identified Dudley as his brother. Dudley reportedly left $50,000 to charity. See *The Diapason,* vol. 4, no. 7 (June 1913), p.7.

3. The specification is given in the *OHS 1967 Convention Program.*

4. The specification is given in *BOC* 33, pp.2–3.

5. The organ for Grace Church is said also to have been a four-manual instrument [433, p.167], but the opus list of his organs classes it as three manuals. Several other organs had four divisions located on three manuals, and that may explain the confusion. In the Chickering Hall organ, for example, the Echo organ was played from the Swell manual. The specification of the St. Thomas Church organ is given in 347a.

6. An interesting sidelight on Hilborne Roosevelt is Webber's account of his friendship with Thomas A. Edison:

> While Mr. Edison was working on his improvements on the telephone, Mr. Roosevelt invented the switch hook that is in use today. When Mr. Edison invented the talking machine, it was the conical foot of a large metal pipe, picked up in the Roosevelt factory, that gave him the idea of amplification. Until then his phonograph was provided with ear phones, but when Mr. Edison walked away with a metal pipe foot under his arm, the familiar horn shown in the engraving "His Master's Voice" became a part of the Edison phonograph. [504, II. p.7]

In 1875 Roosevelt built a little one-manual, two-stop organ for Edison.

7. Inventiveness in the Odell factory was not limited to organs. Webber noted that the remote control of railway switches was first designed in the Odell factory. "They followed the square and tracker idea, translating these devices into steel. Thus was the modern system of railway switch and signal work born" [500, p.329].

8. Webber described this stop:

> It is a wood stop somewhat like what the old builders called a stopped diapason. Its stopper handles are long and are drilled, making it almost a röhrflote. In tonal quality it resembles somewhat a flute and a clarinet played in unison.
> [503, III]

9. See Chester Berry, "Müller and Abel: Successors to the Roosevelt Tradition," in *The Tracker,* vol. 14, no. 2 (Winter 1970), pp.3–5, 14, 18.

XIV. Organs and Builders in Other States

1. The Miller Organ Co. (A. B. Miller and A. H. Miller) of Lebanon, Pennsylvania, was primarily engaged in building reed organs. The company began business in 1873 and continued until the first part of the twentieth century. A. B. Miller built only a few organs. One is a one-manual and pedal organ (c.1885) in St. Paul's United Church, Hamlin, Pennsylvania. Two others

were in St. John's Reformed Church, Lebanon, and St. Jacob's "Kimmerlings" Reformed Church, near Lebanon.

2. Erie, Pennsylvania, also became the home of Anton Gottfried (b.1862). A native of Germany, Gottfried worked for several German builders before coming to America in 1888. He was employed for a time in the Philadelphia branch of the Roosevelt company, and then in 1895 he moved to Erie and opened an organ supply house. His first shop was on the third floor of the Felgemaker factory. Gottfried built organs, but his reputation was established mainly by his ability as a pipe maker, and he supplied pipes to a number of builders [209].

3. Some of the stop names differ in other quotations of the specification [see 166; also *BOC* 18, p.7]. An earlier Notre Dame organ was the 1864 instrument built by Garret House.

4. The specification of this organ is in *BOC* 22, p.8.

5. An earlier source dates Schantz's first pipe organ as 1893, and further states: "From 1903 to 1913 many organs were built both of tracker and pneumatic action" [206].

6. It is possible that this was a reed organ. The source is not clear in this regard.

7. In regard to the Salt Lake City organ, Ayars has said:

> George S. Hutchings is authority for the statement that the firm of Simmons built the action and complicated parts of the interior and did the voicing while the Mormons built the lower bass notes and the case, noted for its Beehives. [13, p.160]

In September 1863, Dwight's *Journal,* vol. 23, no. 12, p.95, contained an entry entitled "A Large Organ in Utah." Its initial statement was: "A large organ, one of the largest in this country, has recently been built by Simmons & Co., to be placed in the Mormon Tabernacle in Salt Lake City. . . ." [See also 18, pp.77–89.]

8. For the stop list and subsequent history of this organ, see the letter to the editor, "Nevada's Oldest Organ is Dying," *The Diapason,* February 1969, p.14.

9. Louis J. Schoenstein, senior retired member of the Schoenstein firm, was most helpful in supplying some of the information not available elsewhere about the history of this company.

10. For a list of Andrews organs see *BOC* 56, pp.4–8.

11. The Methodist Church organ was a two-manual, eighteen-stop Hutchings, Plaisted organ (Opus 114). The Farrand & Votey organ in the Congregational Church was rebuilt and enlarged by the Murray M. Harris Co. in 1905, and was installed in the church's new building. It was again moved in 1930, when the present building was completed. At that time it was installed in the Shatto Memorial Chapel.

Part Five: Organs in the Twentieth Century

XV. *The Orchestral Organ*

1. William Petty has described the studio in which rolls for the Austin Premier Quadruplex Player were cut:

> One of the unique features of the Austin recording studio was the use of multiple consoles enabling several organists to play the individual orchestral

parts of symphonic transcriptions. It was also possible to overdub rolls, that is, play back a completed roll and play along with it while cutting a new roll. The original would be faithfully reproduced along with the added parts. But unlike overdubbing with tape recorders, any number of copies or overdubs could be made with no loss in quality. [422, p.13]

According to Petty, the number of ranks controlled by the player mechanism was thirty, rather than thirty-two [422, p.12].

2. Stanley Williams came to America in 1906 and began working for Wirsching shortly after his arrival. He worked on the construction of the organ he later installed for the Maharajah of Mysore (according to Mrs. Williams, it was installed in 1909). Williams remained associated with Wirsching until 1911, although he spent part of 1910 in Los Angeles, finishing the organ in St. Paul's Cathedral for Murray M. Harris. In 1911 he joined the Los Angeles Art Organ Co. From 1915 to 1923 he was with the Robert Morton company. He then became representative for Kimball. From 1925 until his retirement in 1959 Williams was a representative for Skinner (later Aeolian-Skinner). He was responsible for many of the large, important organs installed in southern California, and was held in high regard by members of the organ profession. He died in June 1971.

3. One of the builders with whom Audsley was associated was Phillip Wirsching. Wirsching produced the instruments for the Audsley-directed Art Organ Company, and Audsley's famous three-manual, sixty-rank organ for Our Lady of Grace Roman Catholic Church, Hoboken, New Jersey (1909), was a Wirsching instrument, with a case made by the Hann-Wangerin-Weickhardt Organ Company [258, p.27]. Wirsching's Opus 94 (1907) was also designed by Audsley. This organ was built for St. Ludwig's Roman Catholic Church, Philadelphia [BOC 41, p.3]. See also pp.305–306.

4. Haskell also applied this principle to string pipes, open wood pipes, and even reeds. Descriptions and diagrams of the Haskell pipe forms may be found in *The American Organist*, III (1920), beginning with the June issue and continuing in subsequent issues of that year.

5. The Temple organ was built by Kimball. It had double-touch, a horse-shoe console, and color-coded stop tabs [243].

6. Harris reorganized in 1906 with Edwin A. Spencer as superintendent. William Fleming was reluctant to share the credit for the big organ with Murray M. Harris. In August 1911 *The Diapason* printed his letter to the editor:

To the Editor of The Diapason: Dear Sir:—In your issue of July 1, 1911, a paragraph reads that the Murray Harris Company built the large organ exhibited at the St. Louis fair. As a matter of fact, the organ was built by the Los Angeles Art Organ Company, in Los Angeles, Cal., under the supervision of the writer and under his patents, and is called the Fleming organ system. Further, the Los Angeles Art Organ Company was awarded the grand prize medal and the writer the gold medal, which can be seen at my address, as the grand prize and gold prize ribbons can be at the Wanamaker store, where the great organ is located. Surely if the Murray Harris Company built the organ that company would have the grand prize medal with diploma. These are facts beyond dispute. Hoping you will see the justice in correcting the statement of July 1, 1911, in your next issue, I am,

Yours truly,
W. B. FLEMING.

7. The specification of the Wanamaker organ in Philadelphia is given in

521; that of the original organ for the St. Louis Exposition in 502, pp.7–8. Another famous Wanamaker organ was the four-manual instrument built in 1921 for the New York store. It was sold in 1955 for $1,200. See *The American Organist*, March 1955, p.96; and *The Diapason*, June 1955, p.20.

8. For report of an extensive enlargement and revision of the gallery organ see *The American Organist*, November 1962, pp.13, 15–16.

XVI. The American Classic Organ

1. One of the largest and most famous of E. M. Skinner's organs after he moved to Methuen was the 1938 instrument for the Washington, D. C., Cathedral. Skinner had built the first of the Cathedral organs for the Bethlehem Chapel in 1911. Plans for a large organ for the main chancel were first drawn up in 1922, and were later revised.

Meanwhile, Skinner had acquired the Boston Music Hall organ along with his Methuen property, and in November 1934 he offered to sell pipes from the old organ for use in the projected Cathedral organ for $6,500. One rank was actually purchased in 1935, but they were not used. By 1937, as plans were finalized, it was evident that the old pipes would not balance with the rest of the organ [127, p.42].

2. The entire specification is given in *The Diapason*, August 1935, p.1; *The American Organist*, December 1935, pp.454–58, and *The Organ* (London), January 1937, pp. 150–58.

3. Harrison's organ was placed in the Boston University School of Fine and Applied Arts. It was destroyed by fire in 1971.

4. This was not the first time an American builder placed a division on the gallery rail, at the organist's back (see pp.150, 476 n.3). However, it may have been the first such division to have been inspired by German examples.

The other divisions of the Cleveland Museum organ were rebuilt by Holtkamp in 1946. In October 1971 a new Holtkamp organ was inaugurated. For a description of this organ, see *Music/ A.G.O.*, January 1972, pp.38–39, 56–57.

5. The specification is given in 507, pp.12–13.

6. The specification for the National Shrine organ is given in 300, pp.8–10. The specification for the Detroit organ is given in *The Diapason*, July 1973, p.1.

7. The specification is given in *The Diapason*, June 1965, pp.1, 27; in *The American Organist*, October 1969, pp.12–13; and in *Music/ A.G.O.*, May 1970, pp.48–49.

8. See also the 113-rank specification for the Highland Park United Methodist Church, Dallas, Texas, in *The Diapason*, January 1973, p.1.

XVII. The Neo-Baroque Organ

1. Charles Fisk considers the characteristics of wind supply in Baroque organs in *The Diapason*, September 1969, pp.18–19. See also David Cogswell's letter to the editor, *The Diapason*, April 1970, p.14.

2. The Casavant firm traces its history back to Joseph Casavant's (d.1874) first experience with organ building in 1837. His two sons, Claver and Samuel, spent three years studying organs and organ building in Europe, returning to Canada in 1879. They established a factory in St. Hyacinthe, the home of Casavant organs since that time. This company had developed an adjustable combination action by 1882 and an electropneumatic action by 1891. Tonally, the Casavant organs followed a moderate path, avoiding the more excessive expressions of early twentieth-century orchestral style.

Index

Abbot, Abiel, 119
Abbott and Sieker, 416
action: mechanical, 407, 411–17; of 19th-century organs, 207–8; pneumatic, 208, 241–42, 276–77
Adams, C. W., 252
Adams, Frank, 351
Adams, George Whitefield, 79, 143
Adams, Gilbert F., 417, 418, 426
Adams, J. N., 251
Adams, Welcome K., 252
advertisements for organs, 79, 98
Aeolian Company, 295, 331
Aeolian-Skinner Co., 368–69, 380–85, 398–99, 416; see also Skinner, Ernest
Albertsen, U. J., 299
Alfred Hertz Memorial Hall of Music, 390–91
Allen, Joel, 79
Alley, Joseph, 140–42
Alsop, Richard, 30
Alton, Ill., organ builders in, 306
American Classic organ, 364–400, 403–5
American Guild of Organists, 206, 348, 408
American orchestral style, 343–56
Anburey, Thomas, 53
Anderson, Charles, 308
Andover Organ Co., 413–17, 420
Andrews, Alvinza, 168–69
Andrews, Charles, 168, 316
Andrews, George, 168, 255, 279–80, 316
Andrews, J. Warren, 348
Antes, John, 12
Appleton Chapel, Harvard University, 115, 116, 173, 217, 249; career, 119–22; characteristics of organs, 121–22; three-manual organs of, 471
Appleton, Chapel, Harvard University, 136–37, 139
Arlidge, Samuel, 175
Armstrong, William H., 16, 52, 86
Art Organ Co., 331–32
The Art of Organ-Building, 339–41, 375
Artiste organ, 331
Ash, Gilbert, 32
Astor & Co., 95

Atlantic City Convention Hall organ, 362–63, 377–78
Audsley, George A.: concept of organ, 274; mentioned, 305, 351, 352, 360, 397; organs by, 309; Art Organ Co. of, 331–32; career, 331–32; The Art of Organ-Building, 339–41, 375; use of electricity, 345; comment on Wanamaker organ, 357–58
Austin, Basil F., 248–49, 351, 368
Austin, Frederick B., 368
Austin, John T., 216, 248–49, 325, 329, 331, 332
Austin Organ Co., 329, 344, 361, 368, 391–92, 400
automatic player organs, 331
Avery, John, 96
Ayars, Christine, 208, 233

Babcock, Mary, 22
Bachmann, Johann Philip: association with Tannenberg, 52; career, 62; organs by, 62–63, 467; mentioned, 87, 171
Backus, Augustus, 169
Baily, Almon, 143
Baker, John, 143
Baker, Robert, 398
Balbiani, Natale, 361
Baltimore, Md.: Cathedral organ, 145–46; organ building in, 179–80, 282–83, 290–92, 420; St. Gregory's Church organ, 291
Baptist Church, Shelburne Falls, Mass., 134
Barckhoff, Carl, 212, 305, 327
Bard, Samuel, 90
Barker, Charles S., 208, 265–66
Barker lever, 208
Barnes, William, 363, 372
Barney, Henry E., 143
Baroque organ, 401–28
barrel organs, 80, 161
Barrington, Ill., Community Church organ, 419
Basset, Massa, 143
Bassett, Ira, 143